opposing viewpoints
SOURCES

environment

environment

vol. 1

David L. Bender, *Publisher*
Bruno Leone, *Executive Editor*
Bonnie Szumski, *Senior Editor*
Janelle Rohr, *Senior Editor*
William Dudley, *Editor*
Karin Swisher, *Editor*
Lisa Orr, *Editor*
Tara P. Deal, *Editor*
Robert Anderson, *Assistant Editor*

Bill Freedman, Ph.D., *Consulting Editor*
*Professor in the Department of Biology and the School
for Resource and Environmental Studies at Dalhousie
University in Halifax, Nova Scotia.*

greenhaven press, inc.

P.O. Box 289009
San Diego, CA 92128-9009

ISBN 0-89908-553-9
ISSN 1048-8006

"Congress shall make no law . . . abridging the freedom of speech, or of the press."

First amendment to the U.S. Constitution

contents

Greenhouse Effect

Nuclear Power

foreword

"It is better to debate a question without settling it than to settle a question without debating it."

Joseph Joubert (1754-1824)

The purpose of Opposing Viewpoints SOURCES is to present balanced, and often difficult to find, opposing points of view on complex and sensitive issues.

Probably the best way to become informed is to analyze the positions of those who are regarded as experts and well studied on issues. It is important to consider every variety of opinion in an attempt to determine the truth. Opinions from the mainstream of society should be examined. But also important are opinions that are considered radical, reactionary, or minority as well as those stigmatized by some other uncomplimentary label. An important lesson of history is the eventual acceptance of many unpopular and even despised opinions. The ideas of Socrates, Jesus, and Galileo are good examples of this.

Readers will approach this anthology with their own opinions on the issues debated within it. However, to have a good grasp of one's own viewpoint, it is necessary to understand the arguments of those with whom one disagrees. It can be said that those who do not completely understand their adversary's point of view do not fully understand their own.

A persuasive case for considering opposing viewpoints has been presented by John Stuart Mill in his work *On Liberty*. When examining controversial issues it may be helpful to reflect on his suggestion:

> The only way in which a human being can make some approach to knowing the whole of a subject, is by hearing what can be said about it by persons of every variety of opinion, and studying all modes in which it can be looked at by every character of mind. No wise man ever acquired his wisdom in any mode but this.

Analyzing Sources of Information

Opposing Viewpoints SOURCES include diverse materials taken from magazines, journals, books, and newspapers, as well as statements and position papers from a wide range of individuals, organizations, and governments. This broad spectrum of sources helps to develop patterns of thinking which are open to the consideration of a variety of opinions.

Pitfalls To Avoid

A pitfall to avoid in considering opposing points of view is that of regarding one's own opinion as being common sense and the most rational stance and the point of view of others as being only opinion and naturally wrong. It may be that another's opinion is correct and one's own is in error.

Another pitfall to avoid is that of closing one's mind to the opinions of those with whom one disagrees. The best way to approach a dialogue is to make one's primary purpose that of understanding the mind and arguments of the other person and not that of enlightening him or her with one's own solutions. More can be learned by listening than speaking.

It is my hope that after reading this anthology the reader will have a deeper understanding of the issues debated and will appreciate the complexity of even seemingly simple issues on which good and honest people disagree. This awareness is particularly important in a democratic society such as ours where people enter into public debate to determine the common good. Those with whom one disagrees should not necessarily be regarded as enemies, but perhaps simply as people who suggest different paths to a common goal.

The Format of SOURCES

In this anthology, carefully chosen opposing viewpoints are purposely placed back to back to create a running debate; each viewpoint is preceded by a short quotation that best expresses the author's main argument. This format instantly plunges the reader into the midst of a controversial issue and greatly aids that reader in mastering the basic skill of recognizing an author's point of view. In addition, the table of contents gives a brief description of each viewpoint, allowing the reader to identify quickly the point of view for which he or she is searching.

Each section of this anthology debates an issue, and the sections build on one another so that the anthology as a whole debates a larger issue. By using this step-by-step, section-by-section approach to understanding separate facets of a topic, the reader will have a solid background upon which to base his or her opinions. Each year a supplement of twenty-five opposing viewpoints will be added to this anthology, enabling the reader to keep abreast of annual developments.

This volume of Opposing Viewpoints SOURCES does not advocate a particular point of view. Quite the contrary! The very nature of the anthology leaves it to the reader to formulate the opinions he or she finds most suitable. My purpose as publisher is to see that this is made possible by offering a wide range of viewpoints that are fairly presented.

David L. Bender
Publisher

introduction

"No single species has ever transformed the biosphere as much as human beings have since the beginning of this century."

Vaclav Smil

Editor's note: Industrial society in the twentieth century has been marked both by damage to the earth's natural environment and by new scientific knowledge of how the environment works. During the 1960s a renewed environmentalist movement drew public attention to the environmental damage caused by industries and human carelessness. The question of how to best protect the environment has thus become a controversial global issue, as nations around the world recognize the costs of environmental destruction. The Environment: Opposing Viewpoints SOURCES *features a broad range of viewpoints on various environmental issues.*

The following excerpt is by Vaclav Smil, an ecologist and professor of geography at the University of Manitoba in Winnipeg, Canada. The selection provides a brief historical overview of environmental problems of the past century and changing human attitudes toward the environment.

Seventy-five years ago the age of the explorer was coming to a close. Although another generation was to pass before the last isolated tribes of New Guinea were contacted by outsiders, successful journeys to the poles—Robert Peary's Arctic trek in 1909 and Roald Amundsen's Antarctic expedition in 1911—removed the designation of terra incognita from the two most inaccessible places on Earth. Four centuries of European voyaging had accumulated a mass of descriptive information about the lands, rivers, oceans and living organisms of the planet, and most of this knowledge had been admirably systematized in such great feats of early science as Carolus Linnaeus's classification of biota, Alexander von Humboldt's sweeping writings and the maps of the British Admiralty.

But our understanding of how the environment actually works was still primitive. To list just a few

Vaclav Smil, "Our Changing Environment," *Current History,* January 1989. © 1990 Current History, Inc. Reprinted with permission.

key examples: flourishing biochemistry was laying the foundations for understanding the complexities of grand biospheric cycles; Charles Darwin's theories were turning attention to the interplays between organisms and their surroundings; and physiologists were offering coherent insights about the nutritional needs of plants, animals and men.

But the blanks dominated: the absence of sensitive, reproducible analytical methods precluded reliable monitoring of critical environmental variables; Wilhelm Bjerknes set down the basic equations of atmospheric dynamics in 1904—but climatology remained ploddingly descriptive for several more decades; the need for an inclusive understanding of living systems was in the air—but the fundamental quantitative tenets of ecology were still unknown.

If science was on the verge of great discoveries, so was the everyday treatment of the environment. New attitudes to protect unique natural settings and the first environmental control techniques were emerging after a century of rapid industrial expansion that treated land, water and air as valueless public property: the final decades of the nineteenth century saw the establishment of the first large natural reserves and parks, and the new century brought primary treatment of urban waste water and the invention of electrostatic cleaning of ash-laden flue gases.

Little Environmental Protection

The two world wars and the intervening generation of economic turmoil were not conducive to gains in environmental protection, but science made some fundamental advances. In 1925, Alfred Lotka published the first extended work that established biology on a quantitative foundation. In 1929, Vladimir Ivanovich Vernadskii ushered in the study of the environment on an integrated, global basis with his pioneering book on the biosphere. In 1935, Arthur Tansley defined the term ecosystem, one of the key terms of modern science. And in 1942, Raymond Lindeman, following Evelyn Hutchinson's earlier ideas, published the first quantifications of energy flows in an observed ecosystem.

Modern Environmental Degradation

Meanwhile, the environment of industrialized countries continued to deteriorate. Three pre-1914 classes of innovations commercialized between the world wars accounted for most of this decline. The thermal generation of electricity, accompanied by emissions of fly ash, sulfur and nitrogen oxides and by a huge demand for cooling water and the consequent warming of streams, moved from isolated city systems to large-scale integrated regional and national networks.

The automobile industry shifted from workshop manufacturing to mass production, which made cars affordable for millions of people. The emissions of unburned hydrocarbons, nitrogen oxides and carbon monoxide spread over urban areas and into the countryside, which was increasingly buried under asphalt and concrete roads. And the synthesis of plastics grew into a large, highly energy-intensive industry generating a variety of toxic pollutants previously never present in the biosphere, introducing huge numbers of nondecaying wastes into the environment.

Post-1945 developments amplified these trends. New environmental risks were introduced as the rich world entered the period of its most impressive economic growth, terminated only by the 1973-1974 quintupling of oil prices. In just 25 years, the consumption of primary commercial energy nearly tripled, electricity generation grew about eightfold, car ownership increased sixfold and production of most kinds of synthetic materials grew more than tenfold.

New environmental burdens were introduced to farmlands and other ecosystems as the rapidly expanding use of nitrogenous fertilizers (derived from synthetic ammonia first produced in 1913) and the growing applications of the just-discovered pesticides (DDT was first used on a large scale in 1944) left nitrates in groundwater and streams and led often to dangerously high insecticide and herbicide residues in plant and animal tissues.

Environmental pollution, previously a matter of regional impact, started to affect more extensive areas around major cities and conurbations and downwind from concentrations of power plants as well as the waters of large lakes, long stretches of streams and coastlines, and many estuaries and bays. More sensitive analytical techniques were recording pollutants in the air, waters and biota thousands of kilometers from their sources.

Only a few remedies were introduced during the 1950's, most notably in combating air pollution. London's heavy air pollution, culminating in 4,000 premature deaths during the city's worst smog episode in December, 1952, led to the adoption of Britain's Clean Air Act, the foundation of the first comprehensive effort to clean a country's air. Throughout the rich world, electrostatic precipitators able to remove more than 98 percent of all fly ash were becoming a standard part of large combustion sources, and black particulate matter started to disappear from many cities and visibility improved; this trend was further aided by the introduction of natural gas in home heating.

Environmental Awareness

The big attitudinal shift came in the 1960's. Rachel Carson's influential warning about the destructive consequences of pesticide residues in the environment was often described as the beginning of new environmental awareness, but the impulses came from many quarters. Accumulating evidence of spreading air pollution was especially important in influencing public opinion: objectionable particulates were removed from the urban air, but invisible pollution began to affect areas far from the most prolific sources of combustion.

Europeans were the first to note this phenomenon. International monitoring networks established in 1948 and Swedish observations started in the early 1960's pointed to worrisome changes in the composition of the continent's precipitation. In 1967, Svante Odén described for the first time the dangers of acid deposition caused by the long-range transport of acid air pollutants followed by degradative changes in lakes and soils in sensitive receptor areas.

The decade of the 1960's also brought many exaggerated claims. . . .

Once the interest in environmental degradation began, the Western media (ever watchful for bad news) and scientists (whose work is so often governed by fashionable topics) kept attention alive with a barrage of new worries. Soon the environmental concerns were adopted by such disparate groups as the leftist student protesters, who discovered yet another reason to tear down the ancien régime, and large oil companies, which discovered that fish thrive around the legs of offshore drilling platforms and advertised accordingly, with two-page glossy spreads.

Checking the Global Environment

The summer of 1970 marked the first attempt at a systematic evaluation of global environmental problems: the Study of Critical Environmental Problems sponsored by the Massachusetts Institute of Technology. The items were not ranked, but the order of their appearance in the summary indicated the relative importance perceived at that time. First came the emissions of carbon dioxide from fossil fuel combustion, then particulate matter in the atmosphere, cirrus clouds from jet aircraft, the effects of supersonic planes on stratospheric chemistry, the thermal pollution of waters and the impact of pesticides. Mercury and other toxic heavy metals, oil on the ocean and the nutrient enrichment of coastal waters closed the list.

Just a month later, President Richard Nixon sent Congress the first report of the President's Council on Environmental Quality, noting that this was the first time in history that a nation had taken comprehensive stock of the quality of its surroundings. Soon afterward his administration established the Environmental Protection Agency by pulling together segments of five departments and agencies; and the environment entered big politics. The same thing happened on the international level, where attention was focused on the first-ever United Nations-organized Conference on Human Environment in Stockholm in 1972. Swedes talked about acid rain, Brazilians insisted on their right to cut down all their tropical forests in their dash to development and the Maoist Chinese claimed to have no environmental problems at all.

The actions taken by OPEC (the Organization of Petroleum Exporting Countries) in 1973-1974, the global economic downturn, and misplaced but deeply felt worries about ruinous shortages of energy turned public attention away from the environment temporarily, but new studies, new revelations and new sensational reporting kept environmental awareness high. Notable 1970's concerns included the effects of nitrous oxide from intensifying fertilization on stratospheric ozone, the carcinogenic potential of nitrates in water and vegetables, and both the short-term effects of routine low-level releases of radionuclides from operating nuclear power plants and the long-term consequences of high-level radioactive waste that had to be stored for millennia.

New Problems

And with the economic plight of poor nations worsened by the higher prices of imported oil came the "discovery" of the continuing dependence of all rural and some urban Asian, African and Latin American populations on traditional biomass energies—wood, charcoal, crop residues, dried dung—and the realization of how environmentally ruinous such reliance can be in societies where recent advances in primary medical care have pushed the natural increase of population to rates as high as 4 percent a year.

Massive deforestation and the ensuing desertification in dry subtropical countries and heavy soil erosion and intensified flooding in rainy environments have other causes as well: inappropriate methods of farming, predatory commercial logging, and often government-sponsored conversion of forests to pastures producing beef for export.

To this must be added the effects of largely uncontrolled urban and industrial wastes, including the release of toxic substances that would not be tolerated in rich countries, appalling housing and transportation conditions in urban areas, the misuse of agricultural chemicals and the continuing rapid losses of arable land to house large population increases and to accommodate new industries. Not surprisingly, when an ambitious American report to the President surveyed the state of the environment in 1980 it devoted much of its attention to the immense environmental burdens of the poor world.

In human terms this degradation and pollution present an especially taxing challenge to China, the world's most populous country. When Chairman Deng Xiaoping's "learning from the facts" axiom replaced Chairman Mao Zedong's "better red than expert," the flood of stunning admissions and previously unavailable hard data provided a depressing comprehensive account of China's environmental mismanagement, whose single most shocking fact may be the loss of one-third of China's farmland within a single generation in a nation that must feed a little more than one-fifth of the world's population from one-fifteenth of the world's arable land.

And the environmental problems of the poor world were even more prominent in another global stocktaking, in 1982, at the Conference on Environmental Research and Priorities organized by the Royal Swedish Academy of Sciences in Rättvik. The meeting's list of ten research priorities for the 1980's was headed by the depletion of tropical forests and the reduction of biological diversity, while the list of management priorities included first of all hazardous chemicals, the depletion of tropical forests and desertification due to overgrazing.

The most recent environmental mishaps and worries have echoed and intensified several recurring concerns. Such accidents as the cyanide poisoning in Bhopal in 1984 and the news about the daunting efforts to clean up thousands of waste sites make hazardous toxic wastes a matter of lasting apprehension, and the Chernobyl disaster in 1986 strengthened the popular fear of nuclear power. At first, an almost unbelievable discovery of a seasonal ozone hole above Antarctica revived the worries about the rapid and intense human-induced change in the atmosphere, a concern further intensified by a new wave of writings and reports on the imminent warming of the atmosphere because of the accumulation of "greenhouse" gases.

The Environmental Challenge

What then is the state of our environment, and what are our prospects? Simple questions may go to the heart of the matter—but simple answers would be highly misleading. Of course, this has not prevented many observers from providing precisely such simple answers during the last 20 years. On the one hand, the environmental catastrophists (a Western intellectual species descended from Robert Malthus) offer vivid descriptions of existing dangers and predict even greater imminent horrors. For some of these doomsayers the question has been not "how shall we live, but indeed if we are going to live at all for very much longer."

On the other hand, the techno-optimists (utopians?) argue that human inventiveness and management skills will soon take care of all environmental ills; they portray a less polluted and ecologically more stable future with less precarious life for a more populated world. . . .

These verbal forays from the mentally antipodal, well-fortified camps of true believers change nothing. Allegiance to one of these groups may confer a feeling of intellectual superiority and righteousness, but a sensible appraisal of the state of the global environment must eschew sloganeering simplifications. There are many environments, many scales, many threats, and many solutions. . . .

A New Understanding

In the long run, the rise of environmental consciousness will have effects comparable to the consequences of the last three great Western transformations—the Renaissance, the Reformation and the Industrial Revolution. A legacy of centuries of predatory attitudes and an adversarial ethos cannot be discarded in a matter of years; yet a new way of understanding is making its way slowly, and often in roundabout ways characteristic of civilization's advance.

No single species has ever transformed the biosphere as much as human beings have since the beginning of this century—and much of this transformation has led to degradation, a trend that cannot continue with impunity. But during the past four generations humans have also learned more than all humans learned in all the preceding millennia about the complexity of the biosphere, about its amazing resilience, about the ways of using and managing the ecosystems in sustainable ways.

Nimble adaptability has been the hallmark of our species. This quality has carried us through enormous environmental upheavals and it has brought longer and richer lives to an ever-increasing number of people. In the coming years, our deepening understanding of the biosphere must be translated into effective action to preserve the integrity of the Earth's environment. The record may not look reassuring, but unprecedented challenges bring extraordinary responses. Apprehension may be in order—but our hope lies in not underestimating our adaptive capabilities. One must always hope that the Linnaean designation of our species—*sapiens*—is correct.

"Compare this October's scene with the same scene photographed five years... ago and the havoc wreaked by acid rain becomes as obvious as the rubble of Lebanon."

viewpoint 1

Acid Rain Harms the Environment

Merritt Clifton and Chris Rose

Editor's note: The following viewpoint is in two parts. The first part was written by Merritt Clifton and the second part by Chris Rose.

I

I live in a war zone. At a glance, it's just the Kemp family farm outside Brigham, Quebec. As October faded and the battle scars became most evident, it still looked like a picture-postcard. Twenty-eight Holstein milkers grazed in green fields. Apple trees awaiting harvest bent beneath their fruit.

But compare this October's scene with the same scene photographed five years, 10 years ago, and the havoc wreaked by acid rain becomes as obvious as the rubble of Lebanon.

A half-hour's drive north of Vermont, the Kemp farm lies in the region Environment Canada says is receiving the most acid rain in North America. Air currents from the south and west merge here, bringing the combined pollution of the Ohio Valley, Great Lakes cities and Toronto-Montreal industrial axis. The rain, snow and fog pH at Environment Canada's Mont Sutton monitoring station rarely tops 5.0, which is 15 times as acidic as it should be.

The statistics, however, tell much less than a keen eye for detail.

Visible Effects

The cows were still out, for instance, after first snowfall, because our hay crop was bad. Our hay crop was bad not because of drought, but because of too much rain—rain that acidified the soil. Acidification killed the microbes that fix nitrogen in the soil. Key trace elements were leached away. We're restoring the chemical balance now by artificial means, but it's a slow and expensive battle

for a small farm sustained the past 150 years by manure and hard labor alone.

Nor were the maple trees simply losing their leaves with the change of seasons. No leaves fell from their crowns because the crowns had been dead all year. Woodpeckers had long since stripped the bark away from what should have been the growing tips of strong branches, seeking the insects that feast upon dead wood.

A healthy maple tree produces syrup for 200, 300, even 400 years. Our oldest maples are around 150. Most are under 40. Few will ever reach their productive prime.

The killer, again, is acid rain. Rain strips the waxy protective coating from leaves, making them vulnerable to sunburn, ozone burn, insects, and fungus. Acidic winter snowpack dissolves toxic metals from rocks and soil, to poison the trees at the roots.

Damage to Trees

Deeper into our woodlot, our birch trees should also have exploded into color—but they were long since naked of foliage. They turned color back in August, some as early as July, less than halfway through their growing season. Acid rain apparently upsets the metabolic trigger that tells the birches when the seasons change. Because they don't grow as long any more, they dry out, becoming brittle. Windstorms that a few years ago left our woodlot unscathed have recently torn swaths of broken birches that we frantically chainsaw into firewood lest they rot and attract more insects to attack the other trees.

So far, our fast-growing evergreens seem unaffected—at a glance. Look closer. Their needles have been combing the acidic morning mists. Their growth tips are skeleton fingers, rattling in the breeze where not long ago they swished and sighed.

Nor is our apple orchard immune. Our apple trees

have survived the worst insect infestations and ground freezes on local record. Suddenly they're dying from what are normally only adverse conditions.

Of course no trout have swum our woodlot brooks for 15 to 20 years. We didn't understand why they disappeared. We know now that acid surge did it—the 20-fold increase in acidity each spring at snowmelt. Young trout can't survive that. Without young trout, there can be no old ones.

Even inside our picturesque old barn, once a hideout for Prohibition-era rumrunners, the effects of acid rain are evident. Where raindrops trickle through between planks, the lime-based whitewash is eaten away.

The Battle

The ancient battle between mankind and the natural environment has been waged here for centuries. The first settlers fought climax forests, long-vanished forms of wildlife and more severe winters than any we've known. Farmers and nature have co-existed here more in armed truce than in mutual cooperation.

Acid rain, however, introduced aerial bombardment. Just as aviation turned the whole world into the front for both terrorism and declared war, so acid rain subjects every forest and field to attack from afar.

Now farmer and nature bear the brunt of this remote struggle among economic and political interests for whom this is just another stretch of no-man's land. We cringe beneath the blitz, knowing it will likely get much, much worse before there's any respite.

II

It was not foresters who first noticed that the forests of central Europe were dying, but parents and children who went each year to the Black Forest in West Germany to collect silver-fir foliage for Christmas decorations. 'At one time sale of these trimmings more than paid our management costs,' a forester told me. 'Then when the people saw they were discolored they stopped coming and we began to realize something was wrong.'

The forest killer was a cocktail of pollutants commonly known as acid rain', a byproduct of the air pollution from car exhausts and industrial processing. The forest decline this causes is called *waldsterben* or the 'forest dying'. It appeared first in the richest and most powerful economies of Europe, striking down firs and spruce in the playground of West Germany—the Black Forest and the Alps of Bavaria. In the past eight years it has also been recognized in most of the rest of northern Europe, Eastern Canada, the US and even Japan. There, downwind of Tokyo and the industrial-technological complex which stretches from Kawasaki to the sea

port of Yokohama, the airborne chemical signature of Japanese industry has left the venerated Japanese cedars thinning and tattered over 20,000 square miles of countryside.

In conifer trees the needles fall years early, often first turning a sickly yellow indicating a shortage of essential metals such as magnesium. As the decline progresses the tree loses its ability to feed itself through photosynthesis (because the leaf area is reduced) and in its weakened state falls victim to diseases. In deciduous species such as the beech and oak the pattern is similar. Official surveys show that over half of Britain's broadleaved trees have lost a quarter or more of their leaf area. In fact Britain's oak and beech are probably the most damaged in Europe.

Like the much-cited canary in the coalmine, the dying forests are potent indicators of what is to become of us, for the chemicals that cause acid rain also attack people. Water on already slightly acid rocks and sands becomes more acid with pollution, releasing toxic metals such as cadmium, lead, mercury and aluminum. This last, it is claimed, accounts for the high rates of Alzheimer's disease (senile dementia) in southern Norway.

"The dying forests are potent indicators of what is to become of us."

Vehicle exhausts spew out oxides of nitrogen and hydrocarbons which include cancer-inducing chemicals. Diesel is particularly rich in such pollution. Together in the air, these chemicals react in sunlight to form ozone, a substance which is essential outside the atmosphere where it protects the earth from harmful ultra-violet rays. Inside the atmosphere, however, it is a pollutant which eats through leaf-cell walls, making them permeable to acidic rainfall, and leaching out key nutrients. Ozone also attacks the lungs of mammals and birds. The American bald eagle used as a mascot at the Los Angeles Olympics died from lung disease caused by air pollution.

Polluting the Countryside

Parents' campaigning organizations in Austria and West Germany have long believed that cot-deaths could be associated with industrial air pollution, just as people who died in the London smogs are now known to have suffered severe lung irritation from sulphuric acid particles. Similarly the US Clean Air Scientific Advisory Committee concludes that current air quality standards do not protect asthmatics. This finding may lead to amendment of the Clean Air Act, requiring substantial extra amounts of sulphur to be cleaned from power station gases.

The issue of air pollution and health is one which should concern us all. It is secondary smoking on the grandest of scales. The advent of tall chimneys, the widespread substitution of electricity for coal as a heating source for houses, and the rapid increase in car ownership and road transport have meant that air pollution once concentrated in urban areas is now spread thinly over the previously clean countryside. Ice cores analyzed from the Arctic and Antarctic show that eventually it reaches there too.

Only recently have the effects of acid rain on trees begun to be recognized, which may be one reason why the implications of acid rain for humans have not really hit home. As Canadian Gilles Gagnon wrote in 1986: 'Each year the beauty of the forest is somewhat diminished but one gets used to it and finds it natural to see trees withering along the roadside'. The same could be said of almost every country in which the insidious decline has taken hold.

Blind to the Signs

When the blight first started to be recognized in West Germany, slogans were daubed on the rocks of the worst affected Black Forest hillsides. 'Do not weep forest,' said one, 'the desert will not last forever'. Others referred to the Christmas carol, *O Tannenbaum*, which celebrates the beauty of the silver fir tree, a tree which not only occupies a central place in German folk-mythology but has been hardest hit by *waldsterben*. Yet within a year or so, the trees were being felled and others planted. After all, they look healthy. The signs were scrubbed from the rocks at the request of the local hoteliers. Acid rain and dying forests, they said, were bad for business. If it couldn't be cured then perhaps it should at least be denied.

"Each year the beauty of the forest is somewhat diminished but one gets used to it and finds it natural to see trees withering along the roadside."

The prospect of a civilization which can happily accept the Black Forest without trees is more than unsettling. On this basis attacks of tree blindness become an act of mass delusion as society turns its back on an apparently insoluble problem. The question is whether we open our eyes before the delusion becomes suicidal.

Merritt Clifton is an environmentalist and a free-lance journalist. Chris Rose is an ecologist who has worked with the environmentalist groups World Wildlife Fund, Greenpeace, and Friends of the Earth.

Acid Rain Does Not Harm the Environment

Warren T. Brookes

On Tuesday evening, July 25, 1989, Ned Potter of ABC News did a three-minute segment purporting to show how acid rain (caused by sulphur dioxide—SO₂—emissions from Midwestern utilities) was killing trees on Camel's Hump Mountain in Vermont.

Aerial photos showed a pattern of dead or dying tall spruce trees. We were informed acid rain was sterilizing the soil. An environmentalist guided us through the devastation. It was potent TV.

It was also a hoax.

When the Camel's Hump story was first brought to national attention in *Natural History* magazine in 1982, soil scientists flocked to see it firsthand. But, in order to examine the dead or dying trees, they had to fight their way up through a veritable jungle of healthy young red spruce trees and new growth.

It was immediately clear there was nothing toxic about the soil. On closer examination, soil scientists from Yale, the University of Pennsylvania and the U.S. Forest Service found the dead or dying trees had one thing in common: They all dated from before 1962. Trees started after that period were generally healthy.

What happened in 1962? Yale's forestry expert Tom Siccama told us, "All we know is that suddenly in 1962, the trees got very unhappy, and it was probably the very severe drought followed by an especially killing winter.

"The one thing it was *not* was acid rain. Look, you don't get that sudden a change from something like acid rain. And why didn't it happen in adjacent areas or states? The people in Vermont who blame this on acid rain must think they live on an island or something," Siccama said.

In fact, Siccama's own research, corroborated by

Andrew Friedland of Dartmouth, shows that over the last few years tree health in that whole region is *improving*, not getting worse.

"We cored hundreds of trees in the area in 1982, and again in 1987, and, in that period, the number of sick trees went down markedly. We just got through coring about 90 trees at Hubbard Brook in New Hampshire and discovered that the rate of growth has more than doubled since 1987 alone," Siccama told us.

Indeed, since 1952, total growing wood volume in the Northeast and New England has risen faster than any other region, including the softwoods the ABC report alleged were dying.

A Hoax

So the entire ABC acid rain story was a fraud, including Ned Potter's concluding statement that "doctors say acid rain is responsible for 50,000 deaths a year." But not even the Environmental Protection Agency (EPA) claims *any* known deaths from sulphur dioxide (SO₂) emissions. The 50,000 figure came from one extreme theoretical estimate in an analysis where half the experts estimated zero health effects.

Sadly, this is exactly the kind of nonsense President Bush has unleashed with his embrace of the "Green revolution": a media race to see who can paint the grimmest pictures.

He also re-energized the EPA, which has a huge power and funding stake in doing the same. These deadly incentives led to an awful lot of BS (bad science).

There is no better example of this than the EPA's wildly scary 1980 report suggesting acid rain was causing a kind of "aquatic silent spring" in Northeast America and Canada:

"It is in the lakes and streams where the most dramatic effects of acid rain have been observed. The increasing acidity of lakes in North America and

Warren T. Brookes, "The Continuing Mythology About Acid Rain," *Human Events*, September 2, 1989. Reprinted by permission of Heritage Syndicate.

Europe has been documented. . . . This has led to a decrease in populations of fish and other aquatic organisms."

This report led to the establishment of a 10-year scientific study of the causes and effects of acid rain, or what is called the National Acid Precipitation Assessment Program (NAPAP).

Unfortunately for the environmentalists, this assessment actually tried to be scientific, that is, to avoid reaching conclusions first and then searching for evidence to support them.

The result in 1987, after more than $300 million was spent in exhaustive study, was to conclude essentially that regional SO_2 concentrations were causing *no* discernible damage to crops or forests at present levels of acid rain emission (about 22 million tons a year, down from 32 million in 1970).

Also, the number of acid lakes and streams was far lower than the EPA had warned, affecting less than 2 per cent of the surface water area even in the Adirondacks, the most heavily impacted region. And the connections between acid rain and acid lakes were statistically too weak to correlate.

No Correlation

The reaction to the interim assessment by the environmentalists and their allies in Congress was fury and the firing of NAPAP's director, Dr. Lawrence Kulp, and the demand that the new director of NAPAP, Dr. James R. Mahoney, "rewrite" the report and produce "an implicit repudiation of the interim assessment."

Yet Mahoney was handed a study by the EPA's own Direct Delayed Response Project (DDRP) with a chart that shows *no* statistical correlation between acid rain deposition and acidic lakes. For New England, the correlation between acid rain and acid lakes is less than 0.16 (statistically insignificant), compared with a correlation of acid lakes with soil chemistry of nearly 0.80.

That data came as no surprise to Dr. Edward Krug, of the Illinois State Water Survey, who authored a 263-page April 1989 study for the U.S. Department of Energy (DOE). This study concludes that aquatic acidification has little, if anything, to do with acid rain and everything to do with land use, soil chemistry and geology.

Lakes and streams get over 90 per cent of their water, not from rain, but from the surface runoff that is filtered first through very acidic surface soils and organic matter and then through bedrock, which tends to neutralize that acidity.

Natural Processes

In those areas where the forest surface is allowed to develop, uncut, unharvested and unburnt, surface soil acidity builds up so much that the bedrock below is hard-pressed to neutralize it all. This is especially true in steep mountainous areas where

water runoff goes more directly from the soil into the lake or stream or in those areas like Cape Cod where the underlying surface is not rock but acidic vegetation such as sphagnum moss.

Paleolimnological (lake sediment analysis) studies in fact show that 90 per cent of the presently acidic lakes in the Northeast and Scandinavia were acidic in pre-industrial times. Even the NAPAP report indicates that aquatic acidification is far less than thought. Krug maintains most of that is re-acidification.

"Contrary to predictions of the acid rain theory, highly acidic surface water can be a natural phenomenon."

What made some of those lakes become less acid by the early 20th Century was hundreds of years of clear-cutting and burning that not only destroyed the acidic buildup of forest floor organic material but also replaced it with ash, which is alkaline. Conversely, when those regions were then allowed to reforest, the re-acidification process began.

As Dr. Krug pointed out in a 1983 article in *Science* magazine, "In New England, the volume of standing wood has increased by about 70 per cent between 1952 and 1976." As recently as 1922, 90 per cent of the Adirondacks and northern New England had been completely clear-cut. Now they are virtually totally reforested.

"Given the effects of vegetation on soil acidification," Krug noted, "there is little doubt that this recovery of landscapes from earlier disturbances can result in increasingly acid surface soil horizons and the thickening and acidification of forest floors.

"Thus mountainous areas of the northeastern United States are not pristine environments that are acted on only by acid rain. These landscapes which were disturbed (cut over and burnt) in the past are undergoing soil transformation processes that produce the greatest increases in natural soil acidity."

Krug also cites controlled experiments which repeatedly show that when highly acid snow melt is leached through less-acid soil, the resulting water has the same acidity as the soil, showing that natural surface acidity is the controlling factor in watersheds, while acid rain effects are at most trivial.

A classic example is Hubbard Brook in New Hampshire, which has remained strongly acidic even as the rain acidity in New Hampshire has in fact declined for 25 years.

Dr. Krug reports that "The highest percentages of highly acidic lakes in North America exist in relatively low- or no-acid deposition areas. This suggests the possibility that, contrary to predictions of the acid rain theory, highly acidic surface water can be a natural phenomenon of these regions."

For example, 12 per cent of Florida lake surfaces are acid, but its rain is only one-sixth as acid as the Adirondacks, which have less than 2 per cent acid lake surfaces.

Krug's best example is southwest Tasmania off Australia, whose climate and topography most clearly resemble Northeast America. Southwest Tasmania enjoys pristine nonacidic rainwater, yet over 28 per cent of the lakes and streams there are highly acidic; but its rainwater is in fact quite alkaline.

As Krug told us, "In statistically weighing possible causes of lake acidification, acid rain does not even show up as a significant variable, let alone correlative."

No wonder the EPA and environmentalists have worked hard and with some success to drum Krug out of his profession and to ignore his valuable DOE study.

Solving the Problem

The astonishing part of the Bush acid rain program is the weakness of both its economics and its science.

Even if you accept the premise that all of the Northeast and Canadian acid lakes resulted from acid rain (which they did not), you could lime all those lakes back to alkalinity for about $250 an acre by helicopter or $50 an acre by boat.

The National Acid Precipitation Assessment Project (NAPAP) has identified only 15,124 acres of acid lake area (under 2 per cent of the total) in the Northeast and Midwest. You could lime all of these lakes every year for under $4 million by helicopter, under $800,000 by boat, or about 1/10th of 1 per cent of the $3-$4 billion cost of the Bush program.

"Acid conditions can result from natural processes in the watershed involving local soils and vegetation."

And, unlike the Bush sulphur dioxide removal program, this would actually *ensure* de-acidification of lakes.

Environmentalists oppose this solution because it would undermine their bureaucratic and ideological agenda and would expose the weak science on which acid rain remediation is based.

In 1987, the National Park Service refused the state of Massachusetts' offer to lime the lakes and ponds in the Cape Cod National Sea Shore, 40 per cent of which are acidic.

The trouble is those ponds and lakes are *naturally* acidic (like over 90 per cent of all acidic lakes). In

this case it is because of the sphagnum moss that lines their bottoms. The Park Service explicitly didn't want to disturb that "natural ecosystem."

As Superintendent Herbert Ohlsen wrote the Massachusetts officials in 1987, "As you know, all of the paleolimnological evidence indicates a 12,000-year history of predominantly acidic lake conditions on outer Cape Cod. We know of no data to support your Division's assumption that significant impact (i.e., pond acidification) is occurring due to current acid rain."

In short, cutting SO_2 emissions will have *no* effect on the acidity of Cape Cod lakes which comprise over half of all acidic lakes in southern New England. Ohlsen told the Audobon Society that "Such acid conditions can result from natural processes in the watershed involving local soils and vegetation, and have been well known for many years."

Warren T. Brookes is a nationally syndicated columnist for the Detroit News.

viewpoint 3

Acid Rain Threatens Human Health

Rose Marie L. Audette

The rap for killing lakes, streams and their dependent fish life has been hung firmly around acid rain's neck. Acid rain has also been charged with killing trees, the phenomenon of "forest dieback" that the Germans call *Waldsterben*.

But acid rain has yet to be indicted on perhaps its most insidious offense: Acid rain is a health hazard.

For humans, the worry is not the acidic rain itself, though you probably wouldn't want to have been in Wheeling, W.Va., when rain as acidic as battery acid fell, or in Jacksonville, Fla., when acidic rain dissolved the paint on 2,000 imported BMW's.

The Dangerous Effects

Rather, scientists and health professionals worry about two more dangerous effects of acid rain:

• The air pollutants that cause acid rain—often called "acid rain precursors"—harm humans. They assault the respiratory systems of healthy adults and take their heaviest toll on the most vulnerable—children, the elderly and those who already have asthma and bronchitis.

• In addition, acid precipitation has been shown to acidify water, increasing the leaching of toxic substances like lead, cadmium, asbestos and aluminum from soil and water pipes into drinking water.

Fran DuMelle, Washington director of the American Lung Association, has been working on clean air issues at the national level since 1979. In that time, she's seen Congress' interest in the health effects of air pollutants "come and go." After an initial bout of hearings in the early 1980s, the health effects question became "quiescent," DuMelle says.

But in the scientific world, research continued. Since 1982, dramatic new evidence has amassed—

evidence that points clearly to acid rain's detrimental health effects. . . .

Sen. George Mitchell (D-Maine) called hearings in February 1987 on the health effects of acid rain before his Environmental Pollution Subcommittee of the Senate Environment and Public Works Committee.

"Current levels of acid air pollution are able to produce substantial adverse health effects in certain segments of the American population and particularly in children," Dr. Philip J. Landrigan, a professor of community medicine and pediatrics at the Mt. Sinai School of Medicine, told the hearing.

Landrigan estimated that acid rain is probably the third largest cause of lung disease after active smoking and passive smoking.

Some 50,000 premature deaths a year in the United States and Canada may result from sulfates and other particulates, according to a key report from the congressional Office of Technology Assessment (OTA), which attempted to provide "reasonable estimates" of acid rain's toll.

Making Rain Acidic

Normal rain is slightly acidic with a 5.6 on the pH scale that measures acidity. In certain troubled parts of the United States and Canada, however, rain is 30 to 40 times more acidic than normal rain, averaging a pH of 4 to 4.3.

The key elements to watch in the acid rain phenomenon are sulfur dioxide (SO_2) and nitrogen oxides (NO_X, which is pronounced like box), both emitted by a number of human sources. In 1980, about 65 percent of SO_2 emissions came from electric utilities' burning of coal and other fossil fuels. For NO_X, 44 percent came from cars, trucks and other "mobile sources" and 29 percent were the products of utility combustion.

Once in the air, SO_2 and NO_X mix with other airborne chemicals and water to form a batch of

Rose Marie L. Audette, "Acid Rain Is Killing More than Lakes and Trees," *Environmental Action*, May/June 1987. Reprinted with permission.

"secondary pollutants," including sulfuric acid, nitric acid, sulfates and nitrates. When SO_2, NO_X or the secondary pollutants drop to earth accompanying rain, snow, sleet or hail, that's acid precipitation.

A related pollutant—though not an acid rain precursor—is ozone, a key ingredient of smog. Ozone forms when NO_X mixes with hydrocarbons from auto emissions and solvent vapors in the presence of sunlight.

Inhaling Pollutants

The concern for human health is that before being "washed" from the air by precipitation, small particles of these various pollutants can be inhaled and become lodged deep in the lungs.

Emissions of both SO_2 and NO_X have risen steeply since World War II—with SO_2 increasing 50 percent and NO_X increasing 400 percent.

Emissions are also higher in the 31 states in the eastern half of the country. Some 80 percent of the total SO_2 is emitted in those states and 65 percent of the NO_X.

Although emission levels have improved since passage of the Clean Air Act in 1970, if current patterns continue, SO_2 will increase 30 percent and NO_X will rise 50 percent from 1980 to 2010. Unless, that is, a national acid rain program is implemented.

Acute air pollution crises were once all too common. A deadly acidic fog settled on London in December 1952. Thirteen died.

Today, air pollution is still killing, but the deaths are from chronic, long-term exposure.

The population most at risk from these air pollutants includes tens of millions of Americans: Infants, children, the elderly, pregnant women, those with heart disease and the 7 percent of the U.S. population with asthma, emphysema or chronic bronchitis.

At Congress' request, the National Institute of Environmental Health Sciences (NIEHS) convened two workshops of scientists in 1983 and 1984 to "assess the state of knowledge of the possible effects of acid rain on human health." Dr. James Fouts, senior scientific advisor to the NIEHS director, is compiling scientific findings in the field. Fouts believes that progress has been made in studying acid rain's health effects.

Similar to Tobacco Research

Fouts compares the state of knowledge to tobacco research in the 1950s, when it was known that cigarette smoke was harmful, but not to what degree. "We've shown in animals that when they breathe these air pollutant constituents, they get in trouble. We can show some decrements in lung function in humans. But we need more studies to pin down the range of responses."

Children are especially at risk, testified Dr. Richard M. Narkewicz at the February hearings on the health effects of acid rain. Narkewicz, a practicing pediatrician in Burlington, Vt. and president of the American Academy of Pediatrics, testified that the "ingredients of acid rain," specifically ozone, sulfates and NO_X, "cause disease in children and aggravate pre-existing respiratory conditions."

Pulmonary disease accounts for one-fifth of all hospitalizations of children under 15. Children have more acute respiratory infections than adults because their immune system isn't fully developed, Narkewicz said, and irritating pollutants make those infections worse.

Narkewicz explained why children are more vulnerable to air pollutants. "Children's airways are much narrower than an adult's. The diameter of the bronchus at the root of an adult bronchial tree averages about one inch; the same bronchus in a child is about an eighth of an inch. A minor irritation caused by acid air pollution, which would produce only a slight response in an adult, will result in a dangerous level of swelling in the lining of the narrow airway of a child. Although children's airways are small . . . they breathe more rapidly and move more of the pollutants past airway and lung surfaces than do adults."

"Children have more acute respiratory infections than adults . . . and irritating pollutants make those infections worse."

Some of the key scientific work on acid air pollutants comes from two Canadian scientists, Dr. David Bates and Dr. Bonnie Stern.

Bates was in London working on emphysema and bronchitis when the 1952 killer fog struck. He was involved in tobacco research in the 1950s. And since 1977, Bates, a professor of medicine at the University of British Columbia, has been studying levels of air pollutants measured by 15 monitoring stations in Ontario Province and their relationship to hospital admissions for pulmonary conditions (asthma, bronchitis and viral and bacterial pneumonia).

He found a "consistent" and "highly significant" relationship between hospital admissions during the summer and levels of sulfates and ozone in the air. "Admissions go up when pollution goes up," Bates says.

These hospitalizations for acute health problems are just "the top of a pyramid," Bates says. "That you can show it at all, means almost certainly that there are much larger effects that you can't prove."

The actual cause of these health problems, Bates cautions, may not be ozone and sulfates, but some other pollutant present along with these pollutants.

Although he found no link between hospital admissions and SO_2 or NO_X levels, the mystery actor could be sulfuric aerosols.

Dr. Bonnie Stern works for the Canadian government's Health and Welfare department. She has been studying what she calls the "acid pollutant mix" of sulfates, particles and ozone.

Her 1983 "summercamp" studies monitored respiratory health by having 1,400 children blow into a machine that measured their lung capacity. Half the group, in a heavy acid deposition area in Ontario, showed a "small but statistically significant decrement in lung function" compared to another group of children in an unpolluted area of Manitoba.

Children in the high-impact area showed short-term decreases in lung function 14 hours after levels of sulfate, particles and ozone rose. Stern cautions that the findings are "suggestive but not conclusive." Although adjusted for parental smoking and socio-economic status, the health differences could result from unexamined differences between the two geographic areas, such as indoor air quality.

The long-term effects of this periodic decrease in lung capacity is not known. Stern suggests that such "repeated assaults on the lungs" could predispose the child to chronic obstructive lung diseases like emphysema and bronchitis later in life, especially if the adult smokes or works in a smelter or chemical factory.

Other Studies

A number of other studies have added pieces to the puzzle. Mt. Sinai's Landrigan summarized some of them at a February 1987 Senate hearing:

• Preliminary evidence from the massive "Harvard Six-City Study" shows that acid air pollution, particularly fine particulates associated with total sulfate particulates, produces respiratory symptoms like bronchitis in school children.

• Controlled studies of human volunteers at the University of Rochester showed that exposing normal adults to sulfuric acid aerosols produced "respiratory dysfunction." Similar effects appeared in asthmatics when they were exposed to even lower pollutant levels.

• A major laboratory study underway at New York University showed that repeatedly exposing healthy animals to "modest exposures" of sulfuric acid mist produced "hyperresponsive airways." If those animals were later exposed to air pollutants or cold air, the animals suffered "bronchoconstriction similar to that seen in asthma."

This data confirms that "current, relatively low levels of air pollution can produce toxic effects in the lung," Landrigan concluded. "These effects are not benign. Nor do they represent a form of adaptation of the respiratory tract to pollutant exposure. They are, in fact, pathologic effects. Whether they have long-term consequences remains to be seen."

Best-documented and best-understood among the effects of acid rain are its impacts on lakes, streams and aquatic life. A 1986 report from the National Academy of Sciences determined that there was "a causal relationship" between acid rain and acidification of lakes and streams. Surveys by the Environmental Protection Agency (EPA) have found that acid rain has increased the acidity of surface waters and shallow groundwaters in many parts of the country.

"Acid rain has increased the acidity of surface waters and shallow groundwaters in many parts of the country."

Another well-known scientific fact is that acidified water is "aggressive," which means it can leach unwanted substances into drinking water. The solubility of a number of toxic metals—cadmium, aluminum, copper, mercury and lead, for example—increases as water's acidity increases. These toxic substances are then more likely to be picked up from corroded water pipes and from the solder that holds those pipes together, as well as from whatever soil the water passes through before reaching reservoirs or seeping into underground aquifers—including, at times, city dumps and toxic landfills.

This leaching is particularly a concern in the northeastern United States where soil is naturally thin, rocky and acidic. "There's no doubt that metals can be leached by acid in acid rain," says Dr. James Fouts of NIEHS. "The question is how much?"

Cadmium. Acid-soluble cadmium can be released from galvanized pipe or copper-zinc solder. Because of its long half-life, cadmium levels build up in the body over time. It is associated with kidney damage. Elevated levels have been recorded in drinking water supplies impacted by acid rain.

Aluminum. As water pH decreases, mobilization of normally insoluble aluminum—which makes up 5 percent of the earth's crust—rises. Aluminum has been connected to Alzheimer's and Parkinson's diseases and some disorders of the central nervous system.

Lead. Where drinking water is corrosive, lead levels have been found to be three times higher in the "first flush" water sample. An EPA study leaked to the press found that nearly 40 million people—one out of every five Americans—has drinking water with lead levels higher than EPA's proposed new standard of 20 parts per billion. Lead has been associated with brain damage in children and increased risk of hypertension and heart attack in adult white males.

A study of New York City's drinking water supply by the Environmental Defense Fund (EDF) focused on the Catskill watersheds, which supply 40 percent of the city's drinking water and are located in an area where rain averages a pH of 4.2 compared to normal rain's 5.6 pH.

"Nitrates in the system have been increasing since at least 1960 and that increase is attributable to atmospheric deposition," says EDF scientist Michael Oppenheimer. Though nitrate levels are currently at 25 percent of the health standard, the study said, they are "rapidly approaching" the limit and will exceed it if acid rain continues.

"Well water has . . . been shown to contain higher levels of lead and copper in areas impacted by acid rain."

The study also confirmed that acid rain causes leaching of toxic substances. "Acid rain has increased the corrosivity of the system's water," Oppenheimer says. "As a result, piping is leaching heavy metals."

Most at risk from leaching may be users of small, private or rural water facilities, which may not routinely monitor or treat water. This is even more true of private systems where families draw water directly from wells or rainwater collection systems. Shallow well water has also been shown to contain higher levels of lead and copper in areas impacted by acid rain.

Rose Marie L. Audette is editor of Environmental Action, *the bimonthly magazine of Environmental Action, Inc., a lobbying and educational organization.*

"Several possible routes have been proposed by which 'acid rain' might constitute a threat to human health. There is no... evidence to support any of them."

viewpoint 4

Acid Rain Does Not Threaten Human Health

Edison Electric Institute

Scientists from industry, universities, and government are engaged in the most extensive and most expensive environmental research effort ever undertaken. Their subject is "acid rain" and related chemical, biological, and environmental phenomena.

The research is paying off. Much more is known today but the subject is so broad and so complex that many of the bits and pieces that make up the fabric of new knowledge about "acid rain" have not been integrated into a coherent picture of the realities that have been uncovered. . . .

The Acid Precipitation Act of 1980 sparked an intensified research effort in both the public and private sectors. New findings began to emerge from the research as early as 1981, and the flow of reports and assessments has accelerated dramatically since then.

Much of the new information creates an understanding about the sources and the impacts of acidic precipitation that differs markedly from the picture drawn earlier.

The consistency of the new findings is impressive. So are the conclusions reported in numerous reviews and assessments prepared by or for government agencies and professional and industry groups. In late 1983, observers at The Hudson Institute reported detecting "an emerging scientific backlash" as increasing numbers of scientists challenged the conventional conclusions about the role of precipitation acidity as the chief culprit threatening sensitive ecosystems.

Differences of opinion on scientific matters are not new. They have occurred for hundreds of years. Indeed, the scientific process involves formulating hypotheses and then developing appropriate proof of the validity or non-validity of the hypothesis. After proof has been offered in the literature, scientific peers review, evaluate and repeat experimental challenges until doubts are resolved.

Highly qualified observers may well differ in their views of scientific matters, but strength of conviction does not establish the facts. Only four centuries ago, astronomers and philosophers "knew" that the heavenly bodies circled the earth, and Copernicus's alternative hypothesis that the earth circles the sun was widely rejected. In 1632, Galileo was sentenced to life imprisonment for publishing calculations that supported the Copernican view.

More recently, experts believed the best way to conquer the harmful smog in Los Angeles was first to eliminate backyard incineration of trash, then to reduce sulfur emissions in the area. After these steps were taken and proved ineffective, it was learned that hydrocarbons and nitrogen oxides were responsible for the chemical processes that generate smog. Restrictions imposed on vehicular emissions of nitrogen compounds eventually led to the relief of the smog problem and proof that the earlier hypothesis was in error.

Challenging Old Concepts

The knowledge of acid rain similarly has changed as new facts and interpretations have emerged. The scientific literature and the technical reviews and assessment documents show the nature and the breadth of the changes in fundamental knowledge. A new understanding has developed about the sources of atmospheric acidity and the role of acidity in environmental matters.

• "The phenomenon of acidic rainfall has . . . experienced 'growing pains' in the form of misrepresentation of facts, assumptions presented as facts, and inconsistency of opinion as a result of special interest groups on all sides drawing premature conclusions."

American Chemical Society. 1982

Edison Electric Institute, *Acid Rain: Answers to Your Questions,* 1988. © Edison Electric Institute, 1111 19th St. NW, Washington, DC 20036.

• "On the basis of currently available empirical data, we cannot in general determine the relative importance for the net deposition of acids in specific locations of long-range transport from distant sources or more direct influences of local sources. We regard the problem of relating emissions from a given region to depositions in a given receptor region to be of primary importance and recommend that high priority be given to research relevant to its solution."

National Academy of Sciences. 1983

• "[D]uring 1982 and 1983, a growing amount of literature began to emanate from diverse scientific sources that directly challenged the concept that acid rain was the chief culprit in those ecosystems and environments. We have been impressed by the many scientists who appear to have had sufficient opportunity to examine the data and claims carefully about acid precipitation, and who are still emerging and expressing their views in public forums. Some of them with considerable expertise in the relevant areas, have found the earlier conclusions about the risk of damage from acid rain somewhat suspect. . . . Although the outcome of what we have chosen to call 'the emerging scientific backlash' will not be known for a while, we believe that all policymakers who are interested in obtaining the best technical information about the effects of acid rain should pay particular attention to the trend of opinions among scientists in the U.S. and Europe during the next few years."

F.E. Armbruster, W.M. Brown and D. Yokelson. Hudson Institute. 1983

The summary is but a sampling of the literature. It is intended to reflect the scope and weight of the evidence now available. As information and understanding spread from individual to individual and from scientists to the general public, it is likely that a more realistic view of "acid rain" will be established. In turn, a broader understanding of the facts should help resolve the issue on the technical evidence rather than by political action. . . .

"Press accounts attributing . . . deaths to acid rain strain the credulity of knowledgeable scientists. . . ."

Does acid rain threaten human health? Several possible routes have been proposed by which "acid rain" might constitute a threat to human health. There is no scientifically accepted evidence to support any of them.

Direct inhalation of acidic particles now seems to be of minor concern, probably because the level of acidity in rain is not much different from that of the mucous lining of the human respiratory tract. There is greater concern about the inhalation of sulfate particles, which are said to aggravate asthma and other respiratory conditions, but the concentrations of sulfate that could cause such effects are far greater than those which occur in locations 100 or more miles from major emissions sources.

Some observers have been concerned about acidified drinking water and the possibility that this might release toxic quantities of metallic ions such as mercury or cadmium from soils, or copper and lead from pipes and plumbing solder. If the acidity of drinking water were responsible for toxic metal contamination, however, it is likely that the acidity would come primarily from the decayed organic matter on the forest floor rather than from precipitation.

No Present Threat

• A California researcher reviewed the evidence of health effects from precipitation acidity and reported: "Upon examination of the most recent evidence in each of these areas, we conclude that sulfates, including sulfuric acid, at levels found in the ambient air, produce no effects on mortality or morbidity even in the most vulnerable subgroups of the population. Indeed, the evidence indicates that sulfates do not begin to show an effect until much higher levels are reached. Consequently, it seems clear, on the basis of the current data, that ambient sulfates do not pose a risk to human health at the present time, and there is no indication that in the future there will be any such health risk from ambient exposure to sulfates."

A.V. Colucci. 1981

• The Interagency Task Force on Acid Precipitation notes that there is a "[p]otential for acidification of surface waters, groundwaters, and wetlands to affect human health, . . . but the linkage to acid deposition, if any, remains unclear."

Interagency Task Force. 1982

• An EPA [Environmental Protection Agency] Assistant Administrator in 1982 commented on a national press story which "incorrectly cites [an Office of Technology Assessment report that] acid rain is killing as many as 51,000 Americans," adding that "EPA has thoroughly evaluated this body of data . . . [and finds that] the collective judgment of most health scientists, including the Clean Air Scientific Advisory Committee, is that available studies do not provide a reliable basis for the kinds of calculations done by OTA.

"Further compounding the problem of what we believe to be unreliable quantitative inferences drawn from available data, press accounts attributing these deaths to acid rain strain the credulity of knowledgeable scientists studying the acid

precipitation phenomenon."
K.M. Bennett. 1982

• The Critical Assessment Review asserts that "indirect health effects that may be causally related to acidic deposition have not been demonstrated in human populations. . . . No adverse human health effects have been documented as being a consequence of metal mobilization by acidic deposition. . . . Acute or chronic diseases in humans have not been related to normal dietary intake of aluminum from food or drinking waters." The potential for problems from aluminum in water used for kidney dialysis was cited.
T.W. Clarkson, J.P. Baker and W.E. Sharpe. 1984

• Harvard School of Public Health investigators concluded: "[The results of human clinical studies] have shown no significant effects from exposure to sulfates or sulfuric acid aerosol at current ambient levels and even at appreciable higher levels."
B.G. Ferris and J.H. Ware. 1983

• In its 1983 report, the Interagency Task Force noted: "[N]o significant indirect human health effects have yet been documented in the United States as being a consequence of the deposition of acid. . . . The National Program's first survey of New England municipal drinking water supplies did not indicate any demonstrable effects from acid deposition."
Interagency Task Force. 1983

Safe Drinking Water
• Arthur D. Little, Inc., studying the health implications of acid rain on drinking water concluded: "[suggestions from the literature] that pipe corrosion problems result predominantly from acid rain are not supported by the evidence presented. . . . At the present time, there is insufficient evidence to support a conclusion that acid rain produces or contributes significantly to adverse health effects by the route of mobilizing the contaminants in drinking water. . . . Based on current practices, for most people in the continental United States, there is likely to be little or no relationship between the quality of their tap water and acid rain."
A.D. Little. 1983

• Work Group I of the U.S.-Canada Memorandum of Intent review found no evidence that human health is directly or indirectly threatened by acidic deposition: "Available information gives little cause for concern over direct health effects from acidic deposition.". . . "Again, no clear evidence of health effects arising from the consumption of drinking water contaminated with metals from acidic deposition are reported in the literature, but some

potential problems are identified.". . . "With respect to the direct inhalation of transported air pollutants for which standards exist, no adverse human health effects are anticipated, providing the ambient air quality standards are not exceeded."
U.S./Canada Work Group 1. 1983

• The New England Water Works Association, completing a study of drinking water supplies in six New England states and in New York's Adirondack region, concluded that the waters "tested in round 1 of the study would not endanger human health when ingested."
F.B. Taylor and G.E. Symons. 1984

• EPA's Dr. John Bachmann, reviewing the current work on human health effects, found "no concrete evidence now exists for acid deposition causing health effects."
Interagency Task Force. 1984

"For most people in the continental United States, there is likely to be little or no relationship between the quality of their tap water and acid rain."

• Despite the widely publicized reference to a controversial Brookhaven National Laboratory estimate that "about 2 percent (a range of 0 to 5 percent) of the deaths per year in the United States and Canada might be attributable to atmospheric sulfate-particle pollution" [see Bennett remarks], the Office of Technology Assessment Report also includes such conclusions as " . . . there is no direct evidence showing detectable effects on human health from maximum likely environmental concentrations of sulfate particles *alone*. . . ." "Nonetheless, scientists generally have been unable to attribute effects to any *single* element of the pollution mix," and "No direct relationship has yet been established between acid deposition and degradation of drinking-water quality."
Office of Technology Assessment. 1984

Edison Electric Institute is an association of electric companies which acts as a liaison between the industry and the federal government.

Pollution Causes Acid Rain

James L. Regens and Robert W. Rycroft

Perhaps, when all is said and done, it is not really so remarkable that acidification could go unnoticed for years—right up to the end of the 1960s. In contrast to environmental influences of many other kinds, acidification is a furtive process—in its early days almost unnoticeable. Our senses of smell and taste are not capable of distinguishing between acidified and unaffected lake or well water. The clear limpid water in an acidic forest lake can also, in many cases, lend it a deceptive beauty. And the trees growing in an acidified forest area look just like trees anywhere else, at least as long as the acidification is moderate.
—*Swedish National Environmental Protection Board (1981)*

What is acid rain and why should we be concerned about it? Acid rain commonly refers to what is identified more precisely as the wet and dry processes for the deposition from the atmosphere of acidic inputs into ecosystems. Thus, all forms of precipitation—not just rain—can be acidic. Indeed, the definition includes acidifying compounds that are deposited in dry form. As a result, *acid deposition* is the scientifically accurate and all-encompassing term for acid rain. For simplicity as well as by conventional usage, however, the term *acid rain* is commonly used to include both precipitation and dry deposition.

Since acids release hydrogen ions in a water solution, the relative acidity or alkalinity of any solution is typically described by the percentage of hydrogen ions that a water solution contains measured on the logarithmic potential hydrogen (pH) scale. Hydrogen ions have a positive electrical charge and are called *cations*. Ions with a negative electrical charge are known as *anions*. A substance containing equal concentrations of cations and anions so that the electrical charge is balanced is *neutral*. A solution that is neutral—that is, neither alkaline (base) nor

acid—has a pH value of 7.0. A substance with more hydrogen ions than anions is acidic and has a value of less than 7.0 on the pH scale. Substances with more anions than cations are alkaline and have a pH that measures above 7.0 on the scale. Thus, as the concentration of hydrogen ions increases, the pH decreases to represent greater acidity. The further a reading is from 7.0, below or above, the more acid or base the substance is. Because pH expresses the negative logarithm of acid concentration, interpreting changes in chemical composition can be confusing for many laypersons. The lower the pH value, the higher the acidity. Each full pH unit drop represents a tenfold increase in acidity. For example, a solution whose pH value equals 4.0 contains ten times as much acid, not just 20 percent more, than one measuring 5.0 on the pH scale. And, it is one hundred times more acidic than a substance with a pH of 6.0.

Manmade Sources

All forms of precipitation—rain, snow, sleet, hail, fog, and mist—are naturally somewhat acidic, and human activities have made them more so. For example, in industrial regions, the pH of rainfall is often around or below 4.0, and it has been measured as low as 2.6. In pure water, the "natural" acidity value often is assumed to be pH 5.6, calculated for distilled water in equilibrium with atmospheric carbon dioxide concentrations. This is a somewhat arbitrary value. The presence of other naturally occurring substances such as sulfur dioxide, ammonia, organic compounds, and windblown dust can produce "natural" values ranging from pH 4.9 to 6.5. However, . . . natural sources such as lightning, microbial activity in soils, and biogenic processes make relatively small contributions to total nitrogen and sulfur emissions in the United States. The ratio of anthropogenic to natural sulfur emissions is on the order of at least 3:1 and it is over 7:1 for nitrogen oxide emissions. Thus, because manmade rather than natural sources for the sulfur and nitrogen oxides released into the atmosphere for conversion to acids predominate in North America and Europe, the atmospheric chemistry suggests that reducing anthropogenic emissions of acid rain's major causes should reduce the aggregate level of acidic deposition, although it may have less impact on some sensitive receptor areas than popular impressions imply.

Robert Angus Smith, a nineteenth-century English chemist, might well lay claim to the title of being the "father of acid rain." In his pioneering studies of precipitation chemistry and its effects, Smith first used the term *acid rain*. Drawing upon data measuring the chemistry of rainfall from England, Scotland, and Germany, Smith demonstrated that variation in regional factors such as coal combustion, wind trajectories, the amount and frequency of precipitation, proximity to seacoasts, and the decomposition of organic materials affected sulfate concentrations in precipitation. His efforts of more than a century ago startlingly mirror the contemporary research agenda. For example, he established a network for collecting and analyzing precipitation samples, discovered that the acidity of rain was dominated primarily by its sulfate content, and, perhaps most interestingly, speculated about whether damages to trees and crops were attributable to acid rain, to the direct actions of gaseous pollutants, or to natural factors. Smith's work, however, was largely ignored and failed to generate immediate follow-up research in spite of the fact that he was the inspector-general of the Alkali Inspectorate for the United Kingdom.

"Scientists asserted that precipitation acidity attributable to . . . industrial processes and utilities, was causing adverse ecological and human health effects."

E.B. Cowling asserts that contemporary concern about acid deposition and its effects originated in three seemingly unrelated areas: limnology, agricultural science, and atmospheric chemistry. Svante Oden, in the first major attempt to integrate knowledge from those disciplines, maintained that analyses of air mass trajectories matched to temporal and spatial changes in precipitation chemistry indicated that sulfur and nitrogen were transported long distances, ranging from 100 to 2,000 kilometers. Oden also asserted that clearly identifiable source and receptor areas existed. His analysis formed the initial basis for concluding that acid deposition is a large-scale regional phenomenon with long-term adverse ecological consequences. Thus, information produced by a complex and rapidly evolving body of research forms the scientific basis for defining the acid deposition problem.

Existing Knowledge

Acid rain first emerged as a public policy concern at the 1972 United Nations Conference on the Human Environment in Stockholm. In a case study prepared for the Stockholm conference, Swedish scientists asserted that precipitation acidity attributable to SO_2 emissions from manmade sources, primarily industrial processes and utilities, was causing adverse ecological and human health effects. Largely in response to the Swedish study, a number of major research efforts were initiated in other countries to address the causes of acid deposition, as well as its direct and indirect ecological effects.

The first of those endeavors to identify adverse ecological effects began in Norway in 1972. The Norwegian Interdisciplinary Research Program, commonly referred to as the SNSF Project, focused on establishing the effects of acid precipitation on forests and fish. The SNSF Project, entitled "Acid Precipitation—Effects on Forest and Fish," was the largest multidisciplinary study in Norwegian history. Its annual budget was approximately 10 million Norwegian kroner, equivalent to U.S. $2 million, from 1972 to 1980. The SNSF Project involved cooperative research undertaken by 12 Norwegian institutions and more than 150 scientists. It produced two major international scientific conferences. The first was held midway through the study at Telemark, Norway, in June 1976. The second conference at Sandefjord, Norway, in March 1980 concluded the SNSF Project and provided a forum to evaluate the state of existent knowledge.

In 1972, another major research project, this one in the atmospheric sciences, was undertaken to address the problem of linking source and receptor areas. Acting under the auspices of the Organization for Economic Cooperation and Development (OECD), eleven European nations launched a cooperative effort to measure the contribution of local and transboundary sources to each participating country's sulfur deposition. Austria, Belgium, Denmark, Finland, France, the Federal Republic of Germany, the Netherlands, Norway, Sweden, Switzerland, and the United Kingdom actively participated in the study. Italy participated on a more limited basis in some of the data collection. Data collected by aircraft sampling and at seventy-six ground monitoring sites for the European Air Chemistry Network (EACN) were reported monthly to the Norwegian Institute for Air Research, which coordinated the study. Transfer coefficients derived from long-range transport models that simulate atmospheric processes were used to estimate the relationship between source emissions and receptor deposition levels. The OECD study concluded that SO_2 emissions could be transported long as well as short distances. In five of the eleven countries participating in the study, more than 50 percent of total sulfur deposition was estimated to come from nondomestic sources. However, because of serious problems with the reliability of national emissions data as well as the accuracy of atmospheric transport models for estimating site-specific deposition inputs, the OECD study's findings are subject to plus or minus 50 percent error for individual receptor estimates. Nonetheless, while meteorological changes and more accurate emissions inventories could alter significantly an individual country's contribution, the study reinforced the conclusion that some proportion of the acid deposition occurring over almost all of northwestern Europe is due to transboundary pollution.

"Areas receiving the greatest yearly average of acid deposition are found within or downwind from . . . regions containing major manmade emissions sources."

During the early 1970s, studies conducted in Canada and the United States produced similar concerns about the possible environmental consequences of acid deposition. Thus, by the mid-1970s, studies noting declining pH and speculating about the possible impact of acidification on aquatic and terrestrial ecosystems had been reported in Sweden, Norway, Canada, and the United States. Since the mid-1970s, other Western European countries such as the United Kingdom, the Federal Republic of Germany, the Netherlands, and Austria have become increasingly concerned as the potential impacts of acid deposition have been identified in both their own and neighboring states.

A Complex Phenomenon

The major contributions to acid rain are sulfur oxides, primarily sulfur dioxide and to a lesser extent sulfur trioxide (SO_3), and various oxides of nitrogen, principally nitrogen dioxide (NO_2) and nitric oxide (NO), commonly labeled NO_X. When a fossil fuel is burned, the sulfur and nitrogen in the fuel combine with oxygen in the atmosphere to form sulfur and nitrogen oxides. In contact with air, SO_2 and NO_X are spontaneously oxidized to form sulfate and nitrate. . . .

Unfortunately, the simplicity of the term *acid rain* also conveys the image of an easily measured and understood phenomenon. In fact, the acid rain problem stems from a series of complex and varied

chemical, meteorological, and physical interactions. . . .

Precipitation chemistry data collected in the 1970s and 1980s indicate that acid deposition occurs throughout eastern North America. The area of greatest acidity is concentrated over eastern Ohio, western New York, and northern West Virginia. W.M. Lewis and L.C. Grant found that rural areas in the western United States at a higher elevation also have low pH rainfall, probably due to significant increases in nitrogen oxide emissions throughout the region. . . .

Adverse Effects

The potential for near continental-scale impacts [exists] if adverse effects are linked to loadings of acidic compounds above a given level or rate, assuming those loadings are not neutralized once they fall to earth. Initial examinations of alkalinity levels in U.S. lakes reinforce such a view. An inventory of sensitive but not necessarily altered lakes conducted by EPA [the Environmental Protection Agency] reveals that more than 10 percent of the lakes surveyed in the eastern United States have pH levels of 6.0 or below, with the Adirondacks and the upper Midwest having the largest proportion of lakes with low acid neutralizing capacity. Similarly, EPA's companion survey of lakes in the West revealed that while fewer than 1 percent of the 10,400 lakes in California, the Pacific Northwest, and the Rocky Mountains have become dangerously acidic, more than two-thirds of the region's lakes had limited acid neutralizing capacity.

One cannot assume automatically that acids are not neutralized in some potentially sensitive areas. Field studies suggest that this may occur in some alpine and subalpine lakes of the Sierra Nevada mountain range in California. Even in areas whose hydrology and geochemistry fail to neutralize acid rain inputs completely, it is important to consider the interaction of acid rain with the acidifying effects of natural soil formation processes and long-term changes in land use practices when establishing the geographical extent of actual or potential damages. Nonetheless, given the acidity levels of precipitation, a policymaker might want information about the possibility of controlling the sources of acid rain.

For eastern North America, sulfur dioxide and nitrogen oxide emissions from manmade sources are estimated to be at least ten times greater than those from natural sources such as ocean-land fluxes and vegetation. Clearly, subject to technological and economic constraints, emissions from manmade sources such as electric utilities, industrial boilers, and motor vehicles can be limited through fuel switching, precombustion cleaning and/or postcombustion flue gas desulfurization. And because the pH of rainfall is more acidic than one might expect due to natural processes, the monitoring data encourage policymakers to seek information about the geographical distribution of manmade sources of precursor emissions. The areas receiving the greatest yearly averages of acid deposition are found within or downwind from, and relatively proximate to, regions containing major manmade emissions sources.

"Emissions can have direct effects, such as the acidification of lakes and streams, plant damage, or reduced forest growth."

Tall stacks at a number of point sources, especially electric utilities, contribute to the likelihood of chemical conversion and the long-range transport of these emissions as acidic compounds. The taller the stack from which the pollutants are emitted, the higher the gases rise into the atmosphere. This reduces ambient concentrations in the vicinity, but increases the potential for those pollutants coming to earth elsewhere. An estimated 429 stacks taller than 200 feet were built in the United States between 1970 and 1979. Most of the tallest, those in excess of 800 feet, were built in the Midwest and Southeast. Prevailing winds from those regions typically move in a northeasterly direction toward New England and Canada. This is consistent with the view that manmade, or *anthropogenic* sources, contribute overwhelmingly to the emissions of acidic precursors.

As a result, assumptions about the relationship between emission sources and receptor areas form the basis for any acid rain control strategy. And because public policies represent a response to perceived problems, this raises the question of the actual or potential adverse effects of acid rain on human health and the environment. As P. Huber notes, "Surely [the] most important question is why anyone cares whether rain, lake or soil acidity is changing." The most obvious, but not necessarily the sole answer, is that if socially valued resources are at risk and damage can be prevented, reduced, or mitigated, then action should be considered.

Environmental Effects

Acid deposition and/or sulfur and nitrogen oxide emissions are said to affect ecosystems and human health both directly and indirectly. Such emissions can have direct effects, such as the acidification of lakes and streams, plant damage, or reduced forest growth, as well as indirect effects on human health or reduced visibility. Critics of additional controls, however, maintain that the "huge acid rain research effort provides ample data showing that the link

between SO_2 emissions and the acidity of rain is far weaker than generally supposed, and, further, that the link between acid rain and ecological damage is even weaker, or nearly nonexistent." What, then, do we know about the environmental impact of acid rain?

Conclusive evidence points to chemical and biological changes, including fish kills, in lakes and streams that have limited capacities to neutralize acidic inputs. This can affect sport fishing, tourism, and other values associated with aquatic resources. As T.D. Crocker and James L. Regens point out, however, the "current economic consequences of these effects are small relative to the economic value of all freshwater sport fishing in North America, and estimates (even with order-of-magnitude errors) of the value of current effects on other categories. Too many substitute lakes and too many alternative outdoor recreational opportunities exist." This underscores current limitations in our knowledge of the magnitude of aquatic damages and the controversy that can accompany efforts to establish quantitative estimates of the value of benefits.

Evidence of damages to nonaquatic ecosystems, especially forests, is largely circumstantial. In part, this reflects limited research. It also reflects the often synergystic nature of effects attributable to air pollution in the ambient environment, which is more analogous to a chemical soup than individual, discrete pollutants exerting effects in a noninteractive fashion. As a result, impacts are plausible, and evidence of nonaquatic effects, especially on forest productivity, is growing. For example, adverse effects on forests may result from the leaching out of soil nutrients or through the mobilization of toxic metals.

Long-Term Effects

As a result, many are concerned about the harmful, long-term effects of acid deposition on trees—particularly spruce, pine, aspen, and birch. H.M. Vogelmann asserts that studies of mature forests in the northeastern United States indicate reduced growth patterns as well as increased mortality for primarily coniferous species in recent decades. Because causal linkages are complex, conclusions about forest effects remain somewhat equivocal. However, acid deposition does appear to be one of various stresses affecting forest ecosystems, although obviously acid rain is not the only potential culprit. A combination of atmospheric pollutants—acidic deposition, sulfur dioxide, ozone— as well as drought, temperature shifts, pathogens, and heavy metals like lead have been implicated.

Unlike the effects on aquatic ecosystems and the possible effects on forests, no clear evidence of a direct link between ambient levels of acid deposition and injury to agricultural crops has been demonstrated. The emerging consensus that acid deposition fails to damage crops is not surprising, since farmers use agricultural practices to manage acidic and alkaline inputs to their soils.

Concern has also been expressed about the impact of acid deposition on outdoor sculpture, historic monuments, buildings, and other structures. Environmentalists refer frequently, because of their emotional appeal, to the damage to priceless artifacts like the Parthenon or the Statue of Liberty. Damage to the Acropolis has been traced primarily to emissions from nearby traffic and from an oil refinery only a few kilometers away. The Statue of Liberty sits in New York Harbor, where the sea water typically measures around pH 8.2 to 8.4, which is highly alkaline. Its damage appears to have resulted from failed insulation that allowed electrolytic corrosion to take place between the statue's copper sheathing and iron framework, as well as from a century's exposure to corrosive sea salts. As a consequence, while field studies have linked materials damage to air pollution, such damage is most prevalent in urban areas with high concentrations of ambient sulfur dioxide. This suggests the impact of primarily local rather than distant sources.

Reducing Emissions

Finally, unlike respirable sulfates or fine particulate matter, acid deposition does not appear to represent a direct threat to human health. Limited health risks may be associated with acid fog episodes or the leaching of metals such as lead into drinking water supplies, although most drinking water supply systems already have treatment facilities for liming to neutralize acid inputs, thereby preventing metals leaching.

"Acid deposition is an environmental problem."

We can use what we already know from the physical and biological sciences to construct a policy rationale for either maintaining existing emissions control programs and expanding R&D [research and development] or initiating additional control measures. First, although the extent as well as the rate at which damage occurs remains uncertain, the widespread recognition that acid deposition is an environmental problem, combined with its salience on the policy agenda, has compelled governments to respond. Second, manmade sources are the overwhelming contributors to acid deposition in eastern North America. While it is expensive, control technology is available to reduce emissions from those sources significantly. Third, a National Academy of Sciences (NAS) report concluded that reductions in sulfur dioxide emissions over a broad

area for several years can be reasonably assumed to produce a proportionate reduction in annual average sulfate deposition for that area if all other factors, including climatic factors, remain constant. Finally, other parameters of air quality in eastern North America—regional visibility, particulate matter loadings, and ambient sulfur dioxide levels—are affected strongly by the causes of acid deposition. As a result, they are likely to be improved if atmospheric loadings of precursor emissions are reduced.

James L. Regens is associate director of the Institute of Natural Resources at the University of Georgia in Athens. Formerly, he served on the Environmental Protection Agency's Task Force on Acid Precipitation. Robert W. Rycroft is director of the graduate program in science, technology, and public policy at George Washington University in Washington, D.C.

"Singling out sulfur dioxide produced by human activities as the major cause of acid rain is not only a gross over-simplification, but probably wrong."

Pollution Does Not Cause Acid Rain

Dixy Lee Ray

The Great Acid Rain Debate has been going on for more than a decade. Public alarm in the United States probably dates from a widely publicized 1974 report which concluded that "the northeastern U.S. has an extensive and severe acid precipitation problem." Does it? Probably not. Is rain really acidic? Yes. Does acid rain, or preferably, acid precipitation, really damage forests, lakes and streams, fish, buildings and monuments? Yes, in some instances, but not as the primary or only cause. Can the adverse environmental effects that have been attributed to acid rain—whatever the real cause—be mitigated by reducing the amount of sulfur dioxide emitted to the atmosphere from industrial sources? No, what evidence there is suggests that it cannot be. Is enough known, and understood, about acid precipitation to warrant spending billions of dollars of public funds on supposed corrective measures? Certainly not.

Clearly, the U.S. Environmental Protection Agency agrees with this assessment, for the agency's administrator, Lee M. Thomas, said in 1986: "Current scientific data suggest that environmental damage would not worsen materially if acidic emissions continued at their present levels for ten or twenty more years. Acid rain is a serious problem, but it is not an emergency."

Past Research

That rain is acidic has been known for a long time. Among the first records are a reference to acid rain in Sweden in 1848 and a discussion on the chemistry of English rain in 1872. Sulfur dioxide was established as a possible cause of damage to trees and other plants in Germany in 1867. The commonly repeated alarm that rainfall has become increasingly acidic over the past twenty-five years rests for its validity on an influential and oft-cited series of articles by G.E. Likens and his co-workers published in the 1970s. Careful evaluation by a group of scientists at Environmental Research and Technology Inc. reveals that Likens's research suffered from problems in data collection and analysis, errors in calculations, questionable averaging of some data, selection of results to support the desired conclusions, and failure to consider all the available data. In a more recent study, Vaclav Smil of the University of Manitoba reached similar conclusions. Besides analyzing Likens's methods of determining rain acidity, Smil examined maps of the distribution of acid precipitation in the eastern U.S. between the mid-1950s and the mid-1960s, prepared by Likens et al. and publicized as providing "unassailable proofs" of rising acidity. "In reality," Smil concludes, "the measurement errors, incompatibility of collection and analytical procedures, inappropriate extrapolations, weather effects and local interferences, make such maps very dubious."

Rain forms when molecules of water vapor condense on ice crystals or salt crystals or minute particles of dust in clouds and then coalesce to form droplets that respond to the force of gravity. As rain falls through the atmosphere it can "pick up" or "wash out" chemicals or other foreign materials or pollutants that may be present. Because water is such a good solvent, even in the cleanest air, rainwater dissolves some of the naturally present carbon dioxide, forming carbonic acid. Hence, rainwater is *always acidic* or if you like, acid rain is normal. There is no such thing as naturally neutral rainwater. Scientific studies generally distinguish between "acid rain," i.e., the acidity of rainwater itself, and "acid deposition," i.e., the fallout of sulfates, nitrates, and other acidic substances. Acid deposition may be "wet" if washed out of the

Dixy Lee Ray, "The Great Acid Rain Debate," *The American Spectator,* January 1987. Reprinted by permission.

atmosphere with rain, or "dry" if gases or particles simply settle out.

How acidic is pure water? Despite the fact that water molecules are very stable, with a chemical composition of two parts hydrogen to one part oxygen (H_2O), the molecular structure or architecture is somewhat asymmetrical; the molecules tend both to clump and to dissociate in response to intermolecular forces. Dissociation leads to a few hydrogen ions carrying a positive charge and an equal number of OH or hydroxyl ions with a negative charge. Under normal conditions, in pure distilled water only a few molecules are dissociated, in fact, about two-ten millionths of one percent. Now 2/10,000,000 of 1 percent is an awkward numerical expression. Therefore, for greater ease in expressing the number of dissociated molecules, which is the measure of relative acidity, a method called pH has been adopted. The pH of pure water is 7, the numerical expression of neutrality. Any pH measure below 7 is acidic, any above 7 is basic or alkaline. The pH scale is logarithmic (like the Richter scale for measuring intensity of earthquakes); therefore a change of one pH unit, for example, from pH 5 to pH 6, is a ten-fold change.

Normal Acidity

Water in the atmosphere normally contains some carbonic acid from dissolved carbon dioxide, and the pH of clean rainwater even in pristine regions of the earth is about pH 5.0 to 5.5. Any lower pH is believed to be environmentally damaging. Lakes, streams, rivers, ponds, indeed all bodies of fresh water may and usually do receive dissolved material, either acidic or alkaline, from runoff and from the soil or earthen basin in which the water stands or flows. Both acid and alkaline lakes are natural phenomena, and exist without intervention by humans.

Getting an accurate measure of the pH of rainwater is more difficult than it may at first seem. Certainly it is no simple litmus test; accurate procedures require careful laboratory analyses. For example, early work—that is, measurements taken before 1968—generally used soft glass containers; it is now known that even when the containers were carefully cleaned and when the analysis was done very soon after collection, the soft glass contributed alkalinity to the sample, and this increased with time in storage. Indeed the range of error attributable to the use of soft glass is sufficient so that it might account for the difference in pH measurements between 1955-56 and 1965-66 reported by Coghill and Likens. Rainwater collection made in metal gauges, a common procedure before the 1960s, also influenced the results. An experiment to test this difference, using a dilute solution of sulfuric acid with a pH of 4.39, gave a reading of pH 5.9 when held for a short time in a metal gauge.

It is also now known that a rainwater sample taken at the beginning of a storm will give a pH reading different from that taken during and at the end of the rainfall; that measurements may differ widely at different locales within a region; and that weather and climate affect the results. With regard to this last phenomenon, it may be that the more alkaline results reported by Likens for the northeast U.S. in the 1950s were related to the drought conditions that prevailed during those years. By contrast, the 1960s were rainy. When dry conditions persist, dust particles are more prevalent, and if they are present in the rain samples, they can neutralize some of the acidity and shift the pH toward the alkaline end of the scale.

"Acid rain can . . . be buffered or neutralized by soil conditions."

For several reasons, then, it now appears that the historical data, on which so much of the alarm and worry has been based, are of insufficient quality and quantity to establish as indisputable a trend toward higher acidity in the rainfall of the northeastern United States.

Complicating the acid rain picture still further are results of samples collected from ice frozen in the geological past, and from rainfall in remote regions of the earth. These results suggest that the relationship between acidity and the industrial production of sulfur dioxide emissions is at best extremely tenuous.

Analysis of ice pack samples in the Antarctic and in the Himalayas indicates that precipitation deposited at intervals hundreds and thousands of years ago in those pristine environments had a pH value of 4.4 to 4.8. Some measurements were as low as 4.2. Examination of Greenland ice pack samples shows that many times in the last 7,000 years the acidity of the rain was as high as pH 4.4. In some cases the periods of extremely high acidity lasted for a year or more. Coal-burning utilities spewing out sulfur dioxide could not have been responsible, but these periods of high acidity do correspond to times of major volcanic eruptions. Also remarkable is the period of low acidity in the ice lasting from 1920 to 1960, when no major volcanic eruptions occurred but industrial pollution increased.

Recent measurements taken by the National Oceanic and Atmospheric Administration on Mauna Loa in Hawaii at 3,500 meters above sea level gave average pH values of 4.9 regardless of wind direction. Moreover, sampling at Cape Matatula on American Samoa, a monitoring site selected for its extreme cleanliness, resulted in measurements from pH 4.5 to 6.0 in the rainwater.

To gather more systematic data on the pH of rain

in remote areas, a Global Precipitation Chemistry Project was set up in 1979. Samples of rainwater were tested from five sites: Northern Australia, Southern Venezuela, Central Alaska, Bermuda, and Amsterdam Island in the southern Indian Ocean halfway between Africa and Australia. The first results were published in 1982. Precipitation was everywhere acidic, pH values averaging between 4.8 and 5.0. Now it is possible to imagine that the Bermuda results could have been affected by long-range transport of sulfate aerosols or other atmospheric pollution from the U.S., or that the Alaskan atmosphere is polluted from coal burning in the Midwest, but that does not appear to be reasonable. At the remaining sites, including American Samoa, clearly man-made emissions could not have caused the measured acidity.

Unexpected Results

Conversely, in some areas where one might expect a low pH, actual measurements of the rainwater reveal higher than anticipated pH values. Twelve sites in Mexico, for example, measured pH 6.2 to 6.8; nine inland sites in India gave a median pH of 7.5 (range 5.8 to 8.9). It turns out that the expected natural acidity of the rain is neutralized by suspended alkaline particles, mainly dust from dry fields, unpaved streets, and so on.

In China seventy percent of the basic energy comes from burning coal; sulfur dioxide releases are very high, particularly in urban areas. Rainwater in Peking is nevertheless close to neutral, most values falling between pH 6.0 and 7.0. Interestingly, the same samples have heavy concentrations of sulfate and nitrate ions as well as suspended alkaline matter, probably dust blown from desert regions. The pH is determined by complex interaction among these aerosols, ions, and particles.

Acid rain can also be buffered or neutralized by soil conditions. Studies at nearly 200 sites in the United States show that in the northern Great Plains high levels of calcium and magnesium ions occur, along with ammonia associated with animal husbandry and fertilizers. These combine to neutralize acidic precipitation. In the western half of North America 75 to 96 percent of all acid anions are so neutralized. By way of contrast, in the northeastern U.S. 52 percent of all acid anions are not so neutralized.

Naturally Acidic Soils

It might be that lower levels of alkaline dust, especially in the northeast, are a consequence of successful air pollution control, resulting in the effective capture of particulate matter from industrial smoke. This possibility was investigated in 1985 by Smil, who reports a great loss of airborne alkaline material between the mid-1950s and mid-1960s. This loss resulted from large-scale replacement of coal as fuel for homes, transportation, and industrial boilers, as well as highly efficient removal of fly ash from flue gases. Although exact and accurate calculations are not possible, reasonable estimates of the largely alkaline particulate emissions were about nine million tons annually in the 1950s; this fell to about four million tons by 1975. Actually the total loss of man-made alkaline material over the northeast was probably much larger than the estimates indicate since emission controls were also applied to the iron, steel, and cement industries. And the amount of barren, dusty land shrank with advancing settlements, paved roads, lawns and considerable re-growth of forests. Another contributing factor to loss of alkaline materials may have been the practice of prompt extinction of forest fires. Wildfires, when left to burn themselves out, result in an accumulation of alkaline ash, which, together with the minerals it contains, acts to buffer natural acidity in the soil and redress the mineral imbalance.

One final point should be made about natural acidity and alkalinity. Soils along the North Pacific coast tend to be quite acidic, a usual feature in areas that had been glaciated. Peat bogs are common; cranberries, huckleberries, blueberries, and Douglas Fir trees—all requiring acid soil—are abundant. For comparison, soils in the arid west and southwest are alkaline, and rarely measure a pH below 9.0. By contrast the soils in New England are among the most acid in the world. Representative Adirondack soil measures pH 3.4. Soils in southeast Canada are similar. That region also was glaciated, and the thin poor soil overlays acid granitic material. In other words, the soils of the northeast United States are by nature acidic, and always have been, environmentalist claims notwithstanding.

"The soils of the northeast United States are by nature acidic, and always have been, environmentalist claims notwithstanding."

There is an extensive and growing body of scientific literature on atmospheric chemistry, much of it highly technical. Gradually, understanding is also growing, but many areas of uncertainty remain. Experts are divided on exactly how acids are formed in clouds, in rainwater, and upon deposition. There is some disagreement too on the relative amount and importance of acid precursors from man-made versus natural sources. Most knowledgeable scientists tend to take a middle view, that the amount of pollutants in the air, particularly of sulfates and nitrates, on a global scale comes about equally from natural and human sources, but even this is a supposition or educated guess.

Sulfur and nitrogen compounds—the "acid" in acid rain—are produced naturally by the decay of organic matter in swamps, wetlands, intertidal areas, and shallow waters of the oceans. How much is contributed to the atmosphere from these sources is not known for certain, but it is considerable. Estimates of naturally produced sulfates and other sulfur compounds are from 35 percent to 85 percent of the total—a rather wide range!—and naturally occurring nitrogen compounds are generally believed to be 40 percent to 60 percent of the total. Some experts go further and claim that nature contributes over 90 percent of the global nitrogen. Considering the additional sulfur that emanates from volcanoes and fumaroles and hot springs and ocean spray, and the nitrogen fixed by lightning, the generally accepted contribution from natural sources may be underestimated.

"Nature is responsible for putting large quantities of sulfates and nitrates into the atmosphere."

The contribution of lightning to the acidity of rain is significant. Two strokes of lightning over one square kilometer (four-tenths of a square mile) produce enough nitric acid to make eight-tenths of an inch of rain with a pH of 3.5. In fact, it has been estimated that lightning creates enough nitric acid so that annual rainfall over the world's land surfaces would average pH 5.0 even without taking into account other natural sources of acidity.

The contribution of volcanoes to atmospheric sulfur dioxide seems never to have been taken seriously; acknowledged, yes—but then dismissed as trivial. Perhaps this is related to the fact that volcanoes are studied by geologists and vulcanologists rather than by atmospheric scientists. Or perhaps it's because volcanic mountains tend to be where meteorologists are not. Predicting exactly when an eruption will occur is notoriously undependable, and obtaining direct measurements or samples of ejecta during eruptions is dangerous and can be fatal. During the daylong eruption of Mt. St. Helens on May 18, 1980, over four billion tons of material were ejected. Although large quantities of gases, including sulfur dioxide, were released to the atmosphere, no direct measurements could be made during the major eruption itself. Before May 18, in the period March 29 to May 14, spectroscopic measurements revealed about forty tons per day of sulfur dioxide. By May 25 measuring was resumed and showed 130 to 260 tons per day. On June 6 this increased abruptly to 1,000 tons per day. From the end of June through December of that year the rates

of sulfur dioxide ranged from 500 tons per day to 3,400 tons per day. Sulfur dioxide, hydrogen sulfide, carbon disulfide, and other sulfur compounds continue to be released from the crater floor and dome, and arise also from fumaroles and the debris of pyroclastic flows.

Sulfur Dioxide

El Chicon, an exceptionally acidic and sulfurous mountain in Mexico, erupted in early 1982, far more violently than Mt. St. Helens. Materials ejected reached the stratosphere and will probably affect the atmosphere for many years. Again no direct measurements were possible, but it is estimated that twenty million tons of sulfur dioxide were released. Also in the northern hemisphere, Mt. St. Augustine in Alaska erupted twice in 1986 with sulfur fumes detectable in Anchorage many miles away. Sulfur fumes continue to seep from both El Chicon and St. Augustine.

In 1973 two scientists, Stoiber and Jepson, reported data on sulfur dioxide emissions from Central American volcanoes, obtained both by remote sensing and by calculation. They conclude that 10,000 metric tons of sulfur dioxide are released to the atmosphere daily. Extrapolating world-wide, they calculate that volcanoes are responsible for emitting annually about 100 million metric tons of sulfur compounds. Thus nature is responsible for putting large quantities of sulfates and nitrates into the atmosphere.

But so, of course, is man. Industrial activity, transportation, and burning fossil fuel for commercial and domestic purposes all contribute sulfate, nitrates, and other pollutants to the atmosphere. Since passage of the Clean Air Act in 1970 there has been an overall reduction of more than 40 percent in factory and utility sulfur dioxide production. But as sulfur dioxide emissions decrease, nitrogen emissions are increasing, primarily from oil burning and oil used in transportation. Industrial society also produces other air pollutants, including volatile organic compounds, ammonia, and hydrocarbons. Any of these may contribute to the formation of acid rain, either singly or in combination. Further, some man-made pollutants can undergo photo-oxidation in sunlight, leading, for example, to the conversion of sulfur dioxide to highly toxic sulfur trioxide. But even this compound, should it be deposited over the ocean, loses its toxicity due to the extraordinarily high buffering capacity of sea water.

Another photo oxidant, ozone, is possibly the most damaging of all air pollutants derived from human activity. Ozone accumulates in quantities toxic to vegetation in all industrial regions of the world. Ozone is a product of photochemical oxidation between oxides of nitrogen and volatile organic substances. The latter may be unburned hydrocarbons (e.g., from automobile exhaust in cars not equipped with catalytic converters) or various organic solvents. Ozone is known to cause severe injury and even death to certain forest trees. The best known cases are the decline of white pine in much of eastern North America and ponderosa and Jeffrey pine in the San Bernardino Mountains of California. Ozone acts synergistically with other pollutants and has been shown to cause damage to agricultural crops when exposure occurs along with sulfur and nitrogen oxides.

Thus, singling out sulfur dioxide produced by human activities as the major cause of acid rain is not only a gross over-simplification, but probably wrong.

Effects on Forests

What about the dying forests? Here again the acid rain activists blame sulfur dioxide produced by industry.

Trees, like every other living thing, are not immortal. They too grow old and die. The decline of a forest may be part of the slow but natural process of plant succession, or it may be initiated by any of several stress-causing factors. Each forest and each tree species responds differently to environmental insults, whether natural or human. As Professor Paul D. Mannion of the State University of New York has said: "If one recognizes the complex array of factors that can contribute to the decline of trees, it is difficult to accept the hypothesis that air pollutants are the basis of our tree decline problems today . . . [although] to question the popular opinion on the cause of our decline problems is not to suggest that pollutants do not produce any effect."

Widespread mortality of forest trees has occurred at times and places where pollution stress was probably not a factor. Declines of western white pine in the 1930s and yellow birch in the 1940s and fifties, for example, were induced by drought, while secondary invasion by insects or other disease organisms is most often the ultimate cause of fatality.

Currently the most widely publicized forest decline problem in the U.S. is the red spruce forest in the northern Appalachian Mountains. Few people now cite the widespread mortality in red spruce between 1871 and 1890. The dieback occurred at roughly the same time in West Virginia, New York, Vermont, New Hampshire, Maine, and New Brunswick, and was then attributed to the invasion of a spruce beetle that followed some other stress. What that was is not clear.

Today the dieback symptoms of the red spruce are most pronounced above 900 meters in an environment that is subject to natural stresses such as wind, winter cold, nutrient-poor soils, and possible high levels of pollutants, heavy metals, and acidity in the clouds that often envelop the forest.

The relative importance of each of these stresses has not been rigorously investigated.

The affected trees grow in one of the windiest locations in North America. It is known that wind can dry out or even remove red spruce foliage, especially if rime ice has formed; it can also cause root damage by excessive tree movements. Tree ring analyses indicate a possible relation between recent cold winters and decline. The abnormal cold extending into spring may have caused the trees to be more susceptible to the adverse effects of pollutants. Arthur H. Johnson and Samuel B. MacLaughlin, who have studied tree rings and the red spruce forest decline, conclude in *Acid Deposition: Long Term Trends* (National Academy Press, 1986) that "there is no indication now that acidic deposition is an important factor in red spruce decline. . . . The abrupt and synchronous changes in ring width and wood density patterns across such a wide area seem more likely to be related to climate than to air pollution." Airborne chemicals might play a role, but they will have to be further assessed.

"American cows burp about fifty million tons of hydrocarbons to the atmosphere annually!"

And then there are the dying forests of Germany. Whereas originally the focus was on acid precipitation and deposition of sulfur dioxide and to a lesser extent nitrogen oxides, emphasis has now shifted to the oxides of nitrogen, hydrocarbons, soil minerals such as aluminum and magnesium, and photo oxidants, chiefly ozone. Sulfur dioxide emissions have been declining in Germany since the mid-1970s, due mainly to the substitution of nuclear energy for coal burning in the production of electricity. But this decline was not accompanied by improvement in the health of forests, suggesting that other factors may be implicated. It is now believed that only in exceptional cases does sulfur dioxide cause direct damage to forests in Germany. But motor vehicle pollution from more than 27 million autos and trucks is among the highest in the world in density per area, and is considered to be a contributing factor to the formation of ozone. Indeed, ozone levels in Germany's damaged forests are often remarkably high. Long-term measurements indicate that the mean value of ozone concentration has increased by one-third over the last twenty years. And the investigators at the Norwegian Forest Research Institute have reached similar conclusions about the importance of ozone in forest declines.

The adoption of the catalytic converter for automobiles in America was primarily to control the release of unburned hydrocarbons in order to reduce the photochemical production of ozone. In this it has functioned well, although it has also led to formation of formaldehyde and larger amounts of acid, especially sulfuric acid. But there is another source of atmospheric hydrocarbons that has not been controlled—cows! American cows burp about fifty million tons of hydrocarbons to the atmosphere annually! There is no known control technology for these emissions. Whether they contribute to ozone formation is also not known, but their presence helps to emphasize the complexity of atmospheric chemistry.

Effects on Lakes and Fish

There are three kinds of naturally occurring acidic lakes: 1) those associated with inorganic acids in geothermal areas (i.e., Yellowstone Park) and sulfur springs (pH 2.0 to 3.0); 2) those found in peat lands, cypress swamps, and rain forests where the acidity is derived from organic acids leached from humus and decaying vegetation (pH 3.5 to 5.0); and 3) those located in areas of weather-resistant granitic or silicious bedrock. Only the last-named are involved in the acid rain question. In these lakes and streams, the absence of carbonate rocks means little natural buffering capacity. This type of naturally acidic lake is common in large areas of eastern Canada and the northeastern United States, where glaciers exposed granitic bedrock during the last period of glaciation. The lakes are called "sensitive" because they may readily become further acidified with adverse impacts on aquatic organisms, of which fish are the most important to man. Indeed the most widely proclaimed complaint about the consequence of acid deposition is the reduction or elimination of fish populations in response to surface water acidification.

But again, this is not a recent phenomenon. Dead lakes are not new. A study by the New York State Department of Environmental Conservation reveals that the stocking of fish in twelve lakes was attempted and failed as early as the 1920s. Of course, many people did catch fish in the 1920s and 1930s in lakes where fish are not available today. But the fact is that during those years many of the Adirondack lakes were being stocked annually by the Fish and Game Commission; fish did not propagate, and the stocking program was discontinued about 1940.

In the United States 219 lakes have been identified as too acidic to support fish. Two hundred and six of these lakes are in the Adirondacks, but they account for only four percent of the lake surface of New York state alone. This, then, is hardly a national problem; it is local. The same applies to southeast Canada, where the highest percentage of acid lakes is located.

Uncertainty continues whether these acid lakes have always had a low pH or whether human

activities have reduced the neutralizing capability of the waters, or the lake basin. A range of human activities could be to blame: use of chemical pesticides to control spruce budworm or black fly infestations, changes in fish hatchery production, change in angler pressure, lumbering, burning of watersheds. On the other hand, declining fish populations were noted in some New York lakes as early as 1918, and bottom sediments deposited eight hundred years ago in Scandinavian lakes are more acid than today's sediments.

To conclude that a decline in fish population is caused by atmospheric acid deposition, it must be established that the lake formerly supported a viable fish population; one or more species of fish formerly present has been reduced or lost; the lake is more acidic now than it was when the fish were present; the increased acid level was not caused by local factors; and other factors, e.g., toxic chemicals, are not present or are unimportant.

Other Explanations

Such data are rare. Studies on three lakes in the Adirondacks—Panther, Sagamore, and Woods Lake, which are remote but close enough together to be affected by the same rainfall—disclosed radically different degrees of acidity, large differences that can be accounted for by the varying geological makeup of the three lake beds and local, surrounding soils and vegetation.

"Modern findings call into question the claim that distant sources of sulfur dioxide are responsible for the growing acidity of waters hundreds of miles away."

Outside the Adirondack Mountains and New York state, many emotional claims have been made about fish kills in Canada, Norway, and Sweden. Most of the losses are reported in the spring; in Scandinavia fish kills have been reported annually in the springtime for more than one hundred years. This recurring natural phenomenon is likely due to oxygen depletion or to snow melt and rain runoff carrying sudden high concentrations of many materials into lakes and streams, and in fact, the acidity of most waters is greatest in the spring. Modern findings call into question the claim that distant sources of sulfur dioxide are responsible for the growing acidity of waters hundreds of miles away.

Using trace elements, Dr. Kenneth Rahn of the University of Rhode Island has found that it is local pollution sources, mostly residual fuel oil burned for domestic, commercial, and industrial purposes in

New England, that are the main cause of added acidity in rain and snow. A meteorological team from the University of Stockholm cautioned the Swedish people not to blame acid rain on emissions from England; they found that local sources accounted for local acid rain. Great Britain, incidentally, has reduced sulfur dioxide emissions by more than 30 percent since 1970 with no effect whatever on the acidity of lakes or rain in Scandinavia. In New York City, EPA scientists traced elevated sulfur dioxide and sulfuric acid in the wintertime to the burning of oil in the 35,000 oil burners of the city's apartment houses. European scientists at the Organization for Economic and Cooperative Development, in Paris, have reached the same conclusion; the most revealing result of an extensive project is that every source region affects itself more than any other region.

Effects on Man-Made Structures

The impact of airborne pollutants and acid rain on deterioration of buildings, monuments, and man-made materials is also predominantly a local phenomenon. It is at least as complex as the effects on the natural environment. And, like forests and lakes, every site is specific and every material different. Few generalizations are possible; fewer still stand up under careful scrutiny. Of course metals corrode, marble and limestone weather, masonry and concrete deteriorate, paint erodes, and so on; but the conditions and substances that lead to loss of integrity vary widely. Perhaps the only statement that can be made is that moisture is essential, that deterioration results more from acid deposition than from acid rain, and that local sources are more important than possible long-range transport of pollutants.

Yet belief persists that acid rain from "someplace else" is destroying cultural monuments. Perhaps the most egregious example is the damage to the granite Egyptian obelisk, "Cleopatra's Needle," located since 1881 in New York City's Central Park. It has been claimed that "the city's atmosphere has done more damage than three and one half millennia in the desert, and in another dozen years the hieroglyphs will probably disappear." A careful study of the monument's complex history, however, makes it clear that the damage can be attributed to advanced salt decay, the high humidity of the New York climate, and unfortunate attempts at preservation. There is no question but that acid deposition causes incremental damage to materials, but far more research is needed before reliable surface protection systems can be developed.

A former governor of Washington, Dixy Lee Ray has also served as chairperson of the Atomic Energy Commission, a governmental body which develops and *controls the U.S. atomic energy program. She was a member of the National Advisory Committee on Oceans and Atmosphere, an advisory group to Congress and the President.*

"If Congress will act on the clean air reforms that I'm offering... every American in every city in America will breathe clean air."

Revising the Clean Air Act Will Reduce Pollution

George Bush

Editor's note: The following viewpoint is taken from a speech delivered in the White House.

In this room are Republicans and Democrats, leaders from both sides of the aisle in Congress, governors, executives from some of the most important companies and business organizations in America; leading conservationists and people who have devoted their lives to creating a cleaner and safer environment. And I've invited you here to make a point. With the leadership assembled in this room, we can break the stalemate that has hindered progress on clean air. And with the minds, the energy, the talent assembled here, we can find a solution.

So let me tell you the purposes of this gathering. First, I'd like to lay on the table my proposals to curb acid rain and cut urban smog and clean up air toxics. And second, I want to call upon all of you to join me in enacting into law a new clean air act. But first, we should remember how far we've come and recognize what works.

The 1970 Clean Air Act got us moving in the right direction with national air quality standards that were strengthened by amendments in 1977. Since 1970, even though we have 55 percent more cars going 50 percent farther, in spite of more utility output and more industrial production, we've still made progress. Lead concentrations in the air we breathe are down 98 percent. Sulfur dioxide and carbon monoxide cut by over a third, particulate matter cut 21 percent. Even ozone-causing emissions have been cut by 17 percent. And still, we have not come far enough.

Too many Americans continue to breathe dirty air. And political paralysis has plagued further progress against air pollution. We have to break this logjam by applying more than just federal leverage. We must take advantage of the innovation, energy and ingenuity of every American.

The environmental movement has a long history here in this country. It's been a force for good, for a safer, healthier America. And as a people, we want and need that economic growth, but now we must also expect environmental responsibility and respect the natural world. And this will demand a national sense of commitment, a new ethic of conservation. And I reject the notion that sound ecology and a strong economy are mutually exclusive.

So I outlined five points of a new environmental philosophy: one, to harness the power of the marketplace; two, to encourage local initiative; three, to emphasize prevention instead of just cleanup; four, to foster international cooperation; and five, to ensure strict enforcement. Polluters will pay.

We know more now than we did just a few years ago. New solutions are close at hand. It's time to put our best minds to work, to turn technology and the power of the marketplace to the advantage of the environment—to create, to innovate, to tip the scales in favor of recovery, restoration and renewal.

Clean Air Guaranteed

Every American expects and deserves to breathe clean air, and as President, it is my mission to guarantee it—for this generation and for the generations to come. If we take this commitment seriously, if we believe that every American expects and deserves clean air, and then we act on that belief, then we will set an example for the rest of the world to follow.

I am proposing to Congress a new Clean Air Act and offering a new opportunity. We've seen enough of this stalemate. It's time to clear the air. And, you know, I think we will. We touched a lot of bases as we prepared this bill, and we've had the benefit of

George Bush, "Remarks by the President in Announcement of the Clean Air Act Amendment," June 12, 1989.

some good thinking on the Hill. And we've met with business leaders who see environmental protection as essential to long-term economic growth, and we've talked with environmentalists who know that cost-effective solutions help build public support for conservation. And we've worked with academics and innovative thinkers from every quarter who have laid the groundwork for this approach.

And I spoke by phone with Prime Minister Brian Mulroney of Canada. I believe he's excited about the prospect, too. I have no pride of authorship. Let me commend Project 88 and groups like the Environmental Defense Fund for bringing creative solutions to long-standing problems, for not only breaking the mold, but helping to build a new one.

And we've had to make some tough choices. And some may think we've gone too far, and others not far enough, but we all care about clean air. To the millions of Americans who still breathe unhealthy air, let me tell you, I'm concerned—I'm concerned about vulnerable groups like the elderly and asthmatics and children—concerned about every American's quality of life. And I'm committed to see that coming generations receive the natural legacy they deserve.

We seek reforms that make major pollution reductions where we most need them. First, our approach is reasonable deadlines for those who must comply. It has compelling sanctions for those who don't. It accounts for continued economic growth and expansion, offers incentives, choice and flexibility for industry to find the best solutions, and taps the power of the marketplace and local initiative better than any previous piece of environmental legislation.

Clear Goals and Deadlines

This legislation will be comprehensive, it will be cost-effective, but above all, it will work. We will make the 1990s the era for clean air.

And we have three clear goals and three clear deadlines. First, we will cut the sulfur dioxide emissions that cause acid rain by almost half—by 10 million tons—and we will cut nitrogen oxide emissions by two million tons—both by the year 2000. We have set absolute goals for reductions and have emphasized early gains. And that means five million tons will be cut by 1995, and the degradation caused by acid rain will stop by the end of this century.

To make sure that coal continues to play a vital role in our energy future, we've provided an extension of three years and regulatory incentives for the use of innovative clean coal technology.

We've set an ambitious reduction target—and applying market forces will be the fastest, most cost-effective way to achieve it. So, we're allowing utilities to take—to trade credits among themselves for reductions they make, to let them decide how to bring aggregate emissions down as cost-effectively as possible. Cleaner fuels, better technologies, energy conservation, improved efficiency in any combination—just as long as it works.

There's a wisdom to handing work to those most qualified to do it. Four hundred years ago Montaigne wrote, "Let us permit nature to have her way. She understands her business better than we do." Well, it's true. Acid rain must be stopped and that's what we all care about.

"We propose bold new initiatives to reconcile the automobile to the environment, ensuring continued economic growth without disruptive driving controls."

But it's also true that business understands its business better than we do. So we're going to put that understanding to work on behalf of clean air and a sound environment. We've provided the goals, but we won't try to micromanage them. We will allow flexibility in how industry achieves these goals. But we stand firm on what must be achieved.

Second, this federal proposal will cut the emissions that cause urban ozone, smog, virtually in half. This will put the states well on the road to meeting the standard.

In 1970, we started on the job. And if Congress will act on the clean air reforms that I'm offering today, by the year 2000 every American in every city in America will breathe clean air. Today, 81 cities don't need federal air quality standards. This legislation will bring clean air to all but about 20 cities by 1995, and within 20 years, even Los Angeles and Houston and New York will be expected to make it.

In the nine urban areas with the greatest smog problems, we propose bold new initiatives to reconcile the automobile to the environment, ensuring continued economic growth without disruptive driving controls. We'll accomplish this through alternative fuels and clean-fueled vehicles. We propose to put up to a million clean-fueled vehicles a year on the road by 1997. But we're also proposing flexibility on the means, even as we remain firm on the goals. A city can either request inclusion in the program or, if they show they can achieve these ambitious reductions through other measures, we will scale back the clean fuel vehicle requirements accordingly.

Also, we're sensitive to the problems of smaller cities, whose own ozone problems are due largely to pollutants that are generated in other areas, other regions, other cities. They will not be penalized for pollution problems outside their control.

Our program incorporates a mix of cost-effective measures to cut emissions from cars, fuels, factories and other sources. But I'm asking the EPA [Environmental Protection Agency] to develop rules like those we're employing on acid rain to allow auto and fuel companies to trade required reductions in order to meet the standard in the most cost-effective way. Our challenge is to develop an emissions trading plan. Their challenge is to meet the standards.

The third leg of our proposal is designed to cut all categories of airborne toxic chemicals by three-quarters within this decade. Our best minds will apply the most advanced industrial technology available to control these airborne poisons. The very best control technology we have will determine the standard we set for those plants. And until now, because of an unworkable law, the EPA has been able to regulate only seven of the 280 known air toxics. The bill I am proposing will set a schedule for regulating sources of air toxics by dates certain.

In addition, it will give the dedicated people of the EPA the right tools for the job, and it will make state-of-the-art technology an everyday fact of doing business, and that's the way it should be.

Reversing Past Errors

In its first phase, this initiative should eliminate about three-quarters of the needless deaths from cancer that have been caused by toxic industrial air emissions, and we plan a second phase to go after any remaining unreasonable risk. People who live near industrial facilities should not have to fear for their health. . . .

The wounded winds of north, south, east and west can be purified and cleansed, and the integrity of nature can be made whole again. Ours is a rare opportunity to reverse the errors of this generation in the service of the next. And we cannot—we must not fail. We must prevail. I ask for your support. We need your support to make all of this into a reality.

After serving as the nation's vice president for eight years, George Bush became the president of the United States in 1989.

Revising the Clean Air Act Will Not Reduce Pollution

Karen Franklin

Never before have Americans had a greater need for safeguards against air pollution. In 1988 alone the number of people breathing unhealthy air in this country increased by 30 million, reaching a sum total of 110 million, say recent estimates from the Environmental Protection Agency (EPA).

President Bush has given Congress his answer to the problem—a mammoth clean-air reauthorization package that he has hailed as the first step toward the "clean air era." Bush announced the outlines of his plan to amend the Clean Air Act in June 1989. "Twenty years from now, every American in every city in America will breathe clean air," he said.

That was before the administration crafted the final wording of its proposal. The bill Congress actually received fell vastly short of fulfilling the president's promise, according to environmental groups and critics in Congress.

Far from accomplishing Bush's stated clean air goals, the proposal would gut a number of provisions in current law, and leave many of the plan's requirements open to abuse by the auto and chemical industries. "The plan is a blueprint for another quarter-century of dirty air," says Casey Padgett, legislative counsel for Environmental Action.

High up on the list of complaints, the administration's proposal suffers from a shortage of mandatory provisions. The bill gives industries "flexibility" in meeting deadlines and determining how they will achieve air-quality standards. And it primarily subjects EPA to discretionary, non-binding guidelines.

Administration officials contend that "flexibility" provides a crucial component of clean air policy. "This bill will be implemented over the next 20 years," explains John Beale, an EPA senior policy analyst who played a hands-on role in writing the legislation. "To adjust to changing economic and technological circumstances, we'll need a reasonable degree of discretion."

Beale rejects skepticism about the administration's intentions. "We don't agree that if something's not mandated, we won't do it," he says. "We've shown our commitment to the environment by drafting this legislation."

Undermining the Proposals

Yet the administration's bill underwent a number of redrafts after Bush's June 1989 announcement, and compromises between EPA and the Office of Management and Budget undermined the original proposal in various ways. Deadlines to meet certain standards were delayed; requirements were relaxed or eliminated; and loopholes were added, according to a staff analysis of the measure prepared by the House Subcommittee on Health and the Environment, chaired by Rep. Henry Waxman (D-Calif.).

Worse than that, all three sections of the Bush legislation—which address ozone smog, toxic emissions and acid rain—would cripple existing law.

The section on smog, for example, would eliminate the current cap on tailpipe emissions imposed on all new cars. Instead, the bill would require only that auto manufacturers meet an "average" level of hydrocarbons, nitrogen oxides and carbon monoxide. Environmentalists fear that the averaging provision would actually increase pollution by allowing as many as half of new cars to exceed air-quality standards. Since each auto must now measure below the tailpipe-emission ceiling, the average already falls 40 percent beneath the current standard, as well as below the Bush-proposed standard, explains Padgett.

The bill also requires the manufacture of one million cars that run on alternative fuels. But neither environmentalists nor industry leaders are impressed

Karen Franklin, "Fouling the Clean Air Law," *Environmental Action*, September/October 1989. Reprinted with permission.

with the "clean fuels" language in the Bush bill.

"Methanol has its own environmental problems," notes William Fay, administrator of the Clean Air Working Group, a leading industry lobby. Ironically, while the bulk of the Bush bill emphasizes a free-market approach, the alternative-fuels provision would dictate that industry enter an untested market. "We don't think mandating methanol is a flexible approach," Fay says. However, the bill also contains a loophole that would allow car makers to delay compliance, possibly indefinitely, if EPA decision-makers foresaw the likelihood of a recession.

Air Toxics

The auto-emissions section is not the only part of the bill drawing fire. The section on toxic emissions also contains significant problems for the environment. Although Bush originally promised to eliminate at least three-fourths of the deaths caused by airborne carcinogenic pollutants, the bill fails to even make the attempt.

"The administration bill has no provisions requiring regulation of the emission sources that, according to EPA, cause 75 percent of the cancer cases attributable to air toxics," notes the House staff report. The legislation, for example, fails to regulate toxic emissions from motor vehicles (50 percent of air-toxic cancer cases) or from localized sources (25 percent) such as the cooling systems of apartment buildings, the report says. Moreover, "the bill would dramatically relax current 1991 bus standards for one of the most dangerous and pervasive air toxics, diesel particulates."

Perhaps the most troubling part of the administration's air toxics plan, it rejects the level of health protection required by current law. Instead of adopting toxic standards that provide "an ample margin of safety," as the Clean Air Act now mandates, the Bush proposal would require protection of public health only in cases of "unreasonable risk," as determined by EPA. Court interpretations of that standard typically require a problematic cost-benefit analysis.

"There are two basic problems with the 'cost-benefit' standard," EA's Padget says. "First, it places a dollar value on human life. And second, the costs of controlling pollution are easy to quantify, while the benefits to public health aren't."

In a third section of the Bush bill, the acid rain language also unravels current pollution-control measures. The Bush proposal exempts most large power facilities from tall-stack regulation, although restricting smokestack height provides one of the only existing safeguards against acid rain.

The package also backs down from earlier promises on reducing pollutants that cause acid rain. After Bush pledged to cut 10 million tons of sulfur dioxide emissions by the year 2000, his bill proposed to cut only nine million tons. Likewise, Bush originally promised to cut nitrogen oxide emissions by two million tons in the next decade, but his bill would only limit *growth* in NO_x emissions. The net outcome would be more pollution.

The administration's thin protections against acid rain would hit hardest in the West, the region likely to see the most construction of new power facilities. Visibility in scenic areas—like the Grand Canyon—would also suffer from Bush's proposal to repeal Clean Air provisions that require protection of air quality in national parks—the "PSD" or "prevention of significant deterioration" mandate.

Despite cost-benefit allowances and other market-flexible strategies, industry groups have expressed misgivings about the expense of the Bush bill. Maintaining that effective pollution control is possible only with a healthy economy, they have objected that the legislation could prove self-defeating due to its high cost, estimated by business leaders as high as $60 billion per year. . . .

"Many of the bill's provisions would actually counteract Bush's stated goal of eliminating air pollution."

The bill goes a long way toward taking the pressure off business. In fact, many of the bill's provisions would actually counteract Bush's stated goal of eliminating air pollution. For example, an "emissions trading" concept would permit a company that produced less pollution than the allowable ceiling to sell off the "difference" to heavy polluters.

Aside from sending the wrong message to industry by allowing pollution permits to be sold like any product or commodity, the policy could prove unworkable from a management standpoint. It would rely on EPA to track complex rights-swapping deals between polluters, which would likely create a nightmare in paperwork. . . .

"For the first time in a decade, we have a president who has pledged clean air," says EA's Padgett. "But instead of the strong plan the president promised, his advisors have offered a polluters' bailout program. We are deeply disappointed."

Karen Franklin is contributing editor of Environmental Action, *the bimonthly magazine of Environmental Action, Inc., a lobbying and educational organization in Washington, D.C.*

Ozone Pollution Is Dangerous

Rose Marie L. Audette

As superbowl hoopla wafted through the San Diego air in January 1988, reporters from round the world monitored the play-by-play. Just outside town, down Interstate 8 in Alpine, Calif. another sort of monitoring was going on.

Inside a small shelter across from a cemetery, a two-foot electronic box quietly measured ozone smog and transmitted the data to a county computer.

Across the country, 608 more ozone monitoring devices sit in schoolyard trailers, in Quonset huts on vacant lots and on building tops. These mechanical sentinels of the polluted sphere have a disturbing story to tell.

While the natural layer of ozone in the upper atmosphere is critical to the preservation of earth-bound life, it's a different story at ground level. Down here, ozone forms when hydrocarbons and nitrogen oxides emitted by vehicles, factories, power plants and hundreds of other sources chemically react with sunlight.

Some 62 metropolitan areas in which about 100 million people live have unhealthy and illegal levels of ozone in their air, according to calculations by the U.S. Environmental Protection Agency (EPA). And though it's mostly created on sunny hot days in urban centers, ozone can be transported hundreds of miles—afflicting suburban neighborhoods and rural areas.

Ozone smog shouldn't still be a national problem. The Clean Air Act ordered states, cities and EPA to reduce ozone smog and other air pollution. And there are control measures on hand that work.

In early 1987, EPA was asked to calculate how many cities with unsafe ozone levels (then numbering 70) would have been in compliance with federal standards if they had implemented a specified list of ozone control measures back in 1982. EPA estimated that up to 50 would have met the health standard.

"It's a clear case of the shut-eyed sentry," says Environmental Action's [EA] clean air lobbyist Dan Becker. "EPA officials could have made the law work, but they shut their eyes. Cities and states alone won't take on powerful polluters or try to change engrained consumer habits."

Those familiar with the ozone problem say some cities have earnestly tried to bring their ozone levels into compliance with federal safety standards, but failed. Other cities devised an adequate plan, but didn't implement all of its provisions. And then there are those who didn't develop an adequate plan in the first place.

"I don't think it's true of any area that they are doing everything they know how to do," says Dave Hawkins, EPA's assistant administrator for air during the Carter administration and now an attorney with the Natural Resources Defense Council (NRDC).

"Bureaucrats on all levels have slackened their efforts," says Hawkins. "It's like a football team that doesn't care enough."

Studies of Effects

Since the 1970s, scientific knowledge of the health risks posed by ozone has increased dramatically. Dr. Larry Folinsbee notes that when he first began studying ozone, around 1974, it was thought that the lowest ozone levels at which human lungs would be affected was about .35 parts per million (ppm) or maybe .3 ppm.

But thanks to improved experimental and measurement methods, it's now known that normal healthy people react adversely to ozone at levels as low as the current EPA standard of .12 parts per million. During "ozone chamber" studies in which volunteers exercise in such air for an hour, these normal healthy people cough, wheeze, feel chest

Rose Marie L. Audette, "It Only Hurts When You Breathe," *Environmental Action*, March/April 1988. Reprinted with permission.

pain, and have trouble taking a deep breath.

Several hours of ozone exposure have been found to cause similar symptoms at even lower levels, says Dr. Folinsbee, a scientist with Environmental Monitoring and Services, a subsidiary of Combustion Engineering.

Folinsbee joined Dr. Bill McDonnell of EPA's research laboratory in North Carolina in a study of ozone effects during 6½ hours of exercise. They found "significant changes in lung function" at .12 ppm, says Folinsbee, some effects at .10 ppm and suggestions of effects at .08 ppm.

The internal mechanism for ozone damage is unclear, says Folinsbee, but he notes that ozone is very unstable, separating once inside the body into O_2 plus a "free radical." These free radicals probably cause changes to cells in the portion of lung where air is exchanged, Folinsbee explains.

With many air pollutants, a specific segment of the population—such as infants, the elderly or those with lung problems—is particularly at risk. But ozone chamber studies haven't identified any such sub-population, says EPA's McDonnell.

Individuals do, however, react very differently. In the 6½ hour study, the average decrease in lung function was 13 percent, but some participants had up to a 40 percent decrease.

While the cause is unknown (allergies don't seem related), the effects are very reproducible, McDonnell says. "If we bring people back, the same people who were sensitive, will be sensitive again."

Ozone's health impacts are also being scrutinized through laboratory animal studies and epidemiological surveys. In a study of children at a summer camp, a five-day haze of ozone smog was found to cause lung problems that lingered for several days. Another study by a Canadian scientist found that when ozone levels rose, so did hospital admissions for asthma, bronchitis and pneumonia. In one animal study, long-term exposure to ozone reduced resistance to infectious disease and prematurely aged the lung.

Ozone is also known to increase the vulnerability of crops and forests to disease and insects. The National Crop Loss Assessment Program, for example, found that smog results in annual yield losses of $1.9 to $4.5 billion for four cash crops—corn, wheat, soybeans and peanuts.

Setting Health Standards

When Congress passed the Clean Air Act of 1970, it required EPA to set health standards for key air pollutants that would protect human health with "an adequate margin of safety."

States were ordered to draw up "State Implementation Plans" (or SIPs) that would clean up their air enough to "attain" the standards by certain deadline dates set by Congress. Those areas that failed faced a number of federal penalties: A ban on constructing large projects that could increase pollution and cutoffs in federal grants for sewage, highway and air projects.

But though many cities are now "non-attainment" areas, few sanctions have been levelled. Instead, Congress has repeatedly rolled back the deadline for meeting the ozone standard: From 1975 to 1982 to 1987 to 1988.

The ozone health threat may be even larger than the list of non-attainment areas. If the ozone chamber studies are right, human health is threatened not only by one-hour exposures at .12 ppm or higher, but also by several hours of exposure at levels below the standard.

Safer Standards

Given this new data, does the .12 ppm standard provide the "adequate margin of safety" required by the Clean Air Act?

Dr. Larry Folinsbee's response to that question? "If that's the only standard we rely on, probably not."

The several-hour ozone threat could be abated by either implementing a more stringent one-hour standard, or by establishing an additional eight-hour standard. "It's a toss-up," says Folinsbee. "You can achieve the same thing by doing either one."

Scientists who serve on an advisory board on clean air issues to EPA forcefully called for rapid movement by EPA on both fronts.

"Human health is threatened . . . by several hours of exposure at levels below the standard."

Despite the number of non-attainment cities, air quality has improved since 1970. According to EPA's most recent air quality report, the average daily ozone level dropped 19 percent from 1976 to 1985. And the average number of days that cities were above the standard dropped 38 percent from 1979 to 1985.

Much of the credit goes to the vehicle emissions program.

As part of the 1970 Clean Air Act, Congress required a 90 percent reduction from 1970 levels in the amount of hydrocarbons, carbon monoxide and nitrogen oxides that could come out of the tailpipe, starting with 1975 car models. To achieve those reductions, most car manufacturers installed catalytic converters, which convert harmful pollutants into more benign compounds. Other pollution control measures were taken, like changing the fuel-air mixture.

The problem now is that there aren't any big sources of ozone precursors left, reductions in which will bring every city into attainment. As EA's clean air lobbyist Dan Becker puts it, "We're dealing with a lot of two and five and 10 percent solutions."

But given the right package of new controls, urban air can greatly improve. "I'm very optimistic that we can bring most areas into attainment within the next five to 10 years," comments another Becker—William Becker, who is executive director of the State and Territorial Air Pollution Program Administrators. Even the nation's worst ozone case—the Los Angeles basin—can reach the standard within 10 to 20 years, he says.

"About half the ozone reductions will have to come from the transportation sector."

About half the ozone reductions will have to come from the transportation sector, environmentalists say, since the biggest share of ozone precursors still comes from vehicles. Emissions standards for hydrocarbons and nitrogen oxides can be "ratcheted down," especially for buses, trucks and diesel vehicles.

Another focus is "I/M"—inspection and maintenance programs, which require periodic inspections of cars and tuneups of those that don't meet a certain emissions level.

If forcefully implemented, I/M programs can be very effective. Cars in Portland, Ore., which has an I/M program, have 24 percent lower hydrocarbon emissions than cars in nearby Eugene, which doesn't have an I/M program.

Gasoline vapors also send hydrocarbons into the air. These vapors are dangerous in their own right—they're a toxic air pollutant. One control strategy is to decrease the "volatility" of the fuel (something oil companies have actually increased in recent years by adding butane to boost octane). Another approach is to control vapor emissions at gasoline terminals, bulk plants and service stations.

But roughly 40 percent of gasoline vapor emissions occur at the gas pump. When gas is pumped into a car's fuel tank, built-up vapors are forced into the air. These fumes can be captured by adding special fittings to the gas station pump (a move gas stations and the oil industry have opposed) or "on-board canisters" to the car itself (which auto makers protest).

Then there are a whole assortment of non-vehicle measures. Organic solvents can be recovered and reused. Hoods and vapor controls can be required of the host of industrial processes that emit volatile organic compounds. Ingredients or processes can be altered; for example, replacing oil-based paints and coatings with water-based alternatives. And nitrogen oxide—which is also an acid rain precursor—can be targeted. Some 29 percent of NOx comes from

power plants, and another 44 percent from vehicles.

With all these alternatives, why do so many cities still have unhealthy ozone-laden air?

Observers point fingers of blame in several directions: At the failure of states and cities to adopt effective controls; at EPA's slack efforts; and at obstacles thrown up by industries desiring emissions reductions to be required of any sector but their own.

In testimony to Congress, Richard Ayres of the National Clean Air Coalition pointed out that EPA has spent 14 years trying to decide whether to require gasoline vapor controls at the fuel pump. Since 1984, Ayres testified, the automotive and oil industries have each spent "huge sums and tremendous energy" trying to prove to EPA that whichever technique would fall on them is less cost-effective.

City and state air agencies have taken heat for the ozone problem, much of it deservedly.

Los Angeles-area residents have come to experience smog as an almost-irreversible act of God. But a study by the American Lung Association's California chapter suggests otherwise.

The Lung Association reviewed the 1982 plan that was supposed to bring the area into attainment by 1987. The "South Coast Air Quality Management District" had promised to adopt 10 measures on mobile sources. Instead, it adopted just two, and even those only partially. Car inspections, for example, were switched from once a year to once every two years.

Insufficient Leadership

Los Angeles had also agreed to adopt 46 measures to cut emissions from stationary sources; only four were adopted on schedule; 18 were scaled back or delayed; and, in early 1987, the rest had yet to be acted on.

But such implementation failures are not always the air agency's fault, says Fran DuMelle of American Lung's D.C. office. In Kentucky, she says, the state air agency wanted to enact an I/M program, but the state legislature refused to approve it for several years in a row. Part of Los Angeles' problem, she notes, is that the air pollution board is composed of local elected officials—elected officials who avoid taking tough action against industries in their hometown.

Air regulators have also been hampered by insufficient leadership from the federal level, says William Becker of the air regulator's association. Becker points out that in the late 1970s, EPA set technology standards, known as CTGs (Control Technology Guidelines) for 29 industries. Since then, the agency hasn't set any.

Becker points to the case of Montgomery County, Md. The air administrator there tried to implement gasoline vapor controls at the pump, a measure that would probably have brought this Washington, D.C. suburb into attainment. But EPA hadn't issued a regulatory ruling defining those controls as "readily available."

Maryland's governor, Becker says, was "besieged by a lobby campaign by the oil industry. And so the legislature passed a law prohibiting the state from adopting any technology that wasn't required by EPA.". . .

Given the 100 million people endangered by ozone smog, new legislation is critical, says former EPA air regulator Dave Hawkins. "Federal agencies and state officials are waiting for a fresh political decision. They want Congress to reaffirm that the government does indeed care about clean air."

Rose Marie L. Audette is editor of Environmental Action, *the bimonthly magazine of Environmental Action, Inc., a lobbying and educational organization.*

The Dangers of Ozone Pollution Have Been Exaggerated

Melinda Warren and Kenneth Chilton

This article takes a hard look at the ozone pollution problem. Ozone, a major component of smog, is formed through a chemical reaction between emissions from automobiles and stationary sources in combination with sunlight. The Environmental Protection Agency (EPA) has set the ozone standard at 0.12 parts per million [ppm], not to be exceeded more than one hour a year. . . .

In 1985, 48 million people were living in counties with measured air quality levels that violated the National Ambient Air Quality Standards (NAAQS) for total suspended particulate (TSP), 40 million in counties out of compliance for carbon monoxide (CO), 8 million in areas with too high nitrogen dioxide (NO_2) levels, 4 million in counties not meeting lead (Pb) standards, and 2 million people in areas out of compliance for sulfur dioxide (SO_2). In contrast, 76 million people were living in counties where ozone (O_3) levels were higher than the NAAQS.

Significant Progress

Nonetheless, significant progress has been made in reducing the levels of the five air pollutants other than ozone for which the EPA has set NAAQS. Ozone was the only criteria air pollutant with a composite average reading for 183 monitoring sites nationwide that exceeded the NAAQS in 1985. From 1976 to 1985, there was a 24 percent reduction in total suspended particulates, a 42 percent reduction in sulfur dioxide; carbon monoxide levels were decreased 36 percent; nitrogen dioxide levels were reduced 11 percent; and lead levels were reduced by an impressive 79 percent.

Progress has also been made in reducing ozone concentrations. The composite average reading

decreased 19 percent between 1976 and 1985. The significance of this change is complicated by the fact that there was a calibration change in the monitoring systems in 1978-79. A major drop was recorded between 1978 and 1979, largely because of that change in measurement. This means that, on average, the ozone level has not been reduced as much as the figures show. A different measure, the number of exceedances of the standard, decreased 38 percent between 1979 and 1985. None of this decrease can be attributed to the calibration change.

Ozone data also show that the 1983 values were higher than those in 1981, 1982, 1984, and 1985. Between 1982 and 1983, the national average ozone level increased sharply, by 12 percent. This is thought to be due to the combination of an increase in volatile organic compound (VOC) emissions (up 3 percent) and meteorological conditions conducive to ozone formation. What this implies is that reported ozone exceedances often are an imprecise measure of the progress made to reduce ozone precursors.

Another study suggests that the ozone problem is much less serious than generally thought. Researchers at the American Petroleum Institute in Washington, D.C., analyzed the scope of the ozone nonattainment problem using Environmental Protection Agency data. The study was critical of the EPA's method of measuring attainment. First, the EPA uses the monitor with the highest readings to determine if an area meets the standard. In most cases, the average reading for all monitors was closer to the readings for the lowest monitor rather than the highest. Second, one year's data, which can be significantly affected by unusual climatic conditions, can, in turn, affect the measurement of attainment over a three-year period. An "exceedance" occurs if ozone levels are above the 0.12 ppm standard for one hour or longer during a 24-hour period. An area then is classified as nonattainment if ozone levels recorded at the highest monitor result in more than three exceedances over a consecutive three-year period.

This method of determining noncompliance ignores the fact that the ozone levels in "nonattainment" areas meet the standard most of the time. A much different picture emerges if average readings from all the monitors in an area are examined. The EPA should look at the exposure levels for the vast majority of the citizens in a "nonattainment" area.

With the exception of Los Angeles, using an average of all monitor readings in an area, the "out-of-compliance" cities are actually within the ozone standard 99.47 percent of the time or better. The well-known purity standard for Ivory soap is only 99 and 44/100 percent! Even Los Angeles is below the 0.12 ppm level 97 percent of the time on average. The highest monitor measured air quality to be below the standard more than 94 percent of the time. Thus, people in the worst nonattainment areas are not exposed on a regular basis to ozone levels above what is considered "safe."

Health Effects

Given the obvious difficulty in meeting the ozone standard and the severity of the sanctions for not doing so, it is necessary to examine the nature of the health problem that it generates. Two methods have been used to measure the effects of ozone on humans—epidemiological studies and clinical studies. Epidemiological studies use statistical techniques to determine the relationship between ozone levels in an area and symptoms reported by a monitored group.

A study by D.I. Hammer in the early 1960s exemplifies the problems encountered with such "uncontrolled experiments." Hammer asked a group of Los Angeles student nurses to keep daily symptom diaries. The symptoms were reported and corresponding ozone levels were analyzed statistically. The group was not informed that they were being studied for effects of pollutants. However, no validation techniques were used to make sure that the levels of pollutants where the nurses lived were the same as at the monitoring station. Statistics on smoking habits, although available, were not used in conjunction with the results reported. Hammer found that the students reported higher incidences of coughing and chest congestion at ozone levels of 0.30 to 0.39 ppm.

An epidemiological study by Shoettlin and Landau looked at the relationship between asthma attacks and photochemical oxidants in Los Angeles. No significant difference was found in the average number of patients having attacks on days measuring above or below the median (0.13 ppm in this study) oxidant level. The authors stated that "all correlations led to the conclusion that there was relatively little association between oxidant levels and attacks of asthma."

Kagawa and Toyoma conducted a study on the pulmonary function of twenty children in an elementary school in Tokyo. The results show that pulmonary function tests were significantly correlated with temperature far more than with any other environment factor.

Clinical studies provide the other source of information on the effects of ozone levels on humans. These studies have been criticized because they typically use small numbers of subjects that have not been randomly selected. For example, Delucia and Adams researched the effects of ozone on six healthy nonsmoking males at rest and with steady exercise at ozone levels ranging from zero ppm to 0.30 ppm. Significant decreases in pulmonary fuction were observed only under conditions of steady exercise at the 0.30 ppm level.

In order to look at the effects on the more sensitive population, Hackney studied a group of thirteen adult male residents of Los Angeles. Of the thirteen, two had a history of asthma and four had histories of allergies. The healthy participants failed to show decreases in basic pulmonary measurements at 0.50 ppm, but the sensitive subjects developed marked respiratory symptoms at 0.37-0.50 ppm.

It would be impossible to summarize the results of the myriad of studies conducted, but there are a few general points that can be made about most of these. First, not all symptoms commonly associated with ozone exposure—eye irritation, decreases in pulmonary function (which includes coughing, chest pain upon deep inhalation and decreased lung volume), aggravation of chronic lung diseases, increased breathing problems for asthmatics, and headaches—are actually attributable to ozone. For example, ozone, in and of itself, does not cause eye irritation. In clinical studies in which the concentration of ozone is several times higher than any likely to be encountered in ambient air, no eye irritation was experienced. Researchers in this field believe that it is more likely that this problem is caused by formaldehyde, acrolein, or peroxyacetyl nitrate.

"Many of the concerns about ozone's effects on persons suffering from lung disease . . . lack substantiation."

Ozone's effects on pulmonary function appear to involve an adaptation mechanism. Results from studies show that, with repeated exposure to O_3, reductions in pulmonary function are greatest on the second day. On each succeeding day, the reductions are less than the day before. On the fifth exposure day small reductions or no changes are observed.

Following a sequence of repeated daily exposures, pulmonary function returns to that prior to repeated exposure. This helps to explain why, in a study of equal exposures to ozone by Canadians and by people from Los Angeles, Canadians were more severely affected than people from Los Angeles.

A survey of clinical studies by Christopher Marraro leads to the general conclusion that small physiological responses occur in the sensitive populations when exposed to ambient air pollution containing about 0.22 ppm of ozone. Another survey of ozone studies by Lawrence White concludes that pure ozone does not seem to affect people at concentrations below 0.30 ppm unless they are exercising so strenuously that the symptoms could be due to the exercise itself.

Many of the concerns about ozone's effects on persons suffering from lung disease also lack substantiation. There have been no consistent findings of symptom aggravation or changes in lung function in patients with chronic lung diseases other than asthma. Also, according to available evidence, people with preexisting lung disease respond to ozone exposure in a manner similar to normal, healthy subjects. There is also evidence that smokers are less responsive to ozone than nonsmokers.

"No one is being forced to live in areas that do not meet the ozone standard."

Even the effects on asthmatics appear less severe than thought to be when the NAAQS was first established for ozone. One recent study showed no decrease in pulmonary function in adult asthmatics either at rest or with light exercise at ozone levels of 0.25 ppm. Adolescent asthmatics were observed for one hour at exposures of 0.12 ppm, and no change in pulmonary function was found. Several other studies have shown that the increase in reported symptoms for asthmatics is statistically insignificant. The results of laboratory tests are by no means definitive; but, in general, it appears that asthmatics react basically the same way to ozone exposure as nonasthmatics.

There also has been some concern that ozone could have a mutagenic effect on humans. Although alterations in chromosomes have been observed in hamsters exposed to 0.20 ppm ozone, no consistent changes have been demonstrated in human subjects at concentrations as high as 0.60 ppm.

In general, epidemiological and clinical studies conducted since the ozone standard was changed in 1979 seem to reinforce the conclusions reached by Lawrence White, a senior staff economist with the Council of Economic Advisers at that time, in *Reforming Regulation: Processes and Problems:*

The ozone-related health effects under discussion were short term and reversible. They involved wheezing, coughing and chest-tightening. They meant temporary discomfort, with complete recovery of an individual's previous state of health shortly after the exposure to ozone ended. Thus far, ozone exposure has not been demonstrated to have long-term debilitating consequences in humans.

Ozone pollution has been identified as a potential cause of crop damage. Because of its requirement to regulate pollutants that could adversely affect human welfare, the EPA has authorized a number of studies to assess the crop losses from current concentrations of ozone. Impacts of ozone range from reduced plant growth to decreased yield to changes in crop quality. Effects on growth and yield have occurred when average ozone levels exceed a concentration of 0.05 ppm for at least two weeks.

Agricultural Studies

Most agricultural studies of ozone's effects have used longer exposure times and a greater frequency of higher ozone levels than normally occur in ambient air. This makes the results of these experiments somewhat suspect. None of the studies compared the estimated crop loss value with compliance costs of effecting changes in ozone concentrations in ambient air. Indeed, there is no reliable method to translate the effects of air pollution standards imposed on urban areas to ozone concentrations in rural areas. There are few air pollution monitors in rural areas, and statistical extrapolations from urban to rural areas are likely to incorporate errors of unknown magnitude.

From a public policy perspective, another key issue is how to evaluate the value of crop losses in a market characterized by price supports and land set-aside payments. As Kopp and Krupnick state in *Agricultural Policy and the Benefits of Ozone Control:*

Conspicuously absent from this literature (on the benefits to agriculture of ozone reduction) is recognition of the fact that agricultural markets are not free and that, in the second-best policy-dominated world of agriculture and a world currently awash in costly crop surpluses, a restrictive ozone control policy that reduces crop damages may not increase social welfare. Further, since the size of crop surpluses depends on the agricultural policy in effect, estimates of the social benefits of alternative ozone control policies depend on assumptions made about agricultural policies. . . .

The point is not that ozone pollution should be ignored but rather that its health consequences need to be kept in perspective. If levels as high as 0.30 ppm (more than two and a half times the standard) are of concern only if individuals are engaged in heavy exercise, then it seems unreasonable to punish cities and citizens with construction bans and federal funding cutoffs for exceeding ozone levels of 0.12 ppm more than one hour per year. The "punishment" simply does not seem to fit the "crime." . . .

Federally mandated solutions . . . would affect the driving public in impractical ways. Mobile sources (autos, buses, and trucks) are responsible for 36 percent of emissions of hydrocarbons and nitrogen oxides, the precursors of ozone, and must be part of the solution. But the degree of coercion required to make a significant decrease in automobile use seems to be politically infeasible. User road fees high enough to cut auto use appreciably would likely be about as popular as the famous interlock system that Congress mandated to force drivers to use seatbelts.

In a free country such as America, no one is being forced to live in areas that do not meet the ozone standard. Yet many of the cities experiencing difficulty in complying with the ozone requirements are growing, not contracting. The Los Angeles area grew by 2 percent a year from 1980 to 1985. Houston has grown 3 percent a year during the same period. It seems that individual citizens are less concerned about the effects of ozone than are their elected representatives.

Washington lawmakers might well consider why so little progress has been made on reducing ozone levels while significant gains have been made in improving levels of the other five criteria pollutants. It just might be that natural sources, meteorological phenomena, and the method of measuring compliance all conspire to make the ozone standard unrealistic. In view of so much uncertainty about both the mechanism of ozone production (and hence the effectiveness of controlling its precursors) and the maximum levels required to protect public health, it seems reasonable to take a more cooperative and less confrontational approach to dealing with the problem of photochemical oxidants. . . .

The Clean Air Act

The Clean Air Act (and the proposed revisions) requires that, in establishing NAAQS, EPA must in effect disregard such vital considerations as cost, technical feasibility and social and economic disruption. Other environmental laws are more flexible and are designed to reduce health threats to acceptable levels. . . .

We recommend that deadlines and sanctions for ozone compliance be removed from the Clean Air Act. By and large, ozone is a local problem. In those areas having the worst smog problems, state and local officials will address the issue without federal coercion. To the extent that plumes of ozone can cross local and state boundaries, some federal role is justified. Determining the NAAQS levels and providing information on effective control technologies for stationary and mobile sources are best done at the national level. The current system of detailed specification of which controls are necessary to constitute an acceptable state implementation plan is too inflexible to meet local needs.

We recommend that states be allowed to present their own good faith plans for reducing ozone levels with as little federal specification as possible. Most areas are well within ozone levels considered to be safe most of the time. The most expedient way to bring the majority of the out-of-compliance metropolitan areas into compliance would be to raise the ozone standard. While there is some debate about healthful concentration levels, most health effects appear at much higher levels than .12 ppm. Nonetheless, we do not recommend changing this target level in the Clean Air Act because the suggestion simply would be too controversial. Instead, we believe that the method of measuring ozone levels should be revised.

"We recommend that deadlines and sanctions for ozone compliance be removed from the Clean Air Act."

Lastly, we recommend that compliance measurement be changed to the average levels recorded at all monitors in an area rather than the highest monitor reading. In short it is time that Congress recognize that something more than extending deadlines and issuing detailed mandates and threats is required to reduce photochemical oxidants in the atmosphere. What is needed is a cooperative approach to ensure cost effective progress toward air quality goals.

The concept of requiring a zero risk environment is untenable. Acceptable risk is a concept that is more realistic and feasible, particularly in an economic environment of international competition. It is foolish to overburden United States companies with regulations in a vain effort to achieve a level of air quality that is needlessly restrictive.

Melinda Warren is a writer and analyst for the Center for the Study of American Business at Washington University in St. Louis, Missouri. Kenneth Chilton is acting director of the Center.

"All types of emissions—residential, commercial, industrial, and agricultural—could be reduced by encouraging 'markets' in air quality."

Free-Market Incentives Would Reduce Air Pollution in Los Angeles

Jo Kwong

The EPA [Environmental Protection Agency] sits perched like a giant atop the San Gabriel Mountains overlooking Los Angeles, sniffing the air disapprovingly and tapping the billy club of Clean Air Act sanctions in the palm of its hand. For two decades, the South Coast Air Quality Management District has faced the task of meeting federal and state air quality standards for an area covering 13,350 square miles. Angelenos have mostly ignored AQMD officials. But now, those officials are saying smugly, if you don't start listening to us, you'll have to deal with Mr. EPA.

With Washington threatening to impose its own measures if Los Angeles doesn't, the AQMD in March 1989 approved a master plan for cleaning up the air. It is being watched closely in cities and states across the nation.

The first stage of the plan alone proposes 120 measures to control emissions. Using lighter fluid on your backyard barbecue during "summer smog episode days" will be an air crime. Only radial tires will be allowed. No more gas-engine lawn mowers or chain saws. Underarm deodorant: banned.

The plan itself, of course, speaks in no such straightforward terms. It proposes "requiring reformulation of [underarm] products with less reactive components" or that "all non-utility internal combustion engines not used for emergency standby be phased out and replaced with electric motors."

The main focus of the plan, though, is vehicle pollutants. It calls for $44 billion or so in new transit and highway facilities, converting most vehicles to solar power or methanol fuel, forcing businesses to locate in residential areas, limiting the number of family cars, and putting 60 percent of the workers in the four-county area on alternative schedules: nine-day, 80-hour or four-day, 40-hour work weeks. The AQMD has made no small Plan.

Some of the technologies required to effect it, admits the AQMD, "may not exist yet." And critics say that many of the measures will not improve the air nearly as much as the AQMD hopes and might even cause more damage. No one really knows, for example, the environmental effects of substituting methanol, which yields the byproduct formaldehyde, for petroleum.

The good news is that the plan will never become law in its present form. Many of the measures await approval from all sorts of governmental entities, from local zoning boards to regulatory agencies. . . . The usual lobbyists will turn out in force to oppose them.

The bad news is that while not all of it will become law, parts of the plan surely will. And the AQMD's approach to cleaning up the air is fundamentally and systematically flawed. The underlying assumption is that regulators can assess overall air quality in the Los Angeles basin; can understand the interactions and operations of everyone and everything that pollutes; can design alternatives to virtually everything in society from gardening to manufacturing, from cosmetics to transportation, taking into consideration the aggregate air pollution effects of these alternatives; and can impose, monitor, and enforce each of their dictates. Even without consideration of cost-effectiveness or least-cost solutions, this is a Herculean task.

The Alternative

Fortunately, there is an alternative to such command-and-control approaches. Most people share the goal of improving air quality and are willing to pay to achieve it—despite the hue and cry from critics about how much the plan will cost (pro and con estimates range from $3.9 billion to $12.8 billion

Jo Kwong, "Wish List in La-La Land," reprinted, with permission, from the June 1989 issue of REASON magazine. Copyright 1989 by the Reason Foundation, 2716 Ocean Park Blvd., Suite 1062, Santa Monica, CA, USA 90405.

annually). The problem with the plan is not that it will cost but that it gives area residents little choice about how to go about achieving cleaner air.

Admittedly, in the absence of regulation, people do not freely incorporate pollution control measures into their lifestyles. Any move to stop treating the air basin as a "free good" is going to cost. But instead of requiring specific technologies or prohibiting particular processes, the AQMD would do far better to establish practical, enforceable air-quality levels and let people search for the least-cost means to achieve them. Under a variety of emission pricing schemes, all types of emissions—residential, commercial, industrial, and agricultural—could be reduced by encouraging "markets" in air quality.

The basic idea behind such markets is to improve air quality by charging polluters for the costs they impose and compensating people who make investments in antipollution equipment and processes. When we have a financial incentive to care about the level of pollution we generate, we will undertake measures to reduce our "pollution bills," just as skyrocketing oil prices induced voluntary conservation.

Suppose, for example, that the AQMD simply required all industries to reduce emissions by 5 percent by some date (varying percentages could be established for sulfur and nitrogen oxides, carbon monoxides, hydrocarbons, and so on). Companies that have already invested in pollution control could be exempted from the first phase. Alternatively, on a sliding scale, the worst offenders could be required to reduce emissions more than less-polluting companies. Polluters would pay for emissions above the specified level.

Market Mechanisms

Rather than dictating each technology or process that every industry must use, such an approach would allow individual firms to decide the least-cost, most convenient ways to reduce air pollution. The polluters, who know more about their own production technology than most regulators, could choose the level of emissions they will produce while taking into consideration the efficiency of alternative processes.

There are other ways, too, to use the pricing mechanism to control pollution. In an emissions trading scheme, polluters who go over the limit can purchase "emission reduction credits" from companies whose pollution levels are below the standards. For example, if Arco has developed a new process that cuts its release of hydrocarbons below the mandated level, it could sell those rights to DuPont if DuPont has not managed to meet the level.

Current EPA regulations allow for such trades, and they are even being used to reduce the aggregate pollution levels in a basin. With each trade, some pollution rights are "retired." To exercise 100 pollution rights, for example, a company must purchase 110 rights and retire 10. Overall pollution in the area is the better for it.

Several companies have emerged to broker trades in air rights. They locate buyers and sellers, appraise the market value (hydrocarbon offsets in the Los Angeles area, for example, currently sell for $500-$1,500 per pound per day), assess the cost of producing an emission credit by installing pollution control, act as liaisons with regulatory agencies, and so on. Since 1976, over 2,000 emission credits have been traded.

"As car owners we are accustomed to paying license plate fees, insurance fees, and so on, but we are not yet paying the pollution costs of our driving habits."

Emission charges and emission trading have tremendous advantages over the command-and-control approach. They certainly offer impressive efficiency by "assigning" the task of pollution reduction to the firms that can do it at least cost. If a charge of $100/ton is implemented, for example, all firms that can reduce emissions by investing less than $100 per ton will do so. Those that can cut emissions at least cost will be the ones that reduce pollution—something no regulator has sufficient information to achieve.

Pollution from vehicles can be addressed in much the same way. As car owners we are accustomed to paying license plate fees, insurance fees, and so on, but we are not yet paying the pollution costs of our driving habits.

The AQMD proposes to deal with the problem by commanding specific behavior: businesses must relocate and workers must change their schedules so that commuting will be reduced; families must get by with fewer cars; etc.

Instead, the regulators charged with cleaning up the air over Los Angeles could establish specified levels of emissions for each business and household based on the number of people of driving age. Those exceeding the limits would have to purchase emission credits from others. This way, those who are adding to the congestion and air pollution would pay extra, and there would be financial incentives for consumers to purchase less-polluting vehicles and for industry to supply them. As the population rises, the AQMD could tighten the exchange rate for credits.

Alternatively, if the volume of traffic is contributing to pollution, the AQMD could go for a number of other measures that would let people choose how to adjust. Instead of trying to change the jobs/housing balance by forcing businesses to locate in residential areas, it could press for the repeal of zoning laws that currently keep them out. Instead of making workers change their schedules, it could get local governments to deregulate taxis, van pools, and shuttle services. Instead of mandating a limit on the number of registered cars in the basin, it could see that highways are converted to toll roads and rush-hour access priced as a scarce resource, giving people incentives to drive less and use less-polluting public transportation.

"There would be financial incentives for consumers to purchase less-polluting vehicles and for industry to supply them."

The proposed Air Quality Management Plan continues the government tradition of setting unrealistic goals for environmental quality and imposing inflexible, top-down mechanisms for achieving them. Past federal legislation set the water pollution goal of "zero discharge" into the nation's waterways. And it has remained just that—a statement of goals. Similarly, the AQMD plan seeks to put the Los Angeles basin in compliance with federal clean-air standards by 2007—using control measures whose emission reductions are highly speculative and whose true costs are yet to be revealed. This plan, too, is likely to become just a statement of goals on the environmental wish list.

Jo Kwong is a research assistant at Capitol Research Center, a Washington, D.C.-based organization which conducts research in public policy. She prepared a study of Los Angeles' Air Quality Management District's proposals for the Reason Foundation, a Santa Barbara, California organization that promotes the free market.

"The array of technological controls, for the most part already implemented and proved effective in Los Angeles, is good news for cities around the world."

viewpoint **12**

Tighter Regulations Would Reduce Air Pollution in Los Angeles

Mark Thompson

Among the first things to suffer was the parsley crop in the Los Angeles Basin during the Second World War. The leaves turned bronze and withered. Orange trees in the area began to produce less fruit at about the same time. And, perhaps most disturbing of all, rubber automobile tires began to crack while they were still new.

The prime suspect was the brownish haze that during the summers in the 1940s had begun to sting people's eyes and shroud the mountains surrounding the basin. The haze, which looked like a mixture of smoke and fog, was dubbed smog. Many Southern Californians put the blame on the region's huge refineries and their smoldering effusion. More than a decade passed—and the problem grew so serious that eye-irritation forecasts were the lead item in daily weather reports—before the experts agreed that smog's key ingredients were supplied in abundance by automobiles.

The Smoggiest City

The term *smog* has stuck, though the air pollution plaguing most American cities is now known to consist of several different problems, including carbon monoxide, particulates, and, most intractable of all, ozone, a highly reactive form of oxygen that hampers lung performance and destroys the molecular bonds in leaves, plastics, and other materials. This colorless gas is a secondary pollutant, produced photochemically: it emerges in the atmosphere when sunlight irradiates a mixture of hydrocarbons and oxides of nitrogen, which are both among the major components of exhaust from engines fueled by gasoline. Smog contains hundreds of other, minor constituents. The chemical stew cooks in the sun, spinning off new substances in chain reactions that go on for days. Researchers so

far have catalogued about a thousand different reactions in smog. These, combined with the vagaries of the weather, make smog a phenomenon so complex that supercomputers can only crudely simulate its behavior.

With its burgeoning population and perpetual sunshine, Los Angeles will most likely never be displaced as the smoggiest city in the nation. But the air in the basin today is cleaner than it has been in half a century. Lead and the compounds that made stinging eyes a hallmark of life in Los Angeles in the 1950s have been virtually eliminated. And in 1986 and 1987 only one inland suburb was hit with a second-stage smog alert—signifying a seriously health-threatening condition that occurs when the ozone level slips above .35 parts per million parts of air (ppm). In 1980 alone twenty-one such alerts occurred. The ozone level is so consistently high, however, that for five months out of every year some inland parts of the basin exceed the maximum federal ozone standard of .12 ppm.

Ozone is not nearly so severe a problem in any other city in the United States, but in 1987 sixty-eight urban areas had ozone levels in excess of the federal standard, which all cities were supposed to have met by the end of the year, under an extended deadline of the Clean Air Act. Sunny, vehicle-clogged foreign metropolises like Mexico City and Athens now have the world's worst air. In Latin America and Europe, where cars are still largely exempt from emissions controls, automobile exhaust is a far greater contributor to the overall air-pollution problem than it is in the United States, according to Michael Walsh, a former director of the Environmental Protection Agency's motor-vehicle program and now an international air-pollution consultant.

Environmental regulators everywhere have found that smog is a wily adversary. It is so complex that some "solutions" have been found to exacerbate

Mark Thompson, "Fighting for Clean Air," *The Atlantic Monthly*, September 1988. Reprinted with permission.

problems downwind. Even more troublesome, the single most important source of smog is the widely beloved automobile. . . .

Smog regulators and scientists have developed enough respect for smog to know that it should be attacked warily. Some of the first attempts at fighting it were disasters. For example, air pumps, required for the first time, in California, on 1966-model cars, were designed to produce hotter combustion that would leave fewer unburned hydrocarbons as waste. Indeed, that's what happened. But the output of nitrogen oxides—created in larger quantities by high-temperature combustion—doubled. (Chemists later learned that one of the nitrogen oxides undergoes a photochemical reaction in the atmosphere to form nitric acid, a substance that forms a brand of acid rain and fog as destructive in some areas as the more-familiar sulfuric-acid variety.)

"Los Angeles has lost confidence that purely technological solutions will be enough."

The mistakes didn't deter California regulators from trying new ideas. The California Air Resources Board was created in 1967 to set emissions standards for mobile sources of pollution. Its increasingly stringent requirements eventually forced most automakers wishing to do business in California after 1975 to equip their cars with catalytic converters designed to cut hydrocarbon emissions. One vehement opponent of the proposed standards was the oil industry—which faced having to scour every bit of lead from tanks and pipelines in order to produce the pure unleaded fuel the devices needed. "I saw a president of a major oil company sit there and say we couldn't use catalysts because the oil industry couldn't switch to unleaded fuel—he said it couldn't be done," recalls an atmospheric chemist who served on a panel of advisers for the ARB when the tough new standards were proposed. "Well, guess what? That company, which shall remain unnamed, sells unleaded fuel."

The three-way catalytic converters now required throughout the United States and Canada, and in several other countries, have drawbacks—primarily the need for regular checkups to be sure they are working, and the expense of replacement if they aren't. But they do cut emissions of hydrocarbons, nitrogen oxides, and carbon monoxide. Catalytic converters may well have saved the city of Los Angeles. "If all the cars on the road today were 1950s cars," says Art Davidson, a spokesman for the South Coast Air Quality Management District, parts of Los Angeles "would actually be uninhabitable in the summer when the ventilation is bad."

Some cities elsewhere in the world are rapidly heading toward that point. "It's hard to get precise air-quality data, but it appears that Mexico City exceeds our federal ozone standard every day of the year," says Michael Walsh, the former director of the EPA's motor-vehicles program. During the temperature inversions that frequently hover over the city in winter, ozone levels soar above the .40 ppm level. "Many people in Mexico City suffer from air pollution," Walsh says. "We're not talking about subtle effects, either."

A number of other cities fall into the same class as Mexico City—Athens, Bangkok, and Santiago, Chile, for example. Many others, including New Delhi, aren't far behind. The streets of the Indian capital are clogged with more than a million vehicles, and 300 more join the throng each day. Their exhaust is every bit as noxious as that produced by the American cars of thirty or forty years ago. "It's getting worse every day," Jag Pravesh Chandra, the head of the Delhi Executive Council and the top elected official in New Delhi, told *The New York Times*. "At this rate, Delhi will become an unlivable city." Though half the air pollution in New Delhi is attributable to vehicle exhaust, India has no auto-emissions regulations at all.

Most of the countries of Europe, where sulfates from burning coal have traditionally been the most troublesome air pollutant, have also long hesitated to attack their significant automotive-smog problems. The European Community capped years of debate on auto-emissions controls by adopting an advisory measure recommending that each member country require three-way catalytic converters on cars with engines of two liters or more—but only about 10 percent of the cars on the road in Europe have engines that large.

California's Program

California's air-pollution-control rules remain the most comprehensive in the world. In more than two decades of steadily tougher auto-emissions regulations almost all of the pollution that can economically be squeezed out of gasoline-powered-engine exhaust has been removed. The South Coast Air Quality Management District was the first agency to mandate such things as vapor-recovery systems on gasoline pumps and emissions controls for dry-cleaning shops. It is now zeroing in on smog-producing emissions from bakeries, swimming-pool heaters, and open-pit barbecues.

In an aggressive program, launched in January 1988 by the AQMD's governing board (which consists of eleven representatives selected by governmental entities in the region), fleet operators, such as bus companies and rental-car firms, will be required to buy cars running on electricity or cleaner-burning fuels starting in 1993. However, methanol, the best alternative currently available, is far from a panacea. Methanol-fueled vehicles emit the same quantity of nitrogen oxides that gasoline-powered ones do. And in lieu of hydrocarbons they spew aldehydes, which are quite reactive photochemically and also probably carcinogenic. Refinements of methanol-fueled engines may mitigate these problems.

The array of technological controls, for the most part already implemented and proved effective in Los Angeles, is good news for cities around the world that have only recently acknowledged their smog problem and that have just begun searching for solutions. But Los Angeles has lost confidence that purely technological solutions will be enough. From now on, the air can only get worse—population growth in the basin over the next twenty years is projected at four to five million—unless the AQMD plunges into a new frontier of regulatory behavior.

Bold Initiatives

Another bold initiative launched by the AQMD board in January 1988 promises to shift the brunt of regulatory attention from cars onto their drivers. Controls on driving are old hat in other parts of the world, where cars have never become most people's sole means of urban transportation. Singapore, for example, bans most private vehicles from large sections of its downtown. Santiago uses a license-plate code system to keep 20 percent of all cars off the roads on any given day. In Los Angeles in 1988, phase one of a car-pool rule was scheduled to begin. Aimed at increasing the car-occupancy rate, hitherto 1.1 passengers per car, the rule forced every business with a hundred or more employees to set up a ride-sharing program and offer its employees positive incentives to join a car pool, take public transportation, or ride a bicycle. The future will hold far more than that in the way of controls on driving. Regulators are discussing the possibility of ordering staggered work hours, banning drive-through service at fast-food restaurants, and even suing the state department of transportation to force it to set aside more freeway lanes for cars with more than one occupant (after considerable wrangling, some lanes have recently been set aside on a few of the most crowded freeways).

"Angelenos won't readily give up the mobility that the automobile offers."

Angelenos won't readily give up the mobility that the automobile offers. Previous AQMD boards have shied away from car-pool rules, multi-passenger (or "diamond") lanes, and other controls that would constrain the Southern California life-style. But the region's smog regulators have overcome difficult obstacles in the past. And the current board, goaded by the threat of sanctions, including growth controls, if the region doesn't continue to move toward meeting the EPA's guidelines, appears undaunted by the toughest opposition yet, in its latest campaign. "We're interested in . . . creating a situation where people do less driving to live their lives," said James Lents, the AQMD executive director, at a press conference. "It's a very new area for us . . . and one that will touch every aspect of life in the Los Angeles Basin."

Mark Thompson is a senior writer for California Lawyer. *He also has written for* The Wall Street Journal *and* The Far Eastern Economic Review.

"Americans should feel secure that we have the safest, most plentiful, inexpensive, nutritious food supply in the world."

Pesticides Are Safe

American Council on Science and Health

In 1910, the typical American farmer produced enough to feed seven people. Today, the typical farmer feeds about 79 people, including 26 in foreign countries.

The reason American farmers of the 1980s can produce over 80 percent more than the preceding generation, and maintain their position as the world's most efficient food producers, is because of modern, scientific farming. This includes using pesticides, fertilizers, new seed varieties and automated equipment.

Yet even with these advancements and the promising future of biotechnology to control pests and increase yields, American agriculture is hard pressed to compete with foreign producers whose labor costs, among other factors, are much lower than ours.

Pesticides Are Necessary

Farmers are competing with more than foreign countries in the production of agricultural products. They also compete with:
- 10,000 species of insects
- 1,500 plant diseases
- 1,800 kinds of weeds
- 1,500 types of nematodes (microscopic soil worms)

These pests can reduce yields and damage crops so severely that the food or fiber is not marketable. Unchecked, they can totally wipe out a crop, sometimes within a matter of hours—before any "natural" methods of pest control can take effect.

In 1986, U.S. farmers spent $4 billion on pesticides. That seemingly huge sum was only about three percent of their total spending for production of goods and services.

American Council on Science and Health, "Pesticides and Food Safety," June 1989.

In California, for example, one strawberry farmer spent about five percent of his production costs on chemicals, the majority of his costs being rent on the land and labor. If he were to pay for hand weeding, the cost for the season would run about $10,000 an acre. By fumigating the soil before planting, he can reduce weeds so that it costs only about $1,200 an acre for follow-up hand weeding. He can typically harvest between 80,000-90,000 pounds to the acre, out of a potential "best case" of about 100,000 pounds an acre. When he tried to do this without chemicals, competition from insects and fungus reduced his production to about 20,000 pounds an acre.

For crops such as lettuce the story is similar. A particular farmer of 300 acres in Monterey County spends 6.25 percent (or $100) of his $1,600-an-acre growing costs on pesticides to control insect damage. The remainder is spent on seed, labor, utilities (including water), insurance and rent. His yield is approximately 800 cartons (or 19,000 heads) to the acre. Without the use of chemicals to control insects he estimates his yield would drop by 30 to 70 percent, depending on insect levels.

These lower costs of production and higher yields mean lower costs to consumers as well as greater availability.

Studies in Iowa and Illinois show that herbicide weed control saved farmers up to 9.2 percent over the cost of mechanical tillage of corn and up to 11.7 percent over mechanical tillage of soybeans. At the same time, herbicide weed control boosted corn yields 9.4 bushels an acre and soybeans 7.9 bushels an acre over yields with mechanical weed control.

Whether it is Midwestern grains or California fruits and vegetables, savings and yield improvements like these may make the difference between a farmer staying in business or not.

Consumers also feel the effects when yields drop due to pest destruction. In the fall of 1987, retail prices for iceberg lettuce nearly quadrupled across the country, to almost $2.00 a head in some areas. The cause was a Fall 1987 invasion of sweet potato whiteflies in California's Imperial Valley and near Yuma, Arizona—both major lettuce growing regions.

The whiteflies spread a virus called "the infectious yellows." The disease did not appear until two to three weeks before harvest, in late October and early November. One University of California agricultural extension scientist said: "The plant would be all nice and green on Friday, but you'd go back to look on Monday and you couldn't believe it was the same thing. The leaves would be all yellow and browning. In a week, it's garbage."

The damage to the lettuce crop sharply drove up prices for substitute crops, too. Prices of romaine and other lettuces almost doubled.

The lettuce crop loss is an extreme example. In Wisconsin tests, however, insect damage prevented green peppers from producing any fruit, reduced the average weight of cabbage heads from 3.5 pounds to one pound and damaged 86 percent of the sweet corn. Although it is unlikely to happen to that extent, such losses on a national basis would increase the consumer price of produce several-fold.

Pest Control and Food

These examples dramatize the economic importance of proper and timely pesticide use as an effective means of pest control. But they do not demonstrate another key benefit of effective pest control: the impact not merely on the external appearance of products, but on their quality.

We don't eat worms when we bite into an apple or an ear of corn. We don't find aphids or insect parts on spinach, lettuce or leafy vegetables. Tiny mites don't make their way into our homes and stomachs via strawberries, soft fruit or citrus. Insect damage is not accompanied by fungi or harmful bacteria.

A minimal amount of cosmetic insect damage on fruits and vegetables does not decrease its taste or nutrition and should by no means be an automatic cause for rejection. However, most consumers would reject the item if they knew that some of the "cosmetic damage" was insect excrement.

Molds, on the other hand, may very well represent a real or potential health threat because research indicates that certain natural blue and green molds cause cancer in laboratory animals. Molds and plant disease are more likely to attack a plant that has sustained insect damage.

An example is patulin, a natural toxin produced by a mold which forms when the skin of apples is damaged by insects such as the codling moth. Patulin causes cancer in laboratory animals and birth defects in chicks. It has been found in commercially available organic apple juice and is tested for by government monitoring programs so that it does not exceed established safety levels. Better control of the

codling moth helps prevent patulin contamination.

Some people believe that any amount of a chemical in the food supply is too much. These people are unlikely to be comforted by the guiding principle in the study of poisons, namely, that the dose makes the poison.

"Some people believe that any amount of a chemical in the food supply is too much."

This accepted principle recognizes that substances have different abilities to cause adverse effects— some are inherently more toxic than others. But toxicity alone is not the factor which determines whether a chemical substance poses a hazard. Only when the dose, or exposure, is significant enough, relative to the toxicity, does it pose a hazard. In some cases, minimal exposure to a highly toxic chemical may present risks on par with high exposure to a minimally toxic chemical.

Some pesticides cause cancer in laboratory animals. The central issue of concern for many consumers is the alleged relationship between cancer and exposure to pesticide residues in food.

In dealing with carcinogens, the scientific consensus 20 and 30 years ago was that we should treat carcinogens differently and assume that even low doses could possibly cause some harm, even though researchers can't measure effects at low levels. The reason is that most carcinogens are also mutagens (substances which damage DNA, the genetic material in cells). It was determined through research on radiation, which is both a mutagen and a carcinogen, that there is a possibility of adverse effects at even low doses.

But, new research is challenging the assumption that carcinogens are automatically mutagens which damage DNA. According to Dr. Bruce Ames, chairman of the Department of Biochemistry at the University of California, Berkeley, whose own work made him a pioneer in linking mutagens and carcinogens, "an astounding percentage of chemicals tested in animal cancer tests are being classified as carcinogens (over 50 percent), and most of these do not appear to be damaging DNA."

The fact that over 50 percent of chemicals fed to laboratory animals cause tumors may add fuel to a current regulatory controversy—the Delaney Clause to the Federal Food, Drug and Cosmetic Act. The provision, adopted in 1958, stated that no substance which caused cancer in animals or humans could be added to food destined for processing. At the time, this "zero risk" policy was thought to be prudent and workable. But, in 1958 there were only about four chemicals known to cause cancer in humans.

If it is true that 50 percent of chemicals tested cause tumors, a "zero risk" policy for man-made food chemicals is unattainable and perhaps unnecessary. Unnecessary because in the 40 or more years since the widespread use of synthetic chemicals in food production, cancer rates—with one exception—have not risen, as some predicted. According to the American Cancer Society:

> There has been a steady rise in the age-adjusted national death rate. In 1930, the number of cancer deaths per 100,000 population was 143. In 1940 it was 152. By 1950 it had risen to 158 and in 1984 the number was 170. The major cause of these increases has been cancer of the lung. Except for that form of cancer, age-adjusted cancer death rates for major sites are leveling off, and in some cases, declining.

Dr. Ames further believes that exposure to man-made carcinogens is not the threat some people believe because: (a) the evidence is that they are not DNA-damaging carcinogens; (b) the exposure to them is trivial relative to the background of natural carcinogens; and (c) evidence is growing that it is "too pessimistic" to assume that enormous doses given to rats can be extrapolated to low-dose human exposure, even for those carcinogens that are mutagens.

Agents causing birth defects that are not mutagens would also be expected to be harmless at low doses, believes Dr. Ames. The human body has numerous defenses against carcinogens in the food supply. Examples of that protective system are the cell lining of the digestive system which is sloughed off daily, the detoxifying enzymes in our livers, and the antioxidants throughout our bodies that protect us against oxidative damage.

Pesticides in Food

When used as intended, some trace amounts of pesticide residues may remain on food and are considered "legal." How and why are these "legal limits" determined?

The premise of our federal food safety laws is that some risk is acceptable. No risk is not the goal. (This premise is not unique to the regulation of food.) The exception is the previously mentioned Delaney Clause to the Federal Food, Drug and Cosmetic Act, which prohibits the addition by man of cancer-causing chemicals (based on animal tests) in processed food. By permitting some theoretical risk, the laws accept the idea that some amount of pesticide may remain in the food and still be considered safe.

The EPA [Environmental Protection Agency] has established maximum allowable residue limits, called tolerances, for about 10,000 chemical-crop combinations involving about 300 pesticide active ingredients. Roughly two-thirds of those active ingredients are in common use in the U.S., with very specialized uses.

These tolerances specify the maximum residue that is permitted in the crop at the time of harvest. These are not the levels likely to be found, but are much lower ones. For this reason, maximum allowable limits estimate maximum risks, not anticipated risk.

The primary purpose of tolerances is to set a standard for enforcement of pesticide laws. If residues exceed their allowable limits, or occur on crops for which they do not have a federally-approved tolerance, the FDA [Food and Drug Administration] and state agencies may seize, quarantine and/or destroy the food.

A 1986 report by the U.S. General Accounting Office has indicated that the FDA needs to develop a quicker and more efficient monitoring system so that foods containing illegal residues are, in fact, not sold to the public.

"The human body has numerous defenses against carcinogens in the food supply."

It should be noted, however, that most toxicologists do not believe that exposures to an occasional "illegal" residue present a significant health risk. This is due to the conservative safety factors used in determining allowable residue limits.

If, for example, the EPA receives a request from a chemical company to set a tolerance for chemical X on peaches, the regulators consider the following major factors:

1. EPA requires information indicating the maximum amount of residue which results from the intended use of chemical X on peaches under maximum application rates, maximum numbers of applications and minimum time between application and harvest. These are worst-case conditions almost unheard of in real practice.

2. At the same time, EPA requires the manufacturer to conduct toxicity tests on animals to determine a No Observable Effect Level in the most sensitive of species. Reducing that dosage by 100 to 1,000 times, which provides a safety buffer to account for animal-to-man extrapolation and extra sensitivity of population subgroups, gives the Acceptable Daily Intake (ADI) level, a figure established by the World Health Organization. The ADI is defined as the daily intake level of pesticide residue which, during a person's lifetime, is not expected to cause appreciable health risk on the basis of all facts known at the time.

3. To determine potential exposure levels, the EPA looks at the worst-case level of chemical X on peaches (based on the maximum use conditions above), and then uses the latest nationwide

Individual Food Consumption Survey of the U.S. Department of Agriculture as a database to determine how many peaches or peach products the population (and its geographic, ethnic and age subgroups) eats each year and in what form. In assessing this, the EPA makes a worst-case assumption that every peach produced in this country has been treated with chemical X and contains the maximum amount of residue.

4. Finally, the EPA considers both the amount of human exposure to chemical X from residues on peaches and the exposure from residues of chemical X on other crops. If the total exposure to chemical X stays below the Acceptable Daily Intake, EPA grants a tolerance, which specifies the maximum residue level allowed for chemical X on peaches. If the total exposure from all sources exceeded the ADI, EPA imposes special restrictions on use of chemical X or denies the manufacturer's request for the new tolerance. A pesticide can only be used on food or feed crops if a tolerance has been approved for this application.

"[Pesticide] residue levels in foods are managed through application restrictions which are legally enforceable."

To improve the method of determining dietary intake of pesticide residues, and thus enable the government to provide better protection from undue or potentially unsafe levels of pesticide residues, the EPA has recently developed the computer-based Tolerance Assessment System. This system uses new government data on food-consumption habits and food-preparation techniques, and allows for determination of food consumption by people with unique dietary patterns, such as infants and others defined according to age, gender, geography, socio-economic and ethnic categories.

Risk estimates can be calculated for daily food consumption patterns (acute exposure) and for annual food consumption patterns (chronic exposure), to better reflect actual exposure, rather than relying on "maximum allowable limits", which rarely occur.

The Tolerance Assessment System also considers the actual pesticide residue levels in food when consumed after processing and refining and allows for measuring exposure to pesticide breakdown products that occur during food processing. And, it will help determine the extent of pesticide exposure from non-food sources, such as water consumption.

Residue levels in foods are managed through application restrictions which are legally enforceable. These restrictions are communicated to the pesticide user through the pesticide label and, in California

where 50 percent of the nation's fruits and vegetables are grown, through a system of "permits" for chemicals that have restrictions on their use. The restrictions limit pesticide applications to crops listed on the label, they dictate the rates and timing of applications, and they tell the farmer how much time must pass between final application and harvest.

When label restrictions are followed, pesticide residues remaining on treated commodities at harvest are below the legal limits. This is true for a number of reasons:

• Allowable limits (called tolerances) are set based on maximum application rates and maximum number of applications, which is a "worst case" scenario that very rarely occurs. Anticipated and actual residues are fractions of the allowable levels. (FDA monitoring has revealed that the actual dietary intake of pesticides is consistently less than one percent of the Acceptable Daily Intake established by the World Health Organization.)

• Part of the pesticide is degraded by sunlight, water, wind, crop growth and microorganisms such as bacteria.

• A portion of the pesticide may be metabolized by the plant itself, converting it into either biologically active or inactive breakdown products.

• Some of the pesticide may reside in parts of the plant that are discarded, such as the outer leaves of lettuce which are thrown away when it is packed in the field.

By the time the consumer receives a commodity at home, the residues have typically broken down even further. After being washed, peeled or cooked, the food contains few, if any residues. Those that do remain are so insignificant that they are generally considered by scientists to be trivial in terms of human health.

For example, for fruits and vegetables treated with the fungicide chlorothalonil, less than one percent of the initial residue remains by the time it is eaten.

Similarly lettuce treated with the insecticide acephate (Orthene) shows a 91 percent decrease in residues between the field and the supermarket shelf. That is one percent of an already "tolerable" amount.

1982-1984 FDA Diet Study

The U.S. FDA Total Diet Study determines how much residue consumers are actually ingesting at the dinner table, rather than what might exist "at the farm gate." It begins by determining the diets of various age groups, the youngest category of which is six to eleven months old.

FDA buys and prepares the food as it would be eaten by these groups. FDA then takes the food and analyzes it for pesticide residues to give an indication of not only which pesticides, but how much residue, the public is actually being exposed to.

These residue intakes are then measured against the Acceptable Daily Intake (ADI). ADI is a figure determined for each pesticide authorized for use on food by the World Health Organization as being safe to ingest every day for 70 years. . . .

Processing and Residues

It is tempting to argue that pesticide residues may concentrate as food moves through the marketing and processing chain to the consumer, and in some cases this may be true. For the majority of chemicals, however, it is not.

For instance, it has been reported that residues of the fungicide benomyl concentrate in tomatoes during processing. Benomyl is used to protect tomatoes from disease. The allowable residue limit is five parts per million (ppm), or five units of benomyl for every million units of crop. Washing removes 80 percent of the residue. Preparation of tomato paste, which involves a four-fold concentration of tomato solids, results in a two-fold concentration of the residue which was on the washed fruit. However, the residue in the concentrated tomato paste is still only about one-tenth of the residue permitted in the raw product.

While in rare cases some concentration may occur, it is far more common for residues to be degraded. . . .

> "Pesticide residues rarely are present at tolerance levels in ready-to-eat food commodities and in many cases may be undetectable by the time the food products reach the consumer."
>
> Lee M. Thomas
> EPA Administrator
> May 1987, EPA Journal

As a final check on the regulation of pesticides, the FDA monitors the food supply to ensure that the allowable limits set by the EPA are not exceeded.

With few exceptions, dietary intakes have consistently been several orders of magnitude lower than the ADI estimated by the World Health Organization. Only one pesticide, dieldrin, has ever approached the ADI. Dieldrin and most other pesticides of a similar chemical composition (organochlorines) were banned in the 1970s.

All shipments of food are not checked for residues because the costs would be prohibitive and the historical evidence of violative residues is so low that doubling or tripling the amount of food tested is unlikely to reveal residue patterns that are different from those currently found.

Priority is given to those pesticides posing the greatest health risk potential and to those most-often-consumed foods that have the greatest potential for containing these chemicals.

The two main purposes of the FDA monitoring program are:

• To enforce maximum allowable residue limits established by the EPA and take regulatory action when illegal residues are found, and to stop shipment of the food where possible and prevent its occurrence again; and

• To determine the incidence and level of pesticide residues in the food supply to provide a check on the effectiveness of regulations and identify emerging problems.

The program is not designed to ensure that the food supply is free of pesticide residues.

Consumers should not assume that because it is permitted, the maximum pesticide residues allowed will be found in food they eat. Those levels are rarely reached, and "illegal" excess residues are even more infrequent.

Annual FDA monitoring of 15,000 samples of food finds less than three percent contain illegal residues. The most likely occurrence of "illegal" residues occurs when a residue shows up on a crop for which no tolerance has been established, even if the residue is considered "legal" on other crops in the exact same amounts.

"Consumers should not assume that because it is permitted, the maximum pesticide residues allowed will be found in food they eat."

Pesticide residues in excess of the tolerance are occasionally caused by misuse. They can occur if too much pesticide is applied to the crop, if the pesticide is applied too close to harvest, or if the crop receives pesticide drift from a neighboring field. They can also occur if the crop accumulates pesticides remaining in the soil from an earlier growing season's application.

The FDA samples a greater proportion of imported foods, mainly fresh produce, for pesticide residues than it does domestically grown food. Foods grown in foreign countries and exported to the United States cannot use a pesticide for which a U.S. tolerance has not been established. The incidence of illegal pesticide residues is about the same as for domestic foods and is not considered to pose a hazard to human health. Shipments are randomly checked at the U.S. border for compliance. If illegal residues are found at the border, the shipment is rejected. And, the next five shipments from the foreign distributor must be certified by a laboratory before they leave the country that they do not contain excess chemicals or chemicals for which a U.S. tolerance has not been established.

California produces half of the nation's fruits and vegetables, and virtually all of its walnuts and almonds. The California Department of Food and Agriculture's (CDFA) 1987 residue monitoring program showed a compliance rate of almost 99 percent on the approximately 12,000 items it tested.

The FDA data on imported food are supported by state monitoring in California, which samples approximately the same number of items a year as the federal government.

CDFA figures are comparable to independent testing programs conducted by private firms on behalf of grocery chains in California. Under an agreement with the CDFA to report all illegal residues, a private testing service representing 65 store locations between 1986 and 1988 reported five cases of illegal residues. Only one of these could be confirmed by state labs and that shipment was destroyed.

CDFA's laboratories can analyze for any pesticide registered for use on food crops in California, and all analyses can be completed within 24 hours.

Using a process to analyze a number of residues at once, it is possible to test for about 100 of the most frequently found pesticides within about four to six hours after arrival at the lab.

Residue analysis for individual active ingredients are performed on chemical/commodity combinations that warrant attention because of high consumption rates, concern about the chemical or suspicion of misuse.

In the rare instance that an illegal residue is found, state officials attempt to remove the item from the channels of trade before it reaches consumers. If it cannot be removed and toxicologists believe that there is a health threat, CDFA issues an announcement to the media about the problem. This is an extremely rare occurrence.

Nutrition's Role

Americans are bombarded with information about what they should and should not eat. The result is a nation confused about its food—an unfortunate situation when you consider that two-thirds of all deaths in America are directly or indirectly related to diet.

The mixed messages about the food supply are frustrating to many health professionals who feel that much of the energy and resources spent worrying about minute or nonexistent pesticide residues on foods such as fruits and vegetables could be better directed at getting ourselves, our families and the public to eat a variety of foods in moderation.

Americans may well benefit from eating more fruits and vegetables. A 1988 statewide survey in California revealed that 78 percent of the people surveyed did not know they should be eating several servings of fruits and vegetables a day. The survey also showed that on any given day, half of all Californians eat no fruit, one-third have no vegetables.

To remedy this situation, a five-year grant from the National Cancer Institute has been awarded to

California to encourage Californians to follow a diet with at least five servings of fruits and vegetables a day.

The ability of the American farmer to produce fruits and vegetables in such great quantities, with resulting low prices to consumers, is a direct result of his ability to control pests effectively and economically.

It is important that consumers do not limit their intake of vital sources of nutrition because of concern about chemical residues. Proper nutrition, through variety, balance, moderation and sanitation, is essential for good health.

"It is important that consumers do not limit their intake of vital sources of nutrition because of concern about chemical residues."

Americans can be proud that they have a food production and distribution system that is efficient and affordable. That is not the case in much of the world.

We can also take comfort in the fact that the vast majority of food scientists and toxicologists believe that our food supply is free from significant levels of pesticide residues. In the opinion of one such expert:

> . . . Based on my nine years experience as Director of the Center for Food Safety and Applied Nutrition at the FDA, as well as 20 previous years working at MIT [Massachusetts Institute of Technology] in nutrition research and policy development, there is absolutely no evidence, in my opinion, that the food supply is unsafe. This is not to say that continual vigilance is not required to ensure that safety, but at the moment there is just no evidence that the food supply represents a hazard. . . .

> Sanford A. Miller, Ph.D.
> Dean, Graduate School of Biomedical Sciences
> University of Texas Health Science Center

We should not, however, be lulled into thinking that we have reached a plateau with regard to safety and that none of our production and regulatory systems needs improving. Improvements in protecting the food supply—be it from the most significant factors (microbial contamination) or from factors of significantly less importance (pesticide residues)—can and should be attempted. The controlling factors are often limited resources and the current limits of science.

A relatively safer food supply is the responsibility of all parties—food producers, processors and handlers; chemical manufacturers and applicators; government agencies; and even consumers. Specifically:

Food industry—Farmers have the responsibility to use the least environmentally damaging pest control techniques they can that provide adequate protection from insects, disease and weeds. And, they are doing just that! Farmers are adopting a whole spectrum of methods, sometimes called Integrated Pest Management (IPM). This ranges from using natural predators and parasites, to good field sanitation to reduce pest populations, to "smarter" applications of chemicals. "Smarter" application means applying them only when close monitoring of fields indicates that non-chemical control methods aren't working well enough to prevent significant damage. In some cases, application rates of chemicals can be reduced and still be effective. Many of the nation's fruit and vegetable growers have reduced pesticide use signficantly (some by 75 percent) using IPM techniques. In the future, biotechnology may also present some pest control options that allow for reduced and more effective pesticide use. And, obviously, the food industry must use chemicals in accordance with the laws that have been designed to prevent excess residues from ending up in the food supply.

Chemical manufacturers—Companies have had since 1978 to upgrade the health data packages for the "older," pre-1978 chemicals on the market. It is a handful of older chemicals, not the ones registered in the past ten years, that are of primary health concern. Yet, submission of upgraded test data has been extremely slow. (A bill passed by Congress in 1988 gives the manufacturers eight years to submit the test upgrades.) Without adequate and reliable health data, the EPA is at a loss to make judgments about the effects of potential exposures to the public.

"Pesticide residues, when they do occur, have consistently been found in amounts far below the maximum allowable levels."

Exposure is another issue. The manufacturers could also work with the farmers and food processors to determine how much of the chemical residue really does or doesn't remain on the food during its stages from farm gate to dinner table. The allowable tolerance limits tell only what the maximum residue could possibly be under maximum use conditions, which rarely occur. It does not give a realistic picture of what is actually there under more realistic use. If a company has a product that doesn't meet today's health standards, it has the responsibility to get it out of the food supply as soon as possible.

Government agencies—A significant part of the pesticide controversy stems from the fact that there are inconsistent definitions of "safe." The concept of "safe" under the Federal Food, Drug and Cosmetic Act (no cancer-causing chemicals allowed to be added to foods that are processed) is different than the concept of "safe" under the Federal Insecticide, Fungicide and Rodenticide Act (risks must be balanced against benefits with regard to chemicals in raw, unprocessed foods). The federal government is struggling with this issue and some observers have suggested a middle path. The EPA could also more strongly encourage, or require, chemical manufacturers to provide realistic residue data and then use that information to review and modify the allowable limits for existing pesticides.

Monitoring for Pesticide Residues

It is questionable whether additional FDA monitoring of the food supply for residues would actually improve its safety, but it might make people feel better. The question is whether we have the luxury of spending money to make people feel better by sampling more food items when, in terms of public health impact, the money might be more effectively spent to address proven public health threats, like cigarette smoking and other dangerous lifestyle factors that substantially threaten the health of Americans.

Consumers—Along with proper nutrition, proper food handling can protect the consumer. For example, cooking meats to 140 degrees F. will kill microorganisms. Cleaning knives and cutting boards which have come in contact with raw meats and chicken before using them for other foods are proven precautions. . . .

Generally speaking, the safety of our food supply is evidenced by relatively few incidents of significant threat to the health of the American public and by numerous examples of mechanisms in place to protect it. Pesticide residues, when they do occur, have consistently been found in amounts far below the maximum allowable levels. Those allowable levels were themselves set to provide a significant safety margin to the public.

Food safety is based on the totality of what one eats. The quality of nourishment and the degree of sanitation are far more important parts of safety than the question of chemical residues. Americans should feel secure that we have the safest, most plentiful, inexpensive, nutritious food supply in the world. There is an elaborate system in place to protect us from the possibility of pesticide contamination.

The American Council on Science and Health is a consumer education organization concerned with issues related to food, nutrition, chemicals, pharmaceuticals, the environment, and health.

Pesticides Are Unsafe

Lawrie Mott and Karen Snyder

When you go to the supermarket, if you are like most Americans, you try to choose foods that are healthy. Instinctively you steer your shopping cart towards the produce section. The average American now eats 26 pounds more fresh fruits and vegetables per year than ten years ago. The typical produce section currently stocks over five times the number of items displayed a decade ago. The increased availability and variety of fresh fruits and vegetables is, in part, due to the extensive use of chemical fertilizers and pesticides. Yet residues of these agricultural chemicals can remain in our food. The fruits and vegetables in your supermarket may contain invisible hazards to your health in the form of residues of pesticides.

All of us are exposed to pesticides on a regular basis. The food we eat, particularly the fresh fruits and vegetables, contains pesticide residues. In the summer of 1985, nearly 1,000 people in several Western states and Canada were poisoned by residues of the pesticide Temik in watermelons. Within two to twelve hours after eating the contaminated watermelons, people experienced nausea, vomiting, blurred vision, muscle weakness and other symptoms. Fortunately, no one died, though some of the victims were gravely ill. Reports included grand mal seizures, cardiac irregularities, a number of hospitalizations, and at least two stillbirths following maternal illness.

During 1986, the public grew increasingly concerned over the use of the plant growth regulator Alar on apples. Primarily used to make the harvest easier and the apples redder, Alar leaves residues in both apple juice and apple sauce. The outcry led many food manufacturers and supermarket chains to announce they would not accept Alar-treated apples.

Also in 1986, approximately 140 dairy herds in Arkansas, Oklahoma, and Missouri were quarantined due to contamination by the banned pesticide heptachlor. Dairy products in eight states were subject to recall. Some milk contained heptachlor in amounts as much as seven times the acceptable level. Those responsible for the contamination were sentenced to prison terms. Several years earlier, it was the news media rather than the regulatory agencies that alerted the public to high levels of the pesticide EDB in muffin and cake mixes, cereals, and citrus. Given these incidents, it is not surprising that three out of four consumers consider pesticides in food a serious hazard, according to a 1987 food industry survey.

Inadequate Government Testing

The National Academy of Sciences issued, in 1987, a report on pesticides in the food supply. On the basis of data in the study, the potential risks posed by cancer-causing pesticides in our food are over one million additional cancer cases in the United States population over our lifetimes. Although some have argued that this theoretical calculation is excessively high, the number was based on the presence of fewer than 30 carcinogenic pesticides in our food supply (many more pesticides applied to food are carcinogens) and does not consider potential exposure to carcinogenic pesticides in drinking water.

The repetition of the Temik, EDB, Alar, and other stories suggests that the government programs designed to protect us from pesticide residues may be inherently flawed. These events also demonstrate the need for information on a series of fundamental issues concerning pesticide residues in food. As it now stands, you have no way of knowing if your food contains dangerous residues or whether the amount of residue you are eating is hazardous. Not only is government testing of food for residues

From *Pesticide Alert: A Guide to Pesticides in Fruits and Vegetables,* by Lawrie Mott and Karen Snyder, copyright © 1987. Reprinted with permission of Sierra Club Books.

spotty and inadequate, not only are some levels of pesticides allowed in food being challenged by leading scientists as too high, but no state or federal government agency really attempts to answer your most basic questions about pesticide residues in food—questions such as what pesticides are found in your food, what level of residue is safe and who should make these decisions. . . .

In the short run, this information can help you make more informed choices. There are some steps you can take to reduce your exposure to pesticides in food, such as buying organically grown produce and avoiding fruits and vegetables imported from nations with weak pesticide regulatory programs.

In the long run, we need to reduce agriculture's reliance on chemicals substantially. Methods to produce food with little or no pesticides have existed for many years. But more research needs to be done to expand these techniques, and the nation's food producers must be encouraged to switch to these methods. You can participate directly in resolving the problems posed by pesticide residues in food. If consumers begin to look for and demand safer food, farmers will be forced to reduce their use of pesticides and make changes that will significantly benefit our health and protect the environment.

By choosing foods with fewer chemicals, you can send a direct message to the food industry that will speed the transition away from hazardous pesticides in agriculture. Even food companies can now take steps to reduce the levels of pesticides in their products. In a March 13, 1986 letter to growers, the H.J. Heinz Company announced that food treated with any of 13 pesticides EPA is reviewing as a potential health hazard will not be used to manufacture baby food. You can also make the government do a better job of protecting our food supply and regulating these chemicals.

Ideal Solution

The ideal solution to the current problems posed by pesticide residues in our food has five different components:

1. Organic food should be made available in regular supermarkets. You should have the right to choose between different types of produce.

2. All produce should be labelled to identify where the food was grown and what pesticide residues it contains. This information would allow you to make more informed choices when purchasing produce.

3. The Environmental Protection Agency (EPA) should regulate pesticide use more stringently, and set tougher limits on pesticide levels in food so that the residues occurring are safe.

4. The Food and Drug Administration (FDA) should improve and expand its monitoring for pesticides in food in order to prevent consumers from eating food containing dangerous residues.

5. Agricultural production methods should be modified to reduce reliance on chemical pesticides. Food should be grown without chemicals used to improve the cosmetic appearance of our fruits and vegetables. Sustainable agriculture—farming that renews and regenerates the land—would be better for our health and the environment.

These changes will not come overnight, though some are already occurring. Several California supermarkets have adopted an independent program to identify pesticides in the produce sold in their stores. Organic produce is available in certain Boston food stores. Some national chain stores have said they would offer organic produce if requested by customers. By our efforts individually and together, we can ensure that these goals become reality.

"Pesticides are applied in countless ways, not just on food crops."

Each year approximately 2.6 billion pounds of pesticides are used in the United States. Pesticides are applied in countless ways, not just on food crops. They are sprayed on forests, lakes, city parks, lawns, and playing fields, and in hospitals, schools, offices, and homes. They are also contained in a huge variety of products from shampoos to shelf paper, mattresses to shower curtains. As a consequence, pesticides may be found wherever we live and work, in the air we breathe, in the water we drink, and in the food we eat. A former director of the federal government's program to regulate pesticides called these chemicals the number one environmental risk, because all Americans are exposed to them.

By definition, pesticides are toxic chemicals—toxic to insects, weeds, fungi, and other unwanted pests. Most are potentially harmful to humans and can cause cancer, birth defects, changes in genetic material that may be inherited by the next generation (genetic mutations), and nerve damage, among other debilitating or lethal effects. Many more of these chemicals have not been thoroughly tested to identify their health effects.

Pesticides applied in agriculture—the production of food, animal feed, and fiber, such as cotton—account for 60 percent of all U.S. pesticide uses other than disinfectants and wood preservatives. Pesticides are designed to control or destroy undesirable pests. Insecticides control insects; herbicides control weeds; fungicides control fungi such as mold and mildew; and rodenticides control rodents. Some of these chemicals are applied to control pests that reduce crop yields or to protect the nutritional value of our food; others are used for cosmetic purposes to enhance the appearance of fresh food.

As a result of massive agricultural applications of pesticides, our food, drinking water, and the world around us now contain pesticide residues; they are literally everywhere—in the United States and throughout the world. In fact, though all these chemicals have been banned from agricultural use, nearly all Americans have residues of the pesticides DDT, chlordane, heptachlor, aldrin, and dieldrin in their bodies. Ground water is the source of drinking water for 95 percent of rural Americans and 50 percent of all Americans. Yet, according to a 1987 Environmental Protection Agency (EPA) report, at least 20 pesticides, some of which cause cancer and other harmful effects, have been found in ground water in at least 24 states. In California alone, 57 different pesticides have been detected in the ground water. The banned pesticide DBCP remains in 2,499 drinking water wells in California's San Joaquin Valley—1,473 of these contaminated wells are not considered suitable for drinking water or bathing because the DBCP levels exceed the state health department's action level. As more states conduct ground water sampling programs for pesticides, more pesticides are expected to be found. Surface water supplies have also been found to contain pesticides. For example, the herbicide alachlor, or Lasso, has contaminated both ground and surface water in the Midwest, primarily as a result of use on corn and soybeans. Meanwhile, the federal government provides financial assistance to cotton and soybean farmers because enormous surpluses of these crops exist in the United States.

The extent of contamination of our food is unknown. The Federal Food and Drug Administration (FDA) monitors our food supply to detect pesticide residues. Between 1982 and 1985, FDA detected pesticide residues in 48 percent of the most frequently consumed fresh fruits and vegetables. This figure probably understates the presence of pesticides in food because about half of the pesticides applied to food cannot be detected by FDA's routine laboratory methods, and FDA samples less than one percent of our food.

"A National Cancer Institute study found that farmers exposed to herbicides had a six times greater risk than nonfarmers of contracting one type of cancer."

The cumulative effect of widespread, chronic low-level exposure to pesticides is only partially understood. Some of the only examples now available involve farmers and field workers. A National Cancer Institute study found that farmers exposed to herbicides had a six times greater risk than nonfarmers of contracting one type of cancer.

Other studies have shown similar results, with farmers exposed to pesticides having an increased risk of developing cancer. Researchers at the University of Southern California uncovered startling results in a 1987 study sponsored by the National Cancer Institute. Children living in homes where household and garden pesticides were used had as much as a sevenfold greater chance of developing childhood leukemia.

Another frightening consequence of the long-term and increasing use of pesticides is that the pest species farmers try to control are becoming resistant to these chemicals. For example, the number of insects resistant to insecticides nearly doubled between 1970 and 1980. Resistance among weeds and fungi has also risen sharply in the last two decades. In order to combat this problem, greater amounts of pesticides must be applied to control the pest, which in turn can increase the pest's resistance to the chemical. For example, since the 1940s pesticide use has increased tenfold, but crop losses to insects have doubled.

Pesticides Harm the Environment

Pesticides can also have detrimental effects on the environment. The widespread use of chlorinated insecticides, particularly DDT, significantly reduced bird populations, affecting bald eagles, ospreys, peregrine falcons, and brown pelicans. DDT is very persistent and highly mobile in the environment. Animals in the Antarctic and from areas never sprayed have been found to contain DDT or its metabolites. Though most of the organochlorines are no longer used in the United States, continuing use in other nations has serious environmental consequences. Other types of pesticides now applied in the United States have adverse effects on the environment.

A February 1987 EPA report, entitled *Unfinished Business*, ranked pesticides in food as one of the nation's most serious health and environmental problems. Many pesticides widely used on food are known to cause, or are suspected of causing, cancer. To date, EPA has identified 55 cancer-causing pesticides that may leave residues in food. Other pesticides can cause birth defects or miscarriages. Some pesticides can produce changes in the genetic material, or genetic mutations, that can be passed to the next generation. Other pesticides can cause sterility or impaired fertility.

Under today's scientific practices, predictions of the potential adverse health effects of chemicals on humans are based on laboratory testing in animals. Unfortunately, the overwhelming majority of pesticides used today have not been sufficiently tested for their health hazards. The National Academy of Sciences estimated, by looking at a selected number of chemicals, that data to conduct a thorough assessment of health effects were available for only ten percent of the ingredients in pesticide products used today.

A 1982 Congressional report estimated that between 82 percent and 85 percent of pesticides registered for use had not been adequately tested for their ability to cause cancer; the figure was 60 percent to 70 percent for birth defects, and 90 percent to 93 percent for genetic mutations. This situation has occurred because the majority of pesticides now available were licensed for use before EPA established requirements for health effects testing.

In 1972, Congress directed EPA to reevaluate all these older chemicals (approximately 600) by the modern testing regimens. Through reregistration, EPA would fill the gaps in required toxicology tests. Roughly 400 pesticides are registered for use on food, and 390 of these are older chemicals that are undergoing reregistration review. By 1986, however, EPA still had not completed a final safety reassessment for any of these chemicals. To make matters worse, scientists are uncovering new types of adverse health effects caused by chemicals. For example, a few pesticides have been found to damage components of the immune system—the body's defense network to protect against infections, cancer, allergies, and autoimmune diseases. Yet testing for toxicity to the immune system is not part of the routine safety evaluation for chemicals. In short, pesticides are being widely used with virtually no knowledge of their potential long-term effects on human health and the human population is unknowingly serving as the test subject.

EPA Regulating Out of Ignorance

The lack of health effects data on pesticides means that EPA is regulating pesticides out of ignorance, rather than knowledge. This poses particularly serious consequences for EPA's regulation of pesticides in food. Pesticides may only be applied to a food crop after EPA has established a maximum safe level, or tolerance, for pesticide residues allowed in the food. However, EPA's tolerances may permit unsafe levels of pesticides for five reasons:

1. EPA established tolerances without necessary health and safety data.

2. EPA relied on outdated assumptions about what constitutes an average diet, such as assuming we eat no more than 7.5 ounces per year of avocado, artichokes, melon, mushrooms, eggplants or nectarines, when setting tolerance levels.

3. Tolerances are rarely revised when new scientific data about the risks of a pesticide are received by EPA.

4. Ingredients in pesticides that may leave hazardous residues in food, such as the so-called, "inert" ingredients, are not considered in tolerance setting.

5. EPA's tolerances allow carcinogenic pesticide residues to occur in food, even though no "safe" level of exposure to a carcinogen may exist.

The EPA is not solely responsible for the flaws in the federal government program to protect our food supply. The FDA monitors food to ensure that residue levels do not exceed EPA's tolerances. Food containing pesticide residues in excess of the applicable tolerance violates the food safety law and FDA is required to seize this food in order to prevent human consumption. However, FDA is not always capable of determining which foods have illegal pesticide residues. For instance, FDA's routine laboratory methods can detect fewer than half the pesticides that may leave residues in food. Some of the pesticides used extensively on food that cannot be regularly identified include alachlor, benomyl, daminozide, and the EBDCs. Furthermore, FDA's enforcement against food with residues in excess of tolerance is ineffective; according to a 1986 General Accounting Office report, for 60 percent of the illegal pesticide residue cases identified, FDA did not prevent the sale or the ultimate consumption of the food.

To understand the potential risks associated with pesticide residues in food, consider the case of the pesticide captan. This chemical is widely used in fruits and vegetables, and is a common residue in food. Although the levels of captan usually found in food are below EPA's tolerances, even these residues may not be safe for four reasons. First, EPA has called this chemical a probable human carcinogen; therefore, any level of exposure may cause cancer. Second, the majority of captan tolerances were set before EPA knew the chemical caused cancer. Third, the tolerances do not cover one of the compound's breakdown products that may also be a carcinogen. Fourth, EPA's determinations of what levels of captan in food should be acceptable do not consider exposure to captan through nonfood sources such as paints, mattresses, shower curtains, and shampoos. Although EPA began a special review of this chemical in 1980 because of concerns about its hazards, by 1987 the Agency still had taken no steps to restrict the use of the chemical or protect the public.

"FDA is not always capable of determining which foods have illegal pesticide residues."

This [article] identifies some of the pesticide residues that are found most frequently in 26 kinds of fresh fruits and vegetables. . . . The data were obtained from the federal government's and California Department of Food and Agriculture's pesticide residue monitoring programs. Because both the state and federal governments' laboratory tests cannot detect about half the pesticides used on food, many agricultural chemicals present in our food may not have been detected. California's results were included because the state program focuses on California grown foods, and California supplies the nation with 51 percent of its fresh vegetables and a significant proportion of its fresh fruit. The FDA does not extensively sample California food, in order to avoid duplication of the state's program. The combined results from both monitoring systems provide a more complete picture of pesticide residues in food nationwide.

TABLE 1
Frequency of residue detection in foods

Commodity	Percent of domestic and imported samples with pesticide residues
Strawberries	63%
Peaches	55%
Celery	53%
Cherries	52%
Cucumbers	51%
Bell Peppers	49%
Tomatoes	45%
Sweet Potatoes	37%
Cantaloupes	34%
Grapes	34%
Lettuce	32%
Apples	29%
Spinach	29%
Carrots	28%
Green Beans	27%
Pears	22%
Grapefruit	22%
Potatoes	22%
Oranges	22%
Cabbage	20%
Broccoli	13%
Onions	10%
Cauliflower	5%
Watermelon	4%
Bananas	1%
Corn	1%

All pesticide residues detected—regardless of the amount—were identified in each type of produce. Most of the residues occurred in amounts below EPA's tolerances. However, even residues below tolerance may not be safe because EPA's tolerance setting system is seriously flawed. Many EPA tolerances were established without adequate health

and safety data, or by relying on inappropriate assumptions about our diet. Therefore, the tolerances may have been set too high. In addition, the Delaney clause of the federal food safety law prohibits the use of cancer-causing food additives *in any amount*. However, the same law permits EPA to allow the presence of carcinogenic pesticides in food. There is no evidence to support this double standard because carcinogenic pesticide residues in food are no less dangerous to human health than other carcinogenic substances added to our food. . . .

What Consumers Can Do

Below are some steps you can take to limit your exposure to pesticides in fresh food. In the long term, the best way to minimize the presence of pesticides in food is by reducing the widespread use of pesticides in agriculture. Consumers can accelerate this transition in agriculture through their power in the marketplace. By demanding food without pesticide residues, or at least with less, consumers will deliver a clear message to our food producers and provide an incentive for farmers to decrease their use of pesticides. Specific advice on removing pesticides from food is difficult to offer because data on this issue are generally scarce.

1. Wash all produce.

In order to decrease exposure to pesticides in food, consumers should wash all fresh fruits and vegetables in water. This will remove *some but not all* pesticide residues on the surface of produce. A mild solution of dish washing soap and water may help remove additional surface pesticide residues.

2. Peel produce when appropriate.

Peeling fruit and vegetable skins will also help to avoid some pesticide residues. Peeling the skin from produce will completely remove pesticide residues contained as surface residues. Residues contained inside the fruit or vegetable will not be eliminated by peeling. Unfortunately, through peeling you may lose some of the valuable nutrients contained in fresh food.

3. Grow your own food.

You may consider growing some of your own food. With a small sunny area you can plant vegetables in a garden, or even planter boxes. For instance, it is relatively easy to grow lettuce, tomatoes or zucchini. Since you are growing the food, you can choose whether you want to apply chemical pesticides, and if you do use pesticides, you can select the safest ones possible.

4. Buy organically grown fruits and vegetables.

Consumers should consider buying organically grown fruits and vegetables. Alternative methods to chemical pest control have been available for many years and their use is increasing in certain crops. Yet these methods have been neglected because chemicals seemed so effective and their ecological and health dangers were not well understood. Most organically grown food is produced entirely without chemicals during the growing, harvesting, shipping or storage stages. Some states, such as California, Oregon, Maine, Massachusetts, Minnesota, Nebraska, Montana and Washington have both strict definitions of what can be called organic food and certification schemes to verify that food sold as organic is organic.

TABLE 2

FDA's imported and domestic food samples

Sample type	Total number of samples	Total number with residues	Percent with residues
Domestic	11,729 (60%)	4,450	38%
Imported	7,686 (40%)	4,922	64%
Total	19,415	9,372	48%

Alternative pest control techniques will not be expanded and used until consumers decide that the current dependence on chemicals is unacceptable. By seeking and buying organically grown food, shoppers are sending an undeniable message about their desire to avoid pesticides—and providing an incentive for farmers to produce organically grown food. Farmers may be more willing to change their agricultural methods if they believe consumers will support their efforts. Further, if growers perceived a larger demand for organic food, they would switch their pest control techniques, and increased amounts of organic food would be available.

The first place to start is your local supermarket. Consumers can request that their regular supermarket sell organically grown produce. All 125 Safeway stores in the United Kingdom, for example, stock organic produce. In 1987, Raley's, a chain of 50 supermarkets in northern California and Nevada, began a program to offer organically grown fruits and vegetables in all its stores. Several major American supermarket chains have said they would offer organic food if the demand existed. Most stores could locate a steady supply of organic food. Some organizations involved with sustainable agriculture have published directories of wholesale suppliers and distributors of organic food. You may want to suggest that your supermarket get such a directory, or directly contact the organization that compiled the directory for a recommendation about the best sources of organic food. The group that certifies organic food in your state, such as the California Certified Organic Farmers, could also identify good suppliers and wholesalers of organic food.

Organic Food Sources

Other sources of organic food include natural food stores and cooperatives. Check your local phone book. Also ask at farmers' markets and U-Pick farms where organic food is available. Your nearest organization for certification of organic growers may also be able to steer you to a source of organically grown fruits and vegetables.

5. Buy domestically grown produce and buy produce in season.

Imported produce generally contains more pesticide residues than domestically grown fruits and vegetables. Produce imported from other nations may contain residues of pesticides that are banned from use in the United States. Also, many food exporting nations in the developing world lack stringent pesticide regulations. You should request that your supermarket label the origin of the produce. Was it grown in the United States or in a foreign country? Produce shipping containers frequently identify the source of the food so it should be easy for supermarkets to provide you with this information.

6. Beware of perfect looking produce.

Consumers should also think twice about pursuing the perfect peach. Nature is not flawless. Many chemical pesticides are used to enhance the cosmetic appearance of fruits and vegetables. Farmers claim they use pesticides because of consumer insistence on perfect looking produce. A brown spot on the surface of an apple does not decrease the nutritional value of the fruit nor does it affect the taste. We must recognize that the price of perfect looking fruits and vegetables often is more pesticide residues.

Lawrie Mott is a senior scientist at the Natural Resources Defense Council (NRDC), an environmental protection organization. Karen Snyder is a research associate at NRDC.

Government Regulation of Pesticides Is Too Lax

William K. Burke

Since it was founded in 1970, the Environmental Protection Agency (EPA) has worked to reassure Americans that the federal government is concerned about their health and environment. But reassuring is not protecting, at least when it comes to regulating pesticides in food.

After 17 years the EPA lacks data on many pesticides consumed daily by U.S. consumers. And now that new studies are being produced the EPA wants to change its pesticide rules. It seems too many highly profitable chemicals now in use will be banned when the agency documents their hazards.

A paradox binds the EPA's efforts to regulate pesticides. Older, more toxic, chemicals continue to be sprayed while newer pesticides are subject to strict standards. The laws are the same for both newer and older chemicals, but the older chemicals have thus far escaped EPA scrutiny because they were first approved for use before residue levels now known to cause cancer were even detectable. And many pesticide uses approved before the EPA was created have continued since then, despite the lack of up-to-date scientific data on health hazards.

The EPA registration process that clears pesticides for use is lengthy, complicated and prone to lawsuits by both manufacturers and environmentalists. As a result, the EPA has traditionally focused its attention on well-known hazards like DDT, and on new chemicals about to enter the market. However, in 1981 the agency initiated a "data call-in" to bring its files on hazards from older pesticides up to date.

The new studies resulted from congressional orders that the EPA use current scientific standards to re-register older pesticides. But, according to agrichemical executives consulted by the National Academy of Sciences (NAS), that new data could

trigger a 1958 law that would ban 24 percent of all pesticides now in use.

That law, the so-called Delaney Clause, prohibits any cancer-causing chemical residues that concentrate in processed food. The clause is named for former Rep. James Delaney (D-NY) who insisted it be inserted into the 1958 Food, Drug and Cosmetics Act.

Until now, lack of data has allowed the EPA to avoid applying the Delaney Clause to older pesticides. But when the agency receives data showing those long-used chemicals cause cancer and concentrate in processed food, they will be forced to ban the pesticides' use in crops destined for processing plants. That would include approximately 55 percent of all foods, according to the NAS.

The prospect of having to ban so many profitable chemicals caused the EPA to ask the NAS for help. A committee of scientists, agrichemical industry representatives and researchers were assembled in 1985 to study current policy and evaluate new methods for regulating toxic pesticides.

The NAS study seemed to resolve the EPA's dilemma. It was exhaustive and properly critical of the EPA's flaws. It also suggested a new policy that could reduce estimated cancer risks from the most dangerous chemicals by almost 98 percent, while preserving the benefits of pesticide use. The NAS's scenario is impressive, but misleading.

The Risk of "Negligible Risk"

The NAS recommended the EPA allow carcinogenic pesticides to be sprayed on crops when the EPA calculated the resulting cancer risk was less than one cancer case per million consumers. The EPA could interpret this so-called "negligible" risk as meeting the Delaney Clause's strict no-carcinogens rule. Newer, less carcinogenic pesticides could then be registered to replace older chemicals.

That NAS recommendation was another manifestation

William K. Burke, "Your Salad Could Be Killing You," *In These Times*, October 14-20, 1987. Reprinted with permission from *In These Times*, a weekly newspaper published in Chicago.

of a Reagan administration policy that allows regulatory agencies to bypass the Delaney Clause if they decide a chemical's cancer risk is low enough. Janet Hathaway, a lawyer with the Natural Resources Defense Council (NRDC), said the NRDC will contest any EPA use of this tactic. "Our view is that you should use the numbers to alert people to [cancer] risk, but you should never use them as consoling mechanisms . . . and say 'gee, no cause for alarm,'" Hathaway said.

Environmental groups like Hathaway's hope that a win in the case of *Public Citizen vs. Young*, a court challenge to the Food and Drug Administration's use of such a "negligible risk" argument to justify continued use of carcinogenic food colorings, will prevent the EPA from using the same tactics. . . .

"It's going to take some gumption to implement this report. Whichever way they go the EPA is going to get sued," said Richard Wiles, who was in charge of the NAS report. If the EPA tries to use the Delaney Clause to ban the known carcinogens now in use, the underfunded agency faces years of costly court battles with the 20 multinational corporations that produce most pesticides. But environmental groups would probably sue to prevent the EPA using the "negligible risk" concept to avoid the law and license new pesticides.

The NRDC and other environmental groups just don't believe EPA pesticide policies will improve by implementing NAS suggestions that actually weaken carcinogen controls by giving the agency the power to disregard the Delaney Clause. "It would be a terrible and tragic mistake to do what the [NAS] report says," Hathaway said.

Dangerous Miscalculations

Poor science riddles EPA's current pesticide policy. For example:

• The agency has no data on synergy—the possible increased hazards from the pesticide combinations found in crops and American diets. Instead the EPA debates pesticide risks one chemical at a time.

• The EPA reports new cancer risks of pesticides by adding them to each American's current one-in-four chance of contracting cancer. "What's an additional one-in-a-million chance added to your current risk?" the agency implies. But saying pesticide risks are separate from other cancer risks like smoking, automobile fumes and radiation is a scientific fiction.

In order to make such an assumption the EPA would need what scientists call a "control" group: a selection of Americans who had never been exposed to carcinogenic pesticides. No such group exists. A chemical-industry scientist admitted almost 25 years ago that all Americans had measurable levels of carcinogenic pesticides in their bodies. Since then pesticide use has increased. The sad truth is that, as Hathaway put it, "no one knows what an

environment free of pesticides and other kinds of synthetic chemicals would yield in terms of cancer risk and mortality."

• "A wide margin of uncertainty surrounds nearly all [the EPA's] numbers," the NAS wrote about the agency's procedures for estimating each chemical's cancer risk. The EPA tests the chemicals on animals, and on the assumption that humans are more sensitive to chemicals. EPA calculations also assume the highest possible rate of pesticide exposure in an average diet.

"The Delaney Clause applies only to residues of carcinogens that tend to concentrate in so-called processed foods."

Of course, no one eats an average diet. If you eat more than the calculated "average" amount of fresh tomatoes treated with carcinogenic pesticides you can significantly raise your own cancer risk while enjoying your daily salad.

• Another major EPA problem is the agency's reliance on chemical manufacturers for health studies. Theoretically chemical corporations provide the EPA with studies done in accredited, independent labs. The studies are then evaluated by EPA scientists. Yet the EPA was forced to halt approval of metalaxyl, a fungicide, after revelations that EPA staff members apparently put the EPA letterhead on a report submitted by the chemical's manufacturer, the multinational CIBA-Geigy.

• The Delaney Clause applies only to residues of carcinogens that tend to concentrate in so-called processed foods. According to the EPA, no meat or dairy products are processed. For example, salami and cheese are called unprocessed and so exempt from Delaney.

Because much of California's tomato crop is processed into paste and sauce, growers are required to meet the stringent Delaney Clause standard. But California's dry conditions require few chemicals to grow tomatoes. Meanwhile, the EPA allows Florida tomato growers to use permethrin, a cancer-causing insecticide. Since most Florida tomatoes are sold and eaten fresh, the EPA exempts them from the Delaney Clause by calling them a separate crop and applying the more lenient standards for carcinogen contents on raw produce.

Critics insist such EPA interpretations favor chemical use over consumer safety. The Florida tomatoes that Americans eat all winter would be illegal if made into spaghetti sauce. But since they are eaten fresh in salads and sandwiches, the EPA says Florida tomatoes' carcinogen content is OK.

Wiles could find no rationale for the agency's

distinctions between processed and unprocessed foods. "Part of the problem is the mix of science and policy. When does the science guy have to go mind his manners and let the policy guy make the call?"

EPA officials often point out they are caught in the middle between environmentalists and industry. "No matter what we do, including nothing, we will be in conflict with somebody," the EPA's Debbie Sisco said. "There is no easy way out of this, someone has got to make a decision." But, especially under Reagan, the EPA has treated chemical companies as clients to be served while excluding environmentalists and consumer advocates from the regulatory process.

The NAS study reflects the EPA's bias toward 20 multinational companies that control the U.S. agrichemical industry. The study assumes that progress in pest control will come primarily from the research-and-development labs of those 20 companies. Even though the report discusses biological controls such as crop rotation and the introduction of pests' natural enemies, its main focus is on how to regulate pesticides while preserving manufacturers' profits.

"If gross sales of agricultural chemical companies are reduced or if net returns become more variable . . . revenues for research and development will decline and overall innovation is likely to fall," the NAS concludes. The threat to these revenues is, of course, potential EPA enforcement of the Delaney Clause.

Environmentalists want the carcinogenic pesticides now in use banned. They also want to prevent any loosening of present law to allow new, supposedly less-carcinogenic chemicals to be approved for use. So how do they think U.S. farmers should protect their crops?

Hathaway suggested the EPA could use its power to influence the structure of U.S. agriculture. "Why are we using carcinogens if there are substitutes available?" she asked. "And if there aren't substitutes available, maybe we shouldn't be using [carcinogens] anyway. . . . It might turn out that certain areas might not be able to grow peanuts, but that's life. It's better to be cautious on the use of these chemicals than to use them willy-nilly and let people suffer the consequences."

An Addiction

For now, pesticide use will flourish on U.S. farms. "You're never going to grow 400 acres of celery in Georgia without insecticides or fungicides," NAS' Wiles said. He noted, however, that the U.S. Department of Agriculture (USDA) estimates 30,000 farmers have switched from pesticide-based farming to natural pest-control methods. But many farmers say they've switched to such natural methods because of economics, not environmental concerns. Chemical farming can quintuple crop costs.

USDA policies promote agricultural chemical use. In 1986, 110 million pounds of pesticides were sprayed on corn and wheat subsequently stored as part of USDA subsidy programs. "Commodity programs are sort of the secret driving force behind the use of a lot of pesticides that don't need to be used," Wiles said. And EPA press releases soothe public concerns about those chemicals' dangers.

"USDA policies promote agricultural chemical use."

Spraying fields with pesticides destroys the predators that control insect pests under natural conditions. Once hooked on chemical solutions, a farmer needs larger doses of stronger pesticides as insects develop resistance to the poisons. And, despite its name, the Environmental Protection Agency has been willing to go to court to protect American farming's chemical addiction.

William K. Burke frequently writes about environmental issues for In These Times, *a weekly socialist newspaper in Chicago.*

"Irrationality not scientific fact has prevailed on the pesticide issue, and the individual consumer has been the loser."

viewpoint 16

Government Regulation of Pesticides Is Too Restrictive

J. Gordon Edwards

For the past 25 years, irrationality not scientific fact has prevailed on the pesticide issue, and the individual consumer has been the loser. Those spreading fear are not just the environmentalist groups who made their reputation by banning DDT and other life-saving and cost-saving pesticides, but also some overzealous scientific groups with political motives.

The problem is typified in a report by the National Research Council of the National Academy of Sciences that calls for restrictions on the use of agricultural chemicals, allegedly because such chemicals are tumor-causing. Released in May 1987, the report is a "worst case analysis" of the type that was abolished by the White House's Council on Environmental Quality in 1986.

The Council on Environmental Quality had determined that only "reasonably foreseeable" effects that are supported by "credible scientific evidence" should be considered in federal reports, and not "worst case" scenarios that breed endless debate and speculation. Unfortunately, the National Research Council ignored this call for a return to the rule of reason, and instead produced a report based on fantasy rather than fact.

The Research Council report lists specific pesticides that may be detected in some agricultural products by means of extremely sensitive analytical equipment. If the council had simply studied adverse human reactions associated with the application of agricultural chemicals on crops, its report would have been very reassuring and would not have provided any frightening headlines.

Instead, the Research Council devised a computer program that calculated the total U.S. acreage of each crop studied and then assumed that every one of those acres would be treated with the maximum legal amount of *all* pesticides approved by the Environmental Protection Agency for use on each crop.

Since every crop is threatened by more than a single species of weed, mold, mite, insect, and nematode, many different herbicides, fungicides, acaricides, insecticides, and nematicides are registered for each. The Research Council computer was padded with the maximum allowable volumes of *each* of these registered pesticides for the crops studied, all at the same time! No crop has ever been treated with such massive amounts of pesticides.

Usually only one pesticide is applied for each kind of serious pest per year, and then only if it appears essential! The California Tomato Growers Association keeps careful records of pesticide applications by its growers. The association reported that *"no pesticides"* were used on more than 70 percent of the tomato acreage in the state, and that no single insecticide was used on more than 40 percent of the total acreage. The National Research Council's calculation of the amounts of pesticides applied per acre of tomatoes was therefore sheerest fantasy!

Unreal Figures

The Research Council's computer program was also fed unreal figures regarding the amount of pesticides in the food that people consume. The computer program assumed that the maximum allowable levels of *every* pesticide registered for use on each food crop *would* be used, and that large proportions of each would be present in *every* bite of that kind of food eaten during the entire lifetime of each person.

Every actual sampling of pesticide residues in commercial foods belies that ridiculous assumption. In California, thousands of food samples are analyzed each year by the state. In 1986, more than 84 percent of the samples contained *no* detectable

J. Gordon Edwards, "Let's Tell the Truth About Pesticides," *21st Century Science and Technology,* May/June 1988. Reprinted with permission.

pesticides, and less than 1 percent had any illegal residues. ("Illegal" means either that a pesticide unregistered for that crop was present, or that a registered pesticide was present at a level exceeding the allowable tolerance level.)

The Research Council computer program further assumed that every person in the United States ingests all of the 15 kinds of foods studied by the council *every day* throughout his or her entire life. Presumably the council anticipated that every day each person eats tomatoes, potatoes, apples, peaches, grapes, oranges, lettuce, beans, carrots, soybeans, corn, wheat, chicken, beef, and pork.

"Pesticides are not presenting the American population with a major health hazard."

The computer then multiplied the legal maximum tolerance level of each chemical in each of these foods by the U.S. Department of Agriculture's calculation of the number of milligrams of that food consumed, per kilogram of human body weight. That multiplication yielded a "Theoretical Maximum Residue Contribution" or TMRC.

For each specific chemical, the TMRC figure was then multiplied by a hypothetical "tumor potency factor." The resultant figure was considered as the "risk of excess tumor development" posed by that particular chemical during a citizen's lifetime.

Based on the false assumption that we all eat all 15 foods every day and that all allowable pesticides are used to the maximum on each crop, the Research Council cranked out a hypothetical estimate of the "Worst Possible Estimate of Oncogenic Pesticide Residues in Food." That estimate, it asserted, indicates the total combined amounts of pesticides, calculated as the TMRCs of *all* registered pesticides from *all* major foods eaten during the lifetime of *all* U.S. residents. According to that "worst possible case" scenario, the council concluded that pesticide residues in our food could cause up to 20,000 excess cancer deaths a year.

More realistic calculations, based on actual levels of pesticides in the actual amounts of food eaten by people every day, were not studied by the National Research Council. When those realistic data are considered, they indicate that there are *zero* excess cancer deaths a year attributable to legally applied pesticides on crops. Dr. Arthur Upton, a member of the Research Council study group, has in fact stated, "Pesticides are not presenting the American population with a major health hazard."

Although the council report refers to "oncogenic pesticide residues in food," and relies upon the 1954 Delaney Clause of the Food, Drug, and Cosmetic Act

as the reason for restricting pesticide use on crops and in our food, there was actually no mention of "oncogenic" hazards in the Delaney Clause. The clause states, *"that no additive shall be deemed to be safe if it is found to induce cancer when ingested by man or animal, or if it is found, after tests which are appropriate for the evalution of the safety of food additives, to induce cancer in man or animal."* Notice that the infamous, shoddily written clause referred only to "food additives." Pesticides applied to crops were specifically excluded from its provisions!

The general counsel of the Department of Health, Education and Welfare at the time quickly pointed out that "the Delaney Amendment does not apply to pesticidal chemical residues in raw agricultural commodities or in foods processed from lawful crops."

The Environmental Protection Agency has frequently observed that the Food, Drug, and Cosmetic Act specifically allowed for legal limits of agricultural chemicals and their by-products to be present in food. These legal limits are referred to as "tolerance" levels permitted for each crop/pesticide combination. The legal tolerance is usually at least *100 times less than the amount that experimenters have found to have no effect on animals.*

The most important words in the Delaney Clause are ignored by the antipesticide activists and are usually omitted from media references to the clause. Those words are *"tests which are appropriate."* Tests on animals using dosages hundreds of times greater than they could ever encounter in real life are certainly *not* appropriate. Even worse, the chemicals have frequently been administered in totally unnatural, inappropriate ways, such as saturation, intravenous injection, fetal intubation, gavage, and so on.

The Tumor Fraud

The Delaney Clause specifically referred to additives that induce "cancer," which was defined at that time as a malignant growth with the tendency to spread to other parts of the body. "Tumors," on the other hand, were nonmalignant growths that do not spread and that often disappear after the massive chemical insults are terminated. (The Food and Drug Administration had defined carcinogenic substances as "those that cause *cancerous* tumors.")

In 1976, to make it easier to invoke the Delaney Clause as an excuse for banning pesticides, Environmental Protection Agency administrator Russell Train, an attorney, redefined "cancer" and "tumor." Train stated that "for purposes of carcinogenicity testing, tumorigenic substances and carcinogenic substances are synonymous."

Leading scientists objected to this unscientific ploy. For example, Dr. Carroll Weil of the Carnegie Mellon Institute wrote, "The main point of contention [regarding the Environmental Protection Agency's cancer policy] is the unacceptable redefinition of 'tumor' to mean 'cancer.'" Despite scientists' opposition, the EPA deleted the words "carcinogenic" and "tumorigenic" from their rulings and began using the word "oncogenic" to designate substances that caused *either* cancerous or benign tumors in test animals.

The word *oncogenic* was then considered sufficient to justify the banning of pesticides by simply invoking the Delaney Clause!

In a deliberate and grotesque misinterpretation of the Delaney Clause, the National Research Council report has now used "oncogenic" in that same manner, in order to hasten bans on many kinds of chemicals. Thus, opponents of agriculture have succeeded in preventing the legal establishment of tolerances for new pesticides, by requiring that they fulfill the current misinterpretations of the Delaney Clause. The Research Council now urges that previously registered crop pesticides (which are *not* food additives) be stripped of registration if they do not fulfill the Research Council's distorted interpretation of the Delaney Clause.

"Hopefully, the specter of lowered farm output, more costly produce, and burgeoning world hunger will cause consumers and legislators alike to reject the misleading National Research Council Report."

What will be the ultimate effects upon the nation's food supply if the will of Congress is subverted by this attempt to "trash" the Delaney Clause? Will the National Research Council's capricious and unsupportable "risk estimates" result in the banning of essential and perfectly safe agricultural chemicals? If so, what harm will that bring to the agricultural industry here and to the "balance of trade" worldwide?

Hopefully, the specter of lowered farm output, more costly produce, and burgeoning world hunger will cause consumers and legislators alike to reject the misleading National Research Council report and demand government actions based on legitimate, realistic estimates of risk, rather than "worst case estimates" with no substantial base of support.

J. Gordon Edwards, professor of entomology at San Jose State University in California, teaches biology and entomology. He is a long-time member of the environmentalist groups the Sierra Club and the Audubon Society, and is a fellow at the California Academy of Sciences.

viewpoint 17

Food Irradiation Is Beneficial

Niel E. Nielson

Most people would prefer their food to be free from disease-causing microorganisms and insect material, and would appreciate a technology that prolongs the shelf-life of fresh foods. Yet, food irradiation to ensure the wholesomeness of fresh and processed foods is under attack from a small group of antinuclear advocates who insist, most unscientifically, that they are protecting people from the alleged unknown effects low-level irradiation may have on food products.

Food Irradiation

These antinukes fail to inform their followers and the public that the established, organized scientific community worldwide encourages use of "food irradiation" done in accordance with published U.S. and international guidelines and regulations.

The focus of those who use the often misleading, all-inclusive term "food irradiation" is the processing of foods with electromagnetic energy at picometer wavelengths (trillionths of meters). It is well recognized in the scientific literature that low doses—that is, extremely small amounts of energy being absorbed—of picowave processing have the ability to disable the reproductive capabilities of essentially all insects, bacteria, parasites, and viruses. Because of this, the expanded, widespread use of this processing technique could be immediately life saving and could immediately, demonstrably, improve public health.

The basis for this assertion has been documented in studies published by the Centers for Disease Control and the U.S. Department of Agriculture, in which it is shown that thousands of lives are lost in the United States alone, annually, from such food-borne infections as salmonellosis and complications

arising from such infections. In addition, there is a large amount of information on the subject that is published in highly respected scientific literature, as well as first-hand experimental and research-based knowledge of the capabilities of low doses of picowaves to kill disease-causing microbes.

Routine applications of doses of picowaves of less than 100 kilorads (this is an amount of energy equivalent to that necessary to raise the temperature of the same amount of water by less than one half a degree Fahrenheit) to foods could reduce total bacterial content in foods by more than 99 percent and could completely disable the reproduction capabilities of 100 percent of the parasites. Since the immune systems of healthy human beings can overcome smaller quantities of disease-causing organisms when ingested, this 99 percent reduction would greatly reduce the numbers of human illnesses resulting from ingesting foods containing disease-causing microorganisms.

Further, based on the findings of the Centers for Disease Control and the Agriculture Department, widespread expanded use of picowave processing of foods could save hundreds of thousands of hospitalizations annually from such food-borne infections.

The Illness Question

The salmonella problem is very real and very complex, and it highlights the importance of the routine use of picowave processing. About 40 percent of the poultry in the United States is infected with salmonella. The problem becomes obscured by the obvious fact that when you properly cook the poultry, you kill the salmonella, so you should not get it from the poultry you eat. You get it from the raw poultry contaminating things that aren't going to get cooked—salads, for example, picking it up from a cutting board, or the kitchen help's hands.

Niel E. Nielson, "Food Irradiation Means Better Health," *21st Century Science and Technology,* July/August 1988. Reprinted with permission.

This is a two-step affair, but the result is the same: People get sick. And that says that you have to prevent the salmonella from getting into the kitchen in the first place. This is the focus of the Department of Agriculture's Food Safety Inspection Service's petition to the Food and Drug Administration to expand use of this technology to include all poultry, and at higher doses.

This is a very important issue: The antinuclear people use the argument that "unknown" illnesses are possible because 50 million people have not been tested for 50 years. The antinukes are saying that they think there is a very remote possibility of food irradiation causing a problem and therefore the technology should not be used. Yet, they completely overlook the fact that people are dying right now who could be prevented from dying if we could use the technology. That means that anyone who gives credibility to the idea that 40 years of testing in the United States and elsewhere is not enough research has lost perspective.

Doubling the Food Supply

Let's look at some of the advantages of this technology, especially for the developing sector.

There is now more food lost to insects and spoilage than would be required to overcome all the malnourishment problems worldwide, if the rest of the infrastructure for transportation, storage, and distribution were also established. If you take the whole world's production, 50 percent is lost before it ever gets on its way to market. In the developing nations, 70 to 90 percent of their own production is lost, thus losing people food and income.

For example, a significant percentage of the fish and seafood harvested in the tropics contains enough bacteria that, if it isn't frozen almost immediately as it is caught and cleaned, it is not going to meet the U.S. Food and Drug Administration standards. As a result, and in some cases as a result of poor handling, the food that could be exported from those countries to the United States is rejected in the range of 3 to 15 percent.

We could prevent a large part of the rejection of good foods—not decomposed foods—by use of routine picowave processing, which would drop down the bacteria count by 90 to 99 percent at only 100 kilorads.

This is a big number—90 percent—if you put it in perspective. In terms of sterility, it is not a big number. But you don't need sterility if you are going to eat the foods right away. All you need to do is knock the bacteria count down by 90 percent.

In the case of fish and seafood, it would be processed, frozen, and then picowaved. In the case of fruits and vegetables, it would be precooled and then picowave processed. This process would prevent insect problems that exist with a lot of these fresh fruits and currently prevent them from being brought to the United States. In many cases, the effective chemical fumigants, like EDB, are banned in the United States; in other cases, the alternative fumigant/disinfestation procedures are ineffective or damage the fruit.

One of the scare stories of the antinukes is that there are unique radiolytic products (URPs) that appear in irradiated food. Now, there has never been a chemical identified in the processing of food by picowaves that is not already in our diets. Every food group has been thoroughly examined looking for evidence of truly unique chemical products and none has ever been found. This is a myth that the opponents of food irradiation like to scare people with, that unique radiolytic products appear in food that has been treated with low-dose radiation. These unique radiolytic products are like UFOs—frequently sighted, but not there.

To date, in the established scientific literature, there has been *no* chemical discovered to result from processing foods with electromagnetic energy at picometer wavelengths that is not already being ingested by mankind routinely in much larger quantities. All such chemicals identified to date have been found to exist in foods naturally, or as a result of several types of widely employed cooking or preserving processes, whether in commercial or domestic kitchens or food production plants.

Obviously, there are proven toxins, carcinogens, mutagens, and so on, and the Food and Drug Administration (FDA) issues standards for their content in foods, regulates the use of such chemicals and the foods that contain them, and takes enforcement actions against food processors and suppliers who do not work within the law.

"There is now more food lost to insects and spoilage than would be required to overcome all the malnourishment problems worldwide."

Also obviously, there are chemicals such as vitamins and minerals about which we are still learning a great deal and the FDA has published (and will publish) recommendations concerning them also. But these chemicals about which we do have knowledge are a very small fraction of the total number of chemicals we ingest each day, and because there are so many different chemicals in foods that have not been thoroughly studied for their impacts upon mankind when ingested, food scientists increasingly employ such techniques as chemiclearance for evaluation of *relative* safety.

In this chemiclearance process, any resulting chemical that is identified as not having been in the foods prior to the processing is compared with all of the known toxins, carcinogens, and so on, and if not found to be among the known problems, a search is made to determine if such a chemical is already in mankind's diet.

Many highly qualified researchers focused for many years, internationally, upon chemicals that appeared to result from picowave processing and did so in every significant food category. They found all of the so-called unique chemical species that were discovered to be already existent in mankind's diet, in one way or another. As a result of all of this, those in this field of study feel very confident of the accuracy of the statement that there is *no* evidence that there will be *any* increase in risk for consumers of picowave processed foods.

"Any further delays in widespread, expanded use of this technology are going to result in a needless continuation of thousands of deaths."

The antinukes who conveniently use the URP argument to further their purposes typically do not have anything to do with public or environmental health. This is an indictment of a lot of people, and there may be some followers to whom I should apologize for making this all-encompassing indictment. But certainly those technologists who encourage those people or who let themselves be used as references for those people, need to be indicted because they are misleading people. They are just not playing it straight.

The established scientific community, as represented by organizations ranging from the National Academy of Sciences to the American Medical Association and the Institute of Food Technologists—the people who really know food science—have all endorsed picowave processing by organization. This means that the majority of the people in these organizations—responsible, recognized scientists—realize that there is no increase in risk and that there are potentially very high benefits. The people who are objecting to the use of this technology have no such accreditation, and yet they would pretend to have a large high-technology following in the field, which in truth they don't.

What they are doing is attacking the established institutions, which the public sponsors and which have gotten us so far advanced in the last 50 to 100 years, in so many ways, including just plain quality of life. There is the underlying theme that the establishment is bad. This permeates all these anti-food-irradiation activities.

In reality, the largest number of the leaders of these antinuclear organizations are doing it for profit for themselves. They are doing it because of the popularity they get, the number of lines of press, the exposure on radio and television. So they are feeding their egos, feeding their pockets from it. However, here the stakes are so high that they can be traced to deaths and needless illnesses, needless misery that is not speculative—it is real.

There is one favorite example that the antinukes like to use—quoted completely out of context. There is an Indian feeding study carried out by the National Institute of Nutrition. This study has been thoroughly repudiated by very well respected scientists worldwide and in India. The work done by India's Nutrition Institute could not be duplicated, which is one of the cardinal requirements of accepting scientific research. Also, their peers in India would not support this study and, in fact, after an investigation of how the study was conducted, came out with a policy statement against it.

A subsequent, much larger and more comprehensive Chinese study reached totally opposite conclusions to those reached by India's National Institute of Nutrition. But when the antinukes quote this study, they do not tell anybody that it's been discredited.

Another thing the antinukes do is distort information. One of these distortions is that irradiation creates peroxides in the food. Well, that is true. Food irradiation creates peroxides. But so does the body—and without them we would not live. These people know that the public did not pay attention in high school when these sorts of topics were discussed. So they play on it.

Machine-Generated Picowaves

The idea of using machine-generated picowaves instead of radioisotope-generated picowaves is gaining in popularity rather quickly around the world. This will cause people to refocus, for so many of the antinuclear factions are focused on the handling and storage of the *radioactive* cobalt-60 or cesium-137. Now we can tell them, "We've eliminated radioactive cobalt; we are using an accelerator to produce picowaves, now what are your concerns?" This throws out the most sensational part of the antinuclear argument.

The bottom line is that once we eliminate the radioisotope question, no argument brought up by the antinukes has merit. This is a bold statement from somebody with a scientific background, but it is true. The antinukes bring up arguments against food irradiation that have been authoritatively defeated, that are irrational, and in the face of overwhelming, established scientific-community rejection of their arguments, they continue to bring them up.

What becomes unquestionably apparent to anyone who believes in the qualifications of the established scientific organizations and has read their endorsements, or has sufficient technical training to do a thorough and objective investigation of the use of this technology, are the following points:

(1) No other food processing technique, whether employing radiation or not, has been as thoroughly studied by so many scientists worldwide.

(2) There is agreement among scientists expert in the field that there is *no* absolutely safe food.

(3) All of the arguments put forth by those who would deprive mankind of use of this technology have proven to be without substance.

(4) The motivations of those who would oppose use of this technology are often for their own personal benefit and have little or nothing to do with food safety.

(5) Thirty years of delays in use of this technology—which was originally recommended for widespread use in 1958 by the food industry, the USDA, FDA, and others—have been costly in terms of the quality of life, or even the continuation of life for millions of victims of many food-borne diseases.

(6) Any further delays in widespread, expanded use of this technology are going to result in a needless continuation of thousands of deaths and hundreds of thousands of illnesses annually from food-borne illnesses in the United States alone.

Niel E. Nielson, a high-technology entrepreneur, was the president of Emergent Technologies, Inc., a San Jose, California food irradiation company.

*"The problems with food irradiation...
range from the creation of unsafe,
possibly carcinogenic by-products in the
food to increased environmental and
worker hazards."*

viewpoint 18

Food Irradiation Is Harmful

Mark Mayell

An armed guard watches as three-foot-square containers are loaded onto a moving conveyor belt. "Caution—High Radiation Area" warn signs that adorn the walls of the small industrial plant. Off to the side is a high-tech control room, complete with consoles arrayed with lights, toggle switches, dials and video screens.

Containers slide by the control room into a maze of concrete walls. At the center of the maze is a room where the walls are over six feet thick. In the middle of this room is a storage tank holding rods of highly radioactive cesium-137, a by-product of nuclear weapons production. The conveyor belt comes to a halt as the containers surround the storage tank. An operator in the control room throws some switches. In the center of the maze, radiation from the cesium-137 swarms into the air, irradiating the containers and their contents. The radiation reaches a level 200 times greater than that which would quickly kill a human being.

Ten minutes later, the conveyor belt starts up and the containers move into a separate storage area. The contents are loaded onto a truck and shipped off for further processing and packaging. Eventually, what was once exposed to cesium-137 will appear as food on the shelves of your local supermarket.

Supermarket? Food? Why should what you eat have anything at all to do with nuclear-weapons by-products and lethal levels of radioactivity? It may seem a strange idea, but scenarios similar to the hypothetical one just described do take place today, and they'll become increasingly commonplace if irradiators, food processors, the nuclear industry and the federal government have their way. Touting food irradiation as an alternative to toxic preservatives, as "a new way to end waste and hunger" and as "the

microwave oven of the 1980s," they hope to see up to half of all foods in the American diet irradiated within the next decade.

Food Fascism

A growing legion of food-irradiation critics disagree. The whole idea of irradiating food is "perfectly ridiculous," says Dr. Sidney Wolfe of the consumer activist Health Research Group in Washington, D.C. It's "food fascism," charges Jeffrey Reinhardt, a co-founder of the San Francisco-based National Coalition to Stop Food Irradiation (NCSFI). It's as absurd as the Defense Department's plans for a nuclear-powered airplane, say others. The problems with food irradiation, critics charge, range from the creation of unsafe, possibly carcinogenic by-products in the food to increased environmental and worker hazards to a further warping of an already dangerously centralized and chemical-dependent agricultural system.

Today, battle lines are forming quickly in what may become one of the most charged public debates of the decade. As Congress and the Food and Drug Administration (FDA) stand poised to allow much greater use of food irradiation in the U.S., consumers and public-health advocates are joining together to try to stop this new technology. Scientists and public-relations campaigns are being marshalled in support of both sides. Already there's a fierce battle raging over the question of whether—and how—irradiated foods should be labeled, and that may be just the first skirmish of a long political conflict.

"Food irradiation is one of the most important issues of the '80s," says Denis Mosgofian, current director of NCSFI, "because it brings together those concerned with natural foods, better nutrition, organic farming, the environment, nuclear power and even the arms race and peace. The issue is not just about food—it's about the by-product use of nuclear technology."

Mark Mayell, "Zapping Your Daily Diet," *East West*, February 1986. Reprinted with permission from *East West: The Journal of Natural Health and Living*, P.O. Box 1200, 17 Station St., Brookline Village, MA 02147. Subscriptions $24/yr. All rights reserved.

Food can be irradiated in any form—packaged, fresh, loose or frozen. If food is sealed in an airtight container and then given a dose high enough to kill all microorganisms, it may have a shelf life of years. For packaged foods, irradiation can eliminate the need for harmful additives, such as nitrates in meat. Since at high enough levels irradiation can kill insects and their larvae, processors may not need to use toxic insecticides and fumigants.

Promoters of the process point to its greatest potential as a means to alleviate world hunger. Up to one quarter of the world's crops spoil before they can be eaten. If a large proportion of these foods could be irradiated, proponents say, starvation in developing countries could be virtually eliminated.

When ionizing radiation in the form of gamma rays strikes food, the result is a sort of biological and chemical mayhem. Cell division is disrupted and slowed down, which will slow the ripening process of fruit, for instance. Thus, by disturbing their metabolism, irradiation can kill bacteria, and at still higher levels can also kill viruses. Ionizing radiation can also disable organisms by destroying their genetic material. It is not necessary to make food radioactive for all this to happen.

> "When ionizing radiation in the form of gamma rays strikes food, the result is a sort of biological and chemical mayhem."

What are left behind in the irradiation process are new biological substances. Some of these biological substances, or *radiolytic products* (RPs), are common in other food processes, such as cooking or canning. These include carbon dioxide, methane and fatty acids. Other substances left behind are *unique radiolytic products* (URPs), and have not been observed outside of the process of food irradiation.

The FDA has already approved a limited number of foods for irradiation treatment. In 1963, it said from 20,000 to 50,000 rads could be used to treat wheat and wheat flour, and in 1964 it approved 5,000 to 15,000 rads for potatoes. Since the standard means of preserving these foods are relatively cheap and safe, there has been no reason for producers to irradiate them. Also, a series of rulings that the FDA made in 1966 and 1967 meant that if these foods were irradiated, they would have to be labeled at the retail level. Since no producer wants to admit on a label that their food has been "Treated with Ionizing Radiation" or "Treated with Gamma Radiation," no one is irradiating wheat or potatoes for U.S. consumers today.

But since 1983, the FDA has made a number of rulings that could greatly expand the availability of irradiated food. In 1983, the FDA approved the use of up to one million rads to irradiate spices and seasonings. Spices are often used as ingredients, and as such don't have to be labeled when irradiated. Today, perhaps one half of one percent of all spices produced in the U.S. are irradiated. McCormick, a major spice producer, may be the only company openly admitting to selling irradiated food in the U.S. today.

The Labeling Controversy

The big breakthrough for food irradiators began on February 14, 1984, when the FDA published in the *Federal Register* proposed guidelines that would allow the irradiation of fruits, vegetables and grains at a level of up to 100,000 rads. The FDA also proposed to eliminate the retail labeling requirement that had been in force since the 1960s. The public was invited to comment on these proposed changes.

The public did comment, too, for almost the next two years, to the tune of some 5,000 letters to the FDA, the overwhelming majority of them opposing food irradiation and favoring honest labeling. Nevertheless, on December 12, 1985, the day before her last day as head of the Department of Health and Human Services, Secretary Margaret Heckler approved for publication an FDA final rule that answers the prayers of food irradiators. The rule both broadens the approved uses of irradiation (allowing fruits and vegetables to be exposed to up to 100,000 rads, and increasing the limit for spices from one to three million rads) and proposes a new labeling requirement that is significantly weaker than what has been in effect for the past 30 years.

Under the new labeling requirement, irradiated foods must still be labeled at the wholesale and retail levels, but no longer is the straightforward "treated with ionizing radiation" the standard. Instead, producers need only put a "radura," a tulip-shaped international symbol, and the word "picowaved" on labels. Moreover, Heckler said that after two years the FDA will consider whether the symbol is well enough known on its own, and "picowaved" can be dropped.

Opponents of food irradiation were livid at what they saw as a gutting of irradiation labeling. The innocent-looking radura could almost be a health food symbol, they pointed out. And picowaved may sound scientific, but don't look for it in any dictionaries. It is a word that was recently coined by Niel Nielson, the president of Emergent Technologies, Inc., a San Jose irradiator. "It's meant to be cute and unthreatening, like 'microwaved,'" says Denis Mosgofian.

The new FDA regulations must be okayed by the Office of Management and Budget before they can be published in the *Federal Register* and become law.

Another food that it is currently legal to treat with irradiation in the U.S. is pork. In July of 1985, the

FDA granted approval to a petition submitted by Radiation Technology of Rockaway, New Jersey, for the use of up to 100,000 rads to destroy the trichinosis parasite in pork. During the short, one-month public comment period that the FDA allowed, critics of the ruling pointed out that pork's high fat content makes it more susceptible to radiation-induced damage, and that there were only 60 reported cases of trichinosis in 1984 anyway.

The Department of Agriculture, which has jurisdiction over meat, needed to put its stamp of approval on the pork irradiation proposal, and on January 15, 1986, they too came through for the irradiators, amending federal meat inspection regulations to permit the use of gamma radiation on pork. Like the FDA, they did some serious waffling on the labeling question, declaring that "decisions with respect to the labeling of such products . . . will be made on a case-by-case basis."

In order to understand why labeling is such a crucial issue in the food-irradiation debate, we must keep one salient fact in mind. That is, given the choice, most consumers would rather not eat food that has been exposed to nuclear radiation.

Overall, the food-irradiation industry is relatively small in the U.S. Analysts put industry revenues at about $3 million per year, mostly due to spices. Radiation Technology, the New Jersey firm, probably does the most business in other foods, such as strawberries and shrimp. These are irradiated for export only. There are a dozen or so companies already formed who hope to do food irradiation, and they're currently waiting for favorable rulings from the FDA. In lieu of food, irradiators are treating disposable medical supplies, baby powder, cosmetics, plastics and Teflon.

"Other important drawbacks to food irradiation include its harmful effect on nutrients, potential environmental hazards and worker safety."

In addition to the growing irradiation industry, the U.S. government is another major actor in this debate with a vested political and economic interest. Both the Department of Defense (DOD) and the Department of Energy (DOE) see food irradiation as the crown jewel in their ongoing "atoms for peace" campaign. The two main sources of gamma radiation, cobalt-60 and cesium-137, are by-products of either nuclear-power processes or nuclear-weapons production.

Figuring out what to do with cesium-137 is a primary function of the DOE's Nuclear By-products Utilization Program. Most cesium-137 in the U.S. comes from the Hanford Nuclear

Reservation in Washington state, where they produce plutonium for various weapons programs.

The connection between nuclear weapons production and food irradiation could be a major liability to the fledgling industry, and some irradiators are hoping cobalt-60 will be a publicly accepted alternative. Over four-fifths of the cobalt-60 used in the world's irradiators comes from Atomic Energy of Canada, a Canadian government-backed company. According to a recent Canadian business report, "Acceptance of gamma processing would mean a great deal to the troubled nuclear industry, which is aggressively marketing the process as a means of selling the by-products of nuclear research."

Is Irradiated Food Safe to Eat?

Perhaps the single most important question with regard to irradiated foods is simply, are they safe to eat? The federal government has spent somewhere between $50 million and $80 million over the past 40 years in an effort to answer that question.

Based on this research, the FDA says that at doses below the 100,000-rad limit being proposed, "the difference between an irradiated food and a comparable non-irradiated food is so small as to make the foods indistinguishable with respect to safety." In effect, the FDA is saying, yes, irradiation causes radiolytic products to form. And some 10 percent of these are likely to be unique radiolytic products. (So far, at least 42 URPs have been identified.) Moreover, foods irradiated at levels above 100,000 rads "may contain enough [URPs] to warrant toxicological evaluation." More study is needed only to determine the safety of, for instance, irradiated meat, fish and poultry. . . .

The government's reading of the scientific findings is hotly disputed by many researchers. One series of objections has to do with the reliability of the studies. Many of the early studies were commissioned by the Army or the Atomic Energy Commission, whose plainly stated support of food irradiation may have caused inconclusive or adverse findings to be discounted.

Offsetting the studies supportive of food irradiation safety are numerous ones demonstrating a variety of ill effects:

• Rats and other test animals experienced an increase in testicular tumors and kidney disease, and a shortened lifespan, while being fed irradiated chicken in tests sponsored by the USDA between 1976 and 1980;

• A recent pair of Russian studies has also found evidence of testicular damage and kidney disease;

• Studies of food irradiation in India have linked it with leukemia and abnormal development of white blood cells (children and monkeys were fed wheat three weeks after it had been exposed to 74,000 rads of radiation);

• Some animals fed irradiated wheat have been known to develop cells that contain more than the usual number of chromosomes.

Safety and labeling questions aside, opponents of food irradiation point to a number of important reasons why the process will never live up to promoters' expectations:

• There are radiation-resistant bacteria, such as the bacteria that cause botulism (botulism-affected foods would in turn be harder for consumers to spot, since other signs of spoilage might have been prevented by the irradiation);

• Irradiation causes what are known as "organoleptic" changes in food, that is, changes in foods' taste, smell and texture. Dairy products and some fruits are especially prone to such changes and are thus inappropriate for irradiation;

• Unpackaged food is not protected from bacterial contamination *after* irradiation;

• Some microorganisms can mutate under radiation, possibly creating new species even more dangerous than the original;

• According to a 1984 EPA [Environmental Protection Agency] report, food irradiation has been tied to increased production of aflatoxins, a deadly carcinogen;

• Even as a sprout inhibitor in potatoes, its most popular use, irradiation is not ideal since it increases potatoes' sensitivity to fungal attack and therefore to rotting;

• As a high-tech, capital-intensive technology, it is particularly unsuited for use in the Third World.

Other important drawbacks to food irradiation include its harmful effect on nutrients, potential environmental hazards and worker safety.

Like canning and freezing, exposing food to a radioactive source is harmful to certain beneficial constituents of food. Studies have shown that irradiation affects vitamins, proteins and amino acids, carbohydrates, nucleic acids and enzymes.

If the food-irradiation industry were ever to treat a significant portion of this country's food supply, the potential for radioactive leaks, spills or even disasters would be significant. Since the process is not economical if foods have to be shipped long distances for treatment, what are being proposed are many hundreds, even thousands, of irradiation facilities spread over the land, concentrated in food-producing areas. All of these would require individual shipments of highly radioactive substances. Residual radioactive wastes would also have to be shipped out or otherwise disposed of.

Consumer Involvement

Faced with the combined efforts of elements in Congress, nuclear weapons producers, the radiation industry and food processors in support of food irradiation, consumers have recently begun to organize on the grassroots level. One common

strategy is passing local labeling laws. In April 1985, an Oregon state legislator introduced the nation's first state irradiated food-labeling law. It would have required all irradiated food sold in the state to bear a label reading: "Warning: This product has been radiated with radioactive isotopes for purposes of preservation; the health effects are unknown." Legislators later changed the focus of the bill from food irradiation to sulfites, but other states have since followed Oregon's lead.

"Given the choice, most consumers would rather not eat food that has been exposed to nuclear radiation."

"We've collected over 5,000 signatures on a food-irradiation labeling petition here in Vermont," says Ken Hannington of the Vermont Alliance to Protect Our Food. Hannington points out that 5,000 signatures are a respectable number for a small state, and he says it will be followed up by a legislative proposal by State Senator Sally Conrad. Vermont's labeling requirements, if passed, would extend even to restaurants. At least one other state, Minnesota, has introduced similar legislation. . . .

As many problems as there are with food irradiation, it might deserve further consideration if there were no alternatives. Fortunately, there are many alternatives—humanity has been preserving its food with various techniques for millennia, and such traditional techniques as cold storage, drying and fermentation work well for certain foods and climes. . . .

A discussion of alternatives brings us to the core of the issue of food irradiation and preservation in general: For what purpose? So that New Englanders can eat Hawaiian mangoes in January? So that any food can be stored indefinitely and then shipped anywhere in the world? So companies can increase their profits? If these reflect our values, food irradiation may be a plausible answer. If, however, we seek our values in more and better fresh food, greater individual and public health, regional and local self-sufficiency in the production and consumption of food, a return to sustainable, ecological agriculture and an environment free of long-term toxic hazards, then there is certainly no need to climb aboard the food irradiation express. Like the nuclear airplane, we must hope that it never gets off the ground.

Mark Mayell is the editor of East West Journal, *a magazine that focuses on natural health and living.*

"A major reason for our parks' decline is the National Park Service itself."

The U.S. Park System Is Endangered

Alston Chase

Most Americans believe that our national parks and monuments remain safely protected. Ever since the creation of our first national park, Yellowstone, in 1872, these parks have represented our highest achievements in natural and historic preservation. The system today comprises 337 sites—including places as diverse as the Statue of Liberty and the vast, undeveloped parks of Alaska—covering more than 79 million acres and visited by nearly 300 million people a year. Together they have become a model that countries around the world have sought to emulate. Similarly, Americans believe that the agency that runs the parks—the National Park Service—is one arm of government that they can trust. Indeed, in a 1978 Gallup poll more than 95 percent of the respondents gave the Park Service a favorable rating.

Yet today the park system is in trouble. In those parks classified as "natural zones," animals and their habitat are disappearing, even though some of the same animals continue to thrive outside the park system. In the Everglades the future of the panther and the wood stork is in doubt, though the latter is rebounding elsewhere; the peregrine falcon is declining in Guadalupe Mountains National Park while staging a comeback in many other places; bighorn sheep are threatened in Death Valley National Monument. Yellowstone has already lost the white-tailed deer, the wolf, and the mountain lion, and has fewer and fewer grizzly bears, beaver, bighorn sheep, and probably mule deer—even though many of these species are doing well just outside the park. Exotic vertebrate species—including goats, rabbits, pigs, burros, and mongooses—have, according to Park Service records, invaded more than 150 parks and monuments, where in many instances they threaten native plants and animals.

A study by William Newmark, a researcher at the University of Michigan, published in the British journal *Nature* in 1987, found that fourteen national parks in western North America had lost a total of forty-two populations of mammals and were in danger of losing more. "Without active intervention by park managers," Newmark wrote, "it is quite likely that a loss of mammalian species will continue."

While the public may have known little about these unfortunate developments, they have increasingly troubled wildlife professionals. The National Park Service, in its State of the Parks Report of 1980, identified 4,345 specific threats to park resources. In 1984 Destry Jarvis, the vice-president of the National Parks and Conservation Association (a citizens' advocacy organization), told a group of park professionals, "Today the national-parks system exists in a state of crisis."

Much of this attention concerns external threats: air and water pollution, growing population pressures, and industrial developments that border some parks. But while encroachment does present a clear and present danger, it is not the only cause of worry. A growing consensus among park professionals holds that a major reason for our parks' decline is the National Park Service itself.

A Double Mission

When the National Park Service was created, in 1916, the enabling legislation directed the Service to "promote and regulate the use of the Federal areas known as national parks, monuments, and reservations . . . the fundamental purpose of the said parks . . . is to conserve the scenery and the natural and historic objects and the wild life therein and to provide for the enjoyment of the same in such manner and by such means as will leave them unimpaired for the enjoyment of future generations."

Alston Chase, "How to Save Our National Parks," *The Atlantic Monthly,* July 1987. Reprinted with permission.

This language has always bothered Park Service officials, for it appears to give the agency two contradictory missions: it directs the Park Service not only to preserve the parks but also to "provide for the enjoyment of same" by the public. How could the mandate of preservation be carried out while the Park Service also promoted public use of our parks? The more the parks were visited, the more damage would be done to them. In attempting to balance use and preservation, many rangers felt, they were playing a zero-sum game.

This ambivalence was aggravated by the fact that for much of its history the agency has had two constituencies with very distinct interests: environmentalists and the recreation industry. The environmental community naturally wished to see preservation take precedence over use, while the recreation industry wanted the reverse. Coincident with these two conceptions of how our parks ought to be used were competing ideas of what parks ought to be. In one—which we might call the landscaping philosophy—national parks were envisioned as larger versions of city parks. They were places of great natural beauty, to be sure, but more important, they were places for people. Rather than presenting to the visitor true wilderness, they offered pleasing, if contrived, vistas, pleasant accommodations, and recreational opportunities. In the landscaping philosophy, parks were cultural entities, the products of artifice. The second view of what national parks ought to be might be called the wilderness philosophy. This was the perception of parks as little pieces of undisturbed, primeval wilderness.

These two ideals called for quite different techniques of park management. Landscaping required the services of landscape architects and maintenance personnel. The wilderness vision, in contrast, required no management at all. If national parks were to be true wilderness, they needed only protection from the impact of people and civilization. Over its history the Park Service has vacillated between these two models, sometimes emphasizing use, sometimes preservation—shifts that have to some degree reflected changes in the lobbying power of the competing interest groups. . . .

Serving Two Interests

So long as the Park Service believed that it had to choose between public use and preservation, it could never formulate a consistent mission for itself. Nevertheless, it did find a formula for management that seemed to serve both the landscaping and the wilderness philosophy, for these two agreed on one critical point: the role of the Park Service, in managing the park system, was principally protective. If parks are managed for people—as the landscaping philosophy dictates—then the Park Service has a duty to protect those people; if parks

are managed to protect wilderness, then the Service has a duty to protect the park from people.

Consequently, whether the Park Service was tending to favor visitation or preservation, it felt that its rangers had to be trained in law enforcement. Currently rangers are far better schooled in law enforcement than in science and ecology. Historically the career ladder has been open to custodial engineers and those trained in police science, but not to ecologists or historians. Not surprisingly, the Park Service budget reflects these priorities: the lion's share of its appropriations goes to "visitor safety and protection," and little is allocated for resource management or research.

"So long as the Park Service believed that it had to choose between public use and preservation, it could never formulate a consistent mission for itself."

These priorities have had critical implications for Service wildlife management. Since 1968 those parks classified as natural zones have been managed in accordance with a policy known as natural regulation or ecosystems management. The idea is that parks, as self-regulating ecosystems, will, if left alone, remain roughly in equilibrium. The best way to preserve the parks, therefore, is to protect them from all outside interference.

Unfortunately, even though this protectionist philosophy—as a reincarnation of the wilderness vision—receives strong support from conservationist public-interest groups, it alone is an inappropriate model for managing our national parks. Never complete ecosystems, these places have been radically altered by civilization and are now tiny islands surrounded by a technological society. The eviction of the Indians, the elimination of predators, the introduction of exotic species of plants and animals, and a century of fire control have thrown even the "wildest" parks into ecological disequilibrium. And once an ecosystem has been truncated and thrown out of balance, it no longer has the capacity to restore itself. Like a seriously ill person whose vital organs are no longer functioning, the natural communities, if left alone, will die. A policy of protection, therefore, will neither arrest further change nor ensure that all that happens is "natural." Rather, over time it will produce historically unprecedented conditions—an entirely new regime of fauna and flora—which we will not have anticipated and which we probably will not like. . . .

What our national parks need, more than protection, is restoration. If the parks are to be preserved, they must first be restored to a semblance of ecological balance. Restoration of the land, moreover, is not a utopian ideal but a developing science. The task of restoration ecology is like searching for and then assembling parts of a puzzle to make a picture. Ecologists find isolated communities of native genetic types and carefully transplant representative individuals of these species to preserves that are reconstructed to replicate their original habitat. . . .

A Mandate from the Start

Restoring and sustaining our national parks is not a new idea. As early as the 1930s thoughtful wildlife ecologists and rangers were aware of the limitations of protectionism. Yet the policies of protection were still prevailing when, in 1962, President John F. Kennedy's Secretary of the Interior, Stewart Udall, created a committee known as the Advisory Board on Wildlife Management and directed the committee to address wildlife problems then afflicting the national park system. The conclusions of this committee—which was chaired by A. Starker Leopold, a professor of zoology at the University of California—were far-reaching, containing both the outline of a philosophy of wildlife management and a statement of purpose for national-parks preservation.

"As a primary goal [of park management]," the committee stated, "we would recommend that the biotic associations within each park be maintained, or where necessary recreated, as nearly as possible in the condition that prevailed when the area was first visited by the white man. A national park should represent a vignette of primitive America."

Yet most of the parks, the Leopold committee noted, had changed dramatically since the white man first came on the scene. . . .

Through [its] evolution the Park Service, while spending more and more money on research, was making little of the effort necessary to save the park system. To make matters worse, the retrograde nature of this trend was obscured by describing park policy in a new and attractive way: its goal, the Park Service decided, should be to "perpetuate the natural ecosystems."

Ecosystems management was supposedly the translation into policy of the Leopold report. Yet the committee explicitly declared that parks are *not* ecosystems: "Few of the world's parks," the report stated, quoting a 1962 report from the First World Conference on National Parks, "are large enough to be in fact self-regulatory ecological units." Nevertheless, by 1968 the Park Service was calling our parks "natural, comparatively self-contained ecosystems." What the Leopold report in 1963 regarded as a challenge—the creation of vignettes of primitive America—the Park Service in 1968 took as a given, though it had done no restoration work at all. By defining intact ecosystems into existence, the

Park Service created a rationale for continuing its policy of protection. If parks were intact ecosystems, then restoration was unnecessary. Nature could be left to take its course. Nor was scientific research required. Parks could be run by people trained as policemen. That this is a kind of voodoo ecology is not lost on professional biologists. Bruce A. Wilcox, the director of the Center of Conservation Biology, at Stanford University, explained in 1986, "A laissez-faire approach to management is simply not tenable any longer." . . .

Neither privatization nor money is, in my opinion, the magic formula that will turn the Park Service into a professional, ecology-minded agency. The preservation of nature, while clearly something that Americans desire, is difficult to price in a way that would offer entrepreneurs a profit incentive. The challenge of preservation is unique—quite different from the goals of managing lands for farming or hunting, for example—and the value of it is intrinsic and difficult to measure. The Park Service has made many of its mistakes in being *too* entrepreneurial in promoting recreation at the expense of preservation. And while Wilderness Endowment Boards may not be entrepreneurial, putting the parks under their control would further feudalize the system, making accountability even more elusive.

"What the Leopold report in 1963 regarded as a challenge—the creation of vignettes of primitive America—the Park Service in 1968 took as a given."

As for giving resource management and research more money, they are, to be sure, starved for funds and have been throughout the history of the agency. But the miser in the system is neither Congress nor the President; it is the Park Service itself. This agency consistently fails to submit appropriations requests for what it should spend on resource management and research. The National Academy of Sciences urged in 1963 that around 10 percent of the Park Service budget be spent on natural-history research. Twenty-four years later, in fiscal 1987, the budget share for such research was less than two percent.

What is needed is a reform of the National Park Service. Such a process would, I believe, entail the following steps:

1. The President should appoint a commission to review the purposes, policies, and performance of the Park Service. This commission should be aided by the National Science Foundation and should include prominent scholars who have not been associated with the Park Service in the past.

2. The Park Service should make clear its own

interpretation of its congressional mandate—something that, surprisingly, it has never done. Following this, the agency should reconsider its present equivocal park-management policy and address directly the apparent conflict between its missions of preservation and providing for public use. It should adopt a more holistic philosophy that is uniquely designed for parks: one that sees them as neither resorts nor pseudo-wildernesses but places of natural and historical importance, designed for appropriate public use. The Park Service should make clear that it is more than a custodian and that its responsibilities include restoration and nurturative management, which imply its sponsorship of intensive research.

"We must recognize that the frontier—and true wilderness—is gone forever."

3. The present distinction between "natural" and "historical" areas should be abolished. The purpose for the parks set forth in the Leopold report—preserving vignettes of primitive America—implies that all parks, even so-called "natural areas," are historic places, established to preserve various features of both our natural and our cultural history. And just as no park is purely a natural area, without any historical relevance, so all "historical" parks have some natural value.

4. If our parks are to preserve the past, they should also reflect, where appropriate, the role that Indians played in these lands. Unfortunately, both the Leopold committee and the Park Service, in implementing the Leopold report's recommendations, have almost entirely overlooked the contributions of the Indians to the primitive ecosystems. Where appropriate, the Indian heritage of our parks should be emphasized, and Indian techniques for modifying the environment should be adopted by resource managers.

5. To give the Park Service more independence and make it more accountable to the American people, it should be established as an independent agency, apart from the Department of the Interior, which is devoted almost entirely to the development of natural resources. As long as the Park Service—with its mission of preservation—remains in Interior, it will be treated as a stepchild.

6. To reduce the power of special-interest groups and enhance the professional stature of the agency, anyone appointed director of the National Park Service should be subject to Senate confirmation, and his or her credentials clearly established.

7. To make management more sensitive to the contributions of science, the ranger corps should be completely professionalized. That is, the Service should create a cadre of resource managers who would be required to have graduate training in relevant academic disciplines in order to advance through the ranks. Resource management should be the primary career ladder that reaches all the way to the top. Qualifications for superintendents and their staffs should not be dissimilar to those we expect college administrators and museum directors to have.

8. Scientific research should be made the centerpiece of all Park Service activities. The number of researchers within the Service should be multiplied at least fivefold. At least one fourth of all researchers should be recruited from academia, and the Park Service should establish clear guidelines for public access to the fruits of government research.

9. To de-balkanize the Service, the chief of research in each national park should report not to the park's superintendent but to the district chief scientist, who in turn should report to Washington. To ensure the accountability of resource managers in the individual parks, resource management, rather than remaining under the aegis of the park's chief ranger, should be made a separate division within each national park, and its chief should be responsible to a regional chief of resource management.

10. To ensure national coordination of resource management, an Office of Ecologic Studies should be established in Washington to direct research throughout the park system and serve as a research facility for natural and historical preservation.

11. To promote field research and provide the best possible information for park-resource managers, multidisciplinary research stations should be established in or near the major parks, and parks in critical condition.

12. To minimize the co-optation of independent scholars doing research in the parks, the process by which such people come to participate in mission-oriented research should be revised. Most needed are long-term studies collecting base-line data on the parks, and equally long-term basic research on ecosystem dynamics. Direction and support for such research should come not from short-term contracts awarded by each park or by Service contracting agents, as are awarded now, but from a funding program administered by peer-review panels composed of nongovernmental scholars, following the pattern of the National Endowment for the Humanities and the National Science Foundation.

Interrelated Problems

Are these reforms likely to happen? To answer this, I think we must take an ecological point of view. Ecology is the science of interconnections. The problems of the parks are interrelated, a consequence of faulty policies and institutional inadequacies, and cultural matters as well.

Our parks represent our past. Very much a part of that past is the frontier. This magic place, as Frederick Jackson Turner noted in 1920, bound the nation together. It represented the qualities we have come to think set us apart as a people: youth, innocence, energy, possibility, freedom, opportunity, and equality.

But to many Americans the frontier has also represented a negative side of the American character: the desire to conquer nature. For three hundred years the land beyond the frontier was a place our forefathers believed they were destined to control. This attitude eventually led to the disappearance of much of this country's wilderness. The lesson many Americans draw from this sad history is that if we want lands to remain wild, we must keep people out of them.

Both positive and negative aspects of the frontier outlook are still very much alive in the American psyche. We all like to think that wilderness still exists, where the land, as the artist Charley Russell once put it, belongs "only to God." And we still fear that human intervention in such places, no matter how well-intentioned, can only lead to harm.

Restoring America

The parks—particularly those classified as natural zones—have been represented to us as such places. They are, we have been told by the Park Service, the last vestiges of wild America. And though the Leopold committee might have considered them illusions of primitive America, in Park Service rhetoric and to many of our countrymen they are the real thing.

In suggesting that our parks are intact ecosystems, therefore, the Park Service has reinforced a peculiarly American myth. Saving our parks, however, can begin only when we reject this myth. We must embark on a program of restoration that treats our parks as places to be nurtured, and we must recognize that the frontier—and true wilderness—is gone forever.

Alston Chase holds a Ph.D. in philosophy from Princeton University in New Jersey. In addition to having taught philosophy at various universities, Chase is a former chairman of the board of the Yellowstone Association. His book Playing God in Yellowstone: The Destruction of America's First National Park *was published in 1986.*

"I firmly believe ... we can pass on to future generations for their enjoyment and use a Park System in better condition than it was made available to us."

viewpoint **20**

The U.S. Park System Is Not Endangered

William Penn Mott Jr.

As a nation, the people of the U.S. possess the largest and most abundant public parks estate in the world. The extent and diversity of our national park resource is in keeping with the great size of this country and the bounties of its natural endowment. They reflect the democratic ideal, the view that the land and the wildlife it nurtures should be held for the use of all, not restricted in private estates, as was once the European custom.

First, some history. By the early 1820's, citizens of the new nation were beginning to move westward across the Appalachian Mountains. The Louisiana Purchase of 1803 and Lewis and Clark's expedition in 1805-06 opened up a vast new territory. Migration beyond the Mississippi River was not far behind. In the 1830's and 1840's, a land rush began.

A few farsighted Americans, fearing the disappearance of wilderness, began to advocate formation of extensive parks. From such concepts developed the idea of reserving national parks, national forests, and wildlife refuges.

The world national park movement is considered to have begun with the acts of a few men. During the late 18th century, trappers worked the northern Wyoming-southern Montana territory—Yellowstone country—emerging with stories of its wonders.

Others heard the fabulous tales and began to explore the remote back country. In 1870, a party named for three of its members—Washburn, Langford, and Doane—visited the Yellowstone area for about a month of camping and observation. One night, as they camped at the junction of the Gibbon and Firehole Rivers, they put aside considerations of private commercial uses and decided to work for preservation of a great new public area. Many believed this began the national parks concept.

William Penn Mott Jr., "The National Park System: Looking Back and Moving Ahead," reprinted from USA TODAY MAGAZINE, May 1987. Copyright © 1989 by the Society for the Advancement of Education.

Following newspaper accounts of the Washburn Expedition, a party of scientists, photographers, and artists visited and brought back undisputable evidence of the area's unique qualities. Congress acted with unusual speed on proposals for setting aside the area. On March 1, 1872, President Grant signed the bill establishing a "public park or pleasuring ground for the benefit and enjoyment of the people." Some 2,000,000 acres of Wyoming and Montana territories became Yellowstone National Park under the Department of the Interior.

Within a few years, other areas were added by Congress. Under the Antiquities Act of 1906, succeeding presidents proclaimed national monuments made up of public lands with outstanding scenic and scientific features. In 1916, the National Park Service was created. By that time, the Department of the Interior had under its jurisdiction 16 national parks and 21 national monuments, mostly carved from vast western public lands.

Impressive Leadership

The parks and monuments were scattered through 15 states and two territories, with each separately administered. They needed cohesive leadership and management. Some parks and their resources were deteriorating to the point that visitors complained. One of these, a Chicago millionaire named Steven T. Mather, wrote a letter to Secretary of the Interior Franklin K. Lane, protesting deplorable conditions in Yosemite and Sequoia National Parks, where Mather had camped in 1914. Lane, a friend from University of California student days, promptly challenged Mather to come to Washington and run them himself. Mather, then 49, a personable, self-made Borax business executive, accepted.

Lane teamed his new assistant with Horace M. Albright, a 26-year-old lawyer and confidential clerk in the Secretary's office. Mather died in 1929 and was succeeded by Albright. The Mather-Albright influence dominated National Park Service management for nearly half a century, from 1916 to 1964. Their friends and proteges who succeeded Albright as director after he resigned in 1933 adhered to the same high standards of public service set by Mather and Albright.

The Congressional act establishing the Service charged it to conserve scenery, wildlife, other natural resources, and historic objects. It envisioned use of the parks for pleasure, but "by such means as will leave them unimpaired for the enjoyment of future generations." To execute this mandate, the Service leadership recruited a corps of professional, civilian park rangers. Mather also strove to make the parks better known and to get high-quality accommodations built in them. He began to contract with private business people as concessionaires to provide food, lodging, and other services, an arrangement that is still in use today.

Congress soon established more areas of the park system, many in the East. That expansion, plus widespread use of the automobile, attracted a steadily increasing number of visitors.

A presidential executive order in 1933 transferred 63 national monuments and military sites from the Forest Service and the War Department to the National Park Service. This action was a major step in the development of today's truly national system of parks—one of historical as well as scenic and scientific importance. . . .

Monumental Scope

The National Park System today includes 337 areas covering almost 80,000,000 acres, located in every state but Delaware and including sites in the District of Columbia, Guam, Puerto Rico, Saipan, and the Virgin Islands. In 1985, recreation visits approached 300,000,000, while total visits, including parkway and highway pass-through visits, were about 400,000,000. Over 16,000,000 overnight stays were recorded in 1985.

So great is the variety of the National Park System that a few paragraphs can give only a hint of its size and character. While the great scenic parks of the West are probably best known, more than half the areas of the System lie east of the Mississippi River, and more than half the areas in the System were reserved primarily for historical, rather than natural, attributes. In size, differences range from large national parks that encompass thousands of square miles to historic sites that cover less than half an acre.

The natural treasures of the System include the giant trees of the California North Coast, great canyons of the Sierra Nevada and the Colorado Plateau, cactus stands of the Sonoran Desert, barrier islands facing the storms of the Atlantic, and hardwood forests of the Appalachians. Active and

extinct volcanoes, fossil beds, coral reefs, limestone and marble caves, and the habitat of the moose, the eagle, the grizzly bear, and the alligator are protected in the parks.

Most of the nation's major historic sites are also the responsibility of the Park Service—among them Independence Hall; battlegrounds such as Saratoga, Yorktown, Gettysburg, and Shiloh; birthplaces and homes of presidents and other celebrated Americans; forts along the migration routes to the West; and dwellings of pre-Columbian Indians.

The diversity of the Park System has been enhanced by additions of the past two decades which included many seashores and lakeshores, wild rivers, and national recreation areas in or near large cities.

"Activities and land uses permitted in the parks vary greatly from park to park, as they must, but are mostly limited to leisure-time and learning pursuits."

Activities and land uses permitted in the parks vary greatly from park to park, as they must, but are mostly limited to leisure-time and learning pursuits. Hiking, picnicking, boating, camping, and fishing are major activities, and winter visits are growing in popularity. Consumptive uses of resources, such as timbering, hunting, and extraction of minerals and fuels, are not allowed in most Park System units.

However, one endeavor common to all parks is the form of teaching the service calls interpretation. This concept was introduced into the parks by Mather, who recognized how much the pleasure of a park visit can be enhanced by some understanding of its geology, history, and plant and animal life. Although places for physical relaxation, the parklands are in a sense academies where minds and spirits are nourished with comprehensive appreciation of the wonders of the natural world. The historic sites help one keep in touch with the inspiring story of the accomplishments of those who have gone before. As one interpretative writer put it, the parks help answer the question, "Who am I?"

Our nation is proud of the national park idea, which is uniquely American, but other nations also were interested early in such conservation. The world's second national park was Royal, in New South Wales, Australia. Gradually, most nations around the globe established parks in some form, although they differ enormously in character, size, and administration. Examples range from the great wildlife parks of Africa, which help preserve numerous species, to Japan's parks that may encompass houses and villages as well as farms and forests, Australia's national parks that are managed by the states, and Sweden's reservations of grand mountains and glaciers. Worldwide, "Yellowstone's Children," as they have been termed, number more than 2,000 national parks and equivalent preserves.

As the U.S. National System has grown, the Park Service has shaped policies and management practices to accommodate heavier visitation and changing social and economic conditions. As the old line would have it, "no one ever promised it would be easy," but it has been a tremendous challenge, forcing us to use all of the creativity and innovative thinking we can muster.

The government is facing a period of belt-tightening and, while the budget of the National Park Service is less than one-tenth of one percent of the over-all Federal budget, the American public pays close attention to any proposed cuts in park visitor services. This close scrutiny of our budget is not surprising when you consider that 300,000,000 visits to the National Park System were recorded in 1985.

Congressional passage of entrance fees legislation would mean a great difference in operation of the National Park System. Similar legislation died in the Congress in recent years, but we worked hard to convince the Office of Management and Budget that fee revenues passed back to the National Park Service would boost the legislation's chances on Capitol Hill and also assure the vitality of park budgets. I believe that the American public will support modest increases, and we are getting support, as well, from national conservation and private-sector groups. The continued quality of our interpretation and visitor service programs are at stake, in deliberations of this proposed legislation, as well as operations and maintenance.

The Philosophy of Interpretation

Interpretation and citizen involvement are among my top priorities. They are at the heart of the Service's 12-point plan. For too long, we have not realized the power of interpretation in helping us achieve the mission of the Service. Every point of public contact represents a tremendous opportunity for us to build public support for the National Park System and to educate our now-predominantly urban population on the natural and cultural values found in the National Park System, and also determine how the public can best appreciate these priceless assets and protect them for future generations to enjoy.

I feel we must emphasize the broader context within which the units of the National Park System are managed. We must "weave" into this a focus of understanding how parks contribute to the quality of life and productivity in our country and throughout the world. Interpretation and visitor service

functions must be "infused" with new ideas and a broader vision of parks.

There is no doubt in my mind that the public support generated by a sound and creative interpretative program is the only long-term protection we can count on to guarantee the preservation of both the National Park System and the National Park Service. In my experience, some of the best ideas and most stimulating thoughts for improved management and development of parks have come from an interested and involved public. We need these groups and individuals to be involved in meaningful ways. They tend to recognize problems as opportunities. They see the world from a different perspective. In an era of accountability, the close involvement of citizen groups to provide constructive criticism, support, and a different way of thinking can be invaluable.

"We will improve the environmental quality of the parks, increase our interpretative training, and increase our research and resource management capability to achieve this goal."

These two points—interpretation and citizen involvement—are important to the future of the National Park System and, for that matter, all Park Systems in the U.S. In the past, the National Park Service has met its challenge with direction and commitment. However, times are changing rapidly, and with these changes we need to sharpen our skills, dedication, and ability to meet complexities of the future. I firmly believe the future is bright and that we can pass on to future generations for their enjoyment and use a Park System in better condition than it was made available to us. We will improve the environmental quality of the parks, increase our interpretative training, and increase our research and resource management capability to achieve this goal.

We intend to develop support for establishing new units not now found in the National Park System. We will utilize budgeted seed money and other than fee acquisition such as land transfer, outside funding, and easements. At this time, we are considering Tall Grass Prairie in Oklahoma, Wild River National Park, somewhere in the Lower 48 states, and the recently opened Great Basin in Nevada.

During my first year as Director of the National Park Service alone, I visited more than 80 sites, and I have found how the national parks offer the public inspiration in many ways. From this special inspiration, we can gain by walking in the invisible footprints of both the great and the ordinary people who have been in these same places, walked the fields, climbed the stairs, and seen the sights just as we can today.

When I visited Bandelier National Monument in New Mexico, I was constantly aware of the Anasazi who had lived, died, worked, and played in the very place where I hiked, stood, and chatted with park employees and visitors. I was following the invisible footprints of the original settlers of our great country.

Inspiration from the Past

Everywhere we go in the National Park System, we can share in the experiences and inspiring moments of those who preceded us. They are not just "gone"; they have opened the way for us, as we can open the way for those who come after us.

How can anyone fail to be inspired knowing that we walk in the invisible footprints of the Father of our Country when we visit George Washington Birthplace National Monument, or come to Gettysburg National Military Park and Cemetery and walk where Lincoln walked when he came to deliver the Gettysburg Address?

Visit Yellowstone and follow the footprints of John Colter, who described that vast, wild place as "The place where Hell bubbled up." Think of Joseph Walker, overwhelmed by unexpected grandeur when he became the first known European man to view the splendor of Yosemite Valley after a rugged trek over the mountains from the East.

At Yorktown, we can feel the immediacy of opposing battlelines so close to each other that a modern freeway would not fit between them.

Go to Mound City Group National Monument in Ohio and follow the invisible moccasin footprints of the Indians whose planning design skills, as well as their manual labor, went into the construction of mound structures that have outlasted not only generations, but entire civilizations.

"By following the footprints of Martin Luther King, Jr., in the National Historic Site in Atlanta, we can renew our understanding of events."

Footprints are the human side of life as it was and is. By following the footprints of Martin Luther King, Jr., in the National Historic Site in Atlanta, we can renew our understanding of events of our own lifetimes. At Independence Hall, we can walk in the familiar steps of Benjamin Franklin and Thomas Jefferson as they were creating and refining the Declaration of Independence and the Constitution of the United States with their fellow members of the Continental Congress or the Constitutional Convention.

We have a dual responsibility here. We are responsible for assuring that future generations, too, can follow the footprints that inspired us so that they may share that experience and gain their own inspiration. We must also create new footprints—the footprints of those committed to preservation, protection, and interpretation so that those historic invisible footprints can be more easily followed and understood.

For future visitors, we, too, will one day be "those who have gone before." We have an obligation to make certain that our efforts lead ever forward and our passage assures opportunity unimpaired for the future experiences of those visitors. That must be our motto: "Ever Forward."

Parks, after all—be they national, state, or local— are among the most important of "nature's physicians" in maintaining the health and welfare of our citizens. More than that, they represent stability. They are our roots.

William Penn Mott Jr. is former director of the National Park Service. He left office in early 1989.

"Timber sales on a National Forest provide multiple benefits, such as wood for the local mill, increased forage for cattle and wildlife, access for dispersed recreation, [and] fire protection."

The Forest Service Effectively Manages National Forests

R. Max Peterson

Eighty years ago the Forest Service was created. At that time, the Forest Service was given a charter to manage the National Forest System lands in the public interest on a sustained basis. This mandate was interpreted as "the greatest good of the greatest number in the long run." Our management philosophy and organization have grown around that mandate from Congress. Even though the overall mission of the agency has not changed significantly over these 80 years, changes have occurred in how the mission is met. Protection and management of the National Forest System for the optimum combination of goods and services over time remains the major mission. The complexity of achieving this mission has increased, the demands for natural resources are greater, and the interest and involvement of the public continues to grow. More people than ever have an increasing interest in the management of public lands. It is important to remember that the National Forests were established to protect and provide a valuable supply of natural resources on a sustained basis in the long term.

Congress has established a direction that clearly demonstrates the importance of these lands to our nation's welfare. Whether one looks at the Organic Act of 1897, the Knutson-Vandenberg Act of 1930, the Multiple-Use Sustained-Yield Act of 1960, the Forest and Rangeland Renewable Resources Planning Act of 1974, the National Forest Management Act of 1976, or other laws, one common theme is the vision or long term management perspective. Even though balanced use of resources in the short term is of high importance, long-term sustained management of the land has been a condition that remains paramount.

Renewable resources such as recreation, range,

timber, watershed, and wildlife and fish, as well as non-renewable resources such as energy and minerals, must be managed, protected, and used in a manner that assures adequate resources available for future generations. To do this, investments must be made now in order to meet future needs. Erosion control measures and improvements for fish and wildlife habitat may not always show positive short-term benefit cost ratios. Investments are being made now to plant trees that will not be harvested for 80 to 100 years. Likewise, capital investments for campgrounds, trails, roads, and bridges are made today even though many of the benefits that justify their construction will not be realized for years into the future. In almost all cases, roads for a particular timber sale have value above and beyond their utility for the removal of trees in the present stand. They provide access for fire protection, public access for recreation, and a transportation network necessary for the future management and utilization of National Forest resources. They are planned, located, designed, and constructed to fit multiple-purpose, long-term needs and not just one initial sale or other project.

The Short-Term Perspective

The current questions regarding the economics of Federal timber sales have been raised in many cases because the long-term perspective has been largely ignored or set aside in favor of judging economic viability by comparing this year's costs to this year's direct receipts. For example, investments and actions related to a timber sale that do not provide a short-term profit based simply on a one-year comparison of total expenditures compared to receipts have been judged by some to be below cost.

It should be noted that Forest Service timber sales can be one vehicle for achieving broad resource management goals. They are used, for example, to improve wildlife habitat, maintain long-term

R. Max Peterson, "Economics of Federal Timber Sales," statement before U.S. House of Representatives Committee on Agriculture, February 26, 1985.

favorable water flows, reduce insect and disease problems, enhance future timber productivity by capturing timber mortality through salvage sales, and to replace stagnant stands with vigorous young growth. In carrying out a timber sale program to meet these multiple objectives, it is likely that specific sales may cost more to make than they initially return even when timber-related costs are properly accounted for. Our intent is that, when such a case exists, the non-timber, multiple-use, as well as future timber, objectives that would be achieved are carefully laid out and explained. There is no doubt that for the overall timber sale program the value of the timber sold does exceed the costs. For example, in fiscal year 1984 the cost of the timber sales program on the National Forests, excluding the long-term investment of road construction, was $303.8 million and the value of the timber sold was $701.4 million. This is true even though the timber sale program includes substantial costs incurred to protect and enhance other values. Road costs, associated with this timber program, totaled $273.1 million in 1984. From 1978 to 1983 the cost of the timber sale program, including roads, amounted to a total of $2.9 billion. The value of the timber harvested was $4.3 billion and the value of the timber sales for future harvest was $8.4 billion.

The timber from these management activities creates employment and helps stabilize or develop local and regional economies. And without an adequate supply of National Forest timber, lumber and wood-product prices would rise significantly, costing consumers substantially more for housing, as well as other wood-related products. This would lead to major increases in consumer expenditures, increase lumber imports, and have some impact on the balance of trade. It is difficult to attribute such benefits to specific individual timber sales, but they do exist and should be recognized in any analysis relating to the pros and cons of selling National Forest timber. . . .

"Utilizing the Forest planning process, we have a method of analyzing the economics of management activities."

Utilizing the Forest planning process, we have a method of analyzing the economics of management activities. Forest plans, some of which have already been completed, provide the analysis and evaluation necessary to determine how the resources of a forest will be managed, what it will cost, and what the environmental consequences will be, including the socio-economic impact and benefits to local communities.

The land management planning process, which

was developed with the assistance of a committee of scientists from outside the Forest Service, not only helps managers determine the best and most cost-effective use of resources, but also allows us to schedule their use so that adequate supplies will continue in the future. The process also identifies which long-term investments should be made and when. Since completion of forest plans is in itself probably the single most important analysis and information base for determining which activities will occur and how those activities will be scheduled on National Forest System lands, we will be briefing members of the Congress as forest plans are finished.

The planning effort throughout the country has resulted in a blending of professional interdisciplinary expertise and public participation, which deals directly at the ground level with the complex issues of management today and in the future, including the economics of those actions.

With this as background, I would like now to review some additional actions that we have taken which respond to the need to provide better information and respond to concerns about the economics of timber sales on National Forest System lands.

Improving Cash Flow

First . . . we are considering a policy that would help improve the cash-flow position of individual National Forest timber sale programs. The policy would make it clear that it is our intent that the total benefits from a timber program on a National Forest should exceed total related costs. The policy analyzed would also provide assurance that the minimum selling price for National Forest timber would be established at a level sufficient to insure that we recover the direct costs of sale preparation and administration. For example, if the direct cost for sale preparation and administration is $20 per thousand board feet, we would establish the minimum price at $20 per thousand board feet. There are some exceptions proposed which would allow some sales at lesser rates when the sale represents the most cost-efficient method of protecting the forest from insect, disease, or fire; attaining identified multiple-use purposes such as wildlife habitat; or retaining reasonable community stability. For the most part the policy would assure that basic direct costs are recovered. Another provision of the policy we are considering would limit increases in the timber sale programs in areas where there has been an unfavorable cost-revenue relationship in the previous five years, reflecting a stagnant market or possibly a supply-demand imbalance. . . .

Second, in response to Congressional direction, we are reviewing accounting procedures to determine if we can more accurately estimate the costs and benefits associated with the timber sale program on a National Forest. A special group has been organized to accomplish this task. . . .

It is already obvious that it is relatively easy to determine costs. However, to quantify the wide array of benefits and impacts of different uses and therefore relate overall costs to benefits is quite complex.

Assisting us in some parts of this effort are personnel from the private foundation of Resources for the Future and Oregon State University. Resources for the Future is working on development of a methodology for identifying and evaluating multiple-use benefits associated with timber management and will develop case studies in application of multiple-use accounting procedures. Oregon State University is making a survey of the private forest industry and is evaluating their accounting systems. . . .

As a part of the investigation stage, we have already found that there does not appear to be any system now in use in any public or private organization that accounts for all the costs and benefits associated with a timber management program which is designed to meet multiple-use objectives.

To keep others informed on the study, we have identified and have been in contact with other agencies, organizations, and individuals that have expressed interest in the economics of the Forest Service timber program. These contacts include the Wilderness Society, Natural Resources Defense Council, National Forest Products Association and the Society of American Foresters, as well as the General Accounting Office, Congressional Research Service, and the Office of Management and Budget. We plan to keep these groups informed and will continue to work with and provide current information to the affected Committees as the study progresses. One of the purposes of the timber accounting system study is to determine if there is a better way to track costs and benefits of timber sale programs for decision purposes. Along those lines, we have provided more information in the Annual Report of the Forest Service for 1984. In it, for example, we included a table which compares by region the cost of the timber program to the value of 1) timber and other products sold, and 2) additional outputs associated with this volume. The table does not include other types of benefits such as employment and taxes, but it shows some important relationships. . . .

Evaluating Forests

Third, we evaluated the relationship of cash flow to the timber sale program on the Black Hills National Forest. From the findings, we have identified several specific opportunities and recommendations that will be reviewed in other areas on a forest-by-forest basis. Through increased uses of economic analysis, opportunities to reduce costs were identified in both timber practices and silvicultural planning. The study resulted in recommendations for improvements in our budgeting practices and land-management planning. It also identified the need to establish specific financial criteria for decision making on a national basis. We are planning to initiate similar evaluations on some other forests in the near future.

"By law, the National Forests are managed on a multiple-use, sustained-yield basis."

By law, the National Forests are managed on a multiple-use, sustained-yield basis. Both the costs and benefits of activities carried out under this mandate are so interrelated that allocation of costs and returns to individual resource activities is, in the final analysis, a matter of judgment with which reasonable people may differ. Other approaches that do not rely on allocation of costs, such as identifying the total benefits achieved by the timber program, are also being evaluated. Timber sales on a National Forest provide multiple benefits, such as wood for the local mill, increased forage for cattle and wildlife, access for dispersed recreation, fire protection and access to capture mortality or treat an insect or disease outbreak. In order to achieve these multiple benefits, higher costs are encountered for sale preparation and administration than would be involved if only wood production were the objective. Because the resulting benefits include those which can be assigned a dollar value, as well as benefits to which no dollar value can readily be given, comparison of costs and benefits is complex and inherently subjective. We continue to work on methods to improve our ability to track costs and benefits in all affected resource areas. . . .

The best process we have for examining both the economic and social consequences of multiple-use forestry decisions is the "Forest Land and Resource Management Plan." The planning process which is underway, as required by the National Forest Management Act of 1976, allows for evaluation of interactions among resources based on various mixes of programs and land-management alternatives. This provides direction, with benefit of extensive public participation, as to how National Forest System land should be managed in the short term to assure that the long-term values are guaranteed.

R. Max Peterson is a former chief of the Forest Service, a division of the U.S. Department of Agriculture.

viewpoint 22

The Forest Service Mismanages National Forests

Randal O'Toole

Environmentalists have achieved much success since the 1960s, yet have fallen far short of their goals. The causes of these shortfalls are usually attributed to shortsighted decision makers and the political power of environmental opponents. But often, it is the environmentalists who are to blame for their incorrect diagnoses of the problems. A prime example of this is the debate over national forest management by the USDA [United States Department of Agriculture] Forest Service.

The 191 million acres of national forests are both the glory and the bane of the environmental movement. Most of the forests were created in the 1890s and 1900s and are today considered one of the greatest legacies of the progressive conservation era. But increasing timber cutting that began in the 1950s caused major public controversies and contributed to the creation of the modern environmental movement.

Gifford Pinchot, the dynamic leader of the Progressive movement, founded the Forest Service with the idea that scientifically trained foresters would manage the national forests in the public interest. One of the most outstanding such foresters was Aldo Leopold, who—together with other Forest Service professionals—literally invented two important concepts: wilderness and wildlife management.

As forest supervisor of New Mexico's Gila National Forest, Leopold approved the designation of the nation's first wilderness area in 1924. With the support of top Forest Service officials, the next twenty years saw the dedication of millions of acres of land to the wilderness concept. Leopold is also credited with being the father of wildlife management. He was among the first to recognize

the importance of habitat to wildlife and later founded the first school of wildlife management at the University of Wisconsin.

The philosopher-king idea of forest management became less enchanting during the 1950s. Depletion of private timber supplies combined with postwar housing demands led to an increasing emphasis on timber management in the national forests. Clearcutting, herbicide spraying, and the declassification of wildlife areas to access their timber aroused public opposition in every region of the country. Debates over these issues have continued to this day.

Believing that the Forest Service is naturally biased toward timber, most environmentalists conclude that prescriptive legislation in some form or another is necessary to resolve these issues. Led by the Sierra Club, opposition to Forest Service policies focused on several demands: congressional designation of wilderness areas to protect them from the Forest Service, a ban on or great reduction of clearcutting in the national forests, protection for old-growth and/or the management of timber on very long rotations, protection of important watersheds, and maintenance of wildlife habitat.

With respect to the national forests, the environmental movement has scored two great victories: the Wilderness Act and the Endangered Species Act. Since passage of the Wilderness Act in 1964, millions of acres of national forest lands have received congressional protection. The Endangered Species Act of 1972 requires the Forest Service and other federal agencies to protect numerous species of birds, mammals, and other wildlife by modifying management practices.

There is no question that the Wilderness Act has succeeded in protecting large amounts of land from timber cutting and other development. Yet, millions of acres of lands that deserve wilderness status are likely to be developed by the Forest Service for

Randal O'Toole, "The National Forests and the Environmental Movement," in *Crossroads: Environmental Priorities for the Future*, edited by Peter Borelli. Washington, DC: Island Press, 1988. Reprinted by permission.

timber sales—mostly at an economic loss. For example, the Forest Service plans to construct roads and log 1.2 million acres of roadless lands in Montana national forests. Such development serves no purpose other than timber harvesting, yet nearly all of the timber sales will lose money. Wilderness bills now being considered by Congress make only a small dent in these proposals.

The Endangered Species Act is not as clearly successful as the Wilderness Act. Whereas some projects have been halted or modified to account for rare species, many believe that the Fish and Wildlife Service, which administers the act, places undue emphasis on individual species rather than habitat protection. Captive breeding programs for the California condor, black-footed ferret, and other species are an expensive and inadequate substitute for sound habitat.

The Yellowstone grizzly bear is a particular example of how the Endangered Species Act has failed to influence national forest management. The bear unquestionably needs solitude more than anything else that people can provide. Yet, plans for forests surrounding Yellowstone National Park call for road construction and timber harvest in hundreds of thousands of acres of prime grizzly habitat. The fact that such timber sales are almost all below cost underscores the misplaced priorities of the Forest Service.

Other than these two laws, the environmental movement has failed to convince Congress of the need for prescriptive legislation regulating national forest management. Congress specifically rejected prescriptive proposals regarding such issues as clearcutting and the age of timber harvest when it passed the National Forest Management Act (NFMA) in 1976. The few prescriptions included in NFMA were already standard Forest Service policy and were included with the approval of the agency.

In any case, the historic record does not indicate that legislation prescribing forest practices will be successful. A federal court ruled in 1974 that the Forest Service was violating an 1897 law forbidding clearcutting. Such violations continued until the law was repealed in 1976. A 1976 court ruling found that a 1904 law prohibiting public entry into the municipal watershed for the City of Portland was violated by large-scale Forest Service timber cutting starting in 1958. That law was repealed in 1977.

A 1972 law limiting timber harvesting in the Hells Canyon National Recreation Area to "selective cutting" (uneven-aged management) was overturned administratively by orders from the Reagan administration to use shelterwood cutting, which, like clearcutting, is even-aged management. Lengthy and expensive court battles can be fought against such actions, but, as the first two experiences suggest, success in the courtroom can be followed by repeal in Congress.

As a substitute for prescriptive legislation, Congress decided that a comprehensive land and resource management planning process should be incorporated into the National Forest Management Act. Accompanied by extensive public involvement, this process was supposed to resolve disputes over clearcutting, wilderness, and other issues. If anything, forest planning has increased polarization and conflicts over national forest management. Most plans have ignored the major issues addressed by NFMA.

"In 1975, debates over national forest management were characterized by shrill emotionalism on the environmental side in contrast to apparently reasoned scientific analysis on the industry side."

For example, although clearcutting was the problem that led to NFMA, few of the 118 forest plans published to date have considered seriously alternatives to even-aged management. Concerns over below-cost timber sales, roadless areas, herbicides, overgrazing, and other issues have been ignored in most if not all plans. In most instances, the plans are little more than justification statements affirming the status quo.

One unintended benefit of the planning process has been the environmentalists' growing mastery of technical and especially economic matters. In 1975, debates over national forest management were characterized by shrill emotionalism on the environmental side in contrast to apparently reasoned scientific analysis on the industry side. Today, the reverse is true, with industry appealing solely to the jobs issue while environmentalists have the support of biological, physical, and economic sciences.

This technical sophistication is changing the standard environmental paradigm. Traditionally, environmentalists have believed that national forest problems are due to the timber bias of Forest Service officials. Recent economic research and analyses suggest that these assumptions are false and that alternative approaches to reforming the Forest Service may be more successful than the traditional environmental goal of prescriptive legislation.

For example, reviews of forest plans have shown that the vast majority of national forests lose money on timber management. When returns to the Treasury are compared to Treasury costs, even forests with valuable old-growth timber often lose money. Yet, a close analysis of below-cost sales shows that they are due not to a Forest Service bias toward timber but to the agency's tendency to maximize its budget.

One old-growth forest that loses money is the Tahoe National Forest in northern California. This forest collected more than $17 million in timber receipts in 1987. This appears impressive because the Forest Service spent only about $4.3 million in tax dollars for timber sales, timber management, and timber-related road construction. Of the receipts, however, $2 million were "paid" by the timber purchaser in the form of road construction. Purchasers are allowed to credit the cost of road construction against the price they bid for timber. An additional $9 million were retained by the Forest Service for postharvest management activities, such as fuel treatment, reforestation, and herbicide spraying. Counties are paid about 25 percent of timber receipts in lieu of taxes, so they received about $4 million. Therefore, the return to the Treasury was only about $2 million. When this is compared with the $4.3 million cost, the Treasury lost more than $2 million.

The Forest Service often claims that such losses are justified by the benefits timber sales provide to other resources, such as roads for recreation and openings for wildlife, and by the need to increase productivity by harvesting slow-growing trees and reforesting with young trees. Forest planning documents reveal, however, that such claims are specious.

Almost all national forest plans indicate that existing forest roads provide more than enough roaded recreation to meet current and future recreation demands. New roads may be used by recreationists, but this use would merely be transferred from another part of the forest; no new value would be created. In most national forests, roadless recreation already is or will be in short supply long before roaded recreation opportunities are used to capacity.

Some wildlife species such as deer and elk benefit from openings that provide a source of food. But most national forests already have sufficient openings, and cover for protection from predators and temperature extremes is more important. Researchers have found that elk avoid timber-related roads in the Rocky Mountains and that deer require old-growth forest in Alaska for food and protection from heavy snows.

Investments that the Forest Service plans to make in growing new trees merely will produce a new crop of below-cost timber. Economic analyses indicate that reforestation on most national forests will return as little as 10¢ to 50¢ for each dollar invested. Below-cost timber sales certainly are not justified by such returns.

Close scrutiny of Forest Service operations shows that below-cost sales are the predictable result of a number of well-intended but poorly designed laws

that give managers an incentive to lose money on timber. The most important of these laws is the Knutson-Vandenberg Act of 1930, which allows the Forest Service to retain funds out of timber sale receipts for reforestation. In 1976, Congress expanded the use of K-V funds to include precommercial thinning, trail construction, and other so-called forest improvements, giving managers a strong incentive to sell timber. Because the cost of arranging timber sales and building timber-related roads is borne by taxpayers, the Forest Service makes no effort to ensure that timber receipts cover these costs. It does require, however, that a minimum bid price includes "necessary" K-V funds. In many timber sales, almost all receipts are placed in the K-V and similar funds, leaving little or none for the Treasury. Taxpayers lost money on the Tahoe National Forest in 1987 because more than half of the forest's timber receipts went into the K-V and related funds.

In 1987, the Forest Service retained more than $300 million out of timber receipts for reforestation and other activities. This is more than the total that Congress appropriated for recreation, watershed, fish and wildlife, and range management combined. Managers see an immediate reward for timber sales because about 75 percent of the timber receipts retained by the Forest Service is spent on the district that earned the receipts. All levels of the bureaucracy encourage timber sales because the remaining 25 percent is spent on "overhead" by the Washington, regional, and forest supervisors' offices. Forest Service specialists in watershed, fish and wildlife, and recreation often support timber sales because K-V funds can be spent on these activities.

"Managers see an immediate reward for timber sales because about 75 percent of the timber receipts retained by the Forest Service is spent on the district that earned the receipts."

The suggestion that Forest Service officials use K-V funds to increase their budgets does not imply that officials are unscrupulous or unethical. Most national forest officials are truly interested in doing what they consider to be best for the land, but through a process of natural selection those managers who believe in activities that increase the agency's budget are the ones who are promoted. After several decades, the Forest Service has become dominated by people who truly, but mistakenly, believe that timber cutting is good for recreation, wildlife, watershed, and other forest resources. . . .

A review of national forest controversies, including wilderness, herbicides, and below-cost sales and grazing, indicates that most are rooted in misincentives created by the Knutson-Vandenberg Act and similar laws. Forest managers can increase their budgets by selling timber, not by creating wilderness, so naturally they will oppose wilderness. Herbicides are funded by K-V collections, and herbicide spraying results in overhead paid to higher offices, so officials tend to support herbicides. Just as K-V funds give managers a powerful incentive to sell timber below cost, the Range Betterment Fund, which gives managers half of all grazing receipts, provides an incentive to lease grazing rights below cost.

"Further progress toward protection of public resources from government-subsidized commodity exploitation will require a new direction from environmental leaders."

This analysis is new to environmental thinking. When the blame for overcutting and overgrazing is laid on managers who are somehow biased toward commodities, prescriptive legislation appears to be the best solution. But if these problems are caused by misincentives created by poorly designed laws such as the Knutson-Vandenberg Act, a completely different solution is required.

This solution is to change the incentives that govern forest management. First, the Knutson-Vandenberg Act and related laws that give managers an incentive to harvest timber and graze domestic animals below cost must be repealed, instead, timber and grazing should be funded out of a fixed share—perhaps two thirds—of net receipts. Then managers will have an incentive to sell timber only where timber sales make money, because below-cost sales will reduce net receipts, thereby reducing the Forest Service's budget.

Because most forests lose money on both timber and grazing, funding activities out of net receipts will reduce environmental conflicts greatly. But some forests, particularly those in the Pacific Northwest and the deep South, make money on timber management, and many other forests have at least some land that can make money. It is not enough simply to remove the incentive for below-cost activities; managers also must be given an incentive to protect recreation, wildlife, and other amenity resources.

One of the best ways to do this is to allow forest managers to charge fees for recreation and give them the same two-thirds share of net recreation receipts. This would more than double funding for recreation and add millions of dollars to the annual budget of

almost all national forests. To protect this income, forest managers would have an incentive to maintain scenic vistas, improve wildlife habitat, protect water quality, and otherwise moderate management of above-cost timber. To enforce collection of fees, recreationists would be required to display on their car or person a visible pemit, much like a parking permit or ski-lift ticket, that indicates they have paid an annual or short-term fee. Experiences with other forms of recreation indicate that such a system would have a low cost and high degree of compliance.

Not all problems can be corrected by changing national forest incentives. Some rare or endangered species such as the grizzly bear will benefit from an end to below-cost sales, but others such as the spotted owl still will require the protection of the Endangered Species Act. Recreation fees provide some incentive to protect water quality, but much national forest water is consumed off the forests, so water quality will continue to require the protection of the Clear Water Act. . . .

The carrot works better than the stick. New incentives for national forest managers will protect many resources better than prescriptive legislation. With support from counties, fiscal conservatives, and other traditional opponents of prescriptive legislation, changing national forest incentives is also more politically feasible than is prescriptive legislation. Improved incentives will resolve numerous environmental conflicts so environmentalists can concentrate their energies on those that remain, such as Pacific Northwest old growth. New incentives could also be applied to the Bureau of Land Management, Corps of Engineers, and other agencies that spend tax dollars on environmentally destructive projects.

Conservationists can take credit for the creation of the national forests and environmentalists can credit themselves for legislative protection of millions of acres of wilderness. But further progress toward protection of public resources from government-subsidized commodity exploitation will require a new direction from environmental leaders. That direction can be found in the area of incentives.

Randal O'Toole is the director of Cascade Holistic Economic Consultants, a nonprofit forestry consulting firm, located in Eugene, Oregon. His book Reforming the Forest Service *was published in 1988.*

"From an ecological point of view, the fire was good for Yellowstone and for its wildlife."

The Yellowstone Fires Were Beneficial

Peter Matthiessen

From Cody, Wyo., the road west to Yellowstone National Park follows the North Fork of the Shoshone River. Despite faltering rain in recent weeks—it was late October, and a fine fall morning, with the crowns of the last green cottonwoods turning to gold—a sign at the edge of the Shoshone National Forest read "FIRE DANGER." Of the national forests that surround Yellowstone—Shoshone and Bridger-Teton, to the east and south, in Wyoming; Gallatin, to the north, in Montana, and Targhee, to the west, in Idaho—the Shoshone was burned as much as any in the great fires of the summer of 1988. But there was no sign of the Clover-Mist fire that in late August 1988 escaped eastward from Yellowstone—one of eight great fires that made up what Yellowstone officials called "the most significant political, ecological and economic event in the park's 116-year history."

Nor was there any blackened forest on the north shore of Yellowstone Lake, although its southern and western sides had burned entirely. Geese, widgeon and mallard dabbled near the shore in the blue water, and a sleek gold and silver coyote, leaving a scent mark, worked the edge of a pine meadow near the lake.

Where the Yellowstone River departs from the great lake at its north end, bright bufflehead and barrow's goldeneye swam in the sunlit river, a late osprey perched in a high tree, a rough-legged hawk in the uncommon dark phase flying overhead was noticeably fat. Hawks and owls fare well in time of fire, which exposes their prey and brings them hurrying from many miles away.

I took the road north toward Yellowstone Falls, passing calm bison at the wood edge, and still there was no sign of fire. Soon the green walls of

lodgepole pine opened out in the broad mountain plains of Hayden Valley. Off this main road, three or four miles to the west, lay what was left of the old garbage dump along Trout Creek, where one summer twilight back in 1957 I watched the grizzlies come in across the sage, scattering the innumerable black bears. I eventually counted 37 grizzlies in view at one time, sniffing at my old convertible, brawling, overturning burning barrels, in one of the most astonishing sights I have ever seen.

A Natural State

For a hundred years, in summer and fall, garbage has been a favored item of bear diet. The sudden closing of this dump and others after 1967, as part of the park's attempt to restore Yellowstone to a "natural" state it had not known since the Indians first came, thousands of years ago, brought hungry bears into the tourist camps with drastic consequences, including human deaths. Since then, by the park's own count, at least 124 "problem" animals have been destroyed, with many others trapped and relocated. The respected field biologists John and Frank Craighead were driven out of Yellowstone by park restrictions before they could complete their 10-year grizzly study; completed instead was the Craigheads' book "Track of the Grizzly," an eloquent and bitter denunciation of bureaucratic arrogance and folly, which had my own strong endorsement on the jacket.

On the mountain prairie by Alum Creek was a herd of several hundred bison, and beyond the creek, along the northwest side of Hayden Valley, the black wall of the North Fork fire. Accidentally started by a woodcutter in Idaho's Targhee Forest on July 22, 1988, it went on to become the largest of the fires and the only one not yet "contained"—surrounded by fire lines—by October 19, 1988, the day of my arrival. On the west side of the road, to Canyon Village and beyond, most trees still standing were black limbless spires, with burned-out logs on bare black earth. A pervasive stench of rain-soaked ash was disagreeably sweet and harsh at the same time.

Here in this scene of desolation, my assumption that the National Park Service must be at fault—whetted at the time of the grizzly controversy and intensified in recent years down in the Everglades—began to undergo a cautious change. I saw no sign of contented elk chomping new green shoots in the blackened forest, as suggested by recent news releases, but this stark scene seemed far less dreadful than press accounts of 200-foot-high flames, charred moonscapes and fleeing citizens had me prepared for. It looked as if high winds had caused the flames to rush here and there in finger patterns, leaving countless patches of green forest within the outer perimeters of each fire. Even in places of most awesome burn, one was never out of sight of live green trees, which would very soon reseed these blackened areas.

Instead of gloom at the seeming "loss," the vast charred prospect, there came instead a heady sense of the earth opening outward, of mountain light and imminent regeneration, which made me recall how oppressive I once found the south part of the park, with its monotone enclosing stands of lodgepole pine. Far from being stunned by the destruction, I felt an exhilaration and relief, as if Yellowstone Park, for the first time in a century, had gotten a deep breath of fresh air. . . .

The Natural Burn Policy

"Natural burn" met its first real test in the dry year of 1979, when a number of lightning fires went along unmolested. The next year, an infestation of the pine-bark beetle added many more trees to the buildup of storm blowdown and dry fuel. In the early 1980's came a drought of seven years that intensified sharply after 1985. Unusually wet springs and summers were unable to offset thin snow packs, which lowered water levels and dried out the land. Then came a record drought year, 1988, when a meager snow pack and a wet spring followed the pattern, but dry, hot, windy summer days did not. The summer of 1988 had the lowest rainfall recorded in the park since 1876, the dusty year of Custer's death on the Little Bighorn. Drought and and wind together brought about the million-acre accident that, according to park critics, had been waiting to happen for a hundred years.

On June 23, 1988, a lightning fire started at Shoshone Lake, in the southwest, and on June 25 what became the Fan fire was reported in the northwest corner of the park. In the next weeks, six other smoke plumes rose from the dark conifers to the blue sky. Because all but two (the North Fork and Hellroaring) were lightning fires, all but two were allowed to burn. Not until after mid-July, when the Shoshone fire and the Fan were already large, and the Clover fire (which had joined the Mist in the northeast) was a good deal larger, did park officials attack the Shoshone, mostly because it had come too close to the park community of Grant Village. People fearing a loss of tourist business were already saying that after three years of low rainfall, the park should have recognized the drought and acted earlier. On July 21, responding to howls of catastrophe from the public and its election-year-politicians, park officials suspended "natural burn" indefinitely, in favor of the greatest firefighting effort in United States history.

Fighting Fire

Those anxious to blame the park for acting too slowly on these great fires might consider that the greatest of them all, the North Fork fire, was fought from the very start. "We threw everything at that fire from Day 1," Denny Bungarz, a North Fork fire boss and veteran from Mendocino National Forest, said at the time. Things got so out of hand that the northeast section of this blaze, for tactical purposes, was considered a separate fire, the Wolf Lake.

Dan Sholly, Yellowstone's chief ranger, and an expert firefighter, was an "incident commander," as fire bosses are now called, of the Wolf Lake fire. At his house in Mammoth Hot Springs, this husky squinting man—he lost his right eye in Vietnam—smiled ironically at that title. "These days," he said, "what you and I would call one hell of a high wind is called a 'wind event.' We had a lot of 'em. In the history of U.S. fires, the single factor that has made things most serious is wind."

In the summer of 1988, the wind scarcely diminished at night, carrying embers across the widest natural firebreaks, such as canyons and rivers. "We saw smoke convection columns like atomic mushroom clouds, 40,000 feet high!" Sholly said.

> "In the summer of 1988, the wind scarcely diminished at night, carrying embers across the widest natural firebreaks, such as canyons and rivers."

"We were criticized for not bulldozing firebreaks to slow the North Fork fire early," he told me. "But at that time the fire was 15 miles from West Yellowstone, with no threat to property. It's not like Santa Monica, where you destroy everything to save million-dollar homes. Anyway, I doubt if dozers would have done much good.

"Not all of the outside crews understood that. The early crews, which we briefed ourselves, were aggressive where necessary but light on the land, but some of the later ones wanted cat [bulldozer] lines right and left, and complained that their hands were tied. This was true especially on the Clover-Mist, which escaped into the Shoshone National Forest, where the Forest Service wanted to protect its timber leases. The rules were different on each side of a boundary that the fire itself paid no attention to."

By mid-August 1988, the firefighting crews gained some control, but a "wind event" on the 19th was followed on August 20, "Black Saturday," by 40-60 mile per hour gales, with gusts still higher, and in that 24-hour period 165,000 acres went up in fire. "We couldn't hold any of the fire lines," Sholly said. "It was truly awesome."

Most of the park villages were closed August 24, and several of the gateway villages were evacuated in early September. From the first light rain on September 10—the turning point—until heavier rain and snow a few days later, the park was closed. . . .

Reseeding the Forest

Don G. Despain, research biologist and plant ecologist at Yellowstone, is devoted to all aspects of this mighty landscape, and as we drove to the burn on the Blacktail Plateau he discussed spruce budworm, mountain pine beetles and other fascinating ecologic factors. "There's so little we really know," he said, all but rubbing his hands, as if he could hardly wait to find out more.

We walked respectfully through the black forest, in char stench and the requiem squawks of ravens. Using his jackknife, Despain dug up a tuft of grass and cut it to demonstrate how the passing fire had penetrated only a half inch, leaving the root crowns still intact. "Over most of the area, the flames went through quickly and the burn was light. This black ground absorbs more sunlight and it warms up faster, and now it's fertilized with ash." He expected a quick return of grasses and heartleaf arnica, fireweed, and other deep-rooted plants.

All around were the burned cones of lodgepole pines, which require the heat of forest fires in order to open and release the winged seeds that scatter on the wind. The myriad seeds were already in place, and he picked up one of the wings to demonstrate how it contracts as it dries and expels the seed. The bases of the burned cones were still intact, a shining pewter gray.

Ash-dusted buffalo chips and gray-blue elk pellets, gold aspen leaves blown in from elsewhere, a gray spider crossing the black ground, unscathed. "Fire-resistant bark," Despain said with a slight smile, pointing at the stark skeleton of a Douglas fir, black cones still clinging to its bony branches, against a smokeless sky.

On all sides were fresh badger holes and the mounds of pocket gophers, both of which were well insulated from the fires. But the mice and moles were probably hard hit, because the leaf litter they depend on for their cover was gone, making them easy prey for the raptors and coyotes. "I once saw a nutcracker take a mammal," Despain said as that bold black and white bird, which usually eats seeds and insects, flew across the clear fall light between black snags. "Swooped in and picked up a mouse we'd just tagged for a mouse study, flew it right over to a tree." He looked happy to see me so astonished by nutcracker lore.

Everywhere on the black ground were tracks of elk and deer and coyote. Wolves were "the missing piece" in the whole ecosystem, Despain said, though he doubts if a few wolves would have much impact on the elk, a fecund creature that can multiply from 4,000 to 10,000 animals in a few years.

In a hollow was a grove of aspen, mostly unburned. For a new grove to establish itself, the seed must remain wet for two weeks and grow without any competition, conditions rarely occurring in the wild. Instead, new aspens sprout profusely from an underground runner system, and the new shoots are important forage for large animals. Like most aspen and willow in the park, these shoots had been damaged by overcropping.

Despain tends to attribute the decline of the aspen not to the alleged overabundance of the elk but to incompletely understood ecological factors. He also believes that the black bear, though now scattered, are as common as they were when their gangs cajoled the tourists at every corner. (Frank Craighead, whom I visited a few days later, says he does not believe this is true.) In these ideas he has little more support from most biologists than he does for his optimistic view that even with the forage loss to drought and fire the large elk herd might adapt itself quite well to a hard winter. He thought it possible that the elk would move to different areas, use different foods.

"It's ecological arrogance to say that we should go out here and manage this—crop the herds, pre-burn the forests, manipulate Mother Nature."

"We don't know as much about ecology as we think we do," Despain said, waving his hand at the great prospect of forest and mountain rivers. "It's ecological arrogance to say that we should go out here and manage this—crop the herds, pre-burn the forests, manipulate Mother Nature, with some idea that everything can be kept just as it was. Impossible! Everything keeps changing, the climate, the animal cycles. The pine bark beetle, beaver, aspen—everything comes and goes!"

Despain shook his head. "Our critics say we could

have stopped some of those early fires, and it's true. Whether that would have made a difference once the rest got going, I doubt very much. The wind and heat built up air currents like small tornadoes, and big embers would fly out ahead, which torched off the next section. This North Fork fire was a natural force, like a volcano or a hurricane. Even when there was no wind, it rumbled like a locomotive, and when the gales came it sounded like a jet plane taking off. It came in from Idaho and did what it was going to do, and there was nothing we could do about it.

"Barbee himself has used the word 'catastrophe,' he told me, because of the human anguish and expense."

"As early as the 1930's, a plant ecologist named George McDougall spoke sharply against suppression of all fires, but it was some time before we heeded his advice, and by the time this bad drought came there was quite a buildup of 'down fuel' on the forest floor. Some people blame that on the spruce budworm, or the pine beetle—we call them 'infestations,' though they've probably been here a lot longer than the grizzly—but the intensity of the crown fire was offset by the insects' thinning effects on the tree crowns."

Despain has been studying the effect of burn and regeneration since 1974, and feels that one great benefit of these fires will be an immense amount of new information and research. "One day when some trees torched right near where we were working, and flying embers ignited one of my nine plots, I was so excited about my experiment that I hollered out, 'Burn, baby, burn!' The press got wind of this and published it as the park's real attitude about the fire . . . and I wasn't allowed near a reporter for two months."

Asked about reports that the fire destruction might require 300 years to heal, Despain said: "The totally burned areas were mostly old forest of spruce and fir, or mature lodgepole. It might take three centuries for a given patch to go from black ground to mature lodgepole, then climax forest. But from an ecological point of view, there is no damage, there's still a forest ecosystem out there, nothing this park was established to preserve is lost. Dead trees may be a loss to house builders, but not to woodpeckers."

Don Despain's optimistic point of view is generally shared by his Park Service colleagues, all the way up to the director, William Mott. "Fire is a stimulant and is as important to the ecosystem as sunshine and rain," the Yellowstone superintendent, Robert Barbee, told the press in late July 1988. "This is not destruction—period!" he said later, an attitude in no

way shared by politicians, nor by the public in general.

"These three states are all in economic decline, and tourism is very important; the tourism and travel people have a lot of clout with the politicans," Barbee said. "As soon as it pinches a little, they will start to holler, and the media will blow that up. Shove a microphone into somebody's face who's scared he's going to lose his house and say, 'The Government thinks this fire's a wonderful thing—what do *you* think?!'" He shook his head. Barbee is a big, genial, ruddy man, who after the most trying summer of his life has not quite lost an ironic sense of humor.

Donald P. Hodel, Secretary of the Interior (which includes and supervises the National Park Service), at first supported what the press (but not the park) had named the "Let-Burn Policy," but on September 10, when he escorted a delegation of Montana and Wyoming politicians and Richard E. Lyng, Secretary of Agriculture (which includes and supervises the United States Forest Service), on a tour of the fires, he appeared to be wincing from the heat. By early October, Hodel was calling the fires a "disaster" and expressing interest in a complete review of firefighting policies, reforestation and a program to feed the needy elk.

Senator Malcolm Wallop, citing the million acres already "lost" in the Yellowstone area, derided the let-burn policy as "absurd," and was joined by his Senate colleague, Alan K. Simpson, in a demand for Mott's scalp. ("I had warned Bill Mott not to seem quite so enthusiastic about the fires, but he didn't listen," Barbee says.) Environmental groups generally defended Mott and dismissed Wallop's opinions as ridiculous, and the Republican Senators were accused of "head-hunting" by their Democratic rivals. Wyoming Governor Mike Sullivan declared ominously to the press: "Now is the time to get the fires out. We can kick butts later." Unquestionably, one of the menaced butts belonged to Barbee, who exclaimed to a reporter: "Why should I resign? This is a natural catastrophe. The myth that policy is responsible for this is just insane."

Fire Debates

By mid-September, with cool damp weather, nine fires were still uncontained. No one mentioned the more than 50 that had been suppressed. Even the extent of the fires was debated. According to *Time* magazine (September 19, 1988), "the fires have ruined 1.2 million acres of Yellowstone and adjoining national forests." The day before, in *The New York Times*, Alston Chase mourned 1.5 million. But what most estimates were based on was the acreage enclosed by the park fire perimeters—approximately 1.1 million acres, or one-half the area of the park. The forest actually burned was about half of that (perhaps one-quarter of the park) and the amount badly burned was about 22,000 acres, 1 percent of the park area, according to the park's chief research officer, John D. Varley.

Barbee himself has used the word "catastrophe," he told me, because of the human anguish and expense—at latest estimate, $120 million in the park alone. "We can't celebrate *that*. But from an ecological point of view, the fire was good for Yellowstone and for its wildlife. It is also of immense educational and scientific value in potential studies of recycling and diversity. Yellowstone is not fixed in formaldehyde and should not be fixed in time. It was *born* in cataclysm! These fires will make it a far more exciting place."

The creatures hardest hit by the fire were the birds and small mammals—most critically, the porcupine and the rare pine marten. The remains of only a few hoofed animals, other than elk, have been located in daily helicopter surveys; no grizzlies were lost, and just one black bear. According to a count made by a park biologist, Frank Singer, on October 23, only 230 or 240 elk, out of 20,000 or more, died during the fires, all of them from smoke inhalation. What concerns Singer more is the loss of perhaps a third of the elks' winter range. Elk mortality in the event of a hard winter might come to 7,000 or 8,000 animals, but Singer, like John Varley, is philosophically opposed to artifical feeding, even in the event of heavy die-off—"what scientists call a 'significant perturbation of the animals,'" Bob Barbee said, teasing Varley. "Not one knowledgeable authority I've ever talked to supports artificial feeding," Varley said.

"The point is, nobody wants feeding except for the uneducated public," Barbee said, "and the media can fan the sentiment, just like the fires: *First They Burn Down All the Forests, Now They're Starving Elk!* That's what they did when we tried to be straight with them, and notified them about one elk herd that was lost to smoke inhalation: *Park Admits Mass Elk Mortality*—something like that." He gave me a wry look. "Media control might work better than fire control—don't answer their questions, just educate 'em, tell 'em what they ought to know."

Support for Park Policy

The Greater Yellowstone Coalition, like Audubon, the Wilderness Society and other conservation groups, generally supports present park policy. And Ed Lewis, its executive director, on his way through Mammoth to his home in Bozeman, after attending a grizzly conference in Jackson Hole, was kind enough to take the time to explain why. We sat in the sun at a picnic table outside the Yellowstone Museum, amid the barnyard smell and wistful bugling of hundreds of elk drifting into Mammoth on their way north to winter range. As they cropped the park lawns and stood about its headquarters, it was as if they were awaiting word about their fate.

Like most national parks, Yellowstone is not a complete ecosystem but an island of wilderness in which many species tend to disappear as their natural wanderings and migrations are cut off. Though Yellowstone and the much smaller Grand Teton National park just south might be called the heart of it, they are only 2.5 million acres out of the 12 million to 14 million acres of the Greater Yellowstone Ecosystem, which includes about 10 million acres of national forest in the three surrounding states as well as nearly 1.5 million run by three national wildlife refuges, the Bureau of Land Management and state and private interests. The larger animals such as bison, elk and grizzly, indifferent to park borders, are chronically in conflict with irate ranchers, ambitious hunters and state agencies.

"The park made the right decision in not using bulldozers, which leave scars that last for a long time."

The G.Y.C., as it is known, was formed in 1983, out of concern for the hydra-headed administration of the Greater Yellowstone Ecosystem, which led policy in all different directions. The management of the grizzly (which Montana hunters would like to see removed from the endangered-species list) was similarly uncoordinated. As Ed Lewis says: "The fires made clear that Yellowstone Park and the surrounding wild lands are inextricably interdependent. The fires totally ignored man's boundaries, following the natural features that define this ecosystem, and they were fought by very different jurisdictions and philosophies.

"What are the alternatives to present policy? Prescribed burning? Most people who really know the park do not believe that the 40,000 to 50,000 acres necessary to offset an event like the summer's could be burned systematically each year. In the autumn, in a normal year, there is too much precipitation; in winter and spring there is just too much snow. In summer you might get a fire going, but once you do, you can't always control it. Anyway, the park's fire policy has been consistently misinterpreted; it's very flexible, and allows for prescribed burns.

"We certainly hope that all these hearings"—he rolled his eyes toward Jackson Hole, where an interagency panel (Forest and Park Service) on fire-management policies had begun meetings a few days earlier—"will not lead us back to the Smokey Bear days of complete suppression, back to the same unnatural fuel buildup, and fires of too great intensity. If all fires had been fought right from Day 1, when they were small and slow, most of them could probably have been stopped, but it's very unlikely that the ultimate result would have been much different. The park made the right decision in not using bulldozers, which leave scars that last for a long time. The impact of the firefighting might have been worse than the impact of the fire.

"Charred areas will probably lead to erosion and sedimentation of the streams, and hurt the fisheries, though those streams should clear up in about two years. There's a definite impact on elk forage and the white-bark pine nut crop, but for the moment, all indications are that the large animals came out of it mostly unharmed. The grizzlies look fat and happy, they are fattening up for winter on elk carcasses, and there'll probably be more carcasses by spring."

A Perception of Stagnation

In general, the Greater Yellowstone Coalition is a strong supporter of park policies and decisions, which might seem to support criticism that such private groups and the Department of Interior form a conservation establishment that tends to encourage Park Service stagnation. And surely, in this torrid summer, the widespread perception of bureaucratic bungling and coverups (as in the grizzly crisis) underlay the accusations that the park was whitewashing its "too little and too late" reaction to the fires. Its cheery ecological prognostications, in the early days, at least, seemed to ignore the human consequences.

"A hard winter . . . might cause heavy mortality in the elk herds, inviting grim news stories of starving elk wandering the snowy wastes of the ruinous fires."

"This was a very unpleasant place to be," Lewis reflected. "Unlike Mount St. Helens, which was quickly over, the fires went on for weeks and weeks and weeks, with stifling smoke and sore throats and anxiety, and tempers ran high. The park just wasn't sensitive to this in its public statements. It tried to make the fire a totally positive thing, and this was one reason there was so much anger."

Like most of Yellowstone's well-wishers, Lewis hopes that the Government review panels will support present park policies in their report, appeasing the public with such recommendations as "more consideration of weather trends" and perhaps "pre-suppression efforts," such as brush-clearing in the vicinity of buildings. He, too, is afraid of a hard winter that might cause heavy mortality in the elk herds, inviting grim news stories of starving elk wandering the snowy wastes of the ruinous fires.

Such stories would surely reignite the public

outrage, and panic the political appointees of the new Administration into ill-advised elk-feeding programs and other programs destructive in the long term to the wildlife for which Yellowstone was first established. Once again, shortsighted politics would harm the long-term welfare of the great deer that even now, as we concluded our discussions, wandered trustingly among man's habitations in these shining mountains.

Peter Matthiessen first conducted research in Yellowstone in 1957 for his book Wildlife in America. *He has recently completed* Men's Lives: Surfmen and Baymen of the South Fork.

"It isn't just 'blackened canopy burn,' it's some of the most beautiful spots in the nation gone forever from our lives and our children's lives."

The Yellowstone Fires Were Devastating

Micah Morrison

The historic fires of '88 were snuffed by the autumn snows that year, but the smoke is thicker than ever. These days, a smoke screen is billowing out from here at the Yellowstone headquarters of the National Park Service (NPS), where federal officials, in a successful damage-control effort, have hoodwinked the President and the press, misled the public, and turned some of the biggest forest fires in recorded memory into nothing more than Mom Nature's little weenie roast.

It's a complicated story, and the NPS is not the only culprit. It's more a story of dishonor than of outright villainy, a story of the cowardly and arrogant behavior endemic to the bureaucratic mind. It's also a story of lazy journalism missing the story once again, crumbling beneath its own sloth and a kill-the-messenger campaign by the NPS. And it's a story of certain environmental groups enjoying a rather too cozy relationship with the Park Service. As a result, the public has been presented with a sanitized version of the fires of '88 and their political and economic repercussions—a curtain is being drawn around events that could reshape not only the boundaries of Yellowstone National Park but also the traditional culture of the American West.

The NPS might as well adopt the tune "Don't Worry, Be Happy" as its anthem for 1989. The fires that swept across nearly one million of the park's 2.2 million acres and through surrounding forests are being portrayed as simply another turn in the ecological cycle. "Welcome to a Changing Yellowstone," announces a special supplement handed to every visitor entering the park. "Yellowstone: A New Beginning" trumpets another glossy publication. The company holding the contract for Yellowstone's lucrative tourist trade, TW

Recreational Services, produced a dreamy 17-minute videotape featuring idyllic landscapes, happy tourists, graceful elk and lumbering buffalo, sparkling streams, and, oh yes, about four minutes of heavily edited fire footage. Thousands of copies were mailed to travel writers and agents, along with copious printed material. The message: forget about the fires, come to Yellowstone.

According to numerous NPS publications and official reports, "meteorological events"—drought, heat, wind—were responsible for the fires. The NPS policy of letting naturally caused fires burn is defended. "Yellowstone: A New Beginning" explains that mapping inside the park's boundaries "indicates that a maximum of 988,925 acres experienced some kind of burning. Of that, 562,350 acres was 'canopy burn,' meaning that the forest was blackened. Another 372,350 acres was 'surface burn,' meaning that only the forest underbrush burned, and most trees will not die. . . . Recovery has started and biologists say much of the burned area will be green and lush come spring." The publication features sixteen color photos, only two of which show burned forest areas.

Help from Fire

The news from the NPS gets better. There is, for example, the case of the lodgepole pines and their heat-sensitive, seed-releasing serotinous cones—cited in virtually every media report. Lodgepole pines form approximately 80 percent of the park's trees. Thankfully, according to the NPS, the "vast forest of lodgepole pines are fire tolerant. Fires caused many cones to open and release their seeds; preliminary surveys at several sites in the park revealed that within a few days after the fire, densities of new seeds on the ground ranged from 50,000 to one million per acre (which equals one to twenty seeds per square foot). Yellowstone's forests have

Micah Morrison, "The Yellowstone Scam," *The American Spectator*, August 1989. Reprinted with permission.

regenerated countless times and are well on their way to doing so again."

With fire heat estimated as high as 1000° Fahrenheit on the surface, some biologists have expressed concern about soil sterilization. Not so, says the NPS. "Soil surveys have shown that no more than one-tenth of one percent of the park received severe enough burn intensity to kill the roots, rhizomes, bulbs, and seeds that lie a few inches under the surface. . . . The fire released nutrients that will enrich the soils, further promoting growth." As for the animals, the NPS reports that "mammal populations sustained only small losses." Humanoids, too, are not abandoning Yellowstone. In June, park officials announced that spring visits were up 23 percent over the previous year.

The only sobering note in all this good cheer, and it is a note sounded over and over, is the role of those damn reporters. "Enormous public confusion resulted from hasty reports in the media," notes one park document. There was "frequent and unfortunate oversimplification and exaggeration," says another. Park Superintendent Robert Barbee has appeared in Washington and a number of European capitals with the message that the media distorted the Yellowstone fires. Apparently, the only group he hasn't met with is local residents.

National Park Service Optimism

When the park launched a May public relations blitz, the media, chastened and apparently unwilling to do any digging on their own, trumpeted the NPS line. "Yellowstone Lives!" announced *U.S. News & World Report*; "From Yellowstone Ashes, New Life and Approach," ran the *New York Times* headline. "As Snow Melts, Yellowstone's Rebirth Begins," said the *Washington Post*. The *U.S. News* approach, written by Michael Satchell, in the May 15, 1989, edition, is a perfect model of the story repeated in newspaper, radio, and television reports across the country. It begins with tiny wildflowers sprouting in blackened meadows, moves on to observe peacefully grazing animals (preferably with a few newborns romping nearby), and then eyes are lifted to the horizon, where "stands of evergreen lodgepole pine, interlaced with lifeless swaths of rust-red and black trees that have perished from heat or flames," keep watch over the placid valley. We are out with park biologist Don Despain, a kind and patient man who seems to spend all his time shepherding journalists. (The Despain tour was repeated for me and, no doubt, hundreds of other reporters.) He opens his Swiss Army knife and digs into a blackened meadow now fresh with a thin coat of new grass. He turns up a few roots beneath a half inch of charred soil. Birds twitter nearby. We marvel over the new grass and cluck about a few burned trees at the outskirts of the meadow. We hear about the seeds from serotinous cones of the lodgepole pines. "By June,"

says *U.S. News*, pine shoots "will be poking up through the ash. Within five years these saplings will be waist high. . . . Grasses and shrubs will also flourish, leaving the forest healthier and more biologically diverse." Yellowstone's chief scientist, John Varley, steps in: "The fires simply have no ecological downside." Varley unceasingly sounds variations on this theme—one local resident compared him to a "tent revivalist." To me it sometimes seemed like a weird mix of an environmental Big Lie and Potemkin Village: Fire is nice. See the green meadow. See the wildflowers. The park is wonderful. Ignore the elk carcass floating in the lake. Don't worry. Be happy.

"Park Superintendent Robert Barbee has appeared in Washington and a number of European capitals with the message that the media distorted the Yellowstone fires."

Yet there is one evil gremlin lurking in the woods, and he isn't carrying a torch. Yellowstone officials and their allies speak of an "ecosystem" that includes the park and millions of acres of adjacent land. The ecosystem argument is not without validity, and we'll come to it in a moment, but here is Mr. Satchell of *U.S. News* exercising his critical acumen from economically moribund Wyoming: last year's "smoke and flames ironically obscured what most experts think is the true threat to the park's future: development." Fire can't destroy the "Greater Yellowstone ecosystem . . .[but the] realistic fear is that the tapestry of America's most ecologically pristine national park will be unraveled, thread by thread, as its creeks are poisoned by mining wastes, endangered grizzlies are shot as they stray over the ecosystem's shrinking boundaries, forest clear-cuts destroy scenic viewscapes and the development squeeze turns Yellowstone into a big-sky version of Central Park."

So, to summarize the NPS account of the fires and the latest media relay: the fires were not nearly as bad as reported. The flames sketched a "mosaic" of burned and green patches across the park. "Renewal" is the theme. The NPS's policy of natural regulation—the phrase "let-it-burn" is frowned upon—has proved sound. A mere half million acres were "blackened" by severe burn, and the other 300,000 burned acres will quickly spring back to life. This is only about 48 percent of the park. Seeds from lodgepole pines will speedily repopulate the forests, and the soil is not sterilized. In fact, the fire was good for the soil. The animals are fine, the tourists are coming back, and the true challenge lies in preserving the Greater Yellowstone ecosystem from the encroachment of "developers."

A nice story, but full of holes. Residents of the "gateway communities" around Yellowstone and some employees of the NPS are furious. They claim that the NPS allowed the fires to get out of control and now is trying to cover up the damage and direct public attention away from the issue. "The National Park Service is trying to bury the controversy," said a year-round resident of the tiny, isolated town of Cooke City, where feelings are especially bitter after the community came within hours of being totally destroyed by the fires. Yellowstone is the major employer in the area and most residents spoke on the condition of anonymity, fearing retribution.

Yellowstone, a federal entity, long has had a running battle with the surrounding small towns. "Does Yellowstone exist for the people in the gateway communities?" pointedly asked Mary Davis, an NPS information officer. She added what seemed to be a veiled warning: "Cooke City is most dependent on us. We keep the road to them plowed, we supply police and fire and ambulance. Sometimes they forget that this park has the word 'National' in its name." Others have been even less kind. One writer called the gateway towns "economic parasites." Another compared them to "spoiled children." Federal authority looms large in the area, and the townspeople are frustrated by their political powerlessness.

NPS reports of the fires are "all a bunch of goddamn lies," said John Griscomb, a Montana businessman. Local people know the countryside well and warned of out-of-control blazes early in the summer of '88. They were ignored. As the fires began to run out of control, the NPS played down local complaints and turned away pleas for action. Now, adding insult to injury, the NPS acts as if nothing happened. "We know some of the fires were inevitable, but some weren't," a Cooke City motel owner told me. "All we want is the truth—and an apology."

"Yellowstone, a federal entity, long has had a running battle with the surrounding small towns."

The truth and an apology—neither will be easy to come by. Based on a recent two-week visit to the region, it is clear to me that the NPS is providing nothing resembling the whole story. Two separate sources in the NPS told me that Park Superintendent Robert Barbee and Chief Scientist John Varley have convened meetings of department heads and instructed them to confront all questioners with "vague, feel good" answers. Other sources confirm that these instructions have been passed on to all employees at orientation meetings. "The entire session," said one person who attended an orientation meeting, "was about how to deal with the media." Reporters have been steered away from heavily damaged areas. Park employees involved in firefighting have been warned not to make waves.

Covering Up the Damage

Only a lengthy investigation of NPS actions during and after the fires and a careful survey of Yellowstone will establish if park officials engaged in a cover-up of actions taken during and after the fires, or simply are putting the best face on a bad situation. In the matter of those serotinous lodgepole pinecones, for instance, it turns out that the study was conducted decades ago. According to a biologist I consulted, only 30 percent of the pines bear effective serotinous cones. Lies—or spin control? I hiked through blasted zones where there was not a cone or pine shoot in sight; other areas showed some pine shoot growth, but an experienced outdoorsman told me that the vast majority of the shoots will not survive. Local residents also claim that the NPS has lied about the number of animals killed during the fires. They repeatedly charge that some of the fires could have been put out early and that the NPS lied about their true size. They ridicule the notion that much of the burned areas will soon spring back to life. And then there are the current glowing reports of increased tourism. Many of the tourists are from nearby towns and counties, driving through for a look. Motel owners I spoke with in early June said bookings were way down, and backcountry guide services say they have been driven close to bankruptcy.

To be sure, Yellowstone lives, and much of it is still spectacularly beautiful. But hike off the road for a while and you may encounter vast stretches of decimated landscape. It isn't just "blackened canopy burn," it's some of the most beautiful spots in the nation gone forever from our lives and our children's lives. Nature, of course, is a savage mistress and sometimes all we can do is stay out of her way. Yet if man is partly or wholly responsible for the destruction in Yellowstone, shouldn't man be called to account? After some of the greatest forest fires in history, should we uncritically accept the explanations of the very people to whom Yellowstone's care was entrusted before the fires? If a Pan Am jet crashes into a mountain, would we let Pan Am issue the official report on the crash?

I walked through the park, drove through it, took an all-terrain vehicle up into some of the adjacent wilderness sectors and talked with backcountry guides and long-time residents who have seen treasured groves and 300-year-old Douglas firs wiped from the face of the earth. Nature's ways they can live with, man's errors they can live with—man's lies and denials and evasions they cannot live with. Something is gone. My foot sinks into black ash on the forest floor, crazy white lines criss-cross the deep powder: markers of death where trees fell and vanished in 1000° heat, leaving only lines of pale ash. Black poles fall away from me on all sides, running down a hill and back up a mountainside, spreading out around the whole valley. I dig down, looking for soil, a root, anything. Nothing will grow here, not for a long time. I look at the black and silent valley, near the origin of the North Fork fire on the west side of Yellowstone. No "mosaic" here. Yes, in other places the fire did jump and burn, and you can see fascinating and grotesque shapes on the mountainsides, as if some ancient Indian god had come flaming down from the sky and commenced a deadly ghost dance. Over across the other side of the park, a guide tells me, Cache Creek has been torn to pieces. Other places too. He stops, unable to continue. There are places, moments, that Barbee and Varley would like to paste a Smiley Face over. Moments when we look upon the fury that has overtaken parts of Yellowstone and, like Lear on the heath, rage against those "sulphurous and thought-executing fires.". . .

Marvelous Recovery

Meanwhile, our kind and environmental President was flying into Yellowstone. A helicopter speeded him over the burn area and set him down in Fountain Flats, near Old Faithful. Barbee and Varley were there. Before the chopper landed, park employees sprayed the area with water to keep down dust and ash. Smiling, Barbee allowed that the Bush visit would help correct the "coast-to-coast misperception" about the fires. Varley led Bush through a thin band of burned trees. Green meadows stretched around them and wildflowers dotted the landscape. Varley showed Bush a bit of ground where pine shoots were poking up. The President was told that the public wrongly perceived the fires as a disaster. The President marveled at the pine shoots. "Are there jillions of others underneath, trying to get up?" he asked Varley. Varley and Barbee grinned. Things were going just fine. The press dutifully recorded everything. "We do not consider it a disaster here at all," a park spokesman said.

Micah Morrison is a correspondent for The American Spectator, *a monthly magazine reporting news and opinions of current affairs. He is working on a book about the Yellowstone fires of 1988.*

"It has been far too easy, when taking out the sixth or seventh bag of trash in a week, to assume that the garbage truck will dump in someone else's backyard.... That mentality will have to change."

A Garbage Crisis Exists

Melinda Beck

At a distance, the yellow, granulated mounds rising 250 feet over Staten Island might be mistaken for sand dunes—if not for the stench. Fresh Kills is the largest city dump in the world, home to most of Gotham's garbage, 24,000 tons each day brought round-the-clock by 22 barges. "We get it all here—your plastics, your Styrofoams, even stoves and refrigerators," says supervisor William Aguirre. "It was a valley when it started [in 1948]. Now it's a mountain." By the year 2000, Fresh Kills will tower half again as high as the Statue of Liberty and fill more cubic feet than the largest Great Pyramid of Egypt—provided it lives that long. The State of New York claims Fresh Kills is leaching 2 million gallons of contaminated gunk into the ground water each day and has threatened to close the dump down in 1991. As a result, city sanitation commissioner Brendan Sexton left this message for newly elected Mayor David Dinkins: "Hi. Welcome to City Hall. By the way, you have no place to put the trash."

Neither do many American communities, from Philadelphia to Berkeley, Minneapolis to Jacksonville. More than two thirds of the nation's landfills have closed since the late 1970s; one third of those remaining will be full by 1994. Federal law prohibits dumping trash into the ocean. Incineration is under attack on economic and environmental grounds. Recycling is gaining popularity, but currently only 11 percent of U.S. solid waste lives again as something else. And still the volume of garbage keeps growing—up by 80 percent since 1960, expected to mount an additional 20 percent by 2000. Not including sludge and construction wastes, Americans collectively toss out 160 million tons each year—enough to spread 30 stories high over 1,000 football fields, enough to fill a bumper-to-bumper convoy of

garbage trucks halfway to the moon.

Municipal waste haulers aren't taking it there—yet. But as their own landfills close and disposal fees soar, many communities are trucking their trash across state lines and into rural areas. Some 28,000 tons of garbage travel the nation's highways each day; New York, Pennsylvania and New Jersey export 8 million tons a year. That practice can be costly, too: Long Island townships each spend an average of $23 million a year shipping garbage out of state. Increasingly, it incenses residents on the receiving end as well. "I'm all for taking care of our garbage needs, but New Jersey can take care of its own," says state Sen. Roger Bedford of Alabama, which has placed a two-year moratorium on accepting garbage not grown at home.

Public Resistance

NIMBY (Not in My Backyard syndrome) is breaking out all over, frustrating efforts to build new landfills, expand old ones and site incinerators, transfer stations and recycling centers. NIMBY has been joined by other acrimonious acronyms of the waste wars: GOOMBY (Get Out of My Backyard), LULU (Locally Undesirable Land Use) and NIMEY (Not in My Election Year). Greater Los Angeles has suffered them all in recent years. Angry citizens have three times blockaded the entrance to Lopez Canyon Landfill, hoping to close the last remaining city-owned dump. Officials of surrounding L.A. County say their canyons won't accept any more of the city's trash and Mayor Tom Bradley helped scuttle the proposed $235 million Lancer incinerator when political opposition to the project grew ferocious. As a result, "we actually have garbage trucks running around town everyday without a place to dump," says local environmentalist Will Baca.

That doesn't faze some unscrupulous drivers. As legal disposal grows more difficult, some private waste haulers simply unload their fetid cargo anywhere, from ghetto streets to forests. Even the Mafia is concerned about the lack of landfill space. Law-enforcement officials say that two New York mob families, which own carting companies, are trying to gain control of valuable Pennsylvania dumps. Worse still, some truckers who haul meat and produce to the East in refrigerated vehicles are carrying maggot-infested garbage back West in the same trucks. Congress is considering banning the practice, which carries serious health risks. "Would you serve potato salad from your cat's litter box?" asked Pennsylvania State University food-science professor Manfred Kroger at congressional hearings.

The garbage crisis didn't appear overnight, of course. Environmentalists first warned of it in the 1970s, and some citizens conscientiously toted cans, bottles and paper to ragtag recycling centers. But there were scant markets for the recycled material and enthusiasm faded like last year's newsprint. The urgency seemed to wane as well: garbage, after all, isn't as frightening as toxic waste or as photogenic as the burning Amazon. Meanwhile, the throwaway society has grown ever more disposable, substituting squeezable plastic ketchup bottles for glass, generating 12.4 billion glossy mail-order catalogs each year and annually buying some 1 billion individual foil-lined boxes of fruit juice, complete with shrink wrapping and a plastic-encased straw on the side.

"Garbage, after all, isn't as frightening as toxic waste or as photogenic as the burning Amazon."

Ann: All I've been thinking about all week is garbage. I mean, I just can't stop thinking about it.

Psychiatrist: What kind of thoughts about garbage?

Ann: I've just gotten real concerned over what's gonna happen. . . . I mean, we've got so much of it. . . . The last time I started feeling this way is when that barge was stranded and you know, it was going around the island and nobody would claim it. . . .

—Opening lines of "sex, lies, and videotape," 1989

The saga of Islip's wandering garbage barge may have been to the trash crisis what the sinking of the Lusitania was to World War I. Ports as far away as Belize turned back the ship laden with 3,000 tons of Long Island filth in the spring of 1987, and nightly news stories starkly reminded Americans that what they toss out must go *somewhere*. Since then, 18 states and scores of municipalities have embarked on ambitious waste-reduction programs. In July 1990, Minneapolis and St. Paul will ban all plastic food packaging that won't degrade or can't be recycled;

Nebraska will ban most disposable diapers in 1993. With amazing speed, recycling has shed its tie-dyed image, attracted big-business investment and political passion. "Nobody knew what the heck curbside recycling was two years ago," says Gary Mielke of Illinois's Department of Energy and Natural Resources; now 500,000 households in his state alone set their glass, paper and aluminum on the street in separate containers. The efforts seem to provide an outlet for a wide range of environmental angst. "People are so tired of hearing about oil spills and nuclear accidents and ozone—things they can't do anything about," Mielke observes. "Recycling is the way they can do their part."

Paper Glut

Alas, it isn't that simple, as Minneapolis discovered in spring 1989. Thousands of residents eagerly turned in their glass, cans and newspapers. But newsprint handlers were so inundated that rather than buying it for $12 a ton, some started charging $20 a ton just to haul it away. Success has threatened newspaper-recycling programs all over the country. Only eight U.S. paper mills are equipped to turn old newspapers into new newsprint, and their capacity is still geared more to the scale of Boy Scout paper drives than mandatory municipal collection. In August 1989 the nationwide glut of newsprint stood at 1 million tons. Industry officials say markets have improved since then, but they complain that too many cities launched into newspaper collection before securing purchasers. Washington, D.C., is among them: papers picked up in its two-month-old recycling program are piling up in a big storage pit. If a buyer isn't found, all those carefully sorted newspapers may simply be hauled off to a dump or an incinerator.

Many other efforts to reduce the nation's trash volume are working at cross purposes as well, leaving citizens who want to help wondering what to do and whom to believe. Sales of degradable disposable diapers are soaring; some communities now require degradable plastic grocery bags. Yet most experts dismiss such items as little more than marketing ploys that won't do much to reduce volume in landfills. Photodegradables decompose only in the presence of sunlight, which doesn't shine inside covered dumps. Many biodegradables rely on microorganisms to digest additives like cornstarch, but disintegration takes place very slowly in dry, oxygen-starved landfills. What's more, if degradables are mingled with recycled plastics, they can weaken the resulting products: picture your fence posts made of recycled plastic sagging in a couple of years. The rush to degradable plastics "is a joke," says Jack Hogan, a group vice president of Spartech Corp., which nevertheless makes the material. "Our company is responding to our customers, who are forced to do this because of legislation. But you and

I will be part of history when they degrade in landfills."

Perhaps no consumer item better symbolizes the crisis—and the contradictions—than the polystyrene foam containers that keep McDonald's hamburgers warm and litter roadsides with such appalling frequency. McDonald's switched from paper to the plastic packaging 10 years ago amid concern over vanishing forests and paper-mill pollution, and was a leader in eliminating ozone-harming CFCs (chlorofluorocarbons) from polystyrene production. Now facing restrictions on the foam containers in nearly 100 communities, the company is scrambling to recycle the material. In October 1989, 100 McDonald's in New England began asking customers to toss their polystyrene into separate trash cans; fledgling recycling centers then pound it into plastic pellets that can be used in such things as Rolodex file holders, cassette boxes and yo-yos. Someday, McDonald's envisions building whole restaurants out of recycled burger boxes. "This material has many, many uses," insists Ray Thompson, a spokesman for Amoco, which makes the boxes. "It only makes sense to enrich our waste stream with *more* polystyrene."

"It's one of those great mysteries of life in America," mutters the cartoon character Shoe as he puts his groceries away. "In just one day, how do two bags of ordinary groceries turn into three bags of garbage?"*

Polystyrene makers insist that their abandoned trays, coffee cups and containers comprise less than 0.25 percent of the nation's trash. The biggest single component—41 percent by weight—is paper products, and their share has grown steadily, thanks in part to reams of computer printouts and competing regional phone books. Yard waste is the next biggest source by weight (18 percent before recycling), followed by metals (8.7 percent), glass (8.2 percent), food (7.9 percent), plastics (6.5 percent) and wood (3.7 percent). Toxic materials make up about 1 percent of the waste stream. They are supposed to be disposed of separately in facilities approved by the Environmental Protection Agency and carefully monitored for leakage. But many hazardous household products—from paint to nail-polish remover—slip through the EPA's guidelines.

"Many hazardous household products— from paint to nail-polish remover—slip through the EPA's guidelines."

Roughly 80 percent of all that stuff ends up in landfills. Some 6,000 remain nationwide, from unruly city dumps to state-of-the-art engineering marvels. Inside, some methane gas is produced but not much else happens. "Practically nothing

decomposes in a landfill," says University of Arizona anthropologist William Rathje, who has made a career excavating dumps from Tucson to Chicago. Rathje has found recognizable hot dogs, corncobs and grapes buried for 25 years, and readable newspapers dating back to 1952. The slow rate of degradation is actually a blessing, he says. If more of the contents did decompose, that would hasten the rate at which toxic inks, dyes and paints mixed with the leachate, posing more of a threat to ground water.

New and Improved Landfills

Landfill operators say that newer facilities pose few environmental dangers. "These are not just holes in the ground," says Bill Plunkett, spokesman for Waste Management, Inc., the nation's largest solid-waste-disposal firm. "They are highly engineered excavations which have expensive leachate- and gas-collection systems." In addition to taking in 2,500 tons of trash each day, Waste Management's 397-acre Settler's Hill landfill in Geneva, Ill., recovers enough methane to power 7,500 homes. The site will include two golf courses, a driving range, ski slopes, trails for horseback riding, jogging, biking, a lake and a picnic area. Still, NIMBY reigns supreme. Even when Waste Management offered $25 million to Chicago's Lake Calumet area for permission to expand a landfill there, residents weren't swayed. "No dumps, no deals," says state Rep. Clement Balanoff. "We have done more than our share."

"The kind of person who is most likely to oppose the siting of [a major incinerator] is young or middle-aged, college educated and liberal. The person least likely to oppose a facility is older, has a high school education or less. . . . Middle and higher socio-economic strata neighborhoods should not fall within the one-mile and five-mile radii of the proposed site. . . ."

—A report prepared by Cerrell Associates for the California Waste Management Board, 1984

Incinerators draw even more ire than landfills these days. "Resource recovery" plants were the bright hope of the 1970s energy crisis, promising to provide steam and electricity while simultaneously reducing trash volume by 90 percent. Some 155 incinerators are now in operation and 29 more are under construction. But an additional 64 have been blocked, canceled or delayed. The problems are partly economic: construction costs can run as high as $500 million, and the energy that incinerators produce is not cost-competitive, even though public utilities are required by law to purchase the power. But what worries residents more are the toxic air pollutants, including dioxins, that some incinerators release. Even the leftover ash can be toxic and should be disposed of as hazardous waste. In Philadelphia's own version of the Islip garbage barge, a ship carrying 28 million pounds of city incinerator ash was rejected by seven countries on three continents over a 22-month period. It was ultimately dumped in 1988, but the ship's owners refuse to say where.

Incinerator operators say that pollution controls such as high-temperature furnaces, scrubbers and bag houses virtually eliminate harmful emissions. They and environmentalists have dueled with scientific studies over how dangerous trashburning can be. L.A.'s Lancer project was stopped after one test found it might cause an additional .118 case of cancer per million people. Detroit officials say the ash from their new $438 million incinerator is no more toxic than what remains in someone's fireplace. Yet the Detroit facility has repeatedly failed state ash tests, and in September 1989 it flunked air-pollution tests with mercury emissions four times Michigan's allowable level. Allen Hershkowitz, senior scientist at the Natural Resources Defense Council, believes that incineration *can* work safely. But he says too many U.S. operators see the environmental concerns as public-relations problems rather than serious calls for upgrading practices. Meanwhile, says Hershkowitz, the fast promises of incinerator operators have "conspired to blind public officials to the opportunities that recycling offers."

The Promise of Recycling

Recycling also holds the edge in creating new jobs, protecting the environment and conserving natural resources. EPA has set a goal of recycling 25 percent of the nation's waste by 1992. But success will depend largely on finding markets for the recycled products. "Most people think they put out the glass, aluminum and paper and they've recycled. In fact, all they've done is separate," says Edward Klein, who heads the agency's task force on solid waste. "Until those commodities are taken somewhere else and used again, you haven't recycled."

What follows is a status report on the potential markets for recyclable materials:

• *Aluminum*: Turning bauxite into new aluminum is 10 times more expensive than reprocessing used cans. That's one key reason more than half of all aluminum beverage cans are recycled today—42.5 billion annually. Even so, Americans still toss out enough aluminum every three months to rebuild the nation's entire airline fleet.

• *Glass*: Reusing old glass also costs less than forging virgin materials. To date, only 10 percent of it is recycled, but markets are growing steadily. Glass bottles can live again as "glassphalt" (a combination of glass and asphalt) and, of course, as other food containers. A California firm, Encore!, has even disproven the old adage that new wine can't come in old vessels. It grosses $3 million a year collecting and sterilizing 65,000 cases of empties

each month and selling them back to West Coast wineries.

• *Yard waste*: Composting America's fertile mounds of leaves and grass clippings could eliminate one fifth of the nation's waste—and as much as one third of L.A.'s total. But aside from backyard gardeners, there hasn't been much call for mulch. Pesticides and lawn chemicals also pose toxicology problems in compost heaps. Still, experts say that markets would grow if more municipalities followed Fairfield, Conn., which opened a $3 million composting center to create topsoil for parks, playgrounds and public landscaping.

• *Plastics*: The $140 billion-a-year plastics industry is at last waking up to recycling. Currently only 1 percent of plastics is recaptured, but manufacturers are scrambling to find new uses, from plastic "lumber" to stuffing for ski jackets. Procter & Gamble is making new Spic and Span containers entirely from recycled PET (polyethylene terephthalate, the stuff beverage bottles are made of) and hopes to turn even used Luvs and Pampers into plastic trash bags and park benches. There are still limitations. The Food and Drug Administration will not permit recycled plastic to serve or store food, since it cannot be decontaminated. Some products—like squeezable ketchup bottles—have up to six layers of polymers, which complicates separating. And some recycled plastic never looks new again. Tom Tomaszek, manager of Plastics Again, a polystyrene recycling center near Boston, says the pellets his plant produces come only in "army green," while manufacturers want white or clear. "The biggest problem," Tomaszek says, "is getting people away from the idea that new is better."

"Industry officials like to boast that nearly 30 percent of all paper products consumed in this country are recycled."

• *Paper*: Industry officials like to boast that nearly 30 percent of all paper products consumed in this country are recycled—26 million tons a year, turning up in cereal boxes, toilet tissue, even bedding for farm animals. Still, that leaves more than 40 million tons clogging landfills and going up smokestacks annually. Tree-poor nations like Taiwan and Korea import some U.S. wastepaper. But matching supply, demand and reprocessing capacity at home will take time and coordination. U.S. recycling mills can actually use more high-quality white paper, like computer printouts, than communities are collecting. For newsprint and magazines, the opposite is true. (Currently, no U.S. mills turn recycled fibers into the kind of glossy, clay-coated paper that *Newsweek* uses.) With burgeoning collection efforts, "we have the potential in this country to increase the supply [of wastepaper] overnight," says J. Rodney Edwards of the American Paper Institute. "But expanding the capacity to use it will take three to five years."

Historically, the American marketplace has been driven by *demand* for products, not *supply* of raw materials. But some lawmakers have concluded that the free market needs adjusting if recycling is to significantly dent the nation's garbage piles. Florida now taxes nonrecycled newsprint at 10 cents per ton. California and Connecticut have passed laws to require newspapers to use a rising percentage of recycled paper in coming years. . . .

Receiving an environmental award from George Bush for his community recycling program, high-school student Allen Graves of North Hollywood, Calif., asked the president, "Does your office recycle?"

"I don't know," said Bush.

Busy, distracted citizens also need incentives to recycle. To that end, New York City plans to fine residents who don't comply with its nascent program: $25 for the first offense, $500 for four offenses in a six-month period, with landlords dunned up to $10,000 if their tenants don't cooperate. San Francisco is relying heavily on public education, reminding residents that recycling one aluminum can, for example, can save enough energy to run a TV for three hours. Nearby Berkeley has even tried gimmickry. Under its Eco-lotto program, city officials selected one household by random each week, rummaged through its trash and promised to award the homeowner $250 if no recyclables had been discarded. If the lucky household wasn't careful, the cash was rolled over into the next week's prize. Sadly, the pot rose to $4,500 before the city found a winner.

The Cost of Creating Garbage

Charging citizens directly for the amount of trash they throw out may prove more effective. In many communities, garbage removal still comes as part of a general-service bill, so residents never know how much it costs. Seattle changed that with "variable can rates" in the 1970s. Today residents pay $13.75 to have a single can of trash picked up four times each month, and $9 for each additional can. Faced with such fees, residents have been buying more recyclables, fewer packaged goods and more large-size boxes. Two thirds of Seattle households also signed up to have private haulers collect their recyclables and yard waste. Combined, those measures have cut Seattle's trash volume by 25 percent. City officials are still considering building an incinerator, but thanks to recycling, they hope it will be a smaller, cheaper one.

Seattle's program is considered a model of modern "integrated waste management"—in short, reducing and recycling as much trash as possible, then burning or burying the rest. Some local environmentalists still bitterly oppose incineration, but organizations from the Environmental Defense Fund to the Office of Technology Assessment say that the nation will need a judicious mix of all four methods to handle its trash in the future. Many experts believe that at best, the nation can recycle only about half of its garbage; recycling itself produces some residues that need to go to landfills. But those, too, can be used more efficiently. One Long Island firm, Landfill Mining Inc., has come up with a technique to "recycle" old dumps: digging through them to unearth reusable material like metal and glass. That allows the landfills to be lined and leaves room for more waste—or incinerator ash. "We can actually recycle the space," says founder Robert Flanagan.

"The nation has only begun to focus its collective ingenuity on source reduction—generating less garbage in the first place."

The nation has only begun to focus its collective ingenuity on source reduction—generating less garbage in the first place. For that, citizens will need to rethink their priorities. It wasn't so long ago that Americans reused string and rubber bands, resharpened razors, threw food scraps into the stock pot and made grease into soap. (At the turn of the century, pigs were also part of waste management in many cities; 100 of them could eat a ton of garbage a day, creating low-cost meat and fertilizer.) The disposable society has brought many conveniences. Single-serving frozen dinners in microwavable trays do facilitate mealtime. Wrapping fast-food utensils in plastic cuts down on germs. Ketchup really does come out faster when the bottle can be squeezed. How much do those conveniences mean to us? Are they worth the price of a landfill or an incinerator next door?

Unfortunately, the trade-offs aren't so obvious. It has been far too easy, when taking out the sixth or seventh bag of trash in a week, to assume that the garbage truck will dump in someone else's backyard, or not to think about it at all. With rare exceptions during wartime, Americans have not been adept at making individual sacrifices for the common good. That mentality will have to change. Otherwise, the dumps will cover the country coast to coast and the trucks will stop in everybody's backyard.

Melinda Beck is a senior editor at Newsweek, *a weekly newsmagazine.*

"When seen in perspective, our garbage woes... are not exceptional, and they can be dealt with by disposal methods that are safe and already available."

A Garbage Crisis Does Not Exist

William L. Rathje

Newspapers. Telephone books. Soiled diapers. Medicine vials encasing brightly colored pills. Brittle ossuaries of chicken bones and T-bones. Sticky green mountains of yard waste. Half-empty cans of paint and turpentine and motor oil and herbicide. Broken furniture and forsaken toys. Americans produce a lot of garbage, some of it very toxic, and our garbage is not always disposed of in a sensible way. The press in recent years has paid much attention to the filling up (and therefore the closing down) of landfills, to the potential dangers of incinerators, and to the apparent inadequacy of our recycling efforts. The use of the word "crisis" in these contexts has become routine. For all the publicity, however, the precise state of affairs is not known. It may be that the lack of reliable information and the persistence of misinformation constitute the real garbage crisis.

But we have learned some things over the years. My program at the University of Arizona, The Garbage Project, has been looking at landfills and at garbage fresh out of the can since the early 1970s, and it has generated important insights. Since 1987, I have visited all parts of the country and spoken with people who think about garbage every day—town planners, politicians, junkyard owners, landfill operators, civil engineers, microbiologists, and captains of industry—as well as many ordinary men and women who help make garbage possible. When seen in perspective, our garbage woes turn out to be serious—indeed, they have been serious for more than a century—but they are not exceptional, and they can be dealt with by disposal methods that are safe and already available. The biggest challenge we will face is to recognize that the conventional wisdom about garbage is often wrong.

To get some perspective on garbage let's review a few fundamentals. For most of the past two and a half million years human beings left their garbage where it fell. Oh, they sometimes tidied up their sleeping and activity areas, but that was about all. This disposal scheme functioned adequately, because hunters and gatherers frequently abandoned their campgrounds to follow game or find new stands of plants. Man faced his first garbage crisis when he became a sedentary animal—when, rather than move himself, he chose to move his garbage. The archaeologist Gordon R. Willey has argued, only partly in fun, that *Homo sapiens* may have been propelled along the path toward civilization by his need for a class at the bottom of the social hierarchy that could be assigned the task of dealing with mounting piles of garbage.

No New Options

This brings us to an important truth about garbage: There are no ways of dealing with it that haven't been known for many thousands of years. These ways are essentially four: dumping it, burning it, converting it into something that can be used again, and minimizing the volume of material goods—future garbage—that is produced in the first place ("source reduction," as it is called). Every civilization of any complexity has used all four methods to varying degrees.

From prehistory through the present day dumping has been the means of disposal favored everywhere, including in the cities. The archaeologist C. W. Blegen, who dug into Bronze Age Troy in the 1950s, found that floors had become so littered that periodically a fresh supply of dirt or clay had been brought in to cover up the refuse. Of course, after several layers had been applied, the doors and roofs had to be adjusted upward. Over time the ancient cities of the Middle East rose high above the landscape on massive mounds, called tells. In 1973 a civil engineer with the Department of Commerce,

William L. Rathje, "Rubbish," *The Atlantic Monthly,* December 1989. Reprinted with permission.

Charles Gunnerson, calculated that the rate of uplift owing to the accumulation of debris in Bronze Age Troy was about 4.7 feet per century. If the idea of a city rising above its garbage at this rate seems extraordinary, it may be worth considering that "street level" on the island of Manhattan is fully six feet higher today than it was when Peter Minuit lived there.

At Troy and elsewhere, of course, not all trash was kept indoors. The larger pieces of garbage and debris were thrown into the streets. There semi-domesticated animals (usually pigs) ate up the food scraps, while human scavengers, in exchange for the right to sell anything useful that they might find, carried much of what was left to vacant lots or to the outskirts of town, where the garbage was burned or simply left.

A Modern System

In most of the Third World a slopping-and-scavenging system that Hector and Aeneas would recognize remains in place. The image of sulfurous "garbage mountains" in the Third World may be repellent, but the people who work these dumps, herding their pigs even as they sort out paper and plastic and metal, are performing the most thorough job of garbage recycling and resource recovery in the world. The garbage mountains point up another important (and often overlooked) truth about garbage: efficient disposal is not always completely compatible with other desirable social ends, such as human dignity and economic modernization. In a liberal democracy these other ends compete for priority, and more often than not win.

Dumping, slopping, and scavenging were the norm in Europe and the United States until the late 1800s. It is difficult for anyone alive now to comprehend how appalling, as recently as a century ago, were the conditions of daily life in all the cities of the Western world, even in the wealthiest parts of town. The stupefying level of filth accepted as normal from the Middle Ages through the Enlightenment was augmented horribly by the Industrial Revolution. As the historian Martin Melosi has noted in his book *Garbage in the Cities* (1981), one of the ironies of laissez-faire capitalism is that it gave rise to a kind of "municipal socialism," as cities were forced, for the first time since antiquity, to shoulder responsibility for such duties as public safety and sanitation. Taking the long view reminds us of one more often-overlooked truth about garbage: Ever since governments began facing up to their responsibilities, the story of the garbage problem in the West has been one of steady amelioration, of bad giving way to less bad and eventually to not too bad. To be able to complain about the garbage problems that persist is, by past standards, something of a luxury.

What most people call garbage, professionals call solid waste. The waste that we're most familiar with, from the households and institutions and small businesses of towns and cities, is "municipal solid waste," or MSW. Professionals talk about what we all throw away as entering the "solid-waste stream," and the figure of speech is apt. Waste flows unceasingly, fed by hundreds of millions of tributaries. While many normal activities come to a halt on weekends and holidays, the production of garbage flows on. Indeed, days of rest tend to create the largest waves of garbage. Christmas is a solid-waste tsunami.

One might think that something for which professionals have a technical term of long standing should also be precisely calibrated in terms of volume. As we shall see, this is not the case with MSW. Nonetheless, there has been a good deal of vivid imagery relating to volume. Katie Kelly, in her book *Garbage* (1973), asserted that the amount of MSW produced in the United States annually would fill five million trucks; these, "placed end to end, would stretch around the world twice." In December of 1987 *Newsday* estimated that a year's worth of America's solid waste would fill the twin towers of 187 World Trade Centers. In 1985 *The Baltimore Sun* claimed that Baltimore generates enough garbage every day to fill Memorial Stadium to a depth of nine feet—a ballpark figure if ever there was one.

"To be able to complain about the garbage problems that persist is, by past standards, something of a luxury."

Calculating the total annual volume or weight of garbage in the United States is difficult because there is, of course, no way one can actually measure or weigh more than a fraction of what is thrown out. All studies have had to take shortcuts. Not surprisingly, estimates of the size of the U.S. solid-waste stream are quite diverse. Figures are most commonly expressed in pounds discarded per person per day, and the studies that I have seen from the past decade and a half give the following rates: 2.9 pounds per person per day, 3.02 pounds, 4.24, 4.28, 5.0, and 8.0. My own view is that the higher estimates significantly overstate the problem. Garbage Project studies of actual refuse reveal that even three pounds of garbage per person per day may be too high an estimate for many parts of the country, a conclusion that has been corroborated by weight-sorts in many communities. Americans are wasteful, but to some degree we have been conditioned to think of ourselves as more wasteful than we truly are—and certainly as more wasteful than we used to be.

Evidence all around us reinforces such

perceptions. Fast-food packaging is ubiquitous and conspicuous. Planned obsolescence is a cliché. Our society is filled with symbolic reminders of waste. What we forget is everything that is no longer there to see. We do not see the 1,200 pounds per year of coal ash that every American generated at home at the turn of the century and that was usually dumped on the poor side of town. We do not see the hundreds of thousands of dead horses that once had to be disposed of by American cities every year. We do not look behind modern packaging and see the food waste that it has prevented, or the garbage that it has saved us from making. (Consider the difference in terms of garbage generation between making orange juice from concentrate and orange juice from scratch; and consider the fact that producers of orange-juice concentrate sell the leftover orange rinds as feed, while households don't.) The average household in Mexico City produces one third more garbage a day than does the average American household. The reason for the relatively favorable U.S. showing is packaging— which is to say, modernity. No, Americans are not suddenly producing more garbage. Per capita our record is, at *worst*, one of relative stability. . . .

The physical reality inside a landfill is considerably different from what you might suppose. I spent some time with The Garbage Project's team digging into seven landfills: two outside Chicago, two in the San Francisco Bay area, two in Tucson, and one in Phoenix. We exhumed 16,000 pounds of garbage, weighing every item we found and sorting them all into twenty-seven basic categories and then into 162 subgroupings. In those eight tons of garbage and dirt cover there were fewer than sixteen pounds of fast-food packaging; in other words, only about a tenth of one percent of the landfills' contents by weight consisted of fast-food packaging. Less than one percent of the contents by weight was disposable diapers. The entire category of things made from plastic accounted for less than five percent of the landfills' contents by weight, and for only 12 percent by volume. The real culprit in every landfill is plain old paper—non-fast-food paper, and mostly paper that isn't for packaging. Paper accounts for 40 to 50 percent of everything we throw away, both by weight and by volume.

The Proliferation of Paper

If fast-food packaging is the Emperor's New Clothes of garbage, then a number of categories of paper goods collectively deserve the role of Invisible Man. In all the hand-wringing over the garbage crisis, has a single voice been raised against the proliferation of telephone books? Each two-volume set of Yellow Pages distributed in Phoenix in 1988—to be thrown out in 1989—weighed 8.63 pounds, for a total of 6,000 tons of wastepaper. And competitors of the Yellow Pages have appeared

virtually everywhere. Dig a trench through a landfill and you will see layers of phone books, like geological strata, or layers of cake. Just as conspicuous as telephone books are newspapers, which make up 10 to 18 percent of the contents of a typical municipal landfill by volume. Even after several years of burial they are usually well preserved. During a recent landfill dig in Phoenix, I found newspapers dating back to 1952 that looked so fresh you might read one over breakfast. Deep within landfills, copies of that *New York Times* editorial about fast-food containers will remain legible until well into the next century.

"Laboratories can indeed biodegrade newspapers into gray slime in a few weeks or months, if the newspapers are finely ground and placed in ideal conditions."

As the foregoing suggests, the notion that much biodegradation occurs inside lined landfills is largely a popular myth. Making discards out of theoretically biodegradable materials, such as paper, or plastic made with cornstarch, is often proposed as a solution to our garbage woes (as things biodegrade, the theory goes, there will be more room for additional refuse). Laboratories can indeed biodegrade newspapers into gray slime in a few weeks or months, if the newspapers are finely ground and placed in ideal conditions. The difficulty, of course, is that newspapers in landfills are not ground up, conditions are far from ideal, and biodegradation does not follow laboratory schedules. Some food and yard debris does degrade, but at a very, very slow rate (by 25 to 50 percent over ten to fifteen years). The remainder of the refuse in landfills seems to retain its original weight, volume, and form. It is, in effect, mummified. This may be a blessing, because if paper did degrade rapidly, the result would be an enormous amount of inks and paint that could leach into groundwater. . . .

Environmental scientists believe that they now know enough to design and locate safe landfills, even if those landfills must hold a considerable amount of hazardous household waste such as motor oil and pesticides. The State of Delaware seems to be successful at siting such landfills now. But places like Long Island, where the water table is high, should never have another landfill. In the congested northeastern states there may simply be no room for many more landfills, at least not safe ones. Some 1,550 twenty-ton tractor trailers laden with garbage now leave Long Island every week bound for landfills elsewhere. But the country at large still has room aplenty. The State of New York recently commissioned an environmental survey of 42 percent of its domain with the express aim of determining where landfills might be properly located. The survey pinpointed lands that constitute only one percent of the area but nevertheless total 200 square miles.

"If there is a prosperous future for recycling, it probably lies in some sort of alliance between wastepaper and scrap dealers and local governments."

The obstacles to the sanitary landfill these days are monetary—transporting garbage a few hundred miles by truck may cost more than shipping the same amount to Taiwan—and, perhaps more important, psychological: no one wants a garbage dump in his backyard. But they are not insuperable, and they are not fundamentally geographic. Quite frankly, few nations have the enormous (and enormously safe) landfill capabilities that this one has. Iraj Zandi, an environmental scientist who teaches at the University of Pennsylvania, said to me during a discussion about landfills, "Have you ever taken a flight from San Diego to Philadelphia? For three thousand miles you look down out of the plane and there's nothing there!"

The yards of America's wastepaper and scrap-metal dealers are located near interstates and in warehouse districts, and they contain piles of crushed automobiles, railroad cars filled with cans, and baled newspaper and cardboard stacked several stories high. These are the trading pits of the recycled-materials markets. There is a big split between those who would recycle to make money and those who would recycle to do good, and I was made painfully aware of it one night at an Association of Recycling Industries convention, where I was scheduled to speak. Talking to a wastepaper dealer, I described with satisfaction the municipal newspaper-recycling program that the city of Tucson had just begun. The dealer looked at me in horror. He said, "You're telling me how well the competition is doing—the ones who are subsidized by the taxpayers to take away our livelihood. Don't you understand? There never has been a shortage of recycled newspapers. The shortage is in demand. Markets fill up just like landfills. There are just so many car panels and cereal boxes that need to be made. I suppose you believe GM [General Motors] is going to say, 'Hey, great! Here's a bunch more newspapers for door panels. Let's make some more cars.' The more Tucson recycles, the less I do."

Years later I count wastepaper dealers and other for-profit recyclers among my friends and also among the most valuable resources available to the

United States for dealing with garbage. The champions of municipal recycling, who in communities across the country have been trying to move in on bottles, newspapers, and cans in the belief that recyclable commodities represent virgin territory, have found that the territory is already inhabited. Recycling by anyone should be encouraged, in my view, but it is important to understand at the outset what kind of recycling works and what kind may end up doing more harm than good. . . .

The fact is that for the time being, despite the recriminations and breast-beating, we are recycling just about as much paper as the market can bear. As noted, the market for recyclable paper is glutted; expansion is possible only overseas. The demand for recyclable plastic and aluminum has not yet been fully met, but Americans have been doing a pretty good job of returning their plastic bottles and aluminum cans, and the beverage industry, which hates it when states pass bottle bills, has pre-empted the issue in most places by opening up successful recycling centers.

Money Spurs Recycling

Suppose there were a lot of room for growth and that the demand for recycled paper, plastic, and aluminum were insatiable. How much garbage would Americans be prepared to recycle? The only factor that could conceivably drive a systematic recycling effort is money. Money is the reason why junk dealers pay attention to some kinds of garbage and not to others, and it is the reason why most people return cans to supermarkets, and newspapers to recycling centers. . . .

There have been studies that have claimed that the people most likely to recycle are those with the most money and the most education, but all these studies are based on people's "self-reports." A look through household garbage yields a different picture. From 1973 to 1980 The Garbage Project examined some 9,000 loads of refuse in Tucson from a variety of neighborhoods chosen for their socioeconomic characteristics. We carefully sorted the contents for newspapers, aluminum cans, and glass bottles (evidence that a household is not recycling), and for bottle caps, aluminum pop-tops, and plastic sixpack holders (possible evidence, in the absence of bottles or cans, that a household *is* recycling). A lot of complicated statistical adjustments and cross-referencing had to be done, but in the end we made three discoveries. First, people don't recycle as much as they say they do (but they recycle just about as much as they say their neighbors do). Second, household patterns of recycling vary over the time; recycling is not yet a consistent habit. Third, high income and education and even a measure of environmental concern do not predict household recycling rates. The only reliable predictor is the price paid for the commodity at buyback centers. When prices rose for, say, newsprint, the number of newspapers found in local garbage suddenly declined.

If there is a prosperous future for recycling, it probably lies in some sort of alliance between wastepaper and scrap dealers and local governments. Where recycling is concerned, municipalities are good at two things: collecting garbage and passing laws to legislate monetary incentives. Wastepaper and scrap dealers are good at something different: selling garbage. Local programs run by bureaucrats and tied to strict cost-accounting measures need predictable prices. Stability in a commodities market is rare. Secondary-materials dealers thrive on daily, hourly fluctuations.

"I am not worried that even if present trends continue, we will be buried in our garbage."

Not long ago I stopped in Berkeley, where a ban was being considered on the use of expanded polystyrene foam—the substance that is turned into coffee cups and hamburger boxes and meat trays. The ban had originally been proposed because chlorofluorocarbons are used in the blowing of foam objects and are believed to contribute to the depletion of atmospheric ozone, and because foam objects are aesthetically repugnant to many people and symbolize the garbage problems we have. At the Berkeley campus of the University of California, I passed Sproul Plaza. It was lunchtime, and the plaza was filled with some 700 or 800 students in various forms of repose; virtually all of them held on their laps what first appeared to be pairs of white wings. The wings turned out to be large foam clamshells, which held hot food. I asked one group of lunchers what they thought about a ban on polystyrene foam. Great idea, they said between mouthfuls, and without irony. The ban has since gone into effect, even though the major producers and users of chlorofluorocarbons agreed to a phase-out.

Source reduction is to garbage what preventive medicine is to health: a means of eliminating a problem before it can happen. But the utility of legislated source reduction is in many respects an illusion. For one thing, most consumer industries already have—and have responded to—strong economic incentives to make products as compact and as light as possible, for ease of distribution and to conserve costly resources. In 1970 a typical plastic soda bottle weighed sixty grams; today it weighs forty-eight grams and is more easily crushed. For another, who is to say when packaging is excessive? We have all seen small items in stores—can openers,

say—attached to big pieces of cardboard hanging on a display hook. That piece of cardboard looks like excessive packaging, but its purpose is to deter shoplifting. Finally, source-reduction measures don't end up eliminating much garbage; hamburgers, eggs, and VCRs, after all, will still have to be put in *something.*

Most source-reduction plans are focused on a drastic reduction in the use of plastic. And yet in landfills foams and other plastics are dormant. While some environmentalists claim that plastics create dioxins when burned in incinerators, a study by New York State's Department of Energy Conservation cleared the most widely used plastics of blame. The senior staff scientist of the National Audubon Society, Jan Beyea, contends that plastics in landfills are fine so long as they don't end up in the oceans. There plastic threatens marine animals, which can swallow or become enmeshed in it. Beyea's big complaint is against paper, whose production, he believes, creates large volumes of sulfur emissions that contribute to acid rain.

Ultimately, the source-reduction question is one of life-style override. The purists' theory is that industry is forcing plastics and convenience products on an unwilling captive audience. This is nonsense. American consumers, though they may in some spiritual sense lament packaging, as a practical matter depend on the product identification and convenience that modern packaging allows. That's the reason source reduction usually doesn't work.

Our "wasteful" life-style is a product of affluence; disregard for the environment is not. Indeed, our short-term aesthetic concerns and long-term practical concerns for the environment are luxuries afforded us only by our wealth. In Third World countries, where a job and the next meal are significant worries, the quality of the environment is hardly a big issue in most people's minds. Concern for the environment can be attributed in major part to the conveniences—and the leisure time they afford—that some activists seem to want to eliminate.

Nothing New

None of this makes us unique, for all our newfangled technologies, Americans are not that different from those who inhabited most of the world's other great civilizations. Our social history fits neatly into the broader cycles of rise and decline that other peoples have experienced before us. Most grand civilizations seem to have moved, over time, from efficient scavenging to conspicuous consumption and then back again. It is a common story, usually driven by economic realities.

In their beginnings most civilizations, both ancient and recent, make efficient use of resources. The Preclassic Maya, who inhabited the rain forests of the southern Yucatan from 1200 to 300 B.C., seem to have lived relatively simple farming lives. They built a few small temples, constructed large houses out of thatch on low dirt platforms, and interred their dead with one or two monochrome pots. Around 300 B.C. something extraordinary happened. A Classic Maya life-style of conspicuous consumption was born. The Classic Maya went in for excessive display: fancy ceremonial clothes and feathered headdresses; tall temples with intricately carved facades; cache offerings of jade and shell mosaics; and lavish burials. This cult of conspicuous consumption spread throughout southern Mesoamerica. Toward the end of major civilizations things are usually quite different. During the Maya Decadent Period temples were small, tombs were reused, and caches contained only a few pieces of broken pottery or chipped obsidian knives. Whatever the stimulus, that which archaeologists in the 1950s saw among the ancient Maya as decadence we can see today as efficient resource utilization. Among the Decadent Maya everything was recycled or reused, and virtually no resources were put away beyond easy retrieval. The Decadent Maya were living on the edge. They had no choice.

"One way or another, Americans will someday stand as exemplars of responsible garbage management."

The United States is still well within a Classic phase, at least in terms of its disposal habits. And I am not worried that even if present trends continue, we will be buried in our garbage. To a considerable extent we will keep doing what other civilizations have done: rising *above* our garbage. (One of the great difficulties I have met in excavating landfills is finding municipal sites that have not already been covered by new facilities.)

A rough consensus has emerged among specialists as to how America can at least manage its garbage, if not make it pretty or go away. Safely sited and designed landfills should be employed in the three quarters of the country where there is still room for them. Incinerators with appropriate safety devices and trained workers can be usefully sited anywhere but make the most sense in the Northeast. And states and municipalities need to cut deals with wastepaper and scrap dealers on splitting the money to be made from recycling. This is a minimum. Several additional steps could be taken to reduce the biggest component of garbage: paper. Freight rates could be revised to make the transport of paper for recycling cheaper than the transport of wood for pulp. Also, many things could be done to increase the demand for recycled paper. For example, the federal government, which uses more paper by far than any other institution in America, could insist

that most federal paperwork be done on recycled paper. Beyond confronting the biggest-ticket item head-on, most garbage specialists would recommend a highly selective attack on a few kinds of plastic: not because plastic doesn't degrade or is ugly or bulky but because recycling certain plastics in household garbage would yield high-grade costly resins for new plastics and make incineration easier on the furnace grates, and perhaps safer. Finally, we need to expand our knowledge base. At present we have more reliable information about Neptune than we do about this country's solid-waste stream.

Exemplars of Responsible Management

One way or another, Americans will someday stand as exemplars of responsible garbage management. This could happen in the not too distant future, when time and resources and society's margin of error run out, and a Decadent America learns painfully to reuse and make do with whatever is at hand. Or it could come sooner, in a palmier and more recognizable time, if Americans, scoffing at history's odds, were to embrace a curious goal: to create the first civilization that became "decadent" before its time.

An archaeologist and anthropologist, William L. Rathje is also the director of The Garbage Project at the University of Arizona, in Tucson.

viewpoint 27

Degradable Plastics Can Reduce Waste

Ann Gibbons

After decades of creating stronger and more durable plastics, chemists have become reverse alchemists: they are designing plastics that disintegrate. Six-pack yokes that crumble, garbage bags that degrade, and medical sutures that dissolve have reached the market.

The plastics industry has plenty of incentive. Pressure has been growing to reduce the amount of waste that clogs landfills, strangles wildlife, and litters beaches. Plastics now account for 7.2 percent of the weight of all municipal refuse and are the fastest-growing type of trash in landfills. The tonnage is expected to double by the year 2000 if Americans continue to increase their use 8 percent annually, as they have for the past 25 years. The mountains of synthetic waste are a legacy for future generations, since plastics normally take some 200 years to degrade.

To limit this legacy, at least 15 states are writing laws that restrict the use and disposal of plastic products. The federal government has banned the dumping of plastics in the ocean, and the U.S. Navy recently canceled a contract to buy 11 million plastic food and trash bags.

Many people see degradable plastics as part of the solution. Congress held hearings on the materials in the summer of 1988 and introduced a flurry of bills to encourage their use.

Yet bugs in the new technology remain to be solved. Degradables cost more to make and usually aren't as reliable as conventional plastics: it's hard to sell garbage bags that fall apart before they reach the landfill. Some of the new plastics don't dissolve entirely, and no one knows how safe the remaining residues are. Environmental groups also fear that the advent of disposables may hinder efforts to recycle longer-lived plastics.

Ann Gibbons, "Making Plastics That Biodegrade," *Technology Review*, February/March 1989. Reprinted with permission from Technology Review, copyright 1989.

The industry itself has invested in the technology somewhat reluctantly. "We're unashamedly market-led," says Roger Lloyd of ICI Biological Products, a division of Imperial Chemical of Britain. For consumers, that means that even if they want plastic products that dissolve, they can't always find them. For example, degradable six-pack yokes that won't strangle fish, birds, and seals are available only in states that require them. But the field promises to grow as more regulations take effect and more consumers demand the new products.

Designing the Technology

The marketplace today boasts more kinds of plastics than metals, with properties as different as lead from gold and aluminum from iron. What these diverse materials share is an underlying strength and flexibility that make them ideal for products ranging from an airplane's nose cone to a disposable diaper lining. Plastics can be devised so they don't rust, rot, mold, or lose their integrity when wet, heated, or frozen.

The chemistry of plastics underlies this indestructibility. They are composed of long chains of repeating hydrocarbon molecules. Those chains, called polymers, are so tightly bound that they are impenetrable to the microorganisms that dissolve paper and most other garbage.

The challenge for chemists is to find a way to weaken those synthetic chains without robbing the plastic of its strength. In pursuing this goal, scientists have focused on three categories of disintegrating plastics: biodegradable, chemically degradable, and photodegradable.

Biodegradable plastics incorporate weakening agents into their chemical structures that allow fungi and bacteria to grab hold and digest the hydrocarbon chains. However, these materials are costly because they are difficult to make, often requiring new steps in the manufacturing process.

Research on biodegradable plastics owes much to Union Carbide chemist James Potts, who screened a variety of materials in the 1960s to see which the bacteria in soil would consume. He discovered that organisms gobbled up natural polymers such as cornstarch, cellulose, cotton, and silk, but that they ate only one class of synthetic polymers: polyesters. These polymers have "ester groups," such as animal and vegetable fats and oils, bound into their chemical backbone. Enzymes from microorganisms seek out an ester group and connect with it, using water to convert it into an alcohol and acid that the organisms can then digest. Biodegradable polyesters also consist of shorter chains and have low melting points, so they can be swollen with water. This softens their molecular structure and makes them more susceptible to the work of enzymes.

Although biodegradable polyesters are too expensive to be used in packaging, the biggest market for plastics, they are valuable in specialty areas such as medicine and agriculture. American Cyanamid Co. manufactures degradable sutures made of polyglocolate acid. Once inside the human body, the sutures slowly dissolve into harmless carbon dioxide and water, disappearing completely after three months. The material costs about $15 a pound to manufacture, compared with the average price of $.65 a pound for conventional plastic.

In the 1970s, the U.S. Forest Service tested Polycaprolactone, a biodedgradable plastic developed by Potts, as a protective sheath for seedlings, according to James Barnett of Timber Management Research in Pineville, La. Rangers used a special tool to fire plastic "bullets" containing seeds into the soil with each step. The containers protected the plants as they took root during their first year of life, and then dissolved. To speed up the pace of reforestation, another company even designed polyester containers with fins that could be fired from airplanes. But the company abandoned the product because the plastic cost too much.

Bone Screws and Farm Mulch

Polyesters have become models for chemists trying to make biodegradable plastics for broader use. At the University of Maryland, William Bailey induces esters to form in conventional plastics derived from petroleum, such as polyethylene used in black trash bags and milk containers.

His technique uses free radicals, unstable atoms that are missing electrons in their outer rings, to break the bonds between molecules. This triggers a chain reaction that tears up the polymers into ester groups, which microorganisms can then attack. He can control how quickly the polymers dissolve—from months to years—by varying the number of esters the free radicals create. Bailey says his material has the strength and flexibility of conventional polyethylene but the biodegradability of a polyester.

He even maintains that he can make the material in the same cheap commercial process used for most conventional plastics, but says he has had trouble capturing the interest of the packaging industry or the government.

"Although biodegradable polyesters are too expensive to be used in packaging... they are valuable in specialty areas such as medicine and agriculture."

Chemists at ICI in Wilmington, Del., rely on a different approach. They have developed a fermentation process to breed bacteria normally found in soil, just as brewers grow yeast for beer. When fed sugar and acid, these bacteria produce a polymer called PHBV (hydroxy butyric valeric acid) as a future source of energy, much as humans store fat. Chemists kill the bugs and harvest the powdery polymer, which they make into resins as strong as conventional plastic.

ICI chemist Tom Galvin says PHBV would be particularly valuable in making agricultural mulch, as well as plates and screws that hold broken bones in place until they heal. Once inside the body or disposed in soil, bacteria would consume the plastic without poisoning the patient or polluting the environment. And because PHBV is entirely natural, the body's immune system would not reject it.

The drawback is that, as with many biologically degradable plastics, the inventors have yet to work out the details of large-scale manufacturing. Companies from diaper makers to tampon manufacturers to packaging firms have expressed interest in PHBV, but at $15 a pound the cost is still too high. An ICI official says his company hopes to reduce manufacturing costs to $2 a pound within the next few years. Since the material isn't derived from petroleum products, its price should remain constant if oil prices rise.

A number of chemists have been using farmers' surpluses and wastes—starch from corn kernels and cellulose from the husks and from wood pulp—to make biodegradable plastics. At Purdue University, Ramani Narayan works with a conventional material such as the polystyrene used to make garbage bags, Styrofoam cups, and milk containers. Since starch and plastic mix about as well as oil and water, he adds an emulsifying agent that helps graft the polystyrene as a side chain onto the starch backbone. The result is a copolymer (made of two polymer chains) with as much as 20 to 30 percent cornstarch or cellulose evenly distributed throughout the plastic. Microorganisms in soil or water that feed on the starch break down the plastic into powder and then consume it within a few years. This approach offers versatility: different plastic polymers can be grafted to the starch or cellulose backbone.

Narayan expects to sell manufacturing rights for products such as fast-food wrappings and garbage bags. But his material has a drawback: it can become moldy if exposed to bacteria in food. He's now working on similar blends using wood pulp, which would not degrade until exposed to iron salts in soil.

In contrast to biologically degradable plastics, those that are chemically degradable do not break down completely. Instead, fillers, often starches, added during the traditional manufacturing process simply cause the material to crumble, leaving behind a residue. Although less effective, these products tend to be cheaper, since the techniques for making them are less delicate and labor intensive.

For example, Canada's St. Lawrence Starch Co. makes a degradable concentrate consisting of a plastic polymer coated with cornstarch. An ester such as corn oil joins the final batch as an oxidizing agent that will help force the polymer chain to break apart. Once a plastic bag made of the material is thrown in soil, bacteria eat the starch, leaving behind a porous structure. Meanwhile, the corn oil reacts with salts in the soil or water to generate peroxides, which attack the bonds in the remaining plastic. Eventually, the pieces become so small that bacteria can digest most of them. Under ideal conditions, about 50 percent of the plastic resin degrades into powder after six months and 100 percent in a few years, according to St. Lawrence Starch.

"Canada's St. Lawrence Starch Co. makes a degradable concentrate consisting of a plastic polymer coated with cornstarch."

Charles Swanson, a research chemist at the U.S. Department of Agriculture's Plant Polymer Research Laboratory in Peoria, is devising a degradable plastic that is up to 60 percent corn. The latter is so well integrated that the plastic absorbs water evenly, so that enzymes have no trouble breaking down the starch. These plastics have been blown into films that have been tested for use as a crop mulch. However, as the starch level rises to allow the plastic to break down more readily, it becomes less durable—to the point that it tears like paper, Swanson says. That's unacceptable for most uses. And Agritech Industries of Gibson, Ill., which has licensed the technology, is having trouble finding the right equipment to make the concentrate in large quantities.

Finally, the third type of degradable plastic does its magic when exposed to light. In photodegradables, "carbonyl groups"—composed of ketones, carbon, and oxygen molecules—absorb ultraviolet light from the sun, triggering a chain reaction that breaks the bonds between molecules. The plastic becomes brittle and crumbles. Most degradable plastic bags, six-pack yokes, and other plastics now on the market rely on this process. However, like chemically degradable plastics, these materials leave behind residue, and may take years to fall apart.

The Big Picture

This raises the question of what exactly consumers get when they buy products that are labeled degradable. All the new plastics need just the right conditions to break down. Photodegradable plastics can solve the litter problem only if they are exposed to sunlight—a problem in landfills and during the winter. Chemically degradable plastics must be buried in dirt or submerged in water to disintegrate. And biodegradable plastics need oxygen and moisture so the bacteria that eat them can survive. Even newspapers, which normally degrade quickly, can still be legible after 10 years in landfills that lack water and oxygen.

The USDA's Swanson maintains that manufacturers' claims of quick degradability are often overly optimistic. "There hasn't yet been a definition of biodegradable," he says. A product may claim to disintegrate, but its label doesn't specify what conditions are needed, how long it takes, or what material remains.

Greg Olson, a microbiologist at the U.S. Bureau of Standards, says his agency has just begun testing degradable plastics, and agrees that there will soon be a need for standards. But the bureau won't be issuing new rules in the near future. First, it must do a market survey to justify them, Olson points out. Then the bureau consults the American Society for Testing Materials to help develop standard testing procedures. The bureau might even produce its own degradable plastic that could be purchased and duplicated by manufacturers. However, any standards would be only voluntary unless EPA [Environmental Protection Agency], Congress, or state governments stepped in.

That's a definite possibility. One bill introduced by Rep. H. Martin Lancaster (D-N.C.) in the summer of 1988 requires EPA to mandate that, within two years, all plastics made in the United States be degradable. Products with no practical alternatives would be the only exceptions.

Some states have taken action rather than wait for the federal government. A notable example is Florida, where sweeping new legislation bans nondegradable six-pack yokes, shopping bags, and the polystyrene foam and plastic-coated paper used to hold food. Some 16 states, including Oregon,

Minnesota, Massachusetts, and New York, require all six-pack yokes to be photodegradable.

Surprisingly, both industry officials and environmentalists agree that such measures are premature and could ultimately prove counterproductive. Chemical companies still want to perfect the technology before relying on it. And environmentalists fear that the residues that remain after many plastics break down could contaminate groundwater supplies, as well as prove hazardous to animals that ingest them. Some industry officials have claimed their end products are safe, but no independent testing of the residue has been done, says Jeanne Wirka of Environmental Action Foundation. Decaying plastics also release gases, such as methane, that can be flammable. Wirka maintains that "it would not be good policy to make a national commitment to degradable plastics without first knowing their environmental impact."

Environmentalists also worry that degradable plastics might interfere with efforts to recycle plastics, a business that is just starting to pick up. Americans recycled 150 million pounds of plastic soft-drink bottles in 1987, up from only 8 million pounds in 1979. Adding degradable plastics to material destined to be recycled could ruin its usefulness.

"Some analysts maintain that the solution lies in new, enlightened management of landfills that combine recycling and degradable technology."

Finally, many environmental groups maintain that the best approach is for consumers to substitute other materials entirely where possible, using paper packaging and cloth diapers, for example. All these concerns mean that even if degradable plastics work perfectly and are found to be safe, they will undoubtedly be just one part of a comprehensive strategy to get rid of waste—used mainly for products such as garbage bags that can't be recycled, or for those that have no good substitutes.

Some analysts maintain that the solution lies in new, enlightened management of landfills that combine recycling and degradable technology. At least 60 percent of what goes into mountains of trash is already biodegradable, EPA studies show. ICI's Lloyd is among a vanguard that says landfills should be operated more like giant compost heaps, with managers taking steps to ensure that degradables rot quickly. "We have to look at creatively managing landfills, not as a bury-and-forget-it approach but as a recycling back to nature," he says. The novel plastics now being developed can be part of this effort.

Ann Gibbons works as a science reporter for the San Diego Tribune, *a daily newspaper.*

Degradable Plastics Cannot Reduce Waste

Jeanne Wirka

It's happening more and more. It's probably happened to you. A friend, eager for your stamp of environmental approval, calls with the news. "I'm doing something about the solid waste problem! I've switched to degradable plastic trash bags!" Sometimes your friend's wonderful news is that he's bought Baby a new kind of diaper—the degradable variety. Or that the neighborhood supermarket is now packing groceries in degradable plastic bags.

There's a hoax afoot.

Promoters of degradable plastics are taking advantage of consumers' desire to do the right thing by marketing an unproven, "feel-good" product that has little, if any, environmental merit. In the process, they are diverting attention from more promising solutions to plastic waste like source reduction and recycling.

So-called "degradable" plastic products with soothing names like "Good Sense" trash bags, "Sun Sack" grocery bags and "TenderCare" diapers are proliferating. And plastic manufacturers are readying degradable bottles, food packages and more for market, awaiting the U.S. Food and Drug Administration's okay to put these new plastics in contact with food.

But there's a wide gap between the claims you will see accompanying these "disappearing" plastics and reality. Experts don't know the answers to basic questions like: Do they really degrade, and, if so, into what? How long will it take? Are the by-products of degradation harmful to the environment? What happens in a landfill, where buried trash is deprived of oxygen and moisture?

When pressed, even their manufacturers will admit that current degradable technologies can play a minute role, at best, in solving our nation's solid

waste woes.

In 1989, a major TV ad campaign was launched by the giant grain conglomerate, Archer Daniels Midland: As a voice-over reviews grim statistics on America's garbage crisis, a host of plastics products, from bottles to bags to burger boxes, tumble into a trash can and turn—poof—to powdery dust. Archer Daniels Midland, or ADM as it likes to be called, recently began manufacturing a cornstarch additive for biodegradable plastics.

While the ad sends a clear message that (with the help of ADM), anything can degrade, that's not what the company says off the airwaves. At industry conferences, ADM officials freely admit that biodegradation only makes sense for products that will enter a composting system, like bags for yard clippings. (Even this claim is dubious.)

The Hypocrisy Trough

Also ponying up to the hypocrisy trough is Mobil Chemical Company, the world's largest supplier of plastics packaging. Mobil has been one of the most outspoken critics of degradable plastics. In a letter to *The Wall Street Journal*, Mobil President Philip Matos wrote:

"We're working to develop real solutions to the solid waste problem. Biodegradability is becoming a buzzword that makes some people feel good, but it is not a solution."

Later, Mobil introduced photodegradable Hefty trash bags. The description on the package reads: "Once the elements have triggered the process, these bags will continue to break down into harmless particles even after they are buried in a landfill."

Mobil has gone even a step further, printing the word "Photodegradable" on its plastic shopping bags even though these bags have not been modified to degrade. Technically, all plastic bags degrade in sunlight, but at a slower rate than bags treated with additives.

Jeanne Wirka, "The Degradable Plastics Hoax," *Environmental Action*, November/December 1989. Reprinted with permission.

Degradable plastics are a consumer rip-off. Consumers are spending up to 15 percent more for "biodegradable" items that won't live up to industry promises. They won't decay in today's landfills, they may not rot away in compost piles, and their usefulness in combatting litter on land and sea is questionable.

But perhaps even more objectionable than the con game being played on environmentally motivated shoppers is the concern that the degradables hype may derail better answers to America's solid waste problems.

Less than two percent of all plastic is now recycled, but efforts in this area have been on the rise in recent years.

Plastics are typically recycled into durable products like indoor/outdoor lumber, shipping pallets, automobile parts and fiberfill for sleeping bags. Many plastics recyclers fear that the additives used in degradables—especially those used in biodegradables—will contaminate the recycling process and impair the quality of end products.

Debra Kaufman, waste reduction coordinator for San Francisco, says recycling companies have told her that "degradable plastics can render useless a whole batch of plastics."

Even bullish ADM is cautious on this issue. "After 17 months, we don't know what it [degradables] will do as far as recycling," admits Jerry Petak, ADM business development manager.

Some proponents of degradables claim there's no conflict between degradability and recycling.

"Some proponents of degradables claim there's no conflict between degradability and recycling."

"If we can't recycle it, let's make it degradable," says Tim Draeger of the National Corn Growers Assocation—one of the most powerful pro-degradable lobbies. Draeger sees "film plastics" like Saran Wrap, garbage bags and candy wrappers as a logical market for degradability, since recycling of such flexible packaging lags behind that of rigid containers.

Many plastics recyclers, however, hope to recycle this flexible packaging in the future. For example, the Rhode Island Solid Waste Management Corporation, a quasi-public agency set up to deal with the state's garbage problems, is looking into collecting film plastics for recycling. And recyclers worry that the list of degradable products will continue to broaden—taking some of the more lucrative plastics out of the recycling loop.

Take plastic milk bottles made of high-density polyethylene, or HDPE.

"It would seriously jeopardize our ongoing recycling program if a degradable milk bottle were introduced," says Marion Gold, who directs recycling programs for the R.I. agency. "HDPE is one of the highest value commodities that we're recycling in Rhode Island."

ADM already has technology to make a degradable milk bottle, according to the company's Jerry Petak.

Don't Throw Away Oil

Besides potential setbacks to plastics recycling, degradables pose other environmental worries. Given scarce global supplies of oil, we should be moving towards conserving and recycling petroleum-based products like plastics, not looking for more effective ways to throw them away.

Moreover, degradable plastics may undermine source reduction aims by requiring extra plastics resin. Dr. Bruce Perleman of Quantum Chemical Company argues that degradable additives weaken plastics products, requiring the addition of extra resin to maintain performance standards.

A prime fear for environmentalists is that degradable technology will make plastics seem environmentally benign, thereby encouraging their continued use and disposal, without solving disposal problems. "Consumers want to do right by the environment," says Lisa Collaton of Environmental Action Foundation's [EAF] solid waste project. "But the degradable plastics industry is telling them that they can do the right thing by continuing to throw something away."

Mobil officials readily admit that the firm is adding to public misperception. "Are we confusing consumers? Yes, we probably are," says Robert Barrett, Mobil's "general manager of solid waste management solutions."

"We have to face that one head on," concurs Michael Levy, a legislative liaison for Mobil. "The more degradable products that are out there, the more they're perceived as a solution."

"But," Levy adds, reining in this corporate responsibility argument, "we're in the business to sell bags."

Some interesting bedfellows have been coupled by the emergence of degradables.

Those pushing degradables fall into several categories. First are the manufacturers of degradable additives like UV-accelerators, pro-oxidants and biodegradable agents. Many of these companies are small ventures that have been around since the 1960s. Second, there are the small entrepreneuring companies that make one or two degradable products.

Recently some "big boys" have joined the degradable game. Realizing that cornstarch could be a key ingredient in biodegradable plastics, the corn growers lobby and Archer Daniels Midland have teamed up with some of the smaller companies to launch a major degradables initiative.

And then, half in and half out of the game, there's the mainstream plastics industry, comprised largely of oil and chemical companies. Officially, most of these companies oppose widespread introduction of degradables, and support a growth in plastics recycling. That's put environmentalists in the distinctly odd position of being on the same side as petrochemical giants like Dow and Du Pont.

"We don't see them [degradables] as offering any solution to the solid waste problem," says Susan Vadney, a spokesperson for the Council on Solid Waste Solutions, the plastic industry's new lobbying, research and PR [public relations] group whose members include Dow, Du Pont, Union Carbide, Amoco Chemical, Exxon Chemical and 18 more.

"But," Vadney continues, "we believe there are applications where degradability serves some worthwhile purpose, such as in surgical sutures, agricultural mulch film and even six-pack rings." In July 1989, the council took out a 12-page ad section in *Time* magazine describing the industry's plastic recycling efforts—and expressing opposition to degradables.

And yet, despite their avowed hesitations and, at times, outright condemnation, plastics manufacturers are sending degradables off to market. Mobil claims it had to introduce "degradable" Hefty bags to protect its market share. Several months earlier, First Brands came out with degradable Glad bags.

"Our business managers responded to what our customers want to buy and what our competitors were doing," says Mobil's Barrett.

"Companies are being driven by market forces," says Vadney of the Council on Solid Waste Solutions. "Public demand is unavoidable. But our hope is that as the public is educated and the facts are on the table, this won't be the case."

Sounds noble—until you think about it. "Consumers glean most product information from ads and product packaging," notes EAF's Lisa Collaton. "How do we convince consumers that degradable plastics won't degrade in a landfill if every time shoppers go to a supermarket, they see trash bags claimed to be degradable on the shelf?"

Voter Pressure

More than the manipulation of market forces is driving the degradables train. Voters (that is, consumers wearing a different hat) are pushing their elected representatives to solve the plastics problem. This pressure, along with a good measure of special interest lobbying, is spurring proposals to mandate degradables in legislatures across the country.

A 1987 law requires the U.S. Environmental Protection Agency (EPA) to study the environmental impact of degradables. Unless the agency finds an overall negative impact, EPA must then issue regulations by October 1, 1990 requiring all six-pack

yokes to be made of degradable resins.

More prodegradable wind seems to be blowing on Capitol Hill. In 1988, the U.S. Senate approved a resolution proclaiming the use of degradables as a national goal. A bill introduced by Sen. John Glenn (D-Ohio) would require the government's supply manager, the General Services Administration, to buy degradable plastics whenever it is possible.

The states are even more active. Sixteen states already require six-pack yokes to be degradable. In 1988, Florida banned shopping bags and food packaging made of polystyrene foam or plastic-coated paper unless they degrade within 12 months. Nebraska has banned not only bags and six-pack rings, but also nondegradable disposable diapers. Iowa's Republican governor Terry Branstad is pushing for a ban on nondegradables in the 1990s. Local governments have also been on the move. In Newark, N.J., grocers are required to bag groceries in either paper or degradable plastic bags.

"We believe there are applications where degradability serves some worthwhile purpose, such as in surgical sutures."

It's not just constituents who are pressuring legislators. Having latched on to cornstarch-based biodegradable plastics as a potential new market for corn, the National Corn Growers Association and other farm groups have been pounding the halls of Capitol Hill and state houses claiming that degradables could boost farm income and reduce taxpayer subsidies.

According to National Corn Growers, widespread use of biodegradable plastic could stimulate corn demand by 150 to 300 million bushels of corn per year, increasing potential uses. But their own 1988 report shows that to use this much corn would require an absurdly large percentage of cornstarch in plastic packaging.

Tim Draeger of National Corn Growers admits that today's "Model T" biodegradables won't use much corn, but he's looking to future technologies. In addition, Draeger and other corn growers argue that the big oil and petrochemical companies like Mobil, Dow and Du Pont are opposed to degradables because they feel threatened by competition from corn as an alternative feedstock. The oil industry denies these accusations, pointing out that only about 1 percent of oil consumed in this country goes to make plastics packaging.

Non-petroleum plastics are, in fact, being researched in university and industry labs across the country. In a process similar to fermentation, Robert Lenz, professor of polymer science and engineering at the University of Massachusetts at Amherst, grows bacteria that produce natural plastics—without any oil at all. But commercial-scale production of "natural" plastics is a long way off.

From an environmental standpoint, natural polymers might be a good thing. Conceivably, they could reduce the toxic pollution created when plastics resins are made from petroleum-based chemicals. But like today's degradables, "biopolymers" probably will not degrade in landfills, only in a compost-like environment.

Some scientists are experimenting with so-called "bioreactive" landfills in which aerobic conditions and moisture are maximized to increase degradation. Besides extending landfill space, methane gas can be recovered as a fuel. These landfills are only in the experimental stages. And many solid waste managers question whether the risks of leachate and gas explosions are worth the potential benefits.

Not Ready for Market

Bottomline assessment for degradable plastics? Given the hints of promising prospects for their future, further R&D [research and development] is justified. But benefits should be carefully weighed. Unless there is a major shift towards composting, or towards operating landfills more like compost piles, even plastics made of 100 percent agricultural products will probably not degrade, although they might help move us away from reliance on petrochemicals.

In any case, these products should not be on the market now. Consumers beware: Degradable products may cost you more, and do little to advance environmental protection.

Jeanne Wirka is a policy analyst for the Solid Waste Alternatives Project for Environmental Action, which is a national political lobbying and education organization concerned with environmental protection.

Incinerators Should Be Used to Reduce Garbage

Allen Hershkowitz

Cities and counties in at least 40 states are operating, building, or considering resource-recovery plants to burn their trash. These facilities create steam that can be used to heat or cool buildings or to generate electricity. However, concern about this technology's potential to cause serious environmental problems is high. Garbage burning generates a range of pollutants, including gases that contain heavy metals and dioxins and that contribute to acid rain. Moreover, incinerators require a new breed of secure landfills that accept only the toxic ash they generate. Thus, citizen groups throughout the United States are battling local officials in an effort to prevent them from building such plants.

After conducting a two-year study of trash-burning plants in Norway, Sweden, West Germany, Switzerland, and Japan, I am convinced that these technologies can be highly efficient in reducing emissions if the waste is properly prepared and pollution-control devices are run by highly skilled workers. However, neither the U.S. government nor individual states have established the full range of standards to guarantee that these steps are taken. The result is that U.S. operators rarely install the needed devices or perform the procedures necessary to ensure the best performance. In fact, plant operators usually consider citizen concern about pollutants a public-relations problem rather than a serious call for reform. Furthermore, plants known to work poorly are not shut down. This situation must be remedied if the United States is to pursue this technology, which is becoming an essential component in dealing with the crisis in municipal waste.

U.S. cities and towns generate more than 410,000 tons of solid waste each day. Landfills, until recently

the method of choice for disposing of this waste, are closing. New York City has shut 14 landfills since 1967 as they have become full and their hazards to public health have become clear. The Fresh Kills landfill on Staten Island, the world's largest and one of only two remaining in the city, violates state and federal law by polluting the nearby Arthur Kill waterway with 4 million gallons of toxic liquid each day. Yet this dump will soon have to accept virtually all the 25,000 tons of solid waste that New York generates each day.

The situation is similar elsewhere. New Jersey officials and industry representatives view the imminent closing of 2 of the state's 13 remaining landfills as a crisis of "unprecedented proportions." All of Seattle's landfills will soon be closed. Michigan has determined that leaching landfills are probably responsible for at least 139 cases of groundwater contamination. The executive director of Mississippi's Department of Natural Resources says that "it will be increasingly difficult, if not impossible, to site a landfill" because of citizen opposition and the threat of groundwater pollution. Only half of the nation's 9,244 municipal landfills have valid operating permits. Communities are beginning to realize that they must take extraordinary precautions to build better landfills, including installing impermeable liners and wastewater collection and treatment facilities. These requirements often make the dumps extremely expensive. Incinerators will not eliminate the need for such landfills, but they can greatly reduce the number required.

The Recycling Option

Many U.S. environmental groups focus on recycling as the solution to the landfill problem. Recycling is already a key component in European and Japanese efforts to handle municipal waste. Yet experience in Japan, which has the world's most

Allen Hershkowitz, "Burning Trash: How It Could Work," *Technology Review*, July 1987. Reprinted with permission from Technology Review, copyright 1987.

successful recycling program, suggests that recycling can take care of 65 percent of municipal solid waste at best.

Machida City, a town with a population of 320,000 about 40 miles south of Tokyo, provides an example of the diligence of Japanese recycling efforts. City officials, including sanitation workers, go door to door at least once a year explaining the purpose of separating wastes, and the municipality distributes brochures about the benefits of recycling to third-grade and fourth-grade children. Like most of Japan's 3,255 municipalities, Machida residents separate their waste into seven general categories: newspapers, combustibles (including organic kitchen wastes, light plastics, and soiled paper), non-combustibles (hard plastics, broken glass, and scrap metal), glass bottles, aluminum and steel cans, hazardous materials (including batteries and other items containing mercury or cadmium), and bulky wastes (such as furniture and bicycles).

"Like most of Japan's 3,255 municipalities, Machida residents separate their wastes into seven general categories."

Over 100 civic groups collect residents' newspapers, glass bottles, and metal cans, and the sale of these items provides income to support their activities. Over 95 percent of all newspapers, 50 percent of glass bottles, and over 70 percent of steel and aluminum cans are recovered. In a program known as *chirigami kokan* (tissue-paper exchange), citizens receive weekly allotments of tissue paper, napkins, and toilet paper in return for their week's worth of newspapers. The town collects hazardous household materials at a citizen's request and stores them on Hokkaido, Japan's northernmost island, until methods for recycling this waste can be found. The town also collects bulky items once a month and sends them to a "recycling cultural center" where handicapped citizens repair them for resale. The center also composts some kitchen wastes for use in its greenhouse. Repaired bulky items and flowers from the greenhouse are sold to help support the center's rehabilitation program. Non-combustibles are sent to the local landfill.

Such an ambitious program is extraordinary by any standards. Yet Machida City must still burn about 1,250 tons of non-recycled waste—about 34 percent of the total—each week. The city does this in an incinerator that supplies steam to heat the cultural center, including its greenhouse and swimming pool.

Thus, even the Japanese have found total recycling impossible. Two key reasons are the heterogeneous nature of municipal waste and the limited market for recycled goods. For example, polyvinyl chloride (PVC), a common resin, has to be separated from other plastic resins such as polyethylene or polystyrene before it can be melted and reused. It can simply be shredded and used as a filler in clothing, but the market for such uses is limited.

As many as 8,000 U.S. communities are recycling one or more commodities, but reductions in waste levels are nowhere near as high as in Japan. Some of the best programs—including those of Davis, Calif., and Camden, N.J., where as many as three of four citizens participate—have reduced waste levels by no more than 25 to 30 percent. Of course, the United States has not made recycling a priority, as indicated by the federal subsidies provided to haulers of virgin materials, and the fact that the government does not monitor the percentage of recyclable commodities that are reused. Still, growing numbers of states and towns are pursuing recycling as an important option in controlling waste, and Oregon, Rhode Island, and New Jersey have made recycling of some wastes mandatory.

The United States could also do more to reduce the amount of waste it generates. The per capita production of garbage is significantly less in Europe and Japan than in this country. The average resident of Oslo, Norway, generates about 1.7 pounds of garbage a day while the average Japanese, Swedish, West German, and Swiss citizen produces about 2.5 pounds a day—a sharp contrast with the U.S. average of 4 to 6 pounds a day. However, efforts to restrict excess packaging, say, even when combined with recycling, cannot eliminate the disposal problem entirely. Communities are finding that they must look to incineration to dispose of at least some of their waste.

The Economics of Incineration

About 70 resource-recovery plants are already in operation or undergoing start-up testing in the United States, 20 more are under construction, and over 100 are planned. A small plant that burns 50 tons per day, such as that being built in Batesville, Ark., can cost $1.2 million, while $570 million is being spent for the 4,500-ton-a-day complex under construction in Broward County, Fla. New York City's Department of Sanitation has estimated that building 8 waste-to-energy plants capable of burning 70 percent of the city's daily garbage will cost $3 billion.

This is a significant investment for most communities, but the sale of energy recovered from the incineration process offsets some of the burden. The garbage is burned in a funnel-shaped furnace and a boiler within or above the furnace produces steam from the hot combustion gases. This steam can be used directly to heat buildings, run air conditioners, or power the turbine of a generator, which makes electricity that is then sold to a utility. Electricity production can range from 11 megawatts from a plant that burns 550 tons of refuse per day to over 100 megawatts from a plant the size of Broward County's.

Municipalities usually contract with manufacturers of resource-recovery plants to build them. The communities may then run the plants themselves or—more commonly—have the manufacturer or another company run them. Such a venture can be quite profitable. The waste-to-energy industry is unique in that operators receive income from both the fuel they burn—towns pay a "tipping fee" for each ton of waste they deposit—and the energy they generate. A plant's manufacturer also sees a 20 to 35 percent pre-tax return on the construction of the facility. In return a community may strike a deal on the use of the energy from the plant. For example, Peekskill, N.Y., receives a $1 million yearly credit from Con Edison, which buys the electricity produced by the town's incinerator.

Resource-recovery plants generate energy much less efficiently than other alternatives such as cogeneration plants. Yet it would be a mistake for towns to regard their incinerators as energy-producing ventures. Rather, they are an important means of disposing of municipal waste.

Recycling Makes Burning Better

Although recycling cannot solve the entire solid-waste disposal problem, it is essential to any incineration scheme. High-volume incinerators are usually a community's most complex investment, and the savings from reducing the amount of waste to be burned can be significant. Reducing plant scale and cost can also shorten the inevitable siting struggle associated with incinerators. Conversely, should incinerators be built before a recycling program is in place, reducing the volume of garbage could be financially disastrous for plant operators and create conflicts with recycling proponents.

"Although recycling cannot solve the entire solid-waste disposal problem, it is essential to any incineration scheme."

Communities that plan incinerators before they adopt a recycling program often find that plant operators will seek permission to import garbage from other areas. This can also exacerbate siting struggles, as shown in Hempstead, N.Y., New Haven, Conn., and Collier County, Fla. Citizens have enough difficulty accepting an incinerator to burn their own community's waste; they often refuse to accept a facility that burns another community's wastes.

Recycling can also be essential in improving the efficiency of an incinerator. Although bottles and metal cans are not combustible, most U.S. communities routinely throw them into the waste stream along with everything else. These materials interfere with good burning and wind up as contaminated ash in the bottom of the incinerator, which must be dumped into landfills. This increases the amount of maintenance a plant requires, depletes scarce landfill space, and inflates disposal costs, which can approach $100 per ton for incinerator ash. The Japanese, who separate most bottles and cans from the rest of their garbage before burning, are amazed that Americans do not do this. U.S. plants generate more than twice the amount of bottom ash that Japanese plants do—10 percent of the waste's original volume.

Metal Emissions

Burning metals can also create serious health problems. Resource-recovery plants can give off as many as 27 metals, including antimony, arsenic, beryllium, cadmium, chromium, lead, mercury, nickel, tin, and zinc. Except for beryllium, lead, and mercury, these substances are not covered by U.S. federal or state air-quality standards. (A few states do try to limit some metal emissions through permit guidelines.) Some of the metals are suspected carcinogens, but standards have not been established because data on their health effects are too scarce. Lead can be especially dangerous since the fine particles typically emitted from incinerators lodge in the lungs, where they are absorbed into the bloodstream and accumulate in bone marrow. High levels of lead are also routinely found in the ash residue from incinerators.

Japan has focused much effort on reducing emissions of hazardous metals, especially mercury, from incinerators. Batteries containing mercury and cadmium are no longer supposed to be burned, for example. The Japanese have also required battery makers to reduce the amount of mercury their products contain by five-sixths.

Glass and metal are not the only substances that cause problems during combustion. Plastics, especially those that contain PVC, can create dioxin and toxic acid gases such as hydrogen chloride when burned. In fact, a report prepared within the New York State Department of Environmental Conservation concludes that U.S. refuse-burning facilities may emit more than 40 times the hydrogen chloride generated by coal-burning facilities. This highly corrosive gas irritates the eyes and respiratory system, contributes to acid rain, and corrodes metal and air-cleaning components in the plant itself. Unfortunately, the U.S. Food and Drug Administration is now proposing to allow more PVC in food packaging, ignoring the problems associated with disposing of this material.

Monitoring devices at three of the eight Japanese

incinerators I visited indicated that levels of hydrogen chloride were "non-detectable," and all these plants removed 95 percent of this substance from the flue gas. The Japanese achieve this by presorting some plastics and employing scrubbers that spray a lime-and-water mixture into the flue gas. The acid gases mix with the lime slurry to form non-acidic, non-toxic calcium salts. Such a system also controls sulfur dioxide, another contributor to acid rain. Monitors at the Japanese plants indicated sulfur dioxide emission levels of 2 parts per million (ppm), a removal efficiency of more than 95 percent. Equally important, all Japanese facilities have on-site treatment plants—powered by energy from the incinerator—to neutralize any contaminated water generated by the scrubbers or other plant components.

Of the 70 high-volume incinerators operating in the United States, only 2—in Framingham, Mass., and Marion County, Ore.—employ a similar scrubbing procedure. The latter plant has reduced hydrogen chloride emissions to the extraordinarily low level of 10 ppm. In contrast, the incinerator in Peekskill, N.Y., emits 500 to 600 ppm of hydrogen chloride, a level typical of scrubberless plants throughout the U.S. As more trash-burning plants come into use, total hydrogen chloride emissions will increase substantially unless scrubbers are installed.

Scrubbers have an added benefit: because they cool the flue gases, they allow any metals to adsorb onto the submicron particles—called fly ash—that are the residue of the burning process. This is important because recycling cannot separate all metals from the waste before it is burned.

Special efforts must be made to control mercury, since it will adhere to the fly ash only at temperatures below 140° C (284°F). Flue gas cooled to that extent will not rise as much from the incinerator and thus will increase the localized effects of whatever pollutants are emitted. Japanese incinerator operators have solved this problem by cooling the flue gas to remove mercury and then reheating it to make it disperse better.

A fabric-filter system (known as a baghouse) or an electrostatic precipitator (ESP) is used to collect the particles that have absorbed metals and other pollutants from the flue gas. The precipitator electrically charges the particles and captures them on a screen of opposite charge.

Dealing with Dioxin

No issue surrounding municipal incinerators is as controversial as emissions of dioxins and furans, and scrubbers can help here, too. The Hempstead, Long Island, incinerator was closed in 1982 partly because of dioxin emissions, and Denmark shut eight of its older plants in 1985 because of fears about the chemicals. These artificial organic compounds . . . are suspected of causing a wide range of illnesses,

from cancer to birth defects. Yet these effects are still subject to dispute, and the United States has not established any standards for incinerator emissions or human exposure. No method for testing dioxin emissions from incinerators is universally accepted, and even the question of whether to sample the flue gas or the fly ash is still being debated.

"Objections to installing scrubbers are particularly misguided since they may pay for themselves in the long run."

Despite this uncertainty, Sweden and other European countries have established strict limits on dioxin emissions. Sweden assumes that an acceptable daily limit is 1 to 5 trillionths of a gram per kilogram (2.2 pounds) of body weight. Swedish tests of mothers' breast milk a few years ago showed that babies were ingesting 50 to 200 times their daily limit. Intense concern over dioxin emissions from 27 resource-recovery plants, which burn half the nation's garbage, led the Swedes to establish a strict goal of .1 nanogram per cubic meter—soon to be mandatory—based on the performances of the best plants.

The only U.S. incinerator that comes close to achieving such results is Oregon's Marion County plant, which employs a scrubber and a baghouse. This plant registers dioxin emissions of .155 nanograms per cubic meter. A state-owned incinerator in Albany, N.Y., that does not use a scrubber or baghouse has registered 16 nanograms per cubic meter—over 100 times the amount emitted by the Marion County plant.

Installing scrubbers and high-efficiency particulate-removal systems can add $5 to $10 to the $20 to $35 tipping fees that plant operators charge for burning each ton of garbage. Many in the resource-recovery industry maintain that such costs are too high. However, these technologies are crucial if hazardous emissions are to be controlled and community concern about municipal incinerators addressed. Objections to installing scrubbers are particularly misguided since they may pay for themselves in the long run. The devices can be connected to heat pumps to capture 15 to 30 percent more heat from the flue gas, which can then be used to create more steam and electricity.

Once the fly ash is collected by the baghouse or ESP, it must be disposed in secure landfills so the dioxin and heavy metals cannot contaminate water supplies. (Bottom ash—about 80 percent of the plant's total residue—does not pose as much of a problem. With good combustion, it is inorganic and not highly toxic, although small amounts of dioxin can be present.) Dioxins and furans adsorb so strongly to fly ash that acid rain and snow do not cause leaching, but they could affect the metals in the ash. Household liquids, including ammonia and turpentine, could also cause pollutants, including dioxins, to leach from the ash. . . .

The U.S. Environmental Protection Agency does not regulate the disposal of incinerator ash because it is still trying to figure out how to test its toxicity. Federal law now exempts municipal waste from being classified as hazardous, and the waste-to-energy industry is arguing that this exemption also applies to incinerator ash. This claim is highly controversial, especially since test results in New York State show that much incinerator ash has hazardous characteristics. Most states seem to be waiting for the EPA to act, with the result that handling practices vary from plant to plant. The most common practice is to mix fly ash and bottom ash and send them to landfills that also accept unprocessed garbage. The assumption is that the bottom ash will act as an alkaline buffer to prevent dioxins and metals from leaching. However, studies designed to determine if this really works and the best combination of bottom and fly ash are widely disputed and often flawed. And few attempts are made to prevent household chemicals from combining with the ash. This policy is extremely shortsighted and further guarantees citizen opposition to garbage-burning plants.

Worker Training

Whether an incinerator achieves low levels of dangerous emissions depends not only on its technology and presorting of the wastes, but also on how well workers are trained and the plant is monitored. Some U.S. incinerator operators try to hire workers with "steam experience"—those who have operated coal- or oil-fueled power plants. This move is based on the erroneous assumption that a municipal incinerator is primarily involved in producing energy rather than disposing of waste. Japanese incinerator workers inevitably describe their main job as preventing pollution, while U.S. workers see their role in terms of providing energy. One shift supervisor at a Delaware plant said, "It's not garbage, it's solid fuel." The high emission levels of most U.S. incinerators attest that this attitude is prevalent.

Burning garbage, which is often wet and composed of many different substances, is more problematic than burning homogeneous fuels such as oil and coal. Workers need special training in controlling emissions and in protecting themselves from contact with harmful bacteria and toxic fly ash.

Employees at resource-recovery plants in West Germany, Japan, and Switzerland are thoroughly trained. Japanese workers spend 6 to 18 months learning how toxic chemicals are stabilized in the furnace and captured in the stack, and they must have an engineering degree and undergo on-site training. Similarly, German incinerator workers attend a training school operated by the Boiler Manufacturers Association. This training includes two years of practical experience and 6 months of theoretical work on combustion efficiency and dioxin formation and reduction. The United States, in contrast, maintains no institute specifically for training workers to burn heterogeneous fuel, although the American Society of Mechanical Engineers is now working to establish such a program. . . .

"Americans have much to learn from their overseas counterparts about handling solid waste without undue risk to human health."

Americans have much to learn from their overseas counterparts about handling solid waste without undue risk to human health. U.S. municipal waste disposal has been one of this century's bargains, but we are beginning to pay the price for past negligence. The technology exists to make waste-to-energy plants an effective way to reduce the volume of material dumped in landfills while limiting hazardous emissions. The next step in protecting the public's health must be to establish an integrated system of solid-waste management keyed by strong regulations that are swiftly enforced.

Allen Hershkowitz is the director of solid waste research for INFORM, an environmental research group based in New York. He is the author of Garbage Burning: Lessons from Europe *and the coauthor of* Garbage Management in Japan.

"The technology exists to recycle as much as 80 percent of our solid waste."

Recycling Should Be Used to Reduce Garbage

Annie Eberhart

On March 22, 1987, Islip, Long Island's "garbage barge" began its highly-publicized search for a place to dump its 3,100-ton cargo of municipal waste. Two months and 6,100 miles later, after being rejected by six states and three countries, the barge returned to New York where a court had ordered the Department of Environmental Conservation to find a disposal site for the outcast trash.

While this "garbage barge" drama played out, another vessel was continuing a much less notorious search that had begun in August 1986. The *Khian Sea*, looking for a place to dump its 15,000-ton cargo of ash from Philadelphia's municipal waste incinerators, traveled first to the Bahamas only to have the island country reject the trash, as did Colombia and a series of other potential sites. In January of 1988, the *Khian Sea* arrived at Gonaives on the coast of Haiti, which had issued it a permit to spread the ash on a government farm. When Haiti tested the ash for nitrogen content and found none, it refused to accept the "fertilizer."

Unfortunately, by the time the ship's operators learned this, they had already hired workers to unload the ash and 4,000 tons had been dumped on the beach. One thousand tons were reloaded but the rest remains on the beach where the wind carries ash inland and the ocean tide carries it seaward. Meanwhile, the *Khian Sea* has left that fiasco behind to return to Philadelphia, according to Jim Vallette of Greenpeace's Waste Exports Campaign, which had been monitoring the boat since the summer of 1987 and brought the ash dumping story to the attention of the media. Neither the city nor the operators of the *Khian Sea*, have located a final resting place for the ash, so the vessel floats in the Delaware Bay.

The Islip garbage barge, with its load of refuse and rubbish, was the perfect media metaphor for America's solid waste disposal crisis: with our landfills filling up, where can we dump our trash? In turn, the *Khian Sea*, bearing a mountain of ash left over from the burning of city garbage not unlike that carried by the Islip barge, is metaphor for new problems created by what many urban planners and industry proponents have hailed as a solution to the first crisis: municipal waste incinerators.

If we can't dump it, burn it: we have no other choice. That is the position being presented to citizens by federal policymakers and municipal leaders who have been coaxed and lobbied by the corporate interests that stand to benefit from large-scale industrial solutions to the waste disposal problem. This polarized view ignores the existence of other solutions such as recycling and waste reduction which their advocates argue are safer, more economical, and ecologically sounder alternatives to incineration.

Nearly 160 million tons of garbage are thrown into U.S. municipal waste systems each year—about 1,280 pounds per person. Much of this trash now goes straight into landfills, but existing dumps are quickly reaching capacity while new ones are becoming increasingly difficult to site because of the scarcity of affordable land, particularly near urban areas, and heightened concerns over their impact on the environment.

Resource Recovery

As an alternative, many municipalities have resorted to mass burn incinerators: huge furnaces which consume unsorted garbage at extremely high temperatures, from 1,800 to 3,000 degrees Fahrenheit, leaving ash that takes up as little as 10 percent of the space of the original trash. These high-tech incinerators also are known as "waste-to-energy" facilities or "resource recovery" plants since they produce energy in the form of steam and/or

Annie Eberhart, "Turn Trash into Ash," *Public Citizen*, May/June 1988. Reprinted with permission.

electricity which can be used to operate the plant or sold to local utilities.

In 1988 the U.S. burned approximately 4 percent of its municipal garbage with 77 operating incinerators. If all the incinerators that are scheduled to come on line by 1990 are actually built, closer to 20 percent of trash will be disposed of through incineration, according to Neil Seldman of the Institute for Local Self-Reliance, a non-profit organization that offers cities technical assistance in designing environmentally and economically sound waste disposal systems.

Citizen Opposition

But in community after community, citizens are opposing the construction of mass burn incinerators because of concerns about adverse environmental effects of incinerator emissions and the leftover ash. They are also wary of the huge financial investments required to build incineration plants. In addition to the hundreds of millions of upfront costs required to construct the huge incineration complexes, citizens are concerned about "risk-shifting"—that they, more than plant operators or investors, will bear the brunt should operating costs turn out to be higher than expected, pollution control costs soar, ash disposal costs accelerate, and revenue from energy production fail to meet anticipated levels.

Furthermore, incineration opponents note that it is a solution which does nothing to discourage the proliferation of garbage and the attitude that disposed-of materials are totally valueless. Opponents point out that substituting incinerators for landfills as the final receptacle for trash merely delays responding to the ultimate issue of how America will dispose of the growing volume of trash produced by a throwaway society.

"Incineration . . . does nothing to discourage the proliferation of garbage."

For much of this century, America disposed of its trash by burning it or by hauling it to open-air dumps or so-called "sanitary landfills" where the debris deposited each day is covered by a layer of dirt or ash. But with the enactment of the federal Clean Air Act in 1970, almost an entire generation of incinerators that had been in use since the early 1950s—some 300 nationwide—were shut down because they did not meet the new air emission standards. As a result, by 1978 nearly 90 percent of trash in the U.S. was being landfilled.

At the same time, the heightened consciousness triggered by the environmental movement of the 1970s led an increasing number of city and state environmental agencies to conduct groundwater monitoring which revealed that landfills were actually potent sources of pollution: rainwater running through decaying materials was discovered to leach toxic heavy metals such as mercury, cadmium, lead, and chromium into the underwater reservoirs which provide the drinking water for many communities. Such pollution was discovered to be caused not only by landfills holding hazardous waste from heavy industry, but also in municipal landfills where rusting appliances, car batteries, chewed-up tires, hospital waste, household solvents, dried-up paint cans, inky newspapers, and used-up pesticide containers are mixed in with paper waste, yard waste, sewage, and other detritus.

Documentation of the polluting capacity of landfills has dramatically reduced the ability of municipalities to site new landfills as older ones reach capacity. According to a survey by the U.S. Environmental Protection Agency (EPA), half of all municipalities will run out of landfill space by 1998 and a third of all municipalities will run out by 1993. Other analysts predict that a national garbage crisis is even closer at hand: Seldman of the Institute for Local Self-Reliance says that half the cities in the U.S. will exhaust their current landfill capacity by 1990.

Landfills Close

As landfills close, pressure on remaining landfills increases exponentially. Philadelphia, for example, has exhausted the capacity of all its local landfills so the trash from this metropolitan area of 6 million must go to other fills, accelerating the rate at which those fills reach capacity. Since landfills closest to large cities fill up faster, garbage is being hauled farther and farther, often to other states and, as Islip's garbage barge illustrates, even to other countries.

Diminishing capacity has made waste disposal the fastest-rising part of many municipal budgets, according to Seldman. Minneapolis saw the cost of disposal rise sixfold in six years, from $5 to $30 per ton. Philadelphia's cost has increased to $90 per ton, up from $20 per ton in 1980. After the closing of a landfill in New Jersey in the summer of 1987, Newark's disposal cost soared from $23 to $125 per ton.

Cost increases of this magnitude put severe pressure on municipal governments and on trash haulers in large cities who must dispose of anywhere from 2,000 to 14,000 tons of trash each day. In 1984, trash haulers drove garbage trucks around the Massachusetts statehouse in Boston to draw attention to the fact that they were running out of affordable places to dispose of the waste they collected.

According to Walter Hang, director of New York Public Interest Research Group's (NYPIRG) Toxics Campaign, in the late 1970s and early 1980s as the drawbacks of landfilling became increasingly apparent, citizens groups promoted recycling as a way to reduce the need for new landfills. But, he adds, activists failed to recognize that large industrial interests had entered the scene to reintroduce the idea of incineration as a one-stop solution to a city's garbage problem. For many city administrators, the idea of a single public works-type project was much easier to embrace than a recycling/waste reduction agenda involving a complex of operating strategies, new waste disposal requirements imposed on consumers and local industry, public education, and the creation of various financial incentives.

"In the 1970s... the U.S. Department of Energy and Environmental Protection Agency spent up to $2 billion to promote 'waste-to-energy' plants."

Indeed, the appeal of incinerators is that they directly replace landfills as a place for haulers to dump raw unsorted garbage, solving a huge disposal problem without requiring many changes in the structure of the waste collection system. To simplicity was added the argument that incineration is now safe: industry proponents say that technological improvements achieved during the 1970s have made incineration almost pollution-free. They contend that the very high temperatures of the boilers destroy all harmful compounds and that other technical improvements, such as smokestack filters and acid scrubbers, protect against air pollutants.

Incineration has also made greater headway than recycling and waste reduction because it exists in a friendlier financial environment. Although the plants are very expensive to build, costing anywhere from $100 to $500 million, financing is supported by various government policies. The U.S. tax code has supported both public and private investment in incinerator plants by making private incinerator owners the beneficiaries of investment tax credits, energy tax credits, and accelerated depreciation rules and by permitting cities to issue tax-exempt bonds to finance construction. Though the incentives for private investors disappeared with the Tax Reform Act of 1986, that has merely encouraged the trend toward total public ownership of new plants.

Support for Incinerators

In the 1970s, in response to the energy crisis, the U.S. Department of Energy and Environmental Protection Agency spent up to $2 billion to promote "waste-to-energy" plants, according to Seldman; recycling, which saves energy rather than produces it, did not receive similar support. Furthermore, federal energy policy guarantees markets for the energy produced through incineration. In 1978 Congress adopted the Public Utility Regulatory Policies Act (PURPA) to encourage the development of alternative energy sources. Though consumer groups, including Public Citizen, support PURPA because it creates markets for safe alternative energy sources, the law does not define nor differentiate between "safe" and "unsafe." It merely requires utilities, within certain limits, to buy the power produced by alternative generators, including mass burn incinerators.

In addition to revenue from generating electricity, incineration plants collect "tipping" fees from garbage haulers. Municipalities have generally not paid "tipping" fees to recyclers who take away trash, demanding that such operations be self-supporting based on their sale of materials. Bonds to underwrite the initial capital costs to start recycling operations are more difficult to obtain because long-term contracts with purchasers of recycled materials, which would guarantee revenue to pay back the bond, are not as available as are the federally-mandated energy contracts with utilities.

These factors have helped make incinerator plants a favored investment for cities and private entrepreneurs alike. Wall Street investment bankers have collected around $194 million in fees since 1982 selling $13.2 billion worth of municipal bonds for garbage incinerators. In one such deal, John Hancock Life Insurance Co. in conjunction with Wheelabrator Environmental Systems Inc. invested $51.7 million in an incinerator in Westchester County, New York. The partnership expects to receive $894.7 million in revenues over the coming years. As Robert Chambers, manager of municipal finance for the Ford Motor Credit Corporation, which also has invested in incinerators, told *Newsday,* "If we felt it was going to go away, we'd find somewhere else to put our money."

The Drawbacks

Despite the bullish attitude of the industry and municipal planners, citizens living near an incinerator—who are also the taxpayers that would bear ultimate responsibility for any defaulted bond issues—have mounted vocal opposition to incinerator proposals on both environmental and economic grounds.

Opponents' primary concern is that incinerators create a major environmental hazard. Once incinerator ash was assumed to be an inert substance, but studies by the EPA as well as by independent organizations such as the Environmental Defense Fund (EDF) have found that the ash contains concentrations of heavy metals that exceed those considered hazardous by environmental statutes. Scientific studies also reveal that the ash contains dioxins and their chemical cousins, furans, some of which are the most carcinogenic substances known. Also, incinerators emit acid gases which contribute to acid rain. Furthermore, depending on the incinerator design and the type of garbage fed into it, trash volume may be reduced only 70 percent, rather than 90 percent as industry claims, leaving unresolved the need for new landfill space.

Emission of dioxin into the air and its presence in leftover ash are perhaps the most troubling and least understood of the health hazards created by incineration. EPA has linked dioxin with the skin disease chloracne, weakening of the immune system, reproductive disorders, liver disease, and kidney cancer. According to Paul Connett, associate professor of chemistry at St. Lawrence University, dioxin concentrates in the food chain: research he conducted revealed that the concentration of dioxin in milk from cows grazing near incinerators was 200 times greater than exposure from inhaling the air in the same vicinity. In 1985, the Swedish government advised mothers living near garbage incinerators not to breastfeed because of high dioxin levels found in their milk.

Dr. Connett points out that while the industry claims its incinerators are pollution-free, only about six of the 77 existing U.S. plants are equipped with the state-of-the-art technology that reduces acid emissions and toxic residues to what the industry itself calls "acceptable" levels. Even if all plants built in the future are "state-of-the-art", older plants will still be in operation. "Some of the plants built in the early '80s are a mess," says Dr. Connett.

"Once a city chooses to build an incinerator it is difficult to change course."

Few states have acted to set emission standards and to regulate ash disposal for the new generation of mass burn incinerators. Under the Clean Air Act, EPA must regulate air pollutants as they are identified, but the agency has yet to set a single standard for emissions from these incinerators. The Resource Conservation and Recovery Act (RCRA) charges EPA with regulation of the disposal of waste, but EPA has not enforced RCRA by requiring incinerator operators to test ash for hazardous content and to ensure safe disposal. RCRA requires that waste be tested for toxicity if there is reason to suspect it might contain poisons. If the tested waste meets the statute definition of hazardous, it must be disposed of in stringently regulated, specially designed chemical dumps which have far higher fees for accepting waste than regular municipal landfills. As a result, incinerator owners avoid testing altogether.

According to EPA officials, the agency has issued "non-binding" regulations for air emissions from mass burn incinerators. The agency is not even working on regulations for testing and disposal of ash, though it is preparing "guidelines."

Citizens' environmental concerns are compounded by economic concerns. Once a city chooses to build an incinerator it is difficult to change course, at least until the bond issue is paid back, which generally takes 20 years. The large financial commitment required can divert resources from, and even counteract, efforts to implement other solutions such as waste reduction or recycling. Since incinerators require a consistent amount of garbage to produce a consistent amount of energy, any policy that would reduce the size of the waste stream likely would be opposed by city managers concerned with generating the revenues to back the municipal bonds that financed the plant. According to the Institute for Local Self-Reliance, one Ohio city actually banned recycling by requiring all garbage be dumped in the city's garbage plant. Though this law was challenged and declared unconstitutional, Brenda Platt, staff engineer at the Institute, reports that almost every community with an incinerator has "flow control" ordinances designed to guarantee sufficient volumes of garbage to support its investment. . . .

In Saugus, Massachusetts, 10 miles north of Boston and home of the oldest metro-sized incinerator and ash landfill, two of five incumbent selectmen were recently ousted because of their support for the incinerator. One of their replacements is school teacher Pete Manoogian, who got involved in politics in 1985 when he found his two-year-old playing with hypodermic needles after a garbage truck spilled a large amount of hospital waste in his neighborhood.

An active opponent of plans to expand the Saugus plant and proposals for incinerators in other parts of the state, Manoogian sees the issue as a race between mass burn and the alternatives. Once in place, the economics of removing or shutting down an existing incinerator are practically impossible, he notes. "I see it all over the country: Build now, ask questions later."

Citizens Groups

While citizens groups across the country work to oppose construction of new plants, environmentalists are working to hold operators of existing plants more accountable. The Natural Resources Defense Council filed suit against the EPA for failing to enforce Clean Air Act provisions on emissions from mass burn incinerators. Likewise, EDF is suing two individual incinerator operators because they are not testing their ash for hazardous content despite the Resource Conservation and Recovery Act (RCRA) which requires them to do so if there is reason to suspect the material may be toxic. EDF claims that there is more than reasonable grounds for suspicion: in a study of ash samples from 25 incinerators, the organization found levels of heavy metals in several samples that were up to six times higher than federal standards.

The Gold in Garbage

Adding a new factor into the incinerator debate is the development of technology that proponents say resolves the problems of the traditional mass burn plant. European companies, involved in incinerator construction for about a decade longer than U.S. firms, have led the way. A new type of incinerator provides for the sorting of trash to remove recyclable materials and to reduce the toxicity of the emissions. The remaining trash is compressed into a pellet fuel (Refuse Derived Fuel, RDF) that can be sold or burned on-site to produce energy. Until 1982 RDF plants were more expensive to build and operate than mass burn incinerators, but, says Seldman, "they experienced a sharp learning curve." As a result, some of the largest incinerator contractors such as Westinghouse, Babcock & Wilcox, and General Electric have moved to RDF as the technology of choice.

Though cleaner than mass burn, RDF still produces ash that must be landfilled and has all the same economic consequences of mass burn plants. In addition, plant operators do not necessarily recycle the material sorted out before burning—most merely landfill it—and many RDF plants have been plagued by equipment failures, unexpected cost overruns, accidents, and greater than expected amounts of leftover ash, according to *Recycling: The Answer to Our Garbage Problem*, a May 1987 report from the Citizens Clearinghouse for Hazardous Wastes, Inc. Activists seeking long-term solutions continue to promote recycling, composting, and reduction of the waste stream as economically and environmentally sound alternatives to landfilling and incineration.

"The key to thinking about the problem is 'value added'," maintains Seldman. "Waste is not waste until you waste it." The challenge, he says, is to build a disposal system based upon separating resources—adding value at each step—instead of mixing refuse at each step in preparation for a mass burn or burial.

A Treasure Trove

As it is, America disposes of a treasure trove of materials. According to *Mining Urban Wastes: The Potential for Recycling*, a May 1987 report by the Worldwatch Institute, the trash of a city the size of San Francisco can yield as much copper as a medium-sized copper mine, as much aluminum as a small bauxite mine, and as much paper as a good-sized timber stand. And resource recovery can be an economic boon, not just from avoided disposal costs. Recycling is labor-intensive, creating jobs, and it increases the availability of materials that can be cheaper than those made from virgin resources.

The value of the resources in garbage is not universally ignored. NYPIRG's Hang says that the two largest exports from New York Harbor are scrap metal and scrap paper, which are shipped to other countries for use as a cheap source of raw materials. The Netherlands, Scandinavia, the Soviet Union, and many developing countries have container deposit laws and parts of Australia, Canada, and Japan also have deposit programs. West Germany and Switzerland have successful voluntary recycling programs in place.

"Oregon, Rhode Island, and New Jersey have taken up the challenge of statewide recycling programs."

The U.S. recycled tremendous amounts of refuse during the Depression and World War II and some sectors of the country have continued or revived those efforts. The aluminum can industry in the U.S. promotes recycling and American consumers have returned over half of the 300 billion cans bought since 1981, according to the Worldwatch Institute. Nine states have container deposit laws. Oregon, Rhode Island, and New Jersey have taken up the challenge of statewide recycling programs and community groups across the country have set up independent recycling centers. In its *Recycling* report, the Citizens Clearinghouse on Hazardous Wastes sums up the challenge: " . . . [T]he technology exists to recycle as much as 80 percent of our solid waste. The issue of what to do is not a technical issue but a political issue."

Annie Eberhart is a former researcher for Congress Watch, a congressional lobby representing consumer interests, especially public health concerns. Congress Watch is organized under Public Citizen, a citizen advocacy organization that uses litigation and lobbying to ensure consumer rights and environmental safety.

"Only market incentives address [the garbage] problem by giving individuals reasons to alter their actions."

Economic Incentives Can Reduce Waste

Michael H. Levin

America's trash crisis—symbolized by Islip's wandering garbage barge and Philadelphia's harborless ash boats—continues to rise in public consciousness, spurred by outcries over incinerators and beached medical debris. It's the latest in a series of such "crises" that began with drives by the Sanitarians of the 1870s for urban refuse collection.

Some aspects of the problem may not be a crisis. Per-capita garbage generation occasionally has been far higher (and more harmful) than our current 3.5 pound national daily average. (It was as high as 4.1 pounds per day in turn-of-the-century New York, for example, not counting manure and dead horses, but including large quantities of noxious coal ash.) Despite headlines, plastics make up less than 10% of our waste stream; attempts to remove them may have little overall effect.

Indeed, requiring Big Mac containers and other packages, bottles or wraps to be "biodegradable" may make things worse. Even newsprint takes decades to decompose when buried away from sunlight. Other discards produce dangerous settling, explosive swamp gas or contaminated runoff when they decompose in landfills. And biodegradable materials may actually undermine recycling efforts, since their life spans are shortened.

Halfway to the Moon

Nevertheless, the crisis is real. America generates 160 million tons a year of solid waste—enough to fill a line of 10-ton garbage trucks stretched halfway to the moon—and this is projected to increase to 200 million tons within a decade as more diapers, razors and other durable goods become disposables. Nationwide, our per-capita waste yield, long the world's highest, has nearly doubled since 1960.

Michael H. Levin, "The Trash Mess Won't Easily Be Disposed Of," *The Wall Street Journal*, December 15, 1988. Reprinted by permission of the author, senior environmental lawyer in the Washington, D.C. office of Nixon, Hargrave, Devans & Doyle.

Municipal landfills now handle as much as 80% of this avalanche. But that route will disappear for the thousands of U.S. communities whose landfills are soon to close for space or health reasons; it may vanish entirely in populous states such as Pennsylvania, which recently announced that at present rates all 77 of its remaining landfills will be filled by 1992.

Meanwhile, new landfills or waste-to-energy facilities grow harder to site. Resulting shortages have tripled disposal fees for many localities, triggering city and state suits to stop or compel acceptance of neighbors' waste. Everyone wants his garbage picked up, but no one wants it put down—at least not anywhere near him.

Curbside recycling is increasingly touted as the answer. At least six states have adopted such recycling laws, usually in the form of household trash-separation requirements. Where not mandated by law, such requirements are often mandatory in fact: Due to voter concerns over noise, traffic and emissions, few landfills or incinerators can be sited today without commitments for substantial recycling.

Mandatory Recycling

But forced recycling won't work either. Cities can scarcely decline to collect improperly sorted garbage. Nor can they have sanitation police pick through trashbins to identify culprits. And markets for separable trash are often volatile, primitive or nonexistent.

Where markets exist, low values by weight for many types of trash make them not worth transporting very far to reach buyers. Moreover, many industries prefer virgin-material suppliers whose output they can control or predict. Much bulky trash—office machines and refrigerators, for example—has grown hard to recycle because it contains suspected hazardous wastes. Curbside separation raises antitrust issues by disadvantaging local haulers, who can ill afford multibin trucks. Books, diapers, coated papers, junk mail, metal foils and construction debris appear beyond recovery. And numerous studies have shown that even if all "realistic recyclables" were recycled, more than 70% of trash would remain.

In short, mandatory approaches may merely yield neat bales in landfills, recycling the problem rather than the waste.

Like groundwater contamination from septic tanks or smog from commuter patterns, the garbage crisis requires changes in life styles, expectations and local economies. Such changes are hard to mandate. Nor will education by itself make much difference: Consumer choices that generate trash are matters of convenience for most people, not moral imperatives.

Only market incentives address this problem by giving individuals reasons to alter their actions—by better matching private interests with public goals. That conclusion was confirmed by the Environmental Protection Agency's draft Agenda for Action on solid waste and the Project '88 Report sponsored by Sen. Timothy Wirth (D., Colo.) and Sen. John Heinz (R., Pa.) and strongly supported by the Environment Defense Fund.

Incentives for Recycling

What incentives are likely to work? That recycling is demand-pulled, not supply-driven, suggests several targets:

• *Reduce the supply of trash.* Fees reflecting waste-disposal costs could be imposed on product manufacturers, then rebated to purchasers of recycled materials or recycling equipment. Fees reflecting products' useful life—with higher levies on throwaway pens, diapers and other disposables—are also an option. Home owners could be billed monthly on a "pay as you throw" basis for the number of cans of trash picked up, as they are now for other utilities, with lower charges if such easily identified items as glass and paper are separated. Bulk postage rates for catalogs and other junk mail might be eliminated. Some European countries have successfully dealt with auto hulks or discarded washing machines by requiring owners to pay annual registration fees and property taxes until the item is properly recycled.

• *Increase demand for recovered materials.* Despite efforts in the 1970s to eliminate price discrimination against recyclables, depletion allowances and some transportation tariffs may still favor virgin materials; such subsidies should be neutralized. Government purchasing standards for recycled materials, together with long-term procurement contracts, could accelerate this trend while discouraging use of materials that make products unrecyclable. Similar government efforts have successfully reduced noise from buses, mowers and other products. Companies or cities could agree to buy the entire output of

recycling facilities, and to pay them bonuses based on the amount and quality of materials supplied.

• *Focus on ends, not means.* The environmental goal is not recycling, but minimizing the waste stream's total impact. Municipalities should encourage innovative methods by seeking cost-effective bids for systems to handle 1,000 tons per day of trash, for example, not simply 1,000-ton-per-day landfills or incinerators. Tax-exempt financing could be made fully available only for comprehensive systems that include recycling, composting, waste-to-energy units and "ash or trash" landfills. And while landfills and incinerators must be made safer, they'll continue to be needed. They should not be blocked by open-ended procedures that encourage killer delays and unpredictably stringent environmental standards, no matter how small the residual risk.

• *Integrate.* One system might require makers of new products to hold tickets showing proper recycling of one item per set quantity of new items made. Under this approach, for example, a bottle manufacturer would have to buy enough tickets—or create them through its own recycling efforts—in one quarter to cover its next quarter's production. Recyclers could sell tickets to the highest bidder; manufacturers would have powerful incentives to maximize recycling. That would allow the market to set ticket prices, while the sources of trash pay for its reduction. . . .

The free lunch for trash is over, barring unforeseen technological advances. Every response to the solid-waste avalanche raises its own difficult issues; none will solve the problem by itself.

"Mandatory approaches may merely yield neat bales in landfills, recycling the problem rather than the waste."

Recycling of colored or printed paper can create hazardous ink sludges; ticket schemes raise fears of monopolization by deep-pocket producers; national rebates may displace private scrap dealers or local deposit programs, yielding little net gain. And because landfills, incinerators and other available choices all have negatives, communities often refuse to act or plan until catastrophe is upon them. But garbage will continue to be generated, whether it's disposed of or not. That argues for approaches that can make a difference, not more rhetoric or crusades.

Michael H. Levin is an environmental lawyer in Washington, D.C. He was director of the Environmental Protection Agency's Regulatory Reform staff and Regulatory Innovations staff from 1979 to 1988.

"Only a sensible combination of recycling, burning, and burying—and its coordination by local, state, and federal government—can prevent this country from being overwhelmed by its own waste."

viewpoint 32

Government Must Enact Legislation to Reduce Waste

Gordon Graff

Plastic packaging is ubiquitous in our daily lives. Plastic bottles for soft drinks and household cleansers, for example, have in recent years edged out bulky, breakable glass bottles. And items such as fast-food containers and wrapping for consumer goods have proliferated. These trends benefit manufacturers and consumers, but they create disposal nightmares for municipal officials as mountains of discarded plastics pile up at dump sites. In many areas, particularly in the urban Northeast, the question of what to do with discarded plastics—and other solid wastes—is assuming crisis proportions. . . .

Solid waste has continued to increase, although only slightly in recent years—according to the Environmental Protection Agency (EPA), the amount of municipal solid waste in the United States grew from 112.8 million tons in 1975 to 126.5 million tons in 1984—but the percentage of the waste made up by plastics almost doubled (growing from 3.9 percent to 7.2 percent) during the same period.

The real cause of the disposal crunch, however, is a steep decline in the number of landfill sites where the wastes may be deposited. Tougher zoning regulations and environmental laws, and the filling of the landfills to capacity, are causing the closure of many sites. . . .

Public officials and legislators are using a variety of approaches to alleviate the shortage. They are enacting deposit laws on beverage containers to discourage disposal. They are authorizing the construction of incinerators that convert the waste to energy. And some communities are implementing curbside pickup of aluminum cans, glass, and plastic bottles for recycling. . . .

Government efforts to boost the level of plastics

recycling have begun—the states of Massachusetts, New Jersey, Michigan, and Ohio are supporting a program of the Plastics Recycling Foundation (Washington, D.C.), and the National Science Foundation has initiated an effort—but more programs that combine public and private resources are clearly needed to develop the necessary technologies and markets as well as to defray startup costs. The plastics industry itself could also contribute more funds for recycling research. For example, Gretchen Brewer of the Massachusetts Division of Solid Waste recently suggested that each of the state's 959 plastics companies voluntarily pledge $1000 to support recycling development efforts.

Greater reliance on bottle-deposit laws, already in effect in many states and municipalities, would spur recycling. So would more measures requiring residents to separate recyclables for curbside pickup. To get full-fledged recycling industries off the ground requires considerable financing, so modest taxes may be in order. Brewer in Massachusetts suggests a one-cent tax per beverage container to be used to finance recycling programs.

Mandatory Recycling

A more obvious way to encourage recycling is to make it mandatory. California's Beverage Container Recycling and Litter Reduction Act, passed in 1986, calls for each beverage container industry to meet a 65 percent redemption rate by specified dates; failure to comply will trigger steep increases in deposits beyond the one-cent per container. In Philadelphia, mandatory recycling enacted in June 1987 sets goals of 25 percent recycling of glass, plastic, metal cans, and paper within two years, 35 percent within three years, and 50 percent within four years.

Of course, the federal government could marshall its considerable purchasing power on behalf of

Reprinted with permission from Gordon Graff, "The Looming Crisis in Plastics Waste Disposal," ISSUES IN SCIENCE AND TECHNOLOGY, Volume IV, Number 2, 1989. Copyright 1989, by the National Academy of Sciences, Washington, D.C.

recycled goods. In fact, the Resource Conservation and Recovery Act (RCRA) of 1976 directs all U.S. agencies to purchase goods containing the maximum level of recycled materials. The hope is that massive purchases of recycled goods by the federal government will stimulate the market for these materials and encourage other players to enter. RCRA also requires procurement guidelines for recycled plastics and other solids, which have yet to be issued.

"Mandatory recycling legislation, however, is not necessarily desirable in the long run."

Mandatory recycling legislation, however, is not necessarily desirable in the long run because it imposes a solution that may not be economical or effective in all localities. Factors such as long distances to reclamation plants, or lack of available markets for recyclables, could make recycling more expensive than landfilling or incineration. The extra expenses, of course, would be borne by the taxpayers. . . .

A Burning Issue

Whatever the potential of recycling, the other alternative to landfill burial—incineration—will still have to figure prominently in future approaches to the solid-waste crisis. Some 74 incineration facilities in the United States convert solid waste into energy. But according to most estimates, these so-called resource recovery plants treat no more than 5 percent of the country's municipal waste. . . .

Regardless of the plant type, heat obtained from burning is used to convert water into steam, which can then be used for home or industrial heating or for driving electrical generators. Electricity production ranges from 10 to 100 megawatts, depending on the unit's capacity and the fuel value of the trash. In the latter regard, advocates of plastics incineration point to the material's high fuel value. Polyethylene, for instance, yields 17,000 to 19,000 British thermal units per pound—a fuel value greater than that of coal. . . .

Their economic attractiveness notwithstanding, incinerators involve a number of liabilities. These include air pollution and the problem of disposing of the toxic ash that remains after burning. Today, the biggest air-pollution fears center on dioxins and other closely related chlorinated compounds called furans. But toxic heavy metals such as mercury, arsenic, cadmium, and lead are also present in smokestack emissions, as are noxious gases that include hydrogen chloride, sulfur dioxide, nitrogen dioxide, and carbon monoxide. . . .

One commonly proposed policy calls for EPA to classify ash from incinerators as a hazardous waste. This would require transporting the ash long distances to federally approved hazardous waste sites, a move that many say would increase disposal costs as much as 10-fold. A better solution would be technological: to equip local landfills with impervious liners and drainage systems that capture and carry away any leachate. The New York State Department of Environmental Conservation, in fact, has already approved this approach. On a national scale, EPA could support the use of lined-landfill technology by issuing standards covering their construction and operation. . . .

In addition to fears of environmental hazards, local residents also worry about the possibility of declining property values; opposition increases directly with the proximity of the facilities to people's homes—the so-called NIMBY ("not in my backyard") phenomenon. State or local governments could help substantially by providing price supports to guarantee that real estate prices will not fall below certain thresholds. Such a system operates successfully in Wisconsin.

Properly run resource recovery plants can be environmentally acceptable, but they must also be profitable. One way to make this more likely is to provide tax incentives that encourage companies to get into the business. Government also can hasten the growth of resource recovery plants by streamlining application procedures for building the units. A single agency could be set up to handle many of the application details that are now handled by a welter of federal, state, and local agencies.

Assigning Priorities

Before building any incinerators, however, it would be a good idea for government planners to assess the actual need for these expensive facilities. Municipalities should launch studies of their present and future situations, and then try to calculate how much solid waste can be dealt with economically and practically through landfilling and recycling programs. Incinerators should be built only to dispose of the remainder; if incinerator construction is premature, in fact, there may be little incentive to recycle, and the costs to the community will rise.

Local studies should result in goals setting forth the percentage of solid waste to be disposed of by each method, together with timetables for compliance. A case in point is the Portland, Oregon metropolitan area, which has targeted 52 percent of its solid waste for recycling, reuse, or reduction; the rest will be burned or buried. Communities in the area have to meet these goals; if they don't, solid waste containing a higher percentage of recyclables will not be accepted at disposal sites. . . .

In the incineration sphere, government should not only set emission and ash-disposal standards, but take steps to see that they are enforced. Modern instrument technology allows continuous monitoring of gases and particles in stack emissions. Some countries, most notably West Germany, plan to funnel such data into the computers of regional environmental agencies. State or local environmental agencies in the United States could demand a similar form of continuous monitoring from incinerator operators. . . .

Consumer Preferences

Of course, the best solution would be to reduce the amount of solid waste generated in the first place. But although foods, beverages, and consumer items in the United States are certainly overpackaged—especially in comparison to the practices in other countries—change would be difficult because consumer preferences and the basic marketing and manufacturing procedures in this country appear so ingrained. Perhaps consumers will eventually come to realize how much extra they must pay, directly and indirectly, to dispose of these wastes, and they will clamor for curbs on excess packaging. In the meantime, only a sensible combination of recycling, burning, and burying—and its coordination by local, state, and federal government—can prevent this country from being overwhelmed by its own waste.

Gordon Graff is a technology and business journalist. He holds a Ph.D. in organic chemistry from New York University, located in New York City.

"In the earth's atmosphere the gases act like the glass in a greenhouse, which lets in sunlight but traps heat."

The Greenhouse Effect: An Overview

Anthony Ramirez

Although the earth has undergone periods of warming and cooling in the past, scientists are now generally agreed that it is about to heat up more—and faster—than ever. By the likeliest scenario, the resulting climatic changes will bedevil farming, shipping, international trade, energy policy, and military strategy. . . .

The threat is clear. Carbon dioxide from the burning of fossil fuels like oil, coal, and gasoline is rapidly accumulating in the atmosphere. So are gases like chlorofluorocarbons (CFCs), which are far less abundant but equally devastating. CO_2, CFCs, and the other gases come almost entirely from a variety of man-made sources like vehicle exhausts and industrial solvents. Only a modest amount derives from natural sources like microbes in the soil. In the earth's atmosphere the gases act like the glass in a greenhouse, which lets in sunlight but traps heat. By absorbing rather than reflecting the infrared radiation that produces heat, they are bringing about the relentless warming of the planet known as the greenhouse effect.

"My feeling is that there's no way to stop it," says Walter Roberts, president emeritus of the National Center for Atmospheric Research (NCAR) in Boulder, Colorado, and an organizer of a year-long United States-Soviet Union conference on global warming. "It may be a little bit smaller or it may be a little bit larger. But the greenhouse effect is going to come." He thinks global dependence on fossil fuels is so vast that it makes serious international cooperation to reduce CO_2 emissions unlikely.

Because no one understands all the variables that alter the earth's temperature, it's not absolutely certain that the greenhouse effect will arrive as predicted or that all its dire projected consequences

will actually occur. Some mitigating factors exist today, and others may emerge as the effect grows. For example, while clouds high in the atmosphere tend to trap heat, low-lying clouds tend to reflect sunlight. Clouds with a high moisture content have an even greater cooling effect.

Ominous Signs

Even so, the signs are ominous. Measured by the global mean temperature, 1987 was the warmest year on record; the 1980s are the warmest decade in a century. A rise in the earth's temperature of at least 2° or 3° Fahrenheit seems inevitable by the mid-21st century, when the concentration of CO_2 in the atmosphere is likely to be some 60% greater than today and double the level that prevailed before the Industrial Revolution. A temperature increase of more than 8° F. is possible.

Just a 2° warming could have dramatic effects. Since that 2° is only an average figure, much larger temperature increases could occur in certain places and seasons. For instance, one NCAR computer simulation projects a hot spot near the Bering Sea that could be nearly 30° warmer in winter than today. It took a worldwide cooling of only about 2°, perhaps due to a drop in solar radiation, to cause the Little Ice Age that wrought havoc in the 14th century. That was only a minor wobble compared with the long-term oscillations that occur over many millenniums. A seemingly small temperature shift means the difference between balmy spells and true ice ages. Civilization has developed in a narrow band of global climate, never more than 2° warmer or cooler, on average, than today's. A warming of 7° over the next 60 years or so would equal the entire rise in global temperature since the glaciers began their long retreat 18,000 years ago.

The greenhouse effect will disturb the climate of the planet, changing such critical variables as rainfall, wind, cloud cover, ocean currents, and the

Anthony Ramirez, "A Warming World: What It Will Mean," *Fortune*, July 4, 1988. Reprinted by permission from FORTUNE Magazine; © 1988 Time Inc. All rights reserved.

extent of the polar icecaps. Although country-by-country consequences are far from clear, scientists are confident of the overall trends. Interiors of continents will tend to get drier and coasts wetter. Cold seasons will shorten, warm seasons lengthen. Increased evaporation will lead to drier soils over wide areas.

The ripple effects through the world economy will be enormous as shifts develop in soil conditions, crop yields, salinity of water supplies, and the availability of river water for generating hydroelectric power. Engineers will be hard put to it to anticipate future stresses on structures they build. "It may become difficult to find a site for a dam or an airport or a public transportation system or anything designed to last 30 to 40 years," says Jesse Ausubel, director of programs at the National Academy of Engineers. "What do you do when the past is no longer a guide to the future?"

Government officials and corporate executives are slowly becoming aware of the hazards of the greenhouse effect, but few are thinking of long-term strategies. Global warming was a minor item on the agenda of the Reagan-Gorbachev summit; the U.S. and the Soviet Union agreed to produce "a detailed study of the climate of the future."

Weyerhaeuser, the giant forest-products company in Tacoma, Washington, worries about its nearly two million acres in Oklahoma and Arkansas, where some climate scientists project a warming, drying trend. The company is trying to breed drought resistance into the tree varieties it will plant there. British Petroleum, which has spent $11 billion on oil and gas operations in Alaska, has a particular interest in the greenhouse problem. Drilling rigs, housing, roads, and the Trans-Alaska Pipeline are all built on permafrost, which could start to thaw in a warming trend. BP has followed the scientific debate about the greenhouse effect, but at this point believes its investment is safe. The reason: BP's facilities rest on gravel pads that insulate the permafrost beneath them.

Both Alaska and Siberia have warmed up about 2.7° in just the past 20 years, according to researchers at the University of East Anglia in England. Says Michael Kelly, a climate researcher at the university and a consultant to BP: "We've now started to warn British Petroleum that 30 years out, greenhouse warming may have moved climate beyond the range of the conditions that have prevailed historically." BP is still studying the East Anglia warning.

Plausible Possibilities

What follows aren't hard and fast predictions of what will happen between the years 2030 and 2070, when carbon dioxide concentrations are expected to double from preindustrial levels. They are "plausible possibilities" suggested by computer models, as

Howard Ferguson, assistant deputy minister of Canada's Atmospheric Environment Service, calls them.

Some of the most obvious effects will appear in agriculture. Through photosynthesis, plants make carbohydrates from CO_2 and water. As carbon dioxide concentrations increase, a plant's stomata, the pores through which gases and water vapor pass, need to open less to take in the same amount of CO_2, so the plant loses less water through evaporation. The upshot: The plant gets bigger.

If some crops grow faster, they could strip soil of nutrients more quickly, forcing farmers to buy more fertilizer. Food quality could deteriorate as CO_2 levels increase, because leaves may become richer in carbon and poorer in nitrogen. Insects feeding off plants stimulated by CO_2 would have to eat more to get their fill of nitrogen. Indeed, hungrier pests and damaging diseases might thrive on the greenhouse effect, forcing farmers to buy more pesticides as well.

"If American agriculture is battered by such punishing summer days, and Soviet agriculture thrives owing to a longer and more temperate growing season, what would that do to the balance of power?"

The social and political consequences of the greenhouse effect are harder to assess. The Dust Bowl of the 1930s pushed millions of Midwesterners west to California; in the 1960s and 1970s, jobs and better weather pulled many millions from the Northeast to the Sunbelt. Says David Rind, a climate scientist with the Goddard Institute for Space Studies in New York City: "You may not get movements to the Southeast and Southwest anymore. It reaches 120° in Phoenix now. Will people still live there if it's 130°? 140°?" According to James Hansen of the Goddard Institute, the maximum temperature in Dallas could exceed 100° on something like 78 days a year; the current average is just 19.

If American agriculture is battered by such punishing summer days, and Soviet agriculture thrives owing to a longer and more temperate growing season, what would that do to the balance of power? "The United States could become a grain importer and the U.S.S.R. could become a grain exporter," says Roberts of NCAR. "At the very least, it would be a major economic, political, and social dislocation."

One of the most discussed—and feared—consequences of the greenhouse effect is a projected rise in sea level, resulting largely from thermal expansion. Like any other liquid, water increases in volume when heated. But most scientists believe the rise will be relatively gentle, on the order of eight to 16 inches, making it a problem mainly for countries with large populations near or below sea level, such as the Netherlands and Bangladesh.

Geographically, the greenhouse effect is likely to have its greatest impact in the high latitudes of the Northern Hemisphere, the broad band from 60° north—roughly the latitude of Anchorage and Stockholm—to the North Pole. A feedback effect accentuates global warming in the higher latitudes. Snow and ice reflect sunlight into space, keeping temperatures from rising. But as the globe warms, the floating Arctic ice cover starts to melt, leaving less snow and ice to reflect sunlight—enhancing the warming, which in turn melts more snow and ice. (In the Southern Hemisphere, sea ice will also melt. But the land-based Antarctic icecap is so massive—it averages two miles thick—that it would take centuries to thaw.)

If the world as a whole warms 3° by midcentury, the higher northern latitudes might become 8° or more warmer in winter. If the global average rises 8°, winter temperatures in the higher latitudes could go up a torrid 19°. "The fabled Northwest Passage would be open," says Walt Roberts of NCAR. "You could sail from Tokyo to Europe in half the time." Maybe so, but British Petroleum and others are beginning to worry about the hazards of pack ice—large, flat masses of ice that predominate in the Arctic Ocean—and icebergs, glacier chunks like the one that sank the *Titanic*, that float off the coasts of Newfoundland and Nova Scotia. The icebergs would endanger ships and floating oil rigs.

Defense Establishments

The Arctic ice cover could also cause problems for the U.S. and Soviet defense establishments. The polar icecap of the Arctic Sea helps both Soviet and American nuclear submarines avoid detection. The effect would be more damaging to the U.S.S.R. Because American submarines are faster and can travel farther than their Soviet counterparts, they are less dependent on hiding places under the icecap.

The Soviet Union would nevertheless appear to benefit substantially from the greenhouse effect. A warming of 8° could add as many as 40 days to the growing season in the U.S.S.R. But a world with twice as much CO_2 in the atmosphere also means a continental interior that is considerably drier; the Soviet Union would have to spend tens of billions on irrigation to take advantage of the longer growing season.

How would the U.S. be affected commercially? Global warming would have strange effects on the Great Lakes, the busiest waterway in the world. Using a computer model that projects an 8° winter warming, the Atmospheric Environment Service says the Great Lakes could be ice-free 11 months of the year, vs. 8.5 months today. That's the good news.

The bad news is that the region will also be drier, so companies shipping such major cargoes as iron ore, grain, coal and limestone will see costs rise 30% or so because lower water levels will mean that deep-draft freighters can no longer navigate the lock systems.

"When climate changes . . . society suffers."

Perhaps the biggest agricultural impact on the U.S. would be in the Midwest, where climate researchers predict a warming, drying trend. Staggering wheat crop losses deepened the Great Depression and prompted the biggest population migration in American history. When temperatures rise as little as 1.8° and precipitation drops 10%, Midwestern crops will suffer. Paul Waggoner, director of the Connecticut Agricultural Experiment Station in New Haven, sees a 2% to 5% cut in the yield of commercially desirable winter wheat.

Western Europe might escape the nastier consequences of global warming because its relatively small landmass is close to the sea and will not undergo the same degree of continental drying as the U.S., Canada, and the Soviet Union. What will happen to European temperatures is being debated. Most scientists think the Gulf Stream, flowing thousands of miles from the Caribbean, should continue to keep Western Europe from freezing to the consistency of Newfoundland, which is at the same latitude. But Wallace Broecker of Columbia University's Lamont-Doherty Geological Observatory in Palisades, New York, warns that the greenhouse effect could disturb the global circulation of the oceans in ways that cannot be predicted. . . .

Research on the effects of global warming in countries of the Third World and the Southern Hemisphere is sketchier. Africa may benefit, at least in rainfall. The rain belt across the equator would move northward, according to research published by Syukuro Manabe, a climate modeler at Princeton's Geophysical Fluid Dynamics Laboratory. That's good news for the parched nations of the Sahel, including Chad, Sudan, and Ethiopia, which have suffered this century's deadliest droughts. Marginal farmland in central China may get more rainfall, increasing crop yields. India and especially Bangladesh, a third of which is only 20 feet above sea level, on average, would be battered by more storms and flooding.

"When climate changes," a United Nations Environment Program (UNEP) report bluntly declared, "society suffers."

Anthony Ramirez is an associate editor at Fortune *magazine.*

"The warming... will continue into the indefinite future unless we take deliberate steps to slow or stop it."

viewpoint 34

The Greenhouse Effect Will Irreparably Damage the Planet

Richard A. Houghton and George M. Woodwell

The world is warming. Climatic zones are shifting. Glaciers are melting. Sea level is rising. These are not hypothetical events from a science-fiction movie; these changes and others are already taking place, and we expect them to accelerate over the next years as the amounts of carbon dioxide, methane and other trace gases accumulating in the atmosphere through human activities increase.

The warming, rapid now, may become even more rapid as a result of the warming itself, and it will continue into the indefinite future unless we take deliberate steps to slow or stop it. Those steps are large and apparently difficult: a 50 percent reduction in the global consumption of fossil fuels, a halting of deforestation, a massive program of reforestation.

There is little choice. A rapid and continuous warming will not only be destructive to agriculture but also lead to the widespread death of forest trees, uncertainty in water supplies and the flooding of coastal areas. When the ice now covering the Arctic Ocean melts, further unpredictable changes in the global climate will ensue. There may be controversy over whether the data are adequate and whether the warming is caused by changes in the atmosphere. Yet there is an unusually powerful consensus among climatologists that the dominant influence on global climate over the next centuries will be a warming driven by the accumulation of heat-trapping gases. The consequences are threatening enough so that many scientists, citizens and even political leaders are urging immediate action to halt the warming.

The fact that heat-trapping gases have been accumulating in the atmosphere is well established. Since the middle of the 19th century the amount of atmospheric carbon dioxide has increased by about 25 percent. The increase has come about because

human activities, especially the burning of coal and oil and the destruction of forests, have released greater quantities of carbon dioxide into the atmosphere than have been removed by diffusion into the oceans or by photosynthesis on land.

The increase in carbon dioxide appears trifling when one considers that the total amount in the atmosphere is a little more than .03 percent by volume. But in spite of its low concentration, carbon dioxide and several other gases present in even smaller amounts have an important role in determining the temperature of the earth. In contrast to both nitrogen and oxygen, which together make up more than 99 percent of the atmosphere, these trace gases absorb infrared radiation, or radiant heat. Since in this regard they act much like the glass over a greenhouse, they are commonly referred to as greenhouse gases.

Because the total amount of greenhouse gases is small, their concentrations are easily changed. An increase in the concentration of any one of them increases the atmosphere's capacity to retain heat and raises the temperature at which the atmosphere comes into equilibrium with the energy it receives from the sun. In recent years investigators have recognized that the atmospheric burden of greenhouse gases other than carbon dioxide, such as methane (CH_4), nitrous oxide (N_2O) and the chlorofluorocarbons (CFC's), is also growing at an increasing rate. By the mid-1980's, in fact, these gases had reached levels at which their combined effect approached that of carbon dioxide.

In this article we emphasize the role of carbon dioxide and methane because they are the principal contributors to the current warming, because their concentrations are strongly influenced by biological processes and because slowing or stopping the global warming will require control of carbon dioxide emissions in particular.

Global warming due to the accumulation of heat-trapping gases, particularly carbon dioxide, was predicted at the turn of the century by Svante Arrhenius in Sweden and Thomas C. Chamberlin in the U.S. Systematic research on the atmospheric accumulation of carbon dioxide began only in 1958. Since then Charles D. Keeling of the Scripps Institution of Oceanography has provided a continuous record of the carbon dioxide level at various stations, the best-known of which is at Mauna Loa in the Hawaiian Islands.

"A global rise in temperature [can] be expected to cause greater releases of carbon dioxide and methane into the atmosphere."

Information on the earth's temperature has been more difficult to accumulate. Strong evidence for global warming became available by late 1988. The most direct evidence lies in temperature records from around the world. James E. Hansen of the National Aeronautics and Space Administration's Goddard Institute of Space Studies and his colleagues have analyzed temperature records going back to 1860. Their analyses suggest that the average global temperature has increased by from .5 to .7 degree Celsius since that year. The greatest increase has taken place in the 1980's; this recent warming is both statistically significant and consistent with their experience based on theory and on models of the global climatic system.

Thomas M. L. Wigley and his colleagues, working independently at the University of East Anglia in England, have also shown the increase in average global temperature. The rise has not been observed in all regions: a recent analysis of climate records by Kirby Hanson and his colleagues at the National Oceanic and Atmospheric Administration shows no trend in temperature for the contiguous U.S. Such regional variation is not unexpected; the contiguous U.S. covers only 1.5 percent of the globe's surface.

The observed rise in global temperature has not been steady and is clearly not simply a response to the accumulation of greenhouse gases. There was, for example, a decline in the mean global temperature between 1940 and 1965 in spite of the continued increase of heat-trapping gases in the atmosphere. Nevertheless, Phil D. Jones, one of Wigley's collaborators, has just recently reported that the global temperature has risen about .5 degree C since the beginning of the century and that the six warmest years on record were 1988, 1987, 1983, 1981, 1980 and 1986 in that order.

If a .5-degree temperature change seems insubstantial, one should remember that in 1816, the "year without a summer," the mean global temperature drop was also less than one degree. It was nonetheless sufficient to cause frosts in June in New England and widespread crop failures. The heat and drought that have afflicted North America and other regions of the earth in recent years are consistent with the predictions of a global warming trend.

There are other indications of an accelerated warming. According to Arthur H. Lachenbruch and B. Vaughn Marshall of the U.S. Geological Survey, the depth to permafrost in the Alaskan and Canadian Arctic has increased in recent decades. The average temperature of Canadian lakes has increased; the annual maximum extent of sea ice surrounding the Antarctic continent and in the Arctic seas appears to be declining; inland glaciers throughout Europe and elsewhere have receded.

These observations are consistent with predictions made by climatologists on the basis of theory aided by general circulation models. Several such global models exist and, although analyses based on them do not agree in detail, the general predictions are consistent with theory and experience. Climatologists expect that the greatest warming will occur at higher latitudes in winter. In these latitudes the warming, according to the models, will probably be at least twice the global average. In addition it is expected that the upper atmosphere will cool as the lower atmosphere warms and that there will be less precipitation and less moisture in the soil at lower latitudes. All these trends have been reported in recent years.

Data such as those are always open to further analyses, interpretation and augmentation. They invariably appear to suffer from inadequacies of measurement and uncertainties about whether the period over which the measurements were taken was long enough to be significant. Investigators are currently improving the data and the analyses, but the fact remains that the observations described above, taken together with the rising concentration of greenhouse gases, constitute strong evidence that the process anticipated nearly a century ago by Arrhenius is under way.

One can learn much about potential future changes in climate by examining past climatic change. A mere 15,000 years ago glaciers covered much of North America and northern Europe. Were changes in the composition of the atmosphere involved in the great climate swings that brought glacial and interglacial periods? The answer is not completely clear, but one of the most important advances in recent years has been the ability to determine atmospheric composition in previous eras from tiny samples of air trapped in glacial ice. In particular, determination of the atmospheric composition during periods of glacial expansion and retreat has been made possible by data obtained from an ice core drilled by a joint French-Soviet team at the Antarctic Vostok station.

The Vostok core, as it is called, was 2,000 meters in length, long enough to sample ice dating through the past 160,000 years. The data show fluctuations in temperature of up to 10 degrees; such fluctuations are derived from changes in the isotopic ratios in the core. It is well established, for example, that the ratio of the two common isotopes of oxygen, ^{18}O and ^{16}O, in cores of marine sediments reflects past temperature changes.

The Vostok data also show how the abundances of atmospheric gases have fluctuated with temperature over the past 160,000 years: the higher the temperature, the greater the concentration of carbon dioxide and vice versa. To be sure, the correlation of carbon dioxide with temperature does not establish whether changes in atmospheric composition caused the warming and cooling trends or were caused by them. Although the carbon dioxide content follows temperature very closely during periods of deglaciation, it apparently lags behind temperature during periods of cooling.

Although there is tight statistical coupling between carbon dioxide and temperature throughout the record, the temperature changes are from five to 14 times greater than would be expected on the basis of the radiative properties of carbon dioxide alone. This relation suggests that quite aside from changes in greenhouse gases, certain positive feedbacks are amplifying the response. Such feedbacks might involve ice on land and sea, clouds or water vapor, which also absorb radiant heat.

Other data from the same Vostok core sample show that methane also closely follows temperature and carbon dioxide. The methane concentration nearly doubled, for example, between the peak of the penultimate glacial period and the following interglacial period. Within the present interglacial period it has more than doubled in just the past 300 years and is rising rapidly. Although the concentration of atmospheric methane is more than two orders of magnitude lower than that of carbon dioxide, it cannot be ignored: the radiative properties of methane make it 20 times more effective molecule for molecule than carbon dioxide in absorbing radiant heat. On the basis of Hansen's radiative-convective model, which includes chemical feedbacks, methane appears to have been about 25 percent as important as carbon dioxide in the warming that took place during the most recent glacial retreat 8,000 to 10,000 years ago.

How can a global rise in temperature be expected to cause greater releases of carbon dioxide and methane into the atmosphere? In the process of photosynthesis terrestrial plants remove about 100 billion tons of carbon from the atmosphere per year, or about 14 percent of the total atmospheric carbon content. An approximately equal amount of carbon is returned to the atmosphere through the processes of plant respiration and decay of organic matter. Because the fluxes are a substantial fraction of the carbon dioxide already in the atmosphere at any time, a change of a few percent in either the photosynthetic or the respiratory flux would soon significantly alter the atmospheric carbon dioxide content. Will global warming produce such an imbalance?

The answer is unclear and probably will remain so until after the climate has changed considerably more than it has already. Nevertheless, the general picture is probably as follows. The rate of photosynthesis is affected by many factors, particularly the availability of light, water and nutrients. It is not, however, very sensitive to temperature change. The rates of plant respiration and decay, on the other hand, do strongly depend on the temperature. A one-degree temperature change in either direction often alters rates of plant respiration by from 10 to 30 percent.

These observations suggest that a global warming will speed the decay of organic matter without appreciably changing the rate of photosynthesis. That will increase the release of carbon dioxide into the atmosphere. A warming will also result in more methane, because methane is produced by respiration in regions where oxygen is not freely available, such as swamps, bogs and moist soils. In recent years there has been a rise in the concentration of atmospheric methane of more than 1 percent per year. The increase is both rapid and significant because, as noted above, methane is 20 times as effective as carbon dioxide in trapping heat. The wet soils where methane is produced as a result of anaerobic decay probably represent the world's major source of methane. The global warming that has already occurred has undoubtedly stimulated anaerobic decay and the production of methane as well as carbon dioxide.

It is possible to estimate the size of the resulting increase in carbon production at least crudely. A significant fraction (from 20 to 30 percent) of global respiration on land takes place in the forest and tundra of the middle and high latitudes, where the warming is expected to be greatest. If we assume that the mean global warming to date has been .5 degree C, and that in the middle and high latitudes the rise has been one degree, then plant respiration in these latitudes and the decay of organic matter in soils has increased significantly. If the increase in respiration is between 5 and 20 percent over 20 to 30 percent of the total area respiring, then total global respiration will increase between 1 and 6 percent above normal. Once again assuming that the annual flux of carbon into the atmosphere is 100 billion tons and that the rate of photosynthesis remains unchanged, the warming that has already taken place has meant an injection of between one and six billion tons of carbon per year. Over the past century from 20 to 30 billion tons of carbon may have been released in this manner.

That estimate is probably high, because the average warming may have been less than assumed and because photosynthetic response will tend to reduce the release of carbon dioxide. Yet the estimate is probably not high by as much as a factor of two, and it serves to emphasize the importance of biotic feedback mechanisms.

How does the value just computed compare with amounts of carbon released by other known processes? The release from the burning of fossil fuels is approximately 5.6 billion tons per year; deforestation adds an amount estimated at between .4 and 2.5 billion tons per year. The total carbon injected into the atmosphere from these two sources added to a temperature-enhanced respiration is not known, but it appears to be more than six billion tons annually and may approach 10 billion.

The release of carbon due to changes in the respiratory rate could fluctuate appreciably; a gradual warming, such as that experienced over most of this century, would change the respiratory rate slowly enough so that year-to-year changes would be inconspicuous. On the other hand, a sudden warming or cooling over a period of several years might result in an observable change in the carbon dioxide content of the atmosphere. In the past 15 years the annual rate of accumulation of atmospheric carbon dioxide has been about 1.5 parts per million, equivalent to a global accumulation of about three billion tons of carbon.

According to data recorded on Mauna Loa and at the South Pole by Keeling, however, during the time period of 1987-1989, the accumulation rate rose to about 2.4 parts per million, equivalent to about five billion tons of carbon. Keeling expects that the surge will prove transitory, as a lesser surge in 1973 and 1974 did. Nevertheless, the implication we assign to the observations at the moment is that the surge is a result of the high temperatures that have marked the 1980's, delayed by the time necessary to warm the soil. Whether this interpretation is correct remains to be seen.

Any climatic change can also be expected to affect the ability of the terrestrial biota, in particular forests and soils, to retain carbon. At warming rates that are lower than the rates at which forests develop, forests may actually expand, and with them the capacity to store carbon. But if the warming rate exceeds the rates at which forests migrate into more climatically favorable regions, widespread mortality of trees and other plants is likely to follow. The net result of such destruction of forests is difficult to predict, but it will probably mean a further release of carbon dioxide through the decay of plants, animals and organic matter in soils.

The amount of carbon dioxide that could be injected into the atmosphere would depend heavily on the rate of climatic change in the forested zones of the middle and high latitudes. Although it is impossible to make any accurate calculation, an upper limit is given by the amount of carbon in these forested latitudes: approximately 750 billion metric tons, or about the same amount of carbon as there is in the atmosphere currently.

Is it possible that a global warming could stimulate the growth of forests? In this case the spread of forests to high latitudes and tundra regions would result in a greater uptake of carbon dioxide from the atmosphere and a greater accumulation of carbon dioxide in the soil. Such a transition is unlikely. Forests require centuries to develop, especially where soils are thin and nutrients are in short supply. They also require climatic stability and sources of seeds. The climatic transitions currently under way, unless they are checked, are rapid by any measure and can be expected to continue into the indefinite future. They do not offer the conditions under which forests are able to develop on new land and remain for long periods.

"The warming, unless consciously checked by human effort, will be rapid and will be felt differentially over the earth."

Might the warming at least stimulate existing forests to store additional carbon in plants and soil? Perhaps. The boreal forest and other coniferous forests may indeed be sufficiently resilient to respond to warming with increased photosynthesis and growth. Whether the carbon taken up by photosynthesis will be stored or simply released through increased respiration remains an open question.

There is also the possibility that the tundra, the treeless plain found in arctic and subarctic regions, will respond to a warming in surprising ways, including an increase in the production of carbon and its storage in peat. The nature of the response will largely hinge on the availability of water. A wetter tundra might store additional carbon in soils; a drier tundra might release it through the decay of organic matter in long-frozen soil or soil that is normally frozen for most of the year. W. Dwight Billings of Duke University believes global warming will speed the decay of peat in tundra soils and precipitate that ultimate breakdown of the tundra known as thermal karst erosion, which allows flowing water to erode the tundra in great acre-size chunks. Not only is the tundra devastated but also substantial amounts of carbon dioxide and methane that were stored in the peat as carbon are released into the atmosphere.

The evidence indicates that under rapid planetary warming respiration rates will increase more than photosynthesis rates. The changes will lead to the release of additional carbon dioxide and methane into the atmosphere. The magnitude of the release will hinge strongly on the rate of warming: the faster the warming, the larger the release. Such behavior is consistent with (but not proved by) the data from the Vostok core.

What will be the consequences of a continued global warming? In 1985 a group of meteorologists meeting under the auspices of the World Meteorological Organization (WMO) and the United Nations Environment Programme (UNEP) demonstrated that without the respiratory feedback mechanisms addressed above, the combined effect of the greenhouse gases would warm the earth by an average of from 1.5 to 4.5 degrees C before the middle of the next century. The conclusion was recently confirmed in a review written by more than 50 scientists who met in Villach, Austria, in 1987 and was published by the WMO and the UNEP.

Seldom has there been such a strong consensus among scientists on a major environmental issue. The warming, unless consciously checked by human effort, will be rapid and will be felt differentially over the earth. Winter temperatures in the middle and high latitudes can be expected to rise by more than twice the world average. If the mean global temperature were to rise by from two to three degrees C by the year 2030, the winter temperature increase in Minneapolis might approach from four to six degrees C, or about one degree per decade. Summer temperatures would also rise, but less severely. A one-degree change in temperature is equivalent to a change in latitude of from 100 to 150 kilometers. The prairie-forest border, which is now south and west of Minneapolis, might be expected to migrate north at a rate of between 100 and 150 kilometers per decade, or between 400 and 600 kilometers by the year 2030.

Such changes are likely to be difficult for most of the world's peoples. First, the changes will be continuous. Unless the warming stops, efforts to adapt to climatic changes are likely to be responses to conditions that no longer exist. Second, the changes in climate will be irreversible for any time of interest to us or our children. There is no way to cool the earth or to lower sea level; we cannot return quickly to an atmosphere with lower concentrations of greenhouse gases. The best we can do is to reduce current emissions. If that step is taken immediately, a further warming of more than one degree can be expected as the full effects of the heat-trapping gases already present are felt.

Finally, the effects are open-ended. Although most modeling to date simulates a doubling of the atmospheric carbon dioxide content, there is simply no reason to assume that the concentrations will stop at twice the current levels. Estimated reserves of recoverable fossil fuels in themselves are enough to increase the atmospheric concentration of carbon dioxide by a factor of from five to 10.

Can anything be done to slow the climatic change that is now under way? The immediate need is to stabilize the greenhouse-gas content of the atmosphere. Regardless of its source, over the past decade carbon has been accumulating in the atmosphere at a rate of about three billion tons annually. (The remainder is being absorbed by the oceans or stored in forests and soils.) If current fluxes were reduced by three billion tons annually, the atmospheric carbon dioxide level would be stabilized for a few years. The stabilization would not be permanent, however. The rate of accumulation in the oceans is determined by how fast they can absorb carbon dioxide from the atmosphere; this in turn depends on the difference in carbon dioxide concentration between the atmosphere and the ocean. As the flux of excess carbon is reduced, the difference is also reduced and the ocean becomes less capable of absorbing excess carbon; carbon dioxide emissions would have to be reduced still further to prevent additional atmospheric accumulation.

The largest source of carbon dioxide emissions is the combustion of fossil fuels, which releases about 5.6 billion tons of carbon into the atmosphere annually. Industrial nations contribute about 75 percent of these emissions; steps toward stabilizing the composition must begin in the industrialized world. A recent study carried out under the auspices of the World Resources Institute and led by José Goldemberg, president of the University of São Paulo in Brazil, suggests that the consumption of energy from fossil fuels in the developed nations could be halved by a program of conservation and improved efficiency alone.

Although developing nations produce less carbon dioxide, their contributions are growing; if economic development follows conventional patterns, their potential contributions are very large. The second step toward the stabilization of greenhouse gases will require innovations in economic development that lessen dependence on fossil fuels.

The other known major source of carbon dioxide is deforestation, predominantly in the Tropics. By 1980 about 11,000 square kilometers of forest were being cleared annually, with the result that in 1980 between .4 and 2.5 billion tons of carbon (as carbon dioxide) were released into the atmosphere. The rate of deforestation has increased over the past decade. If the present release of carbon is near the upper end of the above range, halting deforestation would reduce carbon emissions by the three billion tons per year needed immediately to stabilize atmospheric composition.

Reforestation will also help to stabilize the

composition of the atmosphere. The reforestation of from one to two million square kilometers (about the area of Alaska) will result in the annual storage of one billion tons of carbon. Although this area is large, and productive land in the Tropics is at a premium, there may be as much as 8.5 million square kilometers of once forested land available for reforestation. Of this land, about 3.5 million square kilometers could be returned to forest if permanent agriculture were to replace shifting cultivation. Another five million square kilometers of deforested land are currently unused, and there reforestation could in principle be implemented immediately. Forests established to store carbon would, of course, have to be maintained: neither harvested nor destroyed by toxic effects or change in climate.

Each of the measures to stabilize the atmospheric carbon dioxide level would have salutary effects locally, regionally and nationally, quite apart from its effects on climatic change. An improvement in energy-use efficiency, a step that might have been taken long ago with benefits to all, would bring economic and material advantages to both individuals and nations. An improvement in efficiency would lessen reliance on fossil fuels; this in turn would reduce sulfur and nitrogen oxide emissions, acid deposition and the release of other toxins. Halting deforestation would help to maintain the genetic diversity of the planet, reduce erosion, stabilize local and regional climates, cleanse water and air and preserve opportunities for future generations.

"The greatest problem is gaining the active and effective support of the developing nations, which are poised for a massive increase in fossil-fuel consumption."

No one remedy by itself is likely to stabilize the levels of carbon dioxide and methane in the atmosphere. If the accumulation of carbon dioxide in the atmosphere persists, the carbon burden will have shifted from three billion tons annually to five billion tons and will be that much more difficult to address. The measures that are required can begin at home, although it is clear the world must join in the effort if it is to be effective. There are precedents for international action on similar issues. The Limited Test Ban Treaty of 1962 was an agreement among certain nations to avoid atmospheric tests of nuclear weapons. It has been effective. Nations that did not sign it (France and the People's Republic of China) have yielded to international pressure and now conduct weapons tests underground. The Vienna Convention for the Protection of the Ozone Layer

and the Montreal Protocol, the latter negotiated in 1987, have moved the world far toward the elimination of chlorofluorocarbons.

There is no reason to assume that similar progress cannot be made with carbon-based fuels and deforestation. With that end in view a series of steps has already been undertaken: 50 specialists in international diplomacy and law met recently under the auspices of the Woods Hole Research Center to outline approaches that might work. The greatest problem is gaining the active and effective support of the developing nations, which are poised for a massive increase in fossil-fuel consumption. Development need not, however, follow historical paths. To cite one example, the low-latitude countries stand to gain immeasurably as techniques for exploiting solar energy are perfected. Solar-powered electrolysis of water can produce hydrogen, which in turn can run automobiles and other machinery. There are few places in North America where domestic hot water cannot now be produced by solar energy at little or no cost throughout most of the year. Nor is it to the advantage of nations to allow their forests to be destroyed.

Conferences are under way in the developing nations to explore alternatives to the present course. . . . The conferences will explore the possible responses of developing nations to a world in which conventional energy sources are limited. There are extraordinary opportunities for industrial innovations, particularly in energy efficiency and solar power. But developing countries cannot be expected to shoulder the entire burden; the developed nations, which are responsible for most of the problem, must do their share.

These issues will persist throughout the next century and dominate major technical, scientific and political considerations into the indefinite future.

Richard A. Houghton is an ecologist and a senior scientist at the Woods Hole Research Center in Woods Hole, Massachusetts. George M. Woodwell is also an ecologist and directs the Woods Hole Research Center. They have collaborated for more than twenty years on environmental studies.

"We should expect to experience, and to cope with, all the changes that the [global] warming will bring."

The Greenhouse Effect Is Exaggerated

T.A. Heppenheimer

It was early summer in 1988, and the Northeast was sweltering under an oppressive heat wave. In the Midwest, farmers were battling a serious drought. And at a congressional hearing, the atmospheric scientist James Hansen, director of NASA's [National Aeronautics and Space Administration] Goddard Institute of Space Studies, made headlines by asserting that a worldwide siege of heat and drought was upon us, brought on by man's industrial activities. The dreaded "greenhouse effect" had arrived—perhaps as physical reality, certainly as a political issue. The *New York Times*, the nation's leading herald of environmental crisis, put the story on page one.

While few of Hansen's colleagues share the immediacy of his alarm, most scientists researching the question do agree that a major climate warming is in the offing. Yet in the subsequent months, the response of environmentalists has been rather muted—at least as far as specific policies are concerned.

The reason lies in the way the problem is usually formulated: How do we reverse the greenhouse effect and forestall the warming? To accomplish this sweeping goal, nothing less would do than the complete restructuring of our industrial civilization. A few environmentalists have issued prescriptions along those lines. Richard Houghton and George Woodwell of Woods Hole Research Center, writing in *Scientific American,* called for a "50 percent reduction in the global consumption of fossil fuels, a halting of deforestation, a massive program of reforestation. There is little choice."

Such cutbacks would indeed be required to end the buildup of carbon dioxide, but the cost would be intolerable—a worldwide economic collapse that would make the Great Depression look like a statistical blip. For the most part, therefore, few responsible observers are advocating such drastic actions. Even the Environmental Protection Agency's highly activist recommendations—calling for governments to intervene to hike the prices of fuels and to end deforestation, while promoting tree-planting, energy conservation, and alternative energy sources—would merely slow down the warming, not avoid it.

Sound Policy

We cannot base sound policy on frenzied efforts to retain the climate of the 20th century. Rather, we must seek accommodation to the forthcoming warming. It does little good, as some environmentalists do, to propose that governmental actions can retain the climate to which we are accustomed. That is like saying that government ukases could have kept us in the age of coal, preventing us from ever tapping the world's wealth of petroleum and natural gas. Instead, we must understand the real threats posed by the greenhouse effect and learn to cope.

The problem arises from the worldwide use of coal, oil, and natural gas. When these fuels burn, they release carbon dioxide. This gas builds up in the atmosphere and acts to trap heat in its lower portions, raising global temperatures. (The same process occurs with the atmosphere's naturally present carbon dioxide and water vapor; if they did not trap heat, the sun would warm the earth to a global average temperature of around zero degrees Fahrenheit and the world would be shrouded in ice.)

Industrial activities account for only a small fraction of the world's total flow of carbon dioxide. Every year, some 759 billion metric tons of the gas enter the atmosphere, mainly from decay of vegetation, gases from volcanoes, and exchanges between atmosphere and sea, according to Houghton

T.A. Heppenheimer, "Keep Your Cool," excerpted, with permission, from the January 1990 issue of REASON magazine. Copyright 1990 by the Reason Foundation, 2716 Ocean Park Blvd., Santa Monica, CA 90405.

and Woodwell. As a minor additional source, some 18 billion tons come from fossil fuels. Yet this source is enough to tip the balance toward a global buildup, for only about 748 billion tons of carbon dioxide leave the atmosphere each year, chiefly through plant growth and dissolution in seawater. The net increase, 11 billion tons, can be regarded as entirely manmade.

As early as the turn of the century, and sporadically for several decades thereafter, various scientists suggested that man's activities might be affecting the climate. The first reasonably good study of this issue came only in 1975. That year, Syukuro Manabe and Richard Wetherald of Princeton University published results based on a detailed computer model. Specifically, they looked at the effects of doubling the atmospheric concentration of carbon dioxide, from 300 to 600 parts per million. They concluded that this doubling would raise the earth's mean surface temperature by three to eight degrees. More recent estimates, using improved models, predict a warming of five to nine degrees with this doubled concentration.

Computer models of such complex systems have come under attack for unjustifiably apocalyptic tendencies—the Club of Rome's predictions and the warnings of nuclear winter come to mind. But the greenhouse models appear more reliable. One can test them by demanding that with today's level of carbon dioxide they should accurately reproduce today's observed climate. The slight change of adding extra carbon dioxide to a model then produces a slight change in the climate—a global temperature rise of a few degrees—and this change then is quite believable.

Such temperature increases, occurring over the entire globe, could have dramatic consequences. A project called CLIMAP has compared the climate of the modern era to that at the height of the Ice Age, 18,000 years ago, when Chicago lay buried under glaciers a mile thick. The CLIMAP group used computer models similar to those of Manabe and Wetherald. They concluded that, on average, global temperatures in July of 16,000 B.C. were only nine degrees cooler than in July of recent years.

Prospective Increases in Temperature

If nine degrees make the difference between Ice Age and a comfortable climate, and doubling the carbon dioxide concentration can make a difference of nine degrees, it becomes very important to estimate how long it might take for the atmospheric carbon dioxide to double. Since 1958, Charles D. Keeling of Scripps Institution of Oceanography has monitored month-by-month the atmospheric concentration of carbon dioxide. These measurements have shown a strong, marked rise: from 314 parts per million in 1958 to 348 ppm by 1988. Recent decades have shown a rate of increase

of around 1.5 ppm per year, which would double the carbon dioxide concentration by the year 2150.

A further important clue to prospective change comes from the geological record. The glaciologist Willi Dansgaard has drilled long cores of ice from the Greenland and Antarctic polar caps. These contain records of ancient climates, and of the ancient atmosphere, across hundreds of thousands of years. Air trapped within the ice contains naturally present carbon dioxide, which is readily measured. In addition, the water of the ice contains two "fossil thermometers": isotopes of hydrogen and oxygen, which change their concentrations depending on the temperature.

An ice core drilled at Vostok, Antarctica, by French and Soviet scientists, has given some of the best available evidence on past changes. This core shows a very clear correlation of carbon dioxide with temperature: The isotope ratios in the fossil thermometers, as well as the carbon dioxide concentration, rise and fall virtually in lockstep across the past 160,000 years.

"The greenhouse effect may involve not only industrial civilization but also natural fluctuations."

Interestingly, carbon dioxide levels in recent centuries—prior to the industrial era—were already higher than at any time since around 130,000 years ago. They have gone higher since. So the greenhouse effect may involve not only industrial civilization but also natural fluctuations. And we should be prepared for major climatic changes. The time of high carbon dioxide 130,000 years ago is known in geology as the Eemian interglacial, an era of unparalleled heat, when the warmth-loving hippopotamus lived in, of all places, Great Britain.

The oceans would have to warm perceptibly before the greenhouse effect would truly make itself felt over the continents. This has not happened and may not occur for several decades. Despite the press hysteria, the 1988 heat wave and drought appear to have been caused primarily by a warming in the eastern Pacific known as El Niño, which is due to natural causes. The restoration of normal warmth and rainfall in 1989, in turn, followed a Pacific cooling called La Niña. Neither of these was related to the greenhouse effect. The observed warmings to date are within the range of natural variations, and it may take another decade or two before theory and observation produce general agreement that the greenhouse indeed is at hand.

Nevertheless, there is good evidence for a worldwide increase in mean temperature of about one degree over the past century, with much of this rise having taken place since 1970. Worldwide temperature measurements, recorded over the years, tell of this. In addition, a number of glaciers have retreated. The maximal extent of sea ice, around Antarctica and in the Arctic seas, has declined. In the Alaskan and Canadian Arctic, the depth to permafrost has increased.

The forecasts are admittedly uncertain. Only in recent months have data been published that can permit an adequate understanding of the role of clouds in the earth's climate. Clouds aid in trapping heat from below, but they have the even larger effect of reflecting sunlight back into space, producing a net cooling. Uncertainties concerning the action of clouds are the reason that analysts give a range of possible values for the warming, such as "5 to 9 degrees with a carbon dioxide doubling," rather than a single, more definite value.

Unfortunately, this uncertainty offers little comfort. Michael MacCracken of Lawrence Livermore National Laboratory has compared a variety of computer models with one another and with real-world climate data. He concludes that the warming will amount in any case to several degrees, rather than being one degree or less. That is just what the computations have been showing all along.

Feared Climatic Changes

Despite the uncertainties, we have abundant reason to expect that the next century or so will bring the sort of climatic change that we associate with a passage between geologic epochs. And since it is an ill wind that blows nobody good, it is natural to ask who will be helped and hurt and what the major anticipatable changes may be.

One such feared change—the threat of suffocation due to the using-up of oxygen—is wholly imaginary. Two other changes will be largely beneficial: warming the northern lands and staving off the next Ice Age. Three others will be unpleasant: hot weather, regional droughts, and major changes to ecosystems. Still, they are in line with longstanding trends and past experiences. But one result of the greenhouse warming does indeed pose a major threat. This is the melting of the Antarctic ice sheets, which could raise sea levels worldwide by close to 20 feet.

Taking these effects in turn, one begins with the allegation of a threat to the world's oxygen. This tale comes from environmentalists who are concerned over the widespread burning and deforestation of the Amazon. Some people assert that the Amazon is the world's "lungs," its prime source of new oxygen produced by photosynthesis. To burn the Amazon, then, would condemn us all to perish for want of oxygen to breathe.

There are excellent reasons to seek to save at least a few major tracts of rain forest, for they contain vast numbers of plant and animal species that have

yet to be studied. But to call the Amazon the world's lungs reveals a woeful ignorance of the most basic chemistry. The rain forests produce great quantities of oxygen, true. But they also *consume* equally great quantities of oxygen when their plants die and decay. If the Amazon were a large net source of oxygen, this gas would be chemically balanced by large stores of "fixed carbon": humus, peat, lignite, coal, oil. The Amazon contains little or none of the above. In fact, the oxygen we breathe comes mainly from a source that no human activity could ever touch: the evaporation of seawater. This evaporation produces water vapor that breaks apart in the upper atmosphere, yielding hydrogen atoms that escape into space and oxygen atoms that are heavier and stay behind.

Warming of the northern lands is much more solidly established as a prospect for the future. The global computer models, predicting a worldwide average warming of five or more degrees with a doubling of carbon dioxide, also show that this warming would be substantially greater near the poles. Above the 80th parallel of latitude, the warming could amount to 18 degrees or more.

Agriculture could benefit enormously, both in Canada and the Soviet Union. Over a century or so, these countries might experience economic growth that would vastly enhance their prosperity. The Arctic Ocean might become navigable, with incalculable advantage for the development of Siberia and the other northern lands. The Northwest Passage could become a much-traveled sea route, linking Europe to the Far East. The Scandinavian countries would also prosper, contributing to the growing power of a unifying Europe.

"Staving off the next Ice Age is another valuable consequence of a climate warming."

Staving off the next Ice Age is another valuable consequence of a climate warming. The time between successive ice ages is called an interglacial; we have been living amid such a time for some thousands of years. In 1972, however, a group of researchers gathered at Brown University for a conference with the interesting title, "The Present Interglacial, How and When Will It End?" Reporting on the conference proceedings in *Science*, climate specialists George Kukla and R.K. Matthews stated: "When comparing the present with past interglacials, several investigators showed that the present interglacial is in its final phase . . . and that if nature were allowed to run its course unaltered by man, events similar to those which ended the last interglacial should be expected to occur perhaps as soon as the next few centuries."

One would not wish to write an environmental impact statement for such events. It is sufficient to note that the North American industrial heartland lies within 100 or so miles of the Great Lakes and Long Island—and that these geographic features mark the extent of the glaciers. (The Great Lakes were pressed downward by the weight of the ice, while other glaciers bulldozed material ahead of them to form Long Island.)

We would be eminently justified in doing whatever is necessary to prevent or delay the glaciers' return. And how fortunate we are if to do this we require no surge of global effort, no massive endeavors marshaling the world's concerted energies—nothing more than to continue with the growth of industry, the rise in living standards, and the attendant use of fossil fuels.

"We cut the standing timber, broke the prairie to farmland—and produced a continent where hundreds of millions would live well, where previously fewer than a million had lived meanly."

Still, the climate warmings will bring definite problems to wide areas. Chicago may experience the summer heat of New Orleans, while Boston swelters as if it were Washington, D.C. The greenhouse effect, then, might bring the climate of the Sun Belt to the Frost Belt. But Americans have already experienced an increase in mean temperature that has nothing to do with climate change. Large numbers of people from the Frost Belt have for some time been moving to the Sun Belt, and many more would like to follow. Air conditioning made possible the spectacular postwar boom in the South and Southwest, and it is fair to say that air conditioning would similarly advance as a way of life if summer heat becomes more burdensome in the North.

Regional droughts could pose a more dramatic problem. The word *regional* must certainly be emphasized, for the most elementary physics shows that a warmer world will evaporate more water and hence will produce more rainfall. The Manabe-Wetherald solution, for one, shows a 7 percent increase in total world rainfall. Yet this is hardly a 7 percent solution. Regional rainfall patterns are strongly influenced by seasonal movements of the jet stream and of high- and low-pressure areas. A general climate warming could well bring changes entirely similar to the 1988 El Niño, with its attendant drought and heat.

Rain-fed agriculture is a mainstay in much of the Midwest, and a sudden onset of drought would be ruinous. If the changes took place over decades,

however, they would amount merely to a continuation of trends that have reduced the agricultural workforce to only 3 percent of all persons holding jobs. A boom in Alaskan and Canadian farming would certainly provide opportunities for many people. And the prospect of water shortages might well provide New York and other cities the incentive to rebuild their leaky and obsolete municipal systems.

Elsewhere in the world, one cannot overlook the possibility of intensified drought in already-dry parts of Africa, such as Ethiopia and the sub-Saharan lands. Here, however, the real problem is not climate. Indigenous governments committed to private property and economic growth—and prepared to build highways and railroads—could readily ward off the starvation that brings these lands to the TV screen. And it must be emphasized that, on balance, the worldwide increase in mean rainfall should bring an overall reduction in the extent of such marginal lands.

Then there is the prospect of environmental change, summed up in the question: How fast can trees migrate? Trees in forests are typically adapted to restricted ranges of temperature and hence of latitude. As climates warm, their appropriate ranges would shift northward, and might well do so more rapidly than their seeds could spread by natural means.

We have seen such developments in the last century, and on a particularly vast scale. Today we call such trends "ecocatastrophe," but a century ago they were "taming the wilderness." We cut the standing timber, broke the prairie to farmland—and produced a continent where hundreds of millions would live well, where previously fewer than a million had lived meanly. Since we could produce such sweeping environmental change in the 19th century, we surely will be able to intervene during the 21st—planting seedlings, helping the trees to migrate, and mitigating manmade environmental change with manmade restocking of the forests.

A Major Sea-Level Rise

Still, in so complex a matter as climatic warming, much more is at stake than pleasant northern mildness or effects that, however unpleasant, represent extensions of ongoing trends. The warmings, again, stand to be more severe than in the last major time of high temperatures—the Eemian interglacial of 130,000 years ago. And the geological record of that era shows a clear and present danger.

This danger lies in a major sea-level rise, for the Eemian sea stood at least 20 feet higher than the sea does today. The evidence comes from fossil coral-reef terraces in Hawaii and Barbados. And there is excellent reason to believe that just such a rise in the sea will accompany the carbon dioxide warming.

Such a sea-level rise would be by far the worst effect of a climate warming. The greatest hardships would hit such locales as the Netherlands and New Orleans. Both have large portions of land already below sea level and are protected only by extensive dikes and levees. The inhabitants would have no recourse but to build these works higher, and hope.

"The sea level would rise over centuries, not over days, and would give ever-adaptable humanity time to adjust."

Along the Gulf Coast, nearly a third of Louisiana would be submerged. The same would be true for the flat lowlands of Texas, which include Galveston, Corpus Christi, and parts of the Houston area. All of southern Florida, from Key West to Lake Okeechobee, would drown. So would all its coastal cities; only interior towns such as Tallahassee, Gainesville, Orlando, and Lakeland would be spared.

We would lose Savannah, Georgia; Charleston, South Carolina; four of Virginia's eight largest cities, as well as the Sacramento River flood plain in California that includes the city of that name. In Washington, D.C., the Lincoln Memorial would be swamped. The Mall would be flooded, and it would be possible to launch a boat from the White House lawn and row to just below the Capitol building.

Altogether, the United States would lose some 50,000 square miles of coastal lowlands, with a value of several trillion dollars. Similar losses would afflict every other continent. One must especially think of the hundreds of millions of people who live around the heavily populated deltas and estuaries of the Nile, the Niger, the Ganges, the Yangtze. In China, Egypt, Nigeria, and most certainly in Bangladesh, which already is right at sea level, throughout vast areas—all will be swept away.

Yet even as we contemplate such a natural disaster we must keep in mind that unlike a flood, hurricane, or earthquake, it would not occur quickly. The sea level would rise over centuries, not over days, and would give ever-adaptable humanity time to adjust.

Two distinct causes could contribute to such a sea-level rise. The nearer-term one would come into play as heat from the global warming soaked into the oceans, warming their water and bringing a thermal expansion of the sea. The EPA estimates the resulting sea-level rise at two to seven feet by the year 2100. No such rise has yet been detected; the sea has risen in the past 100 years by only four to six inches.

The rest of the sea-level rise, to the total of 20 feet, could come more slowly and from an entirely different source: the melting of polar ice. Glaciologists today are well aware of a body of ice

that could indeed collapse and send sea levels surging to such an increase. This ice mass appears unstable and may well be at serious risk of melting in a time of global warming. It is the West Antarctic Ice Sheet.

The ice sheet rests upon bedrock up to a mile and a half below sea level. Ordinarily, the sea would tend powerfully to buoy up the ice and cause it to float away, but the ice is protected by fringing shelves of ice more than 1,000 feet thick, which float upon the sea. These act as icy barriers or buttresses that protect the main ice sheet from surging or collapsing into the surrounding seas.

Today, along the ice shelves' outer edges, immense flat-topped bergs continually are breaking off to float northward. This breaking-off is called calving, and a general climatic warming, amplified in the polar regions, could bring an increase in calving that would destroy the protective ice shelves.

In this scenario, once the polar temperature warmed sufficiently, the largest ice shelves would rapidly break up, falling to pieces that would float off as enormous bergs. The main West Antarctic Ice Sheet, lacking its protective barrier, then would surge into the sea. The consequence would be a reduction of West Antarctica to a scattering of islands—and a permanently raised global sea level.

How long might it take for the seas to rise? The question of time scales rests on issues that are particularly uncertain: the time for the seas to warm and the time for major ice sheets to collapse. Several glaciologists have proposed that the last major ice sheet to melt—the Laurentide, which overlay Hudson Bay 8,000 years ago—collapsed over 200 years. Though minuscule on geologic time scales, this period is already far beyond the reach of any conceivable policy or plan in human affairs. If the melting of Antarctica should take longer—500 or 1,000 years—then it would represent nothing more than a long-term trend in the background of the future development of cities and of human civilization. By building seawalls, and by encouraging future growth in the direction of higher ground, communities would cope with the fact that from one generation to the next, sea levels would rise by another foot.

New Energy Sources

Over time, energy sources will also develop, through the natural play of demand and supply, that will reduce the buildup of carbon dioxide. Nuclear power could already substitute for fossil fuels to provide electricity; its lack of carbon dioxide output may in time lead environmentalists to rue the day they opposed it so strenuously.

Over the longer term, solar energy may yet emerge as an economically viable source of electric power. With little fanfare, the prospects for solar cells have been advancing steadily. In the mid-1970s, the cost of their electricity was $15 per kilowatt-hour. Current systems reduce this cost to 30 cents, and some companies are building new facilities that promise a further reduction to 15 cents. That is within reach of the cost range, 6 to 12 cents per kilowatt-hour, that would make solar cells competitive with other future sources of electric power. Early in the next century, solar cells could emerge as the lowest-cost option for producing large blocks of electric power.

Eventually, too, hydrogen derived through electrolysis of water could substitute for the uses of fossil fuels that demand portability—powering automobiles, for instance—and might displace natural gas as a heating source. But, we must remember, in the United States it has taken some 60 years for each new energy source to rise from initial introduction to dominance within the economy. Within the world at large, the transition period has been closer to a century.

Learning to Cope

We should therefore anticipate that the concentration of carbon dioxide in the atmosphere will double, and perhaps more than double, before the rise of new energy sources within free-market economies brings the problem under control. So we should expect to experience, and to cope with, all the changes that the warming will bring—including the rise in sea levels. The geologic record strongly suggests that it is already too late to save the West Antarctic Ice Sheet, that it will inevitably melt as the world adjusts to a new equilibrium. All we may hope for, then, is that the seas will take several centuries to rise, rather than one or two, and that the resulting changes might be accommodated within the ongoing development of human civilization.

We know so little. To cite only the most severe of the effects of warming—the sea-level rise—three pertinent questions carry very large levels of ignorance: What level of climate warming will melt the Antarctic ice sheets? How long will it take? Might an economics-driven transition to new energy sources occur quickly enough to forestall this event?

Until we know the answers to these questions, we have no basis for policy. Nor should we take refuge in the idea that any action that reduces carbon dioxide is necessarily a good thing. Afterall, carbon dioxide is a byproduct of industrial growth and of a prosperous economy. Ill-considered actions against this gas could give us the worst of both worlds: an imperfect reduction in its emissions that barely delays the warming and robs us of the prosperity that might allow us to cope with its effects.

Good intentions are no substitute for knowledge, and fashionable activism cannot fill in gaps of ignorance. Lacking the needed answers, we cannot even accurately assess the future significance of the carbon dioxide that is already in the air. Still less can we propose a global plan designed to save the world. The most we can do is anticipate that we will cope, and muddle through.

"Worldwide prosperity will continue to give humanity the tools to deal with these changes, and to thrive in the face of the resulting difficulties."

Canadian cities will discover air conditioning. Midwestern farmers may move to Alaska. East Coast cities may make it a priority to rebuild their waterworks. Forestry companies and the Department of the Interior will plant warm-weather trees in the Appalachians. Builders will look toward higher ground. Vast engineering works—dikes, seawalls, aqueducts—may come forth against drought and rising seas. And through it all, worldwide prosperity will continue to give humanity the tools to deal with these changes, and to thrive in the face of the resulting difficulties.

T.A. Heppenheimer is a contributing editor for Reason, *a libertarian magazine based in Santa Monica, California.*

"Nuclear energy is the only major, practical energy source that does not emit CO_2."

Nuclear Power Can Alleviate the Greenhouse Effect

Science Concepts, Inc.

Controversy has developed over the theory that man-made additions of greenhouse gases to earth's atmosphere could lead to global climate warming early in the next century.

The greenhouse effect is the phenomenon that keeps the surface of the Earth warmer than outer space. The global warming theory proposes that greenhouse gases from man-made activities could cause excess warming of the atmosphere.

There are five gases which cause the earth's atmosphere to retain heat and could thus contribute to a greenhouse effect: carbon dioxide (CO_2), methane (CH_4), nitrogen oxide (NO_x), and two chlorofluorocarbons ($CFCl_3$, CF_2Cl_2).

Carbon dioxide is estimated to be responsible for one-half of the greenhouse effect, with the other four gases listed above collectively responsible for the other half. Methane is estimated to be responsible for about 20% of the prospective warming, nitrogen oxides about 5%, and CFCs about 25%.

One molecule of chlorofluorocarbon has 10,000 times the atmospheric warming effect of one molecule of CO_2. The chlorofluorocarbons cause a depletion of ozone (O_3) in the upper atmosphere, allowing more heat to reach the earth's surface.

Sources of Greenhouse Gases

About 40% of methane is emitted from natural sources such as wetlands (23%), termites (5%), the oceans (2%), and wild animals (1%). The balance comes from man-made sources; cattle account for 15%, rice paddies 14%, biomass burning 14% and natural gas about 10% of total methane emissions.

About one-half of nitrogen oxide emissions are estimated to come from natural sources, primarily from natural soils; about 26% is estimated to arise

from fossil fuel burning, 5% from biomass burning, and 14% from cultivating and fertilizing soils.

CFCs are manufactured for air conditioning systems, to produce foam materials, and to function as propellants in aerosol cans; 49% of CFC-12 is used for refrigeration, 13% for foams, 32% for aerosols; 8% of CFC-11 is used for refrigeration, 55% for foams, 31% for aerosols.

Climate Effect of Greenhouse Gases

Significant uncertainty remains regarding the timing, magnitude, and likelihood of a greenhouse effect due to the difficulty in establishing computer models that can predict weather and because there is, as yet, no direct observational evidence of any increase in average atmospheric temperature. (There is evidence only of an increase in the atmospheric concentration of gases that can, based on the best current theories, create global warming.)

Proponents of global warming estimate, based on computer modelling, that the combined effect of the five primary greenhouse gases (if current emission trends continue) could lead to an increase in the average global temperature of between 2° and 6° C by 2030.

Some scientists argue that an average global temperature increase of 1.0 to 2.0° C may be "tolerable," probably unavoidable, and potentially easier to manage than attempting to reduce greenhouse gas emissions drastically.

The Little Ice Age (15th-17th centuries) was characterized by an average temperature difference of 1.0 to 1.5° C lower than normal.

The most recent period of high average global temperature (about 2° C higher than today) was in the period between 6,000 and 8,000 years ago.

U.S. electric utilities emit about 7.5% of total world CO_2 emissions—and thus account for about 4% of the man-made global greenhouse gases. About 23% of the world's CO_2 emissions originate in the

Science Concepts, Inc., "Energy Use and Global Warming: Background and Perspective," February 1990. Prepared for the U.S. Council on Energy Awareness. (Science Concepts, Inc. is an affiliate of TMS America.)

U.S. due to fossil fuel combustion. The sources of U.S. CO_2 emissions break down as follows: industry 25%, transportation 31%, homes and businesses 12%, and the electric utility sector 33%. Fossil fuel combustion since the Industrial Revolution is estimated to be primarily responsible for raising the concentration of CO_2 in the atmosphere from about 290 parts per million (ppm) to about 340 ppm today. The global warming theory based on computer modelling suggests that doubling the concentration of CO_2 in the atmosphere would lead to an estimated average increase in the globe's surface temperature of $3.0° \pm 1.5°$ C. Global carbon emissions to the atmosphere from fossil fuel combustion increased from 1.6 billion tons per year in 1950, to 3.1 billion tons in 1965 to about 5.1 billion tons per year in 1980. North America and Western Europe accounted for 68% of CO_2 emissions in 1950, while China and Latin America accounted for 7%. By 1980 the Western world's contribution was 43% and that of China and Latin America had risen to 20%. The following list shows the amount of carbon released from combustion to provide electricity for a 1,000 MW(e) [megawatt electric] power plant, using as a fuel [measured in million tons per year]:

- natural gas   0.9
- oil   1.3
- coal   1.5
- coal-based synfuels   2.5

Considerable uncertainty exists regarding the magnitude of sources and "sinks" for CO_2 in the atmosphere. For example, the estimates for global emissions of CO_2 from tropical forest clearing range from 0.4 to 1.6 billion tons per year, and the ability of the ocean to absorb CO_2 is an estimated 1.8 to 2.5 billion tons per year.

"U.S. electric utilities emit about 7.5% of total world CO_2 emissions—and thus account for about 4% of the man-made global greenhouse gases."

There are two fundamental methods for reducing CO_2 emissions: either use energy sources that emit less, or no CO_2, or improve the efficiency of using CO_2 emitting sources. Reducing emissions of other greenhouse gases may prove more effective and less expensive than draconian measures to reduce CO_2 emissions. The magnitude of the problem of reducing global CO_2 emissions can be put into perspective by noting two basic facts:

- about 90% of the world's energy needs are currently met by burning carbon-based fuels.
- to prevent an increase in the existing concentration of CO_2 in the atmosphere, mankind's CO_2 emissions could not exceed the *estimated* ability

of natural sinks to absorb CO_2. To reduce global CO_2 emissions sufficiently to accomplish this would require a *50% worldwide reduction in fossil fuel* use.

At the same time that fossil fuel use would have to be reduced, the world's appetite for energy is expected to grow to accommodate a global population growing from 5.2 billion in 1989 to more than 6 billion by 2000, and to more than 8 billion by 2025, and to accommodate a continuing improvement in the quality of life for the world. (Most of the population growth will occur in developing nations.) The associated increase in the global economic output per capita is estimated to grow at between 1.4% and 2.9% per year through 2025.

If programs are established to mitigate CO_2 emissions, balancing factors relating to other environmental and economic issues must be considered. In general, programs will need to do two things. First it is necessary to seek means to reduce the CO_2 emissions from current energy consumption patterns (through increased efficiency and fuel substitution). Second it is necessary to seek means to avoid additional CO_2 burdens associated with providing energy to meet economic and population growth.

CO_2 Emissions

Increasing energy efficiency, electrification, growth in nuclear energy, and structural changes in industry have resulted in no significant increase in U.S. CO_2 emissions since 1973.

The total amount of carbon dioxide emitted in the U.S. in 1988 was only 5% greater than in 1973 even though the economy grew 51%. Thus, the amount of carbon dioxide per unit of economic output has been declining in the United States for at least 15 years and is 20% lower today than 10 years ago. The net result of this trend has been that *economic growth has been accompanied by little increase in carbon dioxide emissions.* If the trend towards increasing "CO_2 efficiency" can be accelerated, economic growth may be possible with declining CO_2 emissions. Encouraging or accelerating an existing trend would likely prove the least disruptive and most cost-effective first step towards greenhouse mitigation. In addition, such a policy would have merit regardless of the ultimate proof of the greenhouse theory. Three factors explain the decline in carbon dioxide emissions per unit of economic output:

- Overall energy efficiency has improved.
- The mix of primary fuels has changed; there has been a substantial increase in the share of nuclear energy.
- The mix of fuels used in the marketplace has changed—the role of electricity has grown.

Energy efficiency can mitigate CO_2 emissions by reducing the quantity of fuels burned to accomplish a given task. But even if energy efficiency resulted in no increase in energy use by 2010, fossil fuel burning would still account for 88% of U.S. energy.

While improving energy efficiency is likely to be the most effective cost-effective method for mitigating the CO_2 problem, this is already happening. For the future, it will be important to pursue additional improvements in energy efficiency that are at least as cost-effective as actually producing energy from sources generating no CO_2. The primary measure of energy efficiency, the ratio of primary energy to economic output, is projected to improve in the United States by 11% by 2000. This improvement continues a trend that started almost 100 years ago. Energy required per unit of GNP in 1975 was half the level required in 1925; by 1987 the ratio had dropped a further 25%.

"Reducing electricity consumption . . . would do little to reduce CO_2 emissions."

Improvements in efficiency greater than those already underway, or likely, could prove costly and difficult. The population, economic and industrial growth expected through 2000 are projected to be achieved with only a 10% increase in non-electric fuel consumption for transportation, a 16% increase in the industrial sector and a 4% decline in the residential sectors. However, DOE [Department of Energy] projects that a 9 quadrillion btu, or 30%, *increase* in the energy used to make electricity will occur by 2000. (This trend highlights the importance of continuing electrification and including nuclear energy in the balance of fuels to make electricity.)

Reducing *electricity* consumption should not be confused with reducing *energy* consumption. Increased use of electricity can result in a decreased use of total energy. This arises because the very high efficiency of electric technologies often more than offsets the inefficiency of generating electricity. Reducing electricity consumption in regions of the U.S. where large amounts of electric power are generated with nuclear or hydro power would do little to reduce CO_2 emissions.

Electrification can reduce CO_2 emissions by improving overall energy efficiency, by eliminating the burning of fuels in industrial and residential processes, and by substituting the primary energy needed (for generating the electricity) with fuels that emit low or zero CO_2.

Electrification is a particularly effective means of reducing the use of energy sources which emit CO_2 in manufacturing and heating, as well as for increasing overall energy efficiency. The use of electric processes results in no direct CO_2 emissions at the point of use. This can be combined with the benefits of using electric-generating technologies that have low or no CO_2 emissions.

Electrification plays a major role in reducing fossil fuel use in producing goods and services. Since 1973 GNP growth of 51% has been accomplished with a 5% drop in the direct use of fuels (all of which emit CO_2), but the use of electricity has grown by 54%.

In the industrial sector the direct combustion of fossil fuels (which emit CO_2) has declined by 18% since 1973; at the same time there has been a 33% increase in the use of electricity (which emits no CO_2). The electrification of industry resulted in a reduction in the overall energy required per unit of output. Thus, even if all the additional electricity required had been produced by fossil fuel combustion, there would still have been a decline in CO_2 emissions.

In the residential/commercial sector the direct combustion of fossil fuels (which emit CO_2) has declined by 17% since 1973; at the same time there has been a 66% increase in the use of electricity (which emits no CO_2). The electrification of homes and retail businesses has resulted in a reduction in the overall energy required per person, per household, and per typical business, and only a small increase in the total energy required (i.e., including that used to make the electricity). Thus, even if all the additional electricity required had been produced by combustion, there would have been a net decline in CO_2 emissions.

Nuclear Energy

Nuclear energy (along with hydroelectricity) is the only major, practical energy source that does not emit CO_2. As the U.S. and world need for electrical energy continues to outpace overall demand for energy, the importance of this non-CO_2 emitting energy source will continue to grow.

In 1989, nuclear plants in the United States reduced *total* U.S. CO_2 emissions by almost 9%, and nuclear plants worldwide reduced total global CO_2 emissions by over 7%. Without nuclear power in 1989, U.S. utility emissions of CO_2 would have been 18% higher.

Between 1973 and 1989 in the United States, nuclear energy displaced a cumulative total of 4.3 billion barrels of oil, 1 billion tons of coal, and 6.5 trillion cubic feet of natural gas combustion. Overall, this represents a 6% reduction in total U.S. CO_2 emissions over the same period.

Between 1973 and 1989, nuclear energy worldwide (including the U.S.) displaced a cumulative total of 15 billion barrels of oil, 1.8 billion tons of coal, and 21 trillion cubic feet of natural gas. Overall, this represents a 5% reduction in total worldwide CO_2 emissions over the same period.

Between 1973 and 1989, over 96% of all new electricity produced in the U.S. came from coal and nuclear energy; about 59% and 37%, respectively.

A. THE ENERGY MIX TODAY: 90% of U.S. energy needs are met by fuels which emit CO$_2$

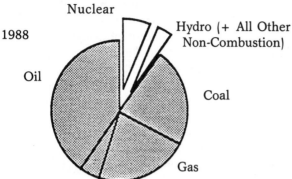

All Other Combustion (incl. Wood)

Nuclear and hydro power account for virtually all non-CO$_2$ emitting energy supply (63% and 36%, respectively); less than 1% comes from non-CO$_2$ emitting renewable sources such as wind, geothermal, and solar.

B. THE FUTURE U.S. ENERGY MIX FOLLOWING AN AGGRESSIVE CONSERVATION PROGRAM

[Nuclear, 2010, Oil, Hydro (+ All Other Non-Combustion), Coal, Gas]

All Other Combustion (incl. Wood)

Conservation alone cannot solve the problem. CO$_2$ emitting fossil fuels would still supply 88% of U.S. energy even if conservation stopped any increase in energy use through 2010, and non-combustion renewable energy tripled.

C. THE FUTURE ENERGY MIX WITH A CRASH RENEWABLE ENERGY + CONSERVATION EFFORT

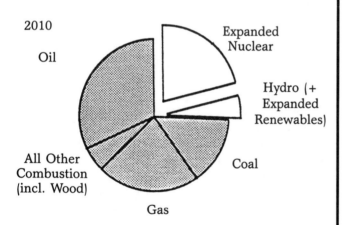

A crash renewable energy program could not make a significant difference. Fossil fuels would still supply 86% of U.S. energy even if conservation stopped energy growth and there was a 20-fold increase in solar, wind, geothermal (non-CO$_2$) energy.

D. THE FUTURE ENERGY MIX FOLLOWING A MAJOR NUCLEAR ENERGY + CONSERVATION EFFORT

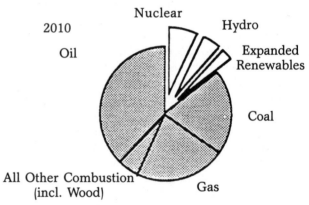

The fossil fuel share would drop to 72% if conservation stopped energy growth along with a 20-fold renewable growth, and there were a 3-fold increase in nuclear—200 new nuclear plants or 10/year through 2010. (7/year came on-line 1984 to 1987.)

This mix of coal and nuclear energy resulted in total CO$_2$ emissions about the same as if the energy had been provided by burning natural gas and about one-half the emissions compared to burning oil.

There is limited potential for substantial expansion of hydroelectricity in the U.S.

Solar energy releases no CO$_2$ directly to the environment, but the technology is not practical or economical for large-scale use. Also, large-scale deployment of solar power would cause substantial environmental impacts and would temporarily *increase* CO$_2$ emissions compared to pursuing nuclear energy.

Today's solar photovoltaic systems are more than $15,000 per kilowatt (compared to estimated cost for ordering a new coal or nuclear plant of about $1,100 and $1,800 per kilowatt, respectively).

The most optimistic goal for solar cells (yet-to-be achieved) would bring capital costs down to about $4,000 per kilowatt, still too expensive for a power plant.

The largest environmental impact associated with the widespread use of solar energy would be the substantial increase in land use. When all aspects of the fuel cycle are taken into account (i.e., including mining, waste disposal, etc.), solar electricity requires about 30 times more land per unit of power delivered than does nuclear energy.

Large amounts of land are already required to meet energy needs. Note that for every square mile of land currently occupied by buildings, cities, residences, and industries, an additional one to two square miles are required to extract, convert, deliver, and manage total energy needs.

"Increasing the demand for natural gas to mitigate CO_2 emissions... will likely exceed domestic supply and require increasing imports by the early 1990s."

Whether solar, hydro, or nuclear facilities are built to produce energy, all require the use of steel, concrete, and other metals. Since the production of metals and concrete result in substantial CO_2 emissions, the quantity of these materials required will determine the amount of carbon dioxide that will be added to the atmosphere just to build these power plants.

Because solar energy is so diffuse and so much land must be covered, solar plants require 15 times more concrete and metal than do nuclear plants (for equal energy delivered). Thus, a large commitment to building solar facilities would add substantially more carbon dioxide to the atmosphere than an equivalent nuclear construction program. (Note that hydro facilities require about four times as much concrete and metal as do nuclear plants, per unit of energy delivered.)

Natural Gas

Burning natural gas results in the lowest CO_2 emissions per unit of energy of all the fossil fuels. However, greatly expanded use of natural gas would likely exceed domestic supply, leading to increased imports and trade imbalances. Increasing production from non-conventional, domestic natural gas sources would be costly.

Current projections for future gas consumption do not incorporate any assumptions about fuel switching to gas to reduce CO_2 emissions and the associated increased gas demand this would entail. While natural gas is the cleanest burning fossil fuel,

it does emit nitrogen oxides (one of the other greenhouse gases and sources of acid rain). Considerable uncertainty also surrounds the greenhouse impact caused by leakage of unburned natural gas (methane).

Current projections are for gas use to increase 16% by 2010. Projections also show a 31% decline in conventional, low-cost domestic gas production. New supplies of gas are projected to come primarily from the following sources: 62% from advanced-technology gas, 19% from imports, 16% from a new Alaska pipeline from the gas fields on Alaska's North Slope. Projections for the availability of advanced-technology gas are premised on higher gas prices (triple today's prices in inflation-adjusted terms), and new initiatives. Cost estimates for the proposed Alaskan Natural Gas Transportation System (from 1982 when the pipeline from the North Slope of Alaska through Canada was considered) ranged from about $50 to $60 billion, which is why natural gas from Alaska's North Slope will be three or four times the cost of domestic gas from the lower 48 states.

Gas Research Institute energy projections assume electricity demand will grow at 1.9% per year. Growth in electric demand averaged about twice this level from 1984 to 1989, and was 4.6% in 1988, and about 2.4% in 1989. Increasing the demand for natural gas to mitigate CO_2 emissions, or to meet growth in electric demand greater than 1.9% per year, will likely exceed domestic supply and require increasing imports by the early 1990s.

Science Concepts, Inc. is a Washington, D.C.-based consulting firm specializing in information development, policy analysis, and communications strategy in the area of energy, resources, and science and technology.

"The risk of climatic change ... cannot be avoided or even significantly reduced through a worldwide expansion of nuclear energy."

viewpoint 37

Nuclear Power Cannot Alleviate the Greenhouse Effect

Donella H. Meadows, Henning Rodhe, and Anders Bjorkstrom

Editor's note: The following viewpoint is in two parts. Part I is by Donella H. Meadows and Part II is by Henning Rodhe and Anders Bjorkstrom.

I

To the proponents of nuclear power, [the 1988] drought is one of the best things that could have happened.

Their logic goes like this. The drought is widely perceived to be a first sign of the greenhouse effect—the global warming caused by a buildup of atmospheric pollutants. Primary among those pollutants is carbon dioxide, which comes from the burning of coal, oil and gas. Nuclear power produces no carbon dioxide. Therefore, to prevent more and worse droughts, sea-level rises, floods and other climatic horrors, we should nuclearize in a big way.

The media have been captivated by this reasoning; recent news-magazine pieces on the greenhouse effect cited nuclear power as the only major energy source that might replace fossil-fuel plants. The problem with this apparently obvious conclusion is that, like many apparently obvious conclusions, it doesn't hold up when you run out the numbers. What does add up, rather than fission, is efficiency of design—a solution that is at once cheaper and more all-inclusive than nuclear energy.

Filling the Breach

Bill Keepin and Gregory Kats, energy analysts at Rocky Mountain Institute in Old Snowmass, Colorado, have figured out exactly what it would take for nuclear power to "fill the breach." They start by supposing that the world's nations come to an unprecedented agreement to replace all current and future uses for coal with nuclear power, and to accomplish that within 40 years. (They choose coal,

rather than oil and gas, because coal is the greatest carbon-emitter of all the fossil fuels, and because nuclear can substitute directly for coal's major use, which is making electricity.) The two analysts also make the deliberately optimistic assumption that it will take only six years to build each nuclear plant and that the cost will be $1,000 per installed kilowatt capacity (which is the reported current cost in France; in the United States the cost is three times higher.)

If the world's energy demand grows at the top of the range of present forecasts, it will increase by 3.5 times between now and 2025. Under that scenario, Keepin and Kats calculate that a substitution of nuclear for coal would require bringing on nuclear power approximately equal to all the world's current energy production. By 2025 the world would need 8,000 large nuclear plants, as opposed to the 350 operating today. New plants would have to come on line at an average rate of one every 1.6 days, at an average cost of $787 billion per year, for 38 years.

Even with this enormous increase in nuclear power, carbon dioxide emissions would grow to be 65 percent higher than they are now. Greenhouse warming would be rampant, and the drought of '88 would probably look like a cool spell.

If energy demand goes up at a slower rate—doubling by 2025—and again nuclear energy was systematically substituted for coal, one new nuclear plant would be required every 2.4 days, at a cost of $525 billion annually. To pay for their share of this buildup, the Third World nations would have to double their current levels of debt (never mind the problem that no one would lend them that much). There would be 18 times as many nuclear plants as there are today. Carbon dioxide emissions would grow until the turn of the century and then slowly fall, but at all times they would be higher than they are now. The greenhouse effect would go on getting worse.

Donella H. Meadows, "Nuclear Power Is Not an Atomic Cure for the Greenhouse Effect," *St. Paul Pioneer Press Dispatch,* August 4, 1988. Reprinted with permission. Henning Rodhe and Anders Bjorkstrom, "How Would Closing Nuclear Plants Affect Climate?" *Forum for Applied Research and Public Policy,* Fall 1988. Reprinted with permission.

Why is nuclear power so ineffective in combating greenhouse warming in these calculations? Because it only provides electricity, which accounts for only one-third of fossil-fuel use. Because fossil-fuel use accounts for only about half of the greenhouse problem—the rest comes from deforestation and from gases other than carbon dioxide. And because even with generous assumptions about construction times and cost, nuclear generation starts from too low a base and takes too much time and money to take over a major part of world energy production.

The massive buildups of nuclear power assumed in the Keepin and Kats calculations could never really happen. Construction times of U.S. plants are more like 12 years than six. Costs around the world are typically two, three, even five times higher than Keepin and Kats assumed. Even if the managerial capacity were available to construct so many plants so fast, the drain of that much capital into nuclear construction would slow or stop the very economic growth that is assumed to require so much power in the first place. And of course the problems of nuclear power—high cost, intractable and dangerous wastes, evacuation planning, threats to public health, decommissioning, diversion of materials into bombs, vulnerability to terrorism, and political unpopularity—all those problems would escalate.

Now for the good news. There are energy scenarios—much easier and cheaper than the high-nuclear ones—that can greatly ameliorate greenhouse warming. They all involve state-of-the-art design to meet energy needs in the most efficient way possible. That doesn't mean what most people think of as conservation—cold rooms, warm beer and general deprivation. It means efficiency—being smart about warming the rooms and cooling the beer, so as to use the least possible amount of energy for the purpose.

"Even with generous assumptions about construction times and cost, nuclear generation starts from too low a base and takes too much time and money to take over a major part of world energy production."

Most efficiency improvements are fast and cheap compared with nuclear power and, unlike nuclear, they apply to every kind of energy use, including transportation. For example, just changing all the light bulbs in America to the most efficient ones now available could shut down at least 40 large coal-fired power plants and save the nation $10 billion a year, an Electric Power Research Institute study concluded.

New office buildings could be constructed in the most energy-efficient way at no increased cost, and over 50 years they would save the equivalent of 85 power plants and two Alaska oil pipelines, Keepin and Kats showed.

If the average fleet efficiency of U.S. cars doubled from the present 18 miles per gallon to 36, automobile carbon emissions could be cut in half (and another half if the fleet reached the 78 mpg of some current five-passenger full-size test vehicles). That could be accomplished within one or two turnover times of the fleet—12 to 24 years—at no cost, and as a side benefit there would be large reductions in urban air pollution and acid rain.

A number of studies have worked out the possible results of a major global commitment to energy efficiency. According to one, the industrialized nations could maintain annual gross-national-product growth rates of 1 percent-2 percent per year and still cut per capita energy use in half. The developing countries could sustain substantial rates of economic growth while holding per capita energy demand at nearly today's rates. The result would be a slight decline in carbon emissions from today's levels. Add a shift to solar energy, stop deforestation and start reforestation, and the greenhouse problem could be reduced dramatically.

Too Expensive

Nuclear power advocates will be quick to point out that nuclear could be added to a conservation scenario to reduce carbon emissions even further. Keepin and Kats do a calculation assuming a sixfold expansion of nuclear power by 2025 (a new plant every 7.5 days at an annual cost of $178 billion) in addition to a major commitment to energy efficiency. In that scenario, carbon emissions are about half of what they are today. About 38 percent of that reduction is due to nuclear substitution for coal.

Which is not, however, an argument for adding nuclear power to the list of possible solutions to the global warming problem, primarily because nuclear is so enormously expensive that it drains money away from better options. At current U.S. costs for nuclear and for efficiency, a dollar spent on efficiency displaces nearly seven times as much carbon as a dollar spent on nuclear, does it sooner and does not generate long-lived radioactive wastes.

Since the same dollar can't be spent twice, it makes much more sense for both environmental and economic reasons to spend it on efficiency. There are so many leaks to plug in the American energy system that efficiency will continue to be our most economic energy option for decades to come—and during that time, solar options, whose costs are already dropping rapidly, will probably become competitive with nuclear.

Some people are so bedazzled by nuclear power (usually because their own finances or status depend on it) that they can think of only one answer to any energy problem. They understate the limitations of nuclear energy (its cost, long lead times, unwieldiness, dangers and wastes), they assume it can produce miracles without stopping to figure the cost of those miracles and they don't see other choices at all. Those of us with no particular stake in the nuclear industry don't need to be so narrow-minded. We don't have to worry about the false dilemma of nuclear power versus global climate change (live near a nuke or turn your grain belt into a desert—you pick). There are other choices that are quicker, cheaper, less environmentally destructive—and much easier to live with.

II

How would an early closing of all the world's nuclear plants affect global climate? The issue has significant policy and environmental implications. The pollutants created by other energy sources (most notably, fossil fuels) used to replace nuclear power could increase the presence of greenhouse gases. This could raise global temperatures. It is probable, however, that a switch from nuclear energy to other energy sources will have no discernible impact on the climate.

Estimates have been made of how global emissions of greenhouse gases would affect the average temperature at the earth's surface (as well as how such changes likely would vary with latitude). However, it is not yet possible to make precise predictions of the changes that can be expected in specific areas.

This study considers greenhouse gas emissions to 2025, or about 37 years into the future (see Table 1). Scenarios for emissions further into the future are too hypothetical and uncertain to be meaningful.

Table 1
Estimated Contributions to Increase in Earth's Temperature 1980 to 2030

Carbon dioxide (CO_2)	0.71°C
CFC-11 ($CFCl_3$)	0.24
CFC-12 (CF_2Cl_2)	0.12
Methane (CH_4)	0.14
Nitrous oxide (N_2O)	0.09
Ozone (O_3)	0.15
Other gases	0.05
TOTAL	1.50

A large part of the gases in question accumulate in the atmosphere. Consequently, the degree of climatic change at a given time is determined primarily by total emissions to that time, rather than by emissions during a particular year.

Most gases that affect climate have a sufficiently long residence time in the atmosphere to become thoroughly mixed over the entire earth. Consequently, emissions have the same ultimate effect regardless of where they occur, which means that total emissions is the factor that determines the degree of climatic change.

Projecting the impact that terminating nuclear power production worldwide would have on global climate depends largely on how much nuclear energy one assumes the world will produce through 2025. Such assumptions are complicated by changing public attitudes toward nuclear power and the considerable uncertainty about the construction of new nuclear energy plants.

This study thus considers scenarios for both high and low energy consumption. It is far from certain that fossil fuels would replace shut down or unbuilt nuclear power plants. Particularly in a longer time frame (more than 20 years), a large part of nuclear power may be replaced by more efficient energy use and by other energy sources. In the scenario for high energy consumption, it is nonetheless assumed that only fossil fuels will replace nuclear power.

High Energy Consumption Scenario

Several scenarios of the world's future energy consumption have been drawn. For nuclear power, estimates for total output in the 2020s vary from about 0.7 billion to five billion killowatt-years per year. (A billion kilowatt-year of electric power equals 8,760 billion kilowatthours). Worldwide, in 1985, about 0.2 billion kilowatt-years of nuclear-powered electricity was generated. In this study, we conclude that more than 1 billion kilowatts of nuclear-powered electricity, or a five-fold increase to the 2020s, is unlikely. As an upper limit for nuclear power use, an increase between 0.2 billion to one billion kilowatts between 1980 and 2025 is assumed. Such an increase would require, at a maximum, more than 1,800 nuclear power plants by 2025, compared with about 400 plants today.

If the increase is assumed to be linear in time, the average rate during this period will be 0.6 billion kilowatts. This implies a total production of about 240,000 billion kilowatthours of electricity.

The production of 240,000 billion kilowatthours, using oil-fired plants, will release 160 billion tons of carbon dioxide into the air. Using coal rather than oil as the basis for the calculations, the contribution would be somewhat greater—about 180 billion tons. Because no more than one-half of these emissions could be expected to accumulate in the atmosphere (the ocean and the plants would absorb the rest), the contribution to the carbon dioxide increase in the atmosphere would be about 90 billion tons.

How much would an additional 90 billion tons of carbon dioxide raise the global temperature? The warming due to carbon dioxide in Table 1 (0.7°C) is for an increase of 340 to 450 parts per million by volume, or from 2,700 to 3,500 billion tons of carbon dioxide. Calibrating a logarithmic equation to these numbers, we find that an additional 90 billion tons of carbon dioxide in the atmosphere will raise the global mean temperature between 0.07°C and 0.09°C.

Carbon dioxide is not the only "greenhouse gas" emitted when fossil fuels are burned, however. Emissions of methane and nitrous oxide from the burning of fossil fuels also will contribute to an increase in temperature, which at most is projected to be 20 percent of that caused by carbon dioxide during the same 37-year period. The total increase in temperature then would be no more than 0.11°C.

Increased concentrations of methane and nitrous oxide affect the atmosphere in more ways than a direct greenhouse effect. Methane contributes to an *increase* in the ozone concentration in the troposphere and the lower stratosphere, while carbon dioxide and nitrous oxide contributes to a *decrease* in the ozone concentration in the stratosphere. Increasing levels of carbon dioxide will lead to an increase in stratospheric temperatures which, in turn, will increase the ozone concentrations at these levels. The climatic impact of these changes probably would not exceed +0.02°C.

"Most efficiency improvements are fast and cheap compared with nuclear power and, unlike nuclear, they apply to every kind of energy use, including transportation."

As a lower limit for how much nuclear energy will be produced during the next 37 years, consider the case in which average annual usage corresponds to the 1985 level. The total amount of energy produced to 2020 would be one-third of the high energy scenario, and would result in a maximum increase in the average global temperature of about 0.04°C—if nuclear power were replaced entirely by coal.

Although it is desirable from a climatic perspective to avoid all burning of fossil fuels, the impact on the global environment of replacing current nuclear power production with fossil fuels would be slight. Calculations show that a total cessation of a projected large-scale global nuclear power program (five times current production by 2025) would increase the average global temperature by about 0.1°C—if all proposed plants were replaced entirely by fossil fuels. Such a change in temperature is not entirely negligible, but it is much less than the increase expected to occur in any case by 2030 (1.5°C according to one group of experts).

Thus, the probability of reducing climatic changes in the foreseeable future cannot be advanced, or even noticeably lessened, through a major worldwide expansion of nuclear power. Consequently, any effort to use the climate issue to advocate an expansion of nuclear power production must be qualified.

What measures then should be taken to solve the climate problem? People already affect the earth's climate and their impact will increase during the coming decades, due to a lack of planning and effective global strategies to deal with this problem.

Therefore, we must determine how we can limit the impact of people on the global climate. It can be seen in Table 1 that carbon dioxide emissions are expected to account for about one-half of the estimated effect on climate to 2030. A large part of carbon dioxide emissions comes from the burning of fossil fuels. These emissions can be reduced by more efficient energy use and by using other energy sources. Renewable energy sources are of great potential value in the long term.

Other Greenhouse Gases

The other half of the estimated climatic impact is related to emissions from agriculture and forestry (methane, nitrous oxide, and some carbon dioxide) and from industrial processes (primarily the production of chlorofluorocarbons). The total impact on climate can only be lessened by rigorously limiting these emissions as well.

It is interesting to note that a phaseout of chlorofluorocarbons would have a greater impact on the greenhouse effect than a substantial expansion of present nuclear energy programs at the expense of fossil fuels. Similarly, a reduction of the methane emission from waste dumps would reduce the risk of climate change significantly. . . .

If all the world's nuclear power were replaced by fossil fuels, the average global temperature in 2025 would increase by about 0.1°C. This figure can be compared with an estimated total increase in temperature in 2030 of about 1.5°C due to emissions from fossil fuel combustion and from certain industrial processes, agriculture, and forestry.

The risk of climatic change, therefore, cannot be avoided or even significantly reduced through a worldwide expansion of nuclear energy. To limit future climatic changes, significant reductions are required in the use of fossil fuels, which would reduce carbon dioxide emissions, and in emissions of other gases from industrial processes, forestry, and agriculture.

Donella H. Meadows is an adjunct professor of environmental and policy studies at Dartmouth College in New Hampshire. Henning Rodhe is a professor and Anders Bjorkstrom a research associate at the University of Stockholm's Department of Meteorology in Sweden.

viewpoint 38

Government Can Alleviate the Greenhouse Effect

Christopher Flavin

National goals to limit emissions of the four main greenhouse gases—carbon dioxide, CFCs [chlorofluorocarbons], methane, and nitrous oxide—are among the most important features of any meaningful global warming strategy. Beyond establishing goals, however, it is important that credible policies be put in place to achieve them, including giving the relevant government agencies responsibility to implement appropriate measures. It is also important to assess progress on an annual basis and, if necessary, make appropriate adjustments.

In the energy arena, those strategies would almost certainly be centered around efficiency and renewables, which will help reduce emissions of methane and nitrous oxide as well as carbon dioxide. Accelerating their development will mean the enactment of a comprehensive package of policies, some local, some national, and still others at the international level. In appraising options it is important to choose those that make economic sense in their own right or help solve other costly problems such as land degradation or air pollution. Unless cost-effective strategies are pursued, nations will go bankrupt long before they stabilize the climate. In Canada, a major government-supported report found that while a 20-percent reduction in carbon emissions could cost the government $108 billion, it would save consumers $192 billion.

The first step is to reverse the policies that bias many countries toward increasing reliance on fossil fuels. Tax codes, research and development programs, and other measures often frustrate efforts to stabilize the climate. In the United States, for example, $2.3 billion is slated to go into "clean coal" research—a program that would move the country

toward even higher levels of carbon emissions. And the 1989 proposal by the Bush administration to develop methanol fuel could commit the U.S. automobile fleet to a highly carbon-intensive fuel source well into the next century.

There is a pressing need to end such counterproductive programs and to develop energy policies that will address various energy and environmental issues in a complementary way. One example is the program developed by the South Coast Air Quality Management District to clean up southern California's air by early in the next century, in part by phasing out gasoline and revamping the region's transportation system. Although global warming played no role in the formulation of the plan, which is aimed at meeting air pollution goals, officials later calculated that it would have as a side benefit a 20-percent reduction in regional carbon emissions.

The Carbon Tax

A key priority is levying a "carbon tax" on fossil fuels. Such a tax would allow market economies to consider the now uncounted global environmental damage that results from fossil fuel combustion. A carbon tax would encourage individuals and companies to choose fuels based on their relative contribution to global warming. Coal would be taxed the highest, oil would be next, and natural gas would follow. Renewable energy sources that do not contribute to the buildup of carbon dioxide would not be taxed at all. A carbon tax has been proposed by Great Britain's environment secretary and is now under discussion internationally.

Picking the correct tax is a complicated exercise. One way of determining the appropriate level is to assess the environmental costs of using a particular fuel, then internalize those costs through taxes. (Beyond global warming, the benefits of reduced air pollution that would come from lowering fossil fuel

Christopher Flavin, "Slowing Global Warming," *Worldwatch Paper 91*, October 1989. Reprinted with permission from Worldwatch Institute.

consumption should be considered in determining such a tax.) Yet, there are no reliable estimates of how much climate change will cost the international economy. Many scientists doubt whether accurate projections of such costs will ever be possible. Suffice it to say that the potential is enormous, likely mounting to the hundreds of billions of dollars. Among human-caused events, only wars are of comparable magnitude.

The most practical approach to establishing the size of a carbon tax is to calculate the costs of limiting emissions, which are almost certainly lower than the possible future costs of warming. Figures developed suggest that large-scale strategies to reduce carbon will cost a minimum of $50 per ton. This in effect represents the cost of avoiding climate change and could be incorporated in the price of fuels. Ideally, such taxes should be agreed on internationally, so that the additional costs do not hit different economies disproportionately. The revenues could be used in part to offset other taxes and in part to develop permanent and stable funding for improving energy efficiency and developing renewable energy sources. It would also make sense to set aside a portion of the funds to help developing countries pay for reforestation and energy efficiency programs. This would, in the words of West Germany's Social Democratic Party, which favors such a tax, "provide an ecological redistribution of taxes."

"A gradually levied carbon tax would avoid the dislocations caused by the OPEC price hikes while encouraging the world to get back onto a course of declining carbon emissions."

If a tax of $50 per ton of carbon were levied worldwide, the total revenues would amount to $280 billion a year. In the United States alone, they would equal about $60 billion ($240 per person); in India the tax would come to $7.5 billion ($9 per person). A tax at this level would raise the price of gasoline by 17 cents a gallon and of electricity by 28 percent. Such a tax—roughly equivalent to the difference between total world energy costs in the early eighties and those today—would spur a surge in efficiency investments similar to the one that led to enormous economic benefits over the last decade. A gradually levied carbon tax would avoid the dislocations caused by the OPEC price hikes while encouraging the world to get back onto a course of declining carbon emissions.

Stepped-up research and development is also essential. Although governments have supported efficiency and renewable technologies for over a decade, their commitment has been inconsistent. This is particularly true in the United States, where research and development budgets for renewables and efficiency soared in the late seventies and then were cut by four-fifths between 1981 and 1988. Despite these reductions, many new technologies, such as wind turbines, highly efficient fluorescent lighting systems, and new insulating materials, have entered the marketplace. The next step is to encourage more widespread use of these emerging technologies.

Closing the Payback Gap

Most of the progress so far in slowing growth in fossil fuel consumption has been stimulated by market forces. For energy efficiency to realize its full potential to revitalize economies and protect the environment, however, major institutional reforms will be needed. The most serious obstacle is what conservation professionals call the "payback gap." While energy producers look to new supply options with payback periods of up to twenty years, energy consumers, from homeowners to factory managers, rarely invest in efficiency measures with payback periods longer than two years. Legislation that encourages consumers to make longer-term investments—perhaps with the aid of utilities—would help close this gap.

Electric utilities can play a crucial role in overcoming these problems—supplying highly efficient bulbs instead of building more generators, for instance, as is already being done in some areas. Utilities are nonetheless probably the energy institutions most in need of reform, because they continue to operate outside the discipline of the market. Since the late seventies, many have been pushed by regulators and legislators to adopt conservation programs by a policy that mimics market forces, "least-cost planning." Using this approach, utilities invest in improving customers' efficiency as long as greater efficiency costs less than new supply. The cheapest options sell first in a market, and they are chosen first in least-cost planning.

Going a step further, a more competitive power industry would foster innovation and the development of technologies that are environmentally preferable. By opening the generation market to competitive bidding for all new power suppliers, policymakers can allow cogeneration and renewable energy projects to sell power to utilities at the "avoided cost" of new utility generation. Some regulators have also begun to include bids from companies that provide "saved energy" that can postpone or offset the construction of new generation facilities. A logical next step is to modify regulations so that utilities' rate of return can be increased when they lower the total economic and environmental costs to consumers by investing in improved efficiency—a win-win situation that ends the current bias toward ever greater electricity sales.

Market incentives are generally more efficient than legislated standards in encouraging change, but mandatory standards do have a role to play. They can ensure that the least efficient or most wasteful practices are eliminated, so that efficiency improvement does not bypass industries and markets where institutional impediments persist. Efficiency standards for automobiles, buildings, and appliances offer enormous energy savings while cutting down on pollution. For example, the 1986 appliance standards passed by the U.S. Congress will save $28 billion worth of electricity and gas and keep over 340 million tons of carbon out of the atmosphere by the turn of the century.

In the developing world, the challenge of raising sufficient funds to invest in efficiency is particularly severe. Already deeply in debt, most Third World countries are chronically short of capital and lack access to many of the highly efficient technologies developed during the eighties. One answer is to redirect a portion of the enormous flow of international lending currently devoted to building power plants and electric lines. This would free billions of dollars that could be invested in improving the efficiency of industry, transportation, and buildings. Recently, the World Bank has begun to consider major loans for improved efficiency, including a proposed $1 billion loan to China. . . .

Curbing CFC Releases

Chlorofluorocarbons, an important class of modern industrial chemicals, are responsible for an estimated 25 percent of the added greenhouse effect during the eighties. In the United States, which is the leading producer of CFCs, these chemicals make up 40 percent of the country's greenhouse emissions. In Japan, CFCs are responsible for over half the country's contribution. Moreover, while growth in the use of CFCs has slowed since the seventies, their concentration is expanding far more rapidly than any other greenhouse gas.

Eliminating CFCs will in some ways be the easiest element of a strategy to slow climate change, and a critical early test of worldwide commitment. Because CFCs are also responsible for depletion of the ozone layer in the stratosphere—which shields the earth from deadly ultraviolet radiation—efforts to limit their use are further along than for the other greenhouse gases. Beginning in the seventies, the United States banned the use of CFCs in aerosol sprays, and several nations followed suit. International efforts to restrict the use of CFCs began in the early eighties, spurred by growing evidence of ozone depletion. After years of negotiations, a large group of countries meeting in Montreal in 1987 agreed to freeze all production of CFCs immediately and cut output by 50 percent by 2000. While this agreement is rightly considered a landmark in environmental diplomacy, evidence has mounted that it is not sufficient to protect societies from ozone depletion or from CFC-induced global warming.

"Market incentives are generally more efficient than legislated standards in encouraging change, but mandatory standards do have a role to play."

It is estimated that, even under the Montreal Protocol, atmospheric concentrations of CFC-11 and CFC-12 will increase by 77 percent and 66 percent respectively by 2040. This could raise the greenhouse burden on the atmosphere by almost one-fifth, even if all the other greenhouse gases were stabilized. This large prospective increase is in part because the protocol makes exceptions for the countries that have lagged in CFC production, such as the Soviet Union and developing nations. This means that the actual emissions reductions by the year 2000 will be less than 40 percent. In addition, there are large quantities of CFCs already contained in refrigerators, air conditioners, and foam products that will gradually find their way into the atmosphere in the years ahead.

Immediate efforts to strengthen the Montreal Protocol and accelerate the elimination of CFCs are priorities in the global warming fight. Because there are already alternatives available for some of the uses of these chemicals, others are being developed rapidly, and technologies to keep them out of the atmosphere are well along, CFC releases can be curbed relatively painlessly. There has been a string of plans announced by corporations and governments to eliminate certain uses of the compounds. In the United States, AT&T has announced plans to switch to substitutes during the early nineties, and General Motors plans to recycle its CFCs. In Japan, Nissan and Seiko Epson have adopted similar policies. The governments of Norway and Sweden have plans to phase out nearly all uses of CFCs by 1994, and the Netherlands will do so by the year 2000. Meanwhile, the U.S. states of Rhode Island and Vermont will ban the use of car air conditioners containing these chemicals by 1992. Irvine, California, will eliminate most uses of CFCs in 1990.

International policymakers are not far behind. The Montreal Protocol included provisions for consideration of accelerating the elimination of CFCs if the evidence warranted. Today, that process has begun, given a boost by concern over global warming and data that indicate that ozone depletion is accelerating. In May 1989, some 82 nations signed the Helsinki Declaration, pledging in principle to phase out five CFCs strongly implicated in ozone depletion by 2000, if additional substitute chemicals are developed. For the first time, a large group of Third World countries was actively engaged in the process, enticed in part by the agreement of industrial nations to establish a fund to assist in obtaining substitutes. Scientists and policymakers are also discussing the need to ensure that the substitute chemicals do not have the heat-absorbing properties of today's CFCs. It may be another year or two before an adequate international CFC agreement is signed, but there is no time for delay. It is unconscionable to allow CFC concentrations to continue to build in the atmosphere when they are so clearly implicated in two of the world's most pressing environmental problems.

"It is unconscionable to allow CFC concentrations to continue to build in the atmosphere when they are so clearly implicated in two of the world's most pressing environmental problems."

It is encouraging that so many governments have begun to mobilize to slow global warming, not waiting for an international agreement to stabilize the climate. The initial wave of euphoria has already begun to fade, however, as many new proposals bog down in the legislative process. The global warming battle has effectively shifted from a blitzkrieg to trench warfare. It will take wide-ranging and sustained efforts at every level of society if this battle is ultimately to be won.

Christopher Flavin is vice president and senior researcher with the Worldwatch Institute, an environmentalist group in Washington, D.C. He is coauthor of Renewable Energy: The Power to Choose.

"If every American cut in half her or his yearly home energy consumption, each would also keep 7,000 pounds of carbon out of the atmosphere."

viewpoint 39

Citizens Can Alleviate the Greenhouse Effect

Dick Russell

Scenario one: *Dateline 2010*. American cities, largely absent of smog, are now lined with trees of numerous varieties. Homes and offices use one-quarter the amount of energy that they consumed only 21 years before, yet an efficiency-conscious economy has helped achieve even greater prosperity. Electric vehicles, powered primarily by the sun, cruise the streets, while the remaining gasoline-fed automobiles now get at least 50 and as many as 120 miles per gallon. Centers for the recycling of paper, aluminum, plastic and other products provide jobs for thousands of people. A network of small but productive farms operating without petrochemical pesticides or fertilizers dots the rural landscape. Public schools, churches and other organizations busily promote additional tree-planting efforts. Abroad, an "Ecology Corps," modeled after the Peace Corps of the '60s, assists in helping developing nations implement similar programs.

Scenario two: *Dateline 2010*. The output of carbon dioxide (CO_2) entering the atmosphere from the burning of coal, oil and natural gas has risen another 38 percent in only 21 years. Millions of lush acres of tropical rain forest that once provided the womb for countless lifeforms and stabilized the Earth's atmosphere by absorbing vast amounts of CO_2 now stand barren, fallen victim to developers. Increased temperatures and shifting weather patterns have transformed the most productive breadbaskets of the world into near-deserts. Around the globe millions are homeless, facing starvation and dying of disease. Nations ravaged by drought and sea level rises frantically seek food, shelter and water for their citizens. Yet no virgin frontiers remain, so there are none to escape to, none to exploit.

Our action or inaction will usher in one of these scenarios. Unfortunately, at the moment the smart money is on the latter. Continued widespread fossil fuel use will trigger nature's response to decades of neglect, and consequently "solve" what some view as the "population problem." Much of the Earth, its atmosphere overwhelmed by CO_2 and other human-produced "greenhouse gases," will face drastic temperature rises. Excessive use of these industrial and agricultural pollutants will transform much of our planetary home into a disaster area.

Scientists can't yet predict the exact time-table and, because the climate is so complex, may never be able to. But they concur that the fuse is already burning.

The hottest end of that fuse is our present addiction to fossil fuels. If the global appetite for burning coal, oil and natural gas continues at its current pace, the atmospheric CO_2 level—which had remained constant for thousands of years—will by the year 2050 be more than double what it was at the onset of the mid-19th century's "Industrial Revolution." Many experts say that unless fossil fuel use is curtailed by more than half around the world, the Earth will undergo temperature rises not experienced since the extinction of the dinosaurs. America is so dependent on fossil fuels that nearly 80 percent of the country's energy flows from their combustion.

Worldwide Mobilization

Altering this course, as Jeremy Rifkin of the Global Greenhouse Network says, "will require an enormous shift in economic, military and political priorities—a shift so extraordinary in scope that it will require a worldwide mobilization effort on a scale never before experienced." Such a shift is not going to occur without massive public education and commitment. Or, as Rep. Claudine Schneider (R-RI) succinctly told Congress, "We need to take personal responsibility for bringing about the change."

Dick Russell, "The Earth Needs You: Part Three of A Greenhouse Effect Series," *In These Times*, February 8-14, 1989. Reprinted with permission from *In These Times*, a weekly newspaper published in Chicago.

How do we begin to work our way out of this mess? Consider the following:

• The U.S. (23 percent) and the Soviet Union (21 percent) are responsible for nearly half of the CO_2 entering the atmosphere from the burning of fossil fuels. In 1988 the U.S. added 1.3 billion tons of carbon to the atmosphere. That was five tons per American.

• The amount of energy wasted annually in the U.S. costs Americans more than the current military budget of about $10,000 per second, or more than $300 billion a year, which is about twice the annual federal budget deficit.

"For homeowners, some energy-saving steps are as simple as turning off lights and TV sets when they're not being used."

• Generation of electricity by power stations produces one-third of the CO_2 emissions in the U.S. But as much energy escapes through American windows as flows through the Alaskan oil pipeline. Buildings use about one-third of the total energy consumed by industrial nations. The technology is now available to construct buildings or convert existing ones that would save enough energy in 50 years to avoid erecting 85 power plants and the equivalent of two Alaskan pipelines.

• About 80 percent of the potential of energy efficiency has yet to be utilized. Studies indicate that efficiency improvements alone could slice in half the projected contribution to global warming from fossil fuel burning by 2050.

• The Department of Energy (DOE) has calculated that 75 percent of the country's projected energy needs by the year 2010 could be economically extracted from such renewable sources as solar, wind, biomass, geothermal and hydropower.

• Transportation ranks a close second to electricity as a CO_2 producer. The average American automobile pumps its own weight in carbon into the atmosphere every year. That adds up to about 200 million tons a year. One out of every six barrels of oil in the world is consumed by passenger cars. The Reagan administration's 1986 lowering of fuel-efficiency standards for new vehicles from 27.5 to 26 miles per gallon has wasted as much oil per year as the federal government hopes to extract from beneath the Arctic National Wildlife Refuge. Increasing the typical car's fuel efficiency to 50 miles per gallon would cut in half the auto-generated CO_2 entering the atmosphere—and, coincidentally, lower the average American's yearly gas-pump bill by about $200 at current prices.

• If all the nation's farmers switched to organic farming methods the soil would stop losing carbon. Instead, it would take so much carbon out of the air that it would roughly balance the total emissions from an efficient American car fleet.

• Thousands of acres of Central American rain forest have been cleared for cattle production, with 90 percent of the beef exported to the U.S., primarily for use in processed foods and pet food and by some fast-food chains. The loss of these forests pours tons of CO_2 into the air. And each cow raised on that land emits 200 to 400 quarts per day of methane, another of the major gases adding to the greenhouse effect. Until recently the restaurant chain McDonald's packaged its products in 1.7 billion cubic feet per year of non-biodegradable styrofoam, made from chlorofluorocarbons (CFCs) whose production also adds to global warming and destroys the stratospheric ozone layer.

• Recovering and recycling the print run of a single edition of the Sunday *New York Times* would leave 75,000 trees standing and continuously reabsorbing, not releasing, more carbon dioxide.

• A can of diet soda offers a single kilocalorie of food energy, yet it takes nearly 2,200 kilocalories of fossil fuel energy to replace instead of recycle the aluminum container.

These staggering statistics, drawn from a variety of sources, clearly point toward alternatives: more efficient use of existing forms of energy, wider use of renewable energy sources and more recycling, less gasoline, less feed-lot-raised beef and less tree-cutting. What makes sense in tackling the greenhouse effect also alleviates just about every other environmental ill, from acid rain to the garbage crisis. It also makes good pocketbook sense. Saving the planet for future generations is not only life-effective, but cost-effective.

Efficient Energy Use

After mortgage or rent, Americans' largest household expense is fuel, which averages about $1,100 a year. A 25 percent reduction in energy use, however, would save about $25 billion annually. It would also make housing more affordable for some two million households, half of them low-income families. These were among the conclusions of a report issued in June 1988 by the Alliance to Save Energy, a coalition of business, government and consumer organizations.

If every American cut in half her or his yearly home energy consumption, each would also keep 7,000 pounds of carbon out of the atmosphere, the Worldwatch Institute has calculated.

The notion of energy efficiency is not new. Long before the greenhouse effect triggered the alarm about the profligate use of energy, the Arab oil embargo and OPEC price hikes of the '70s brought energy efficiency into the American consciousness. At first the electric utility companies scoffed at the ideas of Amory Lovins, Arthur Rosenfeld and other "prophets" of efficiency. The gross national product, the skeptics said, was inextricably tied to growth in energy consumption. Yet in 1986, according to DOE statistics, the nation used only slightly more energy than it did in 1974—while the economy grew by 35 percent during that period.

Greater Efficiency Potential

Yet due partly to the drop in foreign oil prices, energy use has been climbing, up by about 7 percent in the first half of 1988. Nonetheless, improvements in lighting fixtures, windows, insulation, cars and appliances over the past 15 years now save the U.S. about $160 billion annually in energy costs. And the potential for far greater efficiency has only begun to be tapped. For homeowners, some energy saving steps are as simple as turning off lights and TV sets when they're not being used. Others involve an initial outlay of money, but soon pay for themselves. The following are ways to reduce your energy consumption:

Insulation. The total number of cracks and holes in the average house allows to escape about as much energy as a constantly open window, and many office buildings are even less efficient. But now-available "superinsulation" includes an airtight liner in the walls and can more than double a building's insulating capacity. Such airtight buildings can be both efficient and healthful if they are fitted with controlled ventilation that recovers most of the outgoing air. While it does add about 5 percent to the building costs, superinsulation pays for itself in five years in saved energy.

Windows. New "superwindows," which feature heat-reflective film applied to or suspended between window panes, can now insulate three to six times as well as double-glazed windows. Experts claim that windows already can insulate as well as most walls.

Lighting. Compact fluorescent 18-watt lightbulbs can now replace 75-watt incandescent ones and most other sizes. Although many hardware stores don't carry them because of their higher price, the fluorescents in the long run save substantially on electric bills. They last 10 times as long and, according to Lovins, one of these compact bulbs avoids the emission of a ton of CO_2 over its lifetime. New lighting technologies could cut projected carbon emissions by 93 million tons by the year 2010.

Appliances. If every refrigerator in the country were replaced with the best of the mass-produced models, it would be the equivalent of idling 20 coal-fired generating plants. The most efficient new furnaces and air conditioners also use half the energy of the majority of models in use—but even already installed units can be improved as much as one-third. And the Worldwatch Institute recommends a simple practice to relieve energy-guzzling by home air conditioners: plant mature shade trees on the south side of your house.

Home heating. According to the Environmental Action organization, some 18 percent of U.S. CO_2 emissions comes from home systems that burn fossil fuels for cooking, heating and hot water (rather than using electricity). Because an oil-fired system tends to put out more CO_2 than a gas-fired furnace, it must be thoroughly cleaned and tuned each year. This should include vacuuming the heat-exchanging surfaces, replacing the burner nozzle (which should be as small as possible), and a thorough efficiency test (CO_2 percent should be 11).

Other nations, particularly Japan and West Germany, are much more energy-efficient than the U.S. They use half as much energy to produce goods and services (per dollar of GNP), giving them an automatic cost advantage. "If this country were to become as energy-efficient as Japan," notes a study by two public interest groups, Public Citizen and the Safe Energy Communication Council, "it would save $220 billion per year at a cost of only $50 billion per year. The $170 billion difference is about the size of the U.S. [annual] trade and budget deficits."

American electric utilities, prodded by environmental groups, are beginning to take heed. For some time utilities have offered information to their customers about money-saving efficiency investments. But only recently have power companies begun implementing their own "least-cost planning." In Hood River, Ore., the Natural Resources Defense Council teamed up with utility experts in 1981 to kick off a program in which the local electric company installed superinsulating equipment in nearly 3,000 homes. The movement peaked in 1984 when eight California investor-owned utilities spent almost $400 million on energy conservation and load-management programs.

"Many people have already cut down on their electric costs—and kept CO_2 out of the air—by installing their own solar collectors to convert the sun's rays into immediately useful energy."

In New England, which lately has experienced the most rapid electrical-demand growth in the country, local utilities recently inaugurated the nation's most sophisticated efficiency program. Spurred by the Boston-based Conservation Law Foundation, companies have begun spending millions on efficiency improvements rather than for more power generation. A utility plan for Connecticut filed in 1988 will offer customers free installation of weatherstripping and lightbulbs of quadrupled efficiency, subsidies for insulation, and free energy audits for houses, apartments and factories. The goal is to cut in half the state's anticipated growth in electrical demand. A similar effort is underway in Massachusetts.

The Environmental Defense Fund (EDF) proposes that the federal government require utilities planning to expand capacity to reduce their total CO_2 emissions by the same amount that would be produced by adding the new capacity. Presently utilities are planning to build enough additional fossil fuel-powered plants to generate 25,000 megawatts of electricity between now and 1996. According to EDF economist Daniel Dudek, it would take at least 10 million acres of new American forests to absorb the additional CO_2, an area roughly twice the size of New Jersey. Thus far one of the most attractive ways to offset the CO_2 increase, says Dudek, would be to have utilities cooperate with the government under the Conservation Reserve Program (CRP) by paying farmers to plant trees on more of their erodible cropland.

It's a novel idea. The CRP was established by the U.S. Department of Agriculture in 1985, aiming to convert about 40 million to 45 million acres of farmland that are vulnerable to erosion into grassland, orchards or woodland. Farmers in essence "rent" the land to the government. The CRP's goal was to reforest at least five million acres by 1990. But there has been no great rush to plant trees, perhaps because the incentives are too low. So far only about one-quarter of the goal has been achieved. If the utilities, however, upped the ante to farmers and they doubled the newly forested land to 10 million acres, it would cost the utilities between $1 billion and $2 billion—adding only 5.5 percent to the capital investment of a new power plant, Dudek projects.

Alternative Energy Sources

Proposals like EDF's, along with energy efficiency, go hand in hand with the need for intensified development of non-fossil fuel, renewable energy sources. William Chandler, a senior scientist at Pacific Northwest Labs, notes that an energy-efficient economy is much better suited to renewables. Buildings already designed for efficiency, for example, would require only small and affordable solar equipment rather than large and expensive installations.

Presently about 57 percent of the nation's electricity is generated from burning coal. Although it is the most readily available and cheapest fossil fuel, coal is also the dirtiest. It's the primary contributor to acid rain and the greenhouse effect. Coal-fired American utilities, according to the Electric Power Research Institute, account for 7.5 percent of the world's fossil fuel CO_2 output. Natural gas emits less carbon than coal or oil, and increasing its contribution is viewed by many

experts as a bridge away from reliance on the more polluting fossil fuels. The Worldwatch Institute is advocating a tax on carbon whereby coal would be taxed more heavily per unit of energy than natural gas. It suggests that the weatherization of buildings be financed through such a tax.

Roughly 18 percent of the U.S.' electrical capacity now comes from nuclear power plants, and a renewed nuclear thrust is being touted by government and industry as a global warming "solution." Yet aside from safety, proliferation and waste problems, nuclear power's construction costs are exorbitant and the lifespan of nuclear plants is short.

"Americans [are] . . . burning about 100 billion gallons of gasoline annually—and contributing about 13 percent of the global CO_2 that's destroying the atmosphere."

So what about solar, wind and other renewables? Already, despite huge cutbacks under Ronald Reagan for research and development, renewable sources provide close to 10 percent of the country's electricity. Hydropower systems convert the kinetic energy of flowing water into electrical or mechanical energy. Solar collectors absorb relatively low-temperature heat, then transfer it to a gaseous or liquid medium. Photovoltaic cells are thin layers of semiconductor material, usually silicon, that convert sunlight directly into electricity without any mechanical equipment. Wind turbines use the kinetic energy in wind to rotate a shaft linked to a generator. None of these emits carbon dioxide, though hydroelectric dams can pose other adverse effects for local ecosystems.

Many people have already cut down on their electric costs—and kept CO_2 out of the air—by installing their own solar collectors to convert the sun's rays into immediately useful energy. Solar hot water and space heating systems can make an inefficient building at least 40 percent more efficient. Auxiliary solar designs can be incorporated as well: south-facing glass and attached solar greenhouses, awnings or vegetation that regulate sunlight during summer and winter months, thick floors and walls, and natural ventilation, heat circulation and lighting. A well-designed solar home can reduce annual energy bills by a minimum of 75 percent.

Until now solar and other alternative energy sources have not been considered as reliable as conventional ones. Yet in recent years several analysts have demonstrated that, even on a mass scale, renewable sources used in combination could in fact be more reliable than fossil-produced electricity. Lovins summarized detailed technical studies in the November 1983 issue of the *Atlantic Monthly*: ''Stormy weather, bad for direct solar collection, is generally good for windmills and small hydropower plants; dry, sunny weather, bad for hydropower, is ideal for photovoltaics. A diversity of sources, each serving fewer and nearer users, would also greatly restrict the area blacked out if a grid connecting them failed. And when renewable energy sources do fail, they fail for shorter periods than do large power plants.''

Climate Protection Tax

Recent technological advances could make such renewables not only an environmentally sound, but also an economical wave of the future. Take photovoltaic cells, for example, whose cost has fallen 90 percent in the past decade. Most of the solar cells on the market convert only 8 to 13 percent of the sun's rays into electricity. But in 1988 Sandia National Laboratories in Albuquerque, N.M., achieved a goal long considered impossible. It built a photovoltaic cell capable of turning 31 percent of the light striking it into electric power. That is comparable to the 34 percent average efficiency of coal- and oil-fired power generators.

In California 16,000 wind-powered turbines now supply electricity to about 300,000 homes, resulting in 200,000 tons a year less in carbon emissions. New technology makes wind machines far more reliable and cost-effective. Where wind is abundant they can compete handily with fossil fuel power.

Another yet-to-be-harnessed power source is geothermal energy, or heat contained in the crust below the Earth's surface. A geothermal power plant would be designed to tap into this heat, bring it to the surface and release it to drive a turbine generator. The U.S. currently uses about 75 quads of energy annually; it's been estimated that 0.1 million quads of accessible geothermal resources lie primarily under the western third of the nation. But geothermal technology requires water for cooling and drilling, which is likely to become much scarcer in the West due to the greenhouse effect. And it would have to be carefully engineered to be environmentally sound, since salts, heavy metals and hydrogen sulfide would also be brought to the surface.

Someday hydrogen power may prove the ultimate renewable solution. While not an energy source itself, hydrogen can serve as a medium for other sources such as solar. It can be burned, much like natural gas, to provide industrial or space heat, or to generate steam to run electric turbines, and no CO_2 would be emitted.

Eventually hydrogen fuel might be used to power automobiles. Up to 45 percent more energy-efficient than gasoline, hydrogen can be derived from water through a process called electrolysis, which splits water into its basic components, hydrogen and oxygen. Since its combustion product is water vapor, hydrogen is essentially pollution-free.

But hydrogen's cost is exorbitant, and the Clean Energy Research Institute at the University of Miami figures that a full conversion to a hydrogen energy system would take 40 to 50 years. In the interim, what can be done about auto pollution? Besides being the biggest source of urban air toxics, motor vehicles add incredible amounts of CO_2, nitrous oxides and ozone (all greenhouse gases) to the atmosphere. At the end of World War II there were about 50 million cars, trucks and buses worldwide, while today close to 500 million vehicles clog the planet's streets. Americans own 35 percent of these, burning about 100 billion gallons of gasoline annually—and contributing about 13 percent of the global CO_2 that's destroying the atmosphere.

Here again, greater fuel efficiency is not only critical but immediately feasible. The current efficiency of the nation's cars and trucks averages about 18 miles per gallon (mpg). On average, each vehicle produces more than 57 tons of CO_2 during its lifetime. A bill introduced in Congress by Rep. Schneider would mandate minimum auto efficiency standards of 45 mpg within the next 10 years. In Europe and Japan a dozen prototypes get 60 mpg in the city and 80 mpg on the highway. (A 60-mpg car would emit only 17 tons of CO_2 over its average lifetime.) The best, a Renault, averages 78 mpg in the city and 107 mpg on the highway.

''The tremendous potential for recycling has scarcely begun to be tapped.''

Schneider's bill calls for tax rebates of up to $2,000 per car as an incentive for customers to buy more efficient vehicles. It also would increase the current ''gas-guzzler'' tax on high-powered, inefficient ones. Another proposal, put forward by the World Resources Institute in congressional testimony, is a dollar-per-gallon ''climate protection tax'' on gasoline. Presently, the combined federal, state and local fuel taxes total around 22 cents a gallon in the U.S. Americans get off easy compared to Brazil, Japan and most European countries, where gasoline taxes are four to six times higher.

The millions of dollars generated by such a gasoline tax could be earmarked for improvement of mass transit systems and for accelerated development of fuel alternatives to gasoline. Two alcohol-based fuels, methanol and ethanol, both produce fewer regulated pollutants than gasoline. But would they help substantially in reducing the greenhouse effect? Methanol can be derived from coal, natural gas or biomass (energy derived primarily from wood and agricultural wastes). Ethanol can be derived from soy or corn residue. But this type of fuel generation isn't cost-competitive with gasoline. The entire corn crop of the U.S., for example, could supply only one-fourth of the nation's fuel needs. Worldwide, however, enough corncobs and rice hulls are left over from crop production each year to produce 40 billion gallons of ethanol.

"It's simply cheaper not to burn all this fuel in the first place."

Electric vehicles, if their power is generated from renewable sources, may well be the best environmental bet for the future. The biggest obstacle to date for their large-scale distribution has been their lack of battery staying-power. Under current technology, standard lead-acid batteries in experimental vehicles have only a 60-mile range before they need recharging, which takes about eight hours. But a GM van, developed in conjunction with the Southern California Utility company, will go on the market. Able to hold a one-ton cargo or eight passengers, the van will have a top speed of 55 mph, and a two-hour daytime recharge can extend its range to 75 miles.

It could prove ideal for city driving. Though the current cost is about twice that of a conventional van, federal subsidies could help drive down the van's price. The DOE is preparing a van with a 100-mile range. And batteries are being developed that could more than double that range, while requiring less recharging time.

In November 1987 an innovator named Kenneth Kurtz displayed his sleek, three-wheel, open-cockpit electric car to some members of California's Senate Transportation Committee. Starting with a $200 wrecked Volkswagen, Kurtz spent more than five years developing the low, cone-shaped vehicle that he dubbed "Solar Wind." With a dashboard lined with solar cells, it can reach 70 mph speeds.

But until such new technologies become readily available, auto pollution remains a staggering problem. Some planners have gone so far as to suggest banning motor vehicles from areas of high population density, converting entirely to mass transit. Jobs, stores and residences would be more concentrated in revitalized city cores and along mass transit corridors.

Los Angeles, suffocating from the worst air pollution in the nation, has initiated strong measures along these lines. A 20-year air-quality plan contains strategies on how and where future businesses and housing developments may locate, with industrial growth being zoned in proximity to affordable housing. By 1990 all companies with more than 100

employees must offer tangible rewards aimed at persuading workers to car-pool, bus or bike to work.

Besides altering the ways and means of our transportation habits, we have to deal with our trash. Nationwide, in virtually every city and town, the remaining landfill volume capacity is dwindling, and careless past disposal has often severely polluted underground water and fouled the air. One "solution," huge municipal incinerators, is controversial because of its exorbitant costs and possible environmental liabilities. But the tremendous potential for recycling has scarcely begun to be tapped.

Consider what recycling means in terms of saved energy. An EPA [Environmental Protection Agency] study predicts that in the year 2000 the U.S. will landfill or incinerate 48.1 million tons of newsprint, corrugated cardboard, glass, plastic and aluminum. If those 48.1 million tons were recycled instead of tossed out, the National Appropriate Technology Assistance Service says, the nation would save the energy equivalent of 10.1 billion gallons of gasoline. . . .

Before It's Too Late

It is abundantly clear that we can do something about the greenhouse effect. More efficient uses of electrical power and automobile fuel are the obvious first steps. There may be scientific uncertainty about whether global warming is already upon us, but even if there were no greenhouse effect, greater efficiency would save consumers money, make the nation more competitive and improve our energy security.

"It's simply cheaper not to burn all this fuel in the first place," Amory Lovins summarizes. "It's really as if Americans were being offered a couple hundred billion dollars a year to avoid global warming."

But let there be no mistaking the immensity of the task ahead. For what is required amounts to a revolutionary change in the way our society has become accustomed to running. We must face squarely the fact that our civilization has wreaked havoc on the elements that sustain life—the water, the air, the Earth and its creatures. For much too long we have largely acquiesced to the industrialization of our food and energy processes that has brought about this situation.

Now the greenhouse effect looms like a descending curtain over all of us. We can choose to aggressively honor the natural cycles of life, or we can continue to ignore them. The second course, however, assures a future upheaval that will be unprecedented in human history.

Dick Russell writes regularly on environmental issues for In These Times, *a socialist newspaper in Chicago.*

"Business can indeed do its part to solve global warming."

Business Can Alleviate the Greenhouse Effect

Douglas G. Cogan

The year is 2089, the city, Los Angeles, and the basin's 25 million residents are returning to work and school after enduring six weeks of searing 95-degree heat. Yet the weather seems tolerable, compared to the record heat wave of a decade ago, when temperatures soared beyond 100 degrees for most of a summer. Now, like the rest of the world, Los Angeles is cooling off, thanks to sweeping measures instituted in the first half of the century to combat global warming. By the year 2200, give a decade or two, the climate is expected to return to the more favorable conditions of the late 20th century, when the rapid temperature rise was just getting underway.

Already, things are looking up for the City of Angels. There hasn't been a smog alert since that sweltering summer of 2079. The San Gabriel Mountains are visible again behind the city's gleaming skyline. And while the ocean has crept inland a quarter-mile because of a rise in sea level, the beaches are still a mecca for surfers and sun worshippers—who wear more sunscreen now, to ward off ultraviolet rays slipping through a depleted (but also healing) ozone layer.

For the last hundred years, the people of Los Angeles have managed somehow to roll with the punches dealt by Mother Nature and their own city officials. The first blows came in the form of incessant heat waves, smog alerts, and drought in the late 1980s. The municipality countered with an ambitious anti-pollution plan, which rocked the local economy more than the earthquakes of the early 21st century. Now area residents sense that the worst is behind them. Most are even willing to admit that the sacrifices required of them in the last

hundred years have turned out to be changes for the better.

Few can afford the privilege of driving a car to work any more, but average commuting time has been cut from three hours to less than an hour round-trip. With fewer smog alerts, there's more opportunity for exercise and leisure. In the suburbs around Los Angeles, desert flowers are blooming in place of well-tended lawns. That's saving enough water to fill thousands of swimming pools, and, liberated from yard work, people have more time to enjoy them. Even those expensive and ultra-efficient kitchen appliances are paying for themselves with big savings on utility bills—with enough money left over for an occasional night out.

The latest Gallup polls show the people of Los Angeles are more optimistic than ever. They take pride in the fact that their city was the first to overcome environmental problems once thought intractable. Today they describe Los Angeles as a pleasant place to live, and—in contrast to the surveys taken in 1989—a majority of residents now say they wouldn't consider moving elsewhere. Businesses have also stayed in Los Angeles, despite earlier fears that environmental regulations would drive them away. To the contrary, the city has become a major center for technologies and ideas that are leading the world into the 22nd century.

Implementing New Technology

Commerce in Los Angeles is booming. A tour of the region reveals countless examples of products and services for which vast new markets have opened. Covering the roofs of more than a million homes are photovoltaic panels by Westinghouse, Amoco, and Chronar. Inside homes, refrigerators bearing names like Amana, Whirlpool, and Frigidaire use a design that requires no electricity, only a small flame of natural gas to vaporize an ammonia working fluid (which pulls heat from the food

Douglas G. Cogan, "Can Business Solve Global Warming?" *Business Ethics*, September/October 1989. Reprinted with permission.

compartment as it condenses). And these 21st-century refrigerators have more storage space, since their walls are made of ultra-thin, energy-efficient, vacuum panel insulation.

Sears-Kenmore trash compactors are found in more kitchens than ever before. The new models not only crush garbage, they also separate plastic, paper, and glass, making it easier for residents to comply with solid waste ordinances. Waste Management dispatches waste-hauling trucks twice a week to bring household garbage to the local recycling plant. What can't be salvaged is burned in its 100-megawatt waste-to-energy complex.

"Industry could export . . . developing technologies to a world newly aware of its fragility."

Most living rooms are equipped with high-definition televisions made by Zenith, RCA, and Magnavox, which have screens the size of an entire wall, and contain built-in computers and telecommunications equipment. Auto use has become less and less necessary, now that families can order merchandise, "visit" relatives, and bank electronically from their homes.

Fully half the chores that used to require getting out of the house have been eliminated. Even commuting to work has changed dramatically. Companies as diverse as First Interstate Bank, Pacific Enterprises, and Hughes Aircraft now allow many white-collar employees to work at home, or in small satellite offices within walking distance of residential areas. Most other commuters take the basinwide, light-rail system at a cost subsidized by the city government.

Each morning, thousands of Los Angeles commuters still take to the freeways to get to work—but the freeways are no longer free. Commuters hitch up in computer-guided "trains" of automobiles and pay tolls according to the number of miles they travel. The local utility, Southern California Edison, tacks on an extra charge for the amount of energy consumed, since on the freeway cars are propelled by electric magnets instead of gasoline.

Once off the exit ramp, cars return to internal power sources. General Motors cars switch to photovoltaic and battery power packs, while Fords burn high-octane ethanol fuels. Parking anywhere in greater Los Angeles is an added expense these days, since a free-parking ban vent into effect in 2001.

For travel to San Diego or San Francisco, most people take the Amtrak bullet train, which whisks along an elevated track at 175 miles an hour. In the Antelope Valley outside Los Angeles, passengers gaze at a windfarm of hundreds of Zond Systems wind turbines that generate enough electricity to carry the train over a 4,000-foot mountain pass—and pump water from the California Aqueduct back from the other side. Beyond in the desert, thousands of acres of Luz International solar troughs generate electricity for export to cities and towns in the San Joaquin Valley.

Meanwhile, the cogeneration business is on the upswing, with natural gas-fired plants that can reduce air pollution emissions up to 99 percent, compared with conventional coal-fired technologies. GE has a backlog of orders for its gas turbines—used in cogeneration plants—thanks to growing interest by customers in Japan, the Orient and around the world.

GTE/Sylvania is saving as much electricity as GE is producing, through its high-efficiency light bulbs and ballasts. These and other energy-saving measures have enabled Pacific Gas and Electric to cut its peak demand by a full 25 percent, over the last several decades. Simultaneously, PG&E has raised geothermal energy to more than a third of its total generating capacity—with solar, wind, and biomass accounting for much of the rest.

Around the country, similar emphasis on homegrown energy sources has slashed the nation's energy import bill to zero. And a huge export market has opened up for technologies to help other nations do the same. These remarkable circumstances have enabled the United States to relinquish its title as the world's largest debtor nation; now it is on the verge of eclipsing the unified European Community as the world's largest creditor economy.

Real World Prospects

Back in the year 1989, this vision of the world a hundred years hence is not only appealing—it is also plausible. The macro-economic arguments are tenable. Every technology described has already been commercially demonstrated or is now in advanced planning stages (although not always by the same companies as those mentioned).

Perhaps most significantly, the Los Angeles basin has indeed unveiled a revolutionary plan to address its pollution woes, under the watchful eye of California's South Coast Air Quality Management District. By 2007, the regional plan calls for a ban on all gasoline-powered vehicles, a rejuvenated mass transit system, development of paints, aerosols, and other products that emit no smog-producing volatile organic compounds, and installation of emission control devices on pollution sources large and small—ranging from industrial boilers and oil refineries to breweries, bakeries, and restaurants that charbroil food. If fully implemented, the plan would change the fabric of daily life: no more drive-up windows, no more gas-powered lawnmowers, no more lighter fluid for backyard barbecues.

The Los Angeles community is divided over the plan's likely impact. Industry groups say compliance with the plan could cost $14 billion a year and eliminate as many as 150,000 jobs because companies unable to meet the standards will leave the area. Yet the air quality management district puts the price tag at only $2.8 billion annually and says 80,000 additional jobs may be created, as a result of new technologies industry will be compelled to introduce.

"Instead of acting as if it's being picked on," remarks Alan Lloyd, chief scientist for the air quality management district, "industry could export these developing technologies to a world newly aware of its fragility."

How Los Angeles copes with this plan will say a lot about other cities' prospects for realizing the utopian potential of 2089. For if Los Angeles cannot overcome its problems, how could others like Mexico City cope—with twice the population and only a fraction of the financial resources?

Fortunately, help may be on the way. At the economic summit of the G-7 nations in Paris in July 1989, the leaders of the seven richest nations in the free world pledged to make restoration of the environment a top priority. Japan even pledged a multi-billion dollar aid package to help tackle pollution problems in developing nations.

Business Takes Interest

In a world where market-based economic systems are on the rise, however, it may be business—not government—that holds the key to solving global warming. Companies in a range of industries already are scrutinizing the issue carefully. Du Pont, Bechtel, Arco, and New England Electric, to name but a few, have established study committees or have written white papers. Exxon devoted most of a board meeting to discussing implications of the greenhouse effect. And an array of smaller companies are developing innovative products that may play a key role in solving global warming. To the most forward-thinking people in the business community, it's become clear that environmental constraints are rapidly putting an end to business as usual.

Indeed, if U.S. companies fail to seize the opportunities posed by the coming changes, they may lose their early lead in technologies potentially worth billions. It may be that the new technologies outlined above will in fact dominate the marketplace of the future, but American brand names will not be on them. Let's see how the real world stacks up against the trends projected for 2089.

• The American-made photovoltaic panels lining the roofs of Los Angeles homes a hundred years from now could just as easily be made by Sharp of Japan, or Photowatt of France. Japan surpassed the United States as the world's largest producer of photovoltaic modules in 1985. And the world's leading PV manufacturer—Arco Solar—was snatched by Siemens of West Germany, after Atlantic Richfield put it up for sale. On the positive side, two American companies—Chronar and Utility Power Group—have plans to build plants producing 150 megawatts of photovoltaic power in California during the early 1990s—an amount almost five times the total photovoltaic power now produced worldwide.

"Pressures are also building from within corporations to urge companies to pay greater attention to the health of the environment."

• The non-electric refrigerators found in so many kitchens in 2089 could be manufactured by Sweden's Electrolux and marketed in this country by its American subsidiary, White Consolidated Industries. Several years ago Electrolux acquired the Swiss company, Servel, which marketed ammonia-based refrigerators in the United States decades ago, when the technology was popular—before ozone-depleting chlorofluorocarbons (CFCs) were invented. Meanwhile, American appliance manufacturers are in a quandary as to how to meet government efficiency standards in the 1990s without boosting their use of CFCs, which are likely to be phased out by the turn of the century. One company, however, the New Jersey-based Cryodynamics, has developed a nitrogen-based refrigeration system that runs on electricity and is 50 percent more efficient than conventional refrigerators. In 1987, the company signed a licensing agreement to produce 9 million of these units in the world's largest emerging market for refrigerators—the People's Republic of China.

• The high definition television (HDTV) market—which has the potential to revolutionize the way we live and work through its merger of television, computers, and communications—could well be dominated by Japanese companies like Sony, Toshiba, and Hitachi. Since 1970, Japan has put nearly $1 billion into developing this technology, and a European consortium has spent $200 million in just three years. But the United States is finally getting into the act. The Pentagon has committed $30 million for HDTV research, and the American Electronics Association has called for $1.35 billion in federal support for civilian research and development.

• Fuel-efficient cars are certainly not an American hallmark. Mass transit systems continue to take a back seat to U.S. highway development, garnering only one penny of the nine-cent federal gas tax. (Highways get the other eight cents.) Yet fuel efficiency is beginning to get corporate attention. General Motors, for example, has developed a prototype car that gets better than 60 miles a gallon—rivaling the prototypes of its Japanese and European competitors. And Ford has built a prototype electric-powered van and a "flexible-fueled" car that can run on ethanol, methanol or gasoline.

Promising Signs of Change

Fuel-efficient cars, non-electric appliances, solar cells—in a greenhouse world, products like these may well rule the marketplace. If that alone wasn't enough to draw corporations into the environmental future, other forces now converging may help push them in.

At the state level, the National Governors Association has targeted global climate change as its number one priority. On Capitol Hill, there's growing talk about levying a tax on fossil fuels and CFCs—and using the proceeds to trim the whopping federal budget deficit. Even at the international bargaining table, delegates are working to develop a global agreement that limits the release of greenhouse gases—an effort that has won the support of the Bush administration.

Pressures also are building from within corporations to urge companies to pay greater attention to the health of the environment. A case in point is the *Valdez* oil spill. In its aftermath, Exxon agreed to a shareholder request that it appoint a board-level committee to review environmental and worker safety issues, such as acid rain, urban smog, and oil spill preparedness. . . .

Two of Exxon's largest shareholders—the New York City and California public pension systems—are encouraging other oil companies to follow suit. Moreover, church activists announced a shareholder campaign that will ask selected companies to conduct environmental audits of their operations and publicize the results. Through measures like these, environmental issues are being reserved a seat in the corporate boardroom and a desk in the executive suite.

In a still more positive sign, some management teams are beginning to act on their own accord to address environmental concerns. Monsanto, for example, pledged in 1987 to reduce its toxic air emissions by 90 percent—with a long-term goal of zero emissions. Union Carbide and Hoffman-LaRoche have committed themselves to similarly drastic reductions. Du Pont announced early in 1988 it would phase out production of harmful ozone-depleting compounds by the end of the century—though an international treaty calls only for a 50 percent reduction. Now the treaty is likely to be amended to match Du Pont's goal.

And the president of Volvo said publicly that private automobiles could be banned from most urban areas within a decade, if city planners had the will to scale up mass transit systems. Why would a car company president advocate banning cars? Because Volvo also is a leading manufacturer of heavy-duty trucks, passenger buses, and computer systems for mass transit.

In fact, none of these companies is acting strictly from altruistic motives. They know they can profit by responding quickly to changes that are inevitable. For example, Du Pont plans to replace the CFCs it is phasing out with substitute compounds it has spent millions to develop—and hopes to sell for five times the current market price. Similarly, Monsanto has said it doesn't believe its toxic air emissions pose a health hazard, yet it pledged to reduce them because of pending Clean Air Act amendments. "The public has spoken, and it's unmistakable they will no longer tolerate toxic emissions," Monsanto Chairman Richard Mahoney said. "Might as well get on with it."

"As global temperatures approach a level not seen since the age of the dinosaurs, more and more companies will be compelled to get on with the business of solving global warming."

In the years ahead, as global temperatures approach a level not seen since the age of the dinosaurs, more and more companies will be compelled to get on with the business of solving global warming. As Alcan Vice President Hugh Wynne-Edwards observes: "We are in the middle stages of a paradigm shift, a shift from human affairs being managed by thinking from the economy *outward* to the environment . . . to management by thinking from the environment *into* the economy.". . .

Can business solve global warming? Not by itself. But the necessary pieces are coming into place: Appropriate technologies are within reach, consumer consciousness is on the rise, and the profit motive is alive and well. If consensus arises in business that the environment is a priority—and there are hopeful signs pointing in that direction—then the answer will be Yes: Business can indeed do its part to solve global warming.

Douglas G. Cogan is the author of Stones in a Glass House: CFCs and Ozone Depletion, *and is preparing a study on corporate responses to global climate change.*

"We should both reduce CO₂ emissions

"We should both reduce CO$_2$ emissions by ending indiscriminate cutting of our forests and soak up CO$_2$ by establishing new forested areas."

viewpoint **41**

Planting Trees Can Alleviate the Greenhouse Effect

Natural Resources Defense Council

For the first time in history, human activities are altering the climate of our entire planet. In less than two centuries, humans have increased the total amount of carbon dioxide in the atmosphere by 25% from the burning of fossil fuels and the destruction of forests. Carbon dioxide and other pollutants—notably chlorofluorocarbons, nitrous oxide, and methane—trap heat in the earth's atmosphere and warm it due to the "greenhouse effect." Unless we reduce emissions of these greenhouse gases, the stable, hospitable climate on which modern civilization is based could become a thing of the past. In the United States alone, climatic disruptions could eliminate virtually all Eastern forests, undermine the productivity of the Midwestern grain belt, and destroy up to 80% of our coastal wetlands.

Effects in many other nations, whose economic and environmental systems are more fragile, would be even more devastating. The resulting stresses could fracture the economic, social, and political structures that protect the peace and, for the first time in all of human history, hold the promise of providing a full, dignified life for all people.

We must begin to act now to avoid these terrible consequences. U.S. governmental officials must give climate change the same high level of attention that is now reserved for the prospect of nuclear war.

The scientific consensus that we will experience a greenhouse warming has been strong for at least a decade. It is very unlikely that additional research will demonstrate that we face a false alarm or that the consequences of climate change will be benign rather than harmful. Further research is important, but cannot justify the cost of delaying action. As stated by the National Academies of Sciences and Engineering and the Institute of Medicine in a

January 1989 report: "[O]ur current scientific understanding amply justifies" the concern about global warming. They recommended that the President act now to reduce emissions of greenhouse gases. . . .

When we cut trees and their wood decays or burns, CO_2 is released into the atmosphere. Growing trees, on the other hand, absorb CO_2. Improved forest management therefore carries the potential for major reductions in net emissions of CO_2.

The United States should lead the way. We should both reduce CO_2 emissions by ending indiscriminate cutting of our forests and soak up CO_2 by establishing new forested areas. Together, the following actions could reduce the overall U.S. contribution of CO_2 to the atmosphere by approximately 4.5% while providing many other environmental benefits.

Planting Trees on Fragile Croplands

To reduce atmospheric concentrations of CO_2 and set an example for other nations, farmers and the federal government should join in a major effort to establish forest cover on environmentally fragile fields now used to grow crops eligible for federal crop subsidies. By 2000, new forests on ten million acres of rural land—an area roughly half the size of Indiana—could absorb 20 million tons of carbon each year. Other benefits of this forest creation would include soil erosion control, water pollution abatement, diminished pesticide spraying, reduced crop surpluses, and increased farm income.

The Department of Agriculture's Conservation Reserve Program provides a framework for this effort. Under the Program, the Federal Government compensates farmers for establishing long-term grass or tree cover on excessively eroding croplands. Substantial opportunities exist to establish forests on Conservation Reserve Program lands throughout much of the Midwest and the East; the Program is

Excerpted, with permission, from *Cooling the Greenhouse: Vital First Steps to Combat Global Warming*, a booklet published by the Natural Resources Defense Council, May 1989.

already serving this purpose in the South. The cost of creating ten million acres of new forests would be $500 million to $1 billion a year for 15 years. From one-fourth to one-half of this cost would be offset because Conservation Reserve payments to farmers would replace crop subsidies that otherwise would be paid on the same lands.

This rural tree planting program could reduce net annual U.S. CO_2 emissions 1.4% by the year 2000.

Increasing Use of Private Forest Lands

The nation's nonindustrial private forest lands are underused for commercial wood production. The U.S. Forest Service estimates that, by planting trees on unstocked woodlots, converting existing plant cover to marketable timber species, and using environmentally sound forest management procedures such as thinning, annual timber growth on these private forests could be increased by approximately 3.7 billion cubic feet per year. If we can realize just half of this potential over the next few years, the growing trees on these lands will store an additional 22 million tons of carbon a year, and the wood they produce will relieve logging pressures in the National Forests.

Most of the investment necessary to achieve this increased wood production would come from the private sector. However, that investment will not occur unless the federal government systematically points out opportunities for profitable investments and provides technical assistance. To make this possible, Congress and the Forest Service should spend an additional $50 million a year, partly on expanded technical assistance to farmers and other nonindustrial owners through the Forest Service's State and Private Forestry Program and partly for direct financial assistance through the Agriculture Department's Forestry Incentives Program.

In addition, the government should amend the tax laws to permit partial exclusion of taxable income from sales of timber that nonindustrial owners have held for 20 years or longer. These forms of federal support should be tied to development and implementation of sustainable timber management plans on lands with carbon storage potential. The costs to the Government could be offset completely by reductions in uneconomic "below-cost" timber sales and logging road construction in the National Forests.

These efforts to increase wood production could reduce net annual U.S. CO_2 emissions 1.4% by the year 2000.

For the United States to be a credible leader in efforts to end destructive forest practices worldwide, our Government must put its own forestry practices in order. Unfortunately, there are serious deficiencies in management of the 191-million-acre National Forest System. The Forest Service is allowing rapid commercial logging of the diverse old-growth forests of the Pacific Northwest. It would take decades, if not centuries, for new stands of trees to replace the carbon storage lost through clearcutting and milling of the ancient trees now standing. The reforestation backlog in the national forests now exceeds one million acres; and the Forest Service continues to prescribe intensive logging on some lands where timely reforestation is impossible.

The Forest Service also loses hundreds of millions of dollars annually from unprofitable timber sales that typically involve logging of sensitive, remote forest sites. In the Tongass National Forest in Southeast Alaska, for example, our Government is selling majestic 500-year-old spruce trees to loggers and getting back less than ten cents for every taxpayer dollar spent to make the sales.

The Federal Government should implement reforms to correct these abuses. The Forest Service must substantially reduce logging of old-growth forests, prevent logging on fragile sites where reforestation cannot be guaranteed, take all necessary steps to ameliorate the reforestation backlog, and phase out below-cost timber sales. In addition to enhancing our credibility as a world leader, these actions would mitigate U.S. carbon dioxide emissions.

These improvements in National Forest management could reduce net annual U.S. CO_2 emission 0.4% by the year 2000.

"Analyses . . . indicate that planting trees in urban areas is a cost-effective way of offsetting and reducing CO_2 emissions."

Analyses carried out at the Lawrence Berkeley Laboratory in California indicate that planting trees in urban areas is a cost-effective way of offsetting and reducing CO_2 emissions. These findings suggest that each tree planted in an urban area reduces net CO_2 emissions 15 times more than one planted in a rural area.

The reason is that urban trees do more than just absorb CO_2. They also can be placed to shade houses and pavement from the sun, provide natural cooling and reduce the big-city phenomenon known as "heat islands." Heat islands are created by uncovered pavements and other dark surfaces that reduce evaporation and absorb the sun's heat. Outdoor temperatures can be 5-10 degrees Fahrenheit higher than in surrounding areas.

According to American Forestry Association estimates derived from the Lawrence Berkeley studies, an aggressive, nationwide program to plant 100 million trees in urban areas could enable a significant reduction in air conditioning demand and, in turn, the consumption of fossil fuels for electricity. It could offset or reduce some 18 million tons of U.S. carbon emissions, while saving consumers $4 billion in energy costs. The Federal Government, in cooperation with states, local governments, and the private sector, should begin efforts to realize these benefits by the turn of the century.

Urban tree planting could reduce net annual U.S. CO_2 emissions 1.2% by the year 2000. . . .

We have already recommended actions by the United States to halt needless forest destruction and plant trees to absorb atmospheric carbon. It appears that these actions can play a significant role in reducing net U.S. CO_2 emissions. We should persuade other industrialized nations to carry out similar programs. In addition, the United States should take a leading role in halting deforestation in developing nations.

Sustainable Management

Tropical deforestation accounts for about 10-30% of worldwide CO_2 emissions. Actions to halt forest loss and promote afforestation must be an important part of the strategy to minimize global warming. The Worldwatch Institute has estimated that massive, successful programs could cut net CO_2 emissions from tropical forests by two-thirds, thereby offsetting or reducing all man-made CO_2 emissions by perhaps one-fifth. The main emphasis should be on halting the deforestation that is now contributing substantially to the buildup of atmospheric CO_2. The United States must be a leader if these efforts are to succeed.

The Natural Resources Defense Council (NRDC) is an environmentalist organization whose members include lawyers and scientists. In 1988 NRDC launched its Atmosphere Protection Initiative, a coordinated effort to reduce global warming, ozone depletion, acid rain, and urban smog.

"An industrial infrastructure in space could help humanity meet its future energy needs without exacerbating... global warming."

Satellite Solar Power Can Alleviate the Greenhouse Effect

Peter E. Glaser and Gerard K. O'Neill

Editor's note: The following viewpoint is in two parts. Part I is by Peter E. Glaser and Part II is by Gerard K. O'Neill.

I

Most of the discussion about preserving the ecology of our planet has focused on Earth-based solutions. These have been aimed at protecting the environment and providing energy to meet the demands of the planet's expanding population. In the near- to mid-term, these are important and valuable steps. But in the long-term, a key to humanity's continued evolution will be the penetration of space and the economic and scientific exploitation of the solar system's inexhaustible resources and unique physical characteristics.

President Bush outlined some challenging steps toward this goal. His proposal, made on the 20th anniversary of the first lunar landing, called for the establishment of a base on the moon to be followed by a manned mission to Mars. But unlike President John F. Kennedy's earlier proposal to go to the moon, the Bush proposal contained no timetable and no guidelines for financing. He left those issues to the National Space Council, headed by Vice President Quayle.

New Reason for Exploration

Pursuing space missions is important, but not just for economic and scientific reasons. It is also important as a means to meet the future energy needs of this planet without creating further ecological deterioration.

During the first two decades of the space age, the exploration and uses of space were conducted primarily by the United States and the Soviet Union. Now other countries have begun making long-range,

Peter E. Glaser, "Dealing with Global Warming: Power from Space Is Pollution Free," *The New York Times,* October 1, 1989. Copyright 1989 by The New York Times Company. Reprinted with permission. Gerard K. O'Neill, "Solar Power by Satellite Would Solve Ozone Crisis," *Los Angeles Times,* March 7, 1989. Reprinted with permission.

multibillion-dollar plans for space exploration and exploitation. These nations, in many instances, wish to participate in international space missions and to share both in the gains and the costs.

But the real key to entering space is the development of an infrastructure that can be expanded significantly over an extended period. This infrastructure of permanently manned space stations and orbiting industrial parks will be able to support a broad spectrum of scientific investigations, technology development and commercial ventures. A prerequisite for space-based infrastructure will not only be the transportation of material and people, but also the availability of adequate electrical power.

The Soviet Union and Japan already have ambitious plans for generating power in space, at first for use in orbit and subsequently for use on earth. Plans for a long-term Soviet space power development program were presented at the International Astronautical Federation Congress in 1985 and were followed by statements from several leading Soviet space technologists. A recent article in a Soviet scientific journal about that nation's space program written by V.S. Aveyevsky, a Russian expert on manufacturing in space and a winner of the Lenin Prize, stated that "the idea of satellite electric power stations generating energy for consumers in space and on the ground has grown into one of the most fundamental space research programs."

Japan's Space Activities Commission recommended in 1987 that Japan should endeavor to become an important participant in space activities by the beginning of the 21st century. The commission stated that to conduct space activities on a large scale, Japan should promote research and development into the efficient utilization of solar energy for the generation of electricity in space.

The space power systems capable of capturing and converting solar energy and then beaming that energy from orbit to a receiving site in space or on earth were studied by the Department of Energy and the National Aeronautics and Space Administration in the late 1970's and early 1980's. At the time, these power systems were judged to be too expensive because of the high cost of transporting propellants, materials and space structures into orbit from earth.

Since Mr. Bush's speech, there appears to be an opportunity for the United States, and other nations, to develop a lunar base and the lunar resources necessary for large-scale projects like space-based power generating systems. The economic justification for using lunar resources instead of earth resources includes a significant reduction in transportation costs from the moon into an earth orbit, compared with launchings into orbit directly from the earth. Launching materials into an earth orbit from the moon would also alleviate the environmental impacts that would result from multiple earth launchings.

The development of space-based power systems will extend well into the next century. New systems will be needed to supply the power needs of space shuttles, free-flying platforms and space stations in high-earth orbits, and lunar bases. Development of space-based power sources, can—and should—begin with a modest test project to demonstrate the feasibility of new solar energy technologies to collect and beam power between objects in space and to the earth.

A cooperative international test project for space-based power systems provides a unique opportunity to advance this technology. Such a test project could lead to further cooperative efforts among nations that expect to benefit from space-generated power. International participation could also make it easier to obtain agreements on the use of orbits and the portions of the electromagnetic spectrum necessary to transmit energy to earth from space. A test program could also lead to an international consensus on the future course of space power development.

"The world faces a potential catastrophe, which will give little warning before it strikes."

Based on activities already under way in several nations, a power generating program for space could form the basis for the development of space-based industries and support structures. An industrial infrastructure in space could help humanity meet its future energy needs without exacerbating the ecological deterioration resulting from global warming.

The significance of an international test project has

been recognized and recommended as part of the activities for the International Space Year in 1992. It is now time for industry in the United States, in cooperation with NASA, to take the initiative and join with other nations in this test project. The rewards for joining in this project could be as vast as space itself and ultimately could conserve the resources and ecology of the earth.

II

The problem is, by now, widely known: The world faces a potential catastrophe, which will give little warning before it strikes.

It is the irreversible damage to our biosphere from the greenhouse effect. Every year more than 5,000 megatons of carbon dioxide, nearly all from the burning of fossil fuels, escape into the atmosphere. That is far more than can be absorbed by the growth of trees and other plants. In the past 30 years, the burning of fossil fuels has raised the concentration of carbon dioxide in the atmosphere by 10%. A temperate climate depends on the radiating of excess heat through the Earth's atmosphere. But carbon dioxide traps heat. On our neighboring planet of Venus, the greenhouse effect has gone wild. There, a carbon dioxide atmosphere keeps the surface temperature above 800 degrees, hot enough to melt lead.

There is a solution to the problem if nations act cooperatively, something they have proven they can do if disaster is the alternative.

What Are the Options?

Reducing our energy usage is not an option, because the production of goods and services is dependent on maintaining an adequate energy supply. The least-developed industrial nations use only one-hundredth as much energy per capita as the most developed, but suffer a living standard a hundred times lower in consequence. Therefore, we could not reduce energy usage without condemning the majority of the world to unending poverty.

Maintaining the present rate of energy growth in developing nations would require that we generate more than five times the energy in 2039 that we do now. Obtaining it from fossil fuels would raise the global temperature drastically, flood coastal areas and reduce already acutely scarce supplies of fresh water.

A worldwide program, over perhaps a period of 50 years, is needed to convert to clean, renewable sources of energy. Energy used at fixed sites—for industries and homes—can be electric, generated without burning fossil fuels. It is harder to wean transportation, which consumes 25% of all the energy we use, from gasoline and diesel fuel. But fuels like methane, propane and butane can be synthesized using recycled carbon dioxide to put energy into portable form. This becomes practical when central-station electric costs are reduced substantially.

In viewing the alternatives for generating energy without the burning of fossil fuels, we must understand the magnitude of future needs. If nuclear power were to provide all the energy the world needs by the year 2039, there would have to be 63,000 nuclear reactors in operation. The examples of Three Mile Island and Chernobyl will not be forgotten quickly and thus make such an alternative unacceptable to many people. Ground-based solar power cannot be generated in the quantity needed without paving much of the world with solar cells. That would further raise the Earth's temperature by increasing the heat that the ground absorbs. Obtaining power from the temperature difference between surface and deep waters in the tropical oceans would change the global climate profoundly by altering the heat balance at the ocean's surface.

Meets the Criteria

So a fully acceptable system for generating energy must add little to the Earth's heat load, burn no fossil fuels and avoid nuclear fission or fusion. There is only one method that satisfies all these conditions—the conversion of solar energy to electric power in high orbit, where sunlight is intense and continuous.

Twenty years of study and experiments confirm that power in high orbit can be sent efficiently to Earth as low-density radio waves. Antennas in fenced-off regions can transform the radio waves to ordinary electricity. Since more than 90% of the radio-wave energy is converted to electricity, almost no waste heat need be released to the environment. No fuels are required, fossil or nuclear.

"A decade of study and experimentation by government agencies and private foundations confirms that satellite solar power is environmentally benign."

A decade of study and experimentation by government agencies and private foundations confirms that satellite solar power is environmentally benign. It can compete economically with coal-fired and nuclear-power plants if we can avoid having to haul materials out of the Earth's strong gravity. Materials for the power satellites—metals, silicon and oxygen—can come from the moon, whose gravitational grip is less than a twentieth of the Earth's. Those materials are the most abundant elements of the lunar surface and can be mined using known space technology.

The Soviet Union and Japan are particularly aggressive now in working toward satellite solar power. A commercial multination program, modeled on the successful Intelsat and Inmarsat consortia that provide satellite communications, would earn revenues of $250 billion a year, satisfying today's needs for new electric generators. To meet all the energy needs of 2039, the market would be more than $6 trillion a year annually (in today's dollars), larger than America's present gross national product. We as a nation cannot afford to be left out of a commercial program with so huge an export market. Above all, we who live in the biosphere cannot let it die.

Peter E. Glaser is vice president of space operations for Arthur D. Little Inc. He has served on the NASA Task Force on Space Goals and was a member of NASA's Advisory Council for the "Lunar Energy Enterprise Case Study." Gerard K. O'Neill, professor emeritus of physics at Princeton University, founded the Geostar Satellite Corporation. He was appointed in 1985 by President Reagan to the National Commission on Space.

"Nuclear power is still an attractive option."

Nuclear Power Is a Reliable Energy Source

Bernard I. Spinrad

From 1965 to 1975, the use of nuclear power in the United States grew dramatically. However, after 1975 this growth slowed down, and it has now almost stopped. New nuclear power plants are too expensive, and the public does not have confidence in them. Therefore, the product must be improved if it is to be salable. Work toward this end is in progress. The service life of existing nuclear plants must also be extended. These two developments permit some cautious estimates of the status of nuclear power 20 years from now. From about 1990 to 2005 there will probably be a pause in the installation of nuclear plants. During that period the nuclear community will be developing and testing new reactor designs for economic and demonstrably safe nuclear power.

The travail of the nuclear industry began in about 1975, when it became obvious that the shock of the oil price set by the Organization of Petroleum Exporting Countries had brought about an industrial recession and a sudden leveling of demand for electricity. Utilities, faced with unnecessary capital commitments, curtailed the purchase of new generating plants. Nuclear plants suffered the most because most of the plants on order were nuclear, and because nuclear power is capital-intensive.

Economically Attractive

Nevertheless, nuclear power remained economically attractive until 1979. Its generating cost was less than that of coal power, and, in refutation of public opposition, it had an excellent safety record. Therefore, the nuclear industry expected orders to resume as soon as electrical demand began to climb again.

Then the accident at Three Mile Island (TMI) unit

Bernard I. Spinrad, "U.S. Nuclear Power in the Next Twenty Years," *Science*, Vol. 239, pages 707-708, February 12, 1988. Reprinted with permission.

2 occurred. In the aftermath of TMI, major changes were made in nuclear regulations. The number of nuclear plant personnel and the training required of them were greatly increased; extensive backfitting of hardware was also required.

These measures increased the cost of nuclear power, but initially the increase was expected to be modest. However, in the 1980s, plant capital costs escalated. The cost of new nuclear plants reached three to five times what had been originally expected. The price charged for electricity normally includes a "reasonable" return on investment, but at standard rates of return these high costs caused sudden jolts in electricity rates. Some utility commissions began to disallow costs judged to be excessive in setting rates, forcing these costs to be absorbed by stockholders. Only a few, very well-managed nuclear utilities were able to avoid these embarrassments, and nuclear power lost its support in the utility sector.

Many theories as to the cause of this cost escalation have been propounded, most of which blame factors outside the nuclear industry. My theory is that the cause is within the industry. The plant designs now being offered are large, costly, and complicated. Regulatory requirements have been patched into plant designs rather than incorporated into the basic design. The nuclear industry did not see any long-term profit in going beyond incremental design changes for the existing types of nuclear plants. Under these circumstances, the enthusiasm of the design staff waned. Errors began creeping into design and construction, requiring extensive reworking. These problems were combated by hiring larger staffs to do more checking and rechecking, inspection, and paperwork. Nuclear power plant design and construction have become highly bureaucratized—and more expensive.

Nuclear power has also lost its base of popular support. Public confidence plummeted after TMI, and recovery of confidence was frustrated by the Chernobyl accident. A nuclear project will be strongly fought at all government levels. Public interventions and lawsuits will delay the project. The public image of the utility will be hurt, which will jeopardize the utility's case in other disputes. Under these circumstances, the utility can only justify the project to its stockholders and the public if it can guarantee that cheap electricity will be produced; but the recent cost history of nuclear plants does not make such a guarantee feasible. Nuclear power will not be a significant factor in new electricity generation unless or until its economy can be ensured.

A "second nuclear era" seems to be needed if nuclear power is to make a growing contribution to the generation of electricity. The term was coined by Alvin M. Weinberg to denote a period when nuclear power is again publicly accepted and cheap. The environmental benefits of nuclear power are compelling, and if they are associated with both economy and safety they will be hard to oppose. Public response to safety issues becomes muted if the industry being questioned maintains a good safety record for a decade or so. These, then, are the conditions for the second nuclear era. The questions are what types of systems will characterize it, and when will it begin.

"The environmental benefits of nuclear power are compelling, and if they are associated with both economy and safety they will be hard to oppose."

The prevailing view in nuclear circles is that new reactor designs will be needed, but no new reactor types. Types in use today—the light water reactors, the heavy water reactor, the sodium-cooled fast reactor, and the helium-cooled graphite reactor—were selected for valid reasons, and they are the points of departure. They all have attractive intrinsic safety features, but concerns about safety will not be appeased unless safety is clearly apparent. Thus, the design task is to provide transparent safety and economic construction and operation.

One key to economy may be to decrease the size of individual reactor units. This amounts to abandoning economy of scale in favor of economy of standardization and replication. Smaller units would also (i) limit the cost exposure of each incremental unit, (ii) provide a better match to growth of the utility load, and (iii) take greater advantage of the economies and cost management of factory construction, as opposed to field construction. A precedent for smaller units is found in the unit sizes of fossil-fueled plants, which are typically built in

the 250- to 400-MW [megawatt] range, and hardly ever exceed 800 MW.

Another change in philosophy concerns automation. Nuclear plants have been designed for a high degree of human involvement in operation. This is no longer the practice in modern manufacturing, and it is not considered conservative in the sense of safety. Now, the nuclear industry is also starting to consider automation, particularly for situations that do not permit the exercise of operator judgment. Moreover, utilities are installing a variety of computerized, on-line expert systems to guide both maintenance and operations. These automation changes should improve both economy and safety: economy by reversing the trend toward increased staffing, safety by removing a demonstrated weak link—as illustrated by both TMI and Chernobyl—from many of the safety chains.

The Use of Robotics

Another technical opportunity comes from robotics. Human surveillance and servicing of many plant components are costly in terms of radiation exposure and money. The exigencies of TMI led to the use of robots in inspection and cleanup after the accident. These experiences were successful, and plant design for optimum use of robots and teleoperators is now in favor. These techniques will be useful, but the second nuclear era must be based on better reactors. Design programs are under way for several types.

The workhorse reactor type today is the light water reactor (LWR). Advanced LWRs are now under design. They are likely to be smaller (about 600 MW, compared to today's reactors of 1200 MW), more durable (60-year design life rather then 30 years), more conservative with larger safety margins, and, above all, simpler to make proof of safety less equivocal.

Advanced fast reactor design and development is also under way. A consensus has developed in favor of the pool type with all primary components in a single, low-pressure sodium pool, a low power of less than 500 MW per unit, modest breeding, and moderate specific power. Metal, rather than oxide, fuel is now preferred on the basis of experiments at Argonne National Laboratory that showed metal fuel to have impressive safety characteristics. These characteristics permitted the Experimental Breeder Reactor (EBR-II) to survive severe operational accident simulations without damage to fuel or major stress on the system. The pool concept and small size permit emergency cooling by natural circulation of building atmosphere (possibly nitrogen) around the pool tank. Illustrative designs by General Electric and Rockwell International have been published.

Proponents and developers of helium-cooled high-temperature reactors in both the United

States (General Atomic) and West Germany were the first to downsize their concept to small modular units, making conventional pressure vessels and emergency cooling by circulation of air in the building feasible. Finally, the Canadian heavy water reactor line, known as CANDU, could possibly be adapted to U.S. practice; these reactors have compiled excellent operational records.

These advanced and alternative reactor types will need to have their safety, operability, and economy tested by experimental construction and operation. However, with so many possible reactor types, I expect at least one of them to pass this test and to be commercialized. The small unit size of the final product is important in this process, since it would require much less time, money, and extrapolation to go from an experimental plant to a commercial line.

Success in at least one of these programs is the real key to a second nuclear era. I anticipate such a success, but it will take time. A scenario for the process might be as follows: Experimental construction begins in 1992; experience justifies a prototype plant in 1999; and commercial orders begin around 2005. This scenario puts the second nuclear era a full human generation into the future. Most large-scale industrial innovations are realized over that length of time. It took that long for the first nuclear era, which is tailing off now, to bloom, and our present circumstance is indeed one of beginning again.

In the interim, many existing nuclear plants will reach the end of their license periods. They will still be in generally excellent condition, which is a requirement as long as they are licensed. Some components will be at the end of their useful lives and will need refurbishing or replacement, but most of the equipment will be available for continued long-term use. For comparison, fossil-fueled plants are retained in operation as, first, intermediate-load units and, finally, as reserve units. They are only decommissioned when continued maintenance becomes too expensive.

Economic Incentives

The economic incentives for refurbishing nuclear units are compelling. Even if it took $1 billion to refurbish the plant, the fact that the original costs have been fully amortized favors refurbishment over, for example, building a replacement coal plant. Besides, fueling costs for nuclear plants are, and will remain, less than half the fueling costs of coal plants.

The importance of this effort is now appreciated, and a program for extending plant life is under way. Necessarily, the requirements will vary from plant to plant, ranging from requalification of equipment to complex reworking, including in some cases partial reconstruction of the plant. For some plants, running at reduced power would suffice. The variety of work to be done will undoubtedly keep the U.S. nuclear community busy over the next 20 years.

A forecast of the next period in U.S. nuclear power is possible based on the themes of introduction of new reactor designs and the extension of plant life. Nuclear power in the United States is scheduled to grow to about a 95,000-MW generating capacity by about 1995. Not all these plants will remain operational until 2010, but enough will be so that the occasional new nuclear plant in growth areas of the country should maintain a plateau of about 90,000 MW until installation of the new models begins. That should happen around 2010 to 2015, and this is the time I choose for the start of the second nuclear era.

"Nuclear power in the United States is scheduled to grow to about a 95,000-MW generating capacity by about 1995."

Our pause in the installation of new nuclear power plants is being imitated elsewhere in the world, so we cannot expect export business to sustain our domestic nuclear industry indefinitely; instead, we must make innovative changes. Nuclear power is still an attractive option, but it will take ingenuity and perseverance, as well as an impeccable operating record over the next decade, for its potential to be realized.

Bernard I. Spinrad is head of the department of nuclear engineering at Iowa State University in Ames, Iowa.

"Nuclear operations have failed."

Nuclear Power Is Not a Reliable Energy Source

Bruce Biewald and Donald Marron

The time is ripe for a reevaluation of our country's nuclear policy. With only a few straggling units left to go on-line, the nuclear construction industry is essentially dead. Having survived the era of spiralling construction costs and huge rate increases, we now face a number of serious problems caused by the operation of existing nuclear units. The continuing rapid escalation of nuclear operating costs, for example, should encourage us to consider closing those units that are uneconomic. At the same time, we should also consider the vast array of problems that will arise (in the not-so-distant-future) when we begin cleaning up after this first generation of nuclear plants. The potential problems (and costs) associated with nuclear retirement, decommissioning, and waste disposal are huge, yet they remain far from resolved. At the same time, prospects for a second round of nuclear plants are receiving an increasing amount of attention from energy policy makers. . . .

Non-fuel nuclear operating costs have risen since 1970. In *real* terms, industry average non-fuel operating costs have escalated at a rate of 11.6 percent *per year*. Whereas nuclear operating costs were about $20 per kW [kilowatt] in 1970 (in 1987 dollars), they cost about $115 per kW in 1987. Like the escalation of construction costs, this six-fold increase in operating costs can be attributed to a variety of factors. The lack of standardization in plant design and the ever increasing size of nuclear units (with associated increases in complexity) likely caused some of the cost increases. Regulatory burden also played a role, although we should note that many of the new regulations resulted directly from the continued discovery of new technical problems at the plants. The gradual aging of nuclear

plants may also have contributed.

Many pressurized water reactors (PWRs), for example, have experienced water chemistry problems that have eroded pipes in their steam generators. At many plants, these problems have been or will be severe enough to require steam generator replacements at a cost of $100 million or more (estimates for the steam generator replacement at the D.C. Cook plant, for example, put the tab at some $160 million). Boiling water reactors (BWRs) have experienced their own problems with pipes cracking; in a number of cases, BWR pipes have had to be replaced. Such pipe replacements have cost in the $20-$80 million range. While these specific examples are particularly glaring, they are indicative of the general operating problems (and resulting costs) that have permeated the nuclear industry.

Operating Costs

The steady, rapid increase in nuclear operating costs has eroded the operating cost advantages nuclear plants once enjoyed over fossil-fired plants. A 1985 study by the Tennessee Valley Authority (TVA) found, for example, that on average, nuclear operating costs now exceed the operating costs of coal-fired plants. A Department of Energy (DOE) study found, moreover, that the continuing escalation of nuclear operating costs may require that plants be shut down for economic reasons before their physical operating lives are complete.

Nuclear operating costs are compared with oil. The operating cost advantage enjoyed by nuclear plants from the mid-1970s through the mid-1980s has eroded, as the result of steady increases in nuclear operating costs, and the recent decline in oil costs. Note that these data do not include construction costs, which are currently about four times higher for nuclear plants, according to the Electric Power Research Institute.

There are, of course, many other resource

Bruce Biewald and Donald Marron, "Nuclear Power Economics: Construction, Operation and Disposal," reprinted with permission from the May/June 1989 *Science for the People*, 897 Main St., Cambridge, MA 02139, $35 per year.

alternatives to oil and nuclear. Conventional fossil-fueled technologies such as coal-fired power plants and gas-fired combined cycle plants can be considered. Demand-side technologies such as efficiency improvements in lighting, appliances, and building shells are even more promising. The comparison with oil is presented here because oil-fired generation is traditionally considered a high operating cost option; yet now nuclear is in the same price range (even when the enormous construction investments in nuclear power plants are ignored).

Moreover, both oil and nuclear operating costs are expected to increase in the future. The reported pipe thinning and pipe degradation problems at many plants will likely result in large future maintenance and repair costs. The continued aging of nuclear units may add similarly to the increase in future operating costs. In addition, the NRC [Nuclear Regulatory Commission] still faces a backlog of roughly three hundred unresolved safety issues. As the NRC deals with these issues, we may expect further orders and regulations requiring changes (and associated cost increases) at existing plants. Thus nuclear operating costs may well remain high compared to alternatives.

While the escalation of costs has undermined the economic viability of nuclear operations, it is important to note that operations have failed in more than just cost terms. In order to offset their high initial construction costs and other high fixed costs, nuclear plants need to realize significant running cost benefits. These benefits can only come from running the plants at high capacity factors. Back in the halcyon days of nuclear optimism, utility analysts often predicted that units would operate at capacity factors of 75% to 80%. In fact, nuclear capacity factors have averaged below 60%. At such low rates of energy production, it is virtually impossible for many modern nuclear plants to compete with alternatives.

"Rather than being 'too cheap to meter', the nuclear energy produced at many plants has ended up costing far more than it is worth."

Thus, nuclear operations have failed on two fronts. First, the costs of nuclear operations have vastly exceeded utility expectations. These costs continue to escalate at rates that far outstrip the background rate of inflation—a pattern which shows no sign of abating. Second, nuclear units have operated at levels far below the original projections of the industry. The result is that consumers have been stuck paying far more than expected, for much less power than expected. Rather than being "too cheap

to meter", the nuclear energy produced at many plants has ended up costing far more than it is worth. In many cases, the multi-billion dollar investments needed to build the plants have not been justified by subsequent operating benefits, and future benefits will likely be small or nonexistent. As a result, a reevaluation of existing nuclear units may now be in order. . . .

Commercial Nuclear Power

Perhaps the most troublesome problems with commercial nuclear power are yet to come. The "back-end" costs of nuclear power production, spent fuel disposal and decommissioning, have not yet been adequately addressed.

No high-level disposal facility exists to receive and store the spent fuel regularly discharged from operating nuclear plants. The DOE's plans to open a high-level repository by the year 1998 have been frustrated by technical and political difficulties; the current schedule is to begin accepting high-level waste for burial in 2003. Meanwhile, an increasing amount of discharged nuclear fuel is in temporary storage pools at reactor sites.

Decommissioning, the process of dismantling, transporting, and burying the plant itself at the end of its operating life, has yet to be attempted for a full-sized nuclear plant. The amount of radioactive waste at a typical modern nuclear plant after 30 years of operation will amount to about 18 thousand cubic yards of contaminated concrete and steel, containing a total of about 5 million curies of radioactivity (primarily concentrated in the reactor vessel and internal components). In contrast, the largest nuclear plant in the U.S. that has been fully dismantled is the Elk River Reactor, which contained only about 10 thousand curies at the time of its shutdown, after operating for only 4 years.

Current cost estimates for nuclear plant decommissioning are extremely optimistic, based upon theoretical engineering studies developed without the benefit of actual experience. These engineering cost estimates for decommissioning have been increasing steadily since 1976 at an annual rate 15 percent faster than inflation. Decommissioning plans that fail to recognize the likely further increases in the engineering cost estimates are unlikely to be adequate for the requirements of an actual plant decommissioning. Thus, while some initial steps have been made toward recognizing the back-end costs of nuclear power, these costs still pose significant problems for the coming decades.

In light of the recent attention given to global warming theories, some energy policy analysts are looking to a new series of nuclear construction projects as the way to serve our country's growing electricity requirements. Industry advocates argue that standardization and modular plant design for these future plants will avoid the huge construction costs incurred by first generation nuclear plants. They also argue that the plants will be "inherently safe"—impervious to the loss-of-coolant accidents that are the gravest threat of our current generation of nuclear plants.

"Optimistic projections must be met with skepticism, given the sorry performance of the first generation of plants."

These optimistic projections must be met with skepticism, given the sorry performance of the first generation of plants. The proposed future generation will clearly face a series of difficult tests. The safety of the plants, for example, must be ensured. Some analysts have suggested that safety and licensing evaluations could be performed as a combination of theoretical analysis (the basis for current safety standards) and actual proof testing. Such a "license-by-test" practice would certainly be a major improvement over current practices, although it does fail to address some significant safety concerns, such as the impact of plant aging and associated plant deterioration. Environmental concerns must also be addressed. Policy makers have yet to address adequately the range of environmental problems caused by the current stock of nuclear plants. It would seem unwise to start in on a second round of nuclear plants until and unless we solve these current problems, in particular that of nuclear waste.

While the next generation of nuclear plants will (hopefully) be required to satisfy stringent safety and environmental criteria, it is likely that economic concerns will pose the hardest problems. As the reader has probably noticed, we have emphasized economic issues throughout our analysis of the current nuclear generation. This emphasis is intentional, for the failure of the nuclear industry, thus far, lies not in the technology's inherent dangers and environmental problems (which have been, and will remain, a legitimate cause for concern), but, in fact, in its economics (which, of course, have been significantly influenced by public concerns over safety and the environment).

No Limitless, Cheap Energy

The original lure of nuclear power lay in its promise of limitless, cheap energy. The fact of nuclear power, however, has been one of ridiculously expensive energy. The plants have cost too much to build, have cost too much to operate, and have often operated below the levels needed to make them economic. The future costs of waste disposal and decommissioning, moreover, while as yet unknown, will likely be enormous. Proponents of

the next generation of nuclear plants will be hard pressed to demonstrate that their plants will overcome all these economic problems. Advocates argue that standardization and modular design will keep construction and operating costs low. While this may be so, we must wonder how and why it is that the next generation of plants will be able to achieve the level of standardization and cost control to which the first generation aspired, but could never achieve.

Thus as we embark on our second decade following TMI [Three Mile Island], we must remain leery of the optimism of those who tout nuclear power as the technical fix to our current set of economic and environmental woes. While we applaud and encourage the ever broadening interest in global warming and related environmental crises, we remain skeptical at this time that nuclear power should have any significant role in our policy response, particularly when so many problems of the current generation remain unsolved. Even if a second generation of nuclear plants will *eventually* play a role, it will not do so for at least another decade. Global environmental issues demand a response now. Thus the prospects for a second generation of nuclear plants cannot and should not interfere with our immediate policy decisions. Improved energy efficiency, both in terms of end uses as well as in production, remain the key to solving the environmental and economic problems that plague our current energy policy.

Bruce Biewald is an associate scientist with Energy Systems Research Group (ESRG), an organization in Boston, Massachusetts, specializing in energy and environmental research. Donald Marron is a research associate with ESRG.

"It is often contended by opponents of nuclear power that we do not know how to isolate this waste safely and I fear that a large number of people are of this view. It is not correct."

viewpoint 45

Nuclear Power Is Environmentally Safe

Hans Blix

In the past, energy policies were determined mainly on economic grounds—what was the cheapest way to produce heat or electricity. The costs which, in fact, lay in pollution and corrosion were not calculated, partly, no doubt, because there are difficulties in attaching exact price tags to these things. It was only when the alarm bells began to ring loudly about the destruction of lakes and forests, damage to buildings like the Parthenon or to the pyramids, or—lately—the expected change of the global climate that a broader discussion started about the environmental costs of different energy sources. These costs have escalated in a rather short space of time from local ones in the form of smoke pollution or flooded land at hydropower dams, to regional ones in acidified lakes and dying forests, and to the global consequences of the greenhouse effect.

I should like to start with two preliminary points. The first is that, as welcome as the new attention to the environmental aspects of energy is, we cannot turn 180 degrees and ignore other aspects, like economic costs, reliability or the desire for energy independence. The rapidly increasing number of automobiles and trucks in the world cannot use coal or nuclear power, and neither electricity nor hydrogen is yet available for them. They will necessarily continue to burn petrol for some time. Only an increased use of electrically powered trains, trams and trolleybuses could somewhat restrain the pressure for more petrol-powered vehicles. We must also be aware that solar power and wind power will not be economically viable within the next decade or decades. The renewable energies—apart from hydro—today give the world less than 0.5% of its commercial energy. We can decide to invest more

resources in their development, but they will not be significant options when we make decisions on energy for the 1990s and early 2000s.

My second preliminary point is that discussion of one source of energy in isolation is almost meaningless. Our discussion must aim at helping us to choose between available options for an optimal energy mix. We must assess how much energy we should like to use and compare the economic, environmental and other aspects of the different options. . . .

The absence of any emissions of SO_2, NO_x or heavy metals from nuclear power remains a great advantage. Let me give you a few figures on this. Three thousand MW(e) [megawatts] in coal-fired plants—that is the capacity we have been asked to address—would burn about 20,000 tons of coal per day, and it would give rise to about 150,000 tons of SO_2, 75,000 tons of NO_x and 1,200 tons of various toxic metals per year. While a large part of the SO_2 and NO_x today can be prevented from reaching the atmosphere and can be retained on the ground, there is no viable way in which the huge quantities of CO_2 that are formed in the combustion can be prevented from going into the atmosphere.

Let me cite some other figures that are significant. In 1987, all the world's nuclear power stations produced about 6,000 tons of spent fuel, which is highly radioactive. If the same amount of electricity had been generated by coal instead, only the toxic heavy metals (arsenic, mercury, cadmium, vanadium, etc.) released would have amounted to some 100,000 tons. These remain toxic forever.

The Expansion of Nuclear Power

The example of France shows even more concretely that expansion of nuclear power can have an impact on emissions. From 1980 to 1986, SO_2 and NO_x emissions in the electric power sector were reduced by 71% and 60% respectively. This

Hans Blix, "Nuclear Energy and the Environment," paper presented to the Symposium on Energy and Environment, Amsterdam, Holland, May 3, 1989. Reprinted with permission.

contributed significantly to reducing total French SO_2 emissions by 56% and total French NO_x emissions by 9%. That the NO_x emissions did not fall more is explained by increased emissions from more cars during the same period.

Nuclear power does not give rise to any emissions of SO_2, NO_x or CO_2, but it does produce radioactive substances that are dangerous. A comparison of nuclear power with coal-fueled power from the viewpoint of environment and human health should properly examine the whole fuel cycle—from mining to waste disposal and establish damage and risk per quantity of electricity produced. Such inquiries are underway, and I am confident that they will show the wide gap which exists between the common perceptions of the risks of nuclear power and the actual ones. The public's attitude to radiation seems ambivalent. On the one hand, there is fear of use of any radiation for foodstuff preservation and of even low-level radioactive waste disposal facilities. On the other hand, there is acceptance of an ever increasing use of radioisotopes and radiation in agriculture, industry and medicine.

"The average annual dose . . . is less than one hundredth of a percent (0.0002 milliSieverts) of the dose the same individual receives annually from the natural background radiation."

A good overall picture of nuclear power is given in the 1988 report of the United Nations Scientific Committee on the Effects of Atomic Radiation (UNSCEAR). The report points out that the average annual dose to individuals from normal operations for all nuclear power production in the world, including the whole fuel cycle, at the present time is less than one hundredth of a percent (0.0002 milliSieverts) of the dose the same individual receives annually from the natural background radiation (2.4 milliSieverts). I will return later to the additional doses received from the Chernobyl accident.

All operations in all fuel cycles give rise to wastes, for instance, tailings from uranium mining, leakage of methane gas, oil spills in the ocean in the early part of the cycles.

In the nuclear fuel cycle, highly radioactive material arises only after irradiation and use of the uranium in the reactor. The amounts of highly radioactive wastes are small. This is one of the main advantages of nuclear power, as it enables us to dispose of practically all the waste that arises, and certainly all that is hazardous, in a controlled manner. Let me give some data. The operation of a capacity of 3,000 MW(e) in light water reactors will produce about 75 tons of spent fuel annually as a high-level, long-lived radioactive waste. It is often contended by opponents of nuclear power that we do not know how to isolate this waste safely and I fear that a large number of people are of this view. It is not correct. When most countries have decided to store such spent fuel for some 30 to 50 years before either disposing of it as waste or reprocessing it, there are two reasons for this. One is the difficulty of getting political and public acceptance of disposal sites. The other is that by waiting some 50 years, both the radioactivity and the heat produced by the spent fuel will have dropped to about one twenty-fifth of what they were one year after discharge from the reactor. This, of course, simplifies the design of both the waste container and the storage to achieve the safe isolation which is required for a very long time period.

If the 75 tons of spent fuel from one year of 3,000 MW(e) of nuclear plant operation were to be reprocessed rather than stored without reprocessing, the high-level waste could be concentrated in about 9 cubic meters of glass. It gives perhaps some idea about the small volumes we are dealing with when I say that if all the spent fuel in the world from 1987 were to be reprocessed, the high-level vitrified waste would be some 1000-1500 cubic meters, or less than the volume of a two-family house.

Nuclear power plant operation will also give rise to low- and intermediate-level, short-lived wastes, such as filter materials, contaminated clothing, tools and scrap material. This waste needs to be stored and isolated for some hundreds of years. A typical annual quantity from 3,000 MW(e) of light water reactor operation would be about 1500 cubic meters before compacting and concentration. That is equal to a cube with a side of 12 meters, or again about the volume of a two-family house. For this type of waste, some final disposal facilities are already in operation, for instance in Sweden.

Protecting Future Generations

In all countries which have nuclear power plants, there are strict national regulations about waste disposal to protect not only present, but all future generations. It would, for instance, be impossible today to obtain a license for a waste disposal site without having made worst case assumptions including the dissolution of the containers and transport of dissolved radioactive materials by the groundwater to the biosphere and still being able to show that the dose commitment to the future population is low and well below what standards would permit.

It is sometimes suggested that our generation is reaping the benefits of nuclear power, while leaving the financial cost of waste disposal to succeeding generations. However, in several countries there is a legal requirement to add to the price of the nuclear kWh [kilowatt hour] a charge covering the future costs of the management and disposal of the radioactive wastes, and also of future decommissioning of the plants. Contrary to what many believe, these costs are not overwhelming. In Sweden, the addition to the kWh price is two hundredths of a Swedish Crown per kWh, or about 10% of the total price. This sum is placed in an accumulating fund which should be more than sufficient to cover future costs. The estimates of the costs are not very different in other countries.

A concern sometimes voiced about nuclear waste is that we have no experience of the physical behaviour of such waste over the long time periods in question. Two areas of study have, however, given us relevant and interesting experience.

The first shows that in many geological uranium deposits the materials have remained in place for millions of years in spite of being exposed directly to groundwater. The second study has regard to the natural reactor which operated many millions of years ago in a uranium deposit at Oklo in what is presently Gabon. In a rich surface deposit of uranium a chain reaction started "spontaneously" and went on for about 500,000 years, and resulted in some six tons of fission products and two tons of plutonium. It is noteworthy that neither the fission products nor the plutonium have moved more than some centimeters from their place of production, even though they had been directly exposed to the elements without any encapsulation. The two examples I have cited are no cause for complacency about long-lived nuclear waste, but they do contradict the contention that we know nothing about what may happen in the distant future.

Uncontrolled Radioactive Releases

The environmental concerns mostly voiced about the use of nuclear power aim not only at the waste, which I have discussed, but also at the risk of uncontrolled radioactive releases in the case of accidents. There have been two major nuclear power plant accidents. In both cases, the reactor cores were damaged, but they were different in other respects. Like most power reactors in the Western industrialized world, the one at Three Mile Island had a containment and this did function as the safety barrier that it was designed to be. There were no significant releases of radioactivity and no one was injured.

It is years since the Chernobyl accident and a great deal is known about it and about its effects. This reactor did not have a containment around it and large amounts of radioactive substances were released. Some 200-300 persons—operational and fire fighting staff—received high doses and suffered radiation sickness. Twenty-nine of them died of their radiation injuries, but most of the others are back in

productive work after hospital treatment. Over 100,000 persons have been evacuated from their homes and have been settled in other areas. In the restricted zone that was established within a radius of 30 km around the power plant, comprehensive decontamination has been carried out. Some people have moved back, but no general return has been authorized.

"In all countries which have nuclear power plants, there are strict national regulations about waste disposal to protect not only present, but all future generations."

Authoritative figures are now available on how much radioactivity increased in various areas as a result of the Chernobyl accident. UNSCEAR has calculated that the population of Europe, including the European part of the Soviet Union, during the first year after the accident, received on average an additional radiation dose due to fallout that was less than a third of the dose that is received annually from the atmosphere and the environment. Even for the most exposed population, in White Russia, the average additional dose was less than one year's natural dose. These low average values must not, of course, lead us to overlook the fact that a number of people in the vicinity of Chernobyl received much higher doses.

As an industrial accident, the Chernobyl case is unique in some respects, but hardly in the number of deaths or injured. Other ways of generating energy have also taken their tolls. The oil platform that exploded in 1988 in the North Sea took 165 lives. An explosion in a coal mine in the Federal Republic of Germany, likewise in 1988, killed 57 miners. A gas explosion in Mexico City in 1984 left some 450 dead and thousands of people injured. A dam that burst in India in 1979 killed 15,000 people.

No comparison with other accidents will bring back to life the people who died at Chernobyl. However, both in the Soviet Union and in other countries, the accident set in motion many measures designed to reduce further the risk of any accidents. Whether in air traffic or any other human activity, the risks can rarely be reduced to zero, but safety is never a static concept. It is continuously improving. Of particular interest are the measures being taken to ensure that even in the case of a major reactor accident, there will not be radioactive releases. Mechanisms allowing the release of any overpressures in the containment while filtering any radioactive substances are examples of such measures.

Having examined health and environmental

aspects of the use of nuclear power and identified some of the consequences an alternative use of fossil fired generation of electricity would have, I should like to conclude with some comments on how the continued and expanded use of nuclear power can help us to reduce the risk of global warming through the greenhouse effect.

"The continued and expanded use of nuclear power can help us to reduce the risk of global warming through the greenhouse effect."

It is evident that this threat is attracting ever greater public attention and anxiety. Perhaps thereby even far-reaching measures of response will become politically possible. The Declaration adopted in March 1989 at the Hague, by heads of state and governments called for a new international authority with power, if need be, to decide on measures even if these were not unanimously supported and the Soviet Foreign Minister, Mr. Shevardnadze, called during 1988's United Nations General Assembly for consideration of how to turn the United Nations Environmental Programme into an environmental council capable of taking effective decisions to ensure ecological security. Other public statements have called for an international convention against climate change.

These are welcome proposals, but it is important to place the energy policies directly on the world's agenda. Indeed, as you know, about 50% of the greenhouse effect is deemed to be linked to the release of CO_2, most of it from the burning of fossil fuels. Other gases contributing to the effect are CFCs [chlorofluorocarbons], which will need to be reduced anyway because of their impact on the ozone layer, and methane. While research will no doubt intensify to tell us more reliably and in greater detail about the factors that drive the greenhouse effect, it seems to be an accepted proposition that we need to reduce the world's emissions of CO_2, which are at present calculated to be about 20,000 million tons per year from the burning of fossil fuels. The Toronto Conference on the Changing Atmosphere in 1988 proposed a reduction of the CO_2 emissions by 20% from present levels by the year 2005. In absolute terms, this would mean a reduction of about 4,000 million tons per year. Further research might modify this figure, but it is worth noting that if the electricity that was generated by the world's nuclear power stations in 1987 had been generated instead by the burning of coal, this would have resulted in the emission of about 1,600 million tons of CO_2 plus, of course, large quantities of SO_2, NO_x and heavy metals. It does not take any imagination

to realize that an expansion of the use of nuclear power could help to further contain the CO_2 emissions. . . .

When we look to the future, it is very hard to conceive of anything but strong demand for more use of energy, and particularly electricity. . . .

There are wide variations in the present use of electricity in the world—not only between industrialized and developing countries, but also within these groups. Norway tops the users list with 25,000 kWh per capita and year. The Netherlands is at 4,600 kWh, France at 6,200 per capita and year, the USSR and Japan at about 5,500, South Korea at 1,550, China at 420, India at 270 and Bangladesh at 50 kWh per capita and year. No one can doubt that those in the lower part of the league will increase their use. The—justified—call for greater energy efficiency will not stop demands for more energy.

Greater Energy Production

Not surprisingly we find that the *actual plans* of the world's governments are for greater energy production—in particular, electricity generation. In some developing countries, hydropower can still be exploited and will doubtlessly be exploited. For the rest, we can see a strong planned expansion in the use of fossil fuels. China, which is already the biggest user of coal in the world, plans to double its coal production from the levels of the mid-1980s by the year 2000. India plans to triple its coal production in the same period, and these two countries together—with more than a third of the world's population—will use more coal than all the OECD [Organization for Economic Cooperation and Development] countries by the year 2000. For the whole world, present plans point to an increase of around 40% in coal use by the year 2000. This does not exactly augur well for efforts to decrease CO_2 emissions. Most countries are not focussing their discussions on the use of more efficient light bulbs or more windmills or less driving, but on the use of more trucks and cars, refrigerators and air conditioning. To most developing countries, the nuclear option will not be open before the end of the century. If nuclear power is to be relied on to alleviate our burdening of the atmosphere with CO_2, it is therefore to the industrialized countries that we must look. They are in the position to use these advanced technologies—and they are also the greatest emitters of CO_2.

Hans Blix is the director general of the International Atomic Energy Agency in Vienna, Austria.

"Plutonium is already damaging people and the environment on which we depend."

Nuclear Power Is Not Environmentally Safe

Mary Davis

A few years ago my husband and I had the good fortune to live in a village outside Lyon, France. The countryside was idyllic, and I felt a bond with the meadows and wooded hills. Yet I feared for the future of the land; I wondered whether I would ever walk the tree-shaded lanes again.

In the hills above I knew there loomed communication towers for the French nuclear strike force; and some thirty miles to the east, engineers were readying for operation the Superphenix, the world's first commercial-size breeder reactor, a plant fueled by plutonium.

Plutonium has been described by Glenn Seaborg, the scientist who first isolated it, as "diabolically toxic." Inhaling even a minute speck can cause leukemia or cancer of the lungs, liver, or bones. Like other forms of radioactivity, plutonium also produces genetic damage that will be carried from one generation to another. Because plutonium is fissile, it is used in nuclear weapons. It is, in fact, particularly valued for armaments, since a plutonium bomb is smaller and lighter than a uranium bomb with the same power.

Plutonium does not occur in nature. It is an artificial element created by bombarding uranium-238 with neutrons. Once formed, it lasts, for all practical purposes, forever. Twenty-four thousand years must pass before the radioactivity in a given quantity of plutonium decays to a harmless level; two hundred and forty thousand before the radioactivity is negligible. The element can be thought of, in fact, as a physical symbol for the biblical concept that evil came into the world with humankind. Plutonium is a poison that we are foisting on ourselves and on the rest of creation.

Plutonium is produced in fuel rods during the normal operation of electricity-generating reactors. France, a country the size of Texas, has some fifty reactors; five, in addition to the Superphenix, are near Lyon. Plutonium is also made in military production reactors. It cannot be used for weapons while it remains in the fuel rods or targets in which it was created. It is freed from them by a chemical procedure known as reprocessing. The United States currently frees, by reprocessing, only the plutonium made in its military reactors; we plan at present to dispose of our irradiated fuel intact. Such is not the case in Europe or in Japan.

Currently there are two commercial reprocessing plants in operation: La Hague in France and Sellafield in the United Kingdom. More than sixty tons of plutonium have already been separated from commercial fuel in the noncommunist world. Major new reprocessing facilities are scheduled to go into operation in France, the United Kingdom, West Germany, and Japan in the early- to mid-1990s. Therefore, if all goes as planned, a total of 350 to 400 tons of plutonium will have been put into circulation by the year 2000. These figures are frightening, given that thirteen pounds suffice to make a Nagasaki-type bomb.

Breeder Reactors

Some of the plutonium will be used in breeder reactors, like the 1200 MW [megawatts] Superphenix, to generate electricity. The civilian breeder-reactor program was killed in the United States, at least temporarily, by the defeat of funding for the Clinch River breeder in 1983. In Europe and Japan, breeder programs are still in existence. The Superphenix has encountered various start-up problems and was shut down for an indefinite period in the summer of 1987 because of a sodium leak in a barrel used to help move fuel in and out of the reactor. Officials are refusing to abandon the plant and are talking of operating without the barrel, although independent

Mary Davis, "The Plutonium Economy," reprinted with permission from *The Other Side*, © 1988, 300 W. Apsley St., Philadelphia, PA 19144, subscriptions: $27 per year.

scientists question whether this would be safe.

Breeder technology has lured utilities by promising a limitless supply of energy, since, in theory at least, breeder reactors produce more plutonium than they consume. However, because of a sharp drop in the price of uranium, it is now obvious that breeders will not be worthwhile, from an economic point of view, before the next century.

"Reprocessing is actually making waste management more expensive and more complicated."

Meanwhile, another use is being found for plutonium: a fuel known as MOX, made of a blend of plutonium and uranium oxides. Electricity-producing reactors other than breeders are normally fueled only by uranium. However, utilities in Belgium, Switzerland, West Germany, and France have begun using MOX, and utilities in the United Kingdom and Japan are considering doing so. By 1995 Electricity of France will be loading ninety tons of MOX a year into light-water reactors. With the use of MOX in civilian reactors, plutonium will become an item of ordinary commerce.

Unfortunately, many people in the countries moving towards the plutonium economy do not realize the significance of reprocessing, breeders, and MOX. In Europe reprocessing has long been regarded as the answer to the nuclear-waste problem. Many people are unaware that reprocessing is actually making waste management more expensive and more complicated. They do not understand that plutonium is more dangerous than uranium, harmful though it is. This is particularly true in France, which now receives approximately 70 percent of its electricity from nuclear power.

Yet France, along with neighboring sections of Italy, Germany, and Switzerland, is at particular risk. There are scientific reasons for my fears that Lyon and Creys-Malville, the site of the Superphenix, could become household words like Kiev and Chernobyl. The plutonium in breeders, unlike the fuel in standard utility reactors, can form a critical mass and explode. The more likely origin of a major accident, however, is the reactor coolant, sodium. Sodium explodes in contact with water and burns in contact with air. The Superphenix contains water, five thousand tons of sodium, and more than five tons of plutonium. A study conducted for the British Radiological Protection Board in 1977 estimated that the release of 10 percent of the fuel in a breeder approximately the size of the Superphenix would cause six thousand immediate and sixty thousand delayed deaths. The figures are based on a semiurban area like that around Creys-Malville.

Plutonium is already damaging people and the environment on which we depend. The worst case in point is the Sellafield reprocessing plant on the northwest coast of England. This plant constantly pipes liquid radioactive waste into the Irish Sea. Scientists estimate that, since the opening of the facility in 1964, half a ton of plutonium has gone into the water. Furthermore, the plant releases into the air radioactive particles that appear to be linked with a higher than normal rate of leukemia in children. The U.S. Department of Energy's Rocky Flats plutonium facility is another example of the effects of plutonium—excessively high cancer rates downwind of the plant have been documented.

The antinuclear forces in Europe vary in strength from country to country, and the arguments that they use vary. Most speak of the environmental and health threat. Increasingly they are also publicizing the armaments connection. Among the slogans of the French antinuclear movement, for instance, has been the phrase, *"Derrière Malville, nos Euromissiles"*—*"Behind Malville, our Euromissiles."* The activists argue convincingly that the production and use of plutonium to generate electricity is a façade for and a tool of the nuclear-weapons industry.

Military Quality Uranium

A blanket of non-fissile uranium-238 surrounds the fuel of the Superphenix. During operation this uranium will become plutonium of high military quality. France runs only two small military production reactors. Plutonium from the Superphenix, its prototype the Phenix, and an old gas graphite reactor will enable the nation to modernize its nuclear strike force at the expense of consumers of electricity. In Britain and West Germany, there are also links between civilian plutonium and militarization. In fact, the West German Greens accuse their government of promoting the civilian nuclear industry in order to secure the capability of making nuclear weapons, when it decides to do so.

The danger of terrorist attacks and of the loss of civil liberties is an integral part of the weapons connection. The low-enriched uranium burned in utility reactors can be made into bombs, but it is not a first choice for this purpose. Plutonium is more usable for weapons and thus a much more tempting target either for terrorist groups or for nations trying to obtain a nuclear capability. As a result, shipments of plutonium must be closely guarded.

Despite all I have read about the problems that a plutonium society will cause, I was shocked by descriptions of the transport in 1984 of 188 kilograms of fissile plutonium from the La Hague reprocessing plant to Japan. The night of October 4, French activists from the Anti-Plutonium Group of Cherbourg discovered that their homes were under police surveillance. They realized that this was a sign that the plutonium was on its way from the plant to the Cherbourg arsenal where a ship waited. The road was "totally neutralized by gendarmes," the newspaper *Liberation* reported. One hundred police cars and trucks of the gendarmerie and army accompanied the semitrailers. At sea, the ship was protected by a satellite and by vessels of the U.S., French, and Japanese navies.

The secrecy that surrounds plutonium shipments extends to matters other than transport. Governments tend to conceal facts to try to prevent the public from demanding the closure of polluting plants. The British Black Commission studying the relationship between Sellafield and leukemia was given estimates for airborne emissions during the fifties that were too low by a factor of twenty to fifty. The quantities of chemicals released by the La Hague reprocessing plant were not made available to a government-appointed commission studying waste handling, let alone to the public. As plutonium is bought, sold, and transported from place to place, secrecy and armed guards will become increasingly common. . . .

Christian activists believe that stopping the production and use of plutonium is an important aspect of their religious commitment. Christ healed the sick and helped the oppressed. Working to prevent illness and death from radioactive contamination can be as much a part of the Christian mission as binding up wounds. Trying to end policies that are causing individuals to lose their freedom belongs to the Christian tradition also. In a nuclear society all humankind is oppressed. Our lives and health are threatened by human-made situations which are beyond our control—and about which we are often not allowed to know the truth. . . .

"British environmentalists are putting pressure on members of Parliament to shut down Sellafield and protesting plans for a reprocessing plant for breeder fuel."

Nevertheless, resistance continues. In West Germany there will be more demonstrations against Wackersdorf, and the Greens in the Bundestag are asking awkward questions of the administration. British environmentalists are putting pressure on members of Parliament to shut down Sellafield and protesting plans for a reprocessing plant for breeder fuel. In France, where the safe-energy movement is only now recovering from the setback of 1977 and the peace movement has been weak since World War II, groups are concentrating on public

education.

Burnout is a condition that the European activists cannot afford. Pressure against breeders and reprocessing must be maintained; the use of MOX fuel in commercial reactors must be stopped—now, if at all. Mycle Schneider of WISE-Paris reports, "The commercial breeder has no future; but the industry does not declare the breeder to be dead because the industry wants to rescue the reprocessing option. It wants to create another *fait accompli* which is MOX"—an excuse for continuing to extract plutonium from irradiated fuel.

A Plutonium Economy

Can North Americans do anything to help stop the advent of a "plutonium economy"? The U.S. government has the right to intervene directly in many overseas nuclear matters. Because of earlier treaties, foreign countries cannot reprocess much of the irradiated fuel now in storage or transfer the resulting plutonium without our approval. The United States had to grant permission, for instance, for the 1984 shipment of plutonium from France to Japan. Furthermore, by the terms of the U.S.-EURATOM Treaty, we could forbid the militarization of the Superphenix. We could also exert much the same type of pressure as regards nonproliferation on West Germany as we do on Libya and Pakistan. In fact, the West German Greens have asked us to do so.

The United States and Japan recently negotiated a treaty that would give Japan thirty-year blanket approval to reprocess and use as fuel in commercial reactors the plutonium from U.S.-controlled fuel. Japan plans to recover, by the year 2000, eighty-five metric tons of plutonium, most of which will come from fuel supplied by the United States or used in U.S.-supplied reactors. If members of Congress do not reject the treaty within ninety working days of its presentation to them, cargo planes will carry some five hundred pounds of plutonium every two weeks from Europe across Canada to Japan. On the way they will stop for refueling in Alaska.

The Nuclear Control Institute, which is spearheading the attack on the treaty, urges that our government take whatever steps are possible to stop the use of plutonium by utilities abroad. David Albright of the Federation of American Scientists, who first pointed out our position in regard to the Superphenix, emphasizes what we can accomplish with an indirect approach. He believes that we should assist groups opposed to reprocessing and breeders in their own countries and set a positive example by stopping military reprocessing in the United States. Along with other members of the federation, he argues that a mutual Soviet-U.S. ban on producing fissile material would be feasible and verifiable.

I returned to the village near Lyon. Roses were in

bloom along the hedgerows, and my sheepdog friends barked at me from their farm wall. The land near the Superphenix has so far been spared an accident that could be far worse than the contamination from Chernobyl. In the Ukraine there has been much suffering, and there will be more. Nevertheless, good can come from the disaster, if it causes people around the world to rethink their attitudes to nuclear energy and nuclear weapons and to act together to dispel the threat that they pose for all of us.

Alternative Energy

On the roof of the house in which we lived are solar panels for heating hot water; next to the Superphenix is a farm where the owner obtains fuel by turning farm wastes into methane. With our help, the solar panels and the farm—rather than the breeder—can become the symbol of the future.

Mary Davis specializes in nuclear energy and nuclear waste at the World Information Service on Energy (WISE) in Washington, D.C. WISE promotes the development of safe, non-nuclear energy and provides a worldwide network for groups opposed to nuclear energy development.

"Once the public comes to realize that it has been misled about radiological hazards, opposition to all aspects of the nuclear industry will grow."

Nuclear Power Endangers Public Health

John W. Gofman, interviewed by Brian Jacobs

Brian Jacobs: From your own experience with both heart and radiation research, you have witnessed the lag that sometimes occurs between new ideas and their acceptance in the public health community. What accounts for the lag that has occurred between the scientific treatment of certain radiation issues and public policy?

Nuclear Power Generation

John W. Gofman: When governments or other powerful agencies are committed to a particular project—nuclear power generation, for example—and when those same agencies are the sole or even main source of support for research on related health issues, you have the inescapable makings of a conflict of interest. Such agencies know that findings of adverse health consequences pose a challenge to their project. As a result, these agencies are hardly friendly toward health researchers who come up with what one might call "the wrong answer." The scientists supported by these agencies have thus learned which answers are not desired. So either they are silent on certain health issues or they interpret data in the most favorable light.

Let me give you a few examples. I was part of a team studying the health effects of radiation, at the request of the Atomic Energy Commission (AEC). The project was handsomely funded; it was awarded about $3 to $3.5 million a year for almost seven years. In 1969, we issued a report stating that the radiation hazards relevant to cancer induction were some 20 times higher than generally accepted. The AEC declared war on us immediately. Similarly, when Drs. Thomas Mancuso, Alice Stewart, and George Kneale showed that there was an unusually high incidence of cancer at the Hanford plutonium

reprocessing plant among workers receiving higher-than-usual doses of radiation, the AEC immediately defunded their study. It was very useful for the AEC then, as it is for the Department of Energy now, to announce that they were conducting these impressive studies. But they don't want any unfavorable results to issue from them. As a matter of fact, they sometimes prefer that the results not come out at all so they can say the problem is still being studied.

Jacobs: The debates between proponents and opponents of nuclear energy—whether the issue is economics, nuclear waste, or accident probability—ultimately come down to the question of radiological hazards. As such, the radiation issue is a foundation on which all these other issues are built. If that foundation is faulty, as you have just suggested, what are the implications?

Gofman: There is no doubt that the question of radiological hazards is the foundation upon which all other issues of nuclear energy rest, and that foundation is indeed seriously faulty. It is a matter of record, not opinion, that government-sponsored research and governmental and quasi-governmental commissions and committees have consistently been wrong on their estimate of the risk per unit dose of radiation. I am completely confident, based upon the evidence available from numerous epidemiological studies, that such agencies are today underestimating the cancer risk per unit dose by between 18 and 37 times, depending on which governmental reports you use.

A Radiological Hazard

By the way, this error has not arisen by accident. The sponsors of nuclear energy know full well that a serious radiological hazard represents the greatest threat to their enterprise. In their support of health research, therefore, they are not interested in scientific truth so much as they are in confirming

John W. Gofman, interviewed by Brian Jacobs, "On Radiation Hazards and Public Policy," *World Policy Journal*, Vol. IV, No. 2, 1987. Reprinted with permission.

that there is little risk of serious health injury per unit dose. Just look at the track record of independent scientists and that of government-sponsored scientists. Over and over, the independent scientists have been correct and the government scientists have been wrong and have had grudgingly to admit some of their errors.

Jacobs: Could you give an example?

Gofman: Independent predictions 20 years ago stated that virtually all forms of cancer are inducible by ionizing radiation. This was fiercely resisted by government-supported scientists, who demanded that a separate independent study prove that each and every cancer was inducible before they would assign any risk at all. Since that kind of study takes time, the government was able to claim a nonexistent risk for many types of cancer until the epidemiological evidence was in. Sound public policy would have suggested a different approach. Today, finally, government scientists admit the truth of this generalization.

Another example: the current estimates of cancer risk per unit dose, which I say are 18 to 37 times too low, rest largely upon the mistaken claim that the primary cause of cancer at Hiroshima was the neutron dose, not gamma rays. Based upon this error, government scientists constructed models of risk versus dose that led to very low risk estimates for gamma ray exposure. Independent scientists pointed out in 1980 that this was erroneous. And indeed it was wrong, since we now know that neutrons were not even present to any significant degree at Hiroshima. Belatedly, government scientists are acknowledging that they will have to raise their risk of cancer estimates.

"A safe threshold cannot exist for cancer induction by radiation."

After conceding one point after another regarding the risk of cancer from radiation, government-supported scientists are now saying that there could be a safe threshold—a dose below which no cancer at all would occur because repair mechanisms would take care of any injury. It is true that as one goes to lower and lower doses it takes enormous numbers of individuals studied in epidemiological studies to determine whether or not a safe threshold exists. But recently I have proved from a combination of cell biology, physics, and epidemiology that such a safe threshold cannot exist for cancer induction by radiation. I presented my findings at the American Chemical Society meeting on September 9, 1986, but I expect there will be a torrent of resistance to this work before it is accepted simply because it removes one of the last supports of the shaky foundation upon which official assessments of the health risks

of nuclear energy have rested. Some will say that government-supported scientists don't really claim there is a safe threshold. But when a serious accident such as Chernobyl occurs, these scientists are all over the media stating that the doses received are below those that could cause any public health injury. What is this other than claiming a safe threshold?

Cancer Deaths

There are numerous other illustrations, but the central question remains: how does it happen that government-supported scientists can be so wrong so often? Why do they never estimate a risk that turns out to be too high rather than too low? These same scientists are now saying that even if an accident causes 100,000 or one million radiation-induced cancer deaths we should really not look at those numbers; we should instead look at the fact that 100 million people will die anyway from cancer induced by other causes. Since Chernobyl, the press has been full of such statements by so-called experts—experts in immorality, perhaps, but that is about all the expertise that should be credited them. If the public realized how rotten the foundations are upon which government-supported radiation health science rests, objections to all aspects of nuclear energy would increase enormously. Therefore governments consider it very important that the public remain ignorant of the truth on such matters.

But I might add one hopeful note here. It is difficult, over the long run, to hide the truth completely, even with valiant efforts to do so. For example, recently the latest follow-up on radiation-induced cancer deaths among the Hiroshima-Nagasaki population became available. Since this represents a total of 37 years of follow-up, it is what we might call a maturing epidemiological sample. I studied these new results in detail, setting aside all my previous work with prior data from Japan or elsewhere. And I arrived at exactly the same conclusion that I had in 1980, namely that the United Nations Scientific Committee estimate of radiation hazard is 37 times too low and that the U.S. National Academy of Sciences Committee on Biological Effects of Radiation estimate of hazards of radiation is some 18 times too low.

Jacobs: What are the implications of radiological hazards for the economical operation of nuclear power plants? Is it possible to operate plants both safely and economically?

Gofman: If government and industry do not get away with the fraud that low doses are safe, they will be forced to restrict their emissions to far smaller amounts and the costs of operating these plants are going to soar out of sight. Already, one of the chief reasons nuclear power has become increasingly uneconomical is the need to adopt a whole set of additional safeguards to protect against an accident.

It is interesting to note that the law admits a certain contradiction in the claim that nuclear power plants can be operated safely. In this country, the Price-Anderson law limits the liability of utility companies to a trivial fraction of the damage an accident could cause. A Chernobyl-type accident might cause $50 billion worth of damage, yet the current ceiling on liability is $600 million. Most other countries have similar rules in force. Yet if the industry believed one iota of what it says, it would clamor to repeal the Price-Anderson law, thereby proving to the public that it really does have faith in the safety of its own plants. But does it do that? No. Instead, the industry has been clamoring to see that the law is renewed.

I think the industry is very, very worried about an accident. A lot of these companies—the utility companies, the manufacturing companies—have invested up to their eyeballs in this. They've got a horrible amount of money at risk. So they take very careful pains to ensure that if it does happen, they're not going to lose their money. And that tells you a great deal. Now, I don't know what the chance of an accident is. I do know, however, that when so-called experts come out and say they've performed a thorough analysis of the whole system and have come to the conclusion that an accident could occur once every 20 years or every 100,000 years, you can just discard that sort of thing as worthless.

It's sort of like the Maginot Line. After World War I, the French constructed the Maginot Line because they based all their thinking about future conflicts on the one they had just been through. But as a defense in World War II, the Maginot Line proved totally useless. In the case of nuclear power, something goes wrong at Three Mile Island and something else goes wrong at Chernobyl and there is great concern. The experts analyze and analyze and perhaps they remedy the specific problem that caused the difficulty. But in a very complex technology such as nuclear power, accidents of an unforeseen nature can easily occur. I will venture to state that the next nuclear power accident, whenever it is, will arise from causes totally different than those responsible for either Three Mile Island or Chernobyl.

The Economic Consequences

In the end, the economic consequences of barging ahead with a 37-fold underestimate of the health consequences of exposure can be very serious indeed. Once the public comes to realize that it has been misled about radiological hazards, opposition to all aspects of the nuclear industry will grow. The economic consequences of having based your plans for electrical energy on an unacceptable technology could mean an enormous waste of capital resources that could prove ruinous for investors and could lead to severe dislocations of the economy.

Jacobs: The philosopher of science Paul Feyerabend argues that science cannot be left strictly in the hands of scientists. Public exclusion from scientific debate that is termed too technical, he maintains, has served scientists well by minimizing controversy or hiding their ignorance. Does this generalization apply to the radiation issue? Is the controversy too technical to include the public? Or, conversely, should the public be making some of the decisions currently decided by scientists?

Gofman: I agree totally with Professor Feyerabend's comments. My experience has been that scientific issues *can* be explained to the public and that the public quickly comes to ask very penetrating questions. For that reason I have suggested, on innumerable occasions, that the so-called radiation controversy be aired on the floor of Congress, preferably with full television and radio coverage. I doubt that the scientists involved in the effort to hide the dangers of radiation could stand up in such a forum.

"If the public realized how rotten the foundations are upon which government-supported radiation health science rests, objections to all aspects of nuclear energy would increase enormously."

Jacobs: Considering the extent of the Chernobyl accident and the loss of life expected from its fallout, the nuclear establishment seems to have been able to minimize, if not recoup, its political losses. How was it able to do so, and what does this reveal about the general treatment of nuclear energy questions in the industrialized world?

Gofman: I would attribute the containment of political loss in the wake of Chernobyl to a very poor job done by the world press and the electronic media. Good journalism would mandate that, on matters of such great health importance, truly independent opinions be solicited concerning the consequences of the accident. Yet over and over one finds the press accepting statements like, "The consensus of scientists is such-and-such." Generally no probing has been done to validate the statement. Moreover, if hundreds of scientists, totally unfamiliar with the epidemiological evidence and supported by pronuclear governmental agencies, say that something is true, that is meaningless unless evidence can be marshalled. Serious health issues are not resolved by popularity contests, particularly if the poll is taken from a biased set of persons.

Let me illustrate with an example from recent experience. My reading of the evidence has led me to estimate that the total number of cancers that will result from the Chernobyl accident is one million—including those inside and outside the Soviet Union—and that half of those cancers will be fatal. But if you examine media comments, you will generally discover that the Chernobyl accident caused 31 deaths. Of course, what they are talking about is immediate deaths, but this is a gross distortion. In the industrialized world, sadly, the press and electronic media have a great tendency to protect their rear end. They rarely can get in trouble by accepting what so-called experts say. And for this they go to governments, or government-supported sources. On the other hand, they may experience the wrath of God if they go outside these sources. . . .

Jacobs: The International Commission on Radiological Protection (ICRP) is the most influential group in the world in setting radiation standards. Yet throughout the various controversies concerning radiation, such as weapons testing and waste storage, the organization has kept a low profile. When called upon to give his estimates of the deaths Chernobyl will eventually cause, ICRP Chair Dan Beninson gave figures that appear to be gross underestimates. How do you account for this kind of behavior in an organization whose purpose, as its name implies, is to protect populations from radiation exposure?

Protecting Populations

Gofman: I have very grave difficulty with the statement that the ICRP is dedicated to protecting populations from radiation exposure. The selection process that governs membership in the ICRP favors only those persons acceptable to the nuclear establishments of the world's nuclear power nations. ICRP members are never nominated by independent agencies. So, here too, an inherent conflict of interest exists. So long as the ICRP continues to use values between 5,000 and 10,000 person rads [a measure of radiation absorbed] for fatal cancer from radiation exposure, in spite of a mountain of evidence indicating that the true value is in the neighborhood of 260 person rads, I see no reason to interpret any pronouncement from the ICRP as a serious evaluation of the health risks of radiation or of nuclear power. You simply cannot have organizations whose members are chosen as they are for something like the ICRP and whose base of support is what it is.

Jacobs: The accident at Chernobyl has shown that nuclear safety is an issue that concerns those beyond the borders of a country operating a reactor. Sweden, for example, has hastened its retreat from nuclear power. Yet even when the last Swedish reactor has been dismantled, Swedish citizens will still be vulnerable, and perhaps hostage, to other countries' nuclear safety operations. Because radiation plumes respect no political boundaries, is nuclear power a transnational issue? If so, how can it be treated as such?. . .

"In a very complex technology such as nuclear power, accidents of an unforeseen nature can easily occur."

Gofman: On this I would say that the accident at Chernobyl demonstrates most clearly that nuclear power is a transnational issue without any respect for political boundaries. To treat nuclear power as a transnational issue, however, it would be necessary to have all countries involved adhere to the principle of the sacredness of contracts and the principle of respect for the human rights of all people. Obviously, we are far, far away from such a situation. So, frankly, I am not optimistic that there will be any transnational treatment of this issue in any meaningful fashion. The fact that the various governments get together and announce they will increase safety measures and they will provide early warning of accidents that may cross national borders is simply nonsense. That's what the nuclear promoters always do after an accident—vow to do better next time. You see, if nations were forced to compensate for the economic consequences of their own radioactive garbage—not just within a country but everywhere that garbage is spewed—they would have to rethink whether nuclear power is economical at all. We certainly know that governments pick and choose what decisions they like from the World Court, so I see very little hope in that direction.

Now, of course, as long as the deception continues about the true value of the cancer risk per rad of radiation and as long as so-called experts give the authorities refuge with the statements about a so-called safe threshold of radiation, there is even less reason to expect much progress toward dealing fairly with the transnational aspects of the problem. Nor can you expect real transnational justice in handling the problem so long as people downplay the deaths caused by a nuclear accident simply because there are other events and phenomena that cause even more deaths.

John W. Gofman is a physician and nuclear physicist. Gofman was director of the Biomedical Research Division of the Lawrence Livermore National Laboratory, is professor emeritus at the University of California at Berkeley, and was chairperson of the Committee for Nuclear Responsibility. Brian Jacobs is a writer specializing in environmental policy.

"The use of coal and oil has serious health consequences, more serious than those of today's nuclear power plants."

Nuclear Power Does Not Endanger Public Health

The International Atomic Energy Association

The effects of large doses of radiation received at high dose rates are well-documented and understood, but there is less factual certainty about the effects of exposure to low-level radiation. . . .

Ionizing Radiation

The term "radiation" is very broad: it includes visible, infra-red and ultraviolet light, and radio waves. It is also used, however, to mean "ionizing" radiation; that is, radiation which changes the physical state of atoms which it strikes, causing them to become electrically charged or "ionized". In some circumstances, the presence of such ions in living tissues can disrupt normal biological processes. Just as excessive exposure to other forms of radiation can do harm, ionizing radiation may represent a health hazard to man. It is the only form of radiation discussed here.

Some exposure to ionizing radiation cannot be avoided. There are many souces of exposure: they include naturally-occurring radionuclides contained in the earth, building materials, air, food and water, and cosmic rays. The most important man-made sources of exposure are X-rays and radioisotopes used for medical diagnosis and treatment. Others include fallout from nuclear weapons testing and radionuclides emitted from installations where radioactive materials are used (such as radioisotope production facilities and nuclear power plants) in the course of normal operation or if an accident occurs.

Absorbed doses of radiation are expressed in terms of a unit called the *gray* (Gy), which is a measure of the amount of radiation-energy absorbed in any sort of matter. Biologically, not only the amount of radiation is important, but also its type: equal doses of radiation do not necessarily have equal biological effects. Another unit takes these differing effects into account by weighting the absorbed dose by a "quality factor" for each type of radiation. This unit, which is used to measure the *absorbed dose equivalent,* is the *sievert* (Sv).

One sievert of alpha radiation delivered, for example, to the thyroid is reckoned to create the same risk of causing harm as one sievert of beta or gamma radiation. However, different organs have differing sensitivities to radiation, and the magnitude of the risk per unit dose equivalent is therefore different for different organs within the body. Additionally, irradiation of the reproductive organs may create the risk of hereditable damage. The overall risk of exposing the whole body to radiation is therefore the sum of the individual risks of harm to each organ which is affected. If the dose received by each organ is multiplied by an appropriate weighting factor, the sum of the products is the *effective absorbed dose equivalent.* This quantity is also measured in the unit sievert and is an indicator of the radiation risk to the exposed individual.

The sievert is a very large unit, and dose equivalents are more commonly expressed in terms of the millisievert (mSv), one-thousandth as large. On average, the effective dose equivalent an individual receives each year from low-level sources of all kinds amounts to about 2.4 mSv.

The Origins of Radiation Protection

It has long been recognized that large doses of ionizing radiation can damage human tissues. Harmful effects were reported within six months of Wilhelm Roentgen's discovery of X-rays in 1896: for a time workers checked the output of X-ray tubes by exposing themselves to the radiation they emitted and measuring the time required to irritate the skin! More than 300 later died from diseases attributed to their exposure to radiation—about 250 of skin cancer, and more than 50 of blood disorders

Excerpted with permission from "Facts About Low-Level Radiation," published by The International Atomic Energy Agency, Wagramerstrasse 5, A-1400, Vienna, Austria, 1989.

(anaemia and leukaemia). Yet practices now recognized to be hazardous continued. From 1915 onward, for example, hundreds of girls were employed by the Radium Luminous Materials Company, in New Jersey (USA), to paint products such as the dials of watches with a mixture of radium and zinc sulphide. The girls moistened the tips of their brushes by putting them in their mouths: local dentists soon reported a disease they termed "radium jaw", and by the end of 1926 four of the girls had died from bone cancers and aplastic anaemia. . . .

"Effects, if they exist at all, are masked by the 'normal' occurrence of disorders which may or may not be due to radiation exposure."

As more was learned, scientists became increasingly concerned about the potentially damaging effects of exposure to large doses of radiation. Yet people not only ignored the risks they ran, but actively if unwittingly sought them out: for many years people flocked to spas to test the alleged curative properties of radon in spring water, and applied radioactive compresses to relieve their rheumatism and arthritis. (Many people undoubtedly did obtain relief from pain; sufferers do benefit from bathing in heated pools, eating sensibly and breathing the fresh air of a mountain resort for a week or so. But "radioactivity" was the magnet drawing them there.) Even today, spa treatments are promoted in countries where there is strong opposition to other activities involving radiation exposure: it seems that radiation at such spas is considered "different" from radiation from other sources.

The scientific community's growing awareness of the need to regulate exposure to radiation prompted the formation of a number of expert bodies to consider what needed to be done. In 1928, at the second International Congress of Radiology, an independent non-governmental expert body, the International Commission on Radiological Protection (ICRP), was set up. At first, the ICRP was known as the International X-ray and Radium Protection Committee. It brought together experts who had been working in the field, with the aim of establishing basic principles for, and issuing recommendations on, radiation protection. The members of the ICRP were and still are chosen on the basis of their individual merit in medical radiology, health physics, genetics, and other related fields, and care is taken to ensure an appropriate balance of expertise irrespective of nationality. ICRP

recommendations are generally adopted as the basis for national regulations governing the exposure of radiation workers and members of the public. They have also been used by the IAEA [The International Atomic Energy Agency], the World Health Organization, the International Labour Organisation and the Nuclear Energy Agency of the OECD [Organization for Economic Cooperation and Development] in formulating their radiation protection standards. . . .

The effects of radiation at high dose and dose rate are reasonably well documented. Much information has been gleaned by study of the health records of people such as survivors of the bombing of Hiroshima and Nagasaki, and patients who have received large doses of radiation as part of their medical treatments—for example, those who have had radiotherapy for cancer. (The risk that radiotherapy may, in time, be responsible for the induction of further cancers is outweighed by the immediate benefit to the patient.) It is known, for example, that some of the health effects of exposure to radiation do not appear unless a certain minimum, quite large, dose is absorbed. A very large dose delivered over a short time will kill within days.

However, there is still considerable uncertainty about the effects of exposure to radiation at low dose and dose rate. This is because effects, if they exist at all, are masked by the "normal" occurrence of disorders which may or may not be due to radiation exposure. To make a statistically valid study of the effects of radiation on man at the dose levels which are of interest requires the observation of a population of millions, over several generations. Any such analysis is complicated by the fact that it is not possible to isolate a "control" population who is not exposed to radiation. To show conclusively that certain health effects are associated with a given radiation dose, the number of people that must be observed becomes larger and larger as the radiation dose decreases. In the long term, there is a potential for learning from a major epidemiological study of people who were exposed to radiation in the aftermath of the accident at Chernobyl; such a study is now under way in the Soviet Union.

Observable Effects

It is generally agreed that the only observable effect of the exposure of a large number of people to low-level radiation may be the induction of a few cancers in addition to the thousands which occur naturally, years or even decades after the exposure has been incurred. It is often forgotten that cancer is primarily a disease of old age. In countries where life expectancy is in the range of 60-70 years, 20% or more of all deaths are due to cancer, but the average victim is about 65 years old. Secondly, we may be exposed to thousands of substances in our everyday lives—in addition to radiation—which can cause cancer. The list of carcinogens includes items such as nitrosamines in well-done steaks, chimney soot, arsenic, paraffin oil, coal tar, some components of tobacco smoke, ultraviolet light, asbestos, some chemical dye intermediates, fungal toxins in food, viruses and even heat. Only in exceptional cases is it possible to identify conclusively the cause of a particular cancer.

Experimental Evidence

There is also experimental evidence from work with animals and plants that exposure to radiation can have genetic effects, though none which can be attributed to the effect of exposure to radiation have so far been detected with certainty in man. Again, if there were any hereditary effects of exposure to low-level radiation, they could be detected only by careful analysis of a large volume of statistical data, and they would have to be distinguished from those of a number of other agents which might also cause genetic disorders but whose effect may not be recognised until the damage has been done: thalidomide, once prescribed for pregnant women as a tranquilizer, was one example.

Nevertheless, it is presumed that exposure to radiation even at the levels due to natural background may affect human health. It is generally assumed as a practical hypothesis that the probability of an effect is strictly proportional to exposure, right down to zero dose. No evidence to contradict this assumption has been found.

However, there is still debate about the value to be assigned to the risk coefficient—the numerical relationship between probability of cancer induction and dose received. UNSCEAR [United Nations Scientific Committee on the Effects of Atomic Radiation] has published estimates of the risk of cancer for persons exposed to high radiation doses at high dose rates. These estimates have been derived mainly from observations of the Japanese survivors of the bombings of Hiroshima and Nagasaki, and of some groups of patients who have received therapeutic doses of radiation. New data concerning these groups have now been reviewed by the Committee and revised risk estimates are being made. The revised estimates are higher than before; how much higher depends on the methods used to calculate the number of cases of cancer deaths that are still to be expected in the studied populations.

One reason for new estimates being higher than before is that the doses to the Japanese survivors have been reassessed and found to have been lower than had been estimated earlier, thus increasing the estimate of the risk per unit dose. This increase is somewhat reduced by the present method of assessment, which takes into account the length of latent periods and the age structure of the population. . . .

However, it is believed that the cancer risk from X-rays and gamma rays at low radiation doses and dose rates is lower than the values assessed for high doses and dose rates. A correction factor would therefore be needed to calculate this risk from the numbers mentioned above. Such a factor certainly varies very widely but it is assumed that an appropriate range for the correction factor would lie between 2 and 10.

The idea that risk increases in proportion to increases in exposure, or dose, is not unique to radiation. It is equally true for many other agents that induce cancer. Whatever limit is set for exposure to such agents there will still be some risk; only at zero exposure would the risk disappear. In some cases, it may be possible to reduce exposure to zero; in others, it is not. In particular, we cannot avoid natural radiation. Radiation protection practices are aimed simply at keeping all the radiation risks to health as low as is reasonably achievable, social and economical considerations being taken into account, under the constraint that no individual will be subject to an undue risk. This is a central tenet in the ICRP's recommendations.

"Radiation protection practices are aimed simply at keeping all the radiation risks to health as low as is reasonably achievable."

It is against this background that the general philosophy and principles of radiation protection (which are fairly straightforward) and their points of detail (which can be complex) have developed. . . .

Risks in Everyday Life

We all face risks in everyday life. Some of these risks can be avoided (by choosing not to take part in a dangerous sport, for example) and others reduced (say, by giving up smoking). It is, however, impossible to eliminate all risks.

Some risks are imposed on individuals by the society in which they live. The use of coal, oil, and nuclear energy for electricity production, for example, creates some risks which are inescapable, and others which may be reduced by pollution control measures. In general, society accepts such risks, balancing them against the usefulness of electricity as an energy form. The principal risk faced by an individual is that his exposure to carcinogenic pollutants—of which radioactive effluents are only one form—will actually induce cancer. This is not the only potential effect of exposure to pollutants. Respiratory diseases made worse by exposure to oxides of sulphur and nitrogen and other emissions from coal-fired generating plants and domestic fireplaces have killed tens of thousands of people (in London alone, "smog" was responsible for the deaths of about 6000 people between 1950 and 1962). Such emissions are being blamed increasingly as contributors to "acid rain". More is being learned; in comparison, radiation and its effects on health are reasonably well understood.

Clearly, we need to know what risks we are exposed to, and how important each is. It is thought, for example, that tobacco smoke and chemical pollutants in the atmosphere of industrial cities cause roughly 25% of all fatal cancers; another 35% may be attributed to dietary factors, and 20-30% to other environmental causes. A large part, perhaps 90%, of the increase in lung cancer deaths over the past 50 years may be attributable to cigarette smoking. The remaining 10% may be caused by general atmospheric pollutants such as discharges from domestic and industrial furnaces, exhaust fumes from gasoline and diesel engines, dust and fumes from rubber tires, asphalt, paints, industrial chemicals, and so on. Low-level radiation can be only a very small contributor to the total.

"The effects that can be attributed to low-level radiation are also known to be caused by a large number of other agents."

Some people may think that certain activities are unnecessary and that any risk associated with them could be removed simply by eliminating them: for example, banning the production and use of asbestos. The situation is rarely so simple, and an action such as this might even lead to an overall increase in risk. Consider the case of the nuclear power industry. Nuclear power plants and other nuclear installations release small amounts of radioactive material in the course of normal operation. They therefore contribute to our total exposure to low-level radiation—on average, in a western industrialized country, about one-seven-hundredth of the total (a little more than a tenth of one per cent). They may therefore account for about one-seven-hundredth of the health effects attributable to all natural and man-made radiation. If there were no nuclear industry, would the total number of health effects be reduced by this amount?

Whatever one proposes as a possible replacement for nuclear power (including not replacing it with anything) would have some effect on human health. The use of coal and oil has serious health consequences, more serious than those of today's nuclear power plants. So using either (or both) of these energy sources as a replacement would not result in an overall improvement in public health, but rather a decline. Hydro power, where this is available as an alternative, may appear benign; but dam failures have killed thousands. The production and use of energy is risky. It is important to know the risks, to minimize them, and—as far as possible—to avoid them.

Increased Knowledge

More is known today about the risks of exposure to radiation than about those of practically any other physical or chemical agent in our environment.

Uncontrolled, large doses of radiation can kill. Even so, radiation in lesser, but still large, doses is often part of the treatment of cancer patients; the benefit of their exposure outweighs the small risk that the treatment may induce other cancer much later in life.

We are exposed every day to low-level radiation from natural and man-made sources in our environment. Various ways of relating the dose received to health effects have been proposed. It is very difficult to verify any one theory conclusively.

A consensus exists among experts in radiobiology that the number of effects produced by radiation on human health is proportional to the dose of radiation received, for both large and small doses (the linear model). Conclusions reached by a number of studies suggesting that this model underestimates the effects of low-level radiation have not proven convincing, and the consensus remains.

The health effects of exposure to radiation are not unique. The effects that can be attributed to low-level radiation are also known to be caused by a large number of other agents. The risks of radiation exposure to low-level radiation should not be disregarded; but it must be recognized that the risks to health posed by some of these other agents are much greater. Many more are almost unknown.

Founded in 1957, The International Atomic Energy Association is an organization established by the United Nations to promote the peaceful uses of atomic energy. Its headquarters are in Vienna, Austria.

"With their fast growing populations, struggling economies and faltering food production, many poor nations are facing catastrophe unless dramatic steps are taken."

Overpopulation Is a Global Problem

Anne H. Ehrlich and Paul R. Ehrlich

During the nineteenth century, birth rates had begun to decline in western nations, largely in response to social changes related to industrialisation, especially changing attitudes towards children. As more and more people left farming, moved to cities and became involved in manufacturing, children were no longer viewed almost purely as assets, useful as labour on the family farm and serving as a sort of old-age insurance. Instead, they became rather expensive consumers, requiring housing, food and education. People responded to these higher costs, as well as to the children's increasing chance of survival, by limiting their families. This phenomenon—a decline in birth rates following the decline in death rates in industrialising societies—became known as the demographic transition.

In the first half of the twentieth century, as the demographic transition was advancing in western nations, it spread to the industrialising eastern European nations and the Soviet Union. But it was not until after World War II that the reductions in death rates that had occurred earlier in the West spread to non-industrialized parts of the world.

Then, technologies for disease control—especially DDT and other pesticides to attack disease-carrying mosquitoes, and antibiotics to control bacterial infections—were widely disseminated in Asia, Africa and Latin America. These easily applied substances suddenly brought considerable control over malaria and numerous infectious diseases, causing human death rates to plummet, especially among the very young. By the 1970s, mortality rates in many less developed countries were approaching those in industrialised nations.

This death-control technology was imposed from the outside, however; by and large it was not accompanied by industrialisation or other fundamental changes in the societies affected. As a result, there was no sign of a demographic transition; in many countries, there is still no evidence of one. Although death rates plunged, birth rates remained high. Since the rate of population growth is determined by the gap between the birth rate (input to the population) and the death rate (output), the consequence was an unprecedented population explosion in the less developed nations.

Population growth rates in developing nations today typically range between 1.5 per cent and 4 per cent a year, with most of them averaging between 2 and 3 per cent. With an annual growth rate of 3 per cent, a population will double its size in 23 years; at 4 per cent, it doubles in a mere 17 years.

Global Population Size

Since the majority of the world's human beings live in the less developed nations (about three out of every four in the 1980s), the entire world population has also been increasing faster than ever before. Between 1930 and 1976, the global population doubled to four billion souls. During the early 1960s, the worldwide average growth rate was an estimated 2.2 per cent a year, fast enough to double the population in just 32 years. The human population has now passed the five billion mark. Thus, two and a half times as many people now live on Earth as existed when the two of us were born.

Even though the annual percentage rate of growth has lowered significantly since the high point a couple of decades ago, that percentage annual 'interest' (1.7 per cent) is being applied to an ever growing stock of human 'capital'. Consequently, each year sees a record absolute growth in the population. . . .

While the developing nations have been having their turn at the population explosion game, the demographic transition has continued in the industrialised countries. Some European nations, such as the UK and Sweden, have essentially stopped growing. They have about reached zero population growth (ZPG); that is, their birth rates are nearly equal to their death rates. Populations of a few countries—Austria, West and East Germany, Denmark and Hungary—have actually begun to shrink gradually in size, because their death rates are now slightly higher than their birth rates (outputs are greater than inputs). If the present fertility rate of the United Kingdom continues, the British population will soon embark on a slow decline in numbers.

"If replacement reproduction is exactly maintained for long enough, the population will eventually stop growing and remain stationary indefinitely."

In most of the industrialised nations, however, populations are still slowly expanding. In the United States, Japan, Canada and the Soviet Union, among others, rates of natural increase (the excess of births over deaths) are about 0.5 to 0.7 per cent a year. To put this into perspective, if those rates continued unchanged, the populations would double in 100 to 160 years.

But those rates are not likely to remain unchanged, for several reasons. First, reproductive behaviour in modern societies is by no means constant; it fluctuates in response to any number of factors such as economic conditions, wars, participation of women in the work force, and so forth. In addition, there are factors of population structure (the proportions of people of different ages) at play that will cause birth rates in these countries to decline further in the next few decades, even without a significant change in the average person's reproductive behaviour.

The United States, for example, reached a demographic landmark in the early 1970s, when its fertility dropped below 'replacement reproduction'. At the replacement level, each generation of parents just replaces itself in the next generation. With the mortality rates prevailing in modern industrial societies, replacement reproduction implies that each woman in the population will bear an average of 2.1 children in her lifetime, replacing herself and her partner. (The extra fraction compensates for those children who die before reaching reproductive age.) If replacement reproduction is exactly maintained for long enough, the population will eventually stop growing and remain stationary indefinitely.

Why doesn't it stop growing immediately? The reason is that rapidly growing populations, with high birth rates and low death rates, have a very large proportion of young people, who will mature and have children and grandchildren themselves before they reach old age and begin to die in large numbers. In many developing nations, for instance, 40 to 50 per cent of the population are under the age of fifteen; they are the parents of the next generation. Even if the current crop of youngsters produces an average of two children per family, the population will continue to grow throughout their lifetime, just because there are so few people in the older generations who will soon die. Because of this momentum built into the structure of the population, once replacement reproduction is reached, it takes about a lifetime—65 or 70 years— for a previously expanding population to stop growing.

This situation is extreme in less developed countries, where death rates have fallen precipitously while birth rates generally have remained high, vastly swelling the ranks of young people. But in many industrialized countries, especially the United States, the Soviet Union and several former British colonies, the same phenomenon exists because of the post-World War II 'baby boom'. Between 1945 and 1970, birth rates were moderately high in these countries, and accordingly growth rates were 1 per cent a year or more. The baby-boomers of the United States are now entering middle age; even though their fertility is low, they have caused a small 'boomlet', simply because there are so many baby-boomers all having *their* children at once.

The Replacement Level

Since 1973, the average American family size has been somewhat below replacement level—small enough so that if fertility (the average number of births per woman of reproductive age) did not rise again, the US crude birth rate (which is measured not relative to reproductive women but to the entire population) eventually would slowly decline. Meanwhile, the crude death rate (also measured relative to the total population) would rise until it met the falling birth rate. Both changes would be due to an increase in the average age of the population. When the birth and death rates were equal, natural increase would cease.

One other factor can change population growth rates: migration. Even with birth and death rates in balance, a population would continue to grow if the numbers of immigrants exceeded those of emigrants; inputs from all sources must balance outputs for ZPG to be achieved. In the United States today, without immigration, the present low reproductive rate would bring an end to population growth within a few decades, after which there would be a slow population decline.

But that will not happen as long as the United

States has a substantially higher rate of immigration than emigration (inputs higher than outputs). Probably over a million immigrants per year enter the country, many of them illegally (and therefore uncounted). Added to natural increase, this influx of people boosts the current annual US population growth rate to over 1 per cent. A continuation of immigration at this level, or an increase, would appreciably delay the end of population growth and swell the ultimate peak population size. Indeed, a net addition of a million or more immigrants per year would postpone the end of growth indefinitely, unless there were a further drop in fertility.

Clearly, small changes in rates can make a vast difference later on. If there were no immigration after the mid-1980s, and fertility remained the same (about 1.8 children per woman), the US population would reach its peak size around 2030 at less than 250 million, then decline to around 200 million fifty years later. By contrast, if fertility rose to slightly above replacement to an average of 2.2 children per family and net immigration were 1 million per year, the US population would soar past 510 million by 2080, more than doubling in less than a century, and would continue growing until there was a change in one or both vital rates (birth or death) and/or migration.

International Migration

Of course, the people added by immigration to the United States (or any) population are subtracted from somewhere else. Today the great majority of international migrants move to more industrialised nations from less developed nations, thereby somewhat dampening the rapid population growth of the latter. But that dampening is relatively inconsequential in a global context.

Most developing nations are a long way from replacement reproduction, and their populations are almost inevitably destined to expand considerably before their birth rates can be reduced that far. China and a handful of small nations, however, are within striking distance, if not already there, and their fertility will probably have fallen below replacement well before this century is out. Even so, the built-in momentum from the earlier high birth rates will sweep their populations to much larger sizes before natural increase ceases, because of the preponderance of young people—unless there is a substantial change in death rates.

With no rise in death rates, the populations of most developing countries would continue to expand by 30 to 100 per cent after reaching replacement fertility, depending in part on how rapidly and how far their birth rates fell. And, for the majority of developing nations that have yet even to approach that level of fertility, demographic projections anticipate a doubling or tripling of populations before growth finally ends more than a century from

now. Thus, carried mainly by the momentum inherent in the population structures of developing nations, the global population is projected to reach a maximum size of approximately 10 billion (give or take a billion or two)—about twice its present size—before growth ceases.

"Although the economies of the developing nations were expanding at historically unprecedented rates . . . the economic gains were quickly eaten up by population growth."

Since the 1950s, the populations of less developed nations have been expanding rapidly at a remarkably constant average rate (if China is excluded) of about 2.4 or 2.5 per cent a year. For a long time, social scientists complacently assumed that the process of industrialisation would automatically bring about a demographic transition, as had happened earlier in the West. But, to their surprise and dismay, no demographic transition had appeared by the 1970s.

Indeed, although the economies of the developing nations were expanding at historically unprecedented rates—on average, even faster than the also rapidly growing economies of industrial nations—the economic gains were quickly eaten up by population growth. If an economy was expanding by 3.5 per cent a year, and the population by 3 per cent, the net economic growth per person in the population was only 0.5 per cent. In the industrialised world, by contrast, owing to the much slower population growth, economic gains per person were appreciably greater throughout the postwar period, despite a lower rate of economic growth in most industrial nations.

This disparity contributed to a steadily widening economic gap between industrialised and non-industrialised nations. The average individual in developed regions was gaining in wealth much faster than the average person in less developed nations; the already rich were getting constantly richer, while most of the poor were scarcely making headway at all. Indeed, especially since 1972, a good many of the poor have fallen tragically far behind.

The character and meaning of the widening income gap (now almost a chasm) between rich and poor nations is perhaps most starkly revealed in the world food situation—which itself has been transformed since World War II. In the last four decades, worldwide food production has risen substantially—as, of course, it had to in order to feed a population twice as large. Production of grains—which comprise the basic source of nutrition for human beings—has more than doubled in that time.

Thus, on average, there has been a small annual increase in food produced per person in the population. . . .

In spite of heroic increases in global food production over the last several decades, a large proportion of the world's people are still poor and hungry. Even though that proportion has been reduced somewhat, the absolute number of hungry human beings is much higher now than in the late 1940s, just because the total population has nearly doubled. The United Nations Children's Fund (UNICEF) estimates that some 15 million infants and small children die unnecessarily each year from malnutrition and other poverty-related causes.

"By the 1980s, the high costs of overpopulation and the heightening dependence of human beings on non-renewable resources had begun to be felt."

A profound shift has also taken place in the pattern of international trade in food. Before 1940, nearly all the world's regions exported food to other nations. The only important exception was Europe, which imported more food than it exported. Today, western Europe has joined the dwindling list of regions that export more food than they import, whereas the vast majority of nations are now dependent to some degree—and sometimes heavily so—on imported food. Only a handful of countries (primarily the United States, plus Canada, Australia, New Zealand, Argentina, Thailand and the European Community) supply the international grain market for all the rest, including the Soviet Union, eastern Europe, Japan and most of the poor countries.

In addition, until the late 1970s, the primary importers of food were rich countries, which could easily pay for the imports by exporting manufactured goods. In the last decade, though, rapid population growth in the poor countries increasingly outstripped their ability to keep raising food production. Less and less virgin land remained available to open for agriculture, and the scope for increasing productivity on existing farmland (the famous green revolution) was more and more constrained by both biological limitations and the economic realities of poor countries. . . .

With their fast growing populations, struggling economies and faltering food production, many poor nations are facing catastrophe unless dramatic steps are taken. And there is very little sign of such steps materialising, even though the need for them has been increasingly evident for several decades. The poorest of these nations—ones like Chad—are not 'less developed countries', as they euphemistically prefer to be called. Under the current global regime, they would best be considered 'never-to-be-developed' countries, nations that have been written off by arithmetic, if not by intent. The shadow of humanity has so shrouded their landscapes that they seem condemned to perpetual darkness.

The deepening shadows are not restricted to the poorest nations, however; they are merely the most vulnerable. As could be expected, the stresses on the global system have led to collapses in the weakest areas. The enormous, widening gulf between rich and poor peoples, as illustrated by the demographic differences and the food situation, pervades almost every aspect of the human predicament. It colours global politics, causing jittery governments to pile up deadly, expensive and unusable weaponry to protect their land and access to resources, and thus undermines the security of all nations. And the rich/poor division seriously hinders any attempts to address the deepening predicament. Yet that predicament—the overpopulating of Earth by humanity and the squandering of its unique inheritance—is a cause of that same tragic and perilous imbalance.

By the 1980s, the high costs of overpopulation and the heightening dependence of human beings on non-renewable resources had begun to be felt. Staying in the race to produce enough food for more and more people is becoming increasingly difficult. Economies seem to be losing the battle to grow faster than the populations they sustain. Less and less 'virgin' land is available to take over for human use, and natural ecosystems are in full retreat. Earth and its living passengers are taking a beating the likes of which has not been seen in at least 65 million years.

The Lengthening Shadow

As our species is forced by its own actions to burn its capital in earnest, however, the consequences are borne not only by the other life-forms on this lonely space vehicle, but they also fall heavily on our fellow human beings. That lengthening shadow not only darkens the lives of our contemporaries but the prospects of future generations as well.

Anne H. Ehrlich and Paul R. Ehrlich are the authors of many books on the effects of population growth, including Extinction: The Causes and Consequences of the Disappearance of Species *and* Earth.

> *"Population growth has nothing to do with economic growth, infant mortality, or any of the other ugly conditions in which much of the world's population lives."*

Overpopulation Is Not A Problem

R. Cort Kirkwood

Repetition is the mother of learning, and there are some popular beliefs that have no basis in fact, but which many Americans simply accept at face value because the news media have repeated them so many times in so many different ways. One such belief is that spaceship Earth has too many inhabitants, that the developing world's population growth inhibits economic development, and that everyone might run out of food, water and natural resources if something isn't done to stop Africans and Latin Americans from having babies.

The United Nations released an alarmist report saying the world's population will reach 10 billion by 2025 and 14 billion by 3000 if women everywhere don't start using more and better birth control techniques. The headlines were predictable. Ask average people on the street whether population growth is a problem, and they will answer, yes—faster than they can tell you what team Mickey Mantle played for, or who wrote *Huckleberry Finn*.

"The population bogey has been the rare sweet issue everyone could agree upon," says University of Maryland economist Julian Simon, yet a more mythical bogeyman could hardly be found. Though the population controllers such as International Planned Parenthood, The Population Institute, and the Population Crisis Committee have had the media's ear since World War II, thinking economists and demographers have destroyed the theory that population growth inhibits economic growth. How? As the American Enterprise Institute's Nicholas Eberstadt puts it: "That corpus of knowledge simply does not exist. So what you have is pseudoscience. Modern witchcraft."

The ingredients in the population bombers' brew are as strange as those used in witchcraft: eye of newt, crushed bat wings, and whatever else it is they toss in the pot, except the population bombers mix a concoction of Malthusianism, socialism, and economic globaloney that emerges from their kettle as an oracle of doom.

Says Sharon Camp of the Population Crisis Committee: "There are too many people trying to eke out a living at current technology. . . . We don't know what will happen to the natural resource base at a population level of 8, 9, 10, 14 billion."

U.S. Assistance

Without an increase in U.S. assistance for United Nations population programs, Nafis Sadik of the United Nations Population Fund warned, "we will continue to experience high population growth, high infant and child mortality, weakened economies, ineffective agriculture, divided societies and a poorer quality of life for women, children and men."

Barber Conable, president of the World Bank, said in a September 1988 address to the bank's Board of Governors: "The societies in which population is growing so fast must accept that many—perhaps most—of these new lives will be miserable, malnourished and brief. With today's population growth rates, badly needed improvements in living standards cannot be achieved, public resources for necessary services are overstretched, and the environment is severely damaged."

Wrote Loretta McLaughlin in *The Boston Globe*, "It is the pressure of the world's burgeoning population—more than any other single force—that fuels inflation and economic recession. All nations must compete harder for dwindling supplies of the earth's resources; worldwide, more workers must compete for proportionately fewer jobs."

In the same article she quoted Conable's predecessor, Robert McNamara, who best crystallized the population bombers' mantra: "The population problem must be faced up to for what it

R. Cort Kirkwood, "The Population Bomb . . . Defused," *The Freeman*, November 1989. Reprinted with permission.

is—the greatest single obstacle to the economic and social advancement of peoples in the developing world. It is the population explosion, more than anything else, which by holding back the advancement of the poor, is blowing apart the rich and poor and widening the already dangerous gap between them."

It would be truly sad if all these things were true, but they aren't. All the available data suggest that population growth has nothing to do with economic growth, infant mortality, or any of the other ugly conditions in which much of the world's population lives, especially the Third World.

"If prices are a measure of scarcity, then the world's increasing population is hardly a threat."

For example, population planners say too many people will "deplete our limited quantities of food, water and fuel" and other nonrenewable resources. Yet the prices of most commodities (except fuel, thanks to government energy policies and the OPEC [Organization of Petroleum Exporting Countries] cartel), are gradually falling in real terms. If prices are a measure of scarcity, then the world's increasing population is hardly a threat. Population growth statistics really tell observers only one thing: there are more people today than there were yesterday.

Most of the dire predictions are about Africa and Latin America, where huge populations and mass starvation seem to go hand in hand. According to The Population Institute, "There is no simple explanation for why Africa's economic development has been stunted and why Africans today remain so grievously poor. Lack of capital and highly skilled personnel is a factor. . . ongoing civil strife. . . staggering external debts. . . colonial exploitation. . . degradation of . . . its natural resource base. . . . Somewhere in the mix of these factors is the wellspring of Africa's woes." But the real "wellspring of the continent's woes" is never discussed.

Warning that Ethiopia's population of 49 million will double in 23 years, the Institute reports, "The Ethiopian government acknowledges that the country's three percent population growth rate is imperiling its people and their development hopes. . . . There is clearly no way Ethiopia could support that many people. Ethiopia has only two choices: undertake far more vigorous efforts to extend family planning or face even larger-scale suffering in the near future."

But overpopulation is hardly Ethiopia's problem. The Institute and its ideological kin simply ignore Ethiopia's brutal collectivization of agriculture, a throwback to the days of Stalin and the Ukrainian famine even the Soviets have advised the Mengistu regime to stop. The government has deliberately turned mild droughts into nationwide famines and killed thousands of people in forced relocation programs to deprive anti-government guerrillas of crucial rural support.

It is widely known that the Communist authorities use relief food as a lure, stationing supplies near pickup areas for the relocation program. The ultimate goal is to move 33 million people. Not surprisingly, *The Washington Post* reported in 1987, the per capita availability of grain had dropped 22 percent in 10 years, and even though state-owned farms were using 40 percent of all government expenditures, they contributed only four or five percent of total food production. Private farmers—the few that there were—were generating 40 percent of the country's nearly nonexistent gross national product.

Yet The Population Institute says Ethiopia needs more condoms and birth control pills: "Had Ethiopia launched a family planning program in the mid-1960s and had that program been half as successful as many that were begun at that time, the number of births prevented would have been equal to the number of Ethiopians dependent upon food relief during the last famine." That's what you call pseudoscience.

The Institute is also worried about Ghana, "the second fastest growing [population] in western Africa" at 3.3 percent, but credits the Ghanian government with a hands-on approach to family planning.

Socialist Interventions

Yet as Nicholas Eberstadt notes in the Winter 1986 *Wilson Quarterly*, when Ghana was decolonized and Kwame Nkrumah took the reins of power, he systematically destroyed the economy with socialist interventions. He "forced the farmers to sell their cocoa, the nation's chief export, at a fixed price to the government, which then sold it abroad at a profit. The proceeds were poured into Nkrumah's industrial development schemes. By the late 1970s . . . Ghana's small cocoa farmers were getting less than 40 percent of the world price for their crop—an effective tax of over 60 percent. Not surprisingly, Ghana's cocoa output and cocoa exports plummeted."

Next Nkrumah "took aim at industry. Shortly after independence, he nationalized the nation's foreign-owned gold and diamond mines, cocoa-processing plants, and other enterprises. Ghana's new infant industries were also state-owned. The result was inefficiency on a monumental scale. According to one study, between 65 percent and 71 percent of Ghana's publicly owned factory capacity lay idle 10 years after independence. . . . By 1978, tax revenues paid less than 40 percent of the government's budget. Inflation spiraled, climbing by over 30 percent a year during the 1970s. . . . Black Africa's most promising former colony had become an economic disaster."

But The Population Institute concludes, "where population growth is the fastest—Africa—per capita food production is in the sharpest decline."

Some Surprising Comparisons

The Institute's 1988 report on Africa ignores South Africa, which isn't surprising. Its population, one of the continent's highest, has doubled since 1960, yet its per capita gross national product in 1986 was $1,850. Ghana's and Ethiopia's populations have doubled as well, but their per capita GNP's are $390 and $120 respectively. People aren't Africa's problem, government policies are. Even South Africa's racialist apartheid system hasn't done the damage Ethiopia's Communist dictatorship has. In fact, if the government of South Africa ever dismantled the apartheid system, allowing blacks even more economic freedom than they have now, the contrast would be even more dramatic . . . and more embarrassing for the population bombers.

Africa's story is only a snapshot of a worldwide phenomenon. Comparing other countries in the second and first worlds yields similar results. As shown by the table, the differences between Taiwan, Singapore, and China, between North Korea and South Korea, and between East Germany and West Germany are equally startling, especially when population density is brought into the equation. Where China has enough room to put 285 people per square mile, its economy is a failure next to Taiwan's and Singapore's, whose people are packed in like sardines, but whose economies have become known as two of Asia's four "dragons." (The other two being Hong Kong and South Korea.)

These small islands also belie the myth that urban congestion in "Third World mega-cities" such as Mexico City and New Delhi is a threat to public health, education, and housing needs. Need we ask why South Korea, which is more than twice as crowded as North Korea, is doing twice as well economically? Population planners try to explain the differences by saying the successful economies of Asia and Africa benefited from strong, government-backed family planning programs. But the population growth rates of the African countries, East and West Germany, the Koreas, and the Pacific rim countries were pretty much the same from 1960 to 1986. That leaves only one explanation for the differences, one the table doesn't show, one the population bombers don't like to discuss: China, Ethiopia, and the other economic failures are controlled by Communist or socialist central planners, whereas Taiwan, Singapore, and the other economic engines of

progress are largely free market economies.

As Julian Simon has written, "Population growth under an enterprise system poses less of a problem in the short run, and brings many more benefits in the long run, than under conditions of government planning of the economy." Adds Eberstadt, "the overall impact of population change on a society seems to depend on how the society deals with change of all kinds. Indeed, coping with fluctuations in population is in many ways less demanding than dealing with the almost daily uncertainties of the harvest, or the ups and downs of the business cycle, or the vagaries of political life. Societies and governments that meet such challenges successfully as the little dragons did, are also likely to adapt well to population change. Those that do not are likely to find that a growing population 'naturally' causes severe, costly and prolonged dislocations." (*Wilson Quarterly*, Winter 1986) In short, free societies adjust well to population increases, Communist societies do not.

	Population per square mile	GNP per capita
East Germany	399.0	$10,400
West Germany	634.5	12,080
North Korea	448.0	1,180
South Korea	1,095.5	2,370
China	285.0	300
Taiwan	1,385.6	3,748
Ghana	142.9	390
South Africa	68.4	1,850
Singapore	11,608.4	7,410
Ethiopia	92.2	120
Mozambique	45.8	210

Sources: The Heritage Foundation, The World Bank Annual Development Report 1988; Figures from 1986.

The population bombers would be little more than harmless "do-gooders" if their ideas—that people cause inflation, that people consume too much food, that people are a drag on economic development—were not taken so seriously. But they are taken seriously, and the consequences have been disastrous, anti-natalist, even inhuman.

Eberstadt cites a March 1986 *Washington Post* report from Kenya: "hundreds of [rural school] children ran screaming, some scrambling through windows, with the approach of an unfamiliar car: it was thought to contain population workers who would inject them with nonreversible contraceptives. The previous year starving Kenyans in drought-afflicted areas were reported to have refused relief shipments of U.S. corn on the rumor that the corn had been laced with sterilizants."

But the worst application of population control theory is that of the Communist Chinese government, which has been cited by the U.S. House of Representatives for "crimes against humanity" in carrying out its one-family, one-child policy. In collecting 92 accounts from eyewitnesses, human rights activist Dr. Blake Kerr reported the ghastly results in *The Washington Post* (February 26, 1989):

"In the autumn of 1987," two Tibetan monks told Kerr, "a Chinese birth-control team set up their tent next to our monastery in Amdo. The villagers were informed that all women had to report to the tent for abortions and sterilizations or there would be grave consequences. . . . We saw many girls crying, heard their screams as they waited for their turn to go into the tent, and saw the growing pile of fetuses build outside the tent."

Elsewhere in China, in pursuit of its U.N.-backed family planning program, the results are the same: forced sterilization, abortion and outright infanticide. In many cases, doctors perform "abortions" as a child is moving through the birth canal at term, crushing its skull with a forceps or jamming a hypodermic needle filled with formaldehyde into the fontanelle, killing the child just moments before it enters the world. Others who make it past the doctor are often confronted by the nurse, and women have heard their child's first cries on beginning life only to see them snuffed out by that nurse, who is usually armed with what has become know as "the poison shot."

The justification for this mass murder? According to Chen Muhua, head of China's Family Planning Board, "Socialism should make it possible to regulate the reproduction of human beings so that population growth keeps in step with the growth of material production."

"*Effective population control logically demands that we control not only the number of people on earth, but the kind of people who live on it. And that is a recipe for tyranny.*"

Lest you think such exhortations are *sui generis*, look at the words of Friends of the Earth as published in *Progress As If Survival Mattered*:

"Americans should take the lead in adopting policies that will bring reduced population. Ultimately, those policies *may* have to embrace coercion by governments to curb breeding. . . mere unofficial advocacy and purely voluntary compliance are far from enough . . . voluntarism guarantees big families for the ignorant, the stupid, and the conscienceless, while it gradually reduces the proportion of people who, in conscience, limit the size of their families. . . . If the less stringent curbs on procreation fail, someday perhaps childbearing

will be deemed a punishable crime against society unless the parents hold a government license. Or perhaps all potential parents will be required to use contraceptive chemicals, the governments issuing antidotes to citizens chosen for childbearing."

"Unwanted" Pregnancies

The population bombers cannot imagine that an Ethiopian mother might love her children just as much as the sterilization advocate living at the Watergate, that children provide a source of nonmaterial income they don't understand. For them, there are only "unwanted" pregnancies; as George Gilder put it, "mouths, not minds." No wonder they can make pseudoscientific statements like, "500 million women want and need family planning but lack information, access or means to obtain it." In this view, people aren't producers, they're consumers.

If such is the case then the effort to preserve man's finite resources must go beyond mere contraception and the legal elimination of "unwanted" children by abortion. In allocating our supposedly meager resources, judicious authorities would allow only the most learned, polished, and beautiful people to reproduce, for it is they who will use resources most expediently and they who need them most. After all, as devoted friends of the earth say, a system of "voluntarism" would empower the "stupid and ignorant" (the teeming masses of Latin America and Africa?) to waste our dwindling resources.

Effective population control logically demands that we control not only the number of people on earth, but the kind of people who live on it. And that is a recipe for tyranny.

R. Cort Kirkwood is an editorial writer for the daily newspaper, The Washington Times.

Population Growth Damages the Environment

The Washington Spectator

A population explosion in areas that can least afford it—in urban slums and the Third World—threatens world stability. For the first time in history, there are more than five billion members of the human family, and the population is growing at a rate of 89 million a year. Nine out of ten babies born today live in the poorest countries.

The total population is expected to double before stability occurs in the next century, according to the *Christian Science Monitor*. The effects of the overflowing bowl are hunger, poverty, resource depletion, urban deterioration, and economic stagnation.

Zero Population Growth points out: "Globally, over 800 million people suffer from starvation—with 12 million children under the age of five dying each year. . . . Both Mexico and Central America, already facing unemployment rates as high as 30%, can expect a tripling of their [potential] labor force in less than 50 years."

Signs of the times: the Mayor of Washington, while inspecting a shelter for the homeless, was confronted by a woman with 15 children who asked for a better place to live. If population growth keeps on at its present rate, the U.S. will have another 40 million people inside our boundaries by 2000; the figure includes births and legal and illegal immigrants.

Worldwatch Institute reports that the highest birth rates and lowest use of contraceptives occur in sub-Saharan Africa. "Malnutrition and overpopulation are inexorably linked in places like Africa, where devastating drought—combined with the fastest population growth in human history—has led to widespread famine," according to Zero Population Growth.

Nations of the Southern Hemisphere will need 800 million new jobs by the year 2000 to employ their rapidly expanding population. A population explosion in Mexico has converted the capital, Mexico City, into the world's largest city. A third of the 16 million inhabitants live in slums. Other thousands of Mexicans go north in search of jobs.

Reasons Outlined

The reasons for the population explosion are not hard to find:

• In many poor areas, the male sex drive coupled with a macho pride is a major social force. (Macho men count the number of children sired as proof of virility.)

• The lack of female status in Third World countries and in poor, minority groups everywhere override the woman's objections. Worldwatch Institute states: "Surveys confirm that half of the 463 million married women of reproductive age in Third World countries outside of China want no more children. Millions more would like to delay their next pregnancy."

But in these areas, sex is mainly a male sport and female consent is generally overlooked.

• In many poor rural areas, children are seen as farm labor. This explains why China's one-child-per-family program has broken down in agricultural areas.

• Parents, in the Third World particularly, hope that having more children will provide help for them when they grow old and unable to work.

• Large families are encouraged by two major religions, Catholicism and Islam. The position of the Catholic Church may be slowly changing because of pressure from women. In Catholic Italy, for example, half the married women are reported to use contraceptives. On October 8, 1984, 24 nuns signed an advertisement in the *New York Times* stating that opposition to abortion was not "the only legitimate Catholic position."

The Washington Spectator, "Population, The Overflowing Bowl," September 15, 1988. Reprinted with permission.

The Vatican directed the 14 Catholic orders to which the nuns belonged to get them to recant or dismiss them. All but two recanted. Their order, the Sisters of Notre Dame de Namur, began the process for dismissal, but at a meeting in Rome halted the proceedings and then notified the nuns that they would not be dismissed. The letters said: "We will not move to dismissal because we believe that this action would not be in the best interests of the church or congregation at this point." Church sources attributed their stand "in part to letters of protest from about 2,400 members of the order," according to the *Washington Post*.

Heavy Population Growth

• In many areas of heavy population growth, birth control information and devices are not easily available. Some of this lack is due to an order by the Reagan Administration against using foreign-aid funds for this purpose. Senator Bob Packwood (R-Oregon) states that on numerous occasions, "the Administration has attempted to limit the ability of family-planning services to provide women facing unwanted pregnancy with information on the full spectrum of legal actions—including abortion—available to them."

As the *Christian Science Monitor* reports, "U.S. policy emphasizes cutting support to any family-planning group that does not openly reject abortion. One of the ironies of the dispute is that, for the first time, many developing countries are eager to implement family-planning groups."

• "The wave of population increase after WW II is due in part to 'rapidly declining death rates'. Rapid mortality declines in less developed countries were due mostly to the development of medical technologies available to large numbers of people," states the *Population Bulletin*.

As an example, death rates in Mexico were more than 30 per 1,000 population before 1910, rose to nearly 50 from 1910 to 1920, and then declined after 1945. By the early 1960s, the death rate was around 10 per 1,000 population. The birth rate, by contrast, hovered well above 40 per 1,000 population. Most Latin American countries had a similar experience.

What happened, in essence, is that the high mortality of infants, small children and mothers dropped sharply. A cynical comment from sub-Saharan Africa is that the babies saved by medical care and sanitation die later from sickness compounded by malnutrition. Kenyans, for example, live only 54 years on average, while North Americans live for 75.

"By the year 2000, as many as 65 countries may not even be able to feed their own people. In the already politically volatile regions of Central America and the Middle East, where the U.S. has vital security interests, the population will more than double by the year 2025. Economic and political stability will be even more threatened," according to Senator Patrick J. Leahy, D-Vt.

For example, "Nigeria, the Philippines and Peru have all seen per capita incomes drop in the 1980s as production has been outstripped by population growth," according to *State of the World 1987*.

Population growth in Africa and Latin America will top the world average by a large margin. Africa is estimated to add 1.1 billion people, reaching 1.6 billion in 2025, three times the 555 million of 1985. Latin America's estimated gain is 374 million, for a total of 779 million in 2025, almost double the 1985 mark of 405 million.

Also:

• "Timberlands equal to the size of California will vanish by the end of the century, much of the loss due to the increased need for fuelwood and grazing land in developing countries," writes *Development Forum*.

Worldwatch Institute reports: "The loss of forest cover in tropical countries remains rampant. Conversion of forest to cropland is by far the leading cause. Population growth, inequitable land distribution and the expansion of export agriculture greatly reduces the cropland available for subsistence farming, forcing peasants to clear virgin forests to grow food." These areas practice "continuous croppings that are ill suited to fragile forest soils. The soils become so depleted, the peasant must clear more land to survive."

> *"Population growth, inequitable land distribution and the expansion of export agriculture greatly reduces the cropland available for subsistence farming."*

The British monthly, *South*, finds that because of increased demand for food, "on a third of the world's cropland, topsoil is being lost more rapidly than new soil is being formed. . . . Each year, 14.8 million acres of productive land—an area the size of Ireland—turns into desert."

Also, according to *Development Forum*:

• "A total of 21 developing-world cities will have 10 million or more people by the year 2000 . . . leading to incredible strains on already overburdened schools, hospitals, sewage and water systems, and all public services." The latter include police protection and waste disposal.

Worldwatch Institute reports, "Resource demands in numerous cities already exceed the limits of local supplies—whether it be water in Tucson and Mexico City, or firewood in Hyderabad. Especially in Third World areas experiencing unprecedented rates of urbanization, the imbalances will frustrate efforts to improve living standards."

Even in the industrial world, population pressure converts inner-city areas into jungles of crime and violence. Jobs are scarce and poverty is the rule. The *New York Times* gives evidence in an inner-city slum in Detroit: "In 1986, 43 children under 17 were murdered there; in 1987, the figure jumped to 60."

• Population growth may be a significant factor in depleting the Earth's protective ozone layer, according to two atmospheric chemists writing in *Science*. They found a linkage between the growing amount of methane released into the air—a product of population increases—and the destruction of ozone in the atmosphere. Donald R. Blake and F. Sherwood Rowland found that the concentration of methane in the atmosphere has risen 11% since 1978.

The Third World's Condition

Ninety percent of the new babies each year are born in the Third World, where "the number of people living in absolute poverty is increasing," states Dr. Nafis Sadik, director of the UN population program.

The Economist says that the 90% live in "developing countries that find it hard to offer their people a rising standard of education and living. A gulf is widening between regions of the world with slow-growing populations and those with fast-growing ones. . . . Africa has the highest population growth in the world. If things continue as they are, Nigeria will, by the year 2040, have as many people as the whole of Africa today. Kenyans are proliferating faster still—at 4.2% a year." This, in effect, means that the high growth areas will be mired in colossal economic problems. Even today, 15 million people, mostly in the Third World, live on the edge of hunger all the time. For example, "per capita grain production is falling in Africa and Latin America," writes *South*.

State of the World 1987 notes that "between 1987 and 2000, five countries—Brazil, China, Indonesia, India and Mexico—will account for 37% of world population growth, nearly 700 million people." By 2020, Mexico, on our doorstep, will number 138 million, more than are in all of Central America and the Caribbean today. "Within 220 years, the population of Peru, at its present growth rates, would equal that of the entire world today," reports *National Geographic*.

The *Hindustan Times* says that demographers believe that India will overtake China as the world's most populous nation by the middle of the 21st century. "They have reached that conclusion primarily by comparing the failures and successes of the two countries' planning programs." India's population is growing by 15 to 16 million a year, while China hopes to limit births to about 10 million a year.

In Guatemala, "with the annual population growth rate of nearly three percent, the country each year has 200,000 more mouths to feed—twice as many new Guatemalans as there are new Guatemalan jobs," according to *National Geographic*.

In her book *Reproductive Rights and Wrongs*, Betsy Hartmann argues that high birth rates in the Third World will not be brought down until women's rights are recognized. She points to Cuba, which under Castro made women's rights a major goal in contrast with the usual Hispanic macho. Soon after the revolution, the birth rate was 35 per 1,000; today, it is down to 17.

Several nations of Asia and Africa are making an effort to cut the birth rate. China was the pioneer with its goal of one child per family, using the carrot-on-the-stick approach. Families which cooperate get extra perks in housing, jobs and subsidies. Penalties are levied on those who break the rule. In Shanghai, for example, workers who do not belong to a fixed work unit and have more than one child are fined as much as 2,000 yuan ($540), equal to more than a year and a half's salary for the average worker. China's growth rate has been brought down to 1.3 percent.

However, in rural areas, the program is breaking down, reports the *People's Daily*, the leading Communist newspaper. Farmers resist birth control because they claim they need more farm hands to work private acres. Also, China's "floating population" of construction and other itinerant workers are not easily controlled.

As a result, at current growth rates, China's population may reach 1.3 billion by 2000. "Combined with food shortages and price rises, this may counteract the country's efforts to improve its standard of living, writes the *London Financial Times*.

"Even today, 15 million people, mostly in the Third World, live on the edge of hunger all the time."

Bangladesh offers incentives of food, cash and saris to poor women if they agree to be sterilized. This has cut the birth rate from 43 per 1,000 in 1980 to 32 in 1985. Critics complain that the sterilization process is not always carefully performed.

India has adopted a massive education program, but this is not working, as the *Hindustan Times* reports: "India has accepted the logic [of birth control] but falls behind at the implementation stage. Something ought to be done so that we are not No. 1 in this particular race."

In Sri Lanka, the birth rate has been reduced 20% between 1965 and 1983, primarily because of the widespread use of contraceptives. Half the married women of reproductive age use some form of contraception.

Kenya, with the world's highest growth rate, is taking to the air waves to reduce births. A soap opera, "Tushauriane" ("Let's Discuss It," in Swahili), is a melodrama showing the dangers of too many births. One character, a girl of 15, had several pregnancies and becomes seriously ill. The producer says, "Our first concern is to persuade our audience to go for family-planning and health services."

Worldwatch Institute states: "Family planning is the key to improving reproductive health. Each year, up to a million women world wide die from pregnancy-related causes. Fully 99% of these deaths occur in the Third World, where complications arising from pregnancy and illegal abortion are the leading killers of women in their 20s and 30s. At least half of all maternal deaths could be averted through a combined strategy of family planning, legal abortion, and primary health care."

What About the U.S.?

The U.S. is not immune from population problems. We have growing legions of the poor and minorities. If our population growth continues at the present rate—through births and immigrants—we will have another 40 million people by 2000. We are adding "the population equivalent of four Washington, D.C.s, every year, another California every decade," reports Zero Population Growth. In Los Angeles and Phoenix, water supplies are scarce. Chesapeake Bay was once the great spawner of seafood, but overdevelopment has contaminated the water. Every year, more than 44,000 acres of California cropland are converted to urban uses. In 1987, the state's population grew by 662,000.

"The desperate need is to find a way to dramatize the pain that lies ahead if population is not controlled—mass famine, wars over depleted resources, lack of living space and water."

Hunger is on the rise in the U.S. The U.S. Conference of Mayors has reported that the demand for emergency food in 1987 increased by 18% in 25 major cities.

The cost of repairing the damage caused to the world by overpopulation and misuse of the environment could run nearly $150 billion a year over the next decade, according to Lester R. Brown, who directed a study on the earth's physical condition.

There are no easy answers. The desperate need is to find a way to dramatize the pain that lies ahead if population is not controlled—mass famine, wars over depleted resources, lack of living space and water. The need is to open the eyes of humanity to an impending doom before it is too late.

The Washington Spectator *is a publication of The Public Concern Foundation in Fairfax, Virginia. The Foundation investigates political issues and problems worldwide and sponsors symposia on political and foreign affairs, including human rights and the environment.*

"Cutting down or halting future growth of the whole population won't help those in dire straits."

Population Growth Does Not Damage the Environment

Frances Frech

We'll tell you a story. It's a story of a time and place when and where it hadn't rained for several years. Oh, there were a few drops now and then, but never an adequate amount. Too many cattle had grazed in this land; improper farming practices had damaged the protective cover of grass. Now the soil was blowing away in huge clouds of dust, some carried all the way across the continent and far out into the ocean. Places of human habitation were often hidden by drifts of earth as deep as winter snows. Crops grew too poorly to be worth harvesting. Yet in the hardest hit areas, the population would triple in 50 years; in others, it would double, at the very least.

Africa? No. Midwestern United States in the 1930's. States suffering the most damage were Texas, Oklahoma, New Mexico, Colorado, and Kansas, but some on the edges—Wyoming, Arizona, Colorado, the Dakotas, even Minnesota—experienced long term drought and dust storms.

There was hunger and malnutrition in the land in those days. Crop failures plus the Great Depression left millions destitute. There are not any records of actual starvation deaths, but there might have been if, for some, there'd been nowhere else to go, and for others, public and private charitable help.

The Pill hadn't been developed yet, sterilization wasn't acceptable to most people, and abortion was illegal. So, fortunately for those states who were to double and triple their populations later and are doing well now, nobody was screaming for population control in exchange for food.

When the rains came at last and the land was green again, the nightmare was over. Except that the rest of the Depression still had to be lived through, and World War II was waiting in the wings.

American farmers, with government assistance, learned how to manage the land better, to rotate crops, to plant the right kind of crops—grasses—to hold the soil, and to avoid over-grazing. Why couldn't we teach the people of primitive lands what we know about preserving the land? Our own record in "family planning" is extremely poor, after all, with abortion being used to prevent live births in one out of three pregnancies. But we do know how to farm, how to produce and preserve food.

Population Levels

Is Africa over-populated? So much has been published about total population levels in starving countries that the true extent of the numbers affected has been forgotten. In our own Dust Bowl area, the population would later double or triple, as we've said, but it represented less than one-tenth of the U.S. population at that time; today it's about fifteen per cent. The Dust Bowl states were all thinly populated in the first place, ranging from three persons per square mile in New Mexico to about 30 in Oklahoma. Just as those affected by the Dust Bowl didn't represent the whole population of the United States, or even of the individual states, the starving nomadic tribes in Africa don't represent whole countries. Ethiopia, for example, has about 72 persons per square mile, nearly the same as Missouri or Alabama. But in the devastated desert lands there are, perhaps, two persons per square mile. Cutting down or halting future growth of the whole population won't help those in dire straits any more than stopping America's growth in the 1930's would have benefitted Dust Bowl farmers. The big stumbling block in Africa is getting food from where it is to where it isn't. Widely scattered wandering tribes do not have settlements to which railroads and highways can be built.

Africa is a vast, empty, under-populated, undeveloped continent whose resources have barely

Frances Frech, "Out of Africa: Some Population Truths." Published by the Population Renewal Office, 1988. Reprinted with permission.

been touched. But population controllers don't seem to know that resources don't come all polished up and ready to use. It takes people to develop them. In a small, primitive society, it's possible to live on food that grows wild, on the meat of animals that aren't domesticated, on fish. It's possible to live as the animals do, under the shelter of trees or in caves. But as populations grow larger and more sophisticated, it's another matter. Cultivated food crops don't plant themselves, harvest themselves, process themselves, or take themselves to market. People who want to live in houses have to develop the material from which they are built and have to build them, or pay someone else to do so. Trees have to be cut, lumber sawn, bricks made, rocks quarried, concrete manufactured to make the houses in which people live. Coal has to be mined before it can be used for fuel; oil wells have to be drilled, oil refined, stored, transported. Cloth for garments has to be woven or spun from plant or animal fibers—or in modern times, made from chemicals. Almost nothing is used in its natural state. People have to take what's there and turn it into something useable. As societies become more advanced, the work of developing resources becomes more specialized, and no one person does everything. Furthermore, there has to be some need for the products, markets for them, or there's no point in making them. The whole idea that small populations, non-growing populations do better than larger, growing ones has no basis in historical fact.

"The whole idea that small populations, non-growing populations do better than larger, growing ones has no basis in historical fact."

It can't be emphasized strongly enough that resources are useless without development. Half the colonists who landed at Plymouth Rock, and all but a few of the original settlers at Jamestown, starved to death. With a whole continent of natural riches before them, they starved to death because they didn't know how to make use of what was there.

But so many figures are tossed around without comparing them to anything recognizable that the average person is left with the view of Africa as a continent teeming with wall-to-wall human beings, all of them with swollen bellies and matchstick limbs. How many people can picture the true size of the African continent? Would you believe it's larger than the United States, Europe (excluding Russia), and China all put together—and China and the United States, each one alone, is twice the size of Europe (again excluding Russia)? And how many people live in Africa? One-third as many as in the

United States, Europe, and China combined. Over-populated? Not by any stretch of any reasonable person's imagination.

Recent Famines

There have been other famines in recent years, most of them already forgotten. Remember Biafra? That was a nation which broke away from Nigeria in 1967 and a bloody civil war followed. It was predicted that a million Biafrans would starve unless food could be brought in quickly. Because of the war, it couldn't be done. The Biafrans surrendered and the famine ended also. Today it's again a part of Nigeria, and Nigeria isn't on the UN list of starving countries.

Then there was Bangladesh. Bangladesh had broken away from Pakistan in 1971, and for the next three years was pictured as a nation of 70 million people on the brink of extinction. The war ended and the situation promptly improved. The former basket case is doing rather well, with farmers growing two crops a year—rice and winter wheat—instead of one. The people aren't exactly overfed, but they aren't starving any more, either.

And there was Cambodia, again the victim of war. Today there are still some problems with food distribution, but no widespread starvation, as far as we know.

Three common threads run through all of the recent famines: Each was connected to armed conflict which interrupted farming and interfered with distribution. Secondly, the countries were poverty-stricken, with little incentive for farmers to improve production. Thirdly, there was a problem with water. Too little and there's drought; too much and there's flooding. Both have occurred in famine-plagued countries.

With an end to war—if that's ever possible; with stronger but free governments, with incentives to produce, with help from those who know how to control the water situation—irrigation, dams, storage facilities—Africa could bloom. But they would need more people, not fewer, to accomplish what needs to be done.

After the Live-Aid concert there was subsidence of nightly news about starving Africans. Then came the Mexico City earthquake, and with it, a revival of the population controllers' claims that death tolls in disasters are related to overpopulation. Well, one could say that if there were fewer people to be killed, there would be fewer deaths. But this would be true only when there aren't any survivors. For example, in 1883, on the island of Krakatoa, a volcanic eruption and resulting tidal wave killed all of the people on the island. All 36,000 of them. So, of course, if there had been smaller numbers of inhabitants, the death toll would have been less. In catastrophes where there are survivors, however, it's impossible to say how many would have died if the population had been smaller. In Japan in 1923 an earthquake with a magnitude of 8.3 killed 90,000 people. Japan at that time had about half the population she has today. Should a temblor of such magnitude strike that island again, no one can say what the casualties might be. But it's entirely possible there'd be fewer deaths than in 1923. For the Japanese have learned to build earthquake-resistant buildings—smaller, lower, few towering structures.

It can't be estimated what the death count might have been in Mexico City if the population level were smaller, but it could have been just as high as it was. Yet newspaper columnists on the population control side (as most of them are!) have insisted that the Mexican government could have kept it lower by imposing restrictions thirty years ago when that city had 2½ million people instead of allowing her to grow to 18 million.

"With help from those who know how to control the water situation— irrigation, dams, storage facilities— Africa could bloom. But they would need more people, not fewer."

Having been there, we'd be the first to admit that there are too many people in Mexico City. But they weren't all born there. They came in from other parts of Mexico, and they migrated there for the same reasons people come to the cities anywhere else. There are more chances to find jobs and there's more excitement. If other cities were built in Mexico, the problem would be eased, for that nation, with less than 100 persons per square mile, is by no means an over-crowded country.

The Under-Populated South

Mexicans who come to the United States—often illegally—do so to find jobs. It's not for lack of space in Mexico. Indeed, the southern American hemisphere is so under-populated, if Mexicans went south instead of north, it might benefit everybody. So why don't they? A lot of reaons. The United States is richer. It's easier to get across the border— nations to the south are more vigilant, stricter. There are more opportunities for employment. More excitement. More freedom. Too many Latin American countries are under the heels of tyrants.

Some population control advocates maintain that in areas where there have been disastrous floods, the death tolls were caused by overpopulation. People wouldn't live in flood-prone places, they say, if there were room for them elsewhere. What nonsense! Flood plains and river deltas have the richest, most desirable soils. And though it would be ideal if

farmers could live on higher ground, away from the acres they're cultivating, it usually wouldn't be economically feasible to do so. In primitive countries lack of transportation would make it impossible.

Conversely, in the cities, land which undergoes frequent flooding is less valuable, less desirable. Those who live there do so because it's cheaper to buy. "Overpopulation" has nothing to do with it.

In another time, another place, other people faced with disaster might have been told to reduce their numbers as the only way to survive. In the beginning we gave you the story. We were the people.

Frances Frech is the director of the Population Renewal Office in Kansas City, Missouri. The organization studies issues relating to population, including AIDS, Third World development, and population control.

Population Growth Improves Living Standards

Ray Percival

If there is a sure way to invite ridicule it is to deny that population growth is dangerous. Thomas Malthus still carries authority, and his illustrious specter is invoked by what we might call the "neo-Malthusians" to silence impertinent doubt. But Malthus should not be confused with his ghost, and the confusion should not obscure the fact that both Malthus and his ghost are wrong in asserting that population growth rules out a rising standard of living. . . .

Unfortunately . . . the ghostly orthodoxy still stalks the land. Paul Ehrlich, one of its principal exponents, had a penchant for picking figures out of thin air: " . . . a minimum of ten million people, most of them children, will starve to death during each year of the 1970s." The Club of Rome at least packaged its scaremongering in a scientific-looking computer study done at MIT [Massachusetts Institute of Technology], which dutifully declared: "The limits to growth on our planet will be reached sometime within the next one hundred years.". . .

From Malthus's point of view, if half of mankind had been underfed for a significant time, far from exploding, the population "would not grow at all." The misery of inadequate food prevented the population exceeding the food supply. Talk of a senseless explosion of population contradicts Malthus's emphasis on the individual's rational judgment, in which care for the welfare of potential offspring, fear of being reduced in rank, and the thought of the extra work and trouble to support additional offspring all play a role. Anthropologists have shown that all societies practice some form of contraception. The notion that most babies in less-developed countries must be unwanted because their parents do not connect birth with sex or because

they cannot control their primitive urges is nonsense. The neo-Malthusians' appeal to the authority of Malthus has the unintended but charming consequence of undermining their case.

Growth Rates

However, Malthus's theory itself is wrong. Its implications are: a) the theoretical maximum growth rate of population is greater than the theoretical maximum growth rate of food production; b) the long-term growth rate of food and population must be equal. But since plants and most animals have more numerous offspring and shorter gestation periods, they are capable with man's help of multiplying at a higher rate than mankind. Both jayhawks and men eat chickens, but whilst more jayhawks means fewer chickens, more men means more chickens. Malthus's picture of man the parasite just does not fit the facts; man produces more than he consumes.

Between the end of the seventeenth century and the outbreak of the First World War, per-capita income in England increased six-fold despite a six-fold increase in population (the absolute increase in production was thirty- to fifty-fold, far outstripping the rate of growth of the population). Data published by the U.S. Department of Agriculture and by the United Nations show that in the four decades since World War II, world per-capita food production has risen. In these facts we see the most thorough demolition of the Malthusian edifice. The neo-Malthusian ghost fares no better.

Hands up, those who watched on TV: Ten million children starve to death during each year of the Seventies. Ehrlich's prophecy resembled the mumblings of a clairvoyant. It was completely obscure how the predicted minimum figure of ten million deaths per year was derived from theory and data. We can only surmise that the figure was discerned in the cloudy crystal ball that is Ehrlich's

Ray Percival, "Malthus and His Ghost," *National Review*, August 18, 1989. © 1989 by *National Review*, Inc., 150 East 35 Street, New York, NY 10016.

head. Nevertheless, it was a good gamble. If one prophesies a disaster and it occurs, one becomes famous. Yet if the disaster does not occur, the prophet is saved from infamy as another among thousands of flopped prophecies falls into oblivion.

Population and Famine

But we will not allow Ehrlich's mistake the luxury of oblivion this time. Gale D. Johnson argues that during the last quarter of the nineteenth century perhaps twenty to 25 million people died from famine. If Ehrlich's glib formula—more people = more famine—were correct, we could have expected at least fifty million famine deaths in the third quarter of this century. But for the entire twentieth century to the present, there have been at most 15 million famine deaths. And many, if not the majority, of these were due to deliberate government policy, official mismanagement, or war—not to serious crop failure. The Ethiopian famine, occurring in one of the least densely populated regions of the world, is a problem not of population but of repressive government.

But do actual data interest Ehrlich? After all, who wants to be reminded of reality when you're telling your favorite horror story? Ehrlich made much of the time it takes a population to double in size, calculated from the annual rate of growth. He chose doubling time because, as he says in *The Population Bomb*, it is "the best way to impress you with numbers." The magic formula is to pick a doubling time and—as if people bred like flies—simply project it and conclude that within a startlingly short time the earth will be completely carpeted by a two-thousand-story building packed with people. But as any demographer worth his salt will tell you, using the annual rate of growth to project from will exaggerate the prospects for population growth if the birth rate has fallen in the recent past. This is because it takes some decades for a decline in birth rate to show itself in slower population growth. Ehrlich ignored the fact that the birth rate in America had been falling for 13 years before his book was published. By 1975 the *total* number of births was no higher than in 1909.

"Man produces more than he consumes."

The falling birth rate was part of the global demographic transition, a process in which first the death rate and then the birth rate fell from a high to a low level. Even Ehrlich could not completely ignore this most important event in the history of world population. With industrialization, children "became a financial drag—expensive to raise and educate . . . people just wanted to have fewer children." But this means that, contrary to Ehrlich's own argument, population growth is neither explosive nor reckless—ideas he uses to make population growth appear chaotic and frightening and thus set the stage for the state to act as the sole embodiment of rational planning.

In the last decade, the growth rate of the world population has shrunk from 2 per cent to 1.7 per cent, taking it well below replacement level. The UN, whose authority Ehrlich accepts, now expects world population to stabilize at about ten billion near the end of the twenty-first century, and this given *only* the behavior of the population and not external physical constraints. But still the anti-baby crusade continues with the same old refrain about geometric growth leading to disaster. To Ehrlich the macro-mathematics of growth are everything, and he loses sight of the people behind the arithmetic.

A Mathematical Monster

When the human population is seen as a sort of mathematical monster, developments that would strike the non-mathematical as magnificent improvements in man's lot are instead seen as food for the beast. Ehrlich pointed in horror to the dramatic reduction in mortality in less-developed countries (LDCs) as merely an omen of higher growth. But exorcised of the rarefied mathematics of population growth, the dramatic reduction of the death rate in LDCs can be seen for what it really is: the triumph of medicine. It in turn was made possible by the economic development of more-developed countries (MDCs), a process that Ehrlich rejected as "unfair exploitation" of LDCs and as leading eventually to increased death rates through pollution.

It took the seventy years between 1830 and 1900 for average life expectancy in Europe to increase from forty years to fifty years. Thanks largely to the development of insecticides and drugs in MDCs during the 1940s, the same increase in LDCs took only the 15 years between 1950 and 1965. Peter Bauer of the London School of Economics points out that increases in life expectancy in LDCs began first in those places, such as India and Latin America, that had the most contact and commerce with MDCs. This is hardly exploitation in Ehrlich's sense. And if it were, who is exploiting whom? In addition, Ehrlich's prophecy of increased death rates owing to pollution sits uneasily with the fact that people worldwide now live longer.

Besides Ehrlich, the neo-Malthusian ghost also chose to appear in the form of that self-styled "independent college," the Club of Rome. The point of its book, *The Limits to Growth*, published in 1972, was an urgent call for "a non-growing state for society." It went to great lengths to make the message palatable, and even chose the rather exciting term "Global Equilibrium" to replace the grey and boring "no growth." Four years later, after the book had sold four million copies, we find the *New York Times* reporting that, at a meeting in Philadelphia, "Aurelio Peccei, founder of the Club of Rome and former manager of Olivetti, denied the Club was a group of advocates of zero growth."

Zero Growth

To us simple folk the distinction between "non-growing" and "zero growth" is clearly the preserve of the erudite. Was this a face-saving deception, or was the Club of Rome lying in its first report?

For the most telling criticism of *The Limits to Growth* we need look no further than the Club's second technical report, available only a few months after the first, which asserted that with reasonable technological progress continuous growth is feasible, although the Club inconsistently retained the earlier gloomy public stance. One of the crucial defects of the Club's predictions was its neglect of historical price data for minerals. Julian Simon, the author of *The Ultimate Resource*, points out that if mineral resources had indeed become more scarce their prices would have increased. But their real prices on average have been sinking for as long as we can ascertain, indicating that they are now less scarce than they were. If one goes by the long trend, one can expect minerals to become cheaper and cheaper. Furthermore, any shortages on a free market will be accompanied by a rise in the price of the mineral, inducing suppliers to find new sources and substitutes for the mineral, and inducing customers to economize on its use.

Ehrlich and the Club of Rome represent the mistaken ideology of catastrophe. Is there not something to be said for a more modest though still pessimistic position on population growth? The current standard model of population is that of Coale and Hoover. Through Philander Claxton (at one time the highest-ranking U.S. State Department official involved with population matters), the Coale and Hoover model made birth control an important part of U.S. foreign-aid policy. The Coale-Hoover theory focused on economic trends: an increase in the number of consumers and a decrease in saving due to population growth.

Their conclusion was that in India income over the period 1956-86 could have been expected to rise 2.5 times as fast with declining fertility as with continued high fertility. Julian Simon points out that this result is obtained by a) ignoring that in the long run a faster-growing population produces a larger labor supply, which implies a larger output, and b) assuming that capital—land, machines, etc.—does not increase in proportion with the labor force, so that there are diminishing returns to labor. Coale and Hoover simply *assumed* a constant GNP [gross national product] and divided it by more consumers! Subsequent models have given more weight to the

effect of an increased labor force, but they still hold on to the "capital dilution" assumption. The main Coale-Hoover prediction: more children = slower growth.

But as early as 1967, studies by Simon Kuznets had shown that even rapid population growth was no impediment to rapid economic development, as Thailand, Mexico, Panama, Ecuador, and Jordan illustrate. Blaming poverty on population density will not work either: Julian Simon found high density to be associated with high living standards.

The inadequacies of the Coale and Hoover model stand out starkly next to the more complex model developed by Simon. His basic idea is that, in the long run, man produces more than he consumes.

A larger population makes for greater division of labor, economies of scale, and a more extensive market, supporting even very specialized services with minority appeal—how many metaphysical poets or ear specialists could a village support? (And remember, everyone is in a minority for some of his needs and tastes.)

With a larger population, there are more Edisons and Einsteins to contribute to production. In countries at the same level of income, scientific output is proportional to population size; the U.S. is much larger than Sweden, and it produces much more scientific knowledge. How come India and China are not world firsts in the scientific league, then? Well, since they are poor they cannot afford to educate as many people. But their poverty must be attributed to the bumbling brutality of their governments' economic interventions, not to a high proportion of children. There are many countries, such as Costa Rica, Thailand, and Jordan, that have both a high proportion of children in their populations and high levels of education.

"With a larger population, there are more Edisons and Einsteins to contribute to production."

What about the argument that a larger population merely consumes capital? Coale and Hoover naïvely assumed that usable land is a fixed resource. Rises in demand, however, spur people to increase the stock of land and to work the old land more intensively. New crops and methods of cultivation raise output even further, so that output per person is greater than it would have been if there had been no increase in demand. With human beings, scarcity is the mother of abundance. When people want more land, they just go out and create it. In India between 1951 and 1971, cultivated land was increased by 20 per cent. Even now, India is not densely populated. Measured by the number of persons per acre of arable land, Japan and Taiwan—hardly examples of starving populations—are about five times as densely populated. Everyone has heard of Holland's reclamation of land from the sea, and Israel furnishes an instructive example for those who face the barren desert: the Israelis are reclaiming the Negev through the use of hydroponics, an agricultural technique that recycles all water and nutrients, is non-polluting, and needs little land and no soil at all. A desert-tolerant but tasty kind of livestock is also on the menu. . . .

But have we not already stretched our use of land nearly to the limit? No. The Food and Agriculture Organization estimates that there are in the world nearly eight billion acres of arable land lying idle—four times that now being cultivated. Tropical lands allow multiple cropping. If this is taken into account, that four-fold potential increase becomes a ten-fold increase. But as Israel and Holland show, even these untapped potentials do not set an upper limit on how much food could be produced. Imagination is the only limit, and more people means more minds and therefore more imagination.

No Ideal Growth

Julian Simon's research has shown that there is no such thing as an ideal population growth rate. Whether a low, moderate, or high growth rate will maximize future income depends on the economic conditions of the country and the age structure of its population. Two conclusions, however, are unconditional: a) in economic terms, a declining population always does badly in the long run; b) all birth rates above the replacement level raise future income.

"Population growth does not impede but actually contributes to man's rise from poverty and hardship."

The possibility of a declining population, which is showing signs of becoming the next population scare, raises an important question. If we are faced with a declining birth rate, need the state intrude and attempt to boost it by, say, imposing a 5 per cent surtax on persons who are not married before they are 25 years old (as is done in Romania)? No. A declining birth rate means that people (on average) prefer fewer children and more of the goods—pecuniary and non-pecuniary—that they would have had to sacrifice if they had had more children. In any case, the Eastern European attempts to mold family life do not seem to be working. If there is any planning to be done, each family will manage on its own, thank you.

Both the prophets of doom and the sober pessimists have foundered on the rocks of scientific research. It is now time to lay to rest both Malthus and his troubled ghost, in the knowledge that population growth does not impede but actually contributes to man's rise from poverty and hardship. The more people there are, free to exploit their own and the earth's resources, the easier it is to feed them.

Ray Percival is a Ph.D. student in philosophy at the London School of Economics.

"Growth in human numbers is leading to a life-threatening deterioration of environmental systems."

viewpoint **54**

Population Growth Reduces Living Standards

Lester R. Brown, Christopher Flavin, and Sandra Postel

At the annual meeting in Berlin in September 1988, World Bank President Barber Conable urged developing countries to "renew and expand efforts to limit population growth," saying that rapid population increase was contributing to persistent and widespread poverty, which he described as a "moral outrage." Conable's comments reflected growing frustration within the Bank over the inability of many of its member countries to raise living standards. In most countries in Africa, and several in Latin America, average food consumption is falling and living conditions are deteriorating. In many of these countries, the restoration of economic and social progress now depends on quickly reducing population growth.

Population stabilization is the only acceptable goal in a world where growth in human numbers is leading to a life-threatening deterioration of environmental systems. In 13 countries, home to some 266 million people, birth rates have already fallen to the point where births and deaths are in balance. Except for Czechoslovakia, East Germany, and Hungary, all are in Western Europe. They range from tiny Luxembourg to three of the four largest countries in Western Europe—Italy, the United Kingdom, and West Germany.

Birth and Death Rates

Balancing birth and death rates was not an explicit goal in any of these countries. Fertility declined as economic and social conditions improved. As incomes rose and employment opportunities for women expanded, couples chose to have fewer children. The wide availability of family planning services and liberal abortion laws provided the means for them to do so.

The contrasting prospects of these countries and those where populations are projected to double, triple, or quadruple (see Table) is alarming. The experience of recent years indicates that rapid population growth and social progress are not compatible over the long term. Countries either make the shift to smaller families, as China has done, or their life-support systems begin to break down, as is occurring in many African countries. Given the conditions of these systems and the trends in per capita food production and income, many countries may have delayed too long in implementing effective family planning policies. They may now face a choice: adopt a one-child family goal or accept a decline in living standards. It is hard to imagine anything more difficult for a society than striving for acceptance of a one-child family goal except suffering the consequences of failing to do so.

At this point, the only socially responsible step for the United Nations, the World Bank, and the international development community is to call for a sharp reduction in the world growth rate, one patterned after the rapid declines in fertility that occurred in both Japan and China. In effect, each of these countries halved its rate of population growth within a matter of years.

Following the loss of its wartime empire, Japan was faced with the reality of living largely on the resources within its own national borders. Living conditions deteriorated, leading many Japanese couples to want smaller families. This in turn prompted public discussion about population control. The Japanese government responded by legalizing abortion in 1948 and creating a national family planning program to provide contraceptive information and counseling. The result was a drop in fertility "unprecedented in the annals of world demography." Between 1949 and 1956, Japan cut its population growth rate from just under 2.2. percent

Lester R. Brown, Christopher Flavin, and Sandra Postel, *State of the World, 1989.* Reprinted with permission of Worldwatch Institute.

to scarcely 1 percent. Remarkably, Japan made this demographic advance before the advent of modern contraceptives, such as the pill and the intrauterine device.

Projected Population Size at Stabilization and Increase over Current Level, Selected Countries

Country	1988 Population	Projected Population When Stationary State Is Reached	Ratio
	(million)	(million)	
Kenya	23	121	5.3
Uganda	16	82	5.1
Tanzania	24	123	5.1
Nigeria	112	529	4.7
Ethiopia	48	205	4.3
Zaire	33	142	4.3
Sudan	24	101	4.2
Ghana	14	58	4.1
Pakistan	107	423	4.0
Syria	11	42	3.8
Algeria	24	81	3.4
Bolivia	7	24	3.4
Iran	52	169	3.2
Bangladesh	109	342	3.1
South Africa	35	90	2.6
Egypt	53	132	2.5
Peru	21	48	2.3
Philippines	63	137	2.2
Mexico	83	187	2.2
India	817	1,698	2.1

SOURCE: World Bank, *World Development Report 1988* (New York: Oxford University Press, 1988).

Two decades later, the Chinese government also concluded that its fast-falling population/land ratio was threatening its future economic progress. This led to a decision to lower its birth rate. Between 1970 and 1976, China's population growth rate dropped from 2.6 percent per year to 1.3 percent. Although starting from a slightly higher point than Japan, it nonetheless cut its growth rate in half.

These family planning breakthroughs in Japan and China are indicative of what nations can do if they are serious about slowing population growth. Countries that now want to reduce their birth rate can draw upon the experience of these two pioneers. And they have the advantage of a wider range of modern contraceptive technologies.

Given the experience of Japan and China, a global effort to cut world population growth in half by the year 2000 does not seem out of the question. The birth rate for the world of 28 per thousand population in 1988 is lower than the 33 per thousand that prevailed in Japan and China when they launched their fertility reduction campaigns. The 1988 world death rate is 10, midway between the 12 in Japan and the 8 in China when their efforts began. If national governments become serious, it is possible to lower the global birth rate of 28 to 19 by the end of the century, a decline of one third. Assuming that the death rate for the world remains at roughly 10 per thousand, this would cut the rate of world population growth in half, dropping it below 1 percent per year.

Much of this decline would have to occur, of course, where population growth is most rapid—Africa, Latin America, and the Indian subcontinent. Industrial countries, such as the United States, the Soviet Union, and Japan, where population growth is now well below 1 percent per year, can easily follow the industrial societies of Western Europe to zero population growth.

Small Families

Countries that have made the shift to small families typically have four things in common: an active national population education program, widely available family planning services, incentives for small families (and in some cases, disincentives for large ones), and widespread improvements in economic and social conditions.

The starting point for an effective national population education program is a careful look into the future, a set of alternative projections that relate population growth to environmental support systems and economic trends. The model for this continues to be the projections undertaken in China in the mid-seventies as part of the post-Mao reassessment. One of the questions asked was, What will the future be like if each couple has two children? Under this assumption, the country would have added some 700 million people, roughly another India, to its population. When related to the future availability of soil, water, forest, energy resources, and jobs, it became clear that a two-child family would lead to a decline in living standards. China's leaders realized that only a one-child family was compatible with the goals and aspirations of the Chinese people.

This information was then used in public discussions and debates, all the way down to the village level. People were involved in considering whether to accept two or more children per family and a decline in living conditions or to move quickly to a one-child family program and a more promising future. However difficult the choice, China opted for the latter, enabling it to achieve levels of infant mortality and life expectancy that approach those of affluent industrial societies.

Undertaking these studies is an area in which international development agencies can be of major assistance. The key to meaningful projections is the integration of national demographic, economic, and ecological trends. Only when the three are combined can a useful view of the future be achieved. Only then do the choices become clear.

Another step with a potentially high payoff is the provision of family planning services to those not yet reached by existing service networks. Recent surveys in developing countries indicate that many women who wish to limit family size do not have access to family planning services. Few efforts to improve the human condition will pay a higher return on investment than filling this family planning gap.

"Societies that have quickly reduced family size have often relied heavily on a combination of incentives for small families or disincentives for large ones."

Societies that have quickly reduced family size have often relied heavily on a combination of incentives for small families or disincentives for large ones. Countries such as China, Singapore, and South Korea have typically offered free health care and in some cases free education through secondary school if couples agree to have only the one child or two children that circumstances call for. This approach is appealing because the free health care helps assure children's survival and the free education helps enhance their earning power, thus increasing the long-term financial security of parents in societies where people depend on their children in old age.

Any meaningful effort to slow population growth quickly will thus depend on heavy additional investments in the provision of family planning services, improvements in education and health, and financial incentives that encourage couples to have smaller families. Although such a broad-based effort could easily involve additional expenditures of $30 billion per year, it can be viewed by industrial societies, who would help provide financing, as a down payment on a sustainable future, an effort to protect the habitability of the planet.

Population Issues

The formulation of population policies and the design of family planning programs are both handicapped by a lack of information. Although changes in birth rates may have a far greater effect on future economic and social trends in developing countries than any other economic trends will, few such countries regularly collect and publish these data. The U.N. *Monthly Bulletin of Statistics* normally includes data on birth and death rates for only 34 countries, nearly all industrial ones.

If the United Nations could launch a monthly report on population and population-related issues and indicators, it would help fill an information gap that handicaps many family planners. Such a report could include information on national goals to reduce family size and progress in extending family planning services. A monthly population report could also provide national analyses of the characteristics of successful family planning efforts, material on the kinds of contraceptives that work best under various conditions, and country-by-country progress in restoring a balance between births and deaths.

At the national level, it now seems reasonable to expect governments to set family planning goals that will lead to improved living conditions. Some countries may find it necessary to press for one child per couple until the momentum of their population growth is checked. But for the world as a whole, two children may now be a more realistic goal. Accumulating evidence suggests that this is the only population policy that is consistent with restoring a worldwide improvement in living conditions. It is time for international leaders, such as the Secretary General of the United Nations and the President of the World Bank, to urge adoption of such a goal by all governments.

Lester R. Brown, Christopher Flavin, and Sandra Postel are project directors for the Worldwatch Institute's annual report, State of the World. *The Worldwatch Institute is a research organization in Washington, D.C. that focuses on analyzing and solving global problems.*

viewpoint 55

Destroying the Rain Forests Will Lead to Extinction

Peter H. Raven

The world that provides our evolutionary and ecological context is in trouble—trouble serious enough to demand our urgent attention. The large-scale problems of overpopulation and over-development are eradicating the lands and organisms that sustain life on this planet. If we can solve these problems, we can lay the foundation for peace and prosperity in the future. By ignoring these issues, drifting passively while attending to what seem more urgent, personal priorities, we are courting disaster. . . .

Many of our most serious problems are centered in the tropics, where biological diversity is concentrated and where whole ecosystems are being permanently disrupted. Three factors influence this destruction: (1) the explosive growth of human populations; (2) widespread and extreme poverty; and (3) ignorance of modern methods of agriculture and forestry. . . .

Decline of Tropical Forests

Based on 1981 estimates by the Food and Agriculture Organization of the United Nations (FAO), approximately 2.3 million square miles of tropical evergreen forest now exist. This forest is roughly three-quarters the size of the United States exclusive of Alaska—about half the size of the original forest area. In the late 1970s, at least 40,000 square miles of such forest were being cut each year. If that rate of clear-cutting continues, the world's tropical forests will last about 60 years— assuming no population growth or other pressures.

The decline in tropical forests is due, in part, to consumer demand in industrialized countries. For example, the United States obtains much of its timber from tropical forests. Each year, logging

removes about 20,000 square miles of these forests—an area nearly the size of West Virginia. Meanwhile, reforestation is proceeding very slowly in the tropics. Ten trees are cut for each one planted; in Africa, 29 are cut for each one planted. The developed world's consumption of tropical hardwoods has risen 15 times since 1950; consumption in tropical countries has increased only three times.

The clearing of tropical forests for cattle pasture is another reason for the decline of such areas. For example, the growing import of beef by the United States from southern Mexico and Central America since 1962 has been the major factor in the loss of about half of the tropical forests there—all for the sake of keeping the price of a hamburger in the United States about a nickel less than it would have been otherwise.

Yet another factor is the relentless search for fuelwood. Nearly 1.5 billion people—one-third of the world's population—are cutting firewood faster than the wood can be regrown.

Some solutions to these problems have begun to present themselves. For example, by establishing firewood plantations on cut-over lands, tropical nations could incorporate their impoverished people into their economies and convert their forests from non-renewable to sustainable resources. Several formal programs promote solutions of this kind. All major producers and consumers of tropical wood are now parties to the 1986 International Tropical Timber Agreement, and the World Resources Institute's Tropical Forest Action Plan can help ensure both a stable commodity supply and biological conservation.

Nonetheless, taken together, clear-cutting of the forests, shifting agriculture patterns and increased demand for firewood are destroying roughly 80,000 square miles of tropical forest each year—an area approximately the size of the state of Kansas. At this rate, all the world's tropical, evergreen forests will be gone in less than 30 years—even without any growth in population.

But because human populations are in fact growing very rapidly—at the rate of approximately 2.4 percent per year—and because actual rates of destruction differ widely from region to region, much of the forest will disappear, or at least be profoundly altered in nature and composition, much sooner.

The forests most threatened include the tropical, lowland forests of Mexico, Central America, the West Indies, Andean South America, and the southern and eastern Amazon. The forests of Africa and Madagascar outside of the Zaire Basin and all the forests of tropical and subtropical Asia and the Pacific Islands will be similarly affected. For the most part, they will have been consumed or severely damaged within the next 15 years.

Three large blocks of lowland, evergreen forest—those in the northern and western Brazilian Amazon, the interior of the Guyanas, and the Zaire Basin of Africa—are larger and less densely populated than the rest. Consequently, they are being cut more slowly. These forests might, therefore, last past the middle of the 21st century.

We have been emphasizing lowland, evergreen forests—because of their biological richness and because they are the most extensive tropical forests that have persisted to the present day. However, dry deciduous forests, and all the other kinds of tropical forests, were cut and converted to agriculture and cattle grazing long before the tropical, evergreen forests. For example, 500 years ago, the dry deciduous forests that once occurred along the Pacific Coast of Mexico and Central America covered an area approximately twice the size of Texas. Today, only about 2 percent of this once-extensive biome exists in anything resembling its original form. . . .

Impact on Biological Diversity

The most serious, long-term global problem resulting from deforestation will be the loss of a large portion of the earth's biological diversity within a few decades. This process of extinction can be viewed from a scientific, aesthetic or moral standpoint—or simply as the loss of opportunities that otherwise could have been used for human benefit. But it is unquestionably the one problem that will have the most lasting consequences.

Current extinction rates are a thousand times those of the past tens of millions of years. Despite this, it is all too easy to say, "Good-bye, California condor—but so what?" There has been an unfortunate tendency for some of the media to adopt this view. It is often easier to suggest that extinction presents no problem, that everything is fine, than it is to document the extent of the problem.

In fact, the loss of biological diversity is important

to us for many reasons. Only about 150 kinds of food plants are used extensively; only about 5,000 have ever been used. Three species of plants—rice, wheat and corn—supply more than half of all human energy requirements. However, there may be tens of thousands of additional kinds of plants that could provide human food if their properties were fully explored and brought into cultivation. Many of these plants come to us from the tropics.

"Clear-cutting of the forests, shifting agriculture patterns and increased demand for firewood are destroying roughly 80,000 square miles of tropical forest each year."

Further, there are numerous uses for tropical plants other than food. Oral contraceptives for many years were produced from Mexican yams; muscle relaxants used in surgery come from an Amazonian vine traditionally used to poison darts; the cure for Hodgkin's disease comes from the rosy periwinkle, a native of Madagascar; and the gene pool of corn has recently been enriched by the discovery, in a small area of the mountains of Mexico, of a wild, perennial relative. Among the undiscovered or poorly known plants are doubtless many possible sources of medicines, oils, waxes, fibers and other useful commodities for our modern industrial society.

Furthermore, as genetic engineering expands the possibilities for the transfer of genes from one kind of organism to another—indeed, as our scientific techniques become even more sophisticated—we could come to depend even more heavily on biological diversity than we do now.

How fast is extinction proceeding? Although only about 500,000 species of tropical organisms have been named, there are at least 3 million, and perhaps ten times that many, yet to be discovered. While investigating the beetle fauna of the canopy of tropical forests in Panama and Peru, Terry Erwin of the Smithsonian Institution fogged the canopies of the trees with insecticides to obtain comprehensive samples for comparative purposes. Based on these samples, he estimates that the true number of species of insects may approach 30 million, or even more.

Assuming an existence of 3 million species of tropical organisms, the distributions of the better-known groups can be used to project how many of the total species occur only in those forests that will probably be destroyed or severely damaged in the next 15 years. Just under half of the total number of plant species in the world occurs only in forests that are rapidly being destroyed. For plants, that means about 120,000 of the estimated total of about 165,000 tropical species would not survive. Assuming the distribution of other groups of organisms is similar to that of plants, then about 2.2 million species, or somewhat less than half of the total, would be restricted to these forests.

How many of these species can reasonably be expected to survive? The principal basis for making projections of this sort lies in the theory of island biogeography. This theory rests on the empirical observation that, in general, for islands and mainland areas alike, the relationship between species number and area is a logarithmic one, so that a ten-fold increase in area is associated with a doubling in the number of species of a given group. The reciprocal relationship, one now being verified empirically in a number of experiments throughout the world, is that a reduction of area to a tenth or less of its original extent should place at risk half or more of the kinds of organisms that occurred in the larger area.

The biological basis for this relationship is clear. As areas are reduced in size, the population of the organisms in them also is reduced. When a population is small, the chance of species survival is reduced.

The history of bird populations on Barro Colorado Island illustrates the way this process works. This island of about six square miles was formed between 1911 and 1914 by the flooding of the Panama Canal. Set aside as a reserve in 1923, Barro Colorado Island was home at that time to 208 species of breeding birds. It has been protected as a reserve ever since. Sixty years later, at least 45 species of these birds are extinct, despite the fact that Barro Colorado Island is only 600 feet from the mainland, a distance that any of the birds could cross easily.

Organisms found in small areas of vegetation also are more vulnerable to the impact of hunting and poaching; to inbreeding and the consequent loss of genetic variability; to the effects of sun, wind and other factors that can damage the organisms' integrity; and to regional climatic changes, (i.e., precipitation), which can leave the species with nowhere to migrate.

Large-Scale Regional Extinction

There are many instances of regional extinction on a massive scale. For example, there were at least 88 species of land birds in the Hawaiian Islands when the Polynesians arrived; 43 when Captain Cook explored the islands about 1,300 years later (in the late 18th century); and 28 today—two-thirds of which are endangered. The destruction of the lowland forests and the introduction of new species have contributed to the decimation of the native birds and plants, and that process continues rapidly today. The Hawaiian Islands provide a prime

example of the way in which ecosystems are simplified, while pests and weedy species become more widespread throughout the world. . . .

"As areas are reduced in size, the population of the organisms in them also is reduced."

Because the forests where at least half of the 2.2 million species of organisms in the world occur will very probably be reduced to less than a tenth of their original size in the next 15 years, we may safely assume that over a million species also will become extinct during this period. One additional example of the effects of deforestation is western Ecuador, which was almost completely forested as recently as 1950. It is now almost completely deforested. As extensive deforestation spreads to other regions of the country, we can expect the extinction rate to average more than 100 species a day, increasing from perhaps a few species a day now to several hundred by the early years of the next century.

The great majority of these species will not have been collected and, therefore, never will be represented in any scientific collection, never preserved or known in any way. No comparable rate of extinction has occurred since the end of the Cretaceous Period, 65 million years ago. Then, the background level of extinction was perhaps one-thousandth of that now taking place.

From any point of view, the situation is extremely serious. Scientifically, we are losing the opportunity to understand the nature of much of the diversity of life on earth. Aesthetically, we are losing the chance to appreciate fully the results of the process of evolution during the billions of years since life appeared on the planet. Economically, we are denying to ourselves, our children and our grandchildren the opportunity to put to use many of the plants, animals and microorganisms that now exist for our benefit.

Peter H. Raven is director of the Missouri Botanical Garden, located in St. Louis. He is also Engelmann Professor of Botany at Washington University in St. Louis, and home secretary of the United States National Academy of Sciences.

viewpoint 56

Destroying the Rain Forests Will Lead to Global Warming

Rogelio A. Maduro

Full-blown deserts, with moving sand dunes and sandstorms, have emerged in many areas of Brazil and other tropical countries where just 10 to 20 years ago there were lush tropical rain forests. Every year, about 6 million hectares of land are irretrievably lost to desertification and a further 21 million hectares are so degraded that crop production becomes uneconomical. About 3,500 million hectares of land worldwide—an area the size of North and South America combined—are affected by desertification, while the rural population dislocated by serious desertification rose from 57 million people in 1977 to 135 million people in 1984.

The shift from forest to desert is visibly dramatic, but what about the effect on global climate? What happens when the rain forests no longer contribute to the global circulation of water vapor?

The tropical rain forest functions as a solar engine, absorbing more sunshine than any other living land cover, moderating surface temperatures, and reducing heat reflection into the atmosphere. It uses this absorbed energy to combine atmospheric carbon dioxide gas to form all kinds of substances. It is the largest terrestrial net producer of oxygen. It is also the greatest source of terrestrial water vapor into the atmosphere, which provides rain in other areas, sometimes thousands of miles away.

As demonstrated in the now nearly extinct rain forest of Africa, deforestation creates a cycle of desertification, including a rise in temperatures as the albedo effect starts to take place, a result of cutting the green cover—and drought: Rain becomes scarcer when water vapor is no longer being returned into the atmosphere.

A mere 10 countries on the planet possess 75.62 percent of the world's rain forest. The three most

important tropical ecosystems in the world, which provide the vast majority of water vapor transpired from land masses into the atmosphere, are located in the Amazon, the delta of the Zaire (Congo) River, and Indonesia. From here, masses of water vapor are circulated throughout the rest of the globe by jet streams, hurricanes, and other high-energy processes. The greatest amount of global precipitation falls on these tropical rain forests. Disastrously, these areas, especially the Amazon and Indonesia, are where the greatest amount of deforestation is now occurring.

Rain Forest Dynamics

The complex workings of this biosphere and its relation to the atmosphere are largely unknown, but a recent joint study conducted by scientists from the United States and Brazil has provided a wealth of discoveries that are still being evaluated. The expedition, the Global Tropospheric Experiment/Amazon Boundary Layer Experiment (known as GTE/ABLE), was conducted above the Brazilian Amazon rain forest in July and August 1985 and in April and May 1987. It combined, for the first time, local measurements at ground stations, regional measurements aboard aircraft, and global measurements from the Space Shuttle and satellites to study the influence on the troposphere of the world's largest rain forest and its influence on chemistry and meteorology of the Earth's atmosphere.

In a paper summarizing the results, mission scientist Robert C. Harris of the National Aeronautics and Space Administration's Langley Research Center asserted that the data obtained supported hypotheses that:

(1) Tropical rain forest environments are characterized by relatively intense sources of biogenically produced gases and aerosols.

(2) The world's largest rain forest, in the Amazon basin, is a region of frequent atmospheric instability

Rogelio A. Maduro, "The Climatic Consequences of Razing the Rain Forests," *21st Century Science and Technology,* January/February 1989. Reprinted with permission.

with intense thunderstorm activity, resulting in a potential for rapid mixing of biogenic gases and aerosols at high altitudes, where they affect global tropospheric chemistry.

(3) The tropical troposphere is a region of intense photochemical activity where sinks for certain biogenic trace gases (like isoprene, C_5H_8) produce sources of gaseous products (like carbon monoxide, CO) that may be significant to the global budget. . . .

It is also important to consider the effect of the variation in the quantity of vapor condensing in the higher parts of the atmosphere. During evaporation, solar energy is transformed into latent heat, which is released in the highest layers of the atmosphere where the water vapor condenses to form clouds. This energy is partially responsible for the circulation of the upper atmosphere. Part of this vapor is transferred to the polar regions, and upon condensation, releases energy; this is one form of energy transfer from equatorial to polar regions.

The Amazon Rain Forest

The Amazon ecosystem removes ozone from the air in the forest and the air immediately overlying the forest. Concentrations of ozone are typically 40 parts per billion (ppb) in the upper atmosphere over the Amazon, decreasing to 20 ppb in the boundary layer; they go to undetectable levels at night in the forest. Thus, tropical forest ecosystems act as a filter, removing ozone from the air through reactions of hydrocarbon gases emitted by vegetation and by ozone uptake on soil and plant surfaces.

Large convective thunderstorms were observed to transport ozone from above 5 kilometers to the lower atmosphere where ozone removal occurs. Thus, the rain forest ecosystem removes ozone, a chemical poisonous to human and animal life in the forest, while it pumps ozone and chemicals basic to the formation of ozone up into the ozone layer. The destruction of the rain forest may therefore be one of the principal causes of the thinning of the ozone layer.

The GTE/ABLE-2 expedition also revealed that as air coming from the Atlantic Ocean flows over the Amazon to the Andes Mountains and exchanges of gases and aerosols (particles) occur, a series of chemical reactions is set off that eventually affects global air quality and the Earth's radiation budget.

Natural organic carbon makes up more than 80 percent of the aerosol mass. The chemical composition of aerosols changes as inflowing ocean air transects the Amazon Basin, and frequent rainstorms remove sea salt and mix forest aerosols up into the tropical atmosphere. Large convective thunderstorms typical of tropical regions can transport rain forest gases and aerosols to altitudes of greater than 6 kilometers, where they become integrated into the atmospheric circulation. These aerosols play important roles as cloud condensation

nuclei, creating the conditions for rain to occur as water vapor is transported to other areas of the world.

Deforestation plays a critical role in destroying the climate of a region, by reducing humidity and rates of plant evaporation and changing the energy balance. In the Amazon forest, it has been calculated that 25.6 percent of precipitation is intercepted by the vegetation and returns to the atmosphere by direct evaporation, 45.5 percent is transpired by plants, and 25.9 percent is drained through the surface runoff. Therefore, about 75 percent of the precipitation returns to the atmosphere in the form of water vapor through the action of plants, indicating the importance of this type of vegetation cover for the components of the Earth's water budget.

Approximately 6,430 billion tons of water vapor are generated within the Amazon water basin as a whole through the direct action of plants in interception, evaporation, and transpiration. This is the same magnitude of water vapor as that coming from the ocean. There are several hypotheses as to what happens to this water vapor, but no empirical studies of this have been done in the atmosphere. The best working hypothesis, supported by qualitative data from weather satellites, is that the water vapor generated by the Amazon moves toward the west and is replaced by primary vapor generated in the Atlantic Ocean. The Andes Mountains form a natural barrier 4,000 meters high and effectively prevent the exit of water vapor to the Pacific Ocean. This is the reason that the western side of the Andes on the Pacific Coast is so dry, while the eastern slope of the Andes has enormous precipitation rates.

"About 75 percent of the precipitation returns to the atmosphere in the form of water vapor through the action of plants."

The Andes Mountains funnel the water vapor both to the north and to the south, depending on the latitude. Above the Intertropical Convergence Zone, which moves north or south of the equator depending on the season, the rotation of the Earth moves the vapor northward over the Guyana Plateau and the Colombian and Venezuelan plains, the Amazon water vapor ending up in the Caribbean Sea, where most of the storms and hurricanes that hit the East and Gulf coasts of the United States are generated. As could be seen from the satellite images of Hurricane Gilbert, vast amounts of water vapor that fed the hurricane came from convective storms in the Amazon.

Below the Equator, the water vapor is driven south

over the central plateau of Brazil and the lowlands of Bolivia, Paraguay, Argentina, Uruguay, and Brazil. The final destination of the Amazon water vapor is Antarctica, where it may also play a critical role in global climate.

Energy Cycle Changes

Deforestation drastically changes this water and energy cycle. If there is less water available for evapotranspiration, there will be a decrease in relative air humidity, which will alter the energy balance. The incident solar energy, instead of being used for water evaporation, will be used for heating the air.

Modifications of small areas surrounded by forest should not influence the energy and water balance or regional climate as a whole, but when thousands of hectares are involved, drastic local climatic changes occur, as can be witnessed in India and Africa. Several studies have documented the role of deforestation in increasing the temperatures and sharply reducing precipitation in local areas of Africa, Asia, and the Amazon, but no large-scale studies have been done. In India, Indra Kumar Sharma wrote that the unreliability of the rains in the Rajasthan region has increased as a direct result of deforestation: The dry air currents rising off the hot ground dispel weak monsoonal fronts, whereas in contrast, the warm, moist air rising from vegetated areas promotes the buildup of local thunderstorms so that areas of dense vegetation receive 40 percent more than neighboring deforested areas.

Vertical Rain Forest

It would seem, as it did to all early explorers of the Amazon, that the soil must be very rich to grow such a lush forest. Yet, the truth is that tropical rain forests are thriving on the poorest soils on Earth. In tropical moist forests, most of the available nutrients are already bound into plant tissues. While binding the shallow topsoil, the tree root systems and symbiotic fungi (together called mycorrhizae) are efficient recyclers of any organic matter falling to Earth. The tropical rain forests have developed an extremely complex ecosystem that essentially captures all the nutrients necessary without recourse to the soil. The crowns shade the soil from damaging sunlight and protect the soil from compacting and leaching by rain. The many trees and other plant species are the source of food for a large number of animals, including especially fish and invertebrates.

A forest in temperate climates, like that of the United States or Europe, is differentiated "horizontally." First there are shrubs, then small trees, then tall trees; pine trees will dominate certain areas, while maple and oak trees will dominate other areas.

A rain forest is completely different; the differentiation is "vertical." There are five canopies of trees, each with its own specializations. In the constant warm and humid conditions of the forest floor, fallen leaves and twigs and other organic matter rapidly disappear, in contrast to the thick mat of organic materials found in temperate climate forests. Every nutrient—for example, nitrogen, phosphorus, potassium, and calcium—is immediately recycled before it is washed away by the rain. If a leaf falls, the insects, bacteria, and fungi that live in symbiotic relationship with the roots of the trees will digest it immediately, returning the minerals and nutrients necessary for growth back to the canopy. In the canopy itself, there are epiphytes, plants that capture all necessary nutrients and minerals from the surrounding air.

"The tropical rain forests have developed an extremely complex ecosystem that essentially captures all the nutrients necessary without recourse to the soil."

Nitrogen is captured from the atmosphere by bacteria and converted into ammonium, which other microbes convert to nitrates that can then be absorbed by plant roots. Nitrogen is thus recycled by the ecosystem, but the rapid decay of organic matter means that nitrogen is quickly depleted when the forest is cut and burned down.

Much of the phosphorus in tropical soils is chemically bound to the clay. Once in the clay it is very difficult for roots to absorb the phosphates, so roots seek it in the surface, one of the reasons the floors of some tropical forests are carpeted by a thick mat of fine roots at the soil surface. Phosphorus uptake is also facilitated by mycorrhizae, which grow closely associated with root cells. The fine network of the fungus more quickly and thoroughly penetrates the soil and freshly fallen litter than do plant roots. Through these mycorrhizae, plants are able to obtain sufficient phosphate for growth in otherwise nutrient-poor soils.

Desertification

There are two major reasons why the areas where rain forests have been either cut or burned down become desertified so rapidly. The first is the very poor quality of the soils under the forest canopy. The second is the volume of rain that falls—several feet a year. Once the forest cover is removed, severe erosion occurs and whatever nutrients were above ground—like the remains of burned plants—or in the soil itself are leached and washed out in a short period of time. With the root and fungus network no longer in place to capture nutrients released from decaying vegetation, nutrients cannot be regenerated.

Because the soils are unconsolidated—the only thing holding them together, the rain forest, is gone—enormous amounts of erosion take place. The forest mat no longer captures and stores the water, and landslides become very common on the hillsides. It has been calculated that an average hectare of rain forest loses approximately .5 kilograms (1 pound) of soil due to erosion per year. If that forest is cut down, the same hectare may lose up to *14 metric tons* of soil per year.

"The rain forest can reclaim a small plot of land rather quickly. When the area becomes larger, however, the rain forest cannot recover."

Extensive flooding, such as the severe and recurrent flooding in Bangladesh, is caused by the deforestation of Nepal. The same phenomenon is happening to the Amazon River, which is cresting several inches higher every year and now flooding areas that had been dry for centuries. The amount of silt discharged by the Amazon has increased enormously, covering the formerly white beaches of Surinam and French Guyana, several hundred miles to the north, with a thick cap of mud. The change in the discharge of the Amazon has also had unpredictable effects on the marine life of the Atlantic Ocean.

The rain forest can reclaim a small plot of land rather quickly. When the area becomes larger, however, the rain forest cannot recover. Thus, tens of millions of hectares of Brazilian rain forest have now become desertified.

Rogelio A. Maduro is a geologist and a reporter of environmental issues.

"It is the insatiable demand of consumers in developed countries for tropical woods that is contributing to destruction of the Amazon rain forests."

viewpoint 57

Demand for Exotic Wood Spurs Rain Forest Destruction

Bruce Babbitt

The remote headwaters of the Amazon River, long isolated by the Andes on the west and 2,000 miles of waterways to the east, are about to be opened to settlement and commerce—and eventual destruction.

For decades developers have dreamed of opening the western door to the Amazon to move tropical products across the Andes to the seaports of Peru and then across the Pacific to Japan and the rest of Asia. That dream is now coming close to reality. It consists of a modern-day Burma Road that would go up from the Pacific Ocean across 16,000-foot Andean passes, down to the Peruvian jungle town of Pucallpa, and then eastward into the Brazilian city of Rio Branco.

If completed, the western road into the Amazon, known in Brazil as BR-364, will be the world's longest logging road. Japanese and American timber purchasers will be lining up their ships in the Pacific port of Lima to haul away tropical timber with names like mahogany, virola, purpleheart, and adiroba from the last inaccessible reaches of the Amazon basin.

The Jungle Road

The most energetic promoter of BR-364 is Flaviano Melo, governor of Acre, the Brazilian state that borders on Peru. In 1988 Governor Melo traveled to Tokyo and came close to persuading Japanese bankers to finance the project. But before the deal closed the word leaked out, and a public outcry ensued. Even US President Bush got into the act with a few private words to Japanese leaders at the Hirohito funeral. The Japanese backed away.

But Governor Melo is not about to be dissuaded. His objective is to get a road, even a primitive road, blazed through the jungle. For, once a trickle of

settlement and commerce is flowing, the flood will inevitably follow. Then the tide of history will be on his side. And he's almost there.

In Peru there is already a road, albeit a very primitive one, that crosses the Andes from Lima to Pucallpa near the Brazilian border. In Brazil a new road has been pushed westward to Rio Branco. The missing link, all that is needed to realize the dream (or the nightmare) is a 500-mile stretch of wilderness between Rio Branco and Pucallpa.

The race is on between Governor Melo, who is searching the world for lenders, and environmentalists seeking to turn world opinion and Brazilian national policy against the project. If BR-364 is completed, the last wilderness of the Amazon will come within reach of the tree cutters' chain saws.

Insatiable Demand

But the public's hands are also on those chain saws. For it is the insatiable demand of consumers in developed countries for tropical woods that is contributing to destruction of the Amazon rain forests.

Nearly half of the tropical hardwoods exported from third-world countries are consumed in Japan and the United States. The Japanese place great value on rare tropical hardwoods for every manner of furniture and housing, including the traditional Buddhist altar, the Budestan, found in Japanese homes. Even construction materials, such as plywood and cement forms, consume valuable woods where less threatened ones would suffice.

In the United States, tropical hardwoods are in demand everywhere from the corporate boardroom to the neighborhood poolroom. Brazilian rosewoods and mahoganies are a staple of interior decorators and furniture makers. Another tree, the purpleheart, is used for the decorative inlays in pool cues. Rosewood trees are also chopped up and processed

Bruce Babbitt, ''Saving the Forest for the Trees,'' *World Monitor*, September 1989. Reprinted with permission.

for rosewood oil, used in perfumes and cosmetics. Mahogany is still the preferred wood for coffins in many countries.

If consumer demand continues unabated, there is not much hope for the world's remaining rain forests, despite the good efforts of such groups as Save the Rain Forests (US) and the Japan Tropical Forest Action Network. There is, however, evidence that public tastes can be changed, and that in turn public pressure can change governmental policies.

> "If consumer demand continues unabated, there is not much hope for the world's remaining rain forests."

Take the case of the African elephant. In the last several years increasing demand for ivory and relentless poaching have reduced the elephant herds by two-thirds, from 1,500,000 to 500,000. With extinction becoming a real threat, environmental groups mobilized. Full-page ads showing an elephant carcass with its tusks hacked off stirred public response. After Sotheby's advertised a pair of elephant tusks for auction, public pressure caused the tusks to be withdrawn and donated to a museum. A Tennessee bootmaker announced it would discontinue a line of elephant-skin boots.

Then in June 1989 President Bush invoked a law to ban ivory imports, urging other nations to do the same. Japan and Hong Kong, the biggest importers of ivory, quickly followed.

Protection Is Needed

An elephant, evoking childhood memories of Babar and afternoons at the circus, is one thing. Whether it is possible to generate the same protectiveness for trees in a rain forest remains to be seen. But the case for doing so is just as strong. In the Amazon basin and in tropical forests the world over, trees anchor fragile ecosystems that nourish millions of species that cannot be replaced once the forest goes.

In New York a well-known architect, William McDonough, avoids the use of tropical woods. He advises prospective clients that there are plenty of renewable American hardwoods such as ash or black cherry, a tree that, in his words, "grows like a weed." McDonough says that most clients seem grateful to learn that they can have a prestigious office building without becoming an accessory to the destruction of an ecosystem. He says he himself plants a tree on his farm in New York's Hudson Valley—10,000 trees so far—every time he uses the lumber from one.

A modest effort to educate consumers about the implications of using tropical wood could make a big difference, for tropical hardwood imports make up less than 2% of total timber consumption in the United States. That tiny percentage could easily be replaced by renewable domestic hardwoods and renewable softwoods from temperate forests.

Perhaps the day will come when environmentally conscious investment bankers will boycott the closing of any deal that takes place at a rosewood conference table. Or when pool players will examine their cues for the telltale lavender of well-aged purpleheart. And it might then become uneconomical to build roads across the Andes.

Meanwhile, it is urgent that governments act to set limits on the imports of tropical timber. The European Parliament has taken under consideration a measure to ban such imports. But the important players are the United States and Japan. And, although Tokyo issued promising words of intent before the Paris summit of industrialized democracies in July 1989, those two players have yet to act decisively.

Bruce Babbitt is a former governor of Arizona and was a candidate for the Democratic presidential nomination in 1988. He first conducted geophysical studies in the Amazon Basin in 1962 and has made numerous trips to the area since then.

"Consumers must be made aware that when they bite into a fast-food hamburger or feed their dogs, they may also be consuming toucans, tapirs and tropical rainforests."

viewpoint **58**

Demand for Cheap Beef Spurs Rain Forest Destruction

Peter Cox

San Bernadino, California, the year 1954. 'San Berdoo' is a rich boomtown of oddball bikers: the end of the road, transcontinental terminus for Route 66. No jobless, no homeless. In motor city everyone drives to the shopping mall or rides the gleaming freeway, never walks. This is the town that gave you Hell's Angels, high priests of the consumer society on wheels: the town that spawned hamburgers on an unsuspecting world—*fast food for fast times!*

Ray Kroc, kitchen paraphernalia super-salesman from Chicago, wonders why Mac and Richard McDonald buy so much equipment from his company. Flies down to San Berdoo. Meets them. Cash tills ring. 'Visions of McDonalds restaurants dotting crossroads all over the country, paraded through my brain,' he reports. 'Padding a steady flow into my pockets.' The deal is struck. The hamburger's time has come. Today McDonalds takes over $12 billion every year and over 95 per cent of Americans will eat at McDonalds during any year. Jobs too: McDonalds has employed at one time or another 20 per cent of the American working public.

Hamburgers in The Third World

Thirty years ago the citizens of Hamburg, West Germany, hadn't even heard of 'hamburgers'. Now the food religion that McDonalds did so much to popularize has spread throughout the world. And still more growth potential! Seventy per cent of all consumers live in poor countries. They can't afford a car or a colour TV, but enough of those people can be persuaded to find a few cents for a burger to make the potential market extremely juicy. In India '10 per cent of the population can consume on a level with most Americans and Western Europeans,' says management guru Peter Drucker. That's 70

million people—a bigger market than any country in Europe.

And selling to Third World countries is easy too. Target the impressionable kids, the aspiring young, anyone who's prepared to believe that all things fashionably Western must be good. In Hong Kong and Manila some primary schools even have contracts with hamburger chains who sell their products on school premises. Few countries can resist the onslaught. Morocco has banned a major hamburger chain from setting up shop; Indonesia has prohibited the television advertising of fast-food establishments. But most cultures succumb eventually. Powerful stuff, this advertising. Take the latest campaign in the US featuring TV star Cybill Shepherd, who purrs seductively:

'Sometimes I wonder if people have a primal, instinctive craving for hamburgers. Something hot and juicy and so utterly simple you can eat it with your hands. I mean, I know some people who don't eat burgers. But I'm not sure I trust them.'

Got the message? If you don't eat burgers, you ain't a trustworthy American. Other commercials contrast the macho, all-American image of burgers to 'that fancy food they eat in San Francisco'. So you're not just unpatriotic if you don't eat hamburgers— you're probably homosexual too. Macho advertising is one important ingredient in a hamburger. The other is a plentiful source of cheap raw materials.

Which is where trees come in.

The Tree Connection

In their quest for ever cheaper meat supplies, the international beef industry is always looking for usable tracts of grazing land—anywhere in the world. As one rancher puts it: 'It boils down to $95 per cow per year in Montana, $25 in Costa Rica'. So forests are felled, land is cleared, grass planted, cheap beef is produced and consumer demand is satisfied.

Peter Cox, "Fast Food, Chop Chop," *New Internationalist*, June 1988. Reprinted with permission.

But recently, a few consumers have begun to wonder how much their hamburgers *really* cost. Not in dollars and cents but in terms of natural resources consumed or destroyed. Then someone did a simple but very shocking calculation. They reasoned that a hectare of rainforest—the sort of land regularly cleared for ranching in remote areas—supports about 800,000 kilogrammes of plants and animals. When the same hectare has been felled, torched, razed and seeded with grass for grazing, it will produce at most 200 kilogrammes of meat a year—enough flesh to make about 1,600 hamburgers. The pasture doesn't last long however, because the land is quickly leached of its nutrients and left barren by over-grazing. In a few years it becomes useless.

By then of course, more forest has been destroyed and converted to stop-gap pasture land. This makes the *true* cost of a hamburger something in the region of half a tonne of rainforest for each burger—or about nine square metres of irreplaceable natural wealth, forever destroyed for the price of a quick unhealthy snack.

"The West's apparently insatiable desire for cheap meat . . . exerts enormous market pressures on beef producers to exploit the cheapest and most available land."

Some burger companies—McDonalds for example—make it clear that they never have and never will use beef from Central or South American sources. McDonalds uses US domestic beef from dedicated suppliers. Other companies like Burger King, who used to buy beef from Costa Rica, have recently changed their buying policy and now no longer accept beef from Central American sources. The fact remains however, that the West's apparently insatiable desire for cheap meat (whether for burgers, pet food or processed meat products), exerts enormous market pressures on beef producers to exploit the cheapest and most available land—which is often tropical forest.

To Kill a Forest

A forest must be ravaged three times before it dies, for the scrub and remaining undergrowth must be burned for three consecutive years before its life-force becomes spent and the jungle is rendered barren. Then you can plant grass to graze your cattle.

A forest may be destroyed in several different ways. First, roads must be driven deep into its being. Slashing, ramming, mutilating and violating. An image of rape? Certainly. Men have always had a

violent relationship with Mother Nature. Then the timber companies can extract their prizes—mahogany, tropical cedar, whatever sells on the world market. Never doubt its profitability—mahogany trades for $20 per cubic metre in Brazil and $4,000 in London when made into furniture for affluent, but unthinking consumers.

It is wrong to call this type of operation forestry, for it is quite flagrantly the plundering of a priceless natural resource. Nigeria for example, lost four per cent of its forests in the first half of the 1980s, and the best trees have long since been turned into designer furniture or toilet seats for the trend setters. Nigeria now imports *100 times* more wood than it exports.

Forest Settlers

Another irresistible force pitted against the survival of the last rainforests comes from settlers. They are the jobless, the landless, the displaced and the dispossessed—those who dream of escape from grinding poverty. Such as Luis Bernardi, who journeyed penniless from Sao Paulo on Highway BR-364, a dirt track leading to the heart of virgin forest in Brazil's Rondonia state. Fourteen years later, he now owns an eight-bedroom house and 740 acres of land.

As many as 60,000 people make the same journey each month, hoping for similar wealth. 'The Bold Ones March Westwards' say the government-sponsored TV commercials. Such people are unlikely to understand Western concerns about conservation when their own survival and future prosperity is at stake.

'We have the same right to destroy our wilderness as the Americans had in the Far West,' says Adeildo Martins de Lucena, a newspaper editor from the Brazilian border town of Vilhena. The settling of forest areas is frequently the result of impossible pressure for land resources elsewhere, caused by inequitable land distribution in Latin America where 7 per cent of the landowners control 93 per cent of the arable land. Under such circumstances, colonization of wildernesses can relieve pressure for land reform and promote national unity.

Although the new settlers intend to stay and prosper, it doesn't often work out like that. Sometimes they get moved out or even killed by hired gunmen working for absentee landowners who are eager to annex small-holdings into a good-sized cattle ranch. (The average price for a settler's life is $25.) Other times, the land gives out after a few years of producing cash crops. The soil beneath the rainforest canopy is poor. Without protection, it erodes and within a few years is leached of nutrients. So the settlers move on, having cleared the rainforest for the benefit of the incoming ranchers.

While meat production increases, local meat consumption decreases. Two-thirds of Central

America's arable land is now used for beef rearing, whilst domestic per-capita consumption steadily drops. In 1959 Costa Ricans ate 30 pounds of beef per year. By 1979 beef production had doubled, but its inhabitants got less than 19 pounds per annum.

Ethiopia, recently the target of much Western media attention, has suffered a similar fate. From a forest area covering 16 per cent of the land in the 1950s, less than four per cent is now left. Multinationals which were welcomed with generous tax incentives proceeded to develop the best and most fertile areas, evicting the indigenous population, who then struggled to survive on fragile upland areas. The consequent tree felling, overgrazing and land degradation has exacerbated the country's problems. Nevertheless Ethiopia still exports beef to the West: one Italian multinational has been shipping Ethiopian beef to Europe since 1986, although the country of origin is sometimes obscured on labels. 'It has been rejected in some quarters,' the UK importers are quoted as saying, 'because the emotive value makes it too hot for the retailer to handle'.

Fighting Livestock Production

Organizations such as the World Bank, the United Nations Development Fund, the African Development Bank and the Inter-American Development Bank have all provided loans for livestock production and meat processing in developing countries. It is essential that pressure is brought to bear on these development organizations to curtail such catastrophic loan programmes.

"It is Western consumers who by producing a demand for cheap beef make the whole process economically worthwhile."

Some organizations like the Environmental Defense Fund are doing just that, and having a degree of success. A newly formed group, Conservation International, pulled off a coup recently when it purchased $650,000 of Bolivian debt in exchange for a promise to set aside 3.7 million acres for conservation. And after much lobbying, US Treasury Secretary James Baker ordered his representative to the African Development Bank to oppose a loan for a cattle abattoir in Botswana. Such victories are comparatively small but important in as much as they show that something can be done—if we are prepared to try. In the end of course, it is Western consumers who by producing a demand for cheap beef make the whole process economically worthwhile.

In the words of James Nations and Daniel Komer, two staff members at the Texas-based Center for Human Ecology: 'Consumers must be made aware that when they bite into a fast-food hamburger or feed their dogs, they may also be consuming toucans, tapirs and tropical rainforests.'

Have a hamburger you say? You must be choking.

Peter Cox is the author of Why You Don't Need Meat, *a study of meat and its physiological effects, and of* Active Ingredients.

The Brazilian Government Should Stop Rain Forest Destruction

Philip M. Fearnside

Deforestation is rapidly converting Brazil's Amazon forest to low-value, unproductive cattle pasture. To stop this annual loss of about 35,000 square kilometers of forest from the 5-million-square-kilometer Amazonian region, effective policies that slow deforestation must redirect development. Otherwise, the option to use the forest in a sustainable way will be irrevocably lost, because rapid soil degradation, competition with weeds, and disruption of seed dispersal and pollination prevent forest regrowth.

Only production systems that allow the forest canopy to remain intact will prove sustainable in Amazonia. Sustainable production implies harvesting only those forest products that can be easily renewed. One possibility is to protect tracts of Amazonia as extractive reserves, from which only nonendangered flora and fauna could be harvested. Such a harvest would include only nontimber forest products like latex, resins, nuts, and medicinal compounds. However, slowing deforestation is only a means of buying time for more research on the technologies of sustained production and on the economic mechanisms needed to ensure that sustainable systems are adopted by Brazilian settlers and businesses.

Motives for Deforestation

Slowing forest destruction requires more than simply outlawing deforestation, which is the current, completely unenforceable approach embodied in Decree Law 7511 of 7 July 1986. Policymakers also must remove the motives for deforestation. Some of the needed measures are expensive: For example, to reduce the flow of migrants to Amazonia, massive funding would be required to increase employment opportunities in migrant source areas, such as the southern state of Paraná, through agrarian reform and urban industrial development. Other measures, such as changing people's attitudes through education and extension programs, can only produce results slowly. However, many essential measures can have immediate impact at no cost or even at considerable savings to the government.

Land Speculation

One principal force driving deforestation in Brazilian Amazonia today is land speculation. The forest is free for anyone who can claim it. By clear cutting forest for cattle pasture (the cheapest land use to adopt), settlers can gain title to a tract of land and keep other squatters or ranchers from invading the area either before or after title is obtained. Although a tract's beef production may be negligible or zero, such land speculation is highly profitable because a title permits the sale of land to be legally recorded, and titled land can be used as collateral for bank loans. Land values also rise when roads are built. Low capital gains taxes on land sales permit speculators to realize large profits with relatively little effort. This profitability must be removed by levying heavy taxes on capital gains from land sales. Heavy taxes are fully justified because the rapid increase in land values does not stem from the efforts of the landholders but from the expanding road network financed by taxpayers throughout Brazil. Whenever a road is built or improved in Amazonia, the value of nearby land immediately multiplies by as much as a factor of 10, if not more.

Land tenure in Amazonia is established by clearing forest and planting pasture, which is recognized by the National Institute of Agrarian Reform as an improvement, or *benfeitoria*. In reality, however, creating pasture is not an improvement but a form of ecological destruction, because the soil in clear-cut areas of Amazonia becomes compacted and

Philip M. Fearnside, "A Prescription for Slowing Deforestation in Amazonia," *Environment*, May 1989. © 1989 by Philip M. Fearnside.

depleted of available phosphorus in about a decade. Afterwards, pasture is usually abandoned to second growth of little or no economic value. Growth of edible grass for forage declines sharply during the life of the pasture, until the cost of controlling inedible weeds exceeds any economic return from the cattle grazed there.

To control deforestation, classification of pasture as an improvement must be abolished. Otherwise, people claiming title to land will continue to find ways to circumvent forest conservation legislation and will benefit from deforestation and the increases in land value that accompany the granting of legal title.

Financial Incentives

Deforestation is encouraged by special government subsidies for such programs as the agricultural and pig-iron (crude iron cast in blocks) projects approved by the Grande Carajás Program and the ranching projects and sawmills approved by the Superintendency for Development of Amazonia (SUDAM) as well as the Superintendency for the Manaus Free Trade Zone (SUFRAMA). Incentives for deforestation include income tax exemptions, arrangements that forgive half the taxes owed on profits from undertakings elsewhere in Brazil provided the money is invested in Amazonian development, and loans granted at interest rates lower than the Brazilian inflation rate. For example, in 1975 when the inflation rate was about 35 percent, loans were granted at an interest rate of just 7 percent. Recently, the rate of inflation has jumped to 1,000 percent, while the loan rate is only a fraction of this.

In 1979, SUDAM policy was changed to bar new incentives in Legal Amazonia, which covers 5 million square kilometers of mostly lowland rain forest. However, SUDAM still grants new incentives in transition forest areas, and incentives approved before 1979 continue to be paid throughout the region. If these incentives were abolished immediately, the government would benefit economically as much as the country would benefit environmentally.

Brazil's economic difficulties greatly reduced the flow of government subsidies in 1988, but no policy has been established to prevent the resumption of large financial incentives when the economy recovers. Indeed, Brazil's president, José Sarney, has declared his intention of maintaining the incentive programs indefinitely. . . .

Projects receiving incentives have already devastated wide areas of the Amazon forest for little economic return to the public. The profits made by the beneficiaries do not represent productive contributions to the national economy but, rather, speculative gains and, often, the illicit use of the incentive monies themselves. The incentives should be halted summarily, but if beneficiaries are judged to have acquired rights (*direitos adequeridos*) to incentives that already have been granted, any future installments should be given exclusively for restoring tree cover to already deforested areas.

Road Building

Highway construction is a key component of deforestation and one of the most sensitive pressure points where government action can slow forest loss. The government could also save substantial sums of money by not building highways. Road construction encourages forest clear cutting by fueling land speculation, pasture planting, colonist turnover, and new immigration. Deforestation has increased wherever roads are built in Amazonia, as it has along the BR-364 and Transamazon highways.

Road building and improvement projects must be restricted to areas where the land is suitable for agriculture. Otherwise, infertile lands inevitably are settled with virtually no government control. A zoning system to identify good agricultural land is necessary, and it must be based on technical criteria like soil quality rather than on politics or geopolitics. The best example of an ill-advised road improvement is the BR-429 Highway in the state of Rondônia, which will open to settlement the highly infertile valley of the Guaporé River. The road already exists as a seasonally passable track, but local politicians are pressing strongly to have it paved. Although maps made by the Brazilian Enterprise for Agricultural and Cattle Ranching Research of the land adjacent to the road clearly show an utter absence of good, fertile soil, preliminary government zoning maps of Rondônia classified the strip along the road as recommended for agricultural use. Subsequent revisions have classified the area for controlled logging. . . .

"The best example of an ill-advised road improvement is the BR-429 Highway in the state of Rondônia, which will open to settlement the highly infertile valley of the Guaporé River."

The National Council for the Environment's Resolution No. 001 of 23 January 1986 requires that every major government project proposed in Brazil have a Report on Impact on the Environment (RIMA). However, consulting firms paid by the projects' proponents write the reports, and often construction begins before a report is finished, even though the resolution states that a RIMA must be finished and approved before work commences.

Both the legislation and its implementation are deficient and must be improved to eliminate this inherent conflict of interest. More effective means are needed to ensure that the interested parties do not influence the conclusions of the reports. For example, a RIMA should be completed, publicly debated, and duly approved before steps are taken that render the project in question an irreversible *fait accompli*. This legally mandated procedure has failed to occur in several major projects initiated since January 1986, when RIMAs became a requirement. The best known example is the North-South Railway, running from Açaílândia, Maranhão to Anápolis, Goiás: Bids were solicited from contractors within a few days of the announcement of the project and before any environmental evaluation had begun. Another example is the approval of fiscal incentives for pig-iron production in the Grande Carajás region and the construction of the necessary smelters with no environmental study. . . .

On 6 April 1989, President Sarney announced the establishment of *Nossa Natureza* (Our Nature), which includes a $100-million, 5-year program to zone the Amazon basin for both economic use and ecological protection. The program emphasizes increased inspection and enforcement of deforestation restrictions, but it does not remove the underlying motives for clear cutting the forest. For instance, *Nossa Natureza* includes only a temporary suspension of new incentives for ranching and does not eliminate the pig-iron scheme in the Grande Carajás Program.

"Deforestation must be slowed drastically and quickly if sustainable uses of the rain forest are to be retained."

Deforestation must be slowed drastically and quickly if sustainable uses of the rain forest are to be retained. Cheap and effective measures include taxing land speculation; disallowing pasture as an "improvement" for establishing land tenure; halting fiscal incentives and other subsidies for developments involving deforestation; reducing and strictly controlling road building; and strengthening RIMA procedures for major development projects. Unless the Brazilian government soon enacts and enforces these measures, the forests of Amazonia will not be saved.

Philip M. Fearnside is a research professor in the ecology department of the National Institute for Research, located in the Amazon of Manaus, Brazil. He has been involved in research in the Amazon for thirteen years.

"The Bush administration can help save tropical forests... by its support on debt-for-nature issues, and by starting to see forest preservation as integrally tied to the debt crisis."

The U.S. Government Should Stop Rain Forest Destruction

Peter P. Swire

In case anyone is wondering where Peter Max has been since the early 1970s, the answer is "in creative retreat," according to a spokesman. But now Max is back, and he's determined to use his art "to show his concern for planetary issues," especially the preservation of tropical forests. For instance, Max has produced a "quality line of sportswear" that features shirts saying "Save the Rainforest" and "Hug a Tree." The proceeds will be donated to Peter Max's bank account. But don't get the wrong idea; Max says he plans to hold a $1 million auction of his work, and *that* money will go to the Rainforest Action Network, a San Francisco-based organization devoted to linking rain forest activists.

That's a lot of linking. Max is but one of many cultural heroes who have lined up for the hottest political cause since world hunger. The British rock star Sting has done a rain forest benefit concert at the Kennedy Center. And the Grateful Dead, though long known for consciousness raising, had never raised it for any specific political cause until the September 1988 benefit concert for tropical forests at Madison Square Garden. The audience received an extensive information kit, including ready-to-send postcards to officials at the World Bank, at the United Nations Environment Program, in Congress, and in Brazil. Also: quotes from band members, including drummer Mickey Hart's meditation on "a profound understanding of man's biochemical relationship with nature." Suzanne Vega and Roger Hornsby sang at the concert, and Kermit the Frog was featured in a "Save the Rainforests" film.

Tropical chic is particularly evident in Washington, D.C. The Smithsonian is featuring a major exhibition on rain forests, the National Zoo is raising money to start its own tropical forest, and environmental

groups are staffing up on lobbyists and grass-roots activists in the area. Among politicians, tropical forest preservation has moved up the charts to rate mention not only by members of Congress, but by former presidents Ford and Carter and President Bush.

What Can We Do?

There is one problem with all of this. Backers of the rain forest movement are mostly in the United States or other modern industrialized countries. The rain forests are not. They're mostly in developing countries, which face other, more pressing issues, such as feeding their growing populations. So two questions must be answered. First, why is it our business to tell Brazil, Indonesia, and other forested countries what to do with their forests? And, assuming there's an answer to that question, how can we in developed countries convince the forested countries they should listen to us?

The standard answer to the first question is that the whole world is affected by tropical deforestation, so everyone should have a say in what happens to the forests. The best-known spillover effect is global warming, caused by emission of carbon dioxide and other gases. Deforestation (often to create farmland or ranch land, or just for the lumber) contributes to the greenhouse effect in two ways: burning the trees releases carbon dioxide into the environment, and cutting them reduces the number of trees on hand to convert carbon dioxide back into oxygen. The effect of deforestation on warming is substantial, perhaps one-third of the effect of all burning of fossil fuels. Estimates of the rate of tropical deforestation vary from 27,000 square miles per year (a bit larger than West Virginia) to 77,000 square miles (Nebraska). At the latter rate, the tropical forests, now covering about seven percent of the world's land surface, will disappear by 2050. Recent satellite photos that show thousands of fires in Brazil, ruining 31,000 square

Peter P. Swire, "Tropical Chic," *The New Republic,* January 30, 1989. Reprinted with permission of THE NEW REPUBLIC, © 1989, The New Republic, Inc.

miles of virgin forest per year, suggest the higher number may be more accurate.

Unfortunately, the problem of global warming can seem abstract and distant to political leaders struggling with crises of debt, hunger, population growth, and urbanization. More to the point, even if, say, Brazil does recognize the gravity of the greenhouse effect, why should it sacrifice for the entire world? After all, northern countries don't have a long history of such sacrifice. They got rich by cutting their forests and exploiting their minerals. In fact, even since the environmental toll of economic development became evident, northern nations haven't posted a strong record. The United States, for example, has been blocked by political bickering from taking strong action on acid rain. So Third World leaders can justifiably tell us to clean up our own back yard before telling them to clean up theirs. In particular, they can demand that we cut our own, sky-high consumption of fossil fuels, which contributes substantially to global warming.

In short, demanding unilateral action from the Southern Hemisphere in the name of the greenhouse effect is unlikely to do any good. And it may backfire, since U.S. pressure is easily seen as Yankee imperialism.

"Third World leaders can justifiably tell us to clean up our own back yard before telling them to clean up theirs."

To be sure, in trying to drive home the urgency of saving the rain forests, we can always note, correctly, that the greenhouse effect is not the only problem. Consider the loss of "biodiversity." Tropical forests hold over half of all terrestrial species, and perhaps over 90 percent. Deforestation, at current rates, will lead to a greater extinction of species than accompanied the demise of the dinosaurs. It is hard to reduce this issue to costs and benefits. Ecologists warn about the large and unpredictable effects that would follow such a mass extinction. Scientists worry about losing the world's most complex ecosystems before most species there are even catalogued, much less studied. Genetic engineers will feel cheated by the loss of their chief feedstock, new genes, just when biotechnology is opening the tropics' genetic diversity to myriad new uses. And many people find human-caused extinctions wrong for moral and aesthetic reasons (which, of all the concerns about biodiversity, turn out to carry the greatest political clout).

Still, with biodiversity as with the greenhouse effect, the question arises: Why should southern nations especially care? Clearing the forests brings them short-term economic gains—at least to their

cattle ranchers and governing elites—even if it impedes sustainable economic development. But the long-term, more abstract benefits of saving the forests accrue mostly to the north. That's where the bioengineering and pharmaceutical companies are, and that's where most of the biologists and taxonomists and *National Geographic* photographers are.

Given that moral suasion is largely unconvincing and ineffective, how are we to get tropical nations to do what we want? Some have proposed boycotting imports of beef raised on burned-out forest plantations, or wood logged in non-sustainable ways. This approach may sometimes work, but it also risks trade retaliation, and it suggests a moral high ground that we may not, in fact, have. Suppose the tropical countries, or other countries, started boycotting U.S. products whose manufacture entailed the burning of fossil fuels (i.e., most U.S. products). How would we feel about that?

The World Must Pay

The fact is that if the world wants southern nations to stop burning their tropical forests, the world is going to have to pay them to do it. It can either pay them in the same currency, by forging some international environmental agreement under which all nations cut their various contributions to the greenhouse effect, or it can pay them with money. For now, the latter is simpler. And the mechanism for it already exists. The World Bank and the other multilateral development banks (MDBs), such as the Inter-American Development Bank, make more than $24 billion in loans and credits available each year to developing countries. These agencies have been criticized for funding projects that cause great environmental harm. Because the United States and other developed nations provide the funding, they can require the MDBs to pick projects that preserve the forests. There are signs that this is starting already.

The idea of subsidizing the preservation of rain forests has been picked up by some environmental groups in the form of "debt-for-nature swaps" that have offered an attractive deal to debtor nations including Costa Rica, Bolivia, and Ecuador. In these swaps, environmental groups buy up debt in hard-to-get dollars. In return, the debtor government agrees to make conservation investments in the local currency. The symbolism is apt: rather than "borrowing" short-term from their natural resources, the nations reduce debt by preserving those resources. The swaps expand parklands, sponsor environmental education and research, and provide funding for maintaining parklands that otherwise often exist only in theory.

But debt-for-nature swaps remain tiny compared with the economics of the overall debt problem. A far greater help to the rain forests would be an aggressive debt reduction plan that would directly ease the pressure on developing countries to exploit their resources so rapidly. Tropical forest preservation can become a major issue in LDC [less developed country] debt negotiations, joining traditional concerns about promoting democracy and maintaining economic stability. Environmental groups are pushing for such a solution, and Latin American governments are starting to see how effective the greenhouse effect could be in getting them more debt relief than they receive under the Baker Plan's renewed loans.

Reasonable Aid Needed

As the debt-for-nature swaps illustrate, environmental groups have done a fair amount of hard-nosed thinking about saving the rain forests. And the statements attributed to their celebrity patrons, for the most part, have been strikingly well informed. But it's important to remember that conscience alone won't save a single tree, and the forested countries are unlikely to respond favorably to stirring moral pleas or self-righteous demands.

Resisting faddish rain forest proposals is a particular challenge for Congress. A bill introduced by Representative Claudine Schneider of Rhode Island would require a forest conservation plan from every tropical country (a significant bureaucratic burden for some countries), and *all* activities supported by direct U.S. foreign assistance would then have to be consistent with the plan. Saving the rain forests is important, but not important enough to trump all other goals of foreign aid.

Among the better congressional proposals: part of the Agency for International Development (AID) appropriation has been earmarked for rain forest projects, with good results. The next step is to increase the overall level of aid and use it as leverage in the rain forest issues. . . .

"The next step is to increase the overall level of aid and use it as leverage in the rain forest issues."

The Bush administration can help save tropical forests through AID and the MDBs, by its support on debt-for-nature issues, and by starting to see forest preservation as integrally tied to the debt crisis. Bush can also use his bully pulpit to educate Americans about environmental issues. Perhaps a joint appearance with the Grateful Dead at the Kennedy Center?

Peter P. Swire is an attorney for the firm of Powell, Goldstein, Frazer & Murphy in Washington, D.C.

Regulations Are Necessary

Henry C. Kenski and Helen M. Ingram

Until the 1970s, environmental regulations were a low priority on the national policy agenda. In 1960, for example, President Eisenhower successfully vetoed a bill to spend $100 million on a wastewater grant program. In a 1965 Gallup Poll asking which three items should get the most attention by government, only 17 percent of the respondents named reducing air and water pollution, ranking it ninth out of ten suggested areas. No cabinet-level pollution agency existed, and air and water pollution were dealt with separately in bureaus located within Health, Education, and Welfare (HEW). The low status of the environment among the subjects of governmental concern can be explained by perceptions of the high costs of regulations to politically important groups. That pollution has attained the stature it has on today's policy agenda, we believe, is testimony to the seriousness of the problem and the extent of a broad public commitment to solution.

Whatever its merits and level of popular support, any policy must gather more organized support than organized opposition to run the political gauntlet successfully. James Q. Wilson has identified pollution policy as one of those troublesome areas where specific, easily identifiable groups bear the cost of a program that confers widely distributed, diffuse benefits. The groups bearing the costs are likely to feel their burden keenly and thus are likely to organize in opposition, while the general community may see its benefits as less important and fail to be supportive.

Traditional pork barrel policies that distribute highways, post offices, military bases, hospitals, waterways, and dams are examples of policies that offer highly salient direct benefits. Such projects

Reprinted from "The Reagan Administration and Environmental Regulation: The Constraint of the Political Market," by Henry C. Kenski and Helen M. Ingram, in *Controversies in Environmental Policy,* edited by Sheldon Kamieniecki et al., by permission of the State University of New York Press. © 1986 by State University of New York. All rights reserved.

have been coveted because they promise economic development and jobs in construction and operation. Compared to these distributive policies, the offering of pollution policy is unimpressive. As air pollution is not "treated" in public waste treatment facilities, its program does not involve extensive public works to distribute targeted benefits. Action, such as subsidies to industry for scrubbers or taller smokestacks, is essentially private and not likely to be seen as much of a public benefit unless a polluter is otherwise forced to clean up. Neither are waste treatment plants for water pollution control especially attractive distributive goods, as the slow start of their construction under federal grants-in-aid available since 1956 attests. Compared with dams or highways, the boon to the construction industry is small; not much growth or employment is generated, and congressmen find it difficult to point to sewage plants for their constituents with pride. The political role of the waste treatment grant program has been as a sweetener, to make somewhat less onerous the regulatory burden placed on municipalities. It has not been the kind of direct benefit that generates spontaneous support.

Everyone Benefits

From the perspective of aesthetics, human health, and ecology, everyone benefits from improved environmental quality; yet, it is precisely because everyone benefits, as opposed to particular interests, that it is difficult to get action to protect environmental quality. The general problem of common pool resources is that a lesser incentive exists to take action that makes everyone better off, but does not give particular actors a relative advantage. The "free rider" problem suggests that in matters like reducing pollution where benefits cannot be restricted to those who give active support, there is strong incentive to let others do the pushing.

Individuals and groups that might be singled out as beneficiaries are notably lacking in political clout. For instance, the very old, the very young, and the infirm—hardly the best organized citizens' groups—are particularly vulnerable to the adverse health effects of polluted air. Studies have shown that populations with the highest per family gross benefits under the Clean Air Act of 1970 are primarily in low-income areas with large minority populations like Jersey City, New York City, Erie, and Newark. Dirty air in low-income areas must compete with other problems (unemployment, housing, and medical care) of such magnitude that its urgency may well be diluted.

In contrast, the direct costs of air and water pollution regulations are clear and very large to important sectors. Automotive exhaust controls fall heavily upon an industry that directly or indirectly employs as many as one in seven Americans and the economic health of which is already in question. The electrical utility industry, a major stationary source of air pollution, and therefore a primary target of regulation, is economically powerful and located in almost every congressional district. Because most industrial processes involve the use of water in production and cooling, the requirement to obtain water pollution permits and install pollution equipment that meets specified standards has a gigantic impact upon industry. Up until the 1970s business was able to argue successfully through such groups as the National Association of Manufacturers and the Chamber of Commerce that the role of industry as a major taxpayer and producer of employment was too important to be so burdened.

Against Strong Odds

Business has been helped by the executive branch of the federal government in fending off pollution policies. President Eisenhower issued a strong warning against federal involvement in water pollution policy and instead endorsed state and local action, partly at the instigation of the Office of Management and Budget which has been concerned about the implications of pollution policy for budget outlays and tax receipts. Other presidents since Eisenhower have been ambiguous about pollution programs. Neither presidents Kennedy nor Johnson took any real initiatives in air and water pollution. While initially supportive of the environment because of the groundswell of public sentiment, President Nixon was outflanked by Senator Edmund Muskie (D., Maine) in the legislative process and ended up vetoing the 1972 Clean Water Act and impounding funds for the waste treatment grant program. Among recent presidents, only Jimmy Carter was wholeheartedly enthusiastic about environmental regulations, and he came to office long after the major initiatives had been passed by Congress.

Just as the prominence of pollution policy on the national agenda was not the result of presidential leadership, neither can it be attributed to the self-aggrandizement of powerful federal agencies. The agencies with jurisdiction over air and water pollution began within a hostile environment in the Public Health Service, which was more oriented to research and information dissemination than regulation. Pollution agencies were continually shifted and reorganized, and it was not until 1970 that the Environmental Protection Agency (EPA) was established as an independent entity with an administrator appointed by the president.

"Environmental policy involves a strong federal/state partnership that did not emerge overnight."

Pollution regulation emerged to its present position as a major agenda item against strong odds. Its prominence can only be explained by the widespread popular belief that there were benefits to be gained that went beyond the usual individual self-interest. The "environmental decade" witnessed a dramatic shift in public tastes and values. Whether or not they themselves were personally affected, citizens wanted to protect the environment and expected their government to take action. Of course, this shift did not take place outside the political process. Political entrepreneurs exploited public sentiments to get newspaper coverage, built membership of interest groups, influenced appointments to official positions, and affected policy. These entrepreneurial successes in turn, fueled public concern through continued focus on pollution problems. However, had it not been for the public conviction that problems are real and important, the appeals of political entrepreneurs would not have been effective.

The odds against making pollution control a major item on the national policy agenda dictated that the federal government's involvement would grow slowly. A review of the pre-1970 history of air and water pollution policy suggests that in the beginning it was noncoercive and nonregulatory, and that it was only with the failure of the milder, more noninterventionist pieces of legislation that policy escalation occurred. The evolution of policy was pushed by past failures to attain goals, not pulled by some conviction that direct federal regulation was the only or the best type of environmental policy.

Table 1 presents a simplified summary of the evolution of federal air and water pollution policy. In the left-hand column is a hierarchy of policy tools, ranging from those least coercive or regulatory to those that are more so. As the table illustrates, pollution policy began with the least stringent type of regulations. It was not until the late sixties and early seventies that Congress chose to take stronger action.

Table 1. Evolution of Pollution Policy: 1948-1977

Policy Tools	Legislation Adopted in Air or Water Pollution	Specific Provisions
Information to reveal dangers	1948—Water Pollution Control Act	Responsibility of Public Health Service to do research
	1955—Air Pollution Control Acts	Research grants and federal research authority
Subsidy to encourage action	1956—Water Pollution Control Act Amendments	$50 million grants for waste treatment plant construction in small cities
	1963—Clean Air Act	Grants to state and local programs
Exposure to public criticism	1956—Water Pollution Control Act	Conference procedure to publicize interstate problem
	1963—Clean Air Act	Conference procedure for interstate air pollution
Either/or threat of federal action	1965—Water Quality Act	If state failed to act, HEW could set standards
	1967—Air Quality Act	Deadlines placed on states to place standards on pollutants or HEW would set standards
Federal regulation of specific sources	1965—Motor Vehicle Air Pollution Control Act	First national standards, restricted to auto emissions
National regulatory standards	1970—Clean Air Act	National ambient based emission standards, time tables and deadlines
	1972—Clean Water Act	National technology based effluent standards and national pollution permit
Flexibility to states in implementation; Use of economic incentives	1977—Clean Air Act Amendments	Larger role for states in classifying areas for protection of clean air Charges to recapture profits gained through failure to meet standards
	1977—Clean Water Act Amendments	Larger role for states in setting priorities for waste treatment

The breaking point where frustration led to action came first in air pollution and culminated in the 1970 Clean Air Act. This thrust toward greater regulation was continued in the 1972 Clean Water Act. The notion that water might be employed as a carrier of wastes had become thoroughly repugnant to many who believed that water users had the responsibility of returning waters to the receiving water body as clean as technically possible. The 1972 legislation set a 1985 goal of zero discharge and

an interim goal of fishable/swimmable waters by 1983. In contrast with the Clean Air Act, the legislation set technically based, rather than ambient, standards. Environmentalists had become disillusioned with classification schemes that regulated streams differently according to their uses. They sensed a tendency to degrade classifications to suit the performance of polluters. Instead, environmentalists supported the 1972 provisions that required the "best practicable technology" be installed on all pollution sources as specified in a permit for which all polluters were required to apply. The national permit system (NPDES) was to be administered by the EPA until states proved themselves capable of administering it themselves.

A Long-Term Development

Although the Clean Air Act and Clean Water Act in some respects represent a high point of federal involvement, it is important to recognize that environmental policy involves a strong federal/state partnership that did not emerge overnight. It evolved from a fairly noncoercive framework to a system involving increased enforcement authority for various levels of government and financial support to the state to implement laws. Contrary to the views of some state officials and Reagan administrators, the federal government did not enter an arena where states were already exercising authority over pollution control. Quite the contrary. Testimony before the Senate Public Works Committee in 1963 revealed that only fifteen states had comprehensive pollution laws, and no more than six actually enforced controls. Total spending by state and local governments was about $12 million a year to control air pollution, with California spending half the total.

A March 1981 report of the Advisory Commission on Intergovernmental Relations notes that "a more accurate assertion would be that the federal government had given to most states a function which they otherwise had chosen to ignore." In a similar vein, a 1981 Congressional Research Service report for the Senate Committee on Environment and Public Works concludes that "the larger federal role may actually have resulted in greater power and authority at the state level, by having stimulated states to take on new responsibilities."

In short, the system has evolved from being noncoercive and nonregulatory to one in which more direct regulation has increased the powers of both the federal and state governments. Moreover, this evolution has resulted in more complex policies. It is not at all surprising then that the highly complex pieces of legislation with demanding goals such as the Clean Air Act and the Clean Water Act should encounter some very severe problems of implementation. Charles O. Jones has persuasively argued this point with respect to air pollution and has described the phenomenon as speculative augmentation in policy making. His argument is also true of water policy. In some cases, standards went beyond what technology at the time could deliver. Further, pollution legislation placed very heavy burdens on understaffed and underfunded federal and state agencies. The intergovernmental cooperation envisioned proved very difficult to achieve, and deadlines have been set back several times.

In 1977, significant modifications were made in both the air and water acts to decentralize decision making and to address particular implementation difficulties. . . . Despite numbers of opportunities to reconsider, Congress has stayed the regulatory course it adopted in the early 1970s after previous experimentation with the less interventionist tools listed in Table 1.

While the visions in the Clean Air and Water Acts—pure air everywhere to protect human health and water clean enough to swim in—have not materialized, impressive progress has been made in the control of some conventional pollutants, particularly in the air. Evidence suggests that these environmental gains were made without significant economic sacrifice or loss of jobs. At the same time, there has been a gradual discovery that a variety of metals, organic compounds, and toxic substances not specifically targeted in the legislation of the early 1970s pose very real threats. In light of these new challenges, cutting back programs is hardly warranted.

Decline in Air Pollution

While the number of motor vehicles in the United States has increased and the economy has expanded, emissions of most major air pollutants have continued to decline. This is confirmed by data on air and water quality from both the Conservation Foundation and the U.S. Council on Environmental Quality. While these two sources differ in their assessment of the costs of improvement, both agree as to the progress made. Data from twenty-three metropolitan areas show that particulate emissions dropped 56 percent between 1970 and 1980. There has been a 24 percent decline in ambient sulfur dioxide levels from 1974 to 1980. Some cities have made remarkable progress at reducing the number of days a year during which their air is in the unhealthful, very unhealthful, and hazardous ranges. New York had 270 bad days in 1975 and 131 in 1980; Chicago, 240 days in 1974 and 48 in 1980. At the same time, conventional air pollution problems remain serious. . . . Los Angeles still had 221 days of unhealthful or worse air in 1980, an improvement from nearly 300 days in 1974, but still a very bad record.

While charges to the contrary persist, available studies indicate that environmental accomplishments have been made without significant economic sacrifice. Both government and industry have tended to overestimate regulatory costs. After reviewing a number of studies, R. Haveman and V.K. Smith conclude that pollution regulations have had only a small negative impact on the gross national product. Most recent studies reinforce this conclusion. Data Resources found in a 1981 study that the real gross national product was 0.2 percentage points lower, the consumer price index 0.5 percentage points higher, and the unemployment rate only 0.3 percentage points higher with environmental programs than would have been the case without them.

"Environmental accomplishments have been made without significant economic sacrifice."

Despite the improvements of the past, problems remain and there are many new items on the environmental agenda. Improvements in water quality have come more slowly than improvements in air. Until recently, groundwater, which supplies half of the nation's drinking water, was presumed safe. Now we find increasing evidence of contamination from carcinogenic substances. Acid rain has become a subject of great controversy and is suspected of causing damage to forests and lakes in the U.S. and Canada. Over 55,000 chemicals are being manufactured, imported, and marketed and while the majority are probably safe, concerns have been raised about untested and unknown impacts on human health. The problem of disposing of toxic wastes without contaminating the air and water has yet to be solved. Even if the nation could be satisfied with the environmental progress already made, new problems are emerging far too rapidly to let up on the environmental policy effort.

Henry C. Kenski and Helen M. Ingram teach political science at the University of Arizona in Tucson.

"The unintended side effects of 'uncompromisingly tough' environmental standards can be . . . dangerous."

Regulations Can Be Harmful

Richard L. Stroup

On February 22, 1983, EPA Administrator Anne Gorsuch (later Burford) announced that the Environmental Protection Agency would pay $33 million to buy all the homes and businesses of the small Missouri town of Times Beach. This followed weeks of nationally publicized hysteria about the town's streets, which had been contaminated with dioxin more than 10 years earlier. Although there was no evidence that anyone in Times Beach had ever been harmed by the dioxin, Administrator Gorsuch traveled to Times Beach to announce the buyout personally and to demonstrate to the national media her concern with the risks of hazardous waste. Her demonstration was not enough. Less than two weeks later she was forced to resign—accused of, among other things, a callous disregard for such risks.

This extraordinary episode echoed the Love Canal disaster of the Carter administration. In 1978 the New York state health commissioner declared an emergency and urged women and young children to move from certain neighborhoods near a chemical waste site. The governor of New York, up for re-election, called for federal aid. The Carter administration quickly answered the call and provided the state federal aid in purchasing hundreds of homes. Massive publicity led to the evacuation of these homes and to the expenditure of millions of dollars—more than $250 million to date for a cleanup that is still unfinished. Yet, while there were allegations about medical effects, no credible evidence has been found that the chemical waste at Love Canal caused any long-term health problems.

Through Republican and Democratic administrations alike, the politicizing of environmental issues is a constant. Increasingly strict regulation, mushrooming tax and spending programs, and mandated private expenditures have been the result. Judging by the virtual absence of demonstrable benefits, these policies are seriously misdirected. Although long-term health problems from industrial waste sites, for example, are almost impossible to substantiate, we spend $8.5 billion on Superfund. This spending is predicated on the assumption that each and every hazardous waste site must be cleaned up to meet the same standard as drinking water. As a recent EPA study reported, "Overall, EPA's priorities appear more closely aligned with public opinion than with our estimated risks."

The good news is that there is enormous room for improvement in the nation's environmental policies. A positive approach involving less political control could substantially reduce the cost of avoiding environmental risks while providing greater environmental benefits. . . .

The Common Law

Historically, individuals and their property have been protected against the invasion of chemicals and other pollutants primarily by nuisance and tort actions. Our system of individual responsibility under the common law has successfully screened us from the worst possible risks.

The key to the common law approach is accountability. Individuals who make decisions must be accountable for the results; that is, they must face penalties and rewards in line with what they do to society and for it. When people are accountable, they find ways to avoid errors and to react quickly and constructively when errors occur. People who are accountable have the incentive to act *as if* others matter, whether or not they truly care about the welfare of others.

One strength of the common law approach is that the rules of evidence and of standing in court have

Richard L. Stroup, "Environmental Policy," *Regulation,* vol. 12, no. 3, 1988. Reprinted with permission.

developed over the decades to prevent frivolous actions and to balance the interests of plaintiffs and defendants. To decide when and how much a polluter should pay in damages, or whether an alleged danger is severe and imminent enough to warrant prior restraint, a judge must be able to estimate the damages being imposed. Absent such estimates, rational control or compensation measures under any regime of protection are impossible. The primary job of courts is to make individuals accountable for what they do, not for what someone thinks or alleges they do. This is what rules of evidence are for, and they operate far more systematically in the courts than in the political process.

Another advantage of the common law is that it evolves in a process that cannot be controlled by lobbyists for industry, the environment, or any other particular interest. When judges impose prior restraint (injunctive relief) to prevent irreversible harm, they must follow rules developed over centuries to balance considerations of freedom, efficiency, and safety within the community.

Despite these advantages, the common law approach has been under siege from environmental activists for the better part of 25 years.

America's "Green"ing

Environmental activism exploded onto the American scene in the 1960s as politically active groups shifted their attention from atmospheric nuclear testing to chemical pollutants. The movement was fueled by the publication of Rachel Carson's *Silent Spring* in 1962. As in much environmental literature since that time, the rhetoric in *Silent Spring* was eloquent and full of strong emotions, but the supporting evidence was considered by many scientists to be one-sided and misleading. The book elicited fear and indignation and moved people to demand political action. "Those who would pollute and plunder the planet must be stopped!" was the message increasingly heard.

Silent Spring inaugurated the view that a whole new regime of governmental controls was required to protect the earth and its inhabitants from technological disasters. This view is still common and, when an environmental crisis stirs public concern, it is the driving force behind public policy.

For people moved by stirring prose of the sort in *Silent Spring* and fearful of new and developing technologies, the traditional common law system fails to provide adequate safeguards against environmental risks. In their view convincing evidence of environmental damage is unnecessary, and an economical means of preventing it is irrelevant. Any plausible threat of damage must be eliminated. Of course this is easy to say as long as large corporations are perceived to be the main culprits in pollution and they, rather than individuals, are presumed to pay the tab for prevention and cleanup.

Unfortunately the laws that result from this viewpoint are notorious for being expensive *and* environmentally ineffective. The reasons for this are clear. Politicizing environmental control does nothing to produce the information needed for effectively protecting us from pollution. When an agency tells polluters exactly what technology to use or what their emissions should be to protect society best, it is usually acting with neither essential data on pollution effects, nor important data on the cost of alternative control measures.

We are increasingly operating under a new regulatory regime, one partly based on common law principles but modified in important ways by statute. Among the important changes is the heavy burden of proof on anything new. New activities often are allowed only if shown to be almost "risk free"—as exemplified by the Delaney clause of the Food, Drug, and Cosmetic Act. Faced with the *potential* risk of new chemicals, drugs, or genetically altered microorganisms, politicians and bureaucrats are inclined to ban use until safety can be proven. As AIDS sufferers and the families of those who have died waiting for federal approval of new drugs can attest, "zero risk" is actually a very dangerous strategy. The unintended side effects of "uncompromisingly tough" environmental standards can be similarly dangerous. When DDT was banned because its misuse harmed some wildlife, more dangerous pesticides replaced it. (In less wealthy Sri Lanka the situation was worse: Sri Lanka withdrew from the World Health Organization's large-scale DDT spraying program, and the number of cases of malaria rebounded from a low of 110 cases in 1961 to 2.5 million cases in 1968-1969.) We cannot know just how many farm workers have died from DDT substitutes, but since the replacement pesticides are much more harmful to people and must be more frequently applied, the "risk avoidance" banning of DDT introduced far more human risk.

> *"The environment can be cleaner and safer, and we can expend far fewer resources in achieving this goal."*

In general, overly conservative risk-avoidance policies are dangerous to society because they stifle technical and economic progress. Most research and development efforts in biotechnology have shown no clear and present dangers and, indeed, offer the promise of more effective waste cleanups and "softer" (less environmentally threatening) means of controlling agricultural pests and weeds. But again, the atmosphere of fear and even of crisis has meant that research, testing, and use of these techniques has been hampered needlessly by a web of regulations created by the EPA and the U.S. Department of Agriculture.

"There is no evidence that we are in a national environmental crisis justifying emergency measures."

Furthermore, abandoning common law to seek shelter from risk in congressional statutes bestows power on organized special interests. Members of Congress, after all, do not have national constituencies, and helping important constituent groups is the name of the game. It is not surprising that many of the costly policies of the Clean Air Act have been used to fight regional economic battles and to protect the powerful eastern coal industry and its unions. Both the Clean Water Act and the Superfund program have funded massive local spending. Some good has surely come from these efforts. We spend an estimated $80 billion annually to control pollution, and some cities certainly have clearer air, and stretches of river immediately downstream of big new sewage treatment plants are noticeably cleaner. But the price is very high, and evidence of serious health harms prevented (that is, benefits achieved) is typically rare and tenuous. . . .

The environment can be cleaner and safer, and we can expend far fewer resources in achieving this goal.

To strengthen the nation's protection against environmental threats, the administration should take steps to expand local control and strengthen the liability approach. It could do this in several ways. First, the administration should allow more leeway for the states and localities to make their own decisions about pollution control. Citizens are certainly in no mood to allow overly lax pollution control, yet jurisdictions choosing more rigorous control would quickly find the price their citizens were willing to pay. This time-honored variety of approaches among the states is an important part of American life, and is part of the genius of the federal system. In this system experiments are small rather than national in scope; more of them are tried; errors are much less costly; and the information produced is useful for the whole country.

Second, the administration should focus federal resources on technical forensic assistance in tracing, or even finding ways to brand, pollutants as they are emitted, so that accountability could be enhanced. Polluters would more often be made to pay when harm is done, and innocent parties would less often be forced to pay in error. A careful firm storing chemical wastes, for example, would *want* to be able to show that its stored wastes did not show up where damage occurred, and it could if the wastes were branded.

Third, the administration should assist states in reaching agreement on interstate compacts when important pollution damages are shown to be interstate matters.

For their part, states should seek to strengthen the common law through statute. Restoring the right of contract in the voluntary transfer of risk, for example, would help to revitalize the insurance industry, which historically has helped to "regulate" risks in cost-effective ways. Requirements for the posting of bonds would also strengthen the liability approach, for example, by insuring the solvency of a firm producing, processing, or storing hazardous wastes. Greatly lengthening the statute of limitations period for the recovery of damages in pollution cases might be another important measure. Branding chemicals that might escape into the water or air could be a real help. Many other innovations can also be tried at the state level without the need for national consensus or a national commitment.

The challenge in environmental policy is to develop better institutions—ones that will preserve environmental quality where it is most important, and minimize the constraints that would keep us from increasing wealth and prosperity. Only with more of the latter can our society better serve all our needs, including demands for safety and environmental quality.

New Directions

Property rights should be expanded in ways which may seem novel in the United States today. If, for example, whales and commercially valuable fisheries in the oceans were owned, it is likely that ocean dumpers would avoid harming them. If that idea seems far-fetched, consider England and Scotland, where sports and commercial fishing rights are privately owned and transferable. Access is often rented daily or leased for longer terms, and prices vary from a few dollars per month for bait fishing to very high fees for the rarest and finest fly fishing. Long before the environmental movement took hold, owners of fishing rights successfully sued polluters of streams for damages and obtained injunctions against polluting activities. It worked: now they seldom have to go to court. Polluters generally leave those waters (and thus the fish) alone. When resources are owned, political wars are no longer necessary to protect them.

A great deal of education and some strong political leadership will be necessary if environmental policy is to be turned in a constructive direction. Unpopular things need to be said. The public must be persuaded of two fundamental facts. First, there is no widespread environmental crisis requiring action so urgent that scientific investigation should be bypassed. There is no evidence that we are in a national environmental crisis justifying emergency measures. Second, despite colorful rhetoric to the contrary, the risks of rapid technological change have been far outweighed by the benefits received. Cancer, for example, (apart from lung cancer attributable to smoking) is declining while life spans continue to rise. We are a far wealthier and thus far healthier and more resilient society than we would have been had technological change not been allowed, or indeed encouraged.

To reform environmental policy, the administration will have to defeat the kind of sensationalist populism that arouses and sustains groundless fears about chemicals and other pollutants. The same sort of deliberate efforts being made by the press and the government to calm fears about AIDS (while at the same time providing information about the genuine risks posed) are needed to reduce the outrage that shapes environmental policies today. We can afford to buy much more environmental quality with a much smaller sacrifice of economic prosperity.

Richard L. Stroup is a professor of economics at Montana State University in Bozeman. He is a senior associate of the Political Economy Research Center, which advocates free-market strategies to conserve natural resources. It is based in Bozeman, Montana.

"Risk analysis . . . has the potential to alter environmental protection in ways that will save more lives, protect more ecological systems, improve health, and save resources."

Assessing Risks and Costs Can Create Effective Regulations

Milton Russell

The goal of environmental protection must be the safest, healthiest, most ecologically secure environment the people of the United States choose to pay for. Over the past decade and a half, significant progress has been made toward that goal. Major streams of toxic substances have been removed from the air and the water. Ecological systems once threatened are now safe, and others, once dying, are on the mend. However, the rough-and-ready bulldozer approach to environmental protection that worked so well in cleaning up pollution you could smell, taste, touch, and see is not well suited to the thousands of toxic chemicals and metals that can only be detected by advanced scientific instruments, whose risks may range from substantial to vanishingly small, and whose production and use are woven into the very fabric of modern life.

In the face of these new challenges, effective environmental protection demands that we understand the nature of the risks—especially the cross-media risks—of toxic chemicals and the costs of avoiding them. It also demands that environmental professionals develop, and share explicitly with the public, procedures that balance understanding of pollution risks with our understanding of social values the public holds dear. Finally, it requires a more systematic method for managing risks that takes into account every point of potential exposure and includes final disposal of a pollutant. Risk analysis is a key element in these tasks. Its use has the potential to alter environmental protection in ways that will save more lives, protect more ecological systems, improve health, and save resources, which can be used to meet other individual and social goals.

The potential of a risk-based approach has not been realized and will not be as long as current views of the world remain unchanged and current practices continue. Some of these views are deeply ingrained in the public and the scientific community. Public officials, including those of us at EPA [the Environmental Protection Agency], need to do more to transform risk analysis potential into environmental protection reality.

The Risk-Based Approach

A risk-based approach begins with the results of a scientific study that a particular pollutant may present a risk. Then comes the task of deciding what to do about it. The questions proliferate: How sure is the scientific evidence? What is the degree and distribution of risk? What is the investment necessary to reduce it, and does this investment make sense, given all the other demands on our economy? What kinds of social and personal disruptions will regulations bring? On the basis of the answers to these and other questions, a judgment is formed and action follows.

It is important to understand that risk-based approaches are meant to be applied to environmental risks as a whole. That is, when EPA considers a particular risk, say of a toxicant in the water, it should be comparing the investment necessary to reduce that risk with all the other risk-reducing investments it could cause society to make. Clearly, it should be mindful of the risk imposed as a pollutant is transferred between environmental media (from the water into the air, for example).

But here, problems arise as science and risk management crash into the reality of the laws under which EPA operates. Simply put, EPA is not a "whole." The agency is more like a holding company for nine major statutory authorities and several minor ones, each with a constituency jealously guarding its sway. Each of these statutes deals with risk in a different way; some reject the idea that balance is necessary.

The premise of the risk-based approach is that not every good thing can be done. Resources are limited, and choices must be made among desirable ends. In short, however regrettable, some environmental risks are simply not worth reducing, or not worth trying to reduce to zero, given competing ends, including other risk reduction opportunities.

"The profound cultural dichotomy between pollution risk as a consequence of modern life and pollution risk as an evil lies at the root of much environmental debate."

A risk-based approach would seem particularly well suited to dealing with toxic substances that can be measured down to the parts-per-quadrillion level, and whose risks, though determinable, may border on the mystically small. Faced with costs that rise exponentially, the question, "Is more control worth it?" presses strongly on the mind. Just as urgent is the question, "What about the missed opportunities?" If there is no stopping place, no point at which "clean enough" applies, then each pollutant that gains EPA's attention can absorb inordinate agency and social resources. Striking a balance among competing ends, using a risk-based approach, should be more appealing than ever.

But the critics of this approach, perhaps the majority of our citizens, do not agree. I think part of the reason for their objection to a risk-based approach is that environmental protection lies only partially in the domain of the rational. To risk managers, and those comfortable with modern technology, pollution is an externality of production and consumption; its reduction is to be pursued vigorously to the point that maximizes the total public interest.

To others, though, reflecting traditional and deeply held values, pollution is a violation of personal rights; its generation is an evil, and its reduction is a matter of moral principle. For them, to speak of acceptable environmental risk is like being told that each community should tolerate an acceptable number of child molesters. Our culture holds that the sanctity of the individual is predominant; avoiding damage to others is what separates moral man from animals. There is little room in this personal value system, designed to define how one individual should treat another, for acceptance of a social policy that implies that some are unfortunately destined to die sooner so that others might live—or even live just a little better. When you pierce through the fog of posturing and politics and

special interests, the profound cultural dichotomy between pollution risk as a consequence of modern life and pollution risk as an evil lies at the root of much environmental debate.

This division will not soon be bridged, but its sharper edges can be dulled. For their part, risk analysts and policymakers should go further to explain effectively their views in terms others can understand. That means focusing on outcomes for real people and ecological systems and avoiding ideology and scientific or analytical cant.

The operational goals of both world views follow the same value predicate—protecting people and the ecological systems they depend on and hold dear. When the debate is moved to the way of achieving them, there is a chance for fruitful coalescence instead of fruitless conflict.

Scientists also have a role to play in shifting the terms of the debate. Unfortunately, though, the cultural divide between views of pollution is mirrored by a divide similarly wide between the culture of science and that of environmental policymaking.

The scientist's world is cautious; it values certainty in quantitative representation of cause-and-effect relationships, or at least the comfort of collegial consensus. The denizens of that world resist drawing conclusions. These values have served science well, but they can sometimes be dysfunctional when the scientist enters an arena where decisions cannot wait for certainty.

The worlds of science and environmental policymaking come together—and sometimes collide—in risk assessments. Risk assessments are the end product of science and the foundation from which policymaking starts. Assumptions are required; the science behind them may need to be massaged—by the scientists—to come up with answers. . . .

Risk Assessment

For our part, EPA pledges that the scientific foundation of risk assessment will not be undermined by nonscientific interference. Policy-makers will be users of risk assessments in the process of making risk management decisions, not interpreters of science.

The potential for risk-based environmental protection is clear. It is also clear that fulfilling it will require efforts at building bridges across the cultural chasms that now hinder risk-based decisionmaking.

Milton Russell is an assistant administrator of the Environmental Protection Agency and heads its Office of Policy, Planning, and Evaluation.

Assessing Risks and Costs Stymies Effective Regulation

Barry Commoner

Beginning in 1950, new forms of environmental pollution appeared and rapidly intensified: smog, acid rain, excess nitrates and phosphates in the water supply, pesticides and toxic chemicals in the food chain and in our bodies, and dangerous accumulations of radioactive waste. In 1970, pressed by a newly aroused public, Congress created the Environmental Protection Agency to undo the damage. Now, twenty years later, the time has come to ask an important question: How far have we progressed toward the goal of restoring the quality of the environment?

The answer is in fact embarrassing. Apart from a few notable exceptions, environmental quality has improved only slightly—in most cases by about 15 percent in the last decade, according to government data. In some cases it has gotten worse.

Most of our environmental problems are the inevitable result of the sweeping changes in the technology of production that transformed the U.S. economy after World War II: the use of new, large, high-powered, smog-generating automobiles; the shift from fuel-efficient trains to gas-guzzling trucks and cars; the replacement of bio-degradable and less toxic natural products with non-degradable and hazardous petrochemical products; and the substitution of chemical fertilizers for manure and crop rotation. By 1970 it was clear that these changes in the technology of production were the *root cause* of modern environmental pollution.

In the few instances where production technology has been modified in response to environmental concerns—such as eliminating lead from gasoline, mercury from chlorine production, DDT from agriculture, PCBs from the electrical industry, and atmospheric nuclear explosions from military

enterprise—the environment has been improved by 70 percent or more in the last ten to fifteen years. When, instead of changing the production technology, an attempt is made to trap pollutants in an appended control device—an automobile's catalyst or a power plant's scrubber—environmental improvement is, at best, only modest.

Take the example of smog, a pollutant that originates when nitrogen oxide is created as a result of the high temperature in modern automobile engines. But nitrogen oxide is not the inevitable product of gasoline engines; pre-war cars did not produce it. Today we can design a high-powered engine that does not produce smog. To do so, however, would mean retooling our auto manufacturing plants—and that would require a willingness to exert some social control over the means of production. Instead, we have applied palliative measures, and these have failed. For once we have agreed to the concept of an "acceptable" level of smog, it is an easy matter for industry and local governments to either weaken or delay the implementation of that standard. Thus, in December 1987, after already extending the deadline twice, we gave some cities twenty-five additional years to comply with the Clean Air Act.

Unfortunately, our environmental legislation ignores the origin of the assault on environmental quality; it fails to recognize that environmental pollution is an essentially incurable disease that can only be prevented, and instead deals with its symptoms. I want to address some of the unrecognized costs of this approach.

The Regulatory Approach

The present—largely unsuccessful—regulatory effort is based upon a now well-established procedure. First, the EPA estimates the degree of harm caused by different levels of various environmental pollutants. Next, some "acceptable"

Barry Commoner, "Acceptable Risks: Who Decides?" *Harper's Magazine*, May 1988. Reprinted with permission.

level of harm is chosen (for example, a cancer risk of one in a million) and the EPA establishes emission standards that can presumably achieve that risk level. Polluters are then expected to introduce controls (such as auto-exhaust catalysts or power-plant stack scrubbers) that will lower emissions to the required level. If the regulation survives the inevitable challenges from industry (and, in recent years, from the administration itself), the polluters will invest in the appropriate control systems. If all goes well—and it frequently does not—at least some areas of the country and some production facilities will then be in compliance.

Clearly this process is the inverse of our preventive approach to public health. It strives not for a continuous improvement in environmental quality but for the social acceptance of some, presumably low, risk to health. In a way, this represents a return to the medieval approach to disease, in which illness—and death itself—was regarded as a debit on life endured as payment for original sin. In our updated version, we think that some level of pollution and some risk to health is the inevitable price to be paid for the material benefits of modern technology.

This approach presents many problems, but I want to focus on the way it leads to a dangerous confusion of science and policy. The very concept of an "acceptable risk" determined by EPA regulators takes decisions out of the public arena and, ostensibly, into the laboratory. Yet, unbeknownst to the public, the "objective" scientific process that is supposed to protect them is easily corrupted.

Dangerous Thinking

The story behind the news that the cancer risk associated with dioxin has been officially "reduced" provides an example of the sort of dangerous thinking fostered by our current approach to environmental protection.

The EPA has a standard of acceptable exposure to dioxin that dictates when contaminated soil must be removed. The EPA based this standard on a 1985 dioxin risk assessment that established the dosage at which the chance that exposure would lead to cancer is one in a million. The one-in-a-million risk standard is generally seen as acceptable and not likely to change. What *can* be altered is the specific dosage that is expected to generate the one-in-a-million risk.

For Syntex Agribusiness Inc.—the company liable for the dioxin cleanup in Missouri—the issue of an acceptable risk level, of course, involves enormous sums of money. According to Syntex, relaxing the cleanup standard from one part per billion (ppb) to ten ppb would reduce cleanup costs by 65 percent. Predictably, Syntex scientists have developed reasons why the 1985 EPA dioxin risk assessment is wrong. . . . [An] EPA task-force draft report develops

a new rationale for a dioxin cancer risk assessment that shows the risk is sixteen times lower than estimated by the EPA in 1985.

To understand how the EPA came to this judgment, we need to review the scientific debate over the role that dioxin plays in the biological process that leads from exposure to a chemical to the appearance of a cancerous tumor. According to the theory currently accepted by much of the scientific community, this process has two sequential steps. First, a substance—an "initiator"—causes an irreversible genetic change in the exposed cells. In the second phase a "promoter" causes these now predisposed cells to proliferate and produce a cancerous tumor.

Mathematical models, based on animal experiments, have been developed to estimate the risk of cancer in people exposed to given amounts of dioxin. Some models assume that dioxin is a "complete carcinogen," acting as both initiator and promoter. Others assume that its sole role is as a promoter. In general, the risks computed from complete-carcinogen models are considerably greater than the risks computed from promoter-based models. The 1985 assessment assumes that dioxin is a complete carcinogen capable of both effects. The Syntex scientists, not surprisingly, claim that dioxin is only a promoter.

So the question remains: Is dioxin a complete carcinogen or just a promoter? Consider these facts: Rats and mice exposed *only* to dioxin exhibit a significant incidence of cancer; this implies that dioxin is a complete carcinogen capable of both initiation and promotion. However, dioxin lacks the distinctive property of an initiator—it does not cause mutations. But dioxin also lacks the distinctive property of a promoter—there is no clear evidence that it causes cell proliferation. According to the actual evidence, then, dioxin is *neither* an initiator nor a promoter. This means that the initiator/promoter dichotomy is not a sensible way to account for the effect of dioxin on cancer incidence, and that risk assessment models based on *either* of these assumptions are not valid.

"Rats and mice exposed only *to dioxin exhibit a significant incidence of cancer."*

Despite the fact that the EPA never reconciles this paradox in its draft report, there is a way to explain it. Dioxin greatly increases the activity of an enzyme that is necessary in the conversion of potential environmental carcinogens to active agents. Apparently, dioxin can sufficiently increase the activity of small amounts of carcinogens present in food, water, and air to generate the increased tumor incidence observed when only dioxin is given to test animals. In effect, dioxin influences tumor production by enhancing the activity of carcinogens—the danger of which is best estimated from the complete-carcinogen model used in the 1985 EPA risk assessment.

But, clearly, the EPA did not take any of this into account. Instead, they chose the midpoint between the lowest risk assessment (based on the idea of dioxin as a promoter) and the highest (based on dioxin as a complete carcinogen). The result was a new "safe standard" sixteen times higher than the one derived in 1985.

A Parable

The EPA's approach grievously violates scientific procedure. I can best explain my concern with a parable. Let us suppose that there is an animal in a closed room; from previous experience this animal is known to bite, but with an undetermined severity. A scientific task force is called to evaluate the bite risk. Opinions differ. One group says, "If we assume that the animal is a lion, and apply an appropriate mathematical model, we can compute that the risk from its bite is ten in a million." The other group assumes that the animal is a dog, and its model yields a risk of 0.001 in a million. The scientists engage in a bitter debate, and in an effort to resolve it, they manage to provoke some sound from the unseen animal. It neither barks like a dog nor growls like a lion. Finally—since the report is due—they reach a consensus: the risk is midway, logarithmically, between 0.001 and 10, or 0.1.

What's wrong with this approach? First, consider the decision to take the midpoint of the two types of risk estimates. If the animal is a dog, obviously it is not a lion, and vice versa. This leads to the conclusion that at least one of the two classes of risk estimates must be wrong. But since the animal neither barks nor roars, *both* sides are wrong, which destroys the logical bases of both risk models—a defect that cannot be cured by averaging their results.

Eventually, some particularly hardy soul decides to open the door and actually look at the animal. It turns out to be a monkey, which then playfully slides open a door at the back of the room, and turns loose a roaring lion. Let me suggest that this monkey represents the dioxin-stimulated enzyme that releases the serious effects of the complete carcinogen, the lion.

I believe that the draft report on the dioxin health risk fails to meet the rudimentary requirements of scientific discourse. However, it may be that this is not the proper standard for judging the report. It is not entirely clear that we should regard the EPA draft report as a purely scientific document, for the report presents its conclusions as an example of sound "science policy."

What can this possibly mean? Isn't there an inherent contradiction between "science" and "policy"? In the present context, the relevant attributes of science are, first, its demand for rigorous, validated methods, and second, its objectivity, or the independence of the data and analysis from the interests of those affected by the results. Policy, by contrast, is defined in *Webster's* dictionary as "prudence or wisdom in the management of affairs" and "management or procedure based primarily on material interest."

If the dioxin risk assessment is a purely scientific exercise, then its conclusion that the EPA's 1985 risk assessment should be greatly reduced collapses under the weight of its faulty methodology. If it is, instead, a policy document, or some undefined hybrid, then it fails to meet a different obligation: it does not specify what "material interest" governed the outcome of the exercise. Was it the explicit interest of Syntex in reducing its Missouri cleanup costs? Was it the Office of Management and Budget's often-expressed interest in balancing health risks against the cost of ameliorating them? Or was it the interests of the American people in minimizing the risk to their health?

"We need good science, wise policies, and the honesty to distinguish the two."

How can we remedy the environmental failure? We do know that the preventive approach is more likely to produce the desired results than the current palliative approach, which is based on dubious "science policy" estimates of "acceptable risk." The preventive approach has its own considerable difficulties—it requires a willingness to challenge the taboo against even questioning the dominance of private interests over the public interest. But at least the public would be included in that debate—indeed, would know that a debate was going on. Politics should not hide behind the skirt of bad science. We need good science, wise policies, and the honesty to distinguish the two. That is the necessary first step toward realizing what has been this nation's avowed goal since 1970—restoring the quality of the environment.

Barry Commoner directs the Center for the Biology of Natural Systems at Queens College in New York City. He has written extensively on environmental issues.

"The fundamental cause of much of the nation's resource mismanagement, water and otherwise, is ill-considered government intervention. . . . Privatization and market pricing are the answers."

viewpoint 65

The Private Sector Can Protect the Environment

Doug Bandow

When the first European settlement was established on American soil in 1607, environmental preservation was hardly a major concern. The supply of natural resources seemed limitless. As such, the immigrants treated the environment as a free good while hewing out a nation. By the end of the 19th century, writes John Whitaker, former Under Secretary of the Department of the Interior: ''. . . the damage to the land was beginning to show. Vast areas of timber had fallen victim to settlement, lumbering, and forest fires, which in turn led to soil erosion and loss of wildlife. Market hunters had killed off most buffalo, wild turkey, and all passenger pigeons. The 1890 census announced the closing of the frontier, a symbol of American opportunity and abundance for 300 years.'' The nation's environmental cornucopia no longer seemed limitless.

The heavy consumption of resources made sense when they were abundant, but as they became increasingly scarce—and, hence, more valuable—a new approach to the environment became necessary. Had the resources been in private hands and had the legal system been capable of vesting property rights in clean air, for example, the change from carefree consumption to careful conservation might have occurred without government intervention. However, with the advent of the Progressives, federal policy shifted radically from encouraging private ownership to extending public control.

Yellowstone was established as the first national park in 1871. Twenty years later Congress passed the Forest Reserve Act authorizing the president to establish national forest reserves. The Reclamation Acts were passed in 1902, and President Theodore Roosevelt made the environment a federal priority.

In succeeding decades the federal government gradually expanded its environmental role. Forest management, water resource, and soil conservation programs were established; the Army Corps of Engineers undertook water projects, such as Hoover Dam. After World War II environmental concerns turned to air and water pollution.

Strong Measures

Yet the environmental problem only seemed to worsen. Writes Whitaker:

> By 1968, the United States was choking from air pollution. Over 200 million tons of the five main classes of pollutants . . . were being pumped into the nation's air each year. Episodes of heavy air pollution in New York, in Los Angeles, and in the supposedly pristine mountain air of Denver and Salt Lake City caused genuine concern, discomfort, increases in illness and even deaths, especially among older people.

Gradually a consensus developed on the need for strong, new measures to protect the environment. Symbolic of the breadth of this widespread concern was Earth Day, April 22, 1970. On January 1 of that year, President Richard Nixon signed the National Environmental Policy Act into law, establishing the Council on Environmental Quality (CEQ). Later in 1970, Nixon created the Environmental Protection Agency (EPA) and Congress passed the Clean Air Act, followed by nearly two dozen other environmental laws in succeeding years. By the end of the decade, notes the CEQ: ''. . . the federal government was writing and enforcing regulations affecting occupational safety and health, resource recovery, noise, water quality, air quality, pesticides, endangered species, drinking water, toxic substances, hazardous wastes, mine safety, coastal zones, ocean pollution, the outer continental shelf, and the upper atmosphere.''. . .

The federal command-and-control model, which steadily gained strength this century, was built on a

Doug Bandow, *Protecting the Environment: A Free-Market Strategy.* © The Heritage Foundation, 1986. Reprinted with permission.

resource economics philosophy dating from the late 1800s. The "use of natural and environmental resources is dominated by market failures," its theorists argued; the only answer was public control and professional managers. Cracks eventually began appearing in the establishment paradigm. In 1968 ecologist Garrett Hardin published "The Tragedy of the Commons." This now famous essay explained that property held in common by the public "may work reasonably satisfactorily for centuries because [use is] well below the carrying capacity of the land. Finally, however, comes the day of reckoning. . . . At this point, the inherent logic of the commons remorselessly generates tragedy." What he meant by this is that something owned by everyone is, in effect, owned by no one. The result: waste is inevitable, unless someone controls the use of the resource. This tragedy to which Hardin refers precisely fits the overuse of resources observed in America near the end of the 19th century.

Of course, someone does manage the public lands—the federal government. But Uncle Sam's record, in contrast to his rhetoric, gave conservationists, let alone preservationists, little reason to cheer. Federal dams destroy wetlands; federal roads promote logging in potential wilderness areas. While environmentalists had won the battle to establish public ownership of much of America's natural endowment, business had won the war by controlling access to those resources.

Over time, an alternative theory of environmental protection has emerged. Generally known as the New Resource Economics, it recognizes the efficiency of the market process. Incentives matter, goes the argument, and giving business an economic reason to reduce air emissions, for example, would help protect the environment.

Seen as particularly important in the New Resource Economics is the role of private property in internalizing costs. A timber company will clear-cut federal forest land and allow erosion because it does not have to bear the costs of the resulting damage to the property. The government, too, has little incentive to safeguard its holdings because economic value is fundamentally irrelevant to the political and bureaucratic process. In contrast, a private landowner who ignores the environmental impact of his activities will destroy a key asset and ultimately lose money. Write environmental analysts Fred Smith and Robert J. Smith: "No one acts as irresponsibly with their own resources as almost everyone does with the commons."

Internalizing Future Costs

Future costs also are internalized. As long as the right to property is secure over time, its value will include an estimate of the resources' future worth. A private owner of coal-rich land thus will leave the coal in the ground if he believes that prices will rise

in the future. In this way, speculators, who buy up resources and hold them in the hopes that prices will rise, represent the interests of later generations by paying current owners and deferring consumption. There is no political equivalent of the speculator: tomorrow's generations do not vote today.

"The quality of air and water in the U.S. has suffered greatly because these resources are the great common pools in which it is naturally difficult for individuals to establish property rights."

The New Resource Economics also draws on the findings of the Public Choice economists, who have analyzed the incentives of government officials and institutions and their role in making public policy. Markets may fail, say Public Choice theorists, but government is even more likely to blunder; thus, state intervention is justified only if the nonmarket response is likely to lead to a better outcome. Examples of government-promoted progress are rare, since, in practice, an iron triangle of elected politicians, career bureaucrats, and self-seeking interest groups makes government intervention inefficient and destructive.

The political process is unpredictable—electoral majorities are often ephemeral and public concern over an issue can be even more transitory—making for poor conservation practices and development planning. Since the government can assert control over private as well as public resources, "the 'worst case' potential for destruction under the present system is virtually limitless," according to Robert J. Smith. In contrast to the extent that environmental decisions are moved into private hands, the shortcomings of the political process become essentially irrelevant. Then, "even in a 'worst case' scenario, with a developer who, through ignorance or malice, actually does irreparable damage to his land, environmental losses would be held to a minimum—that is, to the extent of the developer's own holdings. He would not be free to claim and destroy additional land or resources under some notion of 'common' ownership, or by grabbing control of the political process," writes Smith.

The free market environmental paradigm has important implications for all environmental policy.

The quality of air and water in the U.S. has suffered greatly because these resources are the great common pools, in which it is naturally difficult for individuals to establish property rights. In 1970, as the environmental movement swept America, Congress passed the Clean Air Act. The EPA was directed to set national ambient air quality standards

(NAAQS) and pollution control specifications for new polluting facilities. States were required to develop enforcement procedures—state implementation plans, or SIPs—to bring their air quality up to the national standards. And the Act set rigorous guidelines for auto emissions. These provisions were supplemented by the Clean Air Act amendments of 1977, which established new requirements for the "prevention of significant deterioration" of air quality in regions meeting the NAAQS, and set guidelines for allowing new development in so-called nonattainment areas, where the NAAQS had not been achieved. . . .

How well has the Clean Air Act cleaned up the nation's air? The Council on Environmental Quality (CEQ) argues that the law has "contributed to perceptible improvements in most areas of the country." And since 1970, most forms of air emissions have been reduced. But economic sluggishness during the 1970s and the reduction in auto travel because of the energy crisis, of course, played a major role in cutting emissions. Moreover, Robert Crandall, an economist at the Brookings Institution, has concluded that there is no clear proof that air quality improved more quickly during the 1970s than in the 1960s, before massive federal intervention, or that the Clean Air Act has reduced the absolute level of emissions.

More important, even if the Clean Air Act has reduced air pollution, emissions could have been cut more, at a lower cost, by any of several alternative approaches. The Clean Air Act's flaws start with the NAAQS, the very underpinning of the legislation. The so-called primary and secondary standards are set to protect those persons most sensitive to air pollution, such as those with respiratory ailments, make no distinction between major and minor health effects, and allow no trade-off between marginal health improvements and economic cost. Moreover, the research underlying the standards is flawed; in almost half the cases "the wrong pollutant is being regulated," according to Charles and Gilbert Omenn.

"The emissions monitoring system is a disaster."

The emissions monitoring system is a disaster. Procedures are unreliable and subject to manipulation. Application procedures for changing the legal status—and thus the relevant federal standards—of states are unnecessarily complicated and statutory timetables are unrealistic. In addition, the rigid pollution control mechanisms required by the Clean Air Act are always costly and occasionally unnecessary for meeting the NAAQS. The EPA attempts to prescribe specific abatement technologies for some 200,000 polluting facilities, yet studies

consistently find that emissions could be controlled for less cost were the regulations more flexible. . . .

MathTech calculated that a marketable pollution rights system, where discharge permits could be traded among polluters, would reduce current regulatory costs by up to 90 percent and still achieve the air quality goal. Economists Bruce Yandle and M.T. Maloney, meanwhile, figured that the petrochemical industry could save 86 percent of current costs if firms could buy and sell emissions rights. And other surveys, including one by the General Accounting Office, identify a comparable savings from market-oriented approaches.

Regulatory Requirements

Perhaps the worst of the regulatory requirements is the 1977 congressional mandate that emission reductions for "fossil-fired stationary sources" (power plants) must be achieved through "technological" means. This means that flue-gas coal scrubbers must be installed, even where fuel substitutions or other measures, such as paying other polluters to reduce their sulfur emissions, would achieve the same air quality. The Congressional Budget Office estimates the annual cost of just this requirement to be $3.4 billion.

In setting stricter technological requirements on new sources, the law perversely discourages new plant construction and creates an incentive for firms to maintain dirtier existing factories. The result, of course, is increased overall emissions. Regulations on auto emissions encourage similar inefficiencies—the law effectively requires all carmakers to meet the very stringent standards applicable to high altitude areas, even though only 3 percent of all autos are used in those areas.

Annual expenditures for air pollution controls have grown 350 percent between 1973 and 1982; the CEQ estimates the total cost of compliance for so-called stationary sources, such as factories, to be $74.3 billion between 1975 and 1984. This does not include spending for auto emissions control systems. The Department of Commerce estimated that total outlays for pollution abatement by industry and government were $25.4 billion in 1984 alone.

Federal water pollution regulation generally parallels regulation of air emissions. The waterways were traditionally considered an appropriate dumping ground for wastes of all kinds. The basis for current water policy is the 1972 Clean Water Act. Its long-range goal was "to restore and maintain the chemical, physical and biological integrity of the nation's waters" by eliminating all discharges by 1985; the more immediate objective was to make waterways suitable for swimming and fishing. The Act subsidized local treatment plants and imposed technology-specific standards for industry; firms had to install Best Practicable Technology by 1977 and Best Available Technology (BAT) by 1983. In 1977 the law was amended to extend deadlines and loosen the technology requirements for industry.

Federal regulation of water pollution has succeeded in the sense that "over the past decade the nation also made substantial progress in improving water quality by controlling large individual pollution sources," according to the 1983 annual report of the Council on Environmental Quality. But costs of compliance with the Clean Water Act have been even more than those for the Clean Air Act; the Commerce Department calculates that in 1980 government and industry together spent $20.3 billion on water treatment. Between 1972 and 1984, estimates Paul Tramontozzi of the Center for the Study of American Business, water pollution abatement activities, including operating and maintenance expenses, cost $205.3 billion; other estimates run even higher.

Like the NAAQS, the national goal of "zero discharges" in waterways permits no trade-off between health risk and cost, even though the marginal expense of removing smaller and smaller amounts of pollutants from water rises exponentially. A federal sewage treatment subsidy program, moreover, induces localities to build needlessly expensive plants that often are difficult to maintain; and it discourages private polluters from adopting less expensive process changes that would reduce total emissions and reclaim higher quality wastes.

As for the mandatory plant technology controls, writes Indiana University economics professor Lloyd Orr, ". . . the very concept of issuing permits to over 60,000 point sources of water pollution with targets for future years based on best practicable and best available technology stirs notions of administrative nightmares." And requiring firms to use certain equipment, instead of encouraging them to cut discharges, creates the same type of inefficiencies as in the field of air pollution.

Time for Market Approaches

The gross inefficiencies of the Clean Air and Clean Water Acts can be remedied only if the federal government changes its focus from input-oriented and technology-specific controls to output-oriented and general emissions regulations. That is, Washington should decide what levels of air and water cleanliness it wants to achieve (something that deserves serious review) and allow firms to meet those standards by whatever means are most efficient.

One way to make the policies more market sensitive would be to impose an effluent fee, essentially a tax on pollution equal to the marginal social cost of each additional unit of emissions. Such a value would be hard to determine, of course, but the government could experiment with different rates. For example, firms could be charged a specific fee per pound of pollutant, with more dangerous

emissions taxed at higher rates; if the level of a particular effluent remained unacceptable, the relevant fee could be increased over time. The virtue of an emissions tax is that it forces firms to internalize all the costs of production, giving "firms a strong and continuing incentive to discover inexpensive ways to abate pollution," states the 1979 annual report of the Council on Environmental Quality.

"Sensitive ecosystems often become merely one more bargaining chip in a government-wide game of pork barrel politics."

A second free market device to reduce pollution of the common pools would be to establish a market in transferable pollution rights. In fact, a form of pollution rights market already has evolved. The so-called bubble concept allows a firm to add facilities and expand operations, increasing effluent levels, so long as adjustments are made elsewhere in the plant to keep total factory emissions within federal standards. Moreover, in nonattainment areas new firms can "offset" their expected levels of pollution by inducing other polluters to reduce emissions elsewhere in the region. In attainment areas, a similar procedure is known as "netting." Some 2,500 such emission offsets have been made around the nation. Despite limitations caused by the inflexibility of the Clean Air Act, writes Neil Orloff, director of the Center for Environmental Research at Cornell University, the practice "has created markets for the discharge of pollutants, and in the process has generated incentives for companies to reduce their emissions beyond what they are otherwise required to achieve."

The political prospects for moving pollution control in a more market-oriented direction are problematic: environmentalists appear to support current policies, in part because they are anti-growth, while many firms seem relatively satisfied with a system that, though expensive, burdens potential new competitors the most. The social benefits of fundamental reform, however, would be enormous, given the massive inefficiencies of the current system.

The federal government is the nation's largest landholder, controlling 720 million acres, or 31.7 percent of the total. Uncle Sam's percentage of ownership ranges from 0.3 percent of Connecticut to 86.5 percent of Nevada. Most of the federal acres are managed for multiple-use purposes, including timbering, grazing, energy production, and recreation. Activities in Wilderness and National Park lands are much more restricted: recreation is the prime use, with leasing mostly forbidden.

Federal control has thrust the most sensitive environmental questions into the political arena. When everyone "owns" a property, everyone has a different opinion on how it ought to be used. In Congress, votes matter more than logic in determining where oil companies may drill and offroad vehicles run. The bureaucratic system, moreover, has its own peculiar set of rewards and punishments. Policies that embody sound management practices usually are not those that expand the agency's budget and satisfy interest groups and members of Congress. As a result, sensitive ecosystems often become merely one more bargaining chip in a government-wide game of pork barrel politics.

Examples of federal ecological mismanagement are legion—and inevitable as long as the land is held in common, so that benefits are collected by a few but the costs are shared by all. America's national park system, for example, is overcrowded and deteriorating. A step toward upgrading the system would be to raise entry fees for visitors to prices closer to market levels.

Privatizing Parks

More fundamentally, the federal government should privatize the park system. Washington could start with an experimental program by auctioning off a few small refuges to profit-making firms or giving them to environmental groups. In either case, park operations would improve: private managers would have an economic incentive to protect their assets and could make decisions free of political interference.

Wetlands are among the most sensitive of ecosystems; they essentially are areas covered by a shallow layer of standing water. About 458,000 acres of wetlands are destroyed every year—thanks in part to the favorable tax treatment of water diversion projects and to agriculture subsidies that encourage farmers to drain and plant otherwise uneconomic land. Federal water projects also contribute to the problem. North Dakota's Garrison Diversion Project, for instance, is a $1.2 billion boondoggle designed to reroute water from the Rockies in Montana to North Dakota, eliminating in excess of 70,000 acres of wetlands in the process. The cheap irrigation water would benefit just a handful of North Dakota farmers who own less than 1 percent of the state's agricultural land.

Imposing a market test on such government operations would eliminate federal subsidies for wetlands despoliation; no private firm would underwrite a project as wasteful as the Garrison Diversion. And more flexible pollution regulations would encourage private firms to maintain wetlands habitat under their control. Tenneco, for instance, has reached an agreement with federal and state agencies that allows it to "bank" credits for environmental improvements on its Louisiana wetlands holdings that may be used to meet regulatory requirements on other projects. At the same time, private interests—currently some 500 different land trusts maintain more than three million acres of mostly wetlands—would continue to protect sensitive ecosystems.

The National Forest System is made up of some 190 million acres; the Bureau of Land Management manages a much smaller forest holding. Throughout this vast expanse, the federal government subsidizes what turns out to be the uneconomic harvest of trees across America by building roads into forest areas, conducting surveys, and otherwise maintaining the land, even where it makes no sense to harvest trees. In 1983 the taxpayers got back a mere two cents for every dollar they invested in lumber leasing in Alaska. Overall, the Congressional Research Service estimates that the nation's public forests ran a net deficit of $2.1 billion between 1975 and 1984. . . .

Some 82 million acres of land are part of the Wilderness Preservation System. . . . The bulk of the wilderness is most valuable as it is—undeveloped. The U.S. Geological Survey, for instance, estimates that only 2.7 million acres of wilderness land have a high probability of being good oil drilling sites. Nevertheless, political pressure remains great to open these areas for development, since private firms do not bear the cost of degrading the land. In at least one case, the government has "undesignated" wilderness land, and the Forest Service is using its road-building program to remove property from being considered wilderness. The land would be better protected in the hands of environmental organizations.

"Private ownership also would be more productive for society in the case of acres with good energy and mineral deposits potential."

Private ownership also would be more productive for society in the case of acres with good energy and mineral deposits potential: only a private owner, who receives the benefits of minerals production and pays the price for environmental degradation, has the incentive to make the best decision on whether or not to lease. In fact, some environmental groups, such as the National Audubon Society, allow oil and gas production, with stringent environmental controls, on their own wildlife preserves.

Wilderness land could be sold or simply given to environmental groups such as the Audubon Society. A less radical reform would be to maintain public ownership of the land but have an independent Wilderness Endowment Board manage the holdings.

Private ownership also offers a solution to wildlife preservation. Instances of official concern over, for example, the diminishing grizzly bear population, which led officials to close about 14 percent of Yellowstone National Park, are far outweighed by such practices as subsidized clear-cutting in federal forests. And this is unlikely to change so long as environmental decisions are political decisions—after all, more ranchers than deer are registered to vote.

In contrast, both philanthropy and profit have moved the private sector to protect wildlife and sensitive ecosystems. During the 1970s, preservation groups acquired more than 1.6 million acres of land, while individuals and businesses, too, have promoted wildlife increasingly to make money. The Deseret Ranch in Utah, for instance, manages deer and elk on its property, where it then sells hunting rights. The International Paper Company has a similar program in Texas.

Roughly half the U.S. population relies on ground water as its primary source of drinking water. Yet so-called overdrafts, where water is pumped out more quickly than it is replaced, pose a serious problem in 35 of the 48 contiguous states. While the U.S. has abundant surface water resources, they are not uniformly distributed; 17 of 196 subregions suffer from potentially inadequate supplies. The problem is particularly acute in the arid southwest. The fundamental problem is government. Water prices have been kept below true market levels; as a result, water is wasted, leading to shortages.

Resolving this requires two market-oriented steps. First, consumers should pay the market price for their water. Between 1960 and 1976, government-controlled water prices fell in real terms in 57 percent of cities surveyed. Simply raising prices would reduce waste.

"It is not too late to advance a conservative ecological program that provides more value at less expense."

Second, water rights should be made transferable. For example, most growers in California's San Joaquin, Central, and Imperial Valleys pay from $6.50 to $91.30 per acre-foot for water from federal water projects that costs $50 to $300 per acre-foot to supply. As a result, farmers waste water and grow crops that are not economic. If, however, those who value the resource more highly—particularly consumers in the Los Angeles basin—could purchase the water from the current users, farmers would sell their supplies rather than waste it. The growers would reap a financial windfall, but still the

consumers would be better off.

The fundamental cause of much of the nation's resource mismanagement, water and otherwise, is ill-considered government intervention; all too often environmental abuse or resource waste is subsidized by those who are supposed to be the environment's protectors. In these cases, privatization and market pricing are the answers. . . .

The Real Enemy

Free markets and environmental protection traditionally have been viewed as mutually exclusive: in the public's eye, at least, it is the profit-seeking big business that threatens the nation's ecological future. Yet in case after case, the real enemy of the environment has proved to be government. . . .

It is not too late to advance a conservative ecological program that provides more value at less expense. And that is a result that should please all Americans, industrialists and environmentalists alike.

Doug Bandow is a columnist with the Copley News Service and a senior fellow at the Cato Institute, a Washington, D.C. public policy research organization.

"Firms make the investment and production decisions that are best for their own profits, and those decisions often conflict with what would be best for the environment."

viewpoint 66

The Private Sector Cannot Protect the Environment

Patricia Horn

A sign two blocks from the Jersey City, New Jersey city hall reads, "This area contains dangerous and contaminated materials that are harmful to human life." A chromium refinery that once occupied the lot contaminated the soil with 46 times the amount of carcinogens that New Jersey deems safe.

In the 16th century, Juan Rodriguez Cabrillo sailed into what is now the bay of Los Angeles and christened it *Bahia de los Fumos*—Bay of Smoke. Today, the smog capital of America more than lives up to that name. For 176 days in 1988, the ozone in L.A.'s air exceeded federal standards.

In March 1989, the Exxon Valdez hit a reef, and 11 million gallons of crude oil poured into Alaska's Prince William Sound, saturating birds' wings with oil, clogging fish's gills, and spoiling hundreds of miles of coastline. The magnitude of that disaster stands out, but similar events happen every day. In 1988, the Coast Guard counted some 5,000 oil and other toxic spills in U.S. waters.

For at least 20 years, our national awareness of the link between pollution and survival has grown with each new crisis—oil spills, dying lakes, contaminated water, overflowing garbage, toxic dumps, and global warming. But despite this Sword of Damocles dangling over us, we have barely begun to provide solutions.

The fact is that our private enterprise economy severely restricts progress against pollution. We rely on private decisions of individual firms to determine the course of our economy. Operating individually, these firms make the investment and production decisions that are best for their own profits, and those decisions often conflict with what would be best for the environment. Operating together, these

firms push government policies that encourage growth, frequently at the expense of the air, land, or water.

The fight against pollution is ultimately a fight to restrict and change the private-enterprise system. It requires the government to intervene more actively in the economy and citizens to exert pressure on private firms.

Hostages to Growth

Capitalism needs growth. The expansion of economic activity creates new markets, products, and technologies that make it possible for businesses to make profits. One of the marvels of capitalism is that, when it works well and each individual firm pursues opportunities in its own niche, the resulting investments lead the whole system to expand. This overall expansion, in turn, creates more opportunities and what the system needs: growth.

According to business leaders and government officials, we all have an interest in economic growth, and therefore in letting business go its way with a minimum of restrictions. Growth means more jobs, higher incomes, and more goods and services. When there are no other options, this is a hard argument to counter.

But growth, it turns out, often involves environmental destruction. When we hand businesses the bill for this destruction, they reply with the specter of stagnation and recession: unemployment, bankrupt companies, and higher prices. Given the present economic system, the threat is real. Kentucky miners have good reason to fear that strict emission standards on coal-fired generators will cost them jobs. Consumers know their electric bills will be even higher if utilities are fully prevented from polluting.

The favorite yardstick of economic welfare and economic progress, gross national product (GNP), reflects capitalism's bias, measuring the aggregate

Patricia Horn, "Natural Enemies," *Dollars & Sense*, October 1989. Reprinted with permission.

value only of the things that are produced and sold in the market. The GNP measure distorts the picture of what is happening to the economy, exaggerating economic growth and ignoring environmental degradation. It fails to take account of the costs of foul air, for example, or of unclean lakes, rivers, and oceans.

These are costs for which no money changes hands, but they are real nonetheless. The quality of our lives diminishes when smog suffocates us and waters are despoiled. Our future economic welfare is also diminished because these acts make future production more difficult and costly. Thus the growth registered by GNP is in many ways illusory.

What if the GNP took account of these social costs? Certainly the U.S. GNP would grow more slowly, if at all. Economist and futurist Hazel Henderson has pointed out that if we do not measure "the social costs of a polluted environment, disrupted communities, disrupted family life . . .[then] we have no idea whether we are going forward or backwards."

When a private firm makes decisions, it only takes into consideration the costs it actually incurs and the income it actually receives. When one firm's decision forces another person or firm to incur costs, those costs have no place in its profit calculations.

Occasionally, a firm's actions confer benefits on others. A classic example of a positive external effect—or positive "externality"—is the case of a honey farm. Farmers raise bees to produce honey and sell it for a profit. In the process, however, anyone who has an orchard or flower garden in the vicinity will benefit without having to pay for the bees' pollination tasks.

It is far easier to come up with examples of negative externalities, and many go by the more common name of pollution. When an Ohio utility burns coal to generate electricity, it emits sulfur dioxide and nitrous oxides. As a consequence, acid rain falls on the Northeast and Canada, killing animal life in lakes and rivers, ruining trees, and slowly dissolving buildings and statues. The tourist, fishing, and logging industries suffer, but the utility doesn't bear the costs.

The Pollution Bill

Traditional economic theory, rooted in 19th-century optimism and the exploitation of vast colonial resources, treats such negative externalities as relatively rare events. In 20th-century reality, however, negative externalities dominate our lives.

In each case, the owners of the polluting company do not pay for the abuse of the environment, the damage to human health, and the drain on public resources caused by their activities. So they don't take account of those costs. If they were forced to pay the true social costs, they would certainly cut back their operations.

If the polluters themselves do not pay, someone else does—through poor health and higher health bills, increased taxes to pay for cleanup, more personal expenses such as bottled water and air filters, higher prices in other industries, and the incalculable cost of a less pleasant world to live in.

"If the polluters themselves do not pay, someone else does."

The part of the pollution bill that we can readily measure is growing rapidly. In Los Angeles, for instance, air-quality authorities estimate that the health cost of smog in the region is $3.65 billion every year, while California agriculture suffers to the tune of $7 billion. An 18-year cleanup under consideration for L.A. carries an officially estimated price tag of $2.8 billion for the first five years—a bargain from a social standpoint. Industry in the city, with its eyes narrowly focused on current profits, is fighting to block the cleanup by arguing that the cost will be much higher.

In recent years, the environmental crisis has worsened to the point where no one can ignore it. In the United States, the hidden costs of profit-driven growth are even higher than in other countries because government regulation and planning are so limited. Even staunch conservatives have finally begun to call for action, but their programs are still mired in reverence for the free market and minimal government involvement.

In June 1989, in a shift from Ronald Reagan's denial of the connection between coal-plant pollution and acid rain, George Bush asked Congress to strengthen the 1970 Clean Air Act. Not surprisingly, Bush's rhetoric went far beyond what the proposal actually provides. Bush's promise that sulfur dioxide emissions would be reduced by 10 million tons is achieved in the bill only by counting some reductions that have already taken place. The bill would actually allow an increase of nitrous oxide emissions over present levels. The changes are touted as a "reduction," however, because they would be less than the amount that would be emitted in the future under present regulation.

Beyond its accounting shortcomings, the real problem with the Bush proposal lies in its basic approach. Firms would be allowed a certain level of emissions, and those firms that achieve lower levels than this standard could sell their "right" to pollute to other firms. So one coal-burning electric utility could emit more pollutants if another, cleaner plant offsets the excess. Allowing companies to buy and sell the right to pollute would supposedly promote economic efficiency. They would pollute the most where doing so brought the biggest profit payoff. Such is the world of the free market.

Even on its own terms, the Bush plan is set up to fail. The problems of enforcement by an underfunded Environmental Protection Agency, for example, are immense. Each firm's pollution levels would have to be checked against its purchases and sales of the right to pollute. Numerous loopholes make it likely that firms will find legal ways to avoid the bill's restrictions.

While the Bush plan may have some impact on air pollution, it cannot work because it attempts to *control* rather than *prevent* pollution. The distinction between the two is critical, as Barry Commoner pointed out in a 1987 *New Yorker* article. Control allows pollutants to be produced but blocks them from entering the air, water, or ground. Prevention stops their production outright. To illustrate the effectiveness of prevention, Commoner cited the 1972 U.S. ban on DDT and related insecticides. By 1983, the average DDT levels in human body fat had fallen 71%.

Efforts aimed at only controlling pollution have been less successful. To reduce carbon-monoxide pollution, the federal government requires car makers to install emissions-control devices in automobiles. But between 1975 and 1985, such emissions fell a scant 14%, and the emission level was again rising at the end of this period. As Commoner concludes, "The few real improvements have been achieved not by adding control devices or concealing pollutants (as by pumping hazardous wastes into deep water-bearing strata), but simply by eliminating pollutants."

Of course, the goal of eliminating carbon-monoxide pollution will be elusive as long as we rely on the internal-combustion engine for transportation. Huge investments in public transportation would be essential to any program aimed at preventing auto-originating pollution. But this solution falls outside the scope of the free market.

Toward a Cleaner Future

We do, of course, need to provide for our economic well-being. People need goods and services, and people need jobs. So how do we go about using nature's gifts wisely?

A small first step would be to establish a better way of assessing our economic progress. The GNP measure gives a high value to private benefits and downplays social costs that are external to the market. In fact, alternative measures of growth are available. Though they are imperfect, many are better than what we use now.

The World Resources Institute, for example, has suggested a measure that would deduct the depletion of resources from any year's GNP. In its 1989 study, *Wasting Assets*, the Institute applies this yardstick to Indonesia. Measured the traditional way, Indonesia's GNP rose an average of 7.1% per year from 1971 to 1984. When the depreciation of only three of the

nation's major resources are subtracted, that figure falls to 4.0%. And Indonesia's domestic investment, a prerequisite for economic development and long-term growth, is actually negative in some years if the costs of depletion are deducted. Many industrialized countries—among them Japan, France, Germany, and Norway—have similar measures that account for environmental destruction.

Of course, an alternative measure of economic activity by itself will not ensure a clean environment. Changing corporate behavior requires organized pressure. Indeed, a citizen movement to force capitalists to fully absorb the cost of their pollution is emerging. The movement has had some success in court. In July 1989, a Washington D.C. federal appeals court overturned government regulations and ruled unanimously that polluters must pay to restore the environment to its original condition: "From the bald eagle to the blue whale and snail darter, natural resources have values that are not fully captured by the market system," the court proclaimed. . . .

"A citizen movement to force capitalists to fully absorb the cost of their pollution is emerging."

The court's decision could add billions to the bills that Exxon and other polluters face. While the enormous costs may bankrupt even the biggest firm, they could also force potential polluters to think twice—or thrice—before engaging in ecological madness.

Patricia Horn is a staff editor at Dollars & Sense, *a monthly magazine.*

"The country is facing clean-up costs in the hundreds of billions of dollars and the staggering medical and environmental implications of decades of indiscriminate dumping."

Toxic Waste Landfills Are Hazardous to Local Residents

Andre Carothers

Kaye Kiker, president of Alabamians for a Clean Environment, is telling stories in her parlor—highlights of her five-year campaign to close down what may be the world's largest hazardous waste landfill, located in Emelle, 20 miles from her house in York, Alabama. I am taking notes and trying to understand why she laughs so easily and speaks so benignly, even positively, of the events since 1982.

Circumstances and her Christian sense of right and wrong have transformed this churchgoing rural housewife into the leader of a vocal and controversial group of local townspeople. ACE, Alabamians for a Clean Environment, now numbers about 300, and it has already established itself as the leading citizens group monitoring the Emelle landfill and its owners, Chemical Waste Management, Inc.

Toxic Waste

At 10:30 p.m., Kaye's phone rings. It is the last of five calls made by James Dailey, the mayor of Emelle, whose 300 residents live next to the 2400-acre toxic waste landfill. Dailey tells Kaye he has been trying to decide whether to evacuate his town, based on reports from his neighbors—and the evidence of his own senses—that an acrid, sickly sweet cloud of undetermined content has settled on Emelle.

As she always does when driving up Route 17, Kaye watches the road in the beam of her headlights for chemical spills. Leaking trucks have dumped thousands of gallons of poison on Sumter County roads, she says. Dailey meets us out front of his brick ranch house and we walk into his kitchen. "Their heads are aching," he says, referring to his neighbors. He has already called the EPA [Environmental Protection Agency] and the Alabama

Department of Environmental Management (ADEM) and the manager of the facility and the sheriff's office, but no one has called back. After waiting half an hour, we drive up to the site.

At the gate of Chemical Waste Management's Emelle Treatment Facility, the night manager tells us that some "incompatible material" from a Mississippi landfill was just poured into the gaping pit ChemWaste has carved in the Alabama chalk. They didn't know what it was, but it smelled "real bad" and they were trying to "neutralize" it.

Kaye seems unsurprised. She is long past taking pleasure in having her concerns proven right. Just four months before, in November of 1986, she and her colleagues from ACE had submitted an inch-thick stack of documents to a hearing conducted by the EPA on the question of whether Chemical Waste Management should be allowed to build a toxic waste incinerator at the Emelle facility. In it, ACE mentioned the lack of a proper notification and evacuation procedure in case of an emergency.

The EPA and ChemWaste had drawn up a plan in accordance with regulations, but a few cursory questions on the part of ACE members revealed it to be a sham. The Sheriff of Sumter County had not read it, the Sheriff's department did not know the location of all the houses bordering on the landfill, none of the residents had ever been briefed on an evacuation plan and half of the local people didn't even know that the "factory" on Route 17 was a hazardous waste landfill.

It was then that I began to understand how it came to pass in Sumter County that the elected mayor of Emelle would turn to the county's leading environmentalist—instead of the civil authorities, the managers of the landfill or the U.S. Environmental Protection Agency—when faced with a question concerning the health and welfare of his constituents.

The whites in Sumter County are not politically

Andre Carothers, "Living Next to the Landfill," *Greenpeace*, July/September 1987. Reprinted with permission.

aware. "If I mentioned apartheid," said one ACE member, "they'd ask me what kind of flower it was." But the presence of the toxic waste business—its culture of deception, arrogance and simple lawbreaking—has changed this rural corner of Alabama forever, uniting blacks and whites and eroding the region's deeply held tradition of trust and deference to authority. It is the coming of age of Sumter County.

A Showcase Facility

The Emelle landfill is all things to all people. To the regulators and the burgeoning "waste management" industry, it's one of the United States' showcase disposal facilities—called the "Cadillac of landfills"—a secure resting place for the torrent of hazardous chemical byproducts of U.S. industry. For others, it's a poison pill for Sumter County, a symbol of industrial profligacy and a superficial band-aid over the nation's toxic waste cancer.

"United States industry produces, at last count, close to 300 million metric tons of hazardous waste each year."

United States industry produces, at last count, close to 300 million metric tons of hazardous waste each year, enough to fill a line of railroad cars stretching around the world, with several thousand miles to spare. Until 12 years ago, disposal of these wastes was virtually unregulated in the United States. Now the country is facing clean-up costs in the hundreds of billions of dollars and the staggering medical and environmental implications of decades of indiscriminate dumping. The United States is in the throes of a reform movement—trying to dig out from under decades of accumulated poison with a spasm of regulation and legislation.

One of the results of this reformation is the phenomenal growth, in both profits and influence, of hazardous waste-handling companies. ChemWaste shares the lucrative commerce in hazardous chemicals disposal with a handful of national or global conglomerates—BFI, Allied Signal, IT, IU International and Rollins Environmental Services.

The Emelle landfill is one of 10 major facilities managed by Chemical Waste Management (ChemWaste), a subsidiary of Waste Management Inc., a global conglomerate with gross earnings of $2 billion in 1986. The Emelle facility receives the poisons from waste generators throughout the country and from other dump sites being "cleaned up" by the federal government. Each barrel of waste it takes in represents a profit for ChemWaste.

Since 1977, ChemWaste has accumulated fines of over $30 million; so extensive is the list of their crimes and misdemeanors that the EPA has set up a special task force to deal with ChemWaste's problems alone. But the massive profits have bought a measure of respectability and not a few EPA officials have moved on to more lucrative positions in ChemWaste hierarchy. The collusion between industry and its regulator is now so close that EPA toxic waste administrator Hugh Kaufman once complained "Sometimes the EPA acts as if it were a wholly-owned subsidiary of ChemWaste Management."

What occurs at the national level has been replayed for Sumter County. "It is apparent," said Montgomery County Attorney General Jimmy Evans, "that ChemWaste, the Alabama Department of Environmental Management and the EPA have all gotten into bed together." The Emelle landfill was barely two years old before it was revealed that Alabama Governor George Wallace's son-in-law bought the land, obtained the relevant permits with surprising ease and immediately sold it to ChemWaste at a profit, over the lifetime of the deal, estimated at $15-$30 million.

In the years that followed, the county learned about the leaking barge, the hidden shipment of PCB-contaminated wastes, the controversy over the cracks in the chalk layer and the PCBs in Bodka creek. Today, local legend mirrors national legend—just as the country has elevated Love Canal, Bhopal, Minimata and Seveso to parables for the toxics age, so has Sumter County adopted the stories emerging from Emelle as regional proverbs. The result has been disaffection and distrust—traits uncharacteristic of genteel rural Alabama.

"I told the folks from ACE two years ago that I didn't trust the EPA or ADEM, and I think a few of them were offended," said Wendell Paris, a black civil rights activist who is involved in the toxics issue, "I don't think it would offend them today." ACE and Wendell's group, the Minority People's Council, are now working together, the first such alliance in Sumter County history.

Industry Arrives

Sumter County, Alabama, lies in one of the poorest sections of the South's economically troubled "black belt." Originally, the black belt was a section of rich dark earth running 300 miles along the Tombigbee River from central Alabama to northeastern Mississippi. The term has since been used to denote a much larger band of the southern United States where poor blacks remain—a legacy of the era of slavery and cotton.

The *Atlanta Constitution* calls the black belt "a third world right in our own back yard . . . avoided by industry, failed by agriculture." The history of successful black labor organizing has intimidated businesses, who are being lured by cheap foreign labor. In the corporate view, says one writer, investing here is "a little like investing in some unstable South American government." Sumter County, 70 percent black, is no exception. Thirty-two percent of County residents live below the poverty line. Farming, the mainstay of the region, is unprofitable—land prices have fallen 15-20 percent since 1981 and almost half the store fronts in downtown York are boarded up.

Not surprisingly, when the toxic waste landfill was proposed in 1977, Sumter County residents didn't see it as the convulsion of a nation trying to bury decades of industrial waste—they saw it as the new business in town. "Unique Industry Coming: New Use for Selma Chalk to Create Jobs" reads the headline in the *Sumter County Record*, dated May 25th, 1977. Below, the landfill is described as "a new facility which could give this area more advantage in attracting other businesses."

At the time, many local residents didn't know what was going on atop the hill out Route 17. "When they first came, the rumor was it would be a brick factory," said James Dailey, "Oh boy, we said, we'll all get jobs at the brick factory." When I met Mayor James Dailey in March 1987, no one from Emelle worked at the dump. "We've been losing businesses, not gaining them," said Dailey, "The only thing that a toxic waste dump attracts is toxic waste."

Economics and Environment

Touting the economic benefits of hazardous waste facilities—known in the trade as locally unwanted land uses, or LULUs—is common practice among waste handling companies and their friends in the EPA. Of the four major landfills located in the southeastern United States, three are in impoverished black counties. According to a report by the Commission for Racial Justice, communities with the greatest number of commercial hazardous waste facilities also had the highest relative number of minority residents. "It is, in effect, environmental racism," says Commission Director Reverend Benjamin Chavies.

Will Collette, a director of the Citizen's Clearinghouse on Hazardous Waste, agrees. "The toxic waste issue is fast becoming the top social justice issue in North America. People are becoming more aware of it now, but Sumter County in 1977 was ripe for the picking."

For James Dailey, it means moving his family and picking up the pieces elsewhere. His handsome red brick ranch house, once appraised at $50,000, is now worth less than $15,000. Property values throughout the area are equally depressed. "No one wants to live next to the dump," he says. Down the unpaved street from Mayor Dailey's house is a small park with a swing, gazebo and a few benches—Emelle's municipal park, courtesy of Chemical Waste Management.

While ChemWaste hasn't engendered an economic renaissance, the taxes it pays are now vital to Sumter County. A host of regional services benefit from the 5-dollar per barrel tax, including the library, historical society, ambulance service and sheriff's department. The students at Sumter Academy were entertained by the ChemWaste Easter bunny and use ChemWaste note pads in school. A ChemWaste representative sits on the panel that judges the Livingston High School science fair. "There's no aspect of this county that is not touched by ChemWaste," says Kaye Kiker, "I don't really know how the county would run without them."

"Touting the economic benefits of hazardous waste facilities . . . is common practice among waste handling companies and their friends in the EPA."

Wendell Paris, civil rights activist and head of the Minority People's Council in Livingston, is bitter. He first became involved in the dump issue when a group of ChemWaste workers brought labels from barrels of waste for him to read, wondering why their shoes were melting and their wives and children falling sick. "Ten years ago ChemWaste came in and started buying people up," he said, "Then they built a day care center and that little park in Emelle. Now the whole county is addicted to toxic waste. They've turned Sumter County into America's pay toilet."

The EPA Was Wrong

When the EPA fired its first volley in the war on toxic waste in 1972, the agency was surefooted and confident. Trusting in their numbers and their science, the bureaucrats drafted national regulations and waited for the results to come in—all EPA had to do was "cut the gorilla loose and the problem would soon be solved," said former EPA administrator William Ruckelshaus. The events of the last few years have dampened the EPA's confidence. "In the drafting of those laws, we made several assumptions," Ruckelshaus told the University of Houston Law Center in 1986. "The trouble is, almost all of them are wrong."

Science proved less than conclusive in identifying the toxic chemicals, predicting their effects and isolating them from the environment. Statistics proved equally unreliable—today no one knows how much waste there is, where it comes from and where it ends up.

Of the 35,000 chemicals in commerce considered by the EPA to be definitely or potentially harmful to human health, health and safety guidelines have been established for roughly 2,000. Meanwhile, 1,000 new ones are added to the global chemical inventory each year. Not only is the EPA unsure of the types and quantities of toxic waste produced by industry, but little is known about the effects of individual toxic chemicals on the environment and nothing on what effects they might have in combination.

As the dimensions of the problem became clear, the glimmer of an alternative policy began to emerge. Since 1984, the EPA has officially advocated "waste minimization"—eliminating or altering industrial processes that produce hazardous waste in order to drastically reduce the volume of the waste stream.

"Reducing the production of the waste means no more incinerators, no more leaking landfills, no more toxics-related cancers or birth defects, no more Emelles."

A successful waste minimization strategy essentially removes the problem. Reducing the production of the waste means no more incinerators, no more leaking landfills, no more toxics-related cancers or birth defects, no more Emelles. It has virtually taken over as the policy of choice for environmental groups and now receives the lion's share of the rhetoric in and out of government. "We are all true believers," said one EPA official.

But in practice, the EPA and its officers around the U.S. act as if they had never heard of their agency's policy. The clearest indicator: no money or time is being devoted to it. According to Joel Hirschhorn, senior associate at the U.S. Congress' Office of Technology Assessment, of approximately $16 billion spent by federal, state and local governments on environmental protection in 1986, only about $4 million were devoted to source reduction—less than one-half of one percent of the agency's toxic waste funding. "With the ultimate solution right under their noses, the EPA is doing nothing," says David Rapaport, toxics campaigner for Greenpeace. "There are no regulations, no plans for regulations, and no way of finding out whether anything is being done. It's a joke."

Education Is the Problem

Perhaps nowhere is the chasm between policy and practice more evident than in the EPA's Region IV office in Atlanta, Georgia. Presiding over the southern states from Georgia to Mississippi and north to Kentucky and North Carolina, it is here that decisions are made that affect, among many other things, Emelle, Mayor Dailey, the health of Sumter County and the financial prospects of ChemWaste Management.

Jack Ravan runs the EPA Region IV office. For Ravan, solving the toxic waste problem is a matter of "capacity" and "education"—building more waste-handling facilities and persuading people to accept them into their communities. "There is little government can actively do to participate in waste minimization. . . . Levels of waste generation are expected to grow," Ravan informed a group of state officials and environmentalists. "Reducing waste generation has passed beyond the stage where improved housekeeping procedures can give substantial results." . . .

In Washington, efforts to "manage" the torrent of wastes continues. ChemWaste is looking to the west coast as a site for a "test burn" aboard its incinerator ship and the EPA is moving to permit land-based incinerators. Jack Ravan held another meeting in the southeast, where federal and state officials discussed the dearth of waste management facilities and Ravan admitted he "had no problem forcing an incinerator down a community's throat." And the EPA drew up its 1986 budget, allocating $400,000 of some $16 billion to waste minimization.

Meanwhile, ACE and its allies are filing a lawsuit challenging ChemWaste's incinerator permit on the grounds that the company did not file an Environmental Impact Statement, as required by U.S. law. They are also helping organize a protest march in Sumter County and the state capital.

To raise money, ACE members are organizing rummage sales. Kaye is selling a stained glass window she made in her workshop. Other ACE members hope to sell quilts they sewed. And Peggy Denniston, whose husband Eric Loftis was almost ousted from the county museum council for his outspoken criticism of ChemWaste, says she might sell a wooden sculpture she carved. It placed second in the Livingston University art show sponsored by the local arts council, and the $40.00 prize is going to the lawsuit fund. Crafted of ten separate pieces of mahogany, it depicts a woman's head thrown back in anguish, the mouth open and screaming. It's called *Emelle, 2000: A Victim of Hazardous Waste.*

Andre Carothers is the editor of Greenpeace *magazine, published in Washington, D.C., by Greenpeace, an international environmental organization well known for its direct, nonviolent actions to save endangered species.*

Toxic Waste Landfills Are Not Hazardous to Local Residents

Gregg Easterbrook

The Pinewood, S.C., "secure" landfill of the GSX Corp. is among the dwindling number of facilities with legal permission to accept the type of wastes once tossed onto the fields of Rose Township, Michigan. Pinewood is modern, well engineered and scrupulously clean. Everybody hates it.

Demonstrators have lain before trucks at Pinewood's gate. Environmentalists nationwide condemn the facility; congressional subcommittees have held inquiries; thousands have attended local protest meetings. One of the largest secure landfills in the country, Pinewood accepts 135,000 tons of hazardous wastes annually. Since 1980 Pinewood has operated on an interim EPA [Environmental Protection Agency] permit. Its application for a final license runs 30 hardbound volumes.

A law passed by Congress in 1984 had at its centerpiece a stringent "land ban." Wastes such as PCBs and dioxins were land-banned immediately: basically, compounds like these may now be disposed of only via neutralization or destruction in high-temperature incinerators, never placed in the ground. For other chemicals the law wielded "hammers," a creative new countermeasure to EPA foot dragging. The EPA was given deadlines by which to promulgate rules on how various toxics should be treated. If the agency failed to act on time it would be "hammered"—further bans would take effect automatically. That got even the Reagan administration's attention, and regulations began to flow.

Five years later most hazardous wastes have been "listed" by the EPA, and cannot be buried unless first treated or solidified. In May 1990 a sledgehammer falls: it will become illegal in the United States to dispose of nearly any untreated chemical.

Gregg Easterbrook, "Cleaning Up." From *Newsweek*, July 24, 1989. © 1989, Newsweek, Inc. All rights reserved. Reprinted by permission.

Most trucks entering Pinewood carry chemicals already on a hammer list. Samples are processed in a lab equipped with chromatographs, spectrometers and other expensive gizmos to see if content matches what the shipper declared on an EPA manifest. Chemicals too hot to handle may be sent to a GSX incinerator in a nearby town. Legal compounds are mixed with clay derivative similar to Kitty Litter or with kiln dust to form low-grade cement. Then they are drummed and lined up in huge gashes in the earth decorously called "cells."

Under most cells are two layers of compacted clay, which is highly resistant to liquids, plus two synthetic liners. Between these are sumps to collect rainwater that may leach through, pumping it up for destruction in the GSX incinerator. Around the cells are ground-water monitors. An inspector from the South Carolina Department of Health and Environmental Control is present at all times; the inspectors rotate, making them harder to buy off.

When filled, a cell is covered with more clay and high-density polyethylene, the polyethylene ridges are welded, the cover landscaped. On the GSX computer is a 3-D record of which waste sits where in the grid in case the cells have to be excavated someday. In theory they will remain forever. At present rates Pinewood will be in operation till the year 2030.

No Need to Worry

Less than 1,000 yards down the hydraulic gradient from the GSX property line is a lovely sportsman's paradise, Lake Marion. The proximity of this water, plus technical details of local soil strata, are the chief reasons environmentalists oppose Pinewood. Scientists paid by GSX swear that even if chemicals escaped the cells it would take nearly a hundred years for them to reach the lake; scientists with environmental groups swear this could happen far faster. Because Lake Marion is infested with marine plants that inhibit sports fishing, its surface has been regularly sprayed with herbicide. Under "hammer" rules, GSX would have to neutralize the same herbicides just to enclose them in welded cells. If chemicals ever do escape Pinewood and migrate to Lake Marion, they will arrive in concentrations vastly lower than what's applied directly to the water on purpose.

As a young reporter in the late 1970s, I covered the original round of toxic-waste horror stories, trooping across many government-sanctioned hazardous landfills. Compared with them, Pinewood is a hospital operating theater. At one facility near Los Angeles there were big pits in the ground; trucks would drive up and pour chemicals straight into them. No treatment, no liners, no sumps, no 3-D computer records. The lab consisted of a dingy trailer with a few test tubes; as an "inspection," the guard placed his hand on a truck's side to feel if it was hot, which would indicate the chemicals within were reacting. Places like Pinewood may only be steps along the way to a fully accountable system for managing society's dangerous byproducts. But they are so much better than what we had just a decade ago that it's not funny.

Ideal Disposal

Any burying of hazardous byproducts in verdant soil may sound barbarous. It is: ideally all waste toxics should be destroyed or chemically broken down, preferably while still inside factory gates. On a practical basis industry can't do that yet; and inert hazardous materials such as heavy metals will probably always go into landfills. One obstacle to ideal disposal is that consumers will pay higher prices if better techniques are applied to every product that contains a hazardous chemical or requires use of one during manufacture, which is to say nearly every product. The acid in flashlight batteries, for example, is an EPA-restricted corrosive; hair mousse contains propane. Companies do not manufacture toxics because they get their jollies that way. Toxics are manufactured because consumers want the products they make possible.

Though businessmen whined piteously about the expense of using improved facilities like Pinewood, most are learning to live with it. "Our customers are an even greater regulatory force on us than EPA," Roger Davis, a GSX vice president, said. "They send auditors here to ensure our site conforms to RCRA [Resource Conservation and Recovery Act], because they're intensely concerned about their liability if we slip up." After Davis crowed about the environmental safeguards at Pinewood, I asked whether the company would have installed them if not for government and public pressure. He answered simply, "No." But GSX and other disposal firms are learning to live with strictness as well. "Now we recognize that the waste industry benefits

from tight regulation. It put the midnight dumpers out of business, so we have no cut-rate competition," Davis added.

New liability standards have persuaded many factory managers not to let anyone else, who might slip up, touch their toxics. Today just 4 percent of industrial hazardous wastes are sent to facilities like Pinewood; the rest is handled at the point of production. Much on-site disposal involves a technique called "deep injection," which sends toxics down to the briny part of the water table, theoretically beneath the zones tapped for drinking water. Deep injection is probably safe, though nobody has paid much attention to it. Nearly all public concern has focused on commercial sites where trucks can be seen entering a gate. Such places are just part of the story: as they shut down, the public may be lulled into thinking that toxics have gone away. They won't have.

Nobody wants a facility like Pinewood nearby because of the Nimby [not in my backyard] Reflex. Contrary to what you've heard lately, this reflex is not all bad. "Nimby has created many positives," says Henry Cole of the Clean Water Action Project. "It forces people to come to terms with where their wastes go, forces society to seek better alternatives." Many environmental offenses were facilitated by the old out-of-sight, out-of-mind complacency. If today's demonstrations against reasonable facilities like Pinewood are overreactions, at least they keep the pressure cranked up on industry and regulators.

"Deep injection is probably safe, though nobody has paid much attention to it."

But Nimby can backfire. Once the public went along with anything; now it opposes everything. Fitted with the quiver of modern due-process precedents that makes blocking easier than doing, Nimby patrols oppose nearly all construction of new waste facilities, which has the effect of locking society into already-existing facilities—the lousy old designs. Because hazardous wastes received intense study in the 1980s, a body of knowledge now exists that could make for control facilities with superior environmental characteristics. But good luck getting permission to put one anywhere. The EPA has even had trouble siting support facilities for Superfund cleanups, an Alice-in-Wonderland arrangement.

Nimby is to some extent a property-value phenomenon, but the active ingredient is terror. Industry once conned people into believing toxics harmless; environmentalists now terrify them into believing that just reading the name of some chemicals is enough to make you keel over.

Twenty years ago environmentalists would have kissed the ground on which the Boston Harbor system now sits. Today the Clean Water Action Project says little but nay about the plant: it's too high tech, the sludge will be hideously toxic, the sponsoring authority isn't interested in punishing industry. The Boston cleanup is remarkable both for what it will accomplish and for enjoying broad voter support, though Bostonians will pay through their noses: annual water bills are expected to rise from $300 to $1,100. This indicates the public has been converted to environmentalism in the most significant sense, willingness to spend. Time to celebrate, it would seem.

> *"Today many frantically oppose any municipal waste remedy other than universal recycling, a debatable proposition."*

Likewise 20 years ago an environmentalist who heard that U.S. cities would like to renounce trash landfills in favor of waste-to-energy plants would have thought he'd lived to see the heavens open. Yet today many frantically oppose any municipal waste remedy other than universal recycling, a debatable proposition. Activists fear that to the extent trash power projects are successful they will undercut recycling by reducing the perception of a "garbage crisis," tortured logic at best. Lancer, a trash power system that might have done wonders for the Los Angeles landfill crunch, was defeated by a sky-is-falling campaign of panic over trace toxic emissions, though similar furnaces have been used in Western Europe without adverse effect on public health.

At the extreme, some environmentalists have evolved a world view in which it's fine for them to enjoy the goods and services of industrial society but horribly selfish for anybody else to. To this contingent, cries that the sky is falling become second nature. The dilemma is that environmental hyperbole often plays a worthy role, spurring the political system toward decisions that are in fact in society's interest. Could you catch the attention of Congress on such technical matters as delayed RCRA regulations if you didn't exaggerate a bit, say by claiming the country was being "poisoned?" Probably not.

Gregg Easterbrook is a contributing editor for Newsweek *magazine and for* The Atlantic Monthly. *He is also a frequent contributor to other periodicals, including the* The New Republic *and* The Washington Monthly.

"Cancer is not the only danger that dioxin poses.... Other effects of exposure... include birth defects and infertility."

viewpoint **69**

Dioxin Is Harmful

Peter von Stackelberg

In the dying days of the summer of 1987, a ramshackle house in an isolated valley in Oregon's Coastal Range became the focus of international media attention. It was long in coming. Since the mid-1970s, Carol Van Strum had almost single-handedly conducted a vigorous campaign to end the use of dioxin-contaminated herbicides in her home state. The decade of struggle, chronicled in *A Bitter Fog*, might well have ended with the completion of the book. Except that Van Strum and her husband of eight years, attorney Paul Merrell, soon realized that the herbicide story was just part of something bigger.

Information on dioxin, a chemical that can be as dangerous as plutonium, was scattered and incomplete, they discovered. Even worse, EPA officials were reluctant to release publicly their own studies, some of which showed a connection between dioxin and paper mills. Using freedom of information laws, Van Strum and Merrell obtained EPA's dioxin studies in 1986 and set to work piecing together a report that pulled the dioxin/paper mill connection from behind, in the author's words, "a smokescreen of government secrecy."

In August 1987, the report, entitled *No Margin of Safety* and published by Greenpeace, burst like a bomb on the pulp and paper industry and its regulators within the Environmental Protection Agency (EPA). Evidence gleaned from thousands of pages of the EPA's own documents demonstrated that pulp mills were spewing dioxins into the air and water, creating what Van Strum and Merrell call a public health emergency.

But that was only the beginning. Someone inside the American Paper Institute (API), the paper manufacturer's trade organization, saw the report

and sent a collection of documents to Greenpeace. These documents substantiated Merrell and Van Strum's charges that senior EPA officials and the industries the agency was supposed to regulate were working together to limit public knowledge about the hazards of dioxin and a host of other dangerous chemicals. According to U.S. District Judge Owen M. Panner, the documents revealed an agreement "between the EPA and the industry to suppress, modify or delay the results of the joint EPA/industry [dioxin] study or the manner in which they are publicly presented."

Increased Contamination

Since at least 1980, EPA scientists and researchers with Canada's environment and health departments have been expressing their concern about the growing dioxin contamination of the environment. They are concerned about the high toxicity of dioxin and its extreme ability to bioaccumulate. Dioxin is the term commonly used to describe a group of about 75 compounds with the same basic chemical structure.

2, 3, 7, 8-tetrachlorodibenzo-p-dioxin (TCDD) is the most studied member of the dioxin family. TCDD is also the deadliest substance ever produced. Its toxicity has been compared to plutonium—the EPA's procedures for handling these two materials are the same.

Industry representatives have argued that low levels of dioxin do no harm, but this contention has never been supported by scientific research. During congressional hearings in 1980, EPA scientists testified that TCDD was so powerful a carcinogen and teratogen that even the lowest measurable doses caused cancer and birth defects during laboratory tests. "EPA considers dioxin a carcinogen and, as all carcinogens, considers there to be a finite risk at any level," said the EPA's Alec McBride. "EPA considers any level as posing a degree of risk."

Peter von Stackelberg, "Whitewash: The Dioxin Coverup," *Greenpeace*, March/April 1989. Reprinted with permission.

Cancer is not the only danger that dioxin poses. The effects of TCDD in all species of animals tested under laboratory conditions included weight loss, liver damage, hair loss, abnormal retention of body fluids and suppression of the immune system. Other effects of exposure to TCDD include birth defects and infertility. The dangers to the unborn in particular were emphasized by the EPA's Don Barnes. In a memo written on March 16, 1987, he said:

"Pregnant women, lactating mothers, developing fetuses and nursing infants constitute a subpopulation of special concern. Human body burdens [of dioxins and furans, a closely related group of highly toxic chemicals that are often found with dioxins] are likely to lead to additional burdens to the fetus and the nursing infant, which are not mimicked in the animal tests. Increases in the mother's body burden as the result of [dioxin/furan] contaminated food would likely lead to additional exposures."

In the late 1970s and early '80s, public concern over dioxin contamination centered on sites like Love Canal and Times Beach. But it soon became evident that dioxins are far more widespread in the environment than two places in New York and Missouri.

Agent Orange

In the forest of Van Strum and Merrell's valley, and in many others up and down the Coastal Range, the spraying of defoliants similar to Agent Orange was commonplace during the 1970s and into the early 1980s. So were health problems that many people complained were the result of that spraying.

"One woman had had fourteen miscarriages in the years she had lived in the valley. Another told of her two miscarriages and of her son born with defective lungs and liver. The young wife of a logger had been unable to complete a pregnancy in the five years they had been married," wrote Van Strum in her book.

In Oregon, Larry Archer and his wife Laura lived near a reservoir that was sprayed with herbicides while she was pregnant with her second child. He was present when the baby was born. Van Strum wrote, "'The baby—it was a girl,' Archer said. 'She was perfect, from her toes to her eyebrows. I mean, her face was perfect too. . . . But that was it. It ended at the eyebrows. That's all there was—just this kind of a bowl, with a kind of tissue over it. She couldn't breathe. There wasn't any brain to tell her to breathe.'"

Van Strum, Merrell and others say the evidence clearly shows a link between herbicide spraying programs, dioxins and birth defects. What concerns them is that dioxins have been detected in places where little or no spraying of herbicides has been done and from a variety of sources. Dioxins are showing up everywhere in the environment—and in the food chain.

Dioxins are always produced when chlorinated compounds are burnt. Municipal incinerators, for example, produce dioxins when they burn garbage containing chlorinated plastics like polyvinyl chloride (PVC). Dioxins are also unwanted by-products in the manufacture of chlorinated chemicals, such as Agent Orange and the wood preservative pentachlorophenol (PCP).

"Dioxins are showing up everywhere in the environment—and in the food chain."

EPA scientists suspected some sort of link between pulp mills and dioxin in 1980. Their suspicion was substantiated in 1983, when fish caught downstream from several Wisconsin River pulp mills were found to contain high (50 parts per trillion) levels of dioxin. The dioxin studies secured by Van Strum and Merrell in 1986 confirmed the cause-and-effect relationship. Samples from sites slated for "control" sampling and predicted to have only "background" dioxin levels consistently revealed high levels of dioxin contamination when downstream from or near pulp mills.

Chlorine in the pulp bleaching process acts to form toxic chlorine-based compounds, including dioxin. Kraft-type pulp mills, where chlorine gas is used in the first stage of the bleaching process, are the biggest culprits. Chlorine gas reacts with compounds in wood lignin to create dioxin precursors and many other chlorinated compounds. These toxic compounds, called organochlorines, are released into the air and water when wastes are dumped. In North America, more than 150 pulp mills are dumping organochlorines, and most likely dioxins, into nearby rivers and lakes. An average-sized pulp mill discharges between 35 and 50 tons of chlorinated compounds every day.

"Dioxin, really, is only the tip of the iceberg when it comes to pulp mill effluents," says Renate Kroesa, Greenpeace's international pulp and paper campaign director. "Up to 1,000 different chlorinated compounds, only 300 of which have been identified, are formed during bleaching and discharged with the effluent. Among the compounds identified, we find many well-known carcinogens that are regulated when they come from chemical industries. But, when they are discharged by the pulp and paper industry, there are no limits."

The islands scattered in the Georgia Strait between the British Columbian mainland and Vancouver Island are close to heaven. Sparkling blue water, the deep green of fir, spruce and hemlock and rocky shores make it a beautiful area. The waters around the islands teem with life. Pods of orcas are not an uncommon sight. Crabs, oysters and shellfish abound. But the beautiful scenery is marred by foul air at Crofton, Vancouver Island, where a pulp mill vents its wastes into the air and water.

Like the canaries that once warned coal miners of deadly gases in their pits, the Crofton blue heron colony serves as a warning of new dangers. From 1987 to 1989 the eggs from the blue heron colony near Crofton failed to hatch. Dioxins were detected in the herons' eggs during studies conducted in 1983 and 1986. The dioxins came from two sources: hexa-, hepta-, and octa-dibenzo-p-dioxins were coming from lumber industries in British Columbia that use dioxin-laden pentachlorophenol wood preservatives; TCDD was coming from the pulp mill. Since PCP use has decreased since 1987, levels of dioxins associated with it have dropped. But the pulp mill operates beyond capacity, so levels of TCDD dioxin have tripled since 1987.

Crofton's paper mill is an example of an industry-wide problem. Dioxins not only find their way into the water. They also contaminate the bleached pulp produced by these mills. What this means is that all bleached paper products—coffee filters, disposable diapers, toilet paper, everything—are potentially contaminated with dioxin. Paper industry executives would prefer to keep this quiet. And they almost did, were it not for the ally who sent the American Paper Institute's internal papers to Greenpeace. . . .

"Although the pulp and paper industry was trying to stifle the release of government information, it discovered some disturbing new revelations."

Although the pulp and paper industry was trying to stifle the release of government information, it discovered some disturbing new revelations about the dangers that dioxin contamination of paper products presented. TCDD, the most deadly of the dioxins, was found in bleached pulp at levels ranging from one part per trillion to 51 parts per trillion (ppt) in the vast majority of the samples taken. Levels of related chemicals were found to range from 1.2 ppt to 330 ppt.

Part of the industry's public relations strategy was to dismiss these levels—"trace amounts" as they have often been called—as being far below any level that presented danger to the public. In a speech to an API industry forum on March 8, 1988, Thomas C. Norris of P.H. Glatfelter Company, an API member, told his colleagues that the results of the industry's testing work into the dioxin problem had been "extremely encouraging."

"First, the dioxin detection levels are quite low," Mr. Norris said. "They range from no detection in the disposable diaper sample to 3.8 parts per trillion in paper towels to 14 parts per trillion in non-barrier food packaging." He went on to say that tests done for the industry had demonstrated only minimal movement of dioxins and related chemicals from paper products to the human body. "We are very encouraged by these results, and the bottom line is that all of the testing work done to date confirms that our paper products are safe," Norris said.

Yet other tests sponsored by the API itself showed that superabsorbent disposable diapers had up to 11 parts per trillion of dioxin in them, paper towels up to 7 parts per trillion, and various types of paper plates up to 10 parts per trillion. A draft report prepared for the industry in June 1987 by the research firm of A.D. Little found that between 50 and 90 percent of the dioxins in paper products "in contact with food oils or water is available for consumption."

The EPA Is Aware

Even more damning words about the hazards of dioxin in paper products were then being written by EPA officials. "If the exposure estimates utilized in the risk assessment are reasonably accurate—and I have no reason to believe they are not," wrote EPA scientist Dr. Fran Gostomski on July 10, 1987, "we are presented with a risk estimate for at least one exposure scenario—ingestion of dioxin from coffee filters—that exceeds the lifetime risk level at which EPA would generally be expected to take regulatory action. In addition, this risk estimate does not take into account the very probable occurrence of simultaneous exposure to multiple sources of dioxin from bleached kraft paper products."

If one were to take milk or cream with that coffee, it would add even more dioxin to the diet. In the summer of 1988, at the International Dioxin Symposium, the Canadian Health Protection Branch of the federal health department presented evidence showing that dioxin in paper milk cartons had migrated into the milk. This despite paper industry assurances that it was impossible for dioxins to migrate from cartons.

Although EPA is aware of the connection between pulp mills and dioxins, the agency has failed to produce regulations that would eliminate dioxin contamination of air, water and paper products. Instead, in April 1988, the EPA decided to do another, bigger study of all 104 pulp and paper mills that use chlorine. . . .

A major political fight may be required to stop the spread of deadly dioxins and other organochlorines. Regulations that include a timetable for zero discharge of these toxics seem far away. EPA policy makers continue to stall; they attempted to reduce their obligation to clean-up dioxin-contaminated sites by announcing in 1988 their intent to increase—by 16 times—the levels of exposure that will be deemed acceptable. Fortunately, EPA's Science Advisory Board agreed at their December 1988 meeting that "there is no firm scientific evidence" for the proposal.

Greenpeace is pushing for standards that will completely eliminate organochlorine discharges by 1993. This can be achieved by abandoning the use of chlorine in the bleaching process. "What is needed is a lot of local participation by people," Paul Merrell says. "That is the only way that the spread of dioxins into the environment from pulp mills will be halted quickly," he adds.

In addition to political pressure, the economic weight brought by changing consumer demand for bleached paper products may be needed to force government and industry in North America to deal with the problem. Greenpeace has asked for the immediate introduction of chlorine-free and/or unbleached paper products, as well as a higher recycling rate of paper products. The North American industry has resisted these demands. Coffee filter producers, for example, claim that they do not have enough unbleached pulp to produce unbleached filters. Yet at the same time the pulp industry is undergoing an enormous expansion program, all geared to producing more chlorine-bleached pulp. Unbleached pulp is cheaper and easier to manufacture.

"For years whiter-than-white paper products have been associated with hygiene by consumers."

For years whiter-than-white paper products have been associated with hygiene by consumers. Now they should be seen as a threat to health and the environment. "Paper is a natural product, made of a potentially renewable resource," says Renate Kroesa. "How can we ever come to terms with living on this planet if we don't even produce paper in an environmentally sound way?"

Peter von Stackelberg is a free-lance writer based in Edmonton, Alberta, Canada.

"Dioxin does not appear responsible for any long-lasting health problems in humans."

viewpoint 70

Dioxin May Not Be Harmful

Science Impact Letter

The piece of paper you are holding probably contains some 13 parts per trillion of dioxin. Please don't drop it; this may not be as bad as you think. Dioxin is one of the most deadly chemicals known to the Environmental Protection Agency, but it is not known to travel from paper into fingers, or to harm you if it did.

Nonetheless, the recent discovery that many products made from paper contain dioxin—including coffee filters, disposable diapers, and the packaging for many food products—has made both consumers and environmental regulators nervous.

If only someone knew for sure. To date we only know that dioxin is pervasive and is astoundingly deadly to guinea pigs, but not so bad for hamsters. Surprisingly—aside from the severe headaches it is causing for the EPA—dioxin does not appear responsible for any long-lasting health problems in humans. The only exception is that, at large doses, it causes permanent acne. At least a reasonable person would say so, after exploring the mountain of evidence. Maybe.

Trace Amounts

Dioxin shows up at trace levels in fish, eggs, poultry and pork, breast milk, water downstream from chemical plants, much of the soil in Missouri, and air rising from incinerator stacks. The average American harbors about five parts per trillion (ppt) of the most hazardous form of dioxin. (One ppt is equivalent to one drop of detergent in enough dishwater to fill a ten-mile-long train of tank cars.) Nobody knows what it is doing to us.

There are 75 distinct forms of dioxin to worry about. Ironically, they aren't even useful: Dioxin is a mere contaminant of industrial and agricultural processes, albeit a pervasive one.

To date, nearly all the attention has focused on the most hazardous form of dioxin to animals, known as TCDD (2, 3, 7, 8-tetrachloro-dibenzo-p-dioxin). It causes liver damage, cancer, and infertility even at low doses, in some species. Less than a thousandth of a gram will kill a guinea pig. But the effects are highly variable. It takes 300 times more TCDD per unit body weight to kill a dog than a guinea pig, and 5,000 times more to kill a hamster. And TCDD doesn't appear to harm humans.

Whenever researchers take a close look at new claims that TCDD is bad for people, the evidence seems to vanish like a statistical mirage. But the potential hazard of dioxin is clearly too important to ignore.

Little Evidence of Harm

In 1983, just to be safe, the EPA bought out the entire town of Times Beach, Missouri, after learning that dioxin-contaminated oil had been used years before to control dust on the town's roads. Four years after evacuation, some former residents of Times Beach still have unusually high levels of dioxin in their bodies. Doctors can find minor abnormalities in some immune tests of some of those people, but no evidence that anyone from Times Beach was permanently harmed by the exposure. So far.

The case against TCDD as a hazard to humans is just barely clear enough to be frustrating. Of course, we don't dare test it by giving it to people; we have to wait for an accident to happen and then send in the doctors and epidemiologists. So far, not enough people have been exposed at once or have shown clear enough effects other than acne to comfort a statistician. Nonetheless, a great deal has been published to add to the mystery.

In the first known dioxin accident, a vat heavily contaminated with TCDD exploded at a chemical plant in Nitro, West Virginia in 1949. Ten years later,

Science Impact Letter, ''Dioxin: An Environmental Enigma,'' January 1988. Reprinted with permission.

half of the 122 workers who developed the characteristic TCDD acne still had it, but after 20 years their death and cancer rates were no higher than normal. Factory workers known to be directly exposed to TCDD have yet to show any serious long-term damage from the exposure, despite blood and tissue levels of TCDD that often measure in the thousands of parts per trillion.

"There have been studies claiming to show that dioxin causes cancer in humans, but all of these studies have been challenged by contrary findings."

In 1976, another chemical tank ruptured in Seveso, Italy, spewing a toxic cloud over a residential neighborhood. Some 22 people were admitted for treatment of severe acne, and some of them showed digestive problems and enlarged livers. No long-term effects have been documented. There were reports of an increase in spontaneous abortions afterwards, but a study of some of the aborted fetuses showed no abnormalities.

Thousands of veterans of the Vietnam War now blame their health problems (or those of their children) on Agent Orange, a defoliant contaminated with dioxin. But a study released in the summer of 1987 by the Centers for Disease Control failed to detect noteworthy TCDD levels in the blood of the men most likely to have served in contaminated areas.

An Air Force study found much higher TCDD levels in some of the 1,200-odd men who handled and sprayed Agent Orange, but as yet there is no consistent, persistent evidence of harm to the men from dioxin exposure. The numbers remain too small and the incriminating evidence too weak to say anything conclusive.

There have been studies claiming to show that dioxin causes cancer in humans, but all of these studies have been challenged by contrary findings of equal weight. Dioxin does not appear to cause a generalized increase in human cancers, and attempts to link it to specific types of cancer have been ultimately disappointing. Some studies seem to show an increased risk of cancer among farmers who used weed-killers, but others just as carefully done fail to find the link. In any case, no good study isolates the risk due to the dioxin contaminant from the effects of the many other dangerous chemicals used in farming.

Nonetheless, the possibility remains that dioxin may have subtle effects, difficult to recognize, even at low levels. At the request of Congress, EPA completed a two-year study to determine the extent of dioxin pollution in the U.S. What it found, true to

dioxin's history, was confusing.

EPA had expected to find some 400 or 500 dioxin trouble spots like Times Beach; it could account for only about 100, most of them also in Missouri. However, river sediments downstream from some paper mills were surprisingly contaminated, as were the fish living over them. Samples of wood pulp from five different plants showed that bleached pulp contained about a dozen parts per trillion of TCDD. This pulp becomes a major part of many consumer products including writing paper, paper towels, filters, toilet paper, and disposable diapers. . . .

In the absence of any research on the point, EPA immediately asked a consulting firm to assess the public health risk from the presence of such vanishingly small amounts of TCDD in paper products. The result was a 67-page document, perhaps one of the most remarkable exercises in guesstimation in the history of science.

Lacking good data, the consultants had to make assumptions about the bleached paper content of various products, the possible level of dioxin contamination they would confer, the surface area of the product a human being would come in contact with, how often and by what manner dioxin would escape from the paper into a person's body, how much dioxin one could expect to encounter by this means, and what effect it might have. . . .

Frustrating Uncertainties

"The final uncertainty associated with this analysis," the report concludes, "would . . . be the product of the uncertainty in the exposure estimates and the uncertainty in the risk factor." In short, an unknown multiplied by an unknown. All this uncertainty was too much for one EPA scientist to tolerate. "It is the conclusion of this reviewer," she wrote in an internal analysis of the reports, "that [the assessment] is not helpful and perhaps should not have been done.". . .

Speaking optimistically, perhaps there is no other form of dioxin more dangerous to humans than TCDD. Maybe we don't need to look as carefully at the other 74 forms. It could be that the studies are so confusing because dioxin really does not pose any serious health risks for humans. If it does cause some harm, it may be many years before we are able to find out.

Since a lack of clear evidence of harm can never be used to prove that something is harmless, no real news about dioxin may be the best we can ever hope for. And—newspaper headlines to the contrary—that's what we have, at least for now.

Science Impact Letter is a monthly newsletter published by Impact Publications in Kensington, Maryland.

"Across the United States, toxics in the air threaten health—both from sudden catastrophic releases and long-term exposure."

viewpoint 71

Toxic Air Pollution Is a Serious Health Threat

Alexandra Allen

"These old rounded hills are the essence of Mother Earth herself, and she has a calming effect on everyone—you, your host, the whole way of life here," reads a brochure beckoning visitors to West Virginia. "You can check your anxieties at the border."

Unless, that is, you happen to be at the border of West Virginia's Kanawha Valley, home to roughly 250,000 people. Packed into this narrow river valley are 13 major chemical plants owned by DuPont, Monsanto and others. The plants produce explosive and toxic compounds used in making pesticides, plastics, paint and more. Along the way, they leak, spill and routinely emit thousands of tons of toxics into the air.

The largest town here is Charleston, the state capital, but the best known may be Institute, where a Union Carbide plant produces methyl isocyanate (MIC), the same substance that killed more than 2,500 people and injured over 100,000 when a massive leak occurred at Union Carbide's plant at Bhopal, India in December 1984. Nine months later, a sudden release of aldicarb oxime at the company's Institute, W.V. plant sent 135 area residents to the hospital.

In the Kanawha Valley and across the United States, toxics in the air threaten health—both from sudden catastrophic releases and long-term exposure. The U.S. Environmental Protection Agency (EPA) estimates that just 15 to 45 of the hundreds of air toxics cause up to 1,700 cases of cancer each year. And in response to a nationwide 1985 congressional survey, the chemical companies themselves admitted that they leak or vent 196 extremely hazardous compounds into the air around their facilities.

It's figures like these—and a disturbing lack of action by EPA—that have made toxic air pollution a key part of Clean Air bills before Congress. A tour of Kanawha Valley makes the need for that legislation clear.

Unsafe Facilities

"We had been told for years how sophisticated Union Carbide was and how safe their plants were," says Dr. Edwin Hoffman, president of People Concerned About MIC, a local citizens group. "Bhopal upset that notion, and Institute changed it altogether."

Even before those accidents, there were indications of a serious health problem in the valley. State health department records show that between 1968 and 1977, the incidence of respiratory cancer among Kanawha Valley residents was more than 21 percent above the national average.

Grim statistics came again in the summer of 1987 when EPA's "Toxics Screening Study" showed airborne concentrations of chloroform, ethylene oxide and butadiene high enough to cause cancer in one resident in 1,000 from a lifetime of exposure. EPA has tried to downplay those results, but they clearly place valley residents at the upper end of U.S. risk levels.

Meanwhile, accidental releases of toxics are a regular occurrence in the Kanawha Valley. Over the first 10 months of 1986, 38 chemical accidents were reported, with releases ranging from 5 to over 5,000 pounds.

So why hasn't more been done to protect the health of valley residents? The answer, it seems, is threefold: The clout that the chemical industry wields as a major employer in this economically hard-pressed region; the insufficient resources of the state's regulatory agency; and the void in federal regulation of air toxics.

Roughly 10,000 people work in the valley's chemical industry at average salaries of $600 per

Alexandra Allen, "Poisoned Air," *Environmental Action*, January/February 1988. Reprinted with permission.

week. Kanawha County's unemployment rate is 7.9 percent, appreciably lower than the statewide rate of 9.1, which is the nation's second highest. "Essentially, the chemical industry's failure to do more to protect residents of the valley amounts to economic blackmail," says David Grubb, director of the West Virginia Citizen Action Group.

Following the Bhopal and Institute accidents, the chemical companies have emphasized enhancement of their public image, while actual emission reductions and safety improvements have come at a slower pace.

A few months after Bhopal, the National Institute for Chemical Studies (NICS) was established in Charleston with money from the chemical industry, local businesses and the state. Intended to serve as a "bridging institution," NICS sponsored a slick March 1987 conference bringing together industry, government and citizens. NICS has ballyhooed the valley's emergency response capability and readiness—a status challenged by Dr. Hoffman and others who point out that there's only one road, a two-lane highway, to evacuate the area.

The company doing the most to reduce emissions in the valley is, not surprisingly, Union Carbide, which announced plans to voluntarily cut toxic emissions from its chemical factories by 30 percent a year for a three-year period, a promise the company made shortly after the Institute accident inspired panic in the hearts of valley residents.

"Following the Bhopal and Institute accidents, the chemical companies have emphasized enhancement of their public image, while actual emission reductions and safety improvements have come at a slower pace."

So far, Carbide seems on target in meeting that goal. No other company has achieved even Carbide's level of reduction. Some companies have made no reductions at all. . . .

Having spent years trying to encourage voluntary emissions reductions, the West Virginia Air Pollution Control Commission recently acknowledged its limited success. The commission announced plans to propose to the state legislature that chemical plants be required to use the 'best available technology' to limit emissions of 13 cancer-causing chemicals.

If it makes its way into law, the program will mark the first time a state requires already operating facilities to retrofit best available controls, according to Carl Beard, director of the commission. Currently, states that regulate air toxics at all—a total of 17—require this only of new plants.

Beard anticipates strong opposition to the proposal, however, from the West Virginia Manufacturers Association, which is dominated by the chemical industry. And Perry Bryant, former environmental coordinator for West Virginia Citizen Action and now a member of NICS' board, expresses serious reservations.

"The fact remains that standards based on technological availability rather than human health protection cannot provide assurance that the air is healthy," comments Bryant. "And while it is a good idea to focus on the most dangerous chemicals, a program aimed at only 13 is entirely too narrow, considering that state inventories have counted over 400 chemicals that are emitted in the valley."

A National Problem

Unheeded warnings from a stream of studies, a local government's strain to find resources to protect its citizens' health . . . this is the story not just of the Kanawha Valley, but of countless communities across the country.

About half of the nation's 12,000 chemical plants are located in the 25 largest metropolitan areas, where some 160 million Americans live. And while chemical factories are the largest source, toxic pollutants are also spewed into the air by petroleum refining, steel refining, metal smelting and other large industries. So-called "area sources"—cars, trucks and small solvent users, such as dry-cleaning and painting operations—are also significant contributors to a toxic soup breathed by millions.

The heaviest public exposure to many toxics, in fact, comes through the air. Each day, people drink at most two liters of water—but they breathe 15,000 to 25,000 liters of air. . . .

Sen. David Durenberger (R-Minn.), a leader of efforts to enact a new national air toxics law, bluntly stated during the summer of 1987 that it is "impossible to pretend that EPA is running an adequate program on air toxics." . . .

Meanwhile, millions of people living near chemical facilities or breathing the toxic soup of our cities can second the words of Perry Bryant when he testified before members of Congress at a public hearing two weeks after the Bhopal air toxics disaster. "Whether through a sudden uncontrolled release of a lethal substance, or the legal routine discharge of known carcinogens, every day we in the Kanawha Valley face the possibility of death from chemical toxics. It is only through your action that we will have a safe place to live and work."

Alexandra Allen is an attorney with the U.S. Public Interest Research Group, an organization in Washington, D.C., that conducts research and lobbies for consumer, energy, and environmental reforms.

"An EPA investigation several years ago shows that people may have more to fear from everyday pollutants... than from the chemical plant next door."

viewpoint 72

The Effects of Toxic Air Pollution Are Exaggerated

Edmund Faltermayer

George Bush campaigned as a foursquare environmentalist, claiming that he wants to be the most ecology-minded occupant of the White House since Teddy Roosevelt. Congress is more than eager to go along. After eight years of inactivity, it is primed to make the air fresher and the world brighter. But does the evidence justify the expense of the President's clean-air proposals? Do the health hazards and the damage to crops, forests, and lakes cry out for legislation that could cost industry and consumers up to $19 billion a year by the mid-1990s?

Compared with other threats—drug gangs, slum schools, the budget and trade deficits—a tainted atmosphere seems less urgent. Besides, this is one enemy that is on the run, thanks to the $34 billion a year the U.S. already spends on pollution abatement. But the progress appears to be slowing. *Some* acceleration of the cleanup makes sense, even though the research so far—some of it frightening—is largely inconclusive.

Among the President's goals:

• Drastically reducing airborne toxic chemicals. About half these substances—a grab bag of 320 poisons—emanate from industry. By applying the best abatement techniques or devices available, factories would reduce their wastes so that cancer deaths associated with them—1,500 to 3,000 a year, the Environmental Protection Agency says—would fall 75% to 90% by the mid-1990s.

• Cutting sulfur dioxide emissions, the main ingredient in acid rain, almost in half by the year 2000. Coal-burning electric utilities in the Midwest and Appalachia would carry out and pay for most of the cleanup. Power companies would also have to reduce nitrogen oxides, another contributor to acid

rain escaping from their stacks.

• Breaking an impasse on ozone. A saint in the stratosphere, where it filters radiation from space, ozone is an irredeemable sinner at ground level, where it is the nastiest ingredient in smog. Some 81 urban areas theoretically face federal "sanctions"—bans on new factories, for one—because they have been unable to reduce maximum ozone readings to an EPA health standard that was set in 1979. The President wants stricter controls on auto tailpipe emissions, from which ozone forms, and on fuel vapors that escape from vehicles and gas stations. His plan would also phase in methanol (which is easily made from natural gas) and other clean-burning motor fuels, and would restrict the use of volatile, ozone-creating chemicals at petroleum refineries, paint shops, and dry-cleaning establishments. Under the cleanup plan all but the three most ozone-prone cities would meet the EPA standard by the year 2000. The exceptions—Los Angeles, Houston, and New York City—would get a reprieve until 2010. . . .

A Flexible Plan

For all its ambition, the Administration's plan is not as drastic as clean-air bills circulating in Congress. Nor does it embrace some of the draconian steps that Los Angeles authorities have called for in a 20-year smog-fighting plan, which may ultimately require electric cars on those ten-lane freeways.

Commendably, the Bush plan allows for flexibility. Power companies, for example, would be allowed to pick their own method for bringing down sulfur dioxide and could even trade pollution permits among themselves. The President also advocates that industry use the cheapest, most cost-effective measures in the early years. Thus, before the big spending must kick in, researchers can learn more about pollution's health risks. And the country can

Edmund Faltermayer, "Air: How Clean Is Clean Enough?" *Fortune,* July 17, 1989. Reprinted by permission from FORTUNE Magazine; © 1989 The Time Inc. Magazine Company.

get a clearer idea of how far and how fast it really needs to go.

It has already come a long way. For more than a decade the EPA has set "air-quality criteria" for six major pollutants, mostly expressed as the maximum allowable parts per million. The six are lead, sulfur dioxide, nitrogen dioxide, particulates, carbon monoxide, and ozone. "Except for ozone," says Dr. Bernard Goldstein, former EPA research chief and now director of New Jersey's Environmental and Occupational Health Sciences Institute, "we have done a reasonably creditable job of cleaning up."

Air Toxics Ignored

You sure can't say that about airborne toxics, which were largely ignored when the country went after the six-pack of pollutants. Because of legal hurdles under present law, the EPA has been able to set emissions standards for only seven of the 320 substances. Air toxics include the benzene that leaks from refineries and cars, solvents like acetone, bits of synthetic rubber, and chemicals with names like 1,2-dibromo-3 chloropropane (just call it DBCP). Also on this rogue's roster are metals—cadmium and mercury—suspended as tiny particles in the air.

After the Bhopal disaster in India, Congress passed a law requiring factories to disclose how much of these toxics they emitted. In March of 1989 the EPA announced the total: 2.7 billion pounds in 1987. "The numbers are staggering," says Senator Frank Lautenberg of New Jersey, who together with Representative James Florio, a candidate for governor of the same state, held a press conference in April of 1989 to dramatize the problem. They stood at what they called "toxic ground zero" amid the refineries and petrochemical plants near Newark Airport, where estimated emissions are 110 times the national average. Lautenberg has introduced one of several bills that would force industry to button up.

The President, too, is indignant, saying at his clean-air announcement: "People who live near industrial factories should not have to fear for their health." The neighbors' increased chances of getting cancer, according to the EPA, may be as high as 1 in 1,000. Still, keep a few facts in mind before making wide detours around Newark. The cancer risks assume day and night exposure over a 70-year lifetime and are based on animal studies open to debate.

An EPA investigation several years ago shows that people may have more to fear from everyday pollutants, such as cigarette smoke and paint thinners, than from the chemical plant next door. For two days some 350 residents of Elizabeth and Bayonne, New Jersey—"ground zero" country for sure—wore monitors so sensitive they registered the effect of a visit to the dry cleaner. The dosage of volatile air toxics from those satanic industrial plants, it turned out, was a fraction of the total inhaled—anywhere from one-half to *one-seventieth*, depending on the pollutant. The total intake of perilous stuff was no greater than in a light industrial city in North Carolina used for comparison, or the farm town of Devil's Lake, North Dakota. Other research suggests that airborne metal dust near factories may be a more serious worry than toxic chemicals.

Even if the health effects of air toxics are hard to nail down, industry lobbyists are not inclined to resist this cleanup. Jon Holtzman, a vice president of the Chemical Manufacturers Association, says health arguments in the debate over toxic air are "inconsequential if the public thinks there's too much." Cancers caused by air toxics are believed to have fallen 50% since 1970, but the President's further cleanup seems like a good idea. At a cost of roughly $2 billion a year when in full swing, it is the least expensive part of his clean-air plan. . . .

Ozone Problem Is Worse

"Pound for pound, ozone is by far the most toxic of the usual outdoor pollutants," says environmentalist physician Goldstein. Sunshine and two parents produce ozone at ground level: nitrogen oxides, which result from any kind of combustion, and volatile organic compounds (VOCs) like gasoline. The destructive offspring is a variant of oxygen composed of three atoms instead of the usual two. It can hardly wait to get rid of the loosely attached extra atom, which oxidizes—or burns—anything from paint to soybean crops to the inside of your lungs.

"Pound for pound, ozone is by far the most toxic of the usual outdoor pollutants."

The tailpipes on today's new cars emit 76% less nitrogen oxides and 96% less VOCs than those of a generation ago. But vehicle traffic has soared, and other ozone outputters—manufacturing companies and utilities—have cut back less or not at all. A typical city's ozone concentrations declined only 9% between 1979 and 1987. With no new legislation, improvement would continue for a while as older cars are scrapped. But with traffic still increasing, total VOC emissions—and ozone—will start to climb around the turn of the century. David Hawkins of the Natural Resources Defense Council, an environmental group, contends that ozone is "a public health emergency."

Anyone coming to the subject cold might wonder what the fuss is about. Some 100 million Americans live in those 81 urban areas that exceed the federal ozone standard, but the numbers overstate the risks. A city "violates" the standard if only one of several

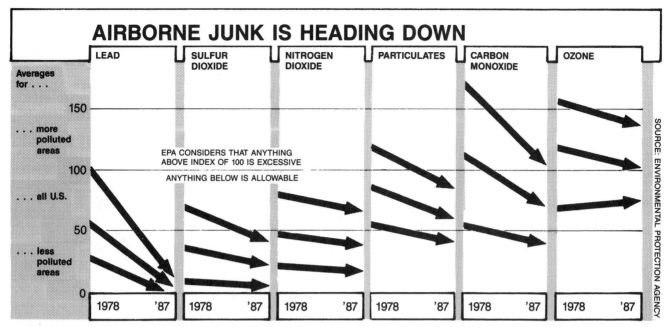

AIRBORNE JUNK IS HEADING DOWN

| LEAD | SULFUR DIOXIDE | NITROGEN DIOXIDE | PARTICULATES | CARBON MONOXIDE | OZONE |

Averages for . . .

. . . more polluted areas

150

EPA CONSIDERS THAT ANYTHING ABOVE INDEX OF 100 IS EXCESSIVE

100

ANYTHING BELOW IS ALLOWABLE

. . . all U.S.

50

. . . less polluted areas

0

| 1978 | '87 | 1978 | '87 | 1978 | '87 | 1978 | '87 | 1978 | '87 | 1978 | '87 |

SOURCE: ENVIRONMENTAL PROTECTION AGENCY

Since the nation declared war on six major pollutants in the 1970s, four have been driven safely below the EPA's standards (indexed here at 100). Carbon monoxide is a problem in congested areas, while ozone, the lung-burning ingredient in smog, remains too high.

monitoring stations has a reading above 0.12 parts per million (ppm) for one hour on two separate days in an entire year. Even in the Los Angeles area, the readings on 35 monitors are below that level 95% of the time. During the 1984 Olympics in Los Angeles, athletes did not complain about smog. So what's the big deal?

To begin with, the Olympians benefited from good weather and strict temporary measures to reduce freeway congestion. Every year thousands of healthy people experience chest pains, coughing, or shortness of breath while playing tennis or golf on summer days in Los Angeles. And the EPA says ozone's damage to crops is costing farmers $2.5 billion a year nationwide. . . .

Eastern and Midwestern ozone may have a partner in crime. Dr. Morton Lippmann, a deputy director of New York University's Institute of Environmental Medicine, . . . suspects that acid aerosols aggravate the lung damage. Is ozone shortening people's lives? Nobody knows, Lippmann says, "but it could be reducing the quality of life at the end of our lives." Fran Du Melle of the American Lung Association adds, "We may be producing a generation of children who will have significantly reduced lung function or chronic lung disease as adults."

Goldstein finds the lack of good statistics deplorable: "We're talking billions for expenditures to cut ozone, when only pennies are needed for research that might give us the answers." For now, jogger Goldstein is putting his running shoes where his mouth is. During heat waves he gets his run in early near his New Jersey home, before the sun sends the ozone climbing.

If his hunches are right, the air cleanup should not just coast along until hundreds more bicyclists have huffed and puffed in smog chambers and thousands of citizens have paraded past epidemiologists. How big a bill should industry and consumers be required to pay? Says economist Paul Portney of Resources for the Future, who has been working on cost-benefit studies of the Los Angeles 20-year plan and who has felt his own lungs burning there: "We may not want to spend every last dime to get ozone down to the EPA standard everywhere. But we will probably want to spend a lot to lower it."

Whatever the right goal, let's also be looking for ways to achieve it at the lowest cost. James Lents, a tall Tennessean in charge of air pollution control for the Los Angeles area, believes his region's plan will prompt an outpouring of money-saving business innovation. Under the proposal, furniture makers must drastically reduce volatile emissions when applying varnish. Lents asks, "What if we come up with a better method of coating the product? Is that bad?"

A debt-laden nation with such a big agenda has no choice but to pinch pennies, even on something as precious as the planet. Especially when the dimensions of some parts of the problem are still as hazy as New York City on a smoggy summer day.

Edmund Faltermayer is an editor for Fortune *magazine. He has written extensively on environmental and energy issues.*

"Radon in homes is a national crisis."

Radon in Homes Constitutes a National Health Crisis

Jason B. Adkins and Daniel H. Pink

Kathy Varady and her husband and four children were each getting more than 100 chest X-rays a day, and they didn't know it. That's because, like the residents of an estimated 4 to 12 million other households across America, their home was filled with high levels of radon, a naturally-occurring radioactive gas that can cause lung cancer.

The Boyertown, Pennsylvania family didn't learn about radon until December 1984 when their neighbor Stanley Watras set off radiation monitors on the way in to work at a nuclear power plant. Authorities discovered that the colorless, odorless gas was seeping out of the soil and into the homes of Watras and some of his neighbors, including the Varadys.

The Varadys' home is now fortified against radon—at a cost of more than $15,000—but they still don't know whether their exposure has affected their chances of developing lung cancer.

The U.S. government has long been aware of radon's dangers but has failed to alert the public. Beyond some initial surveys, pamphlets and a few testing projects, government officials have refused to fund programs to counter the threat. The states have neither the resources nor the expertise to eliminate radon without federal help. In this leadership vacuum, citizens and businesses must grapple with the problem on their own. Radon in homes is a national crisis, a crisis that so far has rallied a meager national response.

EPA's Sluggish Response

"I've known about the radon problems for years and years," former U.S. Environmental Protection Agency (EPA) Administrator Anne Burford told *Public Citizen.*

"Information has always been available within the EPA," added Burford, who blames the press for the lack of public attention. "The reason radon didn't become a public issue [before the Watras incident] was because the media didn't pick it up. Only if it has a human side to it do the media pick up on it."

Yet during Burford's 1981-1983 tenure at EPA, the agency issued no warnings or information about radon. It wasn't until August 1986 that EPA published its first guide for consumers.

What little EPA tried to do on the radon problem was stymied by tightfisted bureaucrats at the Office of Management and Budget (OMB). In 1982, EPA requested $2 million for research on indoor air pollution including radon, but OMB nixed the project.

Uncovering Problems

According to Burford, OMB rejected the budget request because it feared the research would lead to later requests for more funds to remedy any pollution problems it might discover. She recalled that Frederick Khedouri, then associate director of OMB for natural resources, energy, and science and former assistant to Vice President Bush for policy and his deputy chief of staff, told her, "Come on, if we give you $2 million you're liable to uncover a problem and then you'll be coming back for millions more." Mr. Khedouri did not return *Public Citizen's* calls for comment.

EPA paid little attention to radon's hazards to the general population until the Watras incident. According to Richard Guimond, the agency's radon monitoring chief, "The Watras house had the highest known radon level in the world and it wasn't even located on mill tailings, which made us realize the radon problem existed widely and included average homes." [Mill tailings are the unused minerals extracted from uranium ore; the radon in uranium mines has long been associated with miners' increased rates of lung cancer.]

Jason Adkins and Daniel H. Pink, "What You Don't Know Can Hurt You," *Public Citizen*, April 1987. Reprinted with permission.

But in 1980, four years before Watras triggered the radiation alarm, a federal Radon Task Force in which EPA took part concluded that radon was a problem demanding government attention because of "the potential large population at risk." Nonetheless it said that "wide-ranging programs should not be undertaken until more is known about the prevalence of high exposures and ways of controlling them."

"EPA paid little attention to radon's hazards to the general population until the Watras incident."

According to Guimond, Reagan's EPA paid little attention to the report, even to the recommendation that studies be conducted. "If we had started this activity back in 1980," Guimond lamented, "then we'd be much further along than we are today."

Five months after the Watras incident and the ensuing publicity, EPA proposed spending $10.78 million over five years to attack the radon problem. In a never-released July 1985 report, EPA estimated that implementation of its recommendations could prevent "several thousand deaths a year."

The report called for 1) making a national assessment of the radon threat to determine high risk areas; 2) developing mitigation capabilities in conjunction with state and local bodies; 3) developing guidance documents for the states on preventive techniques to eliminate radon contamination in structures; and 4) establishing a national policy for reducing indoor radon exposure.

OMB did not include the report's proposal in either the 1985 supplemental federal budget or the FY [fiscal year] 1986 EPA budget. Sen. Frank R. Lautenberg (D-N.J.), who sits on the Senate Appropriations Committee and chairs the Superfund and Environmental Oversight Subcommittee, accused OMB of "covering up" the report and "waylaying" budget requests for program funding. At an October 1985 hearing on radon held by the House Subcommittee on Natural Resources, Sen. Lautenberg testified that OMB would "rather save money than save lives."

Research Begins

Notwithstanding OMB's position, Congress appropriated funds in 1984 and 1985 that enabled EPA to begin research on mitigation methods and develop measurement standards. In September 1985, EPA Administrator Lee Thomas created a Radon Action Program to assist states in dealing with radon problems in homes.

More than 20 states applied to be included in a preliminary survey of the extent of the hazard, but "due to limited resources," according to Guimond, the agency had to limit the study, which began in the fall of 1986, to just 10 states. . . .

A. James Barnes, deputy administrator of EPA, said that radon "does not lend itself to a regulatory approach" because it is a naturally occurring and therefore "blameless" risk, and also because of the "diversity" of the radon problem, which doesn't affect everyone equally in a given area.

The EPA's budget for radon reflects its belief that a "nonregulatory" approach is best. In fiscal year 1987, it had a $4 million allocation for surveys of the problem, remediation demonstrations and public information programs. . . . By comparison, from 1975 to 1987 the EPA spent close to $500 million on research and remediation of the environmental hazards caused by dioxin. According to Dr. Matthew Zack of the federal Centers for Disease Control (CDC), radon risks are even greater than risks from toxic chemicals such as dioxin because radon gas is found in more toxic concentrations and is more widespread throughout the country. . . .

Ignoring the Evidence

"We've known about the prevalence of dangerous levels of radon gas in homes in the Northwestern United States since 1980 and have tested over 40,000 homes since 1983," said Michael Piper, who heads the Weatherization Program's radon monitoring division at the Bonneville Power Administration (BPA), a part of the Department of Energy (DOE).

The BPA's promotion of energy conservation led it to be concerned about indoor air pollution generally and radon in particular since 1980. BPA has conducted free radon testing in five states and since 1984 has offered up to $1,000 in financial assistance per home for remedial work.

BPA has performed extensive geological research to try to locate radon-prone areas so that local and state officials may be notified of the danger. The BPA also has invested in developing mitigation technologies and has identified some techniques that cost as little as $300 per house.

DOE's budget for radon research is $14 million, up from $4 million in the 1987 budget. With the exception of BPA programs, DOE's interest in radon is limited to "basic science." Dr. Susan Rose, head of DOE's radon research division in Washington, D.C., said the department "performs the epidemiological and geological studies, and explores the relationship of house to soil." By contrast, said Dr. Rose, "EPA is concerned with the practical side of the radon issue—public awareness, the coordination of state activities, and development of remediation techniques.". . .

"The federal government has dragged its feet," said Michael O'Pake, a Pennsylvania state senator active on radon issues. "The necessary political muscle in Washington has not been flexed." As a result, the complex task of dealing with radon has fallen to state governments.

In Wyoming and Colorado, where large concentrations of uranium are found, the state response has been minimal. Wyoming is planning to randomly test 3,700 homes in the state. Health specialists estimate 25 percent of all Wyoming homes will have actionable levels of radon, but state officials say they don't have the money to help affected families fix their homes. Colorado has established a task force to explore the issue, but according to a health department official, the state plans to rely heavily on the private sector to find and solve the problem.

"To counter the [radon] threat will take a coordinated effort of governments on all levels, the housing industry and ordinary citizens."

The state of Washington, where a sizable radon problem has been identified, has earmarked no funds for research or mitigation. Moreover, the state Department of Health Services placed a disclaimer on copies of EPA's "Citizen's Guide" stating that in the department's judgment, "the lung cancer risk estimates are excessively high" and figures on cancer risk due to radon exposure were "done using past epidemiological studies that appear inaccurate or incomplete."

In Maryland, newspaper reports of high radon levels in parts of the state have led hundreds of residents to wonder about their own homes and to seek answers from largely unprepared state officials. The two-year-old Maryland Division of Radon Control receives about 500 phone calls per month on its 800 number. It also publishes a radon fact sheet and a list of reputable testers, and has begun to compile data from homeowners who have tested for radon and reported their results to the state.

Pennsylvania's Programs

Pennsylvania has one of the largest radon investigation programs in the country. The state's residents are particularly at risk from indoor radon pollution because Pennsylvania is situated along the Reading Prong, a radon-laden granite rock formation stretching from eastern Pennsylvania to New England.

In 1985, Pennsylvania offered free radon detectors to homeowners; 22,000 out of 40,000 homeowners living in a high-risk four-county area sent in newspaper ad coupons to receive the detectors. Participants tested their homes and reported the results to the Pennsylvania Radon Monitoring Project. . . .

Since Kathy Varady's unexpected encounter with radon, she has formed a citizen's group in Pennsylvania to lobby government officials and to spread information about radon and its effects. That grass roots activity has been mirrored in Vernon Township, New Jersey, where citizens organized a successful campaign to block a state plan to move radon-contaminated soil from another county to their community.

For the most part, however, there has been little public concern. As Varady explained, "You don't have people standing up and saying, 'Hey, we can't live here. We can't raise our families here.'"

Added Pennsylvania's Sen. O'Pake, "Generally, people aren't responding. They're taking a wait-and-see attitude. There's no real sense of urgency." He suggested that the reason for this is that "if it's naturally occurring, people take it philosophically. It's when it's man-made that people get upset."

Clearly radon gas poses a real threat to millions of Americans. To counter the threat will take a coordinated effort of governments on all levels, the housing industry and ordinary citizens.

Jason B. Adkins and Daniel H. Pink work for Public Citizen, a nonprofit citizen research, lobbying, and litigation organization in Washington, D.C., which was founded in 1970 by Ralph Nader. Adkins is the national director for Buyers Up, which is Public Citizen's heating-oil cooperative. Pink is the outreach coordinator for the Washington, D.C. office of Buyers Up.

"Direct knowledge of lung cancer from residential radon, at any level, does not exist and . . . for the average homeowner there may be no risk at all."

Radon in Homes Does Not Constitute a National Health Crisis

Susan L. Rose

"In the beginning God created the heaven and the earth. And the earth was without form, and void. . . ."

But not without radon. . . . Way back then, even before radioactivity had a name, the earth's crust contained varying concentrations of uranium—the precursor of the now infamous radon gas. Radon, largely ignored in this century, had a second coming in 1984 when researchers discovered Stanley Watras' eastern Pennsylvania home had indoor levels of more than 2,000 picocuries per liter (pCi/l) of radon gas.

This astounding finding—a home with radioactivity levels exceeding those in uranium mines—presented a unique problem for scientists and policymakers. Between 1984 and the "historic" Environmental Protection Agency (EPA) press conference on September 12, 1988, in which radon was declared a nationwide public danger, many policies were considered and many scientifically unsatisfactory choices made.

The nation has paid for and deserves better information upon which to make informed decisions about radon. A media frenzy, which has inadequately portrayed the current state of scientific understanding, has raised public alarm. Misleading terminology, invalid risk assessments, misinterpretation of screening measurements, inadequate attention to smoking as the real radon risk, and lack of effort to convey the enormous uncertainties surrounding the radon issue must be corrected.

No responsible policymaker or public health official would take issue with the risks associated with living in a house such as the Watras'. Everyone agrees on the need to find and fix those homes with significantly elevated levels of indoor radon. At issue is the proper assessment of risk for the vast majority

of U.S. houses in which radon levels fall below 10 pCi/l. The public message has failed to acknowledge that direct knowledge of lung cancer from residential radon, at any level, does not exist and that for the average homeowner there may be no risk at all.

Radon Research Programs

To reduce scientific uncertainties and to provide a sound basis for policy setting, major radon research programs are now under way at the Department of Energy, Centers for Disease Control, National Bureau of Standards, National Cancer Institute, U.S. Geological Survey, and EPA. Research includes:

• Identifying likely radon hot spots.

• Exploring radon entry mechanisms (with mitigation as the goal).

• Understanding the behavior of radon progeny in the home.

• Adequately determining radon variability as a function of climate and building operation.

• Providing better instrumentation for radon/progeny measurements.

• Measuring realistic dose to non-miners.

• Undertaking residential epidemiology studies to evaluate radon/progeny dose effect relationships.

• Understanding the molecular mechanisms that initiate carcinogenesis from radon and copollutants such as smoking.

With all this knowledge being sought with federal dollars, we must let the public know that the residential radon issue is not yet well understood and that we do not really know how many people, if any, will die annually from "radon caused" lung cancer. Indeed, the precise level at which to set the risk is not known.

The single virtue of exaggerating the radon risk may be to increase public awareness and response. This, in turn, theoretically may save lives because some who may otherwise not hear of this villain may now take action. Nevertheless, if U.S. smoking

Susan L. Rose, "Radon: Another Perspective," *Forum for Applied Research and Public Policy*, Spring 1989. Reprinted with permission.

habits remain unchanged (or increase), reducing indoor radon levels to four pCi/l throughout the entire United States would not detectably lessen U.S. lung cancer incidence.

Uranium Miner Studies

Radon risk estimates are based on epidemiologic studies of lung cancer in uranium miners, a far better set than is often the case for regulatory decisionmaking. These data, however, are not as relevant as data would be from residential radon epidemiology studies. Moreover, the many assessments and reassessments of the uranium miner studies are based on the same four or five miner populations with a combined total of only several hundred miner lung cancer cases. Given this small sample, the consensus on the degree of risk should not be surprising.

The problems of extrapolating risk faced by undergound uranium miners to urban and suburban residents are well documented. Miners are healthy males, primarily smokers, breathing an atmosphere quite complex (uranium ore dust, diesel fuels, radon, etc.), have different breathing patterns, and receive their occupational exposure during the middle one-third of their lifespan.

Problems with the Data

Not everyone, moreover, is aware of some additional major problems with the uranium miner data—the source of all the mathematical constructions upon which the indoor radon issue is based:

- None of the study cohorts have been followed to completion.
- There are few, if any, exposure data for individual miners.
- Exposure data for specific mine areas are weak, especially for the early years of exposure.
- The epidemiology studies are complicated by the confounding effects of smoking, age at first exposure, rate, exposure time, inadequate follow-up, small cohort size, weak exposure data, and exposure to other carcinogens in the mines and home.
- Present mine conditions are different from those prevailing during the relevant exposure period. Mining methods have changed.
- Ventilation has greatly increased.
- The incidence of lung cancer is rare before the age of 40.
- The median age associated with lung cancer in miners is about 60 for nonsmokers and 50 plus for smokers regardless of when they begin working in the mines.

The Smoking Factor

The National Academy of Sciences' assessment of risk from radon and other high linear energy transfer (LET) radiations, BEIR IV, provided new statistical tools in its examination of uranium miner studies but included no new data. It also did not include 20,000 deaths in its range of risk—the number the media and EPA are currently using. William Mills, a health physicist and former EPA radiation official, has stated that

> BEIR IV clearly shows that for any given level of radon in indoor air, any risk of lung cancer attributable to radon is 10 times as great in a smoker as it is in a nonsmoker. Based on this report, an estimated 10,000 lung cancer deaths (not 20,000) can be attributable to radon in the U.S. population of 240 million. Of this number, an estimated 7,000 . . . would occur in the 50 million smokers and 3,000 in the 190 million nonsmokers. Even in this nonsmoking population, some of those at risk from radon may be at an enhanced risk due to involuntary exposure to passive smoke.

Lung Cancer

With the estimated risk from radon exposure projected to be so high, we would expect an increased incidence of lung cancer in those places where EPA state surveys have shown elevated levels of indoor radon. . . .

The data raise a perplexing question. Why do states with the greatest radon levels have a lower incidence of lung cancer than the national average?

Smoking provides a better explanation than radon levels. Evidence for this observation is derived by examining female cancer levels in the 1950s before the effects of smoking among American women (from 1920 to 1950) began to show up. During this period, all states have similar incidence of lung cancer, whether "high" radon states or not. Such comparisons admittedly are not based on rigorous scientific data collection. However, in a state where 63 percent of the homes have radon levels greater than four pCi/l, one would expect to see some reflection of this fact in lung cancer incidence.

"Why do states with the greatest radon levels have a lower incidence of lung cancer than the national average?"

Two further observations are in order. As the number of women who smoked increased between 1940 and 1970, so did lung cancer rates. The increase, however, was not consistently related to radon levels. Indeed there was a tendency for "high" level EPA survey states to have smaller increases of lung cancer. This would suggest that if we brought the "high" level states down to the "low" level states, the results would not likely show a significant lung cancer reduction in those states.

That many other pollutants with far less risk are being regulated is often stated as a reason for regulating and controlling indoor radon levels.

Although true, it may indicate that we are overregulating many lesser pollutants that are not serious health hazards but have become health issues due to mathematical extrapolations from animal studies or cellular assays at extraordinarily high doses. While it is reasonable to question what kinds and amounts of risks are acceptable to citizens when exposure is not under their control, we must also question the scientific basis underlying these risks. More policy discussions on this topic need to be undertaken with broader participation by those affected.

Radon risk may be known with more precision than the risk associated with other regulated environmental pollutants. The level of radon risk, however, is similar to lifetime risks of death from many widely accepted lifestyles and occupational hazards (for example, cigarette smoking and automobile driving). The lifetime risk of death is 2 percent from auto accidents, 0.5 percent from a home fall (comparable to the risk posed by indoor radon), 0.5 percent from a home fire, and 30 percent from smoking.

Policies from Abroad

Alternative policy choices may be illustrated through international comparisons. Working with the same scientific data and the same concern for their citizens' welfare, other countries have set their radon action levels much higher than the U.S. level of four pCi/l for existing homes. Moreover, they have implemented simple changes in building codes and building techniques as an easy and prudent policy measure to reduce radon levels in new homes. Over time, Canada, Great Britain, and Sweden, among others, will reduce their total population exposure to radon. Each country has determined that scientific uncertainties in the levels of 0 to 10 (or 20) pCi/l do not warrant stringent action levels (and exorbitant attendant costs) for current homes.

Exposure Measurements

Questions abound about the accuracy of radon measurement. There are large uncertainties in measurement technology and great natural variability in radon levels. These uncertainties do not present major problems when mathematical risks are calculated for radon health effects or when large-scale screening surveys are made. However, when mortgage values, home equity, mitigation costs, and public policymaking (all resulting in billions of dollars of expense) rely on these numbers, they are not acceptable.

The various kinds of measuring devices, the historic use of radon progeny measurement in mines, the conversion problems with techniques that measure radon gas, the randomness of radioactive decay, precision problems at low environmental levels, and differences in international units of measure further complicate radon measurements. The commonly used charcoal canister and track-etch device have so much uncertainty that a house sale can be lost, not because of an elevated radon level but because of the measuring device.

Radon varies greatly from day to day, week to week, and season to season. Thus, a charcoal canister measurement of two days cannot reflect the true radon exposure values over longer periods. Major problems with charcoal canister measurements include the influence of temperature, humidity, air movement, presence of solvents, time in transit (U.S. mail), and counting errors. The relationship of the two-day measurement to an annual exposure (the measure of interest) is, therefore, not possible from charcoal measurements.

Radiation etchable pieces of plastic polymer can be left in place for a year and provide a more reasonable estimate of exposure than charcoal canisters (at least in the room where it is placed). This measurement technique, although more representative of annual exposure than charcoal, is not designed to give a value so exact as to have one's home equity lost. Problems that may be encountered with this technique include significant nonuniformity in batches of the plastic film, counting too small an area of exposed film (thereby yielding wrong results), mistakes in reporting, and using an incorrect duration of exposure.

"The highly publicized EPA state radon surveys . . . were in some states designed specifically to measure areas suspected or known to have elevated radon levels."

The highly publicized EPA state radon surveys that caused so much public concern in 1988 were in some states designed specifically to measure areas suspected or known to have elevated radon levels. Therefore, the surveys were not truly random and must be so acknowledged.

The design—two-day charcoal measurements in a closed house basement—intentionally provided a "worst case" value that cannot and should not be used to derive average annual exposure. Few U.S. residents live 70 years in their basements. For these reasons, valid questions remain about the state surveys' design and public interpretation.

The United States has implemented or is now considering major public policy decisions based on EPA's state surveys. Yet, the only scientifically valid distribution of U.S. radon levels differs by literally millions of "affected" homes from current EPA radon survey estimates. This survey shows that more than one of every 10 U.S. homes have elevated radon readings and need costly remediation. This is a grim but unsubstantiated percentage. Policy decisions and regulations should reflect available scientific information. In this case, the scientific data significantly contradict the total numbers of elevated homes that are now reported in the press.

Only One Absolute

In conclusion, we must try to find some absolutes in the radon issue and address honestly and publicly all the areas of uncertainty. Further scientific research must be brought to bear on those areas of significant public concern and welfare where such great uncertainty exists. At the same time, prudent decisions can be made where the level of scientific knowledge adequately supports the decision. At the moment, the only absolute in terms of an unquestioned, cost-effective lung cancer reduction policy appears to be: *STOP SMOKING!!!*

Susan L. Rose is the radon program manager for the U.S. Department of Energy.

More Government Regulation Will Reduce Hazardous Waste

Claudine Schneider

Beginning in the early 1970s with the Clean Air Act and Clean Water Act and repeatedly in subsequent legislation, Congress has declared that reducing the production of hazardous waste is the best way of dealing with these pollutants. Likewise, the Environmental Protection Agency (EPA) and waste-generating industries endorse a waste management hierarchy in which pollution prevention is the preferred strategy, followed by recycling, treatment, and, as a last resort, disposal.

This consensus, unfortunately, has had little effect on production of hazardous waste. In 1973, EPA estimated that the United States was producing 9 million tons a year. EPA's current estimate is 264 million tons (some of the increase explained by better sampling techniques and reporting requirements). The Office of Technology Assessment's (OTA) estimate is 560 million tons of hazardous waste and perhaps as high as 1 billion tons.

The United States is spending $70 billion a year handling hazardous waste, with industry picking up two-thirds of the cost. On top of that, the government's Superfund will have to pay for the cleanup of 3,000 inadequate dump sites, according to EPA—or 10,000, according to OTA. Meanwhile, health problems resulting from pollution are costing the country additional billions.

Given the cost and aggravation associated with handling waste, broad support for pollution prevention should be well established. In theory, the benefits are enormous. Occupational and public exposure to hazardous chemicals is reduced. Industrial efficiency and competitiveness are enhanced as waste prevention simultaneously cuts raw material inputs, saves energy, and reduces the

volume of waste that has to be stored, treated, or disposed of. Less waste means less expense for buying and operating pollution control equipment. Accidents during rail and highway transportation of waste are reduced. A reduced need for off-site hazardous waste facilities reduces the associated health, environmental, and political problems. Companies can reduce liability risks and costs that otherwise arise from inadequate disposal practices.

In practice, however, progress has been slow because of misguided federal policies and the failure of U.S. industry to recognize the potential economic benefits of waste reduction investments.

Leading the Way

Fortunately, a growing number of companies have adopted a waste reduction strategy and demonstrated that the benefits are more than theoretical, providing a new impetus to act. Minnesota Mining and Manufacturing, the 3M Company, offers one of the most impressive cases to date. In the early 1970s, during the first wave of environmental legislation, 3M's CEO Ray Herzog rejected the common industry complaint that the new pollution control regulations would inevitably lead to higher costs. He challenged his employees to reform company practices—to lower costs while cutting pollution.

What emerged was an approach to pollution abatement that has become a standard at 3M. In 1975, the company established the 3P program— Pollution Prevention Pays—to stress pollution prevention beginning with product development and design of manufacturing processes. The company's comprehensive efforts included reformulating products to replace polluting feedstocks, modifying processes to control by-product formation, and redesigning equipment.

The effort paid off. As of March 1988, the 3P program's 2,261 projects had saved the company

Reprinted with permission from Claudine Schneider, "Hazardous Waste: The Bottom Line Is Prevention," ISSUES IN SCIENCE AND TECHNOLOGY, Volume 5, Number 4, Summer 1989. Copyright 1989, by The National Academy of Sciences, Washington, D.C.

$420 million. In the process, it is also preventing the yearly discharge of more than 120,000 tons of air pollutants, 14,000 tons of water pollutants, 1.6 billion gallons of wastewater, and 313,000 tons of sludge and solid waste. The company's pioneering leadership in designing solutions to this pressing social problem won it the World Environment Center's 1985 International Corporate Environmental Award.

"Examples of successful waste reduction practices are now available for practically every kind of industrial and manufacturing process."

Examples of successful waste reduction practices are now available for practically every kind of industrial and manufacturing process, large and small. Donald Huisingh of North Carolina State University has compiled 74 case studies of pollution generators that have reduced waste by 20 to 98 percent with investments that pay for themselves within five years. For example, the Hill Air Force Base in Ogden, Utah, has dramatically cut waste and costs by shifting from a chemical to a mechanical process for stripping paint from aircraft and ground support equipment. The use of an acidic methylene chloride solution has given way to a modified conventional sandblasting process that uses recoverable plastic beads instead of sand. As a result, solid hazardous waste declined by 95 percent and the 200,000 gallons of wastewater were entirely eliminated. In addition, labor dropped by 90 percent, raw materials costs fell by more than 90 percent, and energy costs have been nearly halved. The savings on operation costs during the first month covered the cost of the new blasting equipment.

Ciba-Geigy took action at its Toms River, New Jersey, plant in response to intense public and government pressure to do something about groundwater contamination. The plant had received the largest environmental fine yet imposed by New Jersey, and EPA had declared it a Superfund site. Company scientists developed a process for producing aminoanthraquinone dyes for cotton without the use of sulfonation, which requires mercury as a catalyst. Ciba-Geigy was thus able to completely eliminate the use of thousands of pounds of hazardous mercury.

In response to a 1976 New Jersey state law, Exxon Chemical Americas installed 16 floating roofs on open tanks of volatile chemicals at its Bayway plant. The company found that the measure resulted in annual savings of 680,000 pounds of organic chemicals worth about $200,000—enough to repay the cost of the new roofs in less than a year. Once it

recognized the economic advantages of the technique, the company proceeded to install more roofs than state regulations required.

Industry's success is reflected in recent studies. Since 1980, OTA has prepared three reports for Congress on the national potential for hazardous waste reduction—*Technologies and Management Controls for Hazardous Waste Management, Serious Reduction of Hazardous Waste,* and *From Pollution to Prevention.* The studies document two principal findings: Waste reduction offers the most reliable environmental protection, and U.S. industry can benefit economically and competitively by practicing waste reduction to reduce its manufacturing, regulatory, and liability costs.

"Producing as much toxic waste and other forms of environmental pollutants as we now do is not inevitable, nor is it demanded by science and engineering," said OTA Project Director Joel Hirschhorn in recent testimony before Congress. "Up to 50 percent of all environmental pollutants and hazardous waste—across air, water, and land environmental media in which they are managed or disposed—could be eliminated with existing technology in the next few years."

The National Research Council independently reached similar conclusions in its 1985 study, *Reducing Hazardous Waste Generation.* "In-plant operations are probably the most effective and economical means of managing hazardous waste," the report concluded. "The committee strongly recommends a major commitment, both philosophically and in funding, to approaches that prevent or eliminate hazardous materials from being discharged as waste."

What's Preventing Prevention?

Despite the mounting evidence that pollution prevention pays, regulatory agencies and private practices have largely ignored waste reduction opportunities. Less than 1 percent of federal and state environmental pollution expenditures are allocated for source reduction efforts. Government spent more than $16 billion battling pollution in 1986, but only $4 million went toward prevention. Roughly $800,000 of EPA's $3 billion budget was spent on waste reduction. After Congress increased funding for waste reduction, EPA requested budget cuts in 1988 and 1989. Despite its rhetorical support for waste reduction, EPA has mainly focused on "waste minimization"—controlling waste by reducing its volume once it has been generated.

Nowhere is this more apparent than in EPA's fragmented hazardous waste control programs. By regulating the minimization of solid waste, liquid waste, and air emissions under separate offices, EPA has unwittingly created the incentive for waste generators to shift waste from a given medium to one that is less stringently regulated. The result is a toxic shell game rather than genuine waste reduction. Air pollution control devices or wastewater treatment plants remove toxic ash and sludge that then pose solid waste problems. Solid waste in landfills or deep wells can lead to water pollution. Pond evaporation can turn solid or liquid waste into air pollution.

Given the regulatory emphasis on end-of-pipe control, it is not surprising that businesses have followed suit. Companies have tended to neglect waste reduction as an option, partly because of lack of awareness of options and partly because complying with waste handling regulations claims most of their time, money, and staff.

"Given the regulatory emphasis on end-of-pipe control, it is not surprising that businesses have followed suit."

In a revealing study of 29 U.S. organic chemical plants, INFORM, an environmental research organization, discovered that waste reduction initiatives were applied to less than 1 percent of their total waste generated. INFORM found that companies generally took waste reduction actions only when forced to do so—mainly when the more routine waste treatment or disposal methods were unacceptable for regulatory or economic reasons. None of the 29 plants had methodically assessed their entire range of operations for waste reduction opportunities. Clearly, waste reduction does not occur automatically. . . .

States Take the Lead

Since 1980, when the Governor's Waste Management Task Force recommended efforts to prevent and reduce hazardous waste generation, North Carolina has persistently promoted waste reduction. The North Carolina Pollution Prevention Program provides on-site technical assistance, outreach to organizations and industry groups, applied research grants to universities and other institutions, and challenge grants (matching funds up to $5,000 of a $10,000 project) to businesses and local governments to tackle very specific problems. By 1986, the program's information clearinghouse had assembled a computerized data base of more than 1,500 references on waste reduction methods, organized by industrial category.

With three professional staff and an annual budget of just $650,000, the program has been highly effective in implementing its policy of "making-it-work." A 1987 volume of 60 case studies documented more than $16 million in annual savings. Looking to the future, the state supported development of a pollution-prevention curriculum

for engineering and industrial technology students and an internship project that enables graduate engineering students to help develop pollution-prevention programs and techniques for industrial firms.

In 1985, North Carolina helped establish the National Roundtable of State Waste Reduction Programs to encourage the development of state programs elsewhere and to exchange information. Forty-two states and Canada belong to the Roundtable, which is chaired by Roger Schecter, the director of North Carolina's Pollution Prevention Program. According to the Roundtable's most recent survey (at the beginning of 1987), California, Georgia, Illinois, Minnesota, New York, and Pennsylvania have also begun comprehensive hazardous waste reduction programs, and Alabama, Florida, Michigan, Texas, and Washington have pilot programs.

The California program, operated out of the Department of Health Services, has had some outstanding successes with its technical assistance program. In Ventura County, just north of Los Angeles, a $150,000 waste reduction program run by the local health department helped 75 companies reduce their hazardous wastes by 70 percent (40,000 tons) over a two-year period. Given land disposal costs of $250 per ton, industry is saving $10 million a year. The program's success has inspired 10 other California counties to start similar programs.

New Federal Initiatives

Given the obvious motivation but limited resources of the states and the critical federal role in regulating hazardous waste, it is clear that a federal-state partnership for waste reduction would have enormous benefits. OTA estimates that a five-year, $250-million federal waste reduction program could pay for itself within a year or two.

With this in mind, the Northeast-Midwest Congressional Coalition—a bipartisan coalition of 17 "frostbelt" states that house a disproportionate share of the nation's toxic chemical dumps—has drafted the Hazardous Waste Reduction Act (H.R. 2800, S. 1429), which Rep. Howard Wolpe (D-Mich.) introduced in June 1987. . . .

To maximize flexibility and innovation in industry actions, the bill takes a nonregulatory approach, which mandates neither the techniques to be used nor the precise level of waste reduction. Instead, it establishes a government priority of fostering comprehensive waste reduction across the nation, particularly through information sharing.

The legislation proposes several steps to institutionalize waste reduction and explicitly authorizes the funds necessary to move EPA from rhetoric to action:

• Create an Office of Waste Reduction to overcome EPA's current organizational problem of regulating pollution by specific media. The Office would institutionalize pollution prevention as very distinct from end-of-the-pipe control of pollutants after they have been created. It would be funded initially with an $18 million annual budget to conduct research on source reduction opportunities, set up a national waste reduction data base, provide state grants, and operate a clearinghouse.

• Establish a federal information clearinghouse to collect case histories of successful waste reduction strategies, general information on waste reduction technologies, and sources of technical assistance. Companies and state programs would be the primary sources and users of the data. The federal government's role would be to consolidate information and make it accessible, and to contribute data collected under Section 313 of the Superfund Amendments and Reauthorization Act of 1986 (SARA), which is the only EPA program that collects chemical-specific data on land, air, and water emissions.

Company trade secrets and other proprietary information would not be threatened because only information of a very general and relative sort is required. Companies would have to report only whether the method of waste reduction used was one of four generic types: technology or process modifications; reformulation or redesign of products; substitution of raw materials; improvements in management, training, or other operational responsibilities. The EPA administrator could modify these categories, but they would remain very general. As backup protection, the bill has a trade secret provision that would allow a company to withhold sensitive data by certifying that its release would give its competitors an economic advantage. . . .

• Provide matching grants to states for technical assistance to businesses seeking to capture waste reduction opportunities. The federal government can capitalize on state interest and knowledge of local industry by allotting $10 million in matching funds for state grants to enable companies to hire technical consultants, to fund R&D and demonstration projects, and to train engineers and technicians in waste reduction techniques. . . .

What Next?

Other initiatives should also be considered. For instance, EPA could incorporate waste reduction into other programs. Section 104(k) of SARA requires states to show that adequate hazardous waste treatment and disposal facilities will be available to handle all hazardous wastes expected to be generated within each state during the next two decades. But this provision makes no mention of waste reduction. EPA should follow the advice of the National Governors Association by introducing "capacity credits," which would allow the states to

substitute verifiable waste reduction improvements for the construction of new facilities. This would prevent states from rushing into the needless construction of treatment, storage, and disposal facilities that could be 10 to 100 times more expensive than source-reduction options.

Another option that deserves a closer look is the waste-end tax, which requires companies to pay a tax based on the volume and danger of the waste produced. A number of colleagues and I proposed a waste-end tax several years ago as the mechanism for funding Superfund cleanups. Instead, Congress chose to impose a feedstock tax on 42 petrochemicals. This was supposed to be easier to administer and was expected to reduce waste by providing an economic incentive to improve the efficiency of production processes.

"The end-use tax includes direct incentives to move up the cleanliness ladder."

Although reducing feedstock use does reduce waste somewhat, significant improvement comes only with changes in production processes and waste management techniques, which are not influenced by a feedstock tax. The end-use tax includes direct incentives to move up the cleanliness ladder by imposing progressively lower rates as a company moves from waste disposal to treatment to recycling to reduction. When the waste-end tax was first proposed, one serious objection was that the difficulty of identifying and measuring waste would create insurmountable administrative difficulties. In the intervening years, about 30 states have implemented a waste-end tax, demonstrating that the problems can be overcome.

States, in fact, are also the source of other innovative policies. Minnesota, for example, has established a 31 percent target for long-range waste reduction, with interim goals set up for each of 14 industrial categories. Such an efficiency goal might be an appropriate action for the nation to undertake; OTA, in fact, has suggested that a 10 percent per year reduction over five years is a feasible national goal. And why not?

Republican Representative Claudine Schneider serves as cochair of the Congressional Competitiveness Caucus and is vice-chair of the Subcommittee on Natural Resources, Agriculture Research, and Environment, which is organized under the House Committee on Science, Space, and Technology.

"Government is itself one of the major obstacles to solving the problem of pollution."

Less Government Regulation Will Reduce Hazardous Waste

Jorge E. Amador

Popular mythology has it that in the struggle against selfish private interests, government stands tall as guardian of the common good.

Consider the environment. In the United States, decades of "landmark" legislation, massive bureaucratic growth, and billions in expenditures have left the impression that the state is the environment's friend.

Appearances deceive. Despite its reputation, government's record on environmental protection is at best mixed. Antipollution legislation has encouraged pollution in the name of abating it. Governments at all levels are among the worst defilers of the environment. Government is itself one of the major obstacles to solving the problem of pollution.

There is a better way to safeguard our health and property from noxious substances. But it requires first weaning ourselves from the notion that the benevolent state is doing it for us.

The Law Is the Problem

"Most governmental regulations are aimed at overseeing the permitted release of toxic chemicals into surrounding neighborhoods during a company's normal operations," acknowledges Representative James J. Florio (D-N.J.), one of the strongest proponents of government intervention in the environment.

The law attempts to manage pollution, not to protect its victims. Those who comply with reporting requirements, get the necessary permits, and stay within prescribed limits may pollute with impunity.

The Federal Water Pollution Control Act proclaims that "the discharge of any pollutant by any person shall be unlawful," except only "as in compliance

with this section and sections 1312, 1316, 1317, 1328, 1342, and 1344 of this title."

Section 1342 of the Act, for instance, authorizes the Environmental Protection Agency to "issue a permit for the discharge of any pollutant, or combination of pollutants . . . upon condition that such discharge will meet either all applicable requirements . . . [or] such conditions as the Administrator determines are necessary to carry out the provisions of this chapter."

The Hazardous Substances Superfund was established in 1980, ostensibly to make polluters clean up toxic-waste spills and dumps. Hailed as a historic victory for the environment, the law exempts "releases in the workplace and releases of nuclear materials or by-products, normal field applications of fertilizers and engine exhausts."

It also excuses spills and dumps from paying cleanup costs incurred by the government if the discharges were in compliance with permits issued under any one of a long list of environmental statutes, including the Clean Water Act, Solid Waste Disposal Act, Marine Protection, Research and Sanctuaries Act, Safe Drinking Water Act, Clean Air Act, and the Atomic Energy Act of 1954.

"It is 'the law' that permits environmental degradation," writes Victor Yannacone, a prominent lawyer in the field of environmental law. "And now when we look to the law for answers to many of our social and environmental problems, we find that the law itself is the cause of many of those problems."

Protection for Polluters

Why does legislation that, we were told, was passed to protect the environment end up protecting polluters instead?

"The first and most obvious set of limitations on legislative power is, of course, the quantum of political constraints under which legislatures must operate," writes another environmental lawyer. Like

Reprinted with permission from Jorge E. Amador, "Take Back the Environment," *The Freeman*, August 1987.

anybody else, lawmakers are affected by what other people tell them. They also have their own preferences. Politicians are ordinary human beings, pushed and pulled by interest groups pursuing competing and often contradictory demands.

Any given vote by the average legislator is the result of a complex balancing process that takes into account these diverse influences. Some want him to stop pollution, others warn that this might ruin the economy. Some represent votes, others offer campaign contributions. The savvy politician tries to keep all sides happy. The result is an Orwellian-named "antipollution" act that actually legitimizes pollution.

Appointed administrators shielded from democratic pressures do little better. Yannacone writes, "If we must find a common denominator for the serious environmental crises facing all technologically developed countries regardless of their nominal form of government, it would have to be entrenched bureaucracies which are essentially immune from criticism or public action."

Subverting the Law

Out of political opposition to the program or sheer bureaucratic inertia, civil servants can subvert the best-intentioned acts of legislators. When Congress renewed Superfund in the fall of 1986, it appropriated $8.5 billion to be spent over the next five years, $1.5 billion of it in the first twelve months. Yet, four months into the fiscal year, only $220 million had been released for Superfund projects.

"One reason," indicated one report, was that the Office of Management and Budget had "not yet approved regulations" drafted by the EPA to guide Superfund spending.

The 1980 Superfund law directed the Department of Health and Human Services to investigate the health hazards of toxic wastes, but, as former EPA policy analyst Fred Smith notes, as of 1986 "almost nothing" had been done.

The law also prohibited persons from challenging an EPA decision on what cleanup method to use. This rule was intended to prevent parties which might be forced to clean up their sites from stalling enforcement for years. But the knife cuts both ways. By initiating preemptive action, the agency can also prevent victims of pollution from seeking more vigorous enforcement of the law. The officials decide how to use this weapon.

The Supreme Court has expanded bureaucratic freedom to bend environmental legislation out of shape. In 1985, the court allowed the EPA to exempt individual industrial plants from full compliance with limits on toxic discharges into sewage treatment facilities, despite apparently clear language in the Clean Water Act that the agency "may not modify" the limits. When provisions can be interpreted into

meaning their opposite, pro-environment legislation can make for open season on the environment.

"It is now clear that the worst offenders in the process of environmental degradation are not the ruthless entrepreneurs dedicated to wanton exploitation of our natural resources," writes Yannacone. Instead, it is "short-sighted, mission-oriented, allegedly public interest agencies." There are some 22,000 sites containing hazardous wastes in the United States. Many are municipal dumps. Military bases alone account for more than 4,000 chemical disposal sites.

"Out of political opposition to the program or sheer bureaucratic inertia, civil servants can subvert the best-intentioned acts of legislators."

Even private pollution is, in very important ways, traceable to public policy. Today, the law protects and encourages polluters at the expense of private interests in healthy bodies and usable property. . . .

In January 1987, a Philadelphia Municipal Court judge ruled in favor of a defense contractor that uses heavy stamping machinery to shape parts for missile casings. The stamping was found to cause irritating and property-damaging vibrations to neighboring homes.

Residents complained of sleepless nights, crying spells, medical bills, and damage to walls. Judge Alexander Macones ruled that the company should not be fined because it provides jobs for 215 people. . . .

Litigation Does Not Work

The courts have developed other restrictions that limit the effectiveness of litigation against pollution. One is the statute of limitations, which for nuisance and trespass actions is dated from the time the original action took place. This is a serious obstacle in pollution cases, where the injurious effects of toxic substances may not become evident until years after the statute of limitations has run out.

Under an action alleging negligence, the statute of limitations has been ruled to begin only when the victim discovers the harm. However, negligence theory has grave shortcomings of its own. Robert Best and James Collins note that "There are four basic elements of any negligence action: A duty or obligation recognized by law requiring conformance to a particular standard of behavior, a breach of that standard, a causal connection between defendant's action or omission and plaintiff's injury, and actual loss or damage to a legally protectable interest."

If the polluter's actions are sanctioned by law, the victim has no recourse, even though he may have suffered harm and may be able to link the polluter to it.

Protection for government-sanctioned pollution has been enshrined in Federal law. The original Superfund legislation, for instance, held that "No person . . . may recover under the authority of this section for any response costs or damages resulting from the application of a pesticide product registered under the Federal Insecticide, Fungicide, and Rodenticide Act."

Congressional Quarterly reports that the new Superfund legislation also bans suits against gas station operators for "costs or damages resulting from release of recycled oil that is not mixed with other hazardous substances, if they are following the regulations and law for handling such oil."

It may be argued that one cannot fault a polluter who was only following the law or taking precautions not to harm his neighbors. This is the basis for the standard of "reasonable conduct" in adjudicating cases.

Though the honest owner of a chemical dump may have dutifully filled all the forms and been careful to use high-quality storage containers, it makes little difference to the unintended victim of his underground leak. We may sympathize with the owner, but his actions injure the victim just the same.

This forms the basis for the idea of strict liability, which recently has gained some ground as a supplement to nuisance, negligence, and trespass.

"Strict liability in tort is based upon the theory that one who realizes profit from the hazards of his or her activity assumes the attending risk and may be held liable for any invasion of the person or property of another, notwithstanding that he or she may be free from all negligence or wrongdoing."

Given the current understanding of strict liability, Best and Collins caution that it "appears unlikely" that the theory will gain as much favor in pollution cases as it has in the field of product liability. Liability is made to hinge on an assessment of whether the activity in question is "abnormally dangerous."

As with nuisance and negligence, the courts have misapplied notions of social utility to provide a basis for defending harm done. Even if it is otherwise "abnormally" dangerous, "though the activity involves a serious risk of harm that cannot be eliminated with reasonable care . . . its value to the community may be such that the danger will not be regarded as an abnormal one.". . .

A Solution

"In our society, the traditional controls have been unable to cope with the continued deterioration of our environment basically because of our failure to recognize pollution for what it is: a form of aggression against society as a whole and our

neighbors in particular," [said Arnold W. Reitze Jr.].

The obstacles seem formidable, but they are not insurmountable. A comprehensive approach to the pollution problem would include the following features:

• Put the environmental protection business out of the government's reach. Place it back in the hands of the people most likely to care—those who are directly affected. As we have seen, "environmental protection" laws often serve to protect polluters, not the environment. Pollution management is left to the shifting discretion of politicians and bureaucrats. Courts take legislation as a cue to strike down common-law remedies and to permit pollution in areas not specifically covered by statute.

• [Make] tort law improvements. In some ways, this requires nothing more than returning to concepts that were in use for centuries before the Industrial Revolution: Collapse the dual law of nuisance back into one to allow private parties to sue over "public" nuisances.

"Put the environmental protection business out of the government's reach. Place it back in the hands of the people most likely to care."

Avoid the quagmire of determining what constitutes an "abnormal" danger or "reasonable" action, and focus instead on the more objective measure of effects. Whether the polluter was careless or law-abiding, the result hurts the same, and it indicts both the polluter and the officials who assured us their regulations would prevent it.

The Superfund law did make one significant improvement by overriding the states' statutes of limitations. It provides that these periods begin to run when harm from the hazardous substances it covers was or should have been discovered.

The doctrine of "joint and several" liability is an incentive to carelessness, as anybody with enough cash, even if only marginally involved in the tort, may be hit for the bulk of the award. Replace it with a system for determining major and minor offenders and the extent of their involvement, then assigning each a corresponding share of the amount to be paid.

• Incorporate the costs to other parties into cost-benefit calculations. Utilitarian analysis has been denigrated as insensitive to the harm suffered by the victims of pollution. This is so only because these costs have not been factored into the formula, tipping the balance toward polluters. Only when polluters pay will the price of technology approximate its actual cost.

There is an intriguing alternative to closing down

the plant or installing devices to stop emissions. The polluter might buy a "license to pollute" from his neighbors. The neighbors would agree to let the plant owner emit specified particles or chemicals in exchange for periodic or lump-sum payments calculated to offset the perceived harm the emissions might cause them. Residents who refused to sell harm to their persons or property would still have recourse to the courts. If greater risks were discovered later, those who sold licenses could demand new or higher fees.

Imperfect Reforms

Even these reforms would not create a perfect world. A victim may not be able to collect from somebody who simply cannot pay. This reflects man's capacity to do more harm than he can possibly make up for.

But the current methods are even less perfect. They encourage pollution, shield the polluter, and leave his victims defenseless. The alternative would reward the scrupulous and encourage industry to adopt safe methods of dealing with hazardous substances. It would bring to the fore the hidden costs of some of today's technology and enable us to decide whether it is worth the price.

Jorge E. Amador is the editor of The Pragmatist, *which provides commentary on current affairs.*

"Americans needn't worry about the water they drink from public water systems."

America's Drinking Water Is Safe

Kristine M. Napier

Water is the universal symbol of life. Throughout time and across the globe it has signified birth, renewal, and purification. The ancient Greeks honored the Titan Oceanus as a powerful creative force. Modern Christians anoint their dead and baptize their living with it. Water blankets three-quarters of our planet and constitutes over half of the human body.

Water is the body's most essential nutrient. Every cell contains it, and as little as a 15 percent loss may be fatal. Water composes 75 percent of all brain and muscle cells. Even rock-hard bone is 25 percent water.

Why is water so essential? In blood, it carries nutrients and oxygen to cells. Through urine, it helps rid the body of toxic wastes. Through perspiration, water helps cool the body. Finally, water is the pool in which thousands of continuous, life-supporting chemical reactions take place.

Thirst, regulated by the sodium concentration of the blood, usually tells us when the body's water supply needs replenishing. A high sodium level turns on receptors in the hypothalamus gland and thus triggers the thirst sensation.

From time immemorial, humans have relied on their senses to guard them from danger. Food and drinks with an unpleasant odor or appearance were usually rejected as unfit for consumption. But modern technology has made the situation much more complicated. What we perceive as safe—or unacceptable—is not always so. For example, water with an objectionable odor due to a small excess of chlorine is likely to be much safer than odorless water that harbors infectious organisms.

Humans have always been concerned with water's microbiological quality. Today's chemophobic society is worried about even minute amounts of many chemicals in drinking water. Although the public is more concerned about chemical contamination, scientists worry more about contamination with disease-causing organisms. . . .

Where Water Comes From

The water we draw from the tap each day comes from either a public water system or a private well. U.S. census data for 1985 indicate that 87 percent of the population receives drinking water from a public water system.

About half of the public water supply comes from surface water: rivers, streams, reservoirs, and lakes. The remainder comes from groundwater, mainly from aquifers under the earth's surface. An aquifer is a water-bearing formation of earth, gravel, or porous rock capable of yielding significant quantities of water. Some geological formations are good aquifers, while others are poor ones. The quality of an aquifer is determined by the soils through which water percolates to reach it and the kind of rock from which the aquifer is formed. These soils and formations contribute dissolved and suspended particles to the water.

Well water, both public and private, is drawn from groundwater sources.

No one wants to drink contaminated water. We want our water safe. Many people, however, equate safe water with "pure" water. But pure water is a human perception. It is not found in nature but made in laboratories. Natural water supplies contain many types of dissolved or suspended solids. These constituents include nutrient minerals such as iron, fluoride, and selenium, as well as organic matter.

Contaminants are substances that change water quality, but do not necessarily render it unsafe for human consumption. Some people call contaminants additives, and distinguish between intentional and unintentional additives. Intentional additives are

Kristine M. Napier, *Assessing the Quality of America's Water*. American Council on Science and Health, December 1988. Excerpted with permission.

substances added to drinking water for some express purpose, such as disinfection. Unintentional additives are substances that accidentally seep into the water supply, such as industrial chemicals or organic material from farms. Whether contaminants (or naturally found constituents) threaten health depends on the nature of the substances and their concentration in the water.

Our ever-improving technology has enabled detection of small and sometimes insignificant amounts of substances in water supplies. In many cases, the limits of technology allow scientists to detect one molecule of a chemical in a trillion parts of water. With this sensitivity, it is possible to detect contaminant molecules in every water supply. Some groups insist on a "zero contaminant" concept. The driving force behind this argument is that even one molecule of a substance may adversely affect human health. Cancer is the most feared adverse health effect.

Scientists cannot examine the effect of one molecule on the human body. But it is clear that everyone is exposed to billions of molecules of carcinogens every day, yet we do not all develop cancer. If people were susceptible to "one molecule," humans would all die of cancer at an early age. But we don't, because our bodies have elaborate defenses against tiny amounts of harmful chemicals.

Thus, even if "zero" levels of potential contaminants were attainable, they are not necessary for good health. To cause trouble, a contaminant must have sufficient concentration. Amounts below this critical concentration (reference point) may be of scientific interest, but should not be of concern for human health.

Becoming Contaminated

Raw water supplies may become contaminated by virtue of the surrounding geology or as a result of nature's or human activities. While contaminants or undesirably high levels of constituents may be found in raw water, the final product from the water treatment plant has been treated and monitored, and with a few exceptions, is safe.

Surrounding geology. As described above, all water is held in its own natural reservoir, either above or below the ground. Some of this natural reservoir, parts of the soil and minerals, leach into the water. Sometimes, however, an area's inherent mineral content is exceptionally high, causing undesirable levels of that mineral to leach into the water supply.

Nature's activities. Like humans, animals center many activities around their water supply. Animal excrement can thus become an undesirable addition to the water supply. Bacterial, viral and/or parasitic contamination may result.

Human activities. Humans use many chemicals that must be manufactured, stored, transported, and/or disposed of. Care taken in each step can prevent

these chemicals from inappropriately entering our ecosystem. But, chemicals are a part of the environment, and may enter the water supply.

Household cleaners and chemicals can enter the water supply. Whatever goes down the toilet or drain will go through a sewage treatment plant, undergo detoxification and be discharged into a body of water. Household cleansers, scrubbers, whiteners, and deodorizers are creating a monumental job for sewage treatment plants.

"Most inorganic substances in the water supply . . . are trace minerals necessary for life and optimal health."

Industrial wastes, including organic solvents, radioactive wastes, and brine are often injected into underground geological formations similar to aquifers. Some injection wells are linked by passageways of geological formations to aquifers bearing usable water. In some areas, valuable aquifers have become permanently polluted by this process.

Wastes disposed of in dumps, pits, ponds, or lagoons can be a source of water contamination. Sometimes undesirable substances from waste percolate through the soil into an aquifer. In other cases, substances may wash across the ground surface, trickling into rivers or lakes.

Petroleum products are often stored in underground tanks. Such tanks may leak, sometimes into an aquifer. This is especially true of older tanks.

Road salt has also been a problem in some areas. The salt is sometimes stored uncovered, resulting in excessive runoff into surface water when it rains or snows. In other cases, the salt is directly over an aquifer. The brine (salt plus water) can percolate through the soil, finding its way to the aquifer. . . .

Clean water is an age-old concern. Hieroglyphic drawings of water-purifying equipment on Egyptian walls date back to the fifteenth century B.C. Hippocrates wrote about public hygiene and the importance of boiling and straining water to prevent disease. The cloth bag he endorsed for straining became known as "Hippocrates' sleeve".

Worldwide, water-borne diseases such as dysentery still claim as many as 25 million lives each year and cause severe illness in millions more. The great majority of this water-carried morbidity and mortality occurs in countries whose water supplies are untreated.

Even with sophisticated water treatment methods and stringent regulations, microbiological contamination still poses a real health threat in the United States. Since the early 1960s, there has been a steady increase in reported outbreaks of water-borne disease, with an average of 41 per year from 1979 to 1983. Salmonellosis, shigellosis, giardiasis, and campylobacteriosis have been the most troublesome infections. Such outbreaks occur in both private well water and public water supplies.

Many infections occur in water supplies the public thinks are the safest. Pristine mountain streams are perceived as "pure" and "natural," but they are easily polluted by microscopic organisms from animal excrement. Water from mountain streams should be disinfected as stringently as water from any other source intended for human consumption. The Environmental Protection Agency (EPA) stresses that infections caused by contaminated water occur exclusively in water systems in violation of current microbiological standards.

Most inorganic substances in the water supply are metals. The vast majority are trace minerals necessary for life and optimal health. Metals come mainly from four sources. They may be natural constituents of water. Industrial processes, such as electroplating and tanning, use metals (especially nickel and chromium). Waste products from these industries may become part of the environment and eventually find their way into the water supply. Metals in household cleaners, many of which are high in nickel, have become an increasing problem because they can enter the sewage system and ultimately the water supply. Finally, metals such as lead and cadmium may be leached from water distribution pipes within the home, especially when the water is soft and acidic.

Overall, metals pose little danger in public drinking water that has passed through the water treatment plant for three reasons. First, some are essential nutrients that contribute to good health. Second, scientists have extensive data about the human health effects of metals, so that setting standards is relatively easy. Scientists use the lowest level known to cause an adverse health effect and add a margin of safety. Thus, only a fraction of the level known to cause harm is allowed in drinking water. Third, many metals are not found in toxic amounts and do not need regulation. Table 1 lists maximum contaminant levels (MCLs) for regulated metals.

Common Concerns

Concern has mounted that raw water contains increasing quantities of metals. While evaluation and treatment of the raw water, along with monitoring of the final product, should ensure safety at the tap, it would be advisable to change certain industrial and household practices that release these metals.

Can selenium pose a health risk in drinking water?

Rarely. Selenium, which is an essential nutrient, occurs naturally in the environment, higher in some areas than others. Although certain industrial processes release selenium, drinking water is rarely

TABLE 1: Primary and Secondary Standards for Drinking Water

Primary standards (mandatory for public water systems)	
Substance	Maximum contaminant level (ppm or mg/liter)
Arsenic	0.05
Barium	1.00
Cadmium	0.01
Chromium	0.05
Lead	0.05
Mercury	0.002
Nitrate	10.00
Selenium	0.01
Silver	0.05
Fluoride	4.00
Trihalomethanes	0.10
Endrin	0.0002
Lindane	0.004
Methoxychlor	0.1
Toxaphene	0.005
2, 4-D	0.1
2, 4, 5-TP Silvex	0.01
Trichloroethylene	0.005
Carbon tetrachloride	0.005
1, 1, 1-Trichloroethane	0.20
1, 2-Dichloroethane	0.005
Vinyl chloride	0.002
Benzene	0.05
1, 1-Dichlorethylene	0.07
Microbiological Total coliforms	(see footnote*)
Turbidity	1 turbidity unit**
Radioactivity combined radium 226 and 228	< 5 picocuries/liter
beta particle and photon radioactivity	an amount not to exceed a total body concentration.
gross alpha particle activity***	< 15 picocuries/liter

*Number dependent upon sample size, method of determination, and other factors. Water companies must consult a chart.

**May go up to 5 units for no longer than 2 consecutive days if microbiological quality of water is maintained.

***Including radium 226, excluding radon and uranium.

Secondary standards (for aesthetic qualities)	
Chloride	250.0 mg/liter
Color	15.0 color units
Copper	1.0 mg/l
Corrosivity	non-corrosive
Fluoride	2.0 mg/l
Foaming Agents	0.5 mg/l
Iron	0.3 mg/l
Manganese	0.05 mg/l
Odor	3.0 threshold odor number
pH	between 6.5 and 8.5
Sulfate	250.0 mg/l
Total dissolved solids	500.0 mg/l
Zinc	5.0 mg/l

Source: 40 *Code of Federal Regulations* 141-143, July 1, 1987.

a source of selenium intoxication. Americans usually consume far more selenium in their diet than they do in their drinking water. The level of selenium in drinking water is regulated by EPA.

Should I be concerned about lead in my drinking water?

At toxic doses, lead causes severe adverse health effects. Recent reports about lead have been confusing. These reports indicate that there may be subtle biochemical changes occurring at lower levels of lead in the body than previously thought. The significance of these subtle changes is not known. But this doesn't mean that lead levels are increasing in air, food, or water. In fact, these levels are decreasing.

"Asbestos may occur naturally in water."

In November, 1986, it was announced that one in five Americans is consuming water with lead at toxic levels. However, the EPA report from which these news accounts originated was based on outdated figures from an unidentified number of tap water samples. These figures were then used to project the possible number of people exposed to lead in drinking water—yielding an unreliable conclusion.

Some homeowners do have a problem with excessive lead in their drinking water. However, the problem is due to contamination within the home. Many older homes have lead pipes, and many new homes, built prior to June, 1986, have copper pipes soldered with lead. Soft and acidic water tends to leach metals, including lead, into water. Water coolers, with their lead soldered pipes, have also been identified as a lead source.

If you have lead pipes, or copper pipes soldered with lead, test your water for lead. If the lead content is high, run your water three to five minutes in the morning or after any prolonged period of non-use (such as overnight). Affected water coolers should also be flushed. Flushing eliminates lead leached from pipes while water has been standing. Do not use hot water for cooking or drinking as it is more corrosive than cold water and leaches more lead from the pipes.

I've heard much about asbestos in drinking water. Should I be concerned?

The general population is exposed to asbestos through air, food, beverages, drug products, and dental preparations. It is well established that workers who breathe asbestos have a marked increase of certain cancers, particularly of the lung, the lining of the lung, and the lining of the abdominal cavity. But, many studies provide good evidence that people exposed to asbestos in drinking water do not have an increased risk of cancer. Drinking water in Duluth, Minnesota; Quebec,

Canada; and several Connecticut towns has contained high asbestos levels for many years.

Asbestos may occur naturally in water or be leached into water from pipes made of asbestos cement. Studies fail to confirm an excess of cancers from asbestos ingested through water supplies.

Some water from the San Francisco area is highly contaminated with asbestos. An increased risk of lung cancer was found in this area. However, scientists question the significance of this finding because asbestos exposure appeared to decrease the incidence of endometrial cancer.

Should I be concerned about nitrates in my drinking water?

Nitrogen build-up may occur in areas of municipal and industrial waste disposal, high fertilizer use, abandoned feed lots, and septic tanks. The nitrate ion is the form of nitrogen usually found in groundwater. Drinking water is not the only source of nitrate we ingest, nor is it the main source. Far more significant levels come from our diet. Excessive nitrate intake can cause health problems, particularly in infants. To prevent excessive intake through water supplies, the EPA carefully regulates water nitrate levels.

Organic Chemical Contamination

Many people fear that our water supply is threatened by various organic chemicals, particularly pesticides and PCBs. However, the best available evidence indicates that no chemical or group of chemicals poses a nationwide health threat via water. In looking at this issue, two concepts should be kept in mind: isolated contamination and defined treatment techniques.

Some chemicals do find their way into isolated water supplies at one time or another. Such chemicals can render that water supply temporarily unfit for use. However, any questionable water supply is not used without further testing and/or use of defined and effective treatment techniques.

Volatile organic chemicals (VOCs) in drinking water.

Although the word "volatile" may sound ominous, it simply means that a chemical easily goes from liquid to gaseous form. Some VOCs are carcinogenic in laboratory animals and may be carcinogenic in humans. Some cause other adverse health effects.

Trichloroethylene (TCE) is a volatile organic chemical commonly used as an industrial cleaner and degreaser. In high doses, TCE causes cancer in several strains of mice under laboratory conditions. However, there is no evidence that it causes cancer in humans. Working near high levels of TCE may result in skin rashes, a change in liver enzymes and/or nervous disorders. TCE in drinking water is not regulated as a human carcinogen, but rather on the basis of chronic health effects in humans.

Pesticides in drinking water.

Many people have a deep-seated concern that

pesticides contaminate drinking water at unhealthy levels. This concern has been stimulated by such headlines as "Ethylene Dibromide: The Anatomy of a Cancer Scare."

Reasonable Concerns

Some degree of concern, however, is warranted. There have been isolated events of water supplies contaminated with agricultural chemicals. Since 1985, the EPA has verified reports from various states on the presence of pesticides in groundwater supplies. These incidents have all been pesticide-specific and limited to certain geographical areas.

In April, 1988, to determine the extent of this problem, EPA began a two-year nationwide survey of pesticides in private and community drinking-water wells throughout the United States. Approximately 600 community and 750 private wells will be sampled for more than 100 commonly used pesticides plus a number of pesticide metabolites. Results of this survey will help determine the frequency of pesticide contamination in drinking water wells. Another goal is to define the relationship between pesticide use and groundwater vulnerability. The estimated cost of the study is $8.9 million.

Exposure to high levels of pesticides may or may not pose a human health threat. Wise use of pesticides, including the manufacture, storage, transportation, and application of pesticides, greatly limits inadvertent exposure. Moreover, we should consider the value of pesticides. Experts believe:

> Stopping the use of pesticides, it has been estimated, would result in a 9% to 50% decrease in crop production. A 9% decrease would be associated with an $8.7 billion increase in crop losses and a 12% increase in the retail price of commodities. A 50% decrease has been estimated to cause up to a 400% to 500% increase in retail food prices.

A 50 percent decrease in crop production would cause severe food shortages in the United States.

Pesticides

Dibromochloropropane (DBCP) was a popular pesticide until 1977. In 1977, all uses were cancelled due to a high incidence of infertility in exposed male workers. DBCP moves through soil freely, not binding to soil particles. It, therefore, has the potential of finding its way into groundwater. However, it has been found in groundwater in less than 10 states. The EPA does not regulate DBCP in drinking water but proposes to do so in the future.

Ethylene dibromide (EDB) is a pesticide whose use was suspended unnecessarily. EDB is used as a gasoline additive, as well as an agricultural fumigant. EDB in large doses causes cancer and birth defects in some laboratory animals under laboratory conditions. There is no evidence of these adverse health effects in humans.

In 1983, EPA issued an emergency suspension of EDB and called it an "imminent hazard" to human health. Groundwater around some areas of EDB use had become contaminated. A closer look at the situation, however, revealed no emergency. The highest level of EDB found in any water supply is 2.0 micrograms per liter. A person who consumed two liters of water daily (most people do not drink this amount), would have ingested 4 micrograms of EDB, assuming the water was contaminated to the maximum amount detected in any water supply. But, even this amount is not known to be harmful. EDB manufacturing workers are exposed to 10 milligrams or more per day without experiencing related adverse health effects.

"Exposure to high levels of pesticides may or may not pose a human health threat."

EDB will soon be regulated in drinking water. The Maximum Contaminant Level Goal (MCLG) is set at zero and the MCL is expected to be 0.00005 parts per million. This is an unrealistic, unattainable level for any water contaminant.

Dioxin is the short name for 2,3,7,8-tetrachlorodibenzodioxin (TCDD), formed during the production of trichlorophenol, which is used to make the disinfectant hexachlorophene and the herbicide 2,4,5-trichlorophenoxyacetic acid. TCDD is also a by-product of combustion processes, such as industrial and municipal incineration, diesel fuel combustion, and coal burning in power plants. Incidents at Love Canal in New York and Times Beach, Missouri, as well as in Vietnam created concern about the health hazards of dioxin. Since TCDD binds tightly to soil and is unable to migrate into groundwater sources, contamination is highly unlikely.

Polychlorinated biphenyls (PCBs), a family of about 200 chemical compounds, are valuable insulators in electrical equipment, due to their chemical stability and flame-retardant characteristics. Widespread use, relative long-term stability, and inappropriate disposal methods have made PCBs ubiquitous in the environment. PCB use is now restricted, reducing the chance of its escape into the environment. PCBs pose little threat to drinking water supplies. Like dioxin, PCBs bind tightly to the soil, rarely reaching groundwater supplies. PCBs also pose little threat to surface water, as they are nearly insoluble in water.

Minute traces of radioactivity are normally found in drinking water supplies. In many cases, the composition of soil and rock formations through which raw water passes determines the composition and concentration of the radioactive components of the water. The radioactive materials normally found in water are only a fraction of the total background radiation present on the earth's surface. Most scientists feel that the radioactive contaminants ingested by drinking two liters of water daily cause no detectable change in the incidence of developmental, teratogenic, and genetic disorders. We receive more radiation from sunlight than from water. Still, EPA regulates radioactive contaminants in our water.

Two tiers of federal regulations protect our drinking water. Four laws protect raw water at its source, and the Safe Drinking Water Act (SDWA) provides for strict quality control at water treatment plants. In addition, many state and local governments have more stringent regulations than the federal government. . . .

Our Water Is Safe

Americans needn't worry about the water they drink from public water systems. . . .

The chances of getting cancer from drinking water are extremely low. Over a 70-year life span, the chance of being in a fatal traffic accident is 3 million times greater than the chance of contracting cancer from drinking water. Drinking water standards for substances believed to be carcinogenic are generally placed at a level that would cause a 1-in-a-million cancer risk over a 70-year life span.

Our society must be prudent, however, about activities that affect the quality of drinking water supplies. Vigorous programs to prevent groundwater contamination should be used. Private and industrial use of chemicals should be prudent, from production to storage to use and disposal. We shouldn't be quick to call for the banning of known or possible animal and human carcinogens. Such action might give rise to even greater health risks, such as using alternative chemicals with unknown and possibly severe effects on human health. The best strategy is one that minimizes risk and maximizes benefit. The presence of a chemical doesn't always represent a health hazard, just as a cloud doesn't always mean rain.

"The presence of a chemical doesn't always represent a health hazard, just as a cloud doesn't always mean rain."

Microbiological contamination of water continues to pose the most severe real threat to human health. Disinfection has greatly reduced the threat of illness and death from such water-borne diseases as typhoid. But vigilance for clean water must be maintained. All water supplies intended for human consumption should pass rigorous tests for microbiological safety. Even mountain streams, often perceived as pure, may harbor serious disease-causing organisms.

Government and private scientists must continue investigating and setting standards to ensure that water quality is maintained while technology in other areas improves our quality of life.

Kristine M. Napier prepared the report on America's drinking water for the American Council on Science and Health, a New York-based consumer education organization that provides information on the environment and health.

"Bad water is the primary source of disease in the United States today."

America's Drinking Water Is Unsafe

Steve Coffel

Our country is facing an ever-deepening, double-barreled water crisis. The purest, most easily developed supplies of usable water have already been tapped, and a growing number of users are fighting over the dwindling remains. The pollution of those remaining reserves is the other barrel of this crisis.

Alarming levels of contamination have been found in ground and surface water used by vast numbers of people. Traces of toxic materials are being found in even the purest groundwater. Lakes and streams in every part of the country are carrying a toxic burden picked up from a host of sources.

The obvious—but not necessarily the most dangerous—pollution that tainted many U.S. waterways in the past has been removed. Raw sewage and toxic discharges from industry and other sources turned many lakes and rivers into lifeless sewers during the 1950s and 1960s. At least no rivers have recently caught fire because of severe pollution, as did Cleveland's Cuyahoga River in 1969. The river became an inferno when the oil slick on its surface ignited, with 200-foot-high flames that burned bridges and curled railroad tracks into giant corkscrews.

Today's water pollution may not be as dramatic, but it is every bit as threatening. In fact, the poisons routinely discovered in our water represent an even greater threat. Many health professionals say *bad water is the primary source of disease in the United States today*. And the cost of toxic tap water goes far beyond money. It is a toll levied against the health of millions of people and of entire ecosystems.

One of the first questions someone moving into an area is likely to ask is, "How's the water?" The response to this familiar query will vary widely, even in different homes within the same community, but the *real* answer is all too often, "Worse than you think."

The Environmental Protection Agency has identified more than 700 toxic compounds in samples drawn from U.S. water systems. The agency estimates that traces of between 300 and 600 organic chemicals are typically present in one source alone, the Ohio River. More than twenty cities use this river for their water supply. These same cities usually return treated waste water to the river. Some 1,800 companies today emit waste water into the Ohio River under the terms of permits dispensed by state water quality agencies.

But the Ohio is only one case in what has become a deluge of bad water. Health-threatening levels of pesticides, herbicides, industrial by-products, metals, and a host of other harmful substances have been found in both surface and groundwater in virtually every corner of the nation. Cancer, reproductive problems, maladies of the immune and nervous systems, and an overabundance of other serious physical disorders have been traced to bad water.

Even if the water that flows from your kitchen tap is clear and sweet-tasting, it may contain dangerous substances. Many toxic materials are hard to detect even with the most advanced testing equipment. Most modern water-supply systems are tested only for the handful of substances regulated under the Safe Drinking Water Act. But there are *thousands* of toxic substances in use in our industrial society, and most of them have a perverse way of finding their way into water supplies. . . .

A Toxic Stream

A river of contaminants enters America's waters every day. The flow of this toxic stream is most vigorous in areas with industrial development and high-density populations. Moving to rural areas, however, is no solution to water quality problems. Agricultural chemicals, petroleum products, mining wastes, septic tanks, and rural industries are just a few of the pollution sources affecting the water outside urban areas. Researchers at Cornell University have found that more than 60 percent of rural wells contain unsafe levels of one or more poisons.

Toxic waste dumps are the most visible source of drinking water contamination. As many as 2,000 of a total of 50,000 toxic waste sites in the United States threaten the health of people living nearby, according to the EPA. Polluted water is the most common route by which toxic materials get into the environment from toxic waste dumps, mine tailings, and other concentrations of poisonous wastes.

More than 20,000 toxic waste sites have been suggested for inclusion in Superfund, the national cleanup program. The Office of Technology Assessment estimates it will cost *several hundred billion dollars*, $100 billion of which will be federal funds, to clean up these sites.

The eighty million tons of toxic wastes generated every year in this country weighs out to about 700 pounds for each citizen. The EPA estimates that only about 10 percent of this mountain of toxic waste is disposed of where it's supposed to be—in a registered disposal facility. The other 90 percent would yield nearly ten tons of wastes per square mile annually, were it to be equally distributed across the nation. . . .

"The water that drains from the country's farms and forests is often laced with pesticides."

The ways in which water can pick up contaminants are as diverse as the uses to which it is put. Here are the major causes of bad water:

The water that drains from the country's farms and forests is often laced with pesticides, herbicides, and excess nutrients and salts. This contaminated runoff does an estimated $2.2 billion damage annually. Runoff from city streets frequently contains petroleum products, lead, toxic chemicals, and even raw sewage. This polluted runoff flows into lakes and streams and—too commonly—ends up in our drinking water. Some of the sources of polluted runoff deserve special mention, as follows:

Almost 50,000 products containing more than 600 potentially dangerous chemicals are used to kill weeds, insects, rodents, and other pests on our country's farms. Herbicides and insecticides are also used extensively in the nation's forests. Thirty-five thousand insecticide formulations with more than 1,400 active ingredients are now in use. The EPA has sufficient data on the health effects of only about 10 percent of these. It is estimated that 1.6 billion

pounds of pesticides are manufactured in the United States each year.

Most agricultural chemicals are members of one of two broad classes: *chlorinated hydrocarbons* and *organic phosphates*. DDT, dieldrin, chlordane, toxaphene, lindane, endrin, aldrin, kepone, and PCBs are chlorinated hydrocarbons, all of which are federally banned, restricted or at least under review. All are potent and long-lasting, and have been linked with cancer, birth defects, neurological disease, and wildlife and environmental damage.

The widely used *organic phosphates*, although they break down more quickly, are actually more toxic to higher life forms than are the chlorinated hydrocarbons. Malathion, parathion, leptophos, and the flame-retardant tris are among the better known organic phosphates. The immediate effects of this family of poisons on humans include drowsiness, confusion, anxiety, headaches, nausea, sweating, and difficulty in breathing. The symptoms are common to so many disorders that poisoning is frequently misdiagnosed. Acute effects include paralysis, convulsions, long-term brain damage, coma, and death.

The majority of the agricultural chemicals now on the market were registered before 1972, when the regulations now in effect were adopted. The Federal Insecticide, Fungicide, and Rodenticide Act of 1972 (FIFRA), which replaced a law with far more lenient standards, calls for testing and re-certification of the 600 active ingredients of agricultural chemicals that already were in use in 1972. Sixteen of the chemicals have been re-certified. A May, 1987, National Academy of Sciences report criticized the EPA for making it more difficult to introduce new pesticides while stalling on the re-registration of the more-damaging old favorites.

The re-registration process, as it is being administered by the EPA, according to the report, is slowing the introduction of possibly safer alternatives to the poisons discussed here. Chemicals are routinely used long after evidence of the threat they pose has become available. And even when the EPA eventually does "ban" a material because of its effects on human health, exceptions are routinely given to users who say they can't get by without the chemical.

Fertilizers Grow More Than Crops

Fertilizers are also responsible for the proliferation of widespread water pollution. Water in 28 percent of Kansas wells contains more nitrates from fertilizers than are allowed under federal guidelines. Water in fifty Iowa communities exceeds the standard. Groundwater across the entire farm belt is contaminated with nitrates and pesticides. Nitrates also get into the water from sewage plants, septic tanks, and industry, also affecting urban areas. Of the 4,300 private wells tested in the Northeast in a recent five-year period, 700 contained nitrates at levels higher than federal guidelines.

Excess nitrates do more than encourage growth that clogs lakes and streams. They also threaten human health. A bacteria that converts *nitrates* to *nitrites* thrives in the alkaline stomachs of infants, especially those under four months old. The nitrites can render the hemoglobin of the infant's blood incapable of carrying oxygen; this condition, known as methemoglobenemia, the "blue-baby syndrome," results from the shortage of oxygen. It can be fatal. Nitrates themselves may be carcinogenic and in adults' digestive tracts they produce nitrosamines, proven carcinogens. One recent study showed that people living in Iowa, Nebraska, and Illinois, areas with excess nitrates in the water, have higher rates of leukemia, lymphoma, and other cancers. Many other areas have similarly elevated nitrate levels.

As irrigation water passes through the soil, it picks up salts, especially in arid climates. Rivers into which this salty water flows become brackish. Evaporation further concentrates the salts.

When water containing high levels of salts is used for irrigation, crystals build up around plants' roots, making it increasingly difficult for them to take up the water. Plant stress, reduced productivity, or death results. Millions of acres of farmlands are seriously threatened by salt pollution. The Colorado River is six times saltier today than it was before the advent of modern irrigation systems.

Increasing salinity also causes problems for cities. Removing the tons of salts that may pass into a supply system each year is an expensive and, so far, seldom-attempted feat. But high salt levels are posing a threat to water users with hypertension (high blood pressure). Salts can also react with other impurities in the water to create even more harmful substances.

Sewage Plants and Landfills

The 228 million tons of municipal solid waste generated each year in the United States take up more than eighteen billion cubic feet. It would make a steaming heap nearly eighty miles high, if stacked on one acre. (If you think Islip, New York, had trouble getting rid of its single barge of municipal waste in 1987, how would you like to try to peddle this one?) Cities are rapidly losing their ability to cope with such mountains of refuse.

Treatment plants often add pollutants to the water at the same time it is being "purified." Chlorine, for example, can react with organic matter in the water to form *trihalomethanes* (THMs), a family of carcinogens. A 1975 survey of eighty cities' water by the EPA initially alerted officials to the problem. One THM, chloroform, was found in *all* the samples. Three other THMs were also found in most of the cities' water. In 1980, a study showed that cancer rates shockingly were higher in cities that chlorinated their water, apparently as a result of the influence of THMs. Users of chlorinated water were found to have a *53 percent* greater chance of contracting colon cancer and a *13 to 93 percent* increase in the risk of getting rectal cancer, according to a report by the President's Council on Environmental Quality.

Some cities have started using other chemicals to remove biological contaminants as a result, but all the alternative treatments also have side effects that can contaminate water. Ozone, chlorine dioxide, and chloramine are the most commonly used chemicals. Dangerous by-products can be produced by reactions of each with water-borne impurities, but generally less than is the case with chlorine.

"Treatment plants often add pollutants to the water at the same time it is being 'purified.'"

Fluoride added to water for its cavity-preventing properties is also cause for concern in some areas. Too much fluoride can cause bone and kidney damage. The EPA is currently reviewing amounts presently considered safe.

A variety of dangerous contaminants can enter water as it makes its way from the treatment plant to your kitchen tap. Many water-supply systems, especially in the Northeast, are old and literally full of holes. As the water mains deteriorate, asbestos, lead, and other toxic metals, as well as a variety of other potentially harmful materials, may be released into the water. Inhibitors added to the water to slow down the corrosion of supply-system pipes can themselves be toxic. Holes in pipes and pipe joints may allow contaminants to enter the system during times when it is shut down for repairs.

Old, corroded metal water mains are still in use in many communities, letting good water escape to be replaced by toxic materials. Water mains made of wood are still in use in many supply systems. The wood mains are typically more than a century old. Although immune to corrosion, such wood pipes are frequently rotten and the metal bands that hold them together are often in very poor condition.

Estimates indicate that there are more than 200,000 miles of asbestos-cement pipe in U.S. water distribution systems. An estimated sixty-five million people in this country use such water systems. A 1979 survey by the EPA found 20 percent of the cities examined had more than one million asbestos fibers in each liter of water, and 11 percent had more than ten million fibers per liter. Sources of the fibers included asbestos-cement pipe, ore processing plants, asbestos-cement roofing tiles (in Seattle), and naturally eroding serpentine rock (in the San Francisco Bay area).

Studies in Canada and California have linked the ingestion of asbestos with an increased risk of cancer in the abdominal tract, although much research remains to be done. It has been found that fiber size has more bearing on asbestos toxicity than does the number of fibers present in the water supply. No standards governing the substance have been established. Asbestos, when inhaled, is a confirmed human carcinogen.

Asbestos-cement pipe's selling points have been its low cost and resistance to corrosion. But recent research has shown that in supply systems with "aggressive" water, even cement pipe will corrode. Water is termed aggressive if it is acidic and contains little calcium chloride, a naturally occurring compound that forms a coating inside pipes and protects them from corrosion.

Acid Rain

Rainwater (and snow) can become acidic as the result of contact with airborne pollutants—mostly sulfur dioxide from the smokestacks of power plants and smelters, and nitrous oxide from the exhaust pipes of automobiles. The resulting acid rain may be as much as forty times acidic as normal rainwater. The dramatic effects of acid rain on the health of fish and forests are relatively well-established. But increased acidity also deteriorates water's quality. The atmospheric pollutants associated with acid rain have also been found in a recent study to be responsible for an increased rate of respiratory ailments. Rain falling on the Catskills in upstate New York is ten to twenty times as acidic as normal. The area is downwind from numerous sources of "acid," principally sulfur dioxide from coal-burning power plants in the Midwest. A recent report by the Environmental Defense Fund concludes that the high acidity in New York City's reservoirs, fed in part by water from the Catskills, may be speeding the deterioration of those reservoirs and supply pipes, leaching additional toxic materials into the water. The two huge supply tunnels that bring water from the Catskills to New York City cannot be shut down for inspection and repair. To do so would leave much of the city without water, a situation officials don't even want to think about. Yet those tunnels, built in 1917 and 1937, may not have much life left.

We've already discussed the hazards of lead pipes. You may be unaware, however, that the newer plastic pipes so popular today can also cause serious problems. A demonstrated resistance to corrosion, low cost, and ease of installation and repair make plastic pipe attractive to utilities replacing old supply lines. They are also used in many homes.

In addition to vinyl chloride (a known human carcinogen), lead, cadmium, and other metals are added to plastic pipe to increase its resistance to heat. Making matters worse, a variety of toxic compounds are employed in the primers and solvent cements used to fasten the pipes together. THMs (trihalomethanes) can form when impurities in the water react with plastic pipe's components.

Research has shown that micro-doses of all these materials can enter water passing through the pipes, but too little investigation has been done to reliably assess the health risk. Plastic pipe has, however, been banned for use in home plumbing systems in California as the result of concern about the quality of drinking water. The fact that plastic pipe is permeable to gasoline and many solvents and pesticides can also mean polluted drinking water if supply-system pipes pass through contaminated ground, as many do.

With only an estimated 10 percent of the more than 300 million pounds of toxic wastes generated each year by American industry being disposed of safely, it's no wonder second-hand industrial chemicals make up a growing part of the water we drink. Communities with problems at least as serious as those experienced in Woburn, Massachusetts and, Love Canal, New York are located virtually everywhere.

The quantities and toxicity of wastes found at abandoned industrial dumps can be shocking. A dump in Toone, Tennessee, has been found to contain *350,000* fifty-five-gallon drums holding more than *sixteen million gallons* of highly toxic materials disposed of by the Velsicol Chemical Company. Benzene, aldrin, endrin, dieldrin, heptachlor, and chlordane were among the toxic chemicals found at the site.

A dozen dangerous pesticides were found in the water of that community. Some wells were found to contain carcinogenic chemicals at levels 2,000 times above the suggested limit. Residents exposed to the chemicals complained of dizziness, nausea, rashes, liver disorders, and urinary tract problems. Many unusual birth defects, including a baby born with an external stomach, were reported. . . .

"Second-hand industrial chemicals make up a growing part of the water we drink."

The discovery of serious pollution of the nation's lakes and streams—surface water—during the 1950s and 1960s led to an unprecedented cleanup during the 1970s. Rivers such as the Hudson, the Potomac, and the Ohio, which had become thoroughly fouled as the result of up to a century of overuse and abuse, were restored, largely through the expenditure of billions of dollars on improved treatment of sewage and industrial wastes.

There are still significant problems with surface water, as we'll see, but the bane of the 1980s (and 1990s) is polluted *groundwater*. This pollution began long ago, of course, but few were aware of it during the time when national concern focused on surface water quality. In reality, ground and surface water are often linked. Contaminated water from lakes and streams can flow into an aquifer, especially when surface water levels are high, and on the flip side, low water in a river can increase the flow of polluted groundwater into it. It has been estimated that one-third of total U.S. streamflow comes from springs—that is, from groundwater. Only during the last decade have we recognized the vulnerability of aquifers to contamination from toxic materials filtering down through the ground and entering from polluted lakes and streams.

"The bane of the 1980s (and 1990s) is polluted groundwater.*"*

The fact that groundwater can't be seen and is difficult and expensive to analyze are primary reasons it took so long for its poor condition to be discovered. The long-held belief that toxic elements are filtered out of polluted water as it soaks through the sand, gravel, or fractured rock above the water-bearing strata has also contributed to this dangerous oversight.

Even now, far too little is known about the movement of water inside aquifers. Toxic materials can be carried many miles, or can stay relatively close to their source, depending on the speed of the water's flow. Toxic chemicals leached from wastes dumped into an eight-acre site that had formerly been a sand and gravel pit near Charles City, Iowa, entered groundwater and were transported *fifty miles* to Waterloo, Iowa. A veterinary medicine manufacturer had, over a period of twenty-five years, dumped more than one million cubic feet of arsenic-bearing wastes at the site. Channels in the fractured limestone underlying the waste dump sloped to the southwest, toward Waterloo. The Cedar Aquifer, from which more than 300,000 Iowa residents get their drinking water, was contaminated as a result.

Impossible to Predict

It is impossible to predict accurately the movement of contaminants in an aquifer without extensive monitoring. One well can be severely contaminated while a neighboring well, drawing water from just outside the plume of pollution, can be unaffected. Contaminants such as gasoline that float on top of the groundwater may foul water when the aquifer is full in the spring, then stick to the materials composing the upper part of the aquifer as the water level falls during the summer. Groundwater contamination will then stop until rising water levels the next spring cause a new surge of water that smells like a service station.

One of the surprises that has come with the discovery of the contamination of the nation's aquifers is that the concentration of pollutants is *far higher* than those found in surface water. For instance, the 300,000 parts per billion of the solvent TCE found in the aquifer near the Friendly Hills neighborhood is almost *two thousand times* the high of 160 ppb that has been measured in surface water. Another solvent, TCA, was measured at 5,440 ppb in groundwater in Maine, *more than one thousand times* the 5.1 ppb maximum measured in surface water. Such large concentrations of toxics can accumulate because the water in aquifers isn't exposed to the purifying effects of sunlight and oxygen.

For the same reason, an aquifer is much slower to recover from pollution. Toxics that would quickly be rendered harmless in surface water can persist for months or years once they have entered an aquifer, which is why such high levels of contamination accumulate in groundwater. Many contaminants can persist even longer. One town on the British coast that had been a whaling center in the mid-nineteenth century was recently found to have polluted groundwater. Analysis revealed the contaminant to be *whale oil* that had soaked into the ground *a century* before!

A Major Source of Water

Nineteen of every twenty gallons of fresh water in the United States is groundwater. Aquifers provide half the drinking water and 40 percent of the irrigation water used in this country, three times what was pumped in the 1950s. Virtually all rural homes draw water from wells, and 75 percent of the nation's cities use at least some groundwater in their drinking water systems. These percentages are certain to increase as available surface water becomes more difficult (and more expensive) to find, so the news of contaminated aquifers is especially serious. . . .

It can be stated unequivocally that every major river in the country is polluted to a serious degree, despite massive efforts in some areas to reverse the threat. And the condition of the nation's aquifers, although not fully known, is very poor in many areas. Clearly, more must be done—and soon—before the nation's sources of drinking water will be safe to use.

Steve Coffel specializes in writing about water resources and renewable energy resources. He has published Solarizing Your Present Home *and* Dome-Builder's Handbook.

Pesticides Contaminate Drinking Water

Larry Fruhling

Lasso, Sencor, Dyfonate, Bladex, Dual—the names are practically household words in the Middle West. As the last snows of winter melt into the rich black soil, farmer-actors promote these chemicals in a blizzard of television commercials.

The advertisements are a ritual of seedtime, as pervasive as the pickup trucks, driven by real farmers, that tool down the county blacktops, towing tanks of nitrogen fertilizer for another fledgling corn crop.

Most of the time, if the weather is reasonably cooperative, the crops develop just as the ads say they will. Rootworms succumb to Dyfonate's poison, and the weeds wither and die under the curse of Aatrex, Lasso, Bladex, and Sencor. The tens of thousands of tons of nitrogen fertilizers produce corn plants that are a dazzling deep green, and they promise another prodigious crop in late autumn, even though the yield will be far beyond the market's capacity to absorb.

For years, Americans were told that the weed- and insect-killing chemicals applied by farmers would do their job without threatening humans or the environment. The herbicides and insecticides were supposed to cling to the topsoil until they broke down into harmless components, and nearly all of the nitrogen fertilizer that wasn't used by the crops was supposed to vaporize into the atmosphere, posing no more of a threat to the environment than, say, a herd of flatulent dairy cows.

Such illusions are rapidly wilting. From the potato fields of Long Island to the orchards of California, residents are discovering that the pesticides and fertilizers upon which modern farming relies are more resilient and enduring—and hazardous—than almost anyone suspected.

Larry Fruhling, "Please Don't Drink the Water," *The Progressive*, October 1986. Reprinted by permission from *The Progressive*, 409 East Main Street, Madison, WI 53703.

Tests of drinking-water supplies in the towns and on the farms increasingly reveal traces of toxic pesticides and higher and higher concentrations of nitrates from fertilizers. What's worse, unlike polluted rivers, which have a certain capacity to cleanse themselves, groundwater may not move a foot in a year's time.

"The supreme worry is that once groundwater is contaminated, it is very difficult to decontaminate," says Dr. Donald Morgan, a toxicologist at the University of Iowa in Iowa City. "It's inevitably kind of a one-way street."

We seem to be moving down that street rather rapidly. In spring 1986, the 319 citizens of Washta, a farm town in northwest Iowa, received the unwelcome news that their public water well contained traces of five weed-killing chemicals—Aatrex, Bladex, Sencor, Dual, and Lasso—along with a tad of the insect-slaying compound Counter. In a well serving nearby Sioux Rapids, five farm chemicals were found. By summer, officials of the Iowa Department of Natural Resources had surmised that more than one quarter of the state's water wells are contaminated by nitrates or pesticides or both.

Nitrate Contamination

Seventeen different agricultural pesticides and herbicides have been detected in the groundwater of twenty-three states, and the list of hazards is expanding all the time. The U.S. Environmental Protection Agency (EPA), rather belatedly, has labeled Lasso a "probable human carcinogen." Studies have linked Bladex to birth defects, after some laboratory animals exposed to the product were born without eyes. And in April 1986, the EPA informed Iowa health authorities that Aatrex—after having been on the market for twenty-seven years, earning millions of dollars for Ciba-Geigy Corporation—"may be carcinogenic."

Then add nitrates to the concoction that is our

groundwater. Nitrates can come from many sources, including animal manures and human sewage-disposal systems. But new studies show that such sources don't hold a candle to nitrogen fertilizers dispensed in huge areas of the Farm Belt.

Most of the groundwater in Iowa, for example, had a low "background level" of nitrates until the tremendous increase in the use of nitrogen fertilizers in the 1960s and 1970s. In an intensively studied 103-square-mile farming area of northeast Iowa, the nitrate level in groundwater was found to have tripled, following exactly a three-fold increase in the application of nitrogen fertilizers on the region's corn crop. In parts of western Iowa, nitrate contamination of groundwater has gone up ten times, reflecting a ten-fold increase in corn farmers' use of nitrogen. And in parts of Nebraska, nitrogen-contaminated groundwater, pulled up by irrigation pumps, provides a ready-made fertilizer.

The Threat to Infants

Physicians have known for years that high nitrate levels in water can kill infants by inducing a reaction that robs a baby's brain of oxygen. For this reason, nitrates in a concentration of more than forty-five parts per million are considered dangerous for infants, according to the World Health Organization and the U.S. Environmental Protection Agency.

That level is now frequently exceeded in the Corn Belt—particularly in the wells used by farmers themselves. Farm wells tend to be closer to the land surface and thus more quickly susceptible to nitrogen and pesticide contamination.

"Blue-baby syndrome" is not the only serious problem caused by nitrates. Some studies have shown a tentative connection between nitrates and certain types of human cancers, and a research team in southern Australia has found a seemingly strong link between nitrates in the drinking water of pregnant women and nervous-system birth defects, including babies born without brains.

The Australian study compared birth-defect rates among expectant mothers who drank rain water, which is essentially free of nitrates, and those who drank from nitrate-contaminated wells and lakes. The data showed that pregnant women whose drinking water contained five to fifteen parts per million of nitrates—well below the health-warning standard that many nations have set—ran three times the risk of bearing malformed infants. The risk was four times greater when nitrate levels exceeded fifteen parts per million.

Since fertilizers, insecticides, and herbicides are so common in everyday farm life, it is difficult to isolate their individual toxic effects and calibrate their cumulative impact. Consider how difficult it would be to calculate the potential harm of water that has, say, a bit of Lasso, a tad of Bladex, a little

Counter, maybe some Aatrex, some nitrates, and perhaps a smidgen of naturally occurring radiation from the rock formations in which your town draws its water supply.

"The long-range effects of drinking chemically contaminated water have not yet been determined."

"Put that mixture in the context of routinely using the water not just for ingestion but also for showering and bathing, and put that in the context of the trace residues of many of these chemicals that appear in foodstuffs, and what does that mean? Well, we don't know," says George Hallberg, an Iowa state geologist. "We don't know."

The long-range effects of drinking chemically contaminated water have not yet been determined. These may not become evident until ten or twenty or thirty years after exposure—not a particularly long span of time for a baby raised on water contaminated by farm chemicals. Remember that three generations of Americans were heavily into smoking before the connection between cigarettes and lung cancer became clear.

"If the chemicals prove to be carcinogenic," says Richard Kelley of the Iowa Department of Natural Resources, "what we have done is to put an entire population at risk."

One of the first organizations to raise serious questions about nitrates and pesticides in groundwater was the Center for Rural Affairs, a family-farm advocacy group in the tiny town of Walthill, Nebraska. "There are no smoking guns, only dead bodies and the smell of gunpowder," the Center noted in a 1984 study.

Causing Concern

Concern over groundwater has increased in the years since the report was issued, says Marty Strange, director of the Center, but there has been little change in the practices of either farmers or chemical manufacturers.

"It's a question of how much epidemiological evidence you need before people believe that the use of agricultural chemicals is harmful to health," Strange says.

Iowa geologist George Hallberg is helping run a study of groundwater contamination in the Big Spring Basin in the northeastern corner of the state. He has the unenviable task of telling farmers they are drinking traces of the toxic chemicals they've been putting in the fields for more than twenty years.

"I've read your stuff and I've heard what you said," one old farmer responded to Hallberg. "You've told me that as far as you know these levels of concentrations won't have any adverse health effects. But you've also told me there's a lot we don't know. But I know what I use these chemicals for. I take them up there to my fields to kill things, and I don't want such chemicals in my drinking water." Soon thereafter, the farmer hired a driller to put down a deeper well, a solution to his problem at least until the chemicals move deeper into the groundwater profile beneath his land.

As public concern grows over the possibly irreversible contamination of groundwater, the makers of farm chemicals are beginning to realize they have a problem. After several years of negotiating, the manufacturers have compromised with environmental groups on accelerated health testing of pesticides and agreed to kick in for some of the costs. Meanwhile, they've gone on a public-relations offensive to salvage as much business as they can for their old-line products currently under suspicion.

"As public concern grows over the possibly irreversible contamination of groundwater, the makers of farm chemicals are beginning to realize they have a problem."

A 1986 issue of *The Bottom Line*, a publication of Dow Chemical Company's agricultural products group, contained an article on groundwater. Following the farm-chemical industry's standard line, *The Bottom Line* averred that a part per billion is a very little bit of anything, and that were it not for newly discovered analytical technology, no one would probably even know if there were parts per billion of pesticides in the water consumed by Farm Belt residents.

The EPA has adopted a typically ineffectual approach to the problem. The Agency's Office of Drinking Water, making its initial stab at determining supposedly safe levels of pesticides in public water supplies, proposed a zero contamination level for the weed-killer Lasso, noting that it has "carcinogenic effects in animals" and seems "highly mobile in the environment." Nevertheless, the EPA's Office of Pesticide Programs continues to allow American farmers to use Lasso by the millions of pounds.

That may sound odd, but naturally there's an EPA bureaucrat who can explain. Congress gave the Office of Drinking Water a mandate to strive for a "philosophical ideal" of purity, says Joseph Cotruvo, director of the criteria and standards division of the EPA's Office of Drinking Water. The longer-established Office of Pesticide Programs, Cotruvo explains, is under orders from Congress to balance a pesticide's possible hazards against its economic benefit in killing weeds and insects.

"We don't live in Utopia," Cotruvo says. "You always have to weigh things."

In late June 1986 a two-month-old South Dakota girl, Lacy Jo Geyer, died of nitrate poisoning. The rural well water which her mother used to prepare formula contained 152 parts per million of nitrates—more than three times the amount considered safe.

"For those who need a body count," says George Hallberg, "here is one to check off."

Larry Fruhling is a reporter for The Des Moines Register *in Iowa.*

"Groundwater pollution rarely occurs when pesticides are properly applied."

Pesticides Do Not Contaminate Drinking Water

Leonard T. Flynn

Pesticides have been used for centuries to combat pests. For example, ancient Romans used burning sulfur to control insects and salt to kill weeds. Modern pesticides vary in their uses and are far more efficient than these crude chemical agents. . . .

Most pesticides are non-persistent and are degraded fairly rapidly (a few weeks or less) by sunlight, soil microorganisms and moisture, so they do not remain in the environment for extended periods. A few pesticides—for example, some organochlorine insecticides—are considered persistent because they maintain their pesticidal potency for some time after application. This often represents an advantage in that fewer applications are needed. Costs for labor and materials can be lower compared to more frequent applications of rapidly degradable pesticides.

Fundamental to the issue of persistence are the toxicity and utility of the pesticide. For example, the organochlorine insecticides have been roundly criticized for their persistence; however, they are generally less toxic than many other insecticides, particularly in their toxicity toward mammals, including humans. . . .

As analytical methods are developed and improved, identification and measurement of smaller and smaller amounts of pesticides, pesticide metabolites and other trace chemicals become possible. Since the 1950s, analytical detectability has advanced from microgram (10^{-6} g) to nanogram (10^{-9} g) to even picogram (10^{-12} g) amounts. As a result, residues previously reported in the parts per million (10^{-6}) range are now measurable in parts per billion (10^{-9}) or even parts per trillion (10^{-12}) concentrations.

With such incredibly minute quantities now being detectable, pesticides and other chemicals can be found almost *anywhere* in the environment, food, water or human or animal tissues. This too often results in fears of the pesticide contamination of the earth and in calls for more restrictions or bans on chemicals . . . a kind of "toxic terror."

The ability to detect, however, has no relation to the biological effects of substances; that is, "residues only matter if they affect organisms," [according to F. Moriarty]. Presence of minute pesticide quantities or other substances rarely presents even the slightest risk to human health. Since any biological effect is related to the size of the residues, the environment is similarly unaffected by minute residues. The extensive testing of and occupational exposure to much higher pesticide levels clearly demonstrate the lack of risk from minuscule amounts of these materials.

A Sufficient Challenge

Indeed, some argument can be made that small amounts of toxic substances are often *beneficial*, according to the concept of hormesis or "sufficient challenge." It has been observed repeatedly in animal studies that the low dose animals often appear to be in better condition than the control (no dose) animals, e.g., by living longer, being larger, having fewer tumors, etc. The phenomenon of sufficient challenge was suggested in the historic "megamouse" study conducted by the National Center for Toxicological Research (NCTR), which was reviewed by a Special Committee of the Society of Toxicology. The study used 24,000 mice exposed to various amounts of the carcinogen 2-acetylaminofluorene (AAF). The Society's review noted that the results suggested "statistically significant evidence that low doses of a carcinogen are *beneficial*," and that if the extrapolation models are correct, "we must conclude that low doses of

Leonard T. Flynn, *Pesticides: Helpful or Harmful?* American Council on Science and Health, September 1988. Excerpted with permission.

AAF *protected* the animals from bladder tumors" (emphasis added).

Groundwater pollution rarely occurs when pesticides are properly applied. Groundwater is particularly critical for agricultural applications; nearly 70% of it is used annually for agricultural irrigation. Obviously, farmers have a strong incentive to avoid poisoning their own water sources. Contamination of neighboring groundwater subjects a careless pesticide applicator to civil and criminal penalties plus lawsuits for damages.

"Public 'chemophobia'—the unreasonable fear of chemicals—has led to bans on useful products."

Trace amounts of pesticides have been detected in groundwater, but this fundamental question has to be addressed: Are the trace amounts detected toxic to humans or animals or otherwise detrimental to the use of the groundwater? Unfortunately, the "sophistication of present-day analytical methods may have outstripped our ability to interpret what they reveal, our ability to determine the significance of low-concentrations (sic) of contaminants on the environment and on public health," [according to V.I. Pye, et al.]

One study of pesticides and groundwater focused on the need for better understanding of toxicology associated with the discovery of trace amounts of pesticides in water. Public pressure to ban pesticides known to be contaminants can easily arise and this sentiment against pesticide usage can severely affect the agricultural sector for minor or specialty crops because the range of alternatives for these crops is narrow.

Public Health Threats

To assure that regulatory actions reflect actual threats to public health or the environment, not thoughtless public panic, the EPA [Environmental Protection Agency] should establish realistic maximum contaminant levels (MCLs) or else provide health advisories to guide state and local officials who must respond to public concerns about groundwater pollution. Since EPA already requires submission of data regarding health effects in its pesticide review program, federal leadership in setting MCLs seems appropriate. The lack of federal MCLs is widely perceived as a critical impediment to state and local health protection programs. The widespread concern [according to P.W. Holden] is that "public apprehension about groundwater contamination will grow to the point where statewide or national bans will become politically expedient, even in cases where pesticide

contamination is a controllable, localized phenomenon.". . .

With the development of increased scientific knowledge plus the use of modern pesticides and fertilizers, the past 40 years have brought more progress in agricultural production than in all previous recorded history. Pesticides have saved millions of lives in all parts of the world due to disease vector control and hygiene programs. Nevertheless, public "chemophobia"—the unreasonable fear of chemicals—has led to bans on useful products and has jeopardized this progress. Despite the enormous improvements in living standards, it seems "mankind still finds new things to make himself miserable," [according to R. Snetsinger]. The news media and other groups too often sensationalize dangers and fail to provide a meaningful perspective on pesticides and pest control issues. As a result, opinions can become polarized. One report by the National Research Council summarized the situation as follows:

> Users of pesticides fear that they will be regulated to the point where pests cannot be effectively controlled, with concomitant losses of food, while opponents of the use of pesticides fear that people are being poisoned and that irreversible damage is being done to the environment.

The environmental and health fears of pesticide opponents appear groundless. In contrast, the concerns of pesticide users that their livelihoods may be jeopardized by bans or other severe limitations do not seem to be unjustified based on recent events. . . .

Ideally, the main thrust of regulation, science and politics should be to improve the methods of pest management. None of our pest control systems is perfect, and because the pests keep evolving, our present techniques may be even less effective in the future. Research and development on a wide variety of fronts must continue in order to stay even and in hopes of pulling ahead. This means encouraging research to develop better pest control tools, including safer and more effective pesticides. Prudence on all sides—environmentalists, industry, researchers, and regulators—would be welcome.

Science and scientists must not be brushed aside by hysteria and the destructive political decrees which follow. We must not forget that "despite the fears and real problems they create, pesticides clearly are responsible for part of the physical well-being enjoyed by most people in the United States and the western world," [as B.L. Bohmont writes].

Leonard T. Flynn is a regulation and science consultant.

Free-Market Incentives Will Reduce Water Pollution

Lawrence Gregory Hines

In the summer of 1969, two railroad bridges over the Cuyahoga River near Cleveland were almost destroyed by fire. This was not remarkable, but its inception was: the fire broke out in the river and spread to the bridges. The source of the fire, the Cuyahoga River, was at that time a turbid, chocolate-brown mass of diluted industrial wastes, sometimes carrying enough oily discharges to be inflammable, but seldom enough oxygen to support life, even that of leeches and sludge worms that are the last aquatic organisms to survive in the lower levels of a heavily polluted river.

Since 1969 the water quality of the Cuyahoga has improved, as has that of Lake Erie, the Detroit River, Galveston Bay, the Merrimack River, and countless other watercourses in the United States. So far, though, the high promise of the federal water pollution control program has not been realized, and its idealistic goals remain well beyond our reach. . . . Eliminating all water pollution would involve an enormous outlay of resources for abatement, with increasing cost per unit of abatement as the goal is approached. . . .

Air and water pollution control in the United States is an outgrowth of earlier programs rather than a comprehensive redesign of the approach when pollution of the environment became critical in the early 1970s. The federal government expanded a system of command and control and increased the subsidies of the construction grants program to impressive levels. Although economic incentives have been employed in the federal programs—construction grants are economic incentives to municipalities and emissions trading is a kind of extension of the market—other economic incentives have been largely ignored. Environmentalists were

initially suspicious of the incentives approach and some influential members of Congress, Senator Edmund Muskie in particular, strongly supported the grants approach and opposed the extension of emissions trading to water pollution. Over the years, however, environmentalists have relaxed their opposition to the use of economic incentives, which they previously viewed as unethical devices that permitted industry to pollute the environment for a price. This change in position in part reflects the failure of existing programs to achieve adequate progress in eliminating pollution in the United States. Normally, though, we think of economic motivation as being responsible for the pollution of the environment by the enterprise system. How can this motivation be turned around to protect the environment? Possibly . . . this is the case where the market has been "lying in the drawer" too long and we need to consider carefully how it may be used to help the environment.

The Market as a Tool

When air, land, and water are free dumping grounds, there is an irresistible economic incentive to take advantage of this gift. Indeed, where an industrial firm locates and the nature of its production process frequently depend upon the opportunities for disposing of its wastes. The Reserve Mining Company, for example, a firm processing low-grade iron ore, located on the north shore of Lake Superior at Silver Bay, Minnesota, so it could dump its wastes into the lake. When the plant was built in 1951, regulation of industrial water pollution was quite limited and few were concerned about the environment. After years of operation, however, it was apparent that annual dumping of 25 million tons of wastes into Lake Superior was impairing the ecology of the lake and the water supply of Duluth, Minnesota. The wastes from iron ore concentration contained asbestos-like fibers that remained in suspension in Lake Superior waters, contaminating the lake for hundreds of miles from Silver Bay.

Early attempts by the U.S. Public Health Service to force the Reserve Mining Company to dispose of its wastes on land were unsuccessful. The enforcement conference approach lacked authority to obtain Reserve's compliance, and a court action by the federal government required more than five years to attain this end. Finally, however, the court ruled against Reserve Mining Company and ordered it to dump its talc-fine wastes on land, thus checking further damage to Lake Superior and internalizing the disposal cost. The Reserve Company now has to truck its wastes to an approved landfill site instead of disposing of them free into Lake Superior. Unfortunately, court action to correct environmental abuse is generally costly, cumbersome, and time-consuming. Is there a better approach to pollution control?

"Although the effluent charge has been seldom used in the United States, it has been employed in Europe with notable success."

The construction grants program of the federal government provides municipalities with an economic inducement to build treatment plants, but this approach is not designed to change behavior or internalize waste disposal costs. The only charges under the present federal water pollution program that internalize pollution costs are the user tax upon industrial firms and sewer fees that municipalities are required to levy upon households and businesses. The major funding of the grants program comes from general revenue sources of both the federal and state governments, while local support is drawn mainly from the general property tax. As a result, the grants program exerts only the most modest disincentive to pollute. The primary purpose of the grants program is to encourage the states to assume an active role in water pollution abatement. For example, the federal water pollution control program required states to classify and upgrade their streams and rivers to qualify for federal pollution abatement grants. These grants were used to build municipal waste-water treatment facilities to improve water quality in the area of the community.

Financing waste-water treatment plants primarily from general revenues provides facilities for improving water quality, but this approach does not change polluters' behavior. To internalize pollution costs, abatement programs should be financed by charges levied upon those responsible for the pollution, householders as well as industry. However,

industrial polluters usually enjoy a wider range of options to abate pollution or modify the processes that generate pollution than do householders, so the effluent charge is generally considered more appropriate as a means of modifying industry behavior.

Effluent Charges in Operation

Although the effluent charge has been seldom used in the United States, it has been employed in Europe with notable success. The first step in taxing pollution is to determine what should be taxed. No single pollution indicator is ideal, since pollution consists of many ingredients, but the criterion that has most frequently been relied upon is biochemical oxygen demand (BOD). As a measure of pollution, BOD leaves much to be desired: it is not quick, like counting dead fish; it is not accurate, like determining the oil spilled by a tanker; and some pollutants are not detected by the test. But it does have wide application to pollution that is organic in nature and biodegradable, such as most forest products and paper mill wastes, human wastes, food industry wastes, livestock operations, and the like. The BOD test is based on the pounds of oxygen that are consumed in the biodegradation of these wastes. (Some wastes are not biodegradable, however, and the BOD measure is not applicable to these pollutants. This is a major disadvantage of the BOD test.) Since biodegradation takes time, the frame of reference usually adopted in the BOD test is the amount of oxygen consumed over a five-day period of decomposition. This is the *oxygen demand* upon which the effluent charge is assessed as a tax per pound of oxygen.

The most notable early use of an effluent charge in the United States was a levy of 1.3 cents per pound of BOD generated by industry in Cincinnati, which was assessed in 1953. As a result of this charge, industrial loadings on the Cincinnati municipal treatment plant fell off by more than one-third and, what is more remarkable, they continued to drop for the next decade. In addition, Springfield, Missouri, and Otsego, Michigan, are both reported to have employed a BOD tax successfully. But the most famous case of effluent taxation is the Ruhr experience.

In the Ruhr Valley of Germany, water management responsibility has been granted by the state to a group of industrial cooperatives. For over fifty years, these cooperative associations have exercised control over water quality, land drainage, water supply, flood control, and waste disposal in the Ruhr Valley. To abate pollution of the Ruhr River, the associations have adopted effluent charges, using the proceeds from these charges to finance treatment facilities. The effluent charge is determined by one of two techniques, depending upon the area involved, and the pollution indicators are somewhat more comprehensive than those employed in the U.S. cases mentioned above. One pollution indicator involves a number of phases but comes down to the question of how much the industrial waste discharge has to be diluted with fresh water for fish to live. The other is based on a five-day population equivalent BOD test but includes some measure of toxic wastes as well as that of degradable materials.

Allen Kneese, of Resources for the Future, who has written extensively on the Ruhr case, points out that some substances, such as phenols, which are neither particularly harmful to fish in small amounts nor demanding of dissolved oxygen, are extreme contaminants of drinking water. Since these kinds of contaminants are not biodegradable, they escape detection by the BOD test. In spite of this inadequacy, however, the Ruhr system has achieved a remarkable abatement of pollution in one of the world's most heavily industrialized regions.

Water Quality

For over ten years, Czechoslovakia has used a variant of a BOD charge to protect the quality of its waters. All discharges of biodegradable wastes are charged a flat fee based on BOD and suspended solids. In addition, BOD and suspended-solid discharges over a given level must pay a surcharge of from 10 to 100 percent of the flat fee. The Czech effluent charges are moderate, however, even when the surcharge is invoked, and are apparently designed to encourage efficient operation of existing treatment systems rather than to induce significant change in industry's abatement processes. Revenue from the charges may be used to subsidize treatment facilities and process changes and to meet water quality standards in areas where they are below desired levels. The Czech system relies mainly on self-monitoring of effluents with random checks by government authority. Criminal penalties are imposed for false reporting and charges are set on a trial-and-error basis. . . .

The most frequently cited drawback of the effluent charge system is the difficulty of measuring the targeted pollutant, such as sulfur dioxide, particulate matter, pesticides, lead, and other undesirable discharges. Most pollutants can be measured, but many require sophisticated equipment that is costly and subject to malfunction. Reliable automatic monitoring of point sources, although developing, has not yet arrived. This at best complicates the application of the effluent charge; at worst, it makes it unworkable. But the advocates of effluent charges contend that the measurement problem is also encountered in the command-and-control approach—that industry emissions have to be measured to see whether point-source requirements are met. This is not quite true, however, since point-source approval depends largely upon the abatement technology employed by the regulated firm.

The market is a versatile tool. It can be used in many ways: why not simply sell the privilege of polluting?

"If producers and others are charged a price to pollute, it will no longer be possible to contaminate the earth, sky, and waters without charge."

To many, the idea of allowing industry to pollute for a price is shocking. But the pay-to-pollute goal is not indiscriminate pollution. Rather, it is emission reduction by bringing pollution under market control. If producers and others are charged a price to pollute, it will no longer be possible to contaminate the earth, sky, and waters without charge. The pay-to-pollute approach has two objectives: (1) to reduce pollution and (2) to ensure that the privilege of *limited* pollution goes to the more productive producers, thus maximizing output for the economy while holding down pollution. Since pollution rights are not normally traded in the market, however, their sale would have to be supervised by a public authority. J.H. Dales, a Canadian advocate of this approach, describes the process as follows:

> Individual holders [of pollution rights] will buy and sell Rights on their own initiative. . . . Firms that go out of business during the year, or that experience a slump in production, or that bring new waste disposal practices into operation, will have Rights to sell; new firms, or those that find that their production is exceeding their expectations, will appear as buyers in the market. Similarly for municipalities; those that build new or better sewage treatment plants will be sellers of Rights, while those that experience growth in their wastes will be buyers. All of these buyers and sellers, through their bids and offers, will establish the price of Rights. The price will no doubt display minor fluctuations from time to time, like other prices; but it will probably show an upward trend over time. That makes sense; if economic growth (which causes pollution) is to continue, and yet pollution is to be checked, the cost of disposing of wastes must rise— and this increasing cost is registered in the rising price of pollution Rights.

The establishment of a market in pollution rights has generally been viewed with distaste and suspicion by hard-core environmentalists. The act of selling the right to pollute is offensive to some because it appears to endorse polluting the environment. Advocates of trading in pollution rights respond that charging to pollute is an effective way to protect the environment, while at the same time ensuring that the economy operates efficiently.

Unless they curb emissions substantially, heavy polluters with relatively low-value output, such as a tannery or a coke manufacturer, may so befoul the water and air of a region that industries of greater economic value—for example, a modern oil refinery or auto manufacturer—may be unable to locate nearby even if equipped with the most advanced abatement equipment. Ideally, a market in pollution rights will permit high-value producers to compete for an optimum location by bidding pollution rights from lower-output polluters.

Flexible Control

When pollution rights are valuable and transferable, both public and private interests are served by the transfer of rights to those producers who need them most. But in addition, pollution rights may also be bought by individuals or groups, such as the Sierra Club, who want them *not* to be used. The purchase of pollution rights to prevent their use is not unlike the practice of The Nature Conservancy, which buys natural areas in the United States that are threatened with commercial development, such as ocean shore wetlands, stands of virgin timber, and portions of wild rivers. The Nature Conservancy employs the market to block development that would normally take place. Since the market is neutral in directing the use of resources—one person's money is as good as another's—it can be used to protect or degrade the environment. A pay-to-pollute system would allow those who wish to protect the environment to express their desires as well as those who are interested only in disposing of wastes. But more important, the approach is a flexible control device: the pollution authority can cut back on pollution by setting the bid price for pollution rights at a level that will encourage abatement rather than allow heavy waste discharge.

Lawrence Gregory Hines is an economics professor at Dartmouth College in Hanover, New Hampshire.

"The improvement of our waters, both fresh and marine, will require more stringent laws and enforcement."

viewpoint 82

Tougher Regulations Will Reduce Water Pollution

David K. Bulloch

The coastlines of the United States are under assault. Gulfs and bays, the waters washing our beaches, and the brackish waters flowing through thousands of miles of estuaries, flats, tidelands, and marshes are inexorably being degraded. No longer do they sustain the thriving and diverse stocks of waterfowl, fish, and shellfish of past years. Beaches and shorelines around industrial areas are fouled with oil, awash with sewage, and littered with garbage.

Critical coastal habitats are disappearing. More than one-half of all our marine wetlands have been destroyed—filled in for ports, marinas, or housing or used as dumps. Some have been choked by spoil from channel dredging. Others have eroded away as dams, dikes, and embankments have diverted upriver fresh water or cut off seawater circulation.

Whole ecosystems are collapsing under a bath of excess nutrients and strange new substances. This chemical bombardment flows from countless pipelines, leaches from dumps and fills, and runs off from streets and farms.

Vanishing uplands, now converted into developments or cleared for agriculture, once held back the rain, absorbing it, filtering it, and slowly releasing it into the streams and rivers that make their way to the wetlands of the nearby coast. These rains now plunge uninhibited into waterways, carrying with them silt, fertilizers, pesticides, and bacteria from farms, and oils, heavy metals, particulates, and trash from city streets.

Along our entire coastline, municipal and industrial waste is pumped either into a convenient estuary or directly into the sea. Many municipal systems are combined with street runoff; during heavy rainfalls these raw waste streams are routinely diverted from the sewage plant directly into coastal or estuarine water with no treatment at all.

This wasting of our waters coincides with the increasing popularity of the pleasures of our coast and its seafood. Per-capita consumption of fish and shellfish is at an all-time high. So too are visits to the beach, recreational fishing, boating, and the demand for nearby living space.

Little Attention

The slow collapse of these marine ecosystems draws little attention. It takes a visible catastrophe for degradation to make the news and, when it does, the story fades quickly. Recurring anoxic bottom water off the Louisiana coast merits barely an inch of type in the national press. A fish kill may rate a picture, especially if the rotting carcasses wash ashore on a popular beach, but little is said about why it happened. Trash on the beach rarely makes the papers. To hit the headlines there must be a twist to the story. In summer 1987, a fifty-mile-long garbage slick from careless barge unloading of New York City trash at their Staten Island Fresh Kills landfill snaked southward along the New Jersey shore. Nothing unusual in that, but this time what washed up included medical waste, the discards of New York clinics. Hypodermic needles and syringes were beached ashore and the media had a field day. Tourists shied away, merchants and realtors saw business sag, and the governor of New Jersey raised hell. The season ended and the flurry died down and all but vanished from the news until the following summer. More medical waste washed up, shutting some New York and New Jersey beaches for three to four weeks during one of the hottest summers on record. Jersey shore business collapsed, down 50 percent by early estimates.

Meanwhile, the relentless decimation going on in the once productive backwaters went unheralded, except for a few routine notices about new shellfish-bed closings.

Fortunately many environmental organizations are fighting and, in some areas, winning the battle for the attention and concern of the public over coastal degradation. Some coastal states, whose economies depend heavily on the integrity of their beaches and fisheries, have moved to slow down the wholesale despoliation of these vital areas.

Federal Legislation

Is it too little, too late? Since 1972 federal legislation has been in force to help stem the destructive tide. Among these laws, the Clean Water Act and the Marine Protection, Research, and Sanctuaries Act regulate the discharge and dumping of wastes into marine waters, put limits on certain kinds and amounts of pollutants, and set standards for sewage treatment.

Although straightforwad in concept, this legislation has been difficult to implement. Federal funding for enforcement and monitoring has fallen short, and state and federal money for upgrading municipal sewage systems has dwindled.

The reluctant conclusions of a study by the Office of Technology Assessment are: "Current programs do not adequately address toxic pollutants or non-point source pollution. . . . Pipeline discharge and non-point source pollution (particularly urban runoff) will increase. . . . Federal resources available for municipal sewage treatment are declining . . . and the ability of states or communities to fill the breach is highly uncertain and . . . [many] factors will make it difficult or impossible to shift disposal of certain wastes out of estuaries and coastal waters."

The waste deluge is only one of the impacts on these waters. The demand for land and easy access to these fragile ecosystems grows every year and is destroying the very basis of its fecundity.

The root of the problem lies in the steady increase in nearshore population and shifts in our life-styles and our technology choices.

The United States population is now just over 241 million people and is shifting from the center of the country to its coastlines. From 1950 to 1984, the number of people living in marine coastal counties increased by over 30 million, a rise of more than 80 percent. Right now over 40 percent of our population lives within fifty miles of saltwater coastline. Long stretches of coastline are now a contiguous ribbon of houses, roads, and storefronts. . . .

Concurrent with the population shift that started shortly after World War II, life-styles and consumption patterns of Americans began to change.

Each U.S. citizen now disposes of three and a half pounds of garbage each day, twice the amount of waste generated by people in any other western country. This throw-away mentality exacerbates local

garbage disposal, burdening solid and liquid waste with toxins and confronting the eye with ever more unpleasant reminders of our folly.

Our technological choices have created long-term ills. High-compression auto engines create new sources of nitrogen oxides, causing smog and acid rain. We have chosen chemical fertilizers over manure, pesticides over biological controls, and new nonbiodegradable products over older ones made from natural materials. . . .

Is the harm we have done irreversible? Yes and no. That we will continue to modify the world around us and seldom restore much of anything to its natural state suggests we have permanently lost most of our former wetlands. As for the poisoning of these waters, all it takes to clean them up is technology, wisdom, and the will to do it. . . .

Some observers think there are more than enough laws now on the books to clean up the country. The stumbling block is the reluctance to implement and enforce them.

Others are not quite so sure. The gist of present environmental law, they say, is reactionary—one of containment and treatment rather than prevention. Massive treatment may be the most practicable course to follow to meet immediate problems, but for the longer run, it will be too expensive and too burdensome on society. It is far easier and cheaper to neutralize, extract, and recycle, or eliminate waste at its source.

Human waste, as well as animal waste, unadulterated by toxins and heavy metals, can be recycled to the land. Fresh water can be better conserved if less is used to carry off waste. Industrial pretreatment, removing organic chemicals and heavy metals before they enter municipal waste streams, would allow more options for water recovery.

"Clean rivers mean less costly and safer drinking water and more water available for other purposes."

Clean rivers mean less costly and safer drinking water and more water available for other purposes. Clean estuaries open possibilities for aquaculture and expanded production of fish and shellfish and the recovery of waterfowl and other marine wildlife.

To accomplish this requires generating and sticking to a series of long-range precepts about how we will change our infrastructure. Just as the old septic systems became outmoded as population densities increased, so has our current waste technology become obsolete given the evolutionary direction of our society. Combined sewage overflows must go. Even the combination of municipal and industrial waste must be called into question in high-density areas. Coupled with crises in air quality and solid-waste control, an overhaul in total policy is quickly becoming a national priority. . . .

"A strong, coordinated, and self-consistent environmental policy must be invoked, implemented, and enforced."

Leading the fight for estuarine waters is a patchwork of private, nonprofit conservation groups. A few have large memberships, but, on average, most are small and operate with minuscule staffs and low budgets. In October 1987, leaders of sixty-five coastal activist groups gathered in Rhode Island for a five-day workshop hosted by Save the Bay and sponsored by the EPA [Environmental Protection Agency] and the Belton Fund. The upshot of the conference was a unified position on major environmental issues and the selection of those needing immediate attention. . . .

Current legislation and regulations are a bewildering potpourri of fragmented and overlapping responsibilities that are neither fully implemented nor enforced. For the present, federal, state, and local laws must be firmly enforced. For the longer term, a strong, coordinated, and self-consistent environmental policy must be invoked, implemented, and enforced.

The three working groups' recommendations go into more detail:

1. *Discharge permits should be issued only after a "need to discharge" has been demonstrated.* The National Pollution Discharge Elimination System (NPDES), through permitting, controls point-source discharges. The agency should issue permits only if no other options are available and, if granted, the grantee should assure the agency that the best possible pretreatment system is in place.

2. *The nation must establish a source-reduction program.* Initiate incentives to reduce toxic waste by process changes and good housekeeping. Fund it from penalties collected by Clean Water Act enforcement.

3. *Comprehensive standards for water, sediment, and sludge should be promulgated to protect our waters.* Under NPDES now, standards exist for only a few dozen pollutants. The EPA plans to regulate only 126 "priority" pollutants. Harmful unregulated pollutants should be brought under Section 307 of the Clean Water Act. So should standards for sediment and sludge; none exist now.

4. *Permits should be based on the above standards with no consideration of mixing zones.* Water quality standards are now based on the effects of dispersed pollutants and do not take into consideration local

damage by concentrated effluent.

5. *Permits should be designed to address all effects of pollutants on a water body.* Currently, combined waste-load "allocation" covers only multiple-point sources and ignores the additional burdens of air fallout, runoff, and sediments.

6. *Comprehensive monitoring programs should be established to evaluate the effectiveness of discharge limitations.* Waters receiving discharges should be monitored by NOAA's [National Oceanic and Atmospheric Administration] Status and Trends program and EPA's National Estuaries program. Note of any ill effects should trigger immediate remedial action irrespective of whether established standards are violated or not.

7. *Permit fees should reflect the true cost of disposal.* Fees should be levied based on the toxicity of the effluent, which should create an incentive for reduction. Fee funds should be applied to clean up existing problems.

8. *Adequate funds from local, state, and federal governments should be raised for the construction of publicly owned sewer systems.* Public law dictates that secondary sewage treatment is mandatory. Currently, many treatment plants go no farther than primary treatment. For some sensitive receiving waters, tertiary treatment may be necessary.

Non-Point Source Pollution

Polluted runoff, urban and agricultural, must be stemmed by "Best Management Practices" (BMPs) such as conservation tillage, animal-waste control laws, street cleaning, etc.

The Federal Construction grants program should be renewed. More Clean Water Act funding is needed. State funding must be encouraged.

9. *Comprehensive strategies must be developed to eliminate adverse effects from sewage runoff.* During rains, combined sewage overflows (CSOs) bypass the treatment plant and dump raw waste. The cost of replacing these older systems is high, but some way of controlling these discharges must be found.

10. *Require implementation of "Best Management Practices" in coastal areas.* To control agricultural runoff, target the offending areas. Mandate and monitor USDA [United States Department of Agriculture] BMPs and be sure BMPs maximize benefits to water quality. Tie farm subsidy support to compliance.

11. *Source-reduction campaigns to reduce non-point pollution should be required.* Agro-urban runoff can be reduced by source reduction. Curb the use of fertilizers and pesticides and provide "how-to" replacement assistance.

12. *Redirect the conservation title of the 1985 farm bill to emphasize water quality and habitat protection in coastal areas.* The Conservation Reserve Program, designed to retire 45 million acres of cropland, is not taking hold in coastal areas. The Department of

Agriculture should extend current contracts from ten to fifteen years and provide incentives to plant trees. CRP should expand to encompass "water quality" lands as well as "highly-erodable" acreage.

A Needed Plan

This nation has no coherent, consistent, and enforced overall plan that addresses either our current or our future waste problems. Nor do we have a firm, deep-felt environmental conscience to guide us.

The improvement of our waters, both fresh and marine, will require more stringent laws and enforcement. It will impose restrictions we are not accustomed to, and costs we've never had to bear before. It will hurt. But land, air, and water are no longer infinitely abundant.

What we once regarded as free has grown scarce and abused. For our own well-being, these new restrictions can come none too soon.

David K. Bulloch is a past president of the American Littoral Society, a New Jersey-based environmental organization which works to preserve America's shorelines.

"Zoos have begun to change the way they do business, thinking of their captive populations as ecological insurance."

viewpoint **83**

Zoos Benefit Wildlife

David M. Kennedy

At Jiddat al Harasis in southern Oman, the Arabian oryx is back. The sand-colored, long-horned antelope was killed off in the wild 20 years ago. Too fleet and wary to have been unduly troubled by millennia of hunters, it had fallen easily to modern Arab princes with Land Rovers and automatic weapons. Ordinarily the demise of the last wild animal is the death knell of a species—as it was in the United States with the passenger pigeon and Eastern elk. But the international zoo community stepped in this time, setting up an intensive breeding program for a few wild oryx from the Arabian peninsula and a few more captive in Arizona's Phoenix Zoo. By the early 1980s more than 300 of these antelopes were living in zoos, and in 1982 14 were released outside the town of Jiddat al Harasis. So far they have flourished and multiplied under the protection of the Sultan of Oman.

The Arabian oryx is not alone in its good fortune. The National Zoo in Washington, D.C., has brought the golden lion tamarin back to its native Brazilian jungle. The small, beautiful New World monkey is faring well on preserves there. British zoos have reintroduced the scimitar-horned oryx to a preserve in Tunisia, and they plan to bring Pere David's deer back to China and Przewalski's horse—the original Mongolian wild horse—back to the Soviet Union.

Only a decade or two ago, most zoos were content with "postage stamp" collections, with one specimen of everything interesting. But because of population growth and urbanization, the global extinction rate has reached 100 species a year and is predicted to hit 100 species a day by the year 2000. Zoos have begun to change the way they do business, thinking of their captive populations as ecological insurance. "It suddenly and powerfully became clear that many

of the living creatures we all held so dear simply would not exist much longer," says William Conway, director of the New York Zoological Society. The American Association of Zoological Parks and Aquariums (AAZPA) has made conservation its top priority, and a similar consciousness dominates British and European zoos.

To achieve their newfound goals, zoos are adopting a variety of strategies. Some, aimed at ensuring the long-term health of captive animals, are essential. Others may be less so—for example, the innovative "landscape immersion" techniques for displaying animals in ecologically realistic enclosures. But all the initiatives play an important role in conservation since they contribute to the public's awareness of the need to preserve wild species in their natural habitat.

"In my mind, the most important task for a zoo is to be a lobbyist for wildlife," says Steve Graham, Detroit's director of zoological parks. "If we can show people a chimpanzee or a Siberian tiger in a very naturalistic setting, and make them appreciate and identify with those animals, then we're far more likely to be able to get their political and financial support for conservation activities."

Preserving Genetic Diversity

The fundamental shift in zoo philosophy is perhaps best reflected in the establishment of the International Species Inventory System (ISIS), a computerized registry of the animals in 220 zoos. Run by AAZPA out of the [Minnesota] Zoo, ISIS records each animal's birth or acquisition from the wild. It also notes the animal's parentage, sex, location, transfer, and death. ISIS represents virtually every American collection and a growing number of foreign ones. Before it was established in 1974, no comparable documentation existed. Many zoos didn't even keep records for their own use.

ISIS is a useful "shopper's guide" to member zoos.

"If you had to call 220 zoos to find a four-year-old armadillo, it'd take you a long time," says ISIS director Nate Flesness. But the system's real purpose is to help zoos construct sound breeding programs for captive species. Zoo animals have been reproducing with great success for several decades. In 1985, 90 percent of the new mammals and 75 percent of the new birds in captivity were zoo-born. Numbers, however, are not enough.

"The pervasive problem confronting conservation efforts today is that, when populations become small, they lose their genetic diversity quickly," says Tom Foose, AAZPA's conservation director. "Gene pools are being converted into gene puddles as populations are reduced and fragmented, both in zoos and in the wild." Lost genetic diversity can cause "depression" in animals, lessening fertility and competitive ability. Genes conveying resistance to certain diseases are often carried by only a few animals in a given population. Normally, these animals and their genes are selected for during epidemics, but if the resistant genes have been lost, the entire population may be doomed.

To avoid these dangers, inbreeding must be minimized and the genetic contribution of unrelated animals maximized. Accomplishing this can be extremely difficult, especially with species such as horses and primates, whose dominant males sire all or most of the young in given groups. Scientists estimate that some Przewalski's horses, a species long confined to zoos, may well have lost 60 percent of their potential genetic diversity. That's because a few stallions have bred with their own progeny and fathered up to 20 times their ideal share of foals. Such highly inbred animals are much less likely to breed successfully.

"Scientists estimate that some Przewalski's horses, a species long confined to zoos, may well have lost 60 percent of their potential genetic diversity."

Captive species should also have a good distribution of age classes as well: some young, some middle-aged, and some old. So many Siberian tigers were bred in U.S. zoos years ago that there was no room for more. Breeding programs were scaled down drastically, and the population became seriously overweighted with older animals. That could make breeding difficult in the future.

Planning is the key to ensuring genetic diversity and adequate age distribution. "These populations have to be managed *across* zoos, not as individual groups of a few animals in one zoo or another,"

Flesness says. By putting the necessary information in one place, ISIS makes such management planning possible.

Using ISIS data, AAZPA members have drawn up about 40 Species Surviving Plans (SSPs). Most SSPs focus on species such as the Arabian oryx, which are already endangered, and species such as the African gorilla, which could soon hit the endangered list. The plans indicate which animals should mate to preserve maximum genetic diversity. They also show how many should mate—and when—to create a good-sized population with optimal age distribution.

Such breeding programs require transferring animals among zoos, and that raises logistical difficulties. Zoos tend to be full, so finding a berth for a new animal often means that other animals must be shuffled around. That may be no big deal with tiny golden lion tamarins, but it is an imposing challenge with Sumatran rhinos. . . .

Breeding Success

Other survival plans have already achieved some marked results. In an effort to breed as many unrelated Siberian tigers as possible, zoos have moved 100 animals. Many of the most prolific breeders were separated because they, like the Przewalski's horses, were contributing too much genetic material to the next generation. The program has already produced a large brood of unrelated offspring.

Just compiling the survival plans has turned up some startling but worthwhile data. For instance, close examination of zoo records on Asian lions reveals that only 4 out of 100 supposedly Asian lions in North American zoos are really that subspecies. Genetic and blood-chemistry analysis confirms that many are the much more common and less valuable African subspecies. The rest are hybrids. Reproduction of these animals has now been completely curtailed, and their spaces, as they become available, will be filled with pure-blooded Asian lions. Fortunately, there is still a small, carefully managed population of these lions in India.

Zoos have developed sophisticated reproductive technologies for breeding animals and preserving genetic diversity. In 1981, for instance, the New York Zoological Society managed to transplant the embryo of a gaur—a wild cow native to Indian and Southeast Asian forests—into a common Holstein cow. The resulting gaur calf was the world's first such cross-species birth. Other zoos followed suit, with the London Zoo birthing two zebra and two Przewalski's horse foals from pony mares. The London Zoo is a leader in artificial insemination techniques as well. In 1986 it achieved five live births from nine tries in blackbuck antelopes. The Cincinnati and San Diego Zoos are among those that have joined the London Zoo and the New York Zoological Society in pursuing techniques for freezing sperm, eggs, and embryos.

The necessity for this research is clear: survival plans or no survival plans, animals are not always willing to breed when and where others would like. "You may buy a male rhino an air ticket and get him somewhere only to find that the female doesn't like him," says Flesness. It's not always a matter of compatibility. After unsuccessfully trying to breed two unrelated gorillas in Buffalo, researchers discovered that the pair had been raised together from infancy and so did not consider each other mate material. Bongos, large and wary African antelopes, give rise to a different kind of predicament. The male bongo can become so violent with the females he rejects that breeding is extremely risky.

Reproductive technologies could also help build up captive populations quickly and without genetic losses. Fertility drugs can stimulate egg production in many mammals, including the female Arabian oryx. If oryx eggs produced with the help of such drugs had been fertilized in vitro and carried to term in a host animal such as the blackbuck, the oryx might have been ready for reintroduction after just a few years instead of 20. Freezing male and female genetic material is another good idea. This material could be banked for use generations hence—insurance against bad population management or a natural disaster.

Technological Drawbacks

However straightforward all these operations sound, working out each one for a new species is a "major step," says Betsy Dresser, research director at the Cincinnati Wildlife Research Federation. Eggs can be collected only at certain points in an animal's estrus cycle. Yet the cycles of most exotic species are not very well understood, so extensive trial and error is necessary. Hormones can promote the acceptance of embryos, but information on which hormones and when they should be used is known for only a few species—chiefly those of economic importance. Different chemicals and different rates of freezing and thawing are required to store the sperm and ova of various species. Again, only painstaking experimentation can determine exactly what to do.

Finally, reproductive technologies are expensive to develop. And zoos cannot devote the kind of funding to oryx research that the dairy industry has to cows. As a result of all these problems, artificial insemination—the simplest of the techniques—is currently routine for only six species: cattle, pigs, turkeys, chickens, horses, and humans. For the foreseeable future, zoos will probably continue to focus on maintaining and managing existing captive collections. . . .

Many zoos are turning to the ambitious approach of landscape immersion. The strategy is to immerse visitors in close facsimiles of the wild. "A sign beside a gorilla exhibit may consciously present a noble creature endangered by habitat destruction in Central Africa, but unconsciously the exhibit seems to present the gorilla as a felon in a barred cage or as an institutionalized deviate in a tile-lined cell," says Jon Coe, a Philadelphia landscape architect active in zoo design.

"Survival plans or no survival plans, animals are not always willing to breed when and where others would like."

The principle behind landscape immersion seems simple, but it marks a radical shift away from what was (and still often is) standard practice. A mere decade ago, most zoos displayed their bears, giraffes, and rhinos in cement grottos; monkeys in steel-wire cages; and gorillas and large cats in indoor tiled cubicles decorated with steel "trees" and whitewall tires.

Today these exhibits could become the exception rather than the rule. Cities such as Seattle, San Diego, Miami, New Orleans, Detroit, Minneapolis, Chicago, New York (the Bronx), and Tacoma, Wash., have instituted changes. Some have built brand-new zoos based on the landscape-immersion concept, while others have rehabilitated their existing zoos with new immersion exhibits.

Several of the first immersion designs were developed for Seattle's Woodland Park Zoo in the late 1970s. A large part of the zoo consists of a huge, open-air African savanna exhibit, where lions, patas monkeys, giraffes, zebras, hippos, springbok gazelles, and several species of birds coexist. What appears to be one uninterrupted expanse is actually a series of displays cleverly segregated by hidden moats and fences. It's obvious that a deep trench keeps the lions from both the visitors and the zebras. (The lions often watch the zebras hungrily anyway.) But it's not easy to see why the monkeys can't mingle with the hippos. Or why they can't walk off their hill and out of the zoo.

The zoo's trees, plants, and grasses—either those native to Africa or close relatives suitable to Seattle's climate—are plentiful and lush. Visitors follow a meandering path along which several exhibits are visible at once. In one location, a family of pale patas monkeys are perched on a knoll, the stern dominant male doing sentry duty high upon a log. Behind them, giraffes stroll and a herd of zebra flashes by at full gallop. (Compatible species, like giraffes and zebras, are not separated.)

While the savanna is a visual feast for visitors, the animals seem to welcome it as well. Woodland

Park's three hippos were inveterate fighters when kept in cramped quarters in the elephant house. But their new enclosure gives them space to be either apart or together, and they've become fast friends. The little patas monkeys keep busy combing through the long grass of their hillside for seeds scattered by keepers. Occasionally these monkeys band together to drive off interloping crows.

The lions roam the whole of their sizable area, which includes an expansive, close-cropped sward and patches of tall grass large enough for several animals to be lost in. The enclosure also features a cliff under which the lions can huddle and several clumps of concrete "rocks," one of which is electrically heated against Seattle's damp. It is possible to spend a lifetime in the old-style zoos without ever seeing lions so much as move. But Woodland Park's lions move all around, chasing patches of sun or each other. No one who's seen them could doubt that they're better off.

Recreating the Kopjes

The kopje exhibit in the San Diego Zoo is another impressive example of landscape immersion. Kopjes are the large rock islands that dot many African plains. Created as the softer earth around them is eroded away over geologic time, kopjes support complex ecologies quite distinct from those of the surrounding grasslands. The San Diego Zoo built one of these islands out of artificial gunnite rock and stocked it with species found in a typical kopje: little badger-like rock hyraxes, pancake tortoises, dwarf mongooses, plated rock lizards, and klipspringers—small, agile antelopes only twice the size of hares. A net over one section keeps indigenous birds in, and visitors can wend their way all through and around the exhibit.

Before the kopje was built, the zoo's klipspringers were far from the most popular animals there. But now that they're out bounding around, they've become a real hit. "You get a whole new world of respect and admiration for these creatures," says David Rice, director of architecture and planning at the Zoological Society of San Diego.

Landscape architects are at the forefront of the new movement, mainly because they know how to make the exhibits work. Zoos don't necessarily want to have nasty bare-dirt plazas for their giraffes. But many managers have never been able to grow grass on the hard-used ground. Coe and his colleagues came to the Woodland Park Zoo, applied the planting and drainage practices appropriate for football fields, and, lo and behold, the grass grew. Synthetic tubing with tiny pores irrigated plants in difficult corners, while strong, thick, permeable fabrics called geotextiles replaced heavy gravel drainage beds.

Landscape immersion owes a lot to stagecraft. "If we want to get our zoo visitors' attention, we shouldn't present potentially dangerous wild animals as tame pets," Coe says. Hidden barriers both maintain the illusion of wide open spaces and create a slight concern that the animals might, in fact, get out. And when nooks and crannies give animals the privacy they sometimes need, the zoo becomes more than a cage-to-cage slide show. Visitors have to do a little looking.

One drawback of the new exhibits is that they tend to take up more space than traditional designs, although sometimes only a little more: Woodland Park's landscape-immersion gorilla exhibit was built in the same space once used for a set of bear grottos. Furthermore, the new immersion exhibits are being built in largely established urban zoos. As a result, they retain their old constituency, while attracting new visitors. Still, many safari-type zoos like San Diego's Wild Animal Park are in trouble because they must be built away from cities, where people are less likely to visit.

Yet according to Woodland Park's representative Hank Klein, visitor response to landscape immersion has been so positive that zoos are almost obligated to provide such exhibits in the future. Furthermore, many people, their consciousness heightened by television wildlife documentaries, are refusing to visit zoos where animals are kept in cramped, uncomfortable-looking cages. In Detroit, Steve Graham persuaded city officials to build a large, showpiece landscape-immersion chimpanzee exhibit—which at $6 million would be close to twice as expensive as a traditional exhibit. He argued that such an attraction would be so popular that it would make fund-raising easier.

"Precisely because they are so popular, the new exhibits may end up contributing directly to conservation goals."

Precisely because they are so popular, the new exhibits may end up contributing directly to conservation goals. "World wildlife conservation and habitat protection are financially supported largely by concerned residents of industrialized nations," Coe says. "In our exhibits, we're trying to present compelling images of beautiful and independent wildlife living in a landscape undisturbed by humankind." Such images should show the public how important conservation is and how much zoos are doing to help.

David M. Kennedy is a staff writer for the John F. Kennedy School of Government at Harvard University in Cambridge, Massachusetts. He is also a frequent contributor to Technology Review, *a monthly science magazine.*

"When we press wild animals into captivity, even for the otherwise righteous aim of preserving endangered species, we do those captive individuals a harm."

Zoos Harm Wildlife

Andrew Linzey

Many would now accept that wantonness or the causing of suffering to animals requires serious moral justification. That so many think this way is in no small measure due to our Christian forebears active in the RSPCA [Royal Society for the Prevention of Cruelty to Animals] and to what has been called the 'moral feat' of the Society in changing attitudes. And yet despite their principal objectives of 'promot[ing] kindness and prevent[ing] . . . cruelty', the RSPCA has increasingly found it necessary to go beyond a simple concern with animal cruelty as such. The Society's current policies oppose a wide range of practices which *may* cause stress or which *may* diminish the quality of an animal's life, or practices like dissection in school biology lessons, which can 'readily lead to desensitization and a lessening of respect for life'. The Society is against non-veterinary mutilations of animals, such as tail-docking and ear-cropping; the selective breeding of animals which 'produces changes in bodily form and/or function'; the sale of puppies and kittens in pet shops; the killing of lobsters, crabs and crayfish by the usual methods; the giving of live animals as prizes and the keeping of animals in schools where 'adequate provision cannot be made for their physical and mental well-being'.

This extension of welfare concern is both inevitable and logical. But it also represents a significant change in moral perspective. The debate about animals is now not simply about whether we should kill needlessly or cause suffering but also about the way we should manage animals in general and how we should respect their God-given lives.

Some Christians are still apt to interpret human dominion over animals as a licence to control them in every situation. While it cannot be denied that Christian teaching gives humans the responsibility of controlling and managing the earth, there are two vital qualifications. The first is that this power must be exercised *under God*. The second is that our manipulation of creation must be in conformity with God's own moral design for the cosmos. Correctly perceived, therefore, humans have no absolute rights. Any 'right' we claim for humans is derived from, dependent on, and must be morally grounded in the will of God. The challenge in this section is to spell out the distinction between moral and immoral management.

Captive Animals

The concern here is with the captivity of *wild* animals. Are wild animals best left alone? Can we justify the keeping of them in zoological gardens or safari parks? We need to begin by understanding the harm done to wild animals by captivity. To deny liberty to a wild animal involves the diminishing of that animal's life. It is an inherent characteristic of wild things to be free. We may reasonably suppose that in almost all cases the denial of this inherent characteristic involves stress, frustration, anxiety and even aggression. One work on the 'failure' of British animal collections, by two people, [Bill Jordan and Stefan Ormrod] with a lifetime's experience, claims that 'many animals remain neglected and live in conditions ranging from poor to what can only be described as absolutely inhumane'. As if the denial of liberty was not enough by itself, many environmental conditions for animals are unsuitable, restricting and boring. Ironically it is the lack of 'normal' stress in the caged environment that helps compound the deprivation. The RSPCA is opposed to 'any degree of confinement likely to cause distress or suffering' and specifically to the 'capture, transportation and acclimatisation of animals' inevitable in the zoo trade.

But quite apart from these humanitarian concerns, there is a theological issue which is frequently overlooked. It is that animals have some right to be free. Not only does Genesis envisage the giving of land as a common possession of man and animals, but also divine 'blessing' is designed to give creatures freedom to be themselves. 'Listen my people,' says the Lord in rejecting blood sacrifices:

> All the beasts of the forest are mine and the cattle in thousands on my hills. I know every bird on those hills, the teeming life of the fields is my care.

In other words, God rejoices in the life of free animals he has made. He does not need them to be offered in sacrifice because they are already his and within his care. There is of course something cursed as well as blessed about the wild creation that lives around us. But wildness is not synonymous with being cursed. Indeed the wildness of nature has its own particular praise to offer:

> All mountains and hills; all fruit-trees and all cedars; wild beasts and cattle, creeping things and winged birds . . . O praise the Lord.

The taming, manipulating and subduing of nature is not self-evidently a Christian pursuit. The precise opposite can be claimed: it could be our responsibility to respect what God has given and let it be.

Potential justifications for keeping wild animals captive are threefold: entertainment, education and conservation. The first is surely the weakest. The harm done to animals cannot be justified, even in utilitarian terms, by whatever entertainment value such parks may possess. But, of course, it is seldom the seemingly altruistic desire to entertain and amuse that is at stake—it is the desire for profit. One worrying feature of the proliferation of zoos in Britain consists in their increasing commercialization. 'For many zoo operators', argue Bill Jordan and Stefan Ormrod, 'the wild animals are simply goods placed on display in exchange for hard cash'. *All* zoos, however high-minded their intentions, also hope to entertain, give pleasure or provide recreation. But to entertain at the animals' expense only compounds the wrong done to them. Are sources of entertainment so scarce, we many ask, that they can be justified even at the cost of animal misery?

"God rejoices in the life of free animals he has made."

The second justification, namely education, takes us a little further, but only a little. For what precisely have humans to learn about wild animals when they are deprived of their liberty? Many of the inmates of our zoos are not 'normal' specimens in the sense that we may view them interacting in their usual environments or with their chosen companions. It is sometimes argued that there can be no substitute for 'seeing the real thing', and that children especially are given an impression of animals that is often positive and admiring. But is there something 'positive' about seeing caged or confined animals? Is it not at least possible to argue that what children in particular 'see' in zoos is damaging to a sense of the dignity of animals? In point of fact, *few* zoos run educational programmes that are worth the name beyond that of 'spot this sort of animal' and 'spot this other sort'. Any educational aspect of zoos is frequently secondary to the desire to make money, to entertain or to win prestige for the individual zoo owner. A Government inquiry into dolphinariums in Britain commissioned the views of unaligned educationalists who concluded that 'the unnatural, anthropomorphic exhibition of animals as performers may be merely showing the majority who witness the displays . . . that the animals' existence is legitimated only by their ability to meet the demands for human entertainment'. Far from being useful, those consulted concluded that such displays were *'anti-educational'*.

The Concern for Conservation

The fourth justification concerning conservation is frequently the most seductive. Surely it is right to make some animals captive, perhaps only for a short time, if the species can be returned to the wild? In point of fact, very few zoos indeed are involved in conservation of this kind, and for obvious reasons. Captivity can very easily make animals the kind of creatures that are not returnable to the wild; prolonged captivity can induce neurosis, impotence, aggression or death. But let us accept that there may be some situations where the enforced capture, transport and captivity of some animals may conceivably lead to their successful transplantation in other regions. Is not the relative deprivation of some animals justifiable in the light of the ultimate goal of conservation?

What this argument assumes is that the rights of some individual animals should be subordinated to those of the species concerned. In other words, for the good of the species, some individuals within it may legitimately suffer deprivation or harm or both. Indeed some conservationists like Aldo Leopold hold that 'a thing is right when it tends to preserve the integrity, stability, and beauty of the biotic community'. Such a view, as Tom Regan indicates, might be labelled 'environmental fascism'. It implies that 'the individual may be sacrificed for the greater biotic good', and if the rights of animals can be thus traded away, what prospect might there be for human beings? This is not to suppose that the rights of animals or humans are absolute. It is only to deny that it is morally satisfactory to subordinate the rights of an individual to those of the species as a matter of course. We may sometimes be justified in infringing the rights of an individual animal where there is a clear and direct situation of conflict between respective right-holders or where such infringement is necessary for the greater good of the *individual* animal concerned. But we treat animals and humans unjustly if we proceed on the assumption that their rights can normally be sacrificed to the interests of others.

But of course conservationists frequently argue that the plight of endangered species is not a 'normal' situation and that extraordinary measures are required to save threatened species. The argument again is not as strong as it looks.

In most if not almost all situations, animals are threatened with extinction because their rights are not respected in the first place. Humans destroy their habitats, hunt them mercilessly and trade in their dead bodies. Endangered species are simply one more sympton of our failure to grasp the claims of animals as individual beings. 'Were we to show proper respect for the rights of the individuals who make up the biotic community,' asks Regan, 'would not the *community* be preserved?' In short: when we press wild animals into captivity, even for the otherwise righteous aim of preserving endangered species, we do those captive individuals a harm that cannot be outweighed by the potential benefit that may accrue to the species concerned. Those who are concerned to let animals be, should first set their sights on preserving the habitats where animals already live. . . .

"In most if not almost all situations, animals are threatened with extinction because their rights are not respected in the first place."

We return to our opening remarks concerning the need for humility as well as vision. What we need is *progressive* disengagement from our inhumanity to animals. The urgent and essential task is to invite, encourage, support and welcome those who want to take some steps along the road to a more peaceful world with the non-human creation. We do not *all* have to agree upon the most vital steps, or indeed the most practical ones. What is important is that we all move some way on, if only by one step at a time, however falteringly. To my mind every pheasant which is left to live rather than shot is a gain. If that is all the humanity one hunter can muster at least we have saved one creature. If we can encourage one researcher to save one mouse, at least that is one mouse saved. If we can persuade an intensive

farmer to refrain from de-beaking one hen then at least some small burden of suffering is lessened in the world. The enemy of progress is the view that everything must be changed before some real gains can be secured. Some may disagree with the major contours as well as the details of the vision I have outlined. Some may argue that such and such a judgement is too hard or such and such an option is too soft. There can be areas of genuine disagreement even among those who are committed to a new world of animal rights. But what is essential for this new world to emerge is the sense that each of us can change our individual worlds, however slightly, to live more peaceably with our non-human neighbours.

A Moral Choice

'I could not but feel with a sympathy full of regret all the pain that I saw around me, not only that of men, but that of the whole creation,' wrote Albert Schweitzer in a telling passage in his autobiography. 'From this community of suffering, I have never tried to withdraw myself.' He concluded: 'It seemed to me a matter of course that we should all take our share of the burden of suffering which lies upon the world.' The vision of Christ-like lordship over the non-human is practically costly. Our moral choices inevitably entail sacrifice and pain. In this way we anticipate, if not actually realize, the future joy of all God's creatures.

Andrew Linzey is chaplain and director of studies at the Center for the Study of Theology at the University of Essex, England. He is a campaigner for animal rights and authored the study Animal Rights, *in addition to other books and articles.*

*"Hunting... is an American tradition.
A tradition of killing, crippling,
extinction, and ecological destruction."*

viewpoint 85

Hunters Harm the Environment

Edward Abbey and The Fund for Animals

Editor's note: The following viewpoint is in two parts. The first part was written by Edward Abbey. The second part was provided by The Fund for Animals.

I

I was born, bred, and raised on a farm in the Allegheny Mountains of Pennsylvania. A little sidehill farm in hardscrabble country, a land of marginal general farms, of submarginal specialized farms—our specialty was finding enough to eat without the shame of going on "The Relief," as we called it during the Great Depression. We lived in the hills, surrounded by scrubby third-growth forests, little coal-mining towns down in the valleys, and sulfur-colored creeks meandering among the corn patches. Few people could make a living from farming alone: my father, for example, supplemented what little we produced on the farm by occasional work in the mines, by driving a school bus, by a one-man logging business, by peddling subscriptions to a farmer's magazine, and by attending every private and public shooting match within fifty miles of home—he was an expert small-bore rifleman and a member, for several years running, of the Pennsylvania state rifle team; he still has a sashful of medals to show for those years. He almost always brought back from the matches a couple of chickens, sometimes a turkey, once a yearling pig.

None of this was quite enough, all together, to keep a family of seven in meat, all the time, through the frozen Appalachian winters. So he hunted. We all hunted. All of our neighbors hunted. Nearly every boy I knew had his own rifle, and maybe a shotgun too, by the time he was twelve years old. As I did myself.

What did we hunt? Cottontail rabbit, first and foremost; we'd kill them, clean them, cut them up;

my mother deep-fried them in bread crumbs and cooked and canned the surplus in Mason jars, as she did tomatoes, string beans, succotash, pork sausage, peaches, pears, sweet corn, everything else that would keep. We had no deep freeze; in fact, we had no electricity until the Rural Electrification Administration reached our neck of the woods in 1940.

So rabbit was almost a staple of our diet; fencerow chicken, we called it, as good and familiar to us as henyard chicken. My father seldom bothered with squirrel, but my brothers and I potted a few with our little Sears, Roebuck single-shot .22s, out among the great ancient white oaks and red oaks that were still standing in our woodlot. Squirrel meat can be good, but not so good as rabbit, and a squirrel is much harder to kill; we missed about ten for every one we hit.

Our only gamebird was the ringneck pheasant, rising with a thrilling rush from the corn stubble. My father bagged a few of those with his old taped-together double-barrel shotgun. Not many. He didn't like to hunt with a shotgun. Wasteful, he thought, and the shells were too expensive, and besides, he disliked chewing on lead pellets. The shotgun was primarily a weapon (though never needed) for home defense. Most of the time he shot rabbits with his target rifle, a massive magazine-loaded .22 with a peep sight. Shot them sitting.

Not a Sportsman

Was that legal? Probably not. I don't remember. But he had a good eye. And he was a hunter—not a sportsman. He hunted for a purpose: to put meat on the table.

My father usually bought a license for deer, when he could afford it, but only because the penalty for getting caught with an untagged deer would have been a small financial catastrophe. In any case, with or without a license, he always killed his deer on the

From ONE LIFE AT A TIME, PLEASE by Edward Abbey. Copyright © 1988 by Edward Abbey. Reprinted by permission of Henry Holt and Company, Inc. The Fund for Animals, "Hunting Fact Sheet #1: An Overview of Killing for Sport," October 1989. Reprinted with permission.

evening before opening day, while those red-coated fellows from the towns and cities were busy setting up their elaborate camps along the back roads, stirring the deer into movement. My father was not a stickler for strict legality, and he believed, as most country men did, that fear tainted the meat and therefore it was better to get your deer before the chase, the gunnery—The Terror—began. We liked our venison poached. (As a result I find that after these many years I retain more admiration and respect for the honest serious poacher than I do or ever could for the so-called gentleman hunter.)

"I retain more admiration and respect for the honest serious poacher than I do or ever could for the so-called gentleman hunter."

My old man practiced what we called "still hunting." On the day before opening, about noon, when the deer were bedded down for their midday siesta, he'd go out with his gun, his cornfodder-tan canvas coat with its many big pockets, and his coal miner's oval-shaped lunch bucket full of hot coffee and sandwiches and mother's stewed-raisin cookies, and he'd pick a familiar spot along one of the half-dozen game paths in our neighborhood, settle down in the brush with his back to a comfortable tree, and wait. And keep on waiting, sometimes into the long autumn twilight, until at last the first somewhat nervous, always uneasy deer appeared. Doe or buck—he always shot whatever came first. You can't eat antlers, he pointed out.

Usually he shot his deer with a "punkin ball" from the battered, dangerous, taped-up shotgun. But at least once, as I recall, he dropped a doe with his target rifle, like a rabbit. Drilled her right between the eyes with a neat little .22-caliber long-rifle bullet. Those deer slugs for the shotgun were expensive.

Then he'd drag the deer into the brush, out of sight, and wait some more, to see if anyone had noticed the shot. When nothing happened, he hung the deer to the nearest tree limb, dressed it out, ate the liver for supper. If he had a license, he would wait through the night, tag the deer, and take it home by wheel first thing in the morning. If not, he slung the carcass over his shoulders and toted it home through the woods and over the hills in the dark. He was a strong, large, and resolute sort of man then, with a wife and five children to feed. Nowadays, getting on a bit—he was born in 1901—he is still oversize, for an old man, but not so strong physically. Nor so resolute. He works only four or five hours a day, alone, out in the woods, cutting down trees, and then quits. He gave up deer hunting thirty years ago.

Why? "Well," he explains, "we don't need the meat anymore."

Now that was how my brothers and I learned about hunting. My brothers still like to go out for deer now and then, but it's road hunting, with good companions, not "still hunting." I wonder if anybody hunts in that fashion these days. I did a lot of deer hunting in New Mexico from 1947 through the 1950s, when I was living on seasonal jobs with the Park Service and Forest Service, often married, trying to write books. As my father had taught me, I usually went out on the day before opening. Much safer then, for one thing, before those orange-vested hordes were turned loose over the landscape, shooting at everything that moves.

Gradually, from year to year, my interest in hunting, as a sport, waned away to nothing. I began to realize that what I liked best about hunting was the companionship of a few good trusted male buddies in the out-of-doors. Anything, any excuse, to get out into the hills, away from the crowds, to live, if only for a few days, beyond the wall. That was the point of hunting.

So why lug a ten-pound gun along? I began leaving my rifle in the truck. Then I left it at home. The last time I looked down the bore of that old piece there was a spider living there.

"We don't need the meat anymore," says my old man. And I say, Let the mountain lions have those deer; they need the meat more than I do. Let the Indians have it, or hungry college students, or unpublished writers, or anyone else trying to get by on welfare, food stamps, and hope. When the money began arriving from New York by airmail, those checks with my name on them, like manna from heaven, I gave up hunting deer. I had no need. Every time you eat a cow, I tell myself, you are saving the life of an elk, or two mule deer, or about two dozen javelina. Let those wild creatures live. Let being be, said Martin Heidegger. Of course, they're going to perish anyway, I know, whether by lion or wolf or starvation or disease—but so are we.

Hunting with a Purpose

Henry David Thoreau, notorious nature lover, was also a hunter and fisherman, on occasion. And among the many things that Thoreau wrote on the matter was this, from *Walden*:

> No humane being, past the thoughtless age of boyhood, will wantonly murder any creature which holds its life by the same tenure he does. The hare in its extremity cries like a child. I warn you, mothers, that my sympathies do not make the usual *philanthropic* distinctions. . . . But I see that if I were to live in a wilderness, I should become . . . a fisher and hunter in earnest.

In earnest. There lies the key to the ethical issue. Earnestness. Purpose. The killing is justified by the need and must be done in a spirit of respect, reverence, gratitude. Otherwise hunting sinks to the level of mere fun, "harvesting animals," *divertissement*, sadism, or sport. *Sport!*

Where did the ugly term "harvesting" come from? To speak of "harvesting" other living creatures, whether deer or elk or birds or cottontail rabbits, as if they were no more than a crop, exposes the meanest, cruelest, most narrow and homocentric of possible attitudes toward the life that surrounds us. The word reveals the pervasive influence of utilitarian economics on the modern mind. Such doctrine insults and violates both humanity and life; and humanity will be, already is, the victim of it.

Now I have railed against the sportsman hunter long enough. I wished only to explain why first my father and then I have given up hunting, for the time being. When times get hard again, as they surely will, when my family and kin need meat on the table, I shall not hesitate to take that old carbine down from the wall and ramrod that spider out of the barrel and wander back once more into the hills.

II

Hunting, it is true, is an American tradition. A tradition of killing, crippling, extinction, and ecological destruction.

In the 19th and 20th Centuries, hunters have helped wipe out dozens of species, such as the bountiful passenger pigeon and the heath hen, and brought a long list of others, including the bison and the grizzly bear, to the edge of extinction. In fact, in its report on the Endangered Species Act of 1973, the U.S. Senate's Commerce Committee stated, "Hunting and habitat destruction are the two major causes of extinction."

As a result of the passage of the Endangered Species Act, the hunting of imperiled species has slowed considerably. But that law has not stopped hunters from maiming and massacring many millions of wild animals every year. Unquestionably, hunting remains America's number one bloodsport.

With an arsenal of rifles, shotguns, muzzle-loaded weapons, handguns, and high-powered bows and arrows, sport hunters kill more than 200 million animals yearly. They cripple, orphan, and harass millions more—all for their pathetic idea of "recreation."

Here are the details of what hunters accomplished [in just one] year.

• Hunters crippled and killed more than 10 million ducks, even though duck numbers are at their lowest levels in decades. In the process, hunters routinely shot protected birds, including threatened and endangered ones, for fun and for failure to identify them properly.

• Hunters killed more than 50 million mourning doves, who are gentle and inoffensive birds. Much of the carnage occurred during September, the month that mourning doves nest their young.

• Hunters often justify their "sport" by claiming that it keeps deer from overpopulating. But hunters gun down predators wherever they find them. Aided by high-powered weapons and sometimes by dogs and baits, hunters killed 30,000 black bears and more than 1,000 brown and grizzly bears. They also slaughtered wolves in Alaska, mountain lions in 11 of the 12 western states where they live, and coyotes (more than 250,000) in each of the 48 contiguous states.

• Native hunters shot non-native ringneck pheasants and bobwhite quail by the millions. Many of these birds are pen-reared and released into the wild just to be shot. Even if the pheasants, native to the Far East, survive the hunters' onslaught, their fate is deadly certain. Soon after release, nearly all the birds succumb to exposure, starvation, or predation because they are physically so ill-equipped to survive.

• From Asiatic deer to African lions to European boars, exotic animals—imported or obtained from auctions or zoos and then bred for "surplus"—are nothing more than living, breathing targets for fee-paying hunters at private shooting preserves. On these so-called preserves, even if the animals did run from hunters, (and they usually don't), they'd have no place to hide. To accommodate the fee-paying and weapon-wielding hunters, preserve operators offer "guaranteed kills." Thus, as desirable "trophies," the animals not only get a prison sentence on fenced-in preserves, but also a firing squad.

"To accommodate the fee-paying and weapon-wielding hunters, preserve operators offer 'guaranteed kills.'"

The hit list also includes deer, elk, moose, musk ox, bison, pronghorn, javelina, turkey, raccoon, rabbit, squirrel, and dozens of others. Almost any creature with four legs or two wings is unfair game for the hunter. Occasionally, two-legged animals also fall victim to hunters. In 1987, 110 people were killed and more than 1,500 injured in hunting accidents. . . .

It's no exaggeration to say that our wildlife, our wild lands, and our wildlife agencies are being held at gunpoint.

Edward Abbey was a noted American author whose books include Fire on the Mountain *and* Desert Solitaire. *The Fund for Animals is an organization based in New York City that works to protect wildlife, fight animal cruelty, and save endangered species.*

"Most hunters, in fact, consider themselves conservationists."

Hunters Help the Environment

George Reiger

A century ago, when John W. Noble, Benjamin Harrison's Secretary of the Interior, sought to praise his President, he called him a "sportsman." Harrison's experiences as a hunter, Noble said, accounted in large measure for his success as a lawyer and politician. In those days, the only true sports were perceived to be hunting and angling. The rest were just games. Teddy Roosevelt was of a similar persuasion, only too pleased to be photographed in 1909 leaning casually against an elephant he had just shot.

Fast forward to December 1988. President-elect Bush is denounced by animal-rights groups because he's gone quail hunting in Texas. "I don't think I could shoot a deer," he assures reporters.

Presidents may feel they have little choice about answering reporters' questions, but today's big-game hunters, all too familiar with the negative feelings of large numbers of Americans toward their sport, tend to clam up. When cornered, they turn the conversation toward their efforts in behalf of wildlife conservation.

Yet the sport has been growing. According to the United States Fish and Wildlife Service, the number of Americans who shoot big game has doubled in the last two decades to about 12.6 million. And the increase reflects not just deer hunters but the high end of the sport—the men and women who pursue game in Africa and around the world. "There are more and more people hunting big game," says Vern Edewaard, president of Safari Club International, a hunting and conservation organization. "First of all, people have more money. And they love the wilderness experience and the chase. Even if you don't get anything, that doesn't negate the hunt."

For Peter L. Horn 2d, the 42-year-old president of

the Princeton Group, a New York textile importer, the "Rolls-Royce of trophy hunting" is the elusive African antelope called the bongo. "There's no easy way to get one," he says. "You're walking 10 to 15 miles a day in a rain forest. It gets to be an obsession." William I. Spencer, retired president of Citicorp, has made seven safaris to Africa and collected four of the Big Five—elephant, Cape buffalo, lion and leopard—but not the rhino. His favority trophy, however, is the bongo. On his first bongo safari, he never even saw one of the animals. It was not until his fourth bongo hunt that he got his prize. Not one in a hundred visitors to his Manhattan office has the least idea how exceptional the trophy behind Spencer's chair is, but those who *do* have an inside track with Spencer.

Africa has always been the mecca of the big-game hunter, but the circumstances of the hunt have changed since Teddy Roosevelt's day. As animals such as the black rhino have been put on the endangered list, they have come off the trophy list. Some countries, like Kenya, have eliminated shooting safaris altogether. In others, the price has soared: a 21-day safari to hunt elephant in Tanzania costs about $21,000. In South Africa, hunting has been privatized. Vast game ranches allow hunters to chase plains animals such as the impala, the eland and the wildebeest.

Big-Game Hunting

Today, more and more big-game hunters are looking beyond Africa. Horn has hunted stag in Hungary, wild boar in Uruguay and jaguar in Guatemala. Garland R. Rolling, a New Orleans banker and attorney, has pursued Kodiak bears in the Alaskan brush and plans to stalk caribou in Newfoundland. In only a year, Lloyd Zeman, the president of Safari Outfitters of Cody, Wyo., has led seven expeditions to the Soviet Union to hunt Siberian snow sheep and other game. "It takes a

George Reiger, "And Still They Go A-Hunting," *The New York Times Magazine*, June 11, 1989. Copyright © 1989 by The New York Times Company. Reprinted by permission.

special kind of person to hunt sheep," he says. "That person has to be able to enjoy hardship."

According to William Spencer, who graduated from a childhood spent shooting prairie dogs on a ranch in Wyoming to African safaris, the sport has other values. "Hunting sharpens your wits, strengthens resolve and teaches humility," he says. "Those are all good qualities for major-league bankers."

"We enjoy competition, and those of us who also enjoy big-game hunting have never found a competitor as unpredictable or challenging as those we find in the wild."

"Show me a successful businessman," says Roy A. Duddy, a 44-year-old lawyer and entrepreneur from Peterborough, N.H., "and I'll show you someone who likes taking risks. We enjoy competition, and those of us who also enjoy big-game hunting have never found a competitor as unpredictable or challenging as those we find in the wild."

Duddy's closest call came when he was on a traditional foot safari in Zimbabwe, searching for elephants with a professional hunter. "We were stalking the patriarch of the herd, a big bull, 11 feet at the shoulder, when the herd started coming at me, knocking down small trees as they ran. You can't really outrun elephants. About the time I heard them breathing down my neck, my professional hunter yelled, 'Shoot that one!' That's when I whirled around and saw the big bull coming right at me."

Duddy tried to make the traditional elephant kill, a shot to the brain. He was using a .577 double-barreled Westley Richards rifle, a collector's piece dating back to 1909. The shot went wide.

"I shouldn't have missed," Duddy says, "but I was off balance and by mistake pulled both triggers simultaneously. The elephants swerved and thundered by four yards away." Duddy gathered his senses and realized that most of his right arm, shoulder and upper torso were badly bruised by the impact of the rifle. "Still," he says, "that was better than being clobbered by six tons of elephant."

Such safari thrills are expensive. A "full-bag" African safari—including a license to shoot plains animals as well as the Big Five—can cost $30,000 or more for three weeks. Even a 10-day trip to hunt elk in Wyoming can cost up to $4,000 depending on food and lodging.

Hunters offer various reasons for their devotion to the sport. Peter Horn, the textile importer, speaks of the romance of Africa—"You can smell Africa, you can feel it"—and the chance to test oneself. "It's like the first time you're in combat," he says. "You don't

know if you're going to turn around and run."

For others, the attraction is not so much the taking of a trophy as the camaraderie of the camp. Jack E. Beal, a contractor who lives in Fort Lauderdale, Fla., met William C. Cloyd, an architect from Canyon Country, Calif., on a sheep-hunting trip in the rugged Pamir Mountains of the Soviet Union in November 1987. "It was 35 below and it never got above freezing," Beal recalls. "The only time I was really warm was in the sleeping bag." Over the course of the hunt, Beal and Cloyd became friends. "You're out there with no TV and no telephone," Beal says, "out there with the stress—the weather, the exertion. You see how the guys react to every possible human emotion: fatigue, frustration, anger, exhaustion. And you get to know them pretty well. Better than their wives."

Says Bartle Bull, a New York lawyer and author of "Safari: A Chronicle of Adventure": "There is nothing like being out in the bush and sitting by the fire with people you love. It's the best thing in the world."

Women on the Chase

Women also gather around the campfire. According to a study by the United States Fish and Wildlife Service, about 1.2 million American women hunt big game. Many come from the South or Southwest, where it's not considered unusual for a woman to use firearms. Polly Anderson Robertson, a 41-year-old hunter and wildlife biologist, is such a woman, brought up in Mississippi and taught at an early age to shoot by her father.

For years, she longed to take a big bear. The black bears of the Mississippi Delta were on the endangered list, so Robertson set her heart on the Alaskan brown bear.

In 1980, she flew north. She trudged up and down hills, enduring damp cold and mosquitoes one day, blistering heat and mosquitoes the next. She passed up possible shots at 30 bears, because they were too small or too distant for a definite kill. When she finally got her bear, it was a giant Alaskan brown taken at less than 80 yards.

"By the time my guide and I had skinned the bear," she recalls, "thousands of stars were twinkling in a jet black sky. Later, the northern lights appeared. It was my birthday, and I realized that I'd gotten my bear and done it in a majestic setting in one of the last great wildernesses on earth."

Many women become hunters to keep their husbands company. Peter Horn had gone on some 30 African safaris before he met his wife-to-be, Deborah Langley, a fashion model. Debbie Horn has now gone on three safaries, and has shot an elephant and a buffalo.

"Women are great on these trips," says Peter Horn. "They are troopers. When you ask them to do something, they do it. Men always think they know better."

Garland Rolling, the New Orleans banker, has a passion for hunting North American game. He also has a passion for conservation. Most hunters, in fact, consider themselves conservationists, a belief that John W. Grandy, the vice president for wildlife and the environment for the Humane Society of the United States, calls self-delusional. "Do we really need to shoot animals to conserve them?" he asks. "How can we call ourselves civilized and go around killing animals so we can put their heads on the wall and say we had fun? Is that a value we want to pass on to our children?"

Some critics, including Grandy, accuse hunters of endangering the very existence of the elephant and the rhino. But, Grandy allows, "In Kenya, over the bulk of West Africa, in Somalia and in Tanzania, the demise is principally due to poaching."

In Kenya, in the 10 years after safari hunting was banned in 1977, professional hunters and outfitters left, and poachers killed about 40 percent of the elephants and 90 percent of the rhinos. "When everybody pulls out, the poachers move in," says Vern Edewaard, president of Safari Club International. "If there were hunters out there, outfitters would be watching the area."

Peter Horn, who has been shot at by poachers in the Sudan, also blames civilization for killing elephants. "Every time they put in a road, a village, a farm, they are stopping the elephants," he says. "Pretty soon, you'll only have elephants in compounds or in zoos." According to Don Causey, the publisher of *The Hunting Report*, "There is a new wave of thinking that is breaking over the conservation community. They are beginning to realize that the real threat to wildlife is the economic pressure on the land." He argues that nations such as Zimbabwe receive income from the sale of hunting permits, which makes the animals a valuable resource and supports the effort to preserve them. "Even if people don't want to think about hunting or see it," he says, "they should accept the overwhelming economic aspect of hunting."

"Some critics . . . accuse hunters of endangering the very existence of the elephant and the rhino."

An advertisement by Friends of Animals decried a planned auction of elephant tusks at Sotheby's "in the midst of an elephant holocaust." Sotheby's subsequently called off the auction.

In the view of Jack S. Parker, a former vice chairman of General Electric and a veteran hunter: "The elephant's plight is a matter of distribution.

They're too abundant in some areas and not abundant enough elsewhere. In South Africa's Kruger National Park, for example, shooters kill about 300 elephants a year to keep the population within bounds. If, instead of paying people to shoot the elephants, they'd allot the job to fee-paying sportsmen, park administrators would be able to raise money they need for other Kruger projects."

Parker has been a trustee and major contributor to the African Wildlife Foundation, which trains Africans for careers in wildlife management and conservation. "We are neither pro- nor anti-hunting in a philosophical sense," says Diana E. McMeekin, the vice president of the foundation. "We believe that it is an important management tool, if it is done properly."

Experts credit South Africa with doing it properly by giving a home to the elephant and the white rhino. "Only in South Africa is the white rhino not on the endangered species list," says Marshall P. Jones, the U.S. Fish and Wildlife Service's representative to CITES, the Convention on International Trade in Endangered Species. "They manage the white rhino quite well."

Fees and Ethics

Hunting has become big business in South Africa and elsewhere, with landowners offering big-game hunting as a way to underwrite their game reserves. One example is the 140,000-acre Timbavati tract in South Africa, which is owned by 32 people who manage their agriculturally marginal land exclusively for wildlife.

Much of Timbavati's income is provided by visitors who spend their days being chauffeured through the bush so they can observe wildlife. Game managers cull animals considered too old to breed, or species that are reproducing faster than the reserve can support.

Once a year, in September, the owners of Timbavati auction off a Big Five hunt to raise funds for habitat reclamation in the reserve. The 1988 hunt went to Maurice A. Cattani, a retired women's garment manufacturer who lives in California. His bid of $72,000 entitled him to spend 21 days on safari. He got his Big Five in only 15 days.

There is still a hunting code of ethics in Africa, left over from British colonial days. A professional hunter serving as a back-up "gun" lessens the chance that a wounded animal will escape. Most hunters take pride in giving what is called "fair chase." According to Bartle Bull, fair chase means "you have to give the animal a fair chance. You have to earn it in energy and risk." Above all, the hunter is expected not to shoot a caged or restrained animal—a practice that, although illegal, is not unknown. As *The Hunting Report* puts it, "You must make very clear what your standards of fair chase are."

"It took me four years to find him," recalls Jack Parker, referring to the bull elephant he shot in Kenya in 1971, six years before hunting was banned. He is one of the few men in modern times to have shot an elephant with tusks weighing more than 100 pounds on a side. "It took me far longer to get a North American Grand Slam on sheep," Parker says, referring to his bagging of a Dall's sheep, a Stone's sheep, a bighorn sheep and a desert sheep, "but it would be easier for me to do that again today than to find another elephant like that."

Bartle Bull, a former publisher of *The Village Voice*, hunted for many years in Africa. He stopped shooting anything but game birds in 1967. "I stopped because I found it distasteful," he says. "It was too easy to kill an animal with trackers, a Land-Rover, a modern professional sporting rifle, a professional hunter. Unless you are going in after a wounded leopard, a wounded elephant. Then it's scary and there's a balance of risk and thrill. But if the thrill is primarily shooting and killing an animal, that's over for me."

Public Perception

Bull believes that, for the most part, people are put off by certain kinds of animal trophies. "If I saw a rhino horn on the wall, I would find it morally offensive and I would say something," he says. "I don't see any way you can justify shooting elephants today. But if I saw an antelope skin, I wouldn't be offended." Antelope, he points out, are plentiful.

"I put trophies in my office," says Peter Horn. "Hundreds of people a week come through, and once in a while someone will say something. But, then again, I don't have stockholders so I don't have to worry."

George Reiger is the conservation editor for Field and Stream *magazine. He is also an angler and a hunter.*

"The only truly effective way to stop the slaughter of elephants is through the complete elimination of the ivory trade."

viewpoint 87

Banning the Ivory Trade Will Save Elephants

Susan S. Lieberman

DATELINE: Nairobi, Kenya, December 1988

The Convention on International Trade in Endangered Species (CITES) held a meeting of its African Elephant Working Group. In attendance were representatives of several conservation organizations, scientists, CITES officials, government representatives (from Europe, the United States, Africa, UK and Japan), and ivory traders. Experts declared at that meeting: "At the present rate, the African elephant will be commercially extinct in 5 years."

It is late afternoon on the African savannah. A family of elephants moves towards a water hole. An old matriarch stands silhouetted against the setting sun. Suddenly, the silence is broken by machine gun fire. One by one the family is gunned down. The roar of gunfire and the screams and bellows of terrified elephants shatter the twilight silence with a terrible dissonance.

Tens of thousands of elephants are slaughtered this way every year to feed the greed of the ivory trade. Current estimates place the carnage at more than 1,000 elephants per week! Most of us have an idealized image of African elephants—of splendor and tranquility against a vast backdrop. The reality, however, is far different: terrible animal suffering, rotting bodies of slaughtered elephants, and mountains of ivory.

Raw Ivory

The tusk of an elephant, or raw ivory, is really an elongated upper incisor tooth, which grows throughout the elephant's life. These tusks are used for feeding, tearing bark, digging for roots, defense, and social display. Ivory can only be obtained from dead elephants. The tusks are turned into ivory

Susan S. Lieberman, "African Elephants: Can We End the Slaughter?" *The Animals' Agenda*, May 1989. Reprinted with permission.

jewelry, trinkets, and carvings. In addition, elephants' skin is made into shoes and purses, and their feet become wastepaper baskets or—if they are from baby elephants—pencil holders.

African elephants have been killed for their ivory since at least the time of the Pharaohs. By the early Middle Ages, elephants had been exterminated from North Africa by ivory hunters. The ivory trade expanded tremendously in the 18th and 19th centuries, and was intimately connected with the slave trade out of Africa. The current ivory trade is a remnant of European colonialism. In the early 1900s, the ivory trade killed more than 100,000 elephants a year, to feed a growing market for piano keys, billiard balls, and trinkets. After World War II, the availability of plastic substitutes caused a temporary decline in the ivory trade. But the luxury ivory market is now on the rise, in spite of the fact that synthetic substitutes are readily available.

In 1980, there were an estimated 1.3 million elephants in Africa. Field research in Central and West Africa puts the total population at close to 400,000, and we cannot afford to delay another nine years in protecting these animals. Most elephant populations in Africa are declining, with the possible exceptions of Zimbabwe, South Africa, Botswana, and Malawi. Elephants are virtually gone in West Africa, where the few survivors are *still* threatened by poaching. Many protected areas and parks have also seen declines in their elephant populations, as a result of poaching. For example, in 1984 only 80 elephants remained in the Niokola-Koba National Park in Senegal. Elephant populations have declined 80 percent in the Central African Republic since 1981, due largely to poaching. In Zaire, there has been a 60 percent decline in elephants within the national park, with worse conditions in surrounding areas. Uganda has lost 90 percent of its elephants since 1984. In unprotected areas, Kenya has lost 91 percent of its elephants; even the protected parks visited by so many tourists have lost more than 72 percent of their elephants.

Though anti-poaching efforts are underway in some African countries, they are rudimentary and underfunded. Sadly, many ill-equipped wildlife officers have been killed by poachers. In a number of countries, military and government officials have been implicated in poaching and ivory trading.

"The decline in average tusk size shows that the large mature elephants have already been wiped out."

While habitat destruction is also a problem, recent scientific studies have shown that poaching for ivory is the most immediate threat to the future of elephants. Rising ivory prices, political instability, and the spread of automatic and semi-automatic rifles throughout Africa have contributed to widespread killing of elephants. The only truly effective way to stop the slaughter of elephants is through the complete elimination of the ivory trade.

In 1972, when the current extensive exploitation of elephants for their ivory was beginning, the average tusk traded weighed about 13 kilograms; the average tusk in trade weighed 8 kilograms in the early 1980s, and 4.6 kilograms in 1986. Today, the average tusk traded weighs only 3 kilograms, and a significant portion of those traded weigh less than half a kilogram. What is happening? Ivory grows throughout an elephant's life, with the greatest growth during an elephant's later years. The decline in average tusk size shows that the large mature elephants have already been wiped out, and the ivory hunters are killing juveniles instead. These young elephants haven't yet reproduced, and their deaths for the ivory trade represents a double tragedy—both for themselves and their species.

In response to declining elephant populations, CITES instituted an Ivory Quota Control System that went into effect January 1986. It set export quotas, requiring member nations to mark tusks with punch dies. CITES also permitted large stockpiles of confiscated illegal raw ivory to enter the "legal" trade in an attempt to control the ivory export trade. The system allows the export of ivory from countries that enforce anti-poaching laws and have reasonable conservation programs.

Both in philosophical intent and in practice, the CITES program is a dismal failure. CITES should function as an advocate for wildlife, protecting wild species from the disastrous effects of commercial trading. Instead, it has become an advocate for the trade itself. More than 90 percent of the ivory entering the U.S. comes in as "worked ivory" (jewelry and trinkets), and most of it arrives from

Hong Kong. Importers in Asia buy raw ivory from Africa, with no regard to where it came from or how it was obtained. The African Elephant and Rhino Specialist Group (AERSG) of the International Union for the Conservation of Nature and Natural Resources (IUCN) has estimated that in 1986, the first year of the quota system, 78 percent of all ivory traded worldwide was poached ivory, and this trade was operating totally outside of the CITES system. This represents the tusks of about 89,000 elephants in one year! In 1985, 4.8 million pieces of worked ivory and 27,346 kilograms of carvings came into the U.S.—most of it from poached elephants. This ivory had a declared value of more than $24 million.

Who bears the greatest blame for the slaughter of elephants for ivory? Is it the villager with an automatic weapon who is paid a few dollars to kill an elephant? Is it the wealthy Asian trader who imports raw ivory into Hong Kong and exports carved trinkets to the U.S.? The guiltiest party is, in fact, the consumer at the end of the line. When people stop buying ivory, there will be no market for ivory, and poachers will stop killing elephants. . . .

End the Wildlife Trade

The African elephant is a powerful symbol of the urgent need to protect wild animals from suffering and death caused by human exploitation. The entire wildlife trade—both in live animals and in luxury products produced from their dead bodies—has expanded greatly over the last decade. The traders and importers hide behind a facade of "sustainable utilization" to justify their unethical activities. But the brutal slaughter of elephants is certainly not sustainable, either numerically or ethically. Unless the ivory market is destroyed, the largest land mammal on this planet will lose its freedom forever; the elephant will go extinct in the wild, with remaining individuals held captive in circuses, menageries, zoos, and "managed" preserves. It is up to all of us to put an end to this merchandising of extinction.

Susan S. Lieberman is associate director of Wildlife and Environment for the Humane Society of the United States, the nation's largest animal protection group.

"Kenya's ban on hunting and efforts to suppress the ivory trade are typical of most of Central and East Africa, and the results have been disastrous."

viewpoint **88**

Banning the Ivory Trade Will Endanger Elephants

Randy T. Simmons and Urs P. Kreuter

On July 18, 1989, Kenyan President Daniel arap Moi set fire to a 12-ton pyre of elephant tusks valued at nearly $3 million. The tusks had been confiscated from poachers and were burned to demonstrate Kenya's dedication to saving the African elephant by ending trade in ivory. Although hunting elephants has been illegal in Kenya for over a decade, the country's elephant population has fallen from 65,000 in 1979 to 19,000 in 1989, a tragedy that Kenyan wildlife experts blame on poaching for the overseas ivory market.

In Harare, Zimbabwe, by contrast, shops openly sell ivory and hides from elephants culled to prevent rapid population growth in the country's game parks. Part of the proceeds of these sales returns to the game parks. Similarly, two dozen peasant villages in Zimbabwe will earn $5 million in 1990 from the sale of elephant-hunting rights on their communal lands to safari operators. The government of Robert Mugabe sees no contradiction between the protection of elephants and the carefully regulated sale of elephant products. On the contrary, Zimbabwe has found that the best way to protect elephants is to give its citizens the opportunity to benefit from their presence. The result: the elephant population has grown from 30,000 to 43,000 since 1979. In neighboring Botswana, where limited hunting is practiced, the elephant population grew from 20,000 to 51,000 in the same period.

There are two conflicting approaches to elephant conservation in Africa today. Kenya's ban on hunting and efforts to suppress the ivory trade are typical of most of Central and East Africa, and the results have been disastrous. From 1979 to 1989, Central Africa's elephant population dropped from 497,400 to 274,800 and East Africa's from 546,650 to 154,720.

Elephants in the game parks were only slightly better protected than those outside. In East Africa's parks, for example, 56 percent of the elephants were killed or died in the past 10 years. Outside the parks, 78 percent disappeared. Some projections show elephants could be extinct in East and Central Africa as early as 2005.

The elephant populations of Zimbabwe, Botswana, Namibia, and South Africa, however, are *increasing*, and now account for 20 percent of the continent's elephants. These Southern African countries all support conservation through utilization, allowing safari hunting and tourism on private, state, and communal lands, and the sale of ivory and hides. The sale of hunting rights and elephant products gives Southern Africans an economic stake in elephant conservation. It also helps finance strict enforcement of poaching laws. South Africa's Kruger National Park, for example, earned $2.5 million in 1988, 10 percent of its annual budget, by selling ivory and hides from 350 elephants culled for ecological reasons to prevent overpopulation. (Without culling, elephant populations will increase at a rate of 5 percent a year.) Similar ecologically-based culling programs and sales have been conducted in Zimbabwe for years and will commence in Botswana in 1990.

A Total Ban

Unfortunately, Kenya's approach to wildlife conservation is dominating international efforts to save the African elephant. A report issued in June 1989 by the Ivory Trade Review Group (ITRG), an international study group funded primarily by Wildlife Conservation International and World Wildlife Fund (U.S.), concluded: "It is the ivory trade and hunting for ivory, and not habitat loss or human population increase, that is responsible for the decline in [African] elephant numbers."

Upon release of the ITRG report, Kenya, Tanzania,

"Herd Mentality: Banning Ivory Sales Is No Way to Save the Elephant," is excerpted from the Fall 1989 issue of *Policy Review*, a publication of The Heritage Foundation, 214 Massachusetts Avenue, NE, Washington, DC 20002.

and international conservation groups called for an immediate worldwide ban on the ivory trade. The United States and the European Community responded with a ban on ivory imports. Japan and Hong Kong, the destinations of most raw ivory, instituted some controls as well. In addition, Kenya and Tanzania requested the secretariat of the Convention on International Trade in Endangered Species of Wild Flora and Fauna (CITES) to list the African elephant on Appendix I. An Appendix I listing would ban all trade in elephant products, including hides as well as ivory.

The African elephant currently is listed on Appendix II, which allows some trade, with permits, in ivory and hide. Permits are allocated under a quota system administered by CITES. The quotas are based on the exporting countries' estimates of a sustainable yield.

"Elephant ivory has been prized for centuries and is now especially valued in the Far East."

Elephant ivory has been prized for centuries and is now especially valued in the Far East. Ivory is made into piano keys and carved into chess pieces, figures, and the Oriental signature stamps known as "chops." Uncarved tusks like the ones burned by Kenya sold for $2.50 a pound in 1969, jumped to $34 in 1978, and now fetch over $90. Since an average elephant's tusks weigh 22 pounds, the value of each elephant's ivory is $2,000. The hide is worth at least as much as the ivory and is made into boots, wallets, and other leather goods.

Even if income from poaching were not available, however, many rural Africans would have a powerful incentive to kill elephants. Unlike the Asian elephant, which has been domesticated as a beast of burden and is therefore considered a valued treasure in many Indian communities, the African elephant competes for scarce resources, and frequently destroys human property. As Norman Myers put it in 1981 as he was leaving Kenya after working 20 years as a wildlife ecologist for international conservation organizations:

> Wildlife in Africa is being elbowed out of living space by millions of digging hoes—a far greater threat than the poachers' poisoned arrows. When zebras chomp up livestock's grass, when elephants drink dry savannahland water supplies, when buffalo herds trample maize crops and when lions carry off prize steers, the animals must go—unless they can pay their way.

East and Central African policies do not allow elephants to pay their way, except through tourism. Tourism does generate income, but not for rural Africa's expanding agricultural population. In countries such as Kenya and Tanzania, where over 80 percent of the people live off agriculture, and human populations are rising at 3 to 4 percent a year, few families are willing to endure hunger so an elephant can live to provide a job for an urban-based tourist guide or a photo opportunity for a foreign tourist.

Competition for Resources

The simple reality is that elephants compete with people for scarce resources, and rural Africans must benefit if conservation is to be successful. The ITRG argument that the decline in elephant numbers is not due to "habitat loss or human population increase" ignores this reality and the incentive it creates for people to engage in poaching or simply to kill off local elephants.

Elephants are not even safe from such human pressures in the parks or wildlife reserves. Rural Africans who want land see a local park as a zoo catering to rich foreigners and resent it greatly. The Serengeti Park in Tanzania, for example, is embroiled in a three-way conflict between wildlife managers, subsistence farmers who want land for crops, and the nomadic Masai cattle herders who regard the park as part of their traditional home. . . .

The policies of East and Central African countries encourage poaching. Rural people have an incentive to eradicate elephants, law enforcement is underfunded and ineffective, and the political will has not been mustered to control corruption among government officials.

The incentives facing would-be poachers are very different in the southern countries. In Zimbabwe, poachers are shot on sight and over $600 per square mile is spent to protect the wildlife estate. Elephants are marketed extensively under concession permits on state-owned safari areas and communal lands, and managed intensively in the national parks. Hunting and photographic opportunities are sold primarily to an international clientele. The price of an average hunt in Zimbabwe, where elephant is the main trophy, is $25,000. With such value at stake, the incentive to protect resident elephants is equivalent to that of protecting domestic livestock.

Ten thousand elephants live on Zimbabwe's communal lands—lands for peasant farmers but without individual ownership of land or wildlife. Rather than rely on prohibitions to protect the elephants, the Zimbabwe Department of National Parks and Wildlife Management gives peasant communities the right to hunt a certain number of elephants. The communities can exercise this right themselves or sell the hunting permits to commercial operators. This has resulted in a much more positive attitude toward wildlife among Zimbabwean villagers.

One Zimbabwean subsistence community curtailed poaching in Gona-re-Zhou National Park and villagers withdrew from some land for wildlife in exchange for hunting permits for elephant and buffalo that overflowed from the park. The permits were sold to a safari operator and part of the proceeds were used to develop community facilities, while the rest was distributed directly to community members who lost crops to animal damage.

In addition to hunting permits, further income is generated for rural communities when animals that destroy property are eliminated by National Parks personnel. The ivory and hide from these animals belong to the community members. Since at least as many destructive animals as trophy bulls are killed each year, the sale of hides and ivory from marauding elephants represent a substantial component of the income to communal members.

The expansion of Southern African elephant herds suggests that proponents of a global ban on ivory trade are asking the wrong question. They ask, "How do we stop the ivory trade in order to remove the incentive for poaching?" They should ask, "How do we make elephants valuable enough that people have an incentive to be careful stewards rather than careless exterminators?"

And why do they ask the wrong question? Perhaps those who wish to save the elephant are simply misled by the no-trade ideology of many American and European environmentalists—a biological imperialism imposed regardless of local realities and values for wildlife. The second possibility is less benign than good intentions gone astray. It is that an international ban is expected to substitute for effective law enforcement at the national level and to cover up or ignore decades of mismanagement and corruption.

"How do we make elephants valuable enough that people have an incentive to be careful stewards rather than careless exterminators?"

Economic theory teaches that a government ban on the supply of a valued commodity can never wholly eliminate demand. It does accomplish three things, however: prices increase, people with a comparative advantage at avoiding detection—usually criminals and corrupt public officials—take over the formerly legal market, and, in the case of a resource owned in common, the resource disappears. Legalizing trade and protecting property rights, however, reverses these outcomes: prices drop as the legal supply grows, there is no premium on criminality and corruption, and property rights encourage wise stewardship of the resource.

Trade bans on wildlife products have failed to protect species for which there is a commercial demand. Many species of Latin American parrots, for instance, are "protected" by a CITES Appendix I listing. Prices skyrocketed after the trade ban and the legal trade was taken over by poachers who make no effort to maintain birds on a sustainable basis. After all, the nest left today will in all likelihood be taken by someone else tomorrow. Native hunters go so far as to chop down nesting trees to get the parrots. The captured parrots are drugged, put in door panels and even hubcaps, and smuggled into the United States, where the few that actually survive are sold on the black market for more than $20,000. The return for trading in protected birds is often greater than what can be made from producing illegal drugs. Rather than reducing the slide in native parrot populations, prohibition has accelerated it. . . .

Conservation Through Commercialization

Contrary to the poor record of trade bans, commercialization has successfully protected a broad variety of species. Seabirds are farmed in Iceland, crocodiles and butterflies are raised in Papua, New Guinea, and Zimbabwe farmers ranch a broad variety of species. Crocodile farming is a multimillion dollar business in Zimbabwe, and is growing in Malawi. The crocodile has an Appendix I listing in most countries, but Zimbabwe has declared a reservation.

The white rhino, also listed on Appendix I, declined from 1,500 animals spread among five countries in 1960 to just 20 animals in 1989. In contrast, the white rhino population increased tenfold in South Africa, during the same time period and now totals about 6,000 in parks, reserves, and on privately owned ranches. White rhinos are hunted in South Africa, and the horns from hunting trophies and natural mortality victims are the sources of several hundred pounds of rhino horn each year. These horns are not presently traded, but would be worth millions of dollars annually that could be spent on additional rhino protection.

An international ban on trade in ivory will increase the price of ivory significantly as the black market tries to satisfy consumer demand. Some countries have already established ivory stockpiles in anticipation of such a price rise. The *Economist* reports that Burundi has stashed 90-100 tons and Hong Kong has 500-700 tons set aside. One effect of the price rise will be to encourage more people to become involved in poaching. Likely candidates include the Southern Somali "Shiftas" who roam and plunder at will in northeastern Kenya. A second effect will be to encourage greater political corruption as the returns from aiding illegal shipments will rise with the price of ivory.

In addition, revenue derived from ecologically necessary culling programs in Southern Africa will be lost, leaving fewer financial resources to protect wildlife from poachers or for controlling expanding elephant herds. Wildlife officials in Zimbabwe believe a ban will make the elephant extinct in communal lands.

Consequently, Zimbabwe, South Africa, Botswana, Malawi, Mozambique, and Zambia have decided not to participate in a ban, and instead are developing a cooperative ivory marketing and control system. This system will include stringent controls and checks to reduce the chances of illegal ivory from other African countries being sold through the system. It will introduce a form of ivory identification, a type of branding, based on chemical analysis, X-ray spectrophotometry, electron microscopy, and other forensic techniques. This identification technology can pinpoint the origin of the ivory. Only that ivory originating in the countries that join the regional marketing system will be allowed to be sold.

Elephants are endangered in certain parts of Africa, not all Africa. Thus, the solution to saving the African elephant lies not in banning ivory trade, but in applying the successful elephant conservation policies of South African nations to East African nations that have mismanaged their resources. Where poaching and facilitation of poaching by corrupt officials occurs, the responsibility lies with the country's government. An international ban on trade in ivory will not solve internal problems and is an abrogation of responsibility to eliminate the true causes of elephant decline.

Managing Wildlife

If the East and Central African nations sincerely wish to save their elephants they must begin by managing wildlife for the benefit of the human inhabitants of their countries. Current conflicts between people and protected areas must be replaced with a custodial and participatory relationship. To do that, rural Africans must be able to make discretionary use of wildlife.

"Commercialization and intensive management of wildlife are difficult concepts for many members of the American wildlife lobby to accept."

Bans on hunting need to be replaced with policies that encourage game ranching, safari hunting, and indigenous use of wildlife. And patrolling efforts need to be funded at levels that make poaching too risky.

Zambia, the only Southern African country with a declining elephant population, is adopting just such a strategy in response to losing 75,000 elephants in the Luangwa Valley to poachers this decade despite a ban on hunting. In a policy reversal, they have started trophy hunting and ivory sales, with the proceeds going to pay for increased policing and to benefit local residents.

Commercialization and intensive management of wildlife are difficult concepts for many members of the American wildlife lobby to accept. But, there is still time to reconsider. With elephant herds expanding in Southern Africa there is no need for those in East and Central Africa to be rushing toward extinction.

Randy T. Simmons is a visiting scholar at the Competitive Institute, a free-market advocacy group, located in Washington, D.C. Urs P. Kreuter is a range scientist who lives in Zimbabwe. He is also a research associate at the Institute of Political Economy at Utah State University, located in Logan.

"It's a given that the boats of the U.S. tuna fleet will kill tens of thousands of dolphins from 1989 to 1991. That's just unacceptable."

viewpoint **89**

The Tuna Industry Needlessly Endangers Dolphins

Kenneth Brower

The beaks of Sam LaBudde's first dolphins strained against the net that had formed a canopy over them. Their flukes churned the ocean white. They thronged at the surface, desperate to force slack in the net sufficient to free their blowholes for a breath. Their shrieks and squeals began high in the hearing range of humans and climbed inaudible scales above. LaBudde wanted to scream himself.

The net was brailed, or hauled in. Its red mesh was scarcely visible, and the dolphins snagged in it seemed to levitate from the sea. High above the deck the great spool of the power block, turning by fits and starts, raised and gathered the seine, conveying the dolphins—some drowned, some still struggling feebly—up toward the block's tight aperture. The net passed through the block, crushing the dolphins, and then slowly descended to the deck. LaBudde stepped forward with his shipmates and began disentangling dead and dying dolphins from the mesh. The dying trembled in their death throes. The dead stared with eyes wide open. LaBudde noticed that the hue of the iris was different in each animal—dolphins are individuals even in death. He noticed his own red arms. A dolphin, the first he had ever touched in his life, had left him bloody to the elbows.

Months later, on land, Sam LaBudde's sleep would be troubled by a recurrent dream in which injured dolphins spoke in cryptic tongues. He might have spared himself the dream, perhaps, had he given vent to his feelings at sea. He could not. LaBudde was not what he seemed—just another crewman on a Panamanian purse seiner in the eastern tropical Pacific. LaBudde was a spy.

For reasons unclear, schools of spotted dolphins, spinner dolphins, and common dolphins travel in company with schools of yellowfin tuna. The association is commonest in the eastern tropical Pacific (ETP)—the warm waters west of Mexico, Central America, Colombia, Ecuador, Peru, and northern Chile. Tuna fishermen have long made use of it, searching for dolphins in order to find fish. Until recently the presence of dolphins simply flagged the location of tuna. . . .

The fish underneath the dolphins were caught by rod, line, and baitless hook. It was a fine old Stone Age method. In the Caroline Islands of Micronesia men in outrigger canoes have fished that way for millennia. The lures are iridescent pearl shell. The hooks are turtle shell or steel. No bait is necessary. The pounding outrigger and hull beat up a froth that attracts the tuna, bringing them right up under the stern. The outrigger pounds the sea, the captain mutters his fish magic, the crew yells itself hoarse, the poles dip and rise as the tuna bite at everything and fly aboard in silvery arcs. The dolphins accompanying the fish, too smart to go for baitless hooks, are not much inconvenienced—unless it is by the loss of their cold-blooded companions and whatever symbiotic advantages the relationship offers them.

The Purse-Seining Technique

All this changed in the early 1960s, with the application of purse-seining techniques to tuna fishing. Since then any dolphins sighted in the ETP have been rounded up with "seal bombs" (underwater explosives that originated in the days of the California sardine fishery, when they were used to discourage seals from raiding the nets) and speedboats and encircled by a mile-long fence of net, its upper edge buoyed by a line of floats—the "corkline"—its lower edge hanging several hundred feet deep. Cables draw the bottom of the seine tight, trapping the dolphins and any tuna swimming underneath. Toward the end of each "set" on

Kenneth Brower, "The Destruction of Dolphins," *The Atlantic Monthly,* July 1989. Reprinted with permission.

dolphins the crew is supposed to follow a procedure called backdown, which is intended to allow the dolphins to escape over the corkline of the net, but often—in darkness or on high seas, from equipment failure, human error, or some unexpected panic by the dolphins—something goes wrong and dolphins die. As a rule only a handful drown, or dozens, but occasionally, in what are called disaster sets, hundreds die, even thousands.

"The 1960s were catastrophic for dolphins. By the end of the decade between a quarter and a half million dolphins were being killed annually in the [eastern tropical Pacific.]"

The 1960s were catastrophic for dolphins. By the end of the decade between a quarter and a half million dolphins were being killed annually in the ETP. Hardest hit were spotted dolphins, next spinner dolphins, and then common dolphins. Since 1960, according to the best available figures, six million dolphins have been killed by purse seiners in the ETP.

But the real number exceeds six million. National Marine Fisheries Service figures make no allowance for mortality among injured, exhausted, or separated animals. Those bloody dolphins Sam LaBudde pulled from the net, for example—animals with broken beaks, or with pectoral fins torn from their sockets—are not counted as dead if they show any signs of life. No allowance is made for shark attacks on hurt, exhausted, or disoriented dolphins as they leave the net, though such attacks are common. No allowance is made for the stress on and fragmentation of dolphin society after months, years, and now decades of repeated sets. "The moot point is, whether Leviathan can long endure so wide a chase, and so remorseless a havoc," Herman Melville wrote. His concern then was for the great cetaceans, but today the same moot point might be made about the small.

The magnitude of the dolphin slaughter of the 1960s, once it became known, was a driving force behind the Marine Mammal Protection Act of 1972. "It shall be the immediate goal," the MMPA stated, "that the incidental kill or incidental serious injury of marine mammals permitted in the course of commercial fishing operations be reduced to insignificant levels approaching a zero mortality and serious injury rate." To reach that goal in the ETP a schedule was established for decreasing the allowable dolphin kill each year, a research program was funded for the development of dolphin-saving gear and techniques, and an observer program was set up.

This is how things stand in the minds of many today—the legislation enacted, the problem solved.

In fact, before the ink was dry on the MMPA, the act was being compromised and eroded. The tuna industry has never ceased its direct assaults and end runs on the law. The government agencies charged with policing the fishermen have been shamefully negligent. The fishermen were given until 1976 before the first quota, an allowable dolphin kill of 78,000, took effect. (This was called a grace period, though that hardly seems the word.) Thus for the first four years of its existence the Marine Mammal Protection Act was nothing of the kind. For the next few years the dolphin kill did decline steadily, as stipulated by the MMPA. (In 1975, before quotas, 166,645 dolphins died in U.S. nets, by the conservative official estimate. In 1977 the official underestimate was only 25,425.)

Then came the Reagan era, and the decline ceased. In 1984, under tuna-industry pressure, the MMPA was amended so that the year's kill quota of 20,500 would apply to every year from then on. The original goal, a dolphin kill "reduced to insignificant levels approaching zero," was abandoned. Under Reagan, funds for research on dolphin-saving gear were greatly reduced, regulations were relaxed, enforcement was softened. Since the MMPA's passage at least 800,000 dolphins have died in U.S. nets alone. The dolphin kill by tuna fishermen in the ETP continues to be the greatest slaughter of marine mammals on earth. . . .

How He Got Started

In 1987, Sam LaBudde dropped by Earth Island Institute, a San Francisco umbrella organization—or seed log, perhaps—for a number of new environmental concerns. One of these, Rainforest Action Network, sounded promising, and he went in to see about a job. Randy Hayes, the founder and director, was on the phone, as usual. Killing time while he waited, LaBudde picked up a copy of *Earth Island Journal*.

"It was the dolphin issue, with the purple cover," he says. "I was just amazed. I was a fisherman, a biologist. I thought I was informed about environmental things. I knew about the depletion of the ozone layer before most people did, and about the destruction of the rain forests. But I had thought whales and dolphins were sacrosanct species, above abuse. Nobody had told me they were being captured in nets, with speedboats and explosives and helicopters."

Why, LaBudde asked, weren't they telling anyone? They were trying, David Phillips and Todd Steiner, of Earth Island, protested. (They had, after all, produced the very article that this stranger . . . was holding in his hand.) Earth Island had the facts on the slaughter, Phillips and Steiner said. They had a lot of dry documentation. What they needed was film. Well, LaBudde wondered, couldn't someone get on a tuna boat? He himself was a former fisherman and NMFS [National Marine Fisheries Service] observer; he could probably get aboard. . . .

Aboard the *Maria Luisa*

In September of 1987 LaBudde drove his old Volkswagen across the border into Mexico. His first night in Ensenada he slept on the beach flats south of town. In the morning he woke to Mexican voices—six or seven women and their children rooting in burning mounds of garbage for food. He rose, brushed off the sand, and drove to the waterfront to look for work. . . .

The tuna captains were curious: why would a former Alaskan fisherman like him, a man who could make $4,000 a month in Alaska, want to work on an Ensenada boat for 30,000 pesos a week—about $15? Because he was tired of American life, LaBudde would answer. He was burned out on the United States and wanted to go to the Andes. On a tuna boat he could work his way closer to those mountains while learning Spanish and practicing a trade he knew. It was not a bad story—there was more than a little truth in all its parts—and LaBudde's résumé was fairly impressive. He had been a commercial fisherman and a machinist. As a mechanic, he pointed out, he had the advantage of literacy in English, the language of the manuals for the American outboard motors that powered the seiner speedboats.

The *Maria Luisa*'s captain finally gave LaBudde an unequivocal no, in spite of that. (The man had good instincts, perhaps.) The boat's owner, a Basque lawyer from Panama, was visiting at the time, and LaBudde went over the captain's head to this man. On the one hand, the move was a good one, for the owner hired him immediately. On the other hand, the captain never forgave him and for the next six weeks at sea hardly spoke to him. . . .

Halfway out of the water, a Costa Rican spinner dolphin, caught by its beak in the mesh, wriggles free and drops back in. The triangular fin cuts under, and the dolphin rejoins its mates in the steadily shallowing belly of the net. Another entangled spinner rises. Its head is pressed awkwardly forward, its dorsal fin bent sideways, its beak half open. It is nearly to the power block when something—the dorsal?—appears to break, and the dolphin and dark fragments of it tumble back into the sea.

The net at first is selective. The youngest spinners, quickest to tire, are the first to be caught in it. For a time mostly the slender bodies of calves are borne up the conveyer of the red mesh. LaBudde's camera rolls on and soon the adults, too, die or surrender and begin the climb. They rise, a dense mass of bodies, until the steepening angle of the net tips them off, four or five at a time, to pitch downward, beak over tailfin, to be caught again by the net's shallower angle at the waterline, to begin the climb once more.

A large male dolphin, completely enshrouded in mesh, approaches the power block. It twists and bucks wildly. The camera notices. The struggles of most dolphins at this stage are much feebler. In this animal the life force seems unusually strong. The camera zooms in. The dolphin passes quickly through the power block. Emerging, it slides down the red mound of brailed net, shoved and guided by the hands of fishermen. A strange thing has happened to it. The amplitude of the big dolphin's struggles has flattened out. Where before its flukes traveled through a wide arc, a reflexive swimming motion, now they beat in a shallow, spasmodic flutter. That moment in the power block was too brief, it seems, to have wrought the change. But that is how it always seems, of course, for mortal creatures passing through that particular door. The fishermen slide the big dolphin, its flukes still fluttering, along the wet deck. They shove it to the top of a sluiceway and send it along to the sharks.

"The first day of the year, we got permission to fish in Costa Rican territorial waters," LaBudde says of this set, in January 1988. "To celebrate we went and wiped out probably five percent of the world's population of these Costa Rican spinners in a single afternoon."

The Costa Rican spinner is the largest of the spinner dolphins, and the rarest. In 1979 the population was estimated at 9,000. The *Maria Luisa*'s set, a decade later, killed two or three hundred of however many Costa Rican spinners remained in the world. When the last of the dead dolphins had been extricated and cast adrift, the fishermen had their catch—ten or twelve yellowfin tuna. . . .

"When the last of the dead dolphins had been extricated and cast adrift, the fishermen had their catch—ten or twelve yellowfin tuna."

Sam LaBudde and his film appeared on ABC and CBS national newscasts, on NBC's *Today Show*, and on local newscasts around the country.

"The networks were not overjoyed when they heard we had eight-millimeter videotape by an amateur," says David Phillips, of Earth Island. "They were surprised at the quality. They bumped it up to a one-inch master without any difficulty. I don't know how Sam learned to get pictures as good as he got. He read the manual as he was bouncing around in the waves on a speedboat. Until Sam, we lacked the indisputable visual evidence. It's very difficult to know what's happening out there. Sam's film has made it a lot more visceral. It's given us an access to the media we've never had. It's galvanized the environmental community, and it's forced the industry to respond."

LaBudde testified and showed his film before Congress at reauthorization hearings for the Marine Mammal Protection Act. Those hearings were a lesson in the subtler workings of the tragedy of the commons in a modern republic. The senators expressed much admiration for progress made by the U.S. industry. They decried the ruthlessness of the foreign fleet. (Not many votes are lost in xenophobia.) "The U.S. industry has an excellent record," said Senator John Breaux, of Louisiana, in whose constituency fishermen are strong. "I'll add my voice to the swelling chorus of praise for the domestic industry," said Senator Pete Wilson, of California. Senator Wilson is a former mayor of San Diego, where the U.S. fleet is based.

Industry at Fault

The senator's swelling chorus of praise is in fact a two-part harmony between the U.S. industry and politicians like himself. The U.S. industry invented purse seining on dolphins and for fifteen years monopolized the technique. The U.S. industry killed millions of dolphins in the early years of tuna seining, and in the years since the MMPA was enacted, the U.S. industry has killed more than 800,000. The U.S. tuna industry has fought every regulation intended to reduce the dolphin kill. In 1980 an NMFS prohibition against "sundown" sets—implemented because the kill rate is up to four times as high at night as it is in daytime—was dropped, under pressure by U.S. industry lobbyists, after being in effect for just eight days. In 1981 the American Tunaboat Association sued to scrap the NMFS observer program. The observers' data, they argued, should not be used for enforcement. They won an injunction that kept all NMFS observers off U.S. tuna boats from 1981 to 1984, when the injunction was overturned on appeal. (At present the U.S. industry is suing to keep women observers off U.S. tuna boats.) In the late 1970s, when forced to do so, the U.S. industry demonstrated considerable inventiveness in coming up with gear and techniques to minimize dolphin kills. That research is stalled, and the U.S. industry has done nothing favorable to dolphins lately.

The separation of the U.S. and foreign tuna industries is in fact a kind of myth. Since 1979 two thirds of the big U.S. seiners have reflagged with foreign fleets. Apparently, little more than the flag has changed. American captains still skipper some of those boats, and available evidence suggests that the new ownership is often only nominal. Three U.S. corporations, H.J. Heinz (which owns Star-Kist), Pillsbury (Bumblebee), and Ralston-Purina (Chicken of the Sea), sell most of the tuna consumed in the United States. Sensibly, they buy their fish where it is least expensive. Yellowfin tuna from the *Maria Luisa* may be sitting in a can on your shelf.

At the MMPA reauthorization hearings several senators expressed their displeasure with the NMFS and its parent agency, the National Oceanic and Atmospheric Administration, for their failure to implement the regulations that would keep that can off the shelf. Senator John Kerry, of Massachusetts, pointed out that the MMPA was amended in 1984 to require foreign nations to demonstrate that they had dolphin-saving programs similar to our own or face a ban on imports of their tuna. Why had the NMFS taken four years to formulate "*interim* final regulations" to that end?

"It's a very delicate operation to get those regulations," explained Charles Fullerton, of the NMFS. "We developed some over a year ago which were not acceptable either to the tuna industry or to the foreign nations. So we went back to the drawing board and developed a whole new set, the ones that are now in interim phase. We'd like to give these a try."

How could a bureaucrat in a regulatory agency so lose track of his mission? The proposed NMFS regulations *were not acceptable to the tuna industry or the foreign nations*—the regulatees—so of course the regulators scrapped them?

"Our basic premise is that it's an unacceptable method of fishing. It should never have been invented in the first place, and it's got to end."

At the reauthorization hearings the environmental community asked for a phase-out, over four years, of tuna seining by dolphin encirclement. What they won was a prohibition—once again—on sundown sets. They won 100 percent observer coverage for trips by the U.S. fleet. They won a set of performance standards, a system by which the skippers most dangerous to dolphins would lose their licenses. They won a requirement that by the end of 1989 foreign countries must reduce their kill rate to double the U.S. rate, and by 1990 to 1.25 times the U.S. rate, or face embargo. Sam LaBudde and his colleagues regard these as the tiniest sorts of victory. No end to the dolphin killing is yet on the horizon.

Kenneth Brower, a frequent contributor to The Atlantic Monthly, *is a writer specializing in wildlife and ecology issues. His books include* Wake of the Whale *and* A Song for Satawal.

The Tuna Industry Does Not Needlessly Endanger Dolphins

StarKist Seafood Company

Dolphin, or porpoise as they also are known, are among the world's most charming mammals. The death of even one is cause for regret. It is only natural, therefore, that people would protest the loss of dolphin lives in the nets of tuna fishermen in the Eastern Tropical Pacific.

But sound solutions are the product of fact, rather than emotion—of advocacy tempered by understanding. This [viewpoint] represents our effort to shed needed light on an issue that is as complex as it is compelling.

Tuna provide humankind with one of its key sources of protein, but in the process of harvesting the catch in the Eastern Tropical Pacific, dolphin sometimes die. That is a fact. However, in the pages that follow, we describe the fishing methods used, the successful strides taken in the past to limit dolphin mortality and new industry and government initiatives to further address the issue. StarKist itself is funding research to speed progress.

Even though tuna fishermen today use helicopters and a wondrous array of electronic gear to locate schools of tuna, they continue to rely on a trained eye and nature's own signs. The activity of sea birds often provides a clue, as does a disturbance on the surface of the water. Tuna also are known to gather under ships or even floating debris.

However, in one of the world's most important fisheries, the Eastern Tropical Pacific, yellowfin tuna exhibit a behavior that is unknown among their fellow creatures. For reasons that remain a mystery to scientists, they often are found to travel under herds of dolphin.

This trait has been known by fishermen for more than 50 years, but until the pole-and-line method of fishing was replaced by netting operations some three decades ago, it was a matter of interest only to ship captains and their crews. Inefficient and labor-intensive, the pole-and-line method did not endanger the accompanying throng of dolphin, while the early approaches to netting clearly did. In those days, many of the dolphin taken incidental to tuna operations died.

Today, thanks in part to the pioneering efforts of three American tuna boat skippers, more than 99 percent of encircled dolphin are released unharmed by U.S. fishermen. The system devised by Anton Misitich and Manuel Neves Jr.—improved upon later by Harold Medina and others—is described in the pages that follow. But so, too, are strategies for further reducing the mortality in the future. Happily, it is a future that is near at hand.

How Are Tuna Netted?

1. Locate the school. Skippers search for signs—sea birds, floating objects, stirrings at the surface of the water or herds of dolphin—then verify the presence of tuna with electronic gear or, sometimes, by a helicopter overflight.

2. Circle the fish. When dolphin are present, speedboats are launched to herd the animals together, much like herding cattle. In this way, the underlying school of tuna is concentrated. Then, another boat is launched and, as it holds one end of the net in place, the mother vessel sails in a mile-wide circle, reeling out the giant net.

3. Close off the bottom of the net. Tuna nets are held on the surface by cork floats, but extend 400 feet down into the ocean. Running through the lower edge of the net is a cable, which is pulled like the drawstring of a purse, closing the net beneath the school of fish, effectively trapping it. However, even after this procedure is completed, the net remains open on the surface of the water, enclosing an expanse of open sea where dolphin swim unhindered.

4. Free the dolphin. About half the net is winched aboard, reducing the open area on the surface of the ocean, and the mother ship, by slowly backing away, pulls what originally is a circle of net into a long oval. As the boat continues to back away, the corkline at the far end of the oval dips beneath the surface, creating an escape route through which crew members in boats and rafts herd the dolphin. The most important thing about the [backdown] procedure is that *it works.* Thanks to its use, the U.S. fleet releases more than 99% of all encircled dolphin.

5. Harvest the fish. When the dolphin are free, power winches pull in the net further so that the tuna can be scooped out by a smaller net called a brailer. On modern U.S. vessels, refrigerated holds can freeze and carry some 1,200 tons of fish.

Working Toward a Perfect System

While no system is foolproof, the purse seine net and the backdown procedure have been perfected so that all dolphin are freed unharmed from more than half of the nets that are set on them by U.S. skippers and, of all dolphin encircled, 99 percent are released unharmed by U.S. fishermen. Still, all agree that fishing methods can and will be improved.

As indicated earlier, the problem was first addressed through the introduction of the purse seine net and backdown procedure. Later, skipper Harold Medina developed an improvement—a section of fine-mesh net, which when added to the seine at the point where the dolphin escape, prevent them from becoming entangled. Then came an even finer mesh panel called the "super apron."

New equipment, techniques and procedures are continually being investigated to further improve the situation. As a result of research conducted by the Porpoise Rescue Foundation (PRF), new "Porpoise Rescue Vehicles," highly maneuverable jet boats designed to facilitate the release of porpoise from nets, are now being placed onboard U.S. vessels. Also now being put into use on U.S. vessels after study by the PRF are "snap rings," which substantially reduce the time that porpoise are encircled, thus lessening the chance of mortality.

"The most important thing about the backdown procedure is that it works.*"*

Aggressive programs are underway to share technology and experience with all U.S. and foreign skippers. In fact, skipper skill and technique is one of the greatest single contributors to dolphin safety today. It is known, for example, that fishermen should avoid currents and wind conditions that can cause the net to be pushed in toward the boat, or the boat into the net. It also is well established that

small rafts can make a big difference when used like a quarter horse to herd dolphin out of the net and keep them away from dangerous areas. Today, crew members on boats and rafts take the extra step of actually getting into the water themselves to lift and push recalcitrant animals out of harm's way.

Progress? Yes. Current statistics from the Department of Commerce establish that no dolphin species is endangered or depleted in the Eastern Tropical Pacific. In fact, all populations were found to be stable and/or growing. Still, as long as there is individual dolphin mortality in nets, the search for improved techniques must continue.

Today, some dolphin are lost as a result of unavoidable equipment failure, wind shifts or other unpredictable environmental conditions. In addition, part of the mortality can be traced to inexperience or a lack of knowledge, specifically among foreign skippers whose governments do not require compliance with U.S. regulations. The good news is that in the United States, the government, the fishing industry and the tuna processors have launched joint initiatives to address these issues.

Government Action

In 1972, primarily in response to the killing of whales, Congress passed the Marine Mammal Protection Act, which banned the direct killing of marine mammals and ruled that specific species must not be allowed to drop "below their optimum sustainable population." From the beginning, tuna fishing operations have been covered by the act, although it was recognized that dolphin deaths in that pursuit are not intentional.

Firm limits on dolphin mortality, based on sound conservation principles, were established some five years later in the form of an annual quota. The task of enforcing these regulations is carried out by the National Marine Fisheries Service, which employs observers and assigns them to travel with ships of the American fleet collecting statistics and actually counting the number of dolphin that die as a result of fishing operations. If the quota is surpassed, fishing activities are halted for the remainder of the year.

Similar data is gathered aboard foreign fishing vessels through the Inter-American Tropical Tuna Commission.

Important amendments to reduce dolphin mortality have been made to the Marine Mammal Protection Act. Regulations developed by the government in cooperation with the industry are now in effect to eliminate all fishing activity involving the release of dolphin that may take place after sunset. So-called "sundown sets" have been determined to be an unreasonable source of incidental porpoise mortality.

Also developed by the government in cooperation with the industry are regulations setting a skipper performance standard that must be met in order to continue to operate a vessel. The standard, which is now under final review expected to be implemented shortly, will ensure that proficiency remains at a high level for those operating vessels that harvest tuna in association with porpoise populations.

In addition, to improve performance by foreign vessels, the U.S. Department of Commerce has established a series of regulations which require foreign fleets to meet comparable U.S. standards in order to export tuna products to the United States.

The ongoing effort to reduce dolphin deaths has involved government agencies, scientists and individual fishermen, but in all these activities tuna boat owners and processors have played a major role. Through the U.S. Tuna Foundation (USTF) and the Porpoise Rescue Foundation (PRF), they have funded much of the study that has taken place in past years and promoted the adoption of improvements in gear and techniques.

"The ongoing effort to reduce dolphin deaths has involved government agencies, scientists and individual fishermen, but in all these activities tuna boat owners and processors have played a major role."

Research has examined not only equipment and procedures but also performance and attitudes. Data from PRF computers quantified what long had been a suspicion—that saving dolphin is not only humane, but *smart*. Bluntly stated, releasing dolphin unharmed through a skillful backdown procedure takes less time than is required to process a catch in which a number of mammals have died. And, the quicker a skipper can pull in a catch and set his nets again, the more profitable the voyage.

The evidence for this emerges from data showing that skippers with the lowest dolphin mortality rates consistently catch the most fish. Indeed, one of the greatest tuna catches in history was scored in 1987, when total dolphin deaths came in more than 30 percent below the established limit. The comparison is particularly dramatic when the record of the U.S. fleet, with its low rate of dolphin deaths per set, is compared to the fleets of foreign nations where statistics show both higher dolphin mortality rates and lower tuna harvests than those of the United States.

As part of its ongoing studies, the PRF consulted with skippers on the most proficient vessels to determine the techniques that account for exemplary records. The PRF also continues to monitor each trip of U.S. vessels to study performance.

Education programs instituted by the PRF and USTF, on behalf of the industry, ensure that the impact and implications of these and other studies are communicated to skippers throughout the U.S. fleet. Active efforts are being undertaken to educate and inform foreign skippers as well. These programs are key as evidence suggests that skipper education programs hold the greatest promise in reducing dolphin losses in the Eastern Tropical Pacific.

The Future for Tuna

Tuna is an important, low-cost, high-protein food source and, for the foreseeable future, dolphin in the Eastern Tropical Pacific must be depended upon as locators of promising schools. However, additional progress in addressing the issue is on the horizon and will continue to be sought.

Playing roles in obtaining this progress will be American and foreign governments, and the tuna industry, including processors, tuna boat owners and skippers. StarKist pledges to be a leading partner in that effort, working through the United States Tuna Foundation and with the Porpoise Rescue Foundation to promote the research and education that will save dolphin lives.

We believe that these efforts will bring positive results because of the strong intentions and good will of those involved and because the simple truth is that releasing dolphin represents a more successful fishing technique than ignoring their safety. It is a powerful message and, in addition to supporting stronger regulations and education programs, we will work to get it across.

StarKist Seafood Company, a division of the H.J. Heinz Corporation, packages and sells tuna.

"The world is fragile and limited. A delicate balance exists between humanity and nature. When this breaks down, as is happening worldwide today, disaster is on the way."

viewpoint 91

Environmental Destruction Is an Impending Disaster

The Washington Spectator

Among the weeds of the Yucatan peninsula at the southern tip of Mexico is an awesome lesson. Here lie the scarred ruins of a great civilization, the Mayan, noted for its splendor. Archeologists have found traces of well-terraced hillsides; drained swamps for growing the staple food, corn; beautiful buildings and a rich cultural life.

Today, nothing remains but ruins. What happened? An extraordinary book, *State of the World 1987*, by Worldwatch Institute, explains: too many people, too little food, too great a diversion of resources and energy by war.

This is not a unique experience. "It is difficult to believe that some 2,000 years ago, northern Africa's fertile fields made it the granary of the expanding Roman Empire. Today, vast deserts cover the region and fully half its grain supplies are imported," reports the *State of the World 1987*.

Today, the desert marches relentlessly southward. Thirty years ago, the scrubland of semi-desert just north of the Niger River was rich with plants, and lions roamed the thick forests. As Byron wrote in sorrow, "Man marks the Earth with ruin."

The world is fragile and limited. A delicate balance exists between humanity and nature. When this breaks down, as is happening worldwide today, disaster is on the way.

Development Forum reports: "The depletion of resources, both renewable and nonrenewable, has contributed to the worst world economic crisis in half a century. . . . The global economy will continue to suffer without more careful management of the natural resources that support it. . . . Under pressure of ever-mounting demand for food, more and more of the world's farmers are mining their topsoil. Soil erosion has now reached epidemic proportions."

Yet, as *State of the World 1987* points out, we may live and prosper on this fertile Earth if we put away the sword, conserve soil and water and balance population with resources. If the problem is neglected, serious food and water shortages will appear, along with unemployment, inflation and such social problems as food riots, revolution, and war between states competing for scarce water. A candidate for disaster lies at our back door: Mexico.

Governments, including our own, habitually ignore the root problem and try to cure the unrest with guns.

A Thoughtful Look

The *New York Times* offers a thoughtful look at the world as it awaits the 21st century: "The pressures of population growth and economic expansion are starting to exceed the ability of Earth's natural systems to sustain it. . . . Human use of the air, water, land, forests and other systems that support life are pushing these systems over 'thresholds' beyond which they cannot absorb such use without permanent change and damage. The result has been declining food and fuel production in many parts of the world, contamination of the atmosphere, and the long-term prospect of a decline in the quality of life."

The keynote address to the American Association for the Advancement of Science in February 1987, by botanist Peter H. Raven, was titled, "We're Killing Our World." He pointed out, according to the *Boston Globe*:

• The five billion inhabitants of Earth are consuming or destroying 40% of the total output of photosynthesis, the source of all nutrition.

• "About half of the rain forests in tropical areas have already been lost to deforestation and other factors, and an area the size of Kansas is being lost every year to clear-cutting for timber, cattle grazing and other reasons."

The Washington Spectator, "Looking Ahead: The State of the World," May 1, 1987. Reprinted with permission.

• The drive by Third World nations to export cash crops is leading to overuse of the soil and the loss of arable land and forests. We are not exempt in the U.S. In the Midwest, about a foot of topsoil has been lost to intensive farming, and the great Ogallala aquifer is being depleted. In the Northeast, forests are deteriorating from acid rain.

Population Pressure

The world's population of five billion is expected to double in the next 35 years. In areas of high population growth, such as sub-Saharan Africa, "environmental stresses are mounting," and along with it is a drop in per capita grain production, says *State of the World 1987*.

The population dilemma is epitomized by China. Despite a vigorous birth-control campaign and strenuous efforts to increase grain production, China must import as much as 10 million metric tons of grain in 1987. Why? The *Washington Post* says, "With only 7% of the world's cultivable land, China has to feed almost a quarter of the world's population."

The effect of high population is described by *State of the World 1987*: "A natural grassland can indefinitely support a set number of cattle or a somewhat larger number of sheep. A fishery will meet the protein needs for a certain number of people, and the forests surrounding a village will supply the firewood for only so large a population. If the numbers depending on these biological supports become excessive, the systems will be slowly destroyed."

There is some awareness of the problem in Congress. Rep. Nancy L. Johnson (R-Conn.) says: "The whole Earth pays the price for overpopulation. Lack of food, housing and jobs causes political instability and social upheaval. Tropical forests are disappearing, grasslands are being overgrazed into deserts, and the air polluted by increased burning of fossil fuels. . . . Nearly half a million women die in childbirth each year, because they bear too many babies too soon. A quarter of the world's families live in makeshift shacks. One billion people don't have safe drinking water."

A case in point is Mexico, with 82 million people, adding 2.1 million each year. During the rest of the 20th century, 15 million young people will enter the job market. The economy staggers under an external debt of $102 billion. Seventeen million people crowd into Mexico City, most of them in the 'ciudades perdidas,' the lost cities without electricity or running water where wealth is measured by the number of children.

State of the World 1987 reports: "A broad-based deterioration of land resources and irrigation water are raising the dependence on imported food. . . . The basic ingredients for internal political conflict and civil strife are in place. The wealthiest 10% of Mexicans received 41% of total income; the poorest 20%, less than 3%. Real wages have declined during the 80s at least a fifth. Fiscal stringencies have forced the elimination of subsidies on tortillas, the cornmeal food staple. Unemployment is rising."

Mexican political scientist Jorge Castenada sees bleak choices for the young: try to move north into the U.S., idle away their time on the streets, or rise in revolt. Another analyst, Sergio Diaz-Briquets, sees rising unemployment among the young, thus "creating stiffer competition among those trying to improve their lot in life, particularly in ossified social systems."

A rise in the numbers of discontented youth is a phenomenon in Latin America, Africa and Asia. Foreign affairs expert Georgia Geyer writes of "unemployed youths roaming the streets in countries where half the population is under 18 years of age, with no prospect of jobs, hungry and looking to irregular leaders to lead them in new and as yet unpredictable movements. There is little question that even more political explosions are on the immediate horizon."

Why, when population pressure is so obvious, do birth rates stay high in Third World countries? The German publication *Der Spiegel* explains: "Mexico's family-planning program is powerless in the face of the macho male, who believes he must have as many children as his wife—or girlfriend—can bear. In Kenya, farmers also consider them [children] as a guarantee for survival and a status symbol. And in many African countries, political power is determined by the size of the tribe, so childbearing is a strict duty." Many Third World parents see children as an assurance that they will be taken care of in their old age. The Roman Catholic Church and the Moslem religion both encourage large families.

"Despite modern technology and feats of engineering, a secure water future for much of the world remains elusive."

"Despite modern technology and feats of engineering, a secure water future for much of the world remains elusive.

"Farmers in several food-producing regions face limited and, in some cases, dwindling water supplies, threatening future food production. . . . Water planners in many corners of the world—in humid climates as well as dry, in affluent societies as well as poor ones—are projecting that within two decades water supplies will fall short of demands," according to the *State of the World 1986*.

In the U.S., depletion of the giant underground Ogallala aquifer "threatens the lucrative High Plains farming economy." Groundwater is the water that lies underground, stored in springs, deep wells, aquifers, an accumulation in some cases of hundreds of years, and is not readily renewable. The Metropolitan Water District of southern California estimates that its supply could fall 14% short of demands by the year 2000. The World Resources Institute adds that "the use of water exceeds average streamflow in nearly every western [U.S.] subregion, and the deficits are being offset with groundwater and imports from adjoining basins."

In the Soviet Union, "there will obviously be a time when the water resources of the Aral Sea will be fully used up and water from Siberia will not yet be available" for the southern areas, according to *Soviet Geography*. Aquifer depletion and falling water tables are "increasingly widespread" across the world, according to *State of the World 1986*.

Looking for Answers

The answers lie in conserving water, removing pollutants and even, possibly, removing salt from seawater.

Of the 122 billion cubic meters pumped from the U.S. groundwater supply each year, 26 billion, or one-fifth, are nonrenewable. Arizona, to meet this challenge, is asking for taxes on groundwater withdrawals.

The greatest use of water is for farming, about 70% worldwide. In much of the Third World, irrigation claims 85-90% of the water. And irrigation systems are generally wasteful; efficiency worldwide averages only 37%. Much water is lost by evaporation and inefficiency.

As an example, irrigation efficiency can be increased by as much as 10% in the Indus region of Pakistan; this would provide enough water to irrigate an additional two million hectares.

Five ways to conserve water are recommended:

• Level the land so that water is evenly distributed when used for irrigation.

• Reduce the loss from evaporation by switching to systems that deliver water close to crops and are about 98% efficient. One type is drip or trickle irrigation, delivering water directly to the crops' roots. In Israel, drip irrigation waters 73,000 hectares, up from 6,000 just 10 years ago. In this country, California and Florida widely use the drip system.

• Schedule irrigation to coincide closely with plant needs, and choose crops that require a minimum of water. Sorghum and wheat use less water than corn and rice.

• Broaden recycling and reuse of water by cities and industries. In the U.S., manufacturing plants took in some 49 billion cubic meters of water in 1978, and each cubic meter was used 3.4 times before being discharged. This saved 120 billion cubic meters—water that did not have to be taken from the nation's supply. An Armco steel mill in Kansas City, Mo., manufacturer of steel bars from scrap, uses nine cubic meters per ton, compared with as much as 100-200 cubic meters per ton in other steel plants.

In the area known as the Federal District, including 70% of Mexico City, treated wastewater provides about 4% of water use, chiefly for parks and the filling of recreation lakes. In Israel, reclaimed water will replace one-fourth or more of the fresh water for farming. By the turn of the century, treated wastewater is expected to supply 16% of the total water needs there.

• Remove pollutants from water supplies. During the debate over the clean-water act, Senator Frank R. Lautenberg (D-N.J.) told of "a growing problem with groundwater contamination. Over 60% of the drinking water in New Jersey comes from groundwater. Drought makes these reserves more critical. Organic compounds, pesticides and heavy metals are found in the groundwater in virtually all areas of the state. Hundreds of wells have been restricted or closed because of chemical contamination." The clean-water bill was passed over President Reagan's veto.

"At the present rate of cropland loss and population growth, there will be half as much cropland available to feed each person by the year 2000."

The *New York Times* predicts, "Poor rural towns in Maine will no longer dump untreated wastes into once-pristine streams and rivers. Tumors will no longer grow on flounder at the bottom of Boston Harbor. Shellfish might one day return to New Jersey's Raritan Bay."

Of all the Earth's resources that are lost, "perhaps the most worrisome is that of topsoil," comments *State of the World 1987*. "Soil erosion is a natural process, but when it exceeds the rate of new soil formation, as it does now on 35% of the world's cropland, then the land's inherent productivity begins to decline." With it is loss of food and higher costs to feed the family. Roughly, 25 billion tons of topsoil disappear every year.

"Desertification now threatens 35% of the planet's land surface and 850 million poor people. About 78,000 square miles turn to desert yearly. About 50 million acres of forest are destroyed each year. The UN estimates that at the present rate of cropland loss and population growth, there will be half as much cropland available to feed each person by the year 2000," according to *Earth First*.

No wonder that the *Christian Science Monitor* editor, Earl W. Foell, writes: "The soil itself—that thin skin that shares our planet's name and, along with air, water and sun radiation, makes Earth habitable, does not get the kind of attention it should from our civilization."

While the greatest damage is in the Third World, our fertile country, which tried to feed the world in the 1970s, is in trouble, too.

A senior Department of Agriculture official tells what happened: "The economic pressure—to generate export earnings, to strengthen the balance of payments and thus the dollar—has been transmitted more or less directly to our natural resource base. As a result, soil erosion today can be described as epidemic in its proportion."

Four to five million acres that should not have been cultivated were added to the plow in the past seven or eight years in North and South Dakota, Montana, and Colorado. In five years, 1977-1982, the U.S. lost some 1.7 million tons of soil each year. Soil tests in the Midwest suggest an average loss of 59 pounds of organic nitrogen an acre over 25 years.

The problem is worldwide. In the Soviet Union, 1.2 million acres of wind-eroded farmland are abandoned annually. One billion tons of topsoil flow out of Ethiopian highlands each year. The loss of four inches of topsoil in one West African area cut corn yields by 52%. In four countries that contain about a quarter of Africa's population—Mozambique, Nigeria, Sudan and Tanzania—crop yields in the mid-1980s were lower than in the early 1950s, partly "because of heavy topsoil loss" and "the extension of agriculture into marginal land," according to the Worldwatch Institute.

More than 250,000 acres of farmland in North Africa are lost to the Sahara Desert every year due to overgrazing, unsuitable farm practices and firewood gathering.

Worldwatch soberly advises: "As world food demand has begun its second doubling since mid-century, pressures on land have become so intense that close to half the world's cropland is losing topsoil at a rate undermining long-term productivity. This loss of topsoil, if unarrested, will undermine the economy.

"Soil erosion will eventually lead to higher food prices, hunger, and, quite possibly, persistent pockets of famine. Although the world has weathered a severalfold increase in the price of oil over the past decade, it is not well equipped to cope with even modest rises in the price of food."

The Loss Of Forests

The World Resources Institute estimates that 27 million acres of tropical forests are lost each year, cut down to clear land for farms, roads and buildings, for firewood and lumber. This creates an immeasurable loss of oxygen, an addition of carbon dioxide in the atmosphere, desertification and a change of weather.

State of the World 1986 reports, "Of all the excessive demands on the Earth's natural resources,

that on forests is the most visible. . . . As of the mid-80s, every country in Africa is losing tree cover. . . . At the same time, forests in industrial areas are beginning to suffer from excessive chemical stress." The *New York Times* tells the toll of acid rain: "Rapidly accumulating evidence indicates that forests throughout the eastern U.S. are in decline, perhaps seriously. Some of the symptoms are similar to those that led to a dramatic decline in Central European forests."

"As evidence piles up of increasing damage to a fragile Earth, we might cease our fool's play of building monstrous weapons and fighting futile wars and, instead, go about repairing and restoring."

As evidence piles up of increasing damage to a fragile Earth, we might cease our fool's play of building monstrous weapons and fighting futile wars and, instead, go about repairing and restoring. The ancient ruins on the Yucatan peninsula should be enough of a goad. The end of a great civilization stands reproachfully among the tangled weeds.

The Washington Spectator *is a publication of The Public Concern Foundation in Fairfax, Virginia. The Foundation investigates political issues and problems worldwide, including human rights and the environment.*

"Resources, far from being limited, are abounding."

Environmental Destruction Is a Myth

Robert W. Lee

Editor's note: In the following viewpoint, Robert W. Lee considers acid rain, the greenhouse effect, ozone depletion, deforestation, overpopulation, and auto emissions, six environmental issues that he believes have been misunderstood and exaggerated.

Neither the cause, nor the extent, of the acid rain "problem" has been definitely established. Environmentalists claim that acid rain is formed when sulfur dioxide (SO_2) and nitrogen oxide (NO_x) pollutants enter the atmosphere and are chemically transformed by sunlight into acids which then fall to earth as precipitation. Coal-burning electric power plants, primarily in the Midwest, produce most of the SO_2, while automobiles are mainly responsible for NO_x emissions.

Volcanoes are another source of atmospheric acid, though environmentalists seldom mention this, since it is difficult to regulate volcanoes. In 1988, some 12 million tons of hydrochloric acid and 6 million tons of hydrofluoric acid were shot into the stratosphere by volcanoes. Scientists consider that amount to be about average, but on occasion it is far higher, as when Alaska's St. Augustine erupted in 1987 and Washington's Mt. St. Helens blew its top in 1980.

Ants (also difficult to regulate) are another source. In 1987, an atmospheric chemist with Bell Laboratories and zoologists from Cornell University reported that ants of the subfamily Formicinae make and store huge quantities of the formic acid that contributes most of the acidity to the rain that falls in remote areas and is found in atmospheric gas and precipitation around the globe. (It is abundant, for instance, in the fog and mists that hang over the rain forests of Central Africa.) According to *Insight* magazine (July 6, 1987), the "ants release the acid

Robert W. Lee, "Six 'Crises': All Leading to World Government," *The New American*, November 20, 1989. Reprinted with permission.

when defending themselves and communicating with each other and upon dying. Since 30 percent of the world ant population belongs to this subfamily, there is significant concern about the acid the ants release," an amount estimated at "600,000 metric tons annually," which is "equal to the combined formic acid contributions of automobiles, refuse combustion and vegetation.". . .

Acid Rain Control

On January 25th 1989, Senator John Kerry (D-MA) introduced a "National Acid Rain Control Act," citing as an example of the problem "Camel's Hump in . . . Vermont" where "there has been a 40-70 percent decrease in the life expectancy of spruce trees over the past 20 years." Seven months later, on July 25th, an ABC News report also claimed that acid rain generated by emissions from utilities was sterilizing the soil and killing trees on Camel's Hump Mountain. According to ABC correspondent Ned Potter, "doctors say acid rain is responsible for 50,000 deaths a year" in the United States.

Syndicated economics columnist Warren Brookes looked into the charges and wrote an important three-part series on acid rain that appeared in the *Washington Post* and other newspapers in August. He found that "the entire ABC acid-rain story was a fraud." The "50,000 deaths" figure, for instance, "came from one extreme theoretical estimate in an analysis where half the experts estimated zero health effects." Indeed, "not even the Environmental Protection Agency claims any known deaths from sulphur dioxide."

In 1982, *Natural History* magazine drew national attention to Camel's Hump. Soil scientists subsequently flocked to the area. According to Brookes, "in order to examine the dead or dying trees, they had to fight their way up through a veritable jungle of healthy young red spruce trees and new growth. It was immediately clear there was nothing toxic about the soil. On closer examination, soil scientists from Yale, the University of Pennsylvania and the U.S. Forest Service found the dead or dying trees had one thing in common: They all dated from before 1962. Trees started after that period were generally healthy."

What had happened in 1962? Yale University forestry expert Tom Siccama speculates that "it was probably the very severe drought followed by an especially killing winter" that year. Siccama is convinced that it was *not* acid rain, since "you don't get that sudden a change from something like acid rain" and it didn't happen in adjacent areas or states.

"An interim report found that relatively few U.S. lakes and streams had become acidified and that damage to crops, forests, and human health was negligible."

In 1980, an EPA report suggested that acid rain was responsible for an "aquatic silent spring" in Northeastern states and Canada. Shortly thereafter, the National Acid Precipitation Assessment Program (NAPAP) was established by the Reagan Administration to study the causes and effects of acid rain. In 1987, after the expenditure of more than $300 million, an interim report found that relatively few U.S. lakes and streams had become acidified and that damage to crops, forests, and human health was negligible. It concluded that no "abrupt change in aquatic systems, crops, or forests at present levels of air pollution" was likely. Environmental extremists and their allies in Congress were furious. Warren Brookes reports that NAPAP's director was fired and his successor was ordered to "'rewrite' the report and produce 'an implicit repudiation of the interim assessment.'" In April 1989, the EPA's Direct Delayed Response Project released a chart showing that there is no statistical correlation between acid rain deposition and acidic lakes.

On June 12th, 1989, President Bush proposed spending about $40 billion dollars over the next decade to reduce by another 10 million tons the annual SO_2 content of emissions generated by Midwestern states that burn coal to generate electricity (their annual output is presently around 22 million tons, down from 32 million tons in 1970). Economist Brookes calculates that the President's plan "will raise Midwest electricity rates 20 to 30 percent and cut coal mine employment in Appalachia by 40 to 60 percent." Even then, the plan is unlikely to achieve its stated goal of significantly

reducing the acidity of the region's lakes and rivers. More than 90 percent of all acidic lakes are naturally so. In April 1989, Dr. Edward Krug of the Illinois State Water Survey released a lengthy study he had prepared for the Department of Energy. It concluded that the acidity of lakes and rivers has little (if anything) to do with acid rain, and is instead related to such factors as land use, solid chemistry, and geology. . . .

Dr. James Hansen, director of the Goddard Institute at the National Aeronautics and Space Administration, is the nation's most outspoken advocate of the thesis that because the concentration of carbon dioxide (CO_2) in the atmosphere has risen 30 percent in the last 100 years, and is expected to rise another 40 percent by the year 2050, the planet will warm up by about 4 degrees Celsius (over 7 degrees Fahrenheit). Dr. Hansen and his disciples contend that such an eventuality would cause major coastal flooding, inland droughts, and sundry other catastrophes.

It is estimated that all of the carbon dioxide injected into the air by the entire human race is less than the amount attributable to volcanoes alone. According to a study reported in *Science* magazine for November 5, 1982, the "estimated gross amount of CO_2 produced (by termites) is more than twice the net global input from fossil fuel combustion." In addition, "Termites are a potentially important source of atmospheric methane; they could account for a large fraction of global emissions." The wood-eating pests have bacteria in their guts that enable them to digest carbon so efficiently that some 90 percent of it is converted to CO_2, methane, and other gases, which they belch into the atmosphere.

Biocycle for July 1987 described another natural source of methane gas. A geophysicist with the New Zealand Institute of Nuclear Sciences discovered that "a lot of methane comes from flatulent sheep. For instance, New Zealand's 70 million sheep emit 2.5 billion gallons of methane into the atmosphere every week."

Global Warming

If the "greenhouse" thesis is correct, our planet should have warmed by 1.3 degrees centigrade during the last century and at least 1 degree centigrade in the last 50 years. Eliminating all automobile driving in North America would save perhaps one-half of a degree of warming. Reducing CO_2 emissions by 20 percent would require that the price of both oil and coal be doubled by taxation. "Fortunately," Warren Brookes reports in a four-part series on global warming that appeared during September 1989, "neither is even close: Over the last 100 years, the statistically inflated warming trend was less than 0.5 degrees centigrade. Most of that happened by 1939 before any CO_2 buildup. In the last 50 years since 1938, there has been practically no net warming at all—and the Northern Hemisphere has actually cooled slightly during two-thirds of the CO_2 buildup.". . .

Dr. James Hansen sought to minimize the importance of the findings by claiming that the United States was too small to reflect a global trend. But Dr. Richard Lindzen, Sloan Professor of Meteorology at the Massachusetts Institute of Technology, told Warren Brookes: "That's absurd. Actually, the smaller the area, the greater the variability. The absence of a trend in the U.S. record leads to the suspicion that all the trends in the global record may in fact be spurious."

Dr. Lindzen notes that recent data from Europe and Canada indicate the absence of a warming trend over land masses, and "most of the Earth's surface is covered by oceans over which we have no fixed-station records."

Greenhouse Propaganda

Propagandists for the "greenhouse" theory usually select 1880 as the base year for their calculations. Dr. Reid Bryson, founder of the Institute for Environmental Studies at the University of Wisconsin, recalls that 1880 was "in the last part of what has been called 'the Little Ice Age' (1500-1880)." Since that year was abnormally cold, it makes today's temperatures seem abnormally warm. Dr. Hugh Ellsaesser of Lawrence Livermore Laboratories points out: "All we probably have seen is a modest recovery from those Little Ice Age lows." If the base year is moved back, say, to 1860, the "warming" melts away.

Urbanization is another important factor. Cities, where trees and grass are replaced with concrete and asphalt, can inflate a region's temperature by as much as a full degree Fahrenheit.

Ironically, the removal of SO_2 from the atmosphere to curb acid rain may contribute significantly to global warming. Warren Brookes explains that SO_2 "not only acidifies rain, it combines with water vapor to form what are known as 'aerosols,' which have the effect of brightening clouds. This makes them reflect more heat away from the earth, thereby cooling it." In the 1960s, when temperatures were falling dramatically in our hemisphere (at the time, many of today's "greenhouse" fright-peddlers were predicting a new ice age), Dr. Reid Bryson attributed the phenomenon in part to "the human volcano" of particulate emissions serving to "backscatter the radiation" of the sun. Needless to say, he was severely criticized for proposing that thesis. But in June 1989, *Nature* magazine printed an article by British climate modeler Thomas Wigley that concluded that the cooling effects of SO_2 "may have significantly offset the temperature changes that resulted from the greenhouse effect."

A recent paper by Dr. Patrick Michaels, chairman of the Department of Environmental Sciences at the University of Virginia, confirms that SO_2 emissions "serve to 'brighten' clouds, reflecting away increasing amounts of solar radiation, and possibly compensating for greenhouse warming." Proponents of the "greenhouse effect" assume that cloud cover contributes to warming, but Dr. Michaels contends that "because of SO_2, that turns out to be dead wrong."

A team of University of Chicago scientists concluded in 1988 that "clouds have a net cooling effect on the earth that is large over the mid- and high-latitude oceans" (i.e., the Northern Hemisphere). Dr. Michaels observes:

> That happens to be precisely in the paths of both the United States and Eurasian coal-burning emission plumes. Careful analysis of cloud brightness by Dr. Robert Cess at the State University of New York shows clear patterns of high and then declining brightness out 2,500 miles or more. But no such trends exist in the Pacific Ocean, where there is no SO_2.
>
> This would explain not only why U.S. and Northern Hemisphere temperatures have failed to respond to CO_2, but also why U.S. daytime temperatures (when brighter clouds have the most cooling effect) have actually declined in the last 50 years, even as the nighttime lows have risen.

Fascinating! If true, the SO_2 emissions that President Bush wants to abolish could actually be helping to make the "greenhouse effect" good for us. Dr. Michaels explains that, if the CO_2-induced warming "takes place primarily at night," then the global-warming doomsayers are "dead wrong," because "[i]ncreases in drought frequency are minimized. The growing season is longer, because that period is primarily determined by night low temperatures . . . many plants, including several agriculturally important species, would show enhanced growth from the fertilizer effect of CO_2." . . .

"The SO₂ emissions that President Bush wants to abolish could actually be helping to make the 'greenhouse effect' good for us."

The ozone layer, a gaseous "blanket" in the upper atmosphere which was discovered around 1880, filters out solar radiation that would otherwise harm life on earth. Any significant reduction in atmospheric ozone, environmentalists claim, could result in increased skin cancer, cataracts, damage to the human immune system, reduced crop yields, and alterations in land and water ecosystems. They contend that the protective ozone shield is being threatened, primarily by the chlorine in chlorofluorocarbons (CFCs), industrial gases on which an estimated $135 billion worth of equipment in the United States alone is dependent. Some 5,000 companies use CFCs to produce goods or services worth $28 billion a year. Approximately one-third of the CFCs in the U.S. are used in refrigeration and air conditioning (including automobile air conditioners); and they are also used in foam insulation, solvents, fire extinguishers, and aerosol cans. CFC-based solvents are critical in cleaning electronic equipment. The U.S. has ratified the 1987 Montreal Protocol on Substances that Deplete the Ozone Layer, which calls for halving the production and consumption of CFCs by 1999. On March 2nd 1989, Senator John Chafee (R-RI) introduced legislation to ban CFCs completely by 1997.

Writing in *Access to Energy* for September 1987, Dr. Petr Beckmann explained how the ozone process works:

> . . . solar radiation splits oxygen molecules into its two component atoms, the latter combining with unsplit molecules into triple-atom molecules, that is, into ozone. The ozone strongly absorbs long-wave ultraviolet radiation, turning most of its energy into heat. This radiation would kill plant life if it reached the earth's surface. If the oxygen-splitting process went on forever, there would be no normal oxygen (O_2) left to turn into ozone (O_3). What returns the ozone back to oxygen consists of two categories. The first is undisputed: ultraviolet (and other) solar radiation, which tears off the extra ozone atom to leave a normal oxygen molecule, and in the process loses some of its deadly energy (the rest is lost as heat to the ozone molecules). This is the effect that shields us.
>
> But there is another category of effects that could change the ozone back to oxygen: chemicals that stray into the stratosphere. . . . There are no less than 150 simultaneous chemical reactions involved that *could* do the trick *if* the culprit is the chlorine, though not necessarily that from CFCs. . . . Nitrogen oxides from both natural sources and fertilizers could do it. Methane could do it. Carbon dioxide could do it.

As noted earlier, some 12 million tons of hydrochloric acid were blown into the atmosphere by volcanoes in 1988. And the salt (sodium chloride) from ocean spray that diffuses upwards in storms and hurricanes is another natural source of atmospheric chlorine. Dr. Beckmann contends that there "is not a soul on earth that knows which of these have what effect (if any) in removing ozone compared with orthodox dissociation by solar radiation." Nevertheless, environmentalists blame industry to justify additional government regulation and taxation.

The Ozone Hole

In 1985, scientists discovered a huge "hole" in the ozone layer above the Antarctic. The "hole" appears annually during September and October, then returns to normal by late November or December. It was slightly larger in 1986, larger still in 1987, and became smaller in 1988. . . . Since the time scale in geophysics is measured in decades, centuries, and

millennia, Dr. Beckmann contends that it is ludicrous to attempt to draw any firm conclusions from the skimpy data to date. The "hole" does not indicate any planet-wide deficiency of ozone. It appears to be simply a seasonal redistribution while the worldwide total remains constant. Dr. Beckmann reports that the "changes of ozone concentration in the layer at a given latitude and at a given time of the year amount to about 0.2 percent per year since 1978; but the seasonal change above Denver is 25 percent, and the variation by latitude is 25 percent between Miami and Vancouver. . . . This tiny positive change is not constant; in the 1960s it was about as large, but negative. Why was the world not threatened by suffocation in the ozone glut then?". . .

"The 'hole' does not indicate any planet-wide deficiency of ozone."

The world's tropical rain forests (the largest is in the Brazilian Amazon) are reportedly being destroyed at a rate of about 53 acres per minute. They contain a tremendous wealth of plant and animal life and are a significant source of the herbs and drugs that humans use to keep healthy. Indeed, the Amazon qualifies as the world's largest pharmaceutical and biochemical factory.

Since forests absorb huge quantities of CO_2 (they now store about 350 billion tons, roughly half of all carbon in the atmosphere), deforestation increases the atmosphere's CO_2 content.

Agricultural expansion is responsible for approximately 30 percent of tropical deforestation, as individuals impoverished by the collectivist economic policies of their governments strive to survive. But the fertility of such land is quickly exhausted, forcing subsistence farmers to clear additional acreage within a year or two. Less government and more free enterprise, resulting in job diversification and rising standards of living, would greatly reduce the need to ravish the rain forests.

On occasion, internationalists have themselves implemented policies detrimental to the forests. Consider, for example, the notorious World Bank-funded Polonoroeste project in Brazil. It was an effort to cut a 900-mile highway into the rain forest, with a network of secondary roads intended to open up much of the Amazon basin to agriculture and industry. In the Spring of 1985, Senator Bob Kasten (R-WI) learned that World Bank loans had already financed the destruction of millions of acres of forest (an area approximately the size of Wisconsin). The Senator investigated and learned that the World Bank had "continued to fund this project for more than two years after it had identified, through its own supervisory missions, that the program was producing environmental devastation of this scale." He also learned that experts had warned from the start that the soil being cleared was insufficient to support planned agricultural operations. Complaints by others were ignored by the World Bank, so Senator Kasten intervened and a few weeks later the project was suspended. "Polonoroeste," he contends, "should never have been approved, much less subsidized by American taxpayers."

Overpopulation

In the days of the Roman Empire there were environmental fright-peddlers proclaiming that population growth was too great and the earth was worn out. In the late 1930s, some educators were telling students that by the time they graduated from college they would be living in darkness, since the exhaustion of fuel supplies would force power plants to shut down. (Our known oil reserves are far greater now than they were then and we have barely touched the earth's vast storehouse of resources.) As Jacqueline Kasun, Professor of Economics at Humboldt State University in California, reports in her important book, *The War Against Population* (Ignatius Press, 1988):

> Resources, far from being limited, are abounding. No more than 1 to 3 percent of the earth's ice-free land area is occupied by human beings, less than one-ninth is used for agricultural purposes. Eight times, and perhaps as much as twenty-two times, the world's present population could support itself at the present standard of living, using present technology; and this leaves half the earth's land surface open to wildlife and conservation areas.

Before Columbus, the Americas were "overpopulated," and some peoples regularly resorted to cannibalism to survive. North America was "overpopulated" when the Indian population was at most 300,000. As the horse and the gun became available, and productive agricultural techniques developed, the problem of "overpopulation" receded even as population grew.

The Plymouth Colony at New England faced famine due to the communistic system of farming that it initially employed. Incentives to produce were hamstrung, as they always are by statist intervention. Once the collectivist system was replaced by the free market, productivity increased and the "overpopulation" problem disappeared. As Dr. Rousas J. Rushdoony has noted: "The world, during its least populous eras, suffered most from hunger and famine." On the other hand, as "statist controls receded in the 19th century, hunger also began to recede, and Western civilization increasingly saw famine banished and hunger successfully dealt with. A far greater population enjoyed far greater supplies of food."

During the 20th century, as statist controls have increased in one country after another (most oppressively under communist regimes), hunger and famine have also increased. In Marxist Ethiopia, for instance, the regime of Lt. Col. Mengistu Haile Mariam abandoned traditional agricultural practices and disrupted food production without providing a viable alternative. As summarized by the Heritage Foundation: "Traditionally, Ethiopian peasants have saved food in good years to prepare for bad harvests. The government outlawed this practice, branding it as hoarding. Peasants traditionally invested money earned from surplus crops in their own farms to expand production. This was denounced as capitalist accumulation. Independent food traders traditionally bought food in food-surplus areas and transported it to markets in food-deficient areas. This was outlawed as exploitation, and government commissions replaced the free market."

"The 'myth of overpopulation is a form of attack on the free market, even though no more lawless and evil use of men and materials exists than under socialism.'"

Dr. Rushdoony finds it amazing that so many people are determined "to see this world as severely limited in its resources: minerals, oil, gas, air, ozone, everything is supposedly being exhausted by 'rapacious' capitalistic man." He points out that the "myth of overpopulation is a form of attack on the free market, even though no more lawless and evil use of men and materials exists than under socialism."

Automobiles provide the sort of individual mobility and privacy that statists deplore. As noted economist Hans F. Sennholz has observed, the "automobile means high standards of living, great individual mobility and productivity, and access to the countryside for recreation and enjoyment. In rural America it is the only means of transportation that assures employment and income. Without it, the countryside would surely be depopulated and our cities far more congested than now." It is hardly a surprise that the automobile has been targeted for massive environmental regulation. During Robert Redford's "greenhouse glasnost" get-together in August 1989, Michael Deland, chairman of President Bush's Council on Environmental Quality, bluntly asserted that we must cool our "love affair" with the automobile. On March 19, 1989, Senator James Jeffords (R-VT) introduced legislation that would, under the guise of reducing CFCs, completely ban after 1993 the sale or export of domestically produced automobiles equipped with air conditioners that use CFC coolants. On February 22, 1989,

Representative Claudine Schneider (R-RI) introduced legislation that would manipulate the car market by granting a tax rebate of up to $2,000 to those who purchase "efficient" vehicles, while hiking the existing tax on "gas guzzlers." Environmental guru Paul Ehrlich of Stanford University suggested during the Smithsonian Institution conference in September 1989 that gasoline should be taxed to raise the price to at least $2.30 a gallon. Even if "it didn't cut consumption," Ehrlich noted, "it would at least reduce the deficit" by transferring more money from the private sector to government.

Some cars driven by environmental hypocrites have carried bumper stickers reading, "Fight smog. Get a horse." The implication that horses would, or ever did, provide a cleaner atmosphere than automobiles is ridiculous. As Dr. Rushdoony points out, the age of transportation by horse was an environmental nightmare:

> Milwaukee, in 1907, had a population of 350,000 people, and a horse population of 12,500. It had a daily problem of 133 tons of manure. . . . In 1908, when New York's population was 4,777,000, it had 120,000 horses. Chicago in 1900 had 83,330 horses.

The streetcar and some automobiles had alleviated the need for horses to some degree, but, with 3.5 million horses in U.S. cities (and another 17 million in the countryside, many of which would come into cities when farmers were delivering produce or purchasing supplies), what was life like? Rushdoony continues: "In the winter or spring, the manure turned to slush, and it meant walking (and slipping and falling) into liquefied manure in bad weather. Americans then were not as calm and sedate as romantics would believe. The weather then led to more bad tempers than we can imagine today. What the well-dressed man and woman said on being plastered by liquefied manure by a passing carriage, or on slipping and falling into the foul slush, is best left to the imagination. It was not a pretty picture."

Horse Pollution

The situation did not improve much in the summer, when the "sun dried the manure, and the carriage and wagon wheels soon turned it into a floating dust to be breathed by all, and to coat clothing and furniture with a foul covering. People complained about breathing 'pulverized horse dung,' and a summer breeze was a disaster. Summer rains only brought back a manure mush."

And what about noise pollution? "Iron horse shoes on cobblestone pavements, four shoes to a horse, and sometimes two and four horses to a wagon, made a tremendous racket, night and day. Automobiles and trucks are silent by comparison. The noise also involved the shouts and profanity of teamsters trying to get the maximum effort out of their over-worked animals." Also, "without the automobile, urban sprawl was not nearly as possible

then as now, and cities were more compact and concentrated. This meant that every form of pollution was also more concentrated and had a corresponding effect on city dwellers."

"The automobile did not increase pollution. Rather, it helped limit it severely."

In short, Rushdoony concludes, the "coming of the twentieth century technology and the automobile did not increase pollution. Rather, it helped limit it severely. Bad as smog is, a very strong case exists for the very important fact that the air over cities is now definitely cleaner."

Robert W. Lee is a contributor to The New American, *a conservative weekly magazine.*

The Federal Government Can Save the Environment

Al Gore

How can we possibly explain the mistakes and false starts President Bush has been making on environmental policy? His administration's decision to censor scientific testimony on the seriousness of the greenhouse effect—and initially to oppose an international convention to begin working out a solution to it—may well mean that the president himself does not yet see the threat clearly. Apparently he does not hear the alarms that are awakening so many other leaders from Margaret Thatcher to Mikhail Gorbachev.

Humankind has suddenly entered into a brand new relationship with the planet Earth. The world's forests are being destroyed; an enormous hole is opening in the ozone layer. Living species are dying at an unprecedented rate. Chemical wastes, in growing volumes, are seeping downward to poison groundwater while huge quantities of carbon dioxide, methane and chlorofluorocarbons are trapping heat in the atmosphere and raising global temperatures.

How much information is needed to recognize a pattern? How much more is needed by the body politic to justify action in response?

If an individual or a nation is accustomed to looking at the future one year at a time, and the past in terms of a single lifetime, then many large patterns are concealed. But seen in historical perspective, it is clear that dozens of destructive effects have followed the same pattern of unprecedented acceleration in the latter half of the 20th century. It took 10,000 human lifetimes for the population to reach two billion. Now in the course of one lifetime, yours and mine, it is rocketing from two to 10 billion, and is already halfway there.

Yet, the pattern of our politics remains remarkably unchanged. That indifference must end. As a nation and a government, we must see that America's future is inextricably tied to the fate of the globe. In effect, the environment is becoming a matter of national security—an issue that directly and imminently menaces the interests of the state or the welfare of the people.

National Security

To date, the national security agenda has been dominated by issues of military security, embedded in the context of global struggle between the United States and the Soviet Union—a struggle often waged through distant surrogates, but that has always harbored the risk of direct confrontation and nuclear war. Given the recent changes in Soviet behavior, optimism is growing that this long, dark period may be passing. This may in turn open the international agenda for other urgent matters and for the release of enormous resources, now committed to war, toward other objectives. Many of us hope that the global environment will be the new dominant concern.

Of course, this national security analogy must be used very cautiously. The U.S.-Soviet rivalry has lasted almost half a century, consumed several trillions of dollars, cost close to 100,000 American lives in Korea and Vietnam and profoundly shaped our psychological and social consciousness. Much the same could be said of the Soviets. Nothing relieves us of our present responsibilities for defense or of the need to conduct painstaking negotiations to limit arms and reduce the risk of war.

And yet, there is strong evidence the new enemy is at least as real as the old. For the general public, the shocking images of 1988's drought, or of beaches covered with medical garbage, inspired a sense of peril once sparked only by Soviet behavior. The U2 spy plane now is used to monitor not missile silos but ozone depletion. Every day in parts of southern

Al Gore, "We Need a Strategic Initiative for the Environment," *The Washington Post National Weekly Edition*, May 22-28, 1989, © The Washington Post.

Iowa, where it hasn't rained for more than a year, National Guard troops are being used to distribute drinking water. In the not-too-distant future, policies that enable the rescue of the global environment will join, perhaps even supplant, our concern with preventing nuclear war as the principal test of statecraft.

However, it is important to distinguish what would—in military jargon—be called the level of threat. Certain environmental problems may be important but are essentially local; others cross borders, and in effect represent theaters of operations; still others are global and strategic. On this scale, the slow suffocation of Mexico City, the deaths of forests in America and Europe or even the desertification of large areas of Africa might not be regarded as full-scale national security issues. But the greenhouse effect and stratospheric ozone depletion *do* fit the profile of strategic national security issues.

Radical Responses

When nations perceive that they are threatened at the strategic level, they may be induced to think of drastic responses, involving sharp discontinuities from everyday approaches to policy. In military terms, this is the point when the United States begins to think of invoking nuclear weapons. The global environmental crisis may demand responses that are equally radical.

At present, despite some progress made toward limiting some sources of the problem, such as CFCs, we have barely scratched the surface. Even if all other elements of the problem are solved, a major threat is still posed by emissions of carbon dioxide, the exhaling breath of the industrial culture upon which our civilization rests. The implications of the latest and best studies on this matter are staggering. Essentially, they tell us that with our current pattern of technology and production, we face a choice between economic growth in the near term and massive environmental disorder as the subsequent penalty.

This central fact suggests that the notion of environmentally sustainable development at present may be an oxymoron, rather than a realistic objective. It declares war, in effect, on routine life in the advanced industrial societies. And—central to the outcome of the entire struggle to restore global environmental balance—it declares war on the Third World.

If the Third World does not develop economically, poverty, hunger and disease will consume entire populations. Rapid economic growth is a life-or-death imperative. And why should they accept what we, manifestly, will not accept for ourselves? Will any nation in the developed world accept serious compromises in levels of comfort for the sake of global environmental balance? Who will apportion

these sacrifices; who will bear them?

The effort to solve the nuclear arms race has been complicated not only by simplistic stereotypes of the enemy and the threat he poses, but by simplistic demands for immediate unilateral disarmament.

Similarly, the effort to solve the global environmental crisis will be complicated not only by blind assertions that more environmental manipulation and more resource extraction are essential for economic growth. It will also be complicated by the emergence of simplistic demands that development, or technology itself, must be stopped for the problem to be solved. This is a crisis of confidence which must be addressed.

The tension between the imperatives of growth and the imperative of environmental management represents a supreme test for modern industrial civilization and an extreme demand upon technology. It will call for the environmental equivalent of the Strategic Defense Initiative: a Strategic Environment Initiative.

I have been an opponent of the military SDI. But even opponents of SDI recognize this effort has been remarkably successful in drawing together previously disconnected government programs, in stimulating development of new technologies and in forcing a new analysis of subjects previously thought exhausted.

We need the same kind of focus and intensity, and similar levels of funding, to deal comprehensively with global warming, stratospheric ozone depletion, species loss, deforestation, ocean pollution, acid rain, air and water and groundwater pollution. In every major sector of economic activity a Strategic Environment Initiative must identify and then spread increasingly effective new technologies: some that are already in hand; some that need further work; and some that are revolutionary ideas whose very existence is now a matter of speculation.

"We need . . . focus and intensity, and . . . funding, to deal comprehensively with global warming, stratospheric ozone depletion, species loss, deforestation, ocean pollution, acid rain, air and water and groundwater pollution."

For example, energy is the life blood of development. Unfortunately, today's most economical technologies for converting energy resources into useable forms of power (such as burning coal to make electricity) release a plethora of pollutants. An Energy SEI should focus on producing energy for development without compromising the environment. Priorities for the near term are efficiency and conservation; for the mid-term, solar power, possibly new-generation nuclear power, and biomass sources (with no extraneous pollutants and a closed carbon cycle); and for the long term, nuclear fusion, as well as enhanced versions of developing technologies.

In agriculture, we have witnessed vast growth in Third World food production through the Green Revolution, but often that growth relied on heavily subsidized fertilizers, pesticides, irrigation and mechanization, sometimes giving the advantage to rich farmers over poor ones. We need a second green revolution, to address the needs of the Third World's poor: a focus on increasing productivity from small farms on marginal land with low-input agricultural methods. These technologies, which include financial and political components, may be the key to satisfying the land hunger of the disadvantaged and the desperate who are slashing daily into the rain forest of Amazonia. It may also be the key to arresting the desertification of Sub-Saharan Africa, where human need and climate stress now operate in a deadly partnership.

Needed in the United States probably more than anywhere is a Transportation SEI focusing in the near term on improving the mileage standards of our vehicles, and encouraging and enabling Americans to drive less. In the mid-term come questions of alternative fuels, such as biomass-based liquids or electricity.

The Transportation Sector

Later will come the inescapable need for re-examining the entire structure of our transportation sector, with its inherent emphasis on the personal vehicle. The U.S. government should organize itself to finance the export of energy-efficient systems and renewable energy sources. That means preferential lending arrangements through the Export-Import Bank of the United States and the Overseas Private Investment Corp.

Encouragement for the Third World should also come in the form of attractive international credit arrangements for energy-efficient and environmentally sustainable processes. Funds could be generated by institutions such as the World Bank, which, in the course of debt swapping, might dedicate new funds to the purchase of more environmentally sound technologies.

Finally, the United States, other developers of new technology and international lending institutions should establish centers of training at locations around the world to create a core of environmentally educated planners and technicians—an effort not unlike that which produced agricultural research centers during the Green Revolution.

Immediately, we should undertake an urgent effort to obtain massive quantities of information about the global processes now underway—through, for example, the Mission to Planet Earth program of NASA [National Aeronautics and Space Administration].

And we also must target first the most readily identifiable and correctable sources of environmental damage. I have introduced a comprehensive legislative package that incorporates the major elements of this SEI: It calls for a ban, within five years, on CFCs and other ozone-depleting chemicals, while promoting development of safer alternatives; radically reducing carbon dioxide emissions and increasing fuel efficiency; encouraging massive reforestation programs; and initiating comprehensive recycling efforts.

"We also must target first the most readily identifiable and correctable sources of environmental damage."

Although Congress is recognizing the challenge, there remains a critical need for presidential leadership, for President Bush to show that as a nation we have the vison and the courage to act responsibly. And in order to accomplish our goal, we also must transform global politics, shifting from short-term concerns to long-term goals, from conflict to cooperation. But we must also transform ourselves—or at least the way we think about ourselves, our children and our future. The solutions we seek will be found in a new faith in the future of life on earth after our own, a faith in the future that justifies sacrifices in the present, a new moral courage to choose higher values in the conduct of human affairs, and a new reverence for absolute principles that can serve as guiding stars for the future course of our species and our place within creation.

Al Gore is a Democratic senator from Tennessee.

"In villages, neighborhoods, and shantytowns around the world, people are coming together to challenge the forces of environmental and economic decline."

viewpoint **94**

Grass-Roots Movements Can Save the Environment

Alan B. Durning

Women on the banks of the Ganges may not be able to calculate an infant mortality rate, but they know all too well the helplessness and agony of holding a child as it dies of diarrhea. Residents along the lower reaches of the Mississippi may not be able to name the carcinogens and mutagens that nearby chemical factories pump into the air and water, but they know how many of their neighbors have suffered miscarriages or died of cancer. Forest dwellers in the Amazon basin cannot quantify the mass extinction of species now occurring around them, but they know what it is to watch their primeval homeland go up in smoke before advancing waves of cattle ranches and developers.

These men and women in Bangladesh, Louisiana, and Brazil understand environmental degradation in its rawest forms. To them, creeping destruction of ecosystems has meant deteriorating health, lengthening workdays, and failing livelihoods. And it has pushed many of them to act. In villages, neighborhoods, and shantytowns around the world, people are coming together to challenge the forces of environmental and economic decline that endanger our communities and our planet.

In the face of such enormous threats, isolated grass-roots organizing efforts appear minuscule—10 women plant trees on a roadside, a local union strikes for a non-toxic workplace, an old man teaches neighborhood children to read—but, when added together, their impact has the potential to reshape the earth. Indeed, local activists form a front line in the worldwide struggle to end poverty and environmental destruction. These grass-roots groups include workplace co-ops, suburban parents committees, peasant farmers unions, religious study groups, neighborhood action federations, tribal

nations, and innumerable others. Although widely diverse in origins, these groups share a common capacity to utilize local knowledge and resources, to respond to problems rapidly and creatively, and to maintain the flexibility necessary to adapt to changing circumstances. In addition, although few groups use the term sustainable development, their agendas often embody this ideal. They want economic prosperity without sacrificing their health or the prospects for their children.

All by itself this new wave of local activist organizations is nowhere near powerful enough to shift modern industrial society onto a more sustainable course of development. The work required—from slowing excessive population growth to reforesting the planet—will involve an unprecedented outpouring of human energy. Yet community groups, whose membership now numbers in the hundreds of millions worldwide, may be able to show the world how to tap the energy to perform these acts.

Fledgling Environmental Movements

Grass-roots action is on the rise everywhere, from Eastern Europe's industrial heartland, where fledgling environmental movements are demanding that human health no longer be sacrificed for economic growth, to the Himalayan foothills, where multitudes of Indian villagers are organized to protect and reforest barren slopes. As environmental decay accelerates in industrial regions, local communities are organizing in growing numbers to protect themselves from chemical wastes, industrial pollution, and nuclear power installations. Meanwhile, in developing countries, deepening poverty combined with often catastrophic ecological degradation has led to the proliferation of grass-roots self-help movements.

In the Third World, especially, traditional tribal, village, and religious organizations—first disturbed

Alan B. Durning, "Action at the Grassroots: Fighting Poverty and Environmental Decline," published in 1989 by Worldwatch Institute. Reprinted with permission.

by European colonialism—have been stretched and often dismantled by the great cultural upheavals of the 20th century: rapid population growth, urbanization, the advent of modern technology, and the spread of Western commercialism. Community groups have been formed in many places to meet the economic and social needs these traditional ties once fulfilled.

In the face of seemingly insurmountable problems, community groups around the planet have been able to accomplish phenomenal things.

• In Lima's Villa El Salvador district, Peruvians have planted a half-million trees; built 26 schools, 150 day-care centers, and 300 community kitchens; and trained hundreds of door-to-door health workers. Despite the extreme poverty of the district's inhabitants and a population that has shot up to 300,000, illiteracy has fallen to 3 percent—one of the lowest rates in Latin America—and infant mortality is 40 percent below the national average. The ingredients of success have been a vast network of women's groups and the neighborhood association's democratic administrative structure, which extends down to representatives on each block.

"Asia has by many accounts the most active grass-roots movement."

• In Dhandhuka, on the barren coastal plain of India's Gujarat state, a generation of excessive fuelwood gathering and overgrazing has led to desertification, which in turn has triggered social and economic disintegration. As cattle died of thirst, the children lost their milk, making them easy victims for the diseases that prey on the malnourished. Conflicts erupted over water that seeped into brackish wells, and in the worst years, four-fifths of the population had to migrate to survive. As in much of the world, fetching water in Dhandhuka is women's work. Thus it was the women who decided, upon talking with community organizers in 1981, to build a permanent reservoir to trap the seasonal rains. Migrant laborers described irrigation channels lined with plastic sheets they had seen elsewhere, and the villagers reasoned that a reservoir could be sealed the same way. After lengthy discussion and debate, the community agreed to the plan, and in 1986, all but a few stayed home during the dry season to get the job done. Moving thousands of tons of earth by hand, they finished the pool before the rains returned. The next dry season they were well-supplied, which inspired neighboring villages to plan their own reservoirs.

Asia has by many accounts the most active grass-roots movement. India's self-help movement has a prized place in society, tracing its roots to Mahatma Gandhi's pioneering village development work 60

years ago. Gandhi aimed to build a just and humane society from the bottom up, starting with self-reliant villages based on renewable resources. Tens if not hundreds of thousands of local groups in India now wage the day-by-day struggle for development.

Across the region, community activism runs high. Three million Sri Lankans, for instance, participate in Sarvodaya Shramadana, a community development movement that combines Gandhian teachings with social action tenets of Theravada Buddhism. Sarvodaya mobilizes massive work teams to do everything from building roads to draining malarial ponds.

After Asia, Latin American communities are perhaps the most active. The event that sparked much of this work was the 1968 conference of Catholic Bishops in Medellin, Colombia, where the Roman Catholic Church fundamentally reoriented its social mission toward improving the lot of the poor. Since that time, millions of priests, nuns, and laypeople have fanned out into the back streets and hinterlands from Tierra del Fuego to the Rio Grande, dedicating themselves to creating a people's church embodied in neighborhood worship and action groups called Christian Base Communities. Brazil alone has 100,000 base communities, with at least three million members, and an equal number are spread across the rest of the continent.

Latin American political movements also laid the groundwork for current community self-help efforts. A decade ago, the rise and subsequent repression of Colombia's National Association of Small Farmers gave peasants experience with organizing that led to the abundance of community efforts today, including cooperative stores and environmental "green councils." In Nicaragua, the national uprising that overthrew the dictatorship of Anastasio Somoza in 1979 created a surge of grass-roots energy that flowed into thousands of new cooperatives, women's groups, and community-development projects.

Self-Help Organizations

Self-help organizations are relative newcomers to Africa, though traditional village institutions remain stronger here than in other regions. Nevertheless, in parts of Africa where political struggles have led to dramatic changes in political structures, local initiatives have sprung up in abundance. In Kenya, the *harambee* (let's pull together) movement began with independence in 1963 and, with encouragement from the national government, by the early '80s was contributing nearly one-third of all labor, materials, and finances invested in rural development. With Zimbabwe's transfer to black rule in 1980, a similar explosion in community organizing began, as thousands of women's community gardens and informal small-farmer associations formed.

A noteworthy characteristic of community movements throughout the Third World is the central role that women play. Women's traditional nurturing role may give them increased concern for the generations of their children and grandchildren, while their subordinate social status gives them more to gain from organizing.

Unfortunately, the map of Third World local action has several blank spaces. Independent community-level organizations concentrating on self-help are scarce or non-existent in the Middle East, China, north Africa, large patches of sub-Saharan Africa, and northeastern India. Likewise, remote regions in many countries lack grass-roots groups. Some of these absences are a result of cultural, religious, or political factors, as in China, where state-sanctioned local groups monopolize grass-roots development. Northeastern India and sub-Saharan Africa, by contrast, are home to some of the poorest people on earth. The absence of local groups there may reflect a degree of misery that prevents energy from being expended on anything beyond survival.

Outside the Third World, grass-roots movements are also on the rise. In the Soviet Union and Eastern Europe, where officially sanctioned local organizations are numerous but largely controlled by state and party hierarchies, the political openness of this decade has brought a wave of independent citizens groups.

Environmental issues and grass-roots politics play a major role in the new nationalist movements rocking the USSR. In February 1988, thousands of Armenians, tired of bearing the brunt of pollution from the scores of local chemical facilities, demanded cancellation of a proposed plant near their capital city, Yerevan. Eight months later, 50,000 Latvians, Estonians, and Lithuanians linked arms in a human chain stretching 150 kilometers along the shore of the severely polluted Baltic Sea to protest Soviet planners' blatant disregard for the ecology of their homelands.

"Outside the Third World, grass-roots movements are also on the rise."

In those regions where nuclear power is still on a growth course—Japan, France, and Eastern Europe—anti-nuclear movements have grown dramatically since the 1986 explosion at Chernobyl. Intense popular opposition seems to follow nuclear power wherever it goes. In the Soviet Union, public protests have led to plans to close one operating nuclear reactor and to cancellation of at least five planned plants. In Japan, an unprecedented groundswell—the first nationwide movement on an environmental issue in the country's history—has enrolled tens of thousands of citizens with no past experience in political activism. Women in particular are joining in large numbers, apparently sensitized

by fears of radioactive food imported from Europe after Chernobyl.

In Western industrial nations, community-based organizations set their sights on everything from local waste recycling to international trade and debt issues. The ascent of the German Green Party in the early '80s was partly a product of an evolution in this movement from local to national concerns. Inspired by their German counterpart, Green parties have sprung up in 16 European countries and already hold parliamentary seats in more than half of them.

Paralleling a steady rise in neighborhood organizing on local social and economic issues, the U.S. environmental movement experienced a marked grass-roots expansion in the early '80s. Local concern focuses particularly on toxic waste management, groundwater protection, and solid waste problems.

Issue-Oriented Activism

Issue-oriented environmental activism is not peculiar to industrial lands. Just as grass-roots self-help movements have spread through the slums and countrysides of many developing nations, vocal advocates for environmental protection have emerged in most capital cities. Malaysia, India, Brazil, Argentina, Kenya, Mexico, Indonesia, Ecuador, Thailand, and other developing countries have all given birth to activist groups—largely since 1980. Sri Lanka alone has a congress of environmental groups with 100 members. Environmental movements and grass-roots development movements have also begun to work together.

Despite the heartening rise of grass-roots action, humanity is losing the struggle for sustainable development. For every peasant movement that reverses the topsoil erosion of valuable agricultural land, dozens more fail. For each neighborhood that rallies to replace a proposed garbage burner with a recyling program, many others remain mired in inaction. Spreading today's grass-roots mobilization to a larger share of the world's communities is a crucial step toward putting an end to the global scourges of poverty and environmental degradation.

All local groups eventually collide with forces they cannot control. Peasant associations cannot enact national or international agricultural policies or build roads to distant markets. Women's groups cannot develop and test modern contraceptive technologies or rewrite bank lending rules. Neighborhood committees cannot implement citywide recycling programs or give themselves a seat at the table in national energy planning. The greatest obstacle to community action is that communities cannot do it alone. Small may be beautiful, but it can also be insignificant.

The prospects for grass-roots progress against poverty are further limited in a world economy in which vested interests are deeply entrenched and power is concentrated in a few nations. Thus reforms at the international level are as important as those in the village.

The largest challenge in reversing global ecological and economic deterioration is to forge an alliance between local groups and national governments. Only governments have the resources and authority to create the conditions for full-scale grass-roots mobilization. In the rare cases where national-local alliances have been forged, extraordinary gains have followed. South Korea and China have used village-level organizations to plant enormous expanses of trees, implement national population policies, and boost agricultural production. Zimbabwe has trained more than 500 community-selected family planners to improve maternal and child health and control population growth. In the year after the 1979 Nicaraguan revolution, a massive literacy campaign sent 90,000 volunteers into the countryside; in one year, they raised literacy from 50 to 87 percent. Even under Ferdinand Marcos' repressive rule in the Philippines, the National Irrigation Administration amazingly transformed itself into a people-centered institution, cooperating with peasant associations.

> *"The largest challenge in reversing global ecological and economic deterioration is to forge an alliance between local groups and national governments."*

Full-scale community-state alliances can come about only when a motivated and organized populace joins forces with responsive national leadership. But herein lies the greatest obstacle to mobilizing for prosperity and ecology: Few leaders are committed to promoting popular organizations. Because government's first concern is almost always to retain political power, independent-minded grass-roots movements are generally seen as more of a threat than an ally. Unrepresentative elites rule many nations and all too often they crush popular movements rather than yield any of their privilege or power. Inevitably, self-help movements will clash with these forces, because like all development, self-help is inherently political: It is the struggle to control the future.

Essentially, grass-roots action on poverty and the environment comes down to the basic question of people's right to shape their own destiny. Around the world, community organizations are doing their best to put this participatory vision into practice, and they are simultaneously posing an even deeper question. In the world's impoverished south, it is phrased, "What is development?" In the industrial north, "What is progress?" Behind the words, however, is the same profoundly democratic refrain: What kind of society shall our nation be? What kind of lives shall our people lead? What kind of world shall we leave to our children?

The Lesson

Whether these scattered beginnings launched by grass-roots groups eventually rise in a global groundswell depends only on how many more individuals commit their creativity and energy to the challenge. The inescapable lesson for each of us is distilled in the words of Angeles Serrano, a grandmother and community activist from the slums of Manila. "Act, act, act. You can't just watch."

Alan B. Durning is a researcher at the Worldwatch Institute in Washington, D.C. The Institute analyzes global problems, including the environment.

"Environmental scientists are blazing new, bold, and imaginative trails to discover the interactions that bind the elements of land, water, biota, and energy into planet Earth."

viewpoint **95**

Scientific Advances Can Save the Environment

Thomas F. Malone and Robert Corell

Environmental scientists are blazing new, bold, and imaginative trails to discover the interactions that bind the elements of land, water, air, biota, and energy into planet Earth. Understanding these interactions is imperative if future generations are to inherit a habitable planet, because human activity has expanded and developed to the point where anthropogenic environmental changes are jeopardizing continued human existence. Science stands at the threshold of an unprecedented opportunity to study and learn the far-reaching implications of both anthropogenic and natural environmental changes.

A comprehensive study of the global environment is within reach. Such a study would give humanity the knowledge base necessary to intervene on its own behalf—to reverse the trends of global environmental degradation and to bequeath to future generations a benign Earth. The complex and vital nature of this endeavor demands careful deliberation. A rationale for such a study, titled "Mission to Planet Earth," was set forth in *Environment* in 1987. It rested on five central considerations:

• A revolution under way in the sciences is leading to the treatment of the physical, biological, chemical, and geographical parts of the global system as an integrated and responsive whole.

• Scientific understanding of each part and the interactions among the parts is approaching a stage at which describing the controlling physical, chemical, and biological processes in quantitative form (i.e., with mathematical models) will be possible.

• Scientists are developing with unprecedented speed the necessary technological tools (*in situ* and

space-based measurements, computers, and communications) for a holistic analysis of Earth's system. These tools could enhance the ability of science to predict changes in the environment.

• With exponential growth in population, agriculture, and industry, human activity is becoming a powerful factor, or forcing function, for global change.

• The capacity of the global life-support system to sustain a technologically advanced and exponentially expanding civilization is likely to collapse within the foreseeable future.

Mission to Planet Earth

The rationale for a "Mission to Planet Earth" has been significantly transformed since 1987. Opportunities to respond to this scientific and technological revolution are still open and have, in fact, expanded on their own merits. The compelling need now, however, is to increase the knowledge base underlying major policy decisions on societal and national behaviors that affect global well-being. A new era, characterized by a grand convergence of natural sciences, social sciences, engineering, public policy, and international relations, is emerging.

Many national and international research organizations have incorporated the "Mission to Planet Earth" rationale into their language and programs. At a meeting in Berne, Switzerland, in September 1986, the General Assembly of the International Council of Scientific Unions (ICSU) decided to establish the International Geosphere-Biosphere Programme: A Study of Global Change (IGBP). Since that meeting, organization and planning have proceeded with remarkable speed. IGBP represents a herculean effort by scientists worldwide to give humanity the knowledge base to fashion policies that will reverse the global environmental decline.

What has pulled scientists out of their separate

Thomas F. Malone and Robert Corell, "Mission to Planet Earth, Revisited," *Environment*, vol. 31, no. 3, pp. 6-11, 31-35, April 1989. Reprinted with permission of the Helen Dwight Reid Educational Foundation. Published by Heldref Publications, 4000 Albermarle St. NW, Washington, DC 20016. Copyright © 1989.

laboratories to call for and organize this effort? Several recent developments have pushed global change and environmental policy issues on center stage. One such development is the frequent scientific prediction of a rise in global temperature of several degrees centigrade as a result of increased emissions to the atmosphere of greenhouse gases, which trap long-wave radiation emanating from Earth's surface. The possibility that human activity, especially fossil fuel use, could exacerbate the atmosphere's greenhouse effect was recognized as long as a century ago. Not until a 1985 meeting of Earth scientists in Villach, Austria, however, did the scientific community become sufficiently impressed with all the evidence for the probable magnitude of the greenhouse effect to call for political action. . . . In the summer of 1988, James Hansen, a scientist with the National Aeronautics and Space Administration (NASA), intensified the policy debate while testifying before the U.S. Congress by implying that the first sign of greenhouse warming had already been detected in the climate records.

"Scientists have repeatedly verified the manifestations of global change."

Another development that has pushed global change into the limelight is the sharp seasonal decrease of the stratospheric ozone layer over the Antarctic and signs of incipient decline over the Arctic. The ozone layer screens out the sun's harmful ultraviolet radiation. The warning by scientists in 1974 that chlorofluorocarbons (CFCs) drifting up into the stratosphere constitute a threat to the ozone layer turned out to be remarkably prescient. By 1987, the evidence for ozone depletion was so persuasive that international agreement was quickly reached on the Montreal Protocol to limit the production of CFCs. Already a number of countries have announced plans to accelerate the protocol's implementation by banning certain CFCs entirely by the year 2000.

A third development is the annual loss of more than 10 million hectares of forest cover in the tropics. In industrialized countries, millions of hectares of forest are destroyed each year by fire, and many more millions of hectares are jeopardized as a result of acid deposition. Worldwide, the rate of forest loss is about 1 acre (or 0.4 hectares) per second. At the same time, more than 5 million hectares of new desert are formed each year as a consequence of land mismanagement in semi-arid regions. Finally, the rate of extinction of plant and animal species has reached alarming and probably irreversible levels. This loss is robbing future generations of valuable resources for food, industry, and medicine. All of these developments have

helped to heighten the public's awareness of global change.

Scientists have repeatedly verified the manifestations of global change. Plans to cope with these disastrous changes are being formulated worldwide. Thus, research like that proposed in "Mission to Planet Earth" has been elevated to new importance by a greater perception on the part of the public and policymakers that human activity is rapidly approaching a level at which human-induced change of the global environment will be on a scale equivalent to change produced by natural forces. Some indications that there will be definite winners and losers in the global change game have sparked additional enthusiasm for worldwide conservation and research. More fuel for this fire has been the perception that the human carrying capacity of Earth may soon be stressed to a point where catastrophic consequences should be expected in regions currently characterized by high population density and growth.

The very threat of such consequences has raised issues of social equity and international security, and a stirring of political will for environmental causes is evident:

• In the United States, two dozen bills concerning the environment were cosponsored by more than 400 senators and representatives during the 100th Congress (1987 and 1988).

• In his 1988 campaign for the U.S. presidency, George Bush promised to convene an international conference on global warming during his first year in office.

• In fall 1988, in a speech to The Royal Society, Great Britain's Prime Minister Margaret Thatcher labeled protection of the balance of nature as one of the "great challenges of the late twentieth century."

• At their December 1987 summit meeting in Washington, D.C., General Secretary Mikhail Gorbachev and President Ronald Reagan agreed to a collaboration on issues of climate and environmental change.

• In his December 1988 address to the United Nations General Assembly, Gorbachev remarked that "international economic security is inconceivable unless related not only to disarmament but also to the elimination of the threat to the world's environment."

World Environment Day

• In his 1988 World Environment Day message, Mostafa Tolba, Executive Director of the United Nations Environment Programme (UNEP), warned that "it may take another 15 years before scientists can give reliable predictions of what warming will mean in each region. But by then it may be too late to act." He called on political and industrial leaders to cooperate with one another and with climate scientists to finance more international research and coordination that will produce more information more quickly.

In 1988, greater attention to climate change issues by the news media was both a cause and effect of the new public awareness. The National Geographic Society devoted the December 1988 issue of its magazine to the theme "Can Man Save This Fragile Earth?" *Time* magazine broke tradition and set aside identification of the man or woman of the year to dedicate its New Year's issue to "Planet of the Year: Endangered Earth." Beyond just diagnosing the ills of the planet, *Time* proposed a 19-point action agenda for all nations and 8 steps that the United States should take to address Earth's environmental crisis. In fact, three major U.S. news magazines—*Time, Newsweek,* and *U.S. News and World Report*—devoted cover articles to global change during 1988. More recently, the very critical nature of global change was well summarized by the U.S. National Academy of Sciences' recommendations to the Bush administration. . . .

Forcing functions of global change, including solar and orbital changes, solid-Earth processes, and, in particular, human activities that influence the Earth system on a planetary scale, must be analyzed and understood. Variations in solar activity influence climate change over scales of decades, centuries, and millennia. The solar energy flux can affect not only the physical environment but also such biological processes as photosynthesis and respiration. Solid-Earth processes such as volcanic eruptions and marine vents affect the global climate and may cause extinctions.

Changes in a human activity like land use can cause global change by disturbing carbon storage, nutrient cycles, the hydrologic cycle, atmospheric composition, and the reflection of solar energy from the Earth's surface. As global population grows and humans convert more and more natural resources into goods and services, anthropogenic perturbations of the environment can only increase. (Figure 1 shows projected population growth through the year 2120.) The rate of change itself may be a forcing function because the rate of change can affect the kind of change; short-term but extreme perturbations of Earth's system can cause more dramatic changes than do long-term, gradual perturbations.

The Flux of Energy

Scientists must pay more attention to the interactions of physical, chemical, and biological components of the system and to the flux of energy, water, and chemicals throughout all of Earth's domains, instead of concentrating on pieces of the system as if they were static and isolated. Understanding these interactions is critical in part because global change is nonlinear: It occurs as a threshold response to a continual force, just as the back of the proverbial camel breaks suddenly with

the addition of one more straw. Moreover, the change effected upon the atmosphere by the ocean will in turn affect the ocean (as well as other domains). Special attention must be paid to the cycling of chemicals (carbon, nitrogen, sulfur, phosphorus, and trace gases) through the physical, biological, industrial, and agricultural systems. A network of geosphere-biosphere observatories in selected ecosystems is envisioned to serve as regional research and training centers. As understanding of Earth processes is enhanced, attention will be turned to developing quantitative models capable of projecting global change into the future.

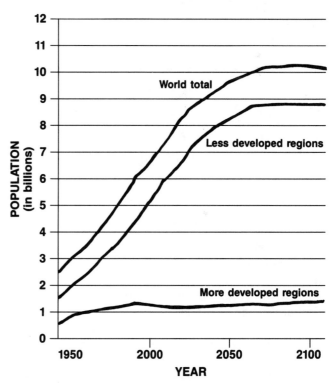

FIGURE 1

Projected population growth for developed and less developed regions through the year 2120.

Notes: More developed regions include Europe, North America, Australia, Japan, New Zealand, and the USSR. Less developed regions include Africa, Asia, Latin America, and Oceania.

SOURCES: Department of International Economic and Social Affairs, *World Population Prospects as Assessed in 1980, Population Studies No. 78* (New York: United Nations, 1981); and Department of International Economic and Social Affairs, *Long-Range Population Projections of the World and Major Regions, 2025-2150, Five Variants, as Assessed in 1980, 1981* (New York: United Nations, 1981).

Global change will cause important, large-scale modifications in the availability and distribution of renewable and nonrenewable resources. Although the force behind the change may be global in scale (like global warming), predictions of resource availability are needed on a regional scale. . . .

An important contribution to global-change research planning was the massive report *Earth System Science* released in January 1988 by the Earth System Sciences Committee of the NASA Advisory

Council. The Committee's mandate was to define a comprehensive, integrated program to obtain a scientific understanding of the entire Earth system and of the functions and interactions of its component parts. Such understanding could enable scientists to predict both natural and anthropogenic global changes over time scales of decades to centuries. The committee made detailed recommendations on five substantive topics:

• space-based and *in situ* long-term measurement of the global variables that define the vital signs of the Earth system and control its changes;

• fundamental description of Earth and its history;

• process studies and research focused on key Earth-system problems;

• development of Earth-system models to integrate data sets, guide research programs, and simulate future trends; and

• development of an information system to facilitate data reduction, data analysis, and quantitative modeling. . . .

"Scientists must pay more attention to the interactions of physical, chemical, and biological components of the system and to the flux of energy, water, and chemicals throughout all of Earth's domains."

The IGBP initiative at the international level is being supported by imaginative proposals emanating from many of the 70 scientific organizations adhering to ICSU. For example, the Committee on Global Change of the U.S. National Research Council recommended that U.S. contributions to IGBP include the development of an integrated EOS [Earth Observing System] with space- and ground-based observatories and proposed initial research priorities that included studies of:

• water, energy, and vegetation interactions, to develop models of the coupling between climate and terrestrial ecosystems;

• fluxes of trace gases and nutrients between terrestrial ecosystems, the atmosphere, and the oceans;

• biogeochemical dynamics in the ocean, to understand and predict the effects of global change on ocean biogeochemical cycles and their feedback effects on global change;

• Earth history, to construct models of past climate change that could stand as a basis for validating models of future global change; and

• human interactions with global change, with special attention to land-use changes that affect both physical and biological parameters and to the

residues from industrial/agricultural processes that perturb the global environment. . . .

In close coordination with the National Research Council and ICSU, a U.S. strategy for global change research was developed by federal agencies and transmitted to Congress by the Director of the Office of Science and Technology Policy in the Executive Office of the President. . . . The budget message proposed funding global change research with $190.5 million—an increase of 41 percent. The U.S. Global Change Research Program aims to provide a sound scientific basis for national and international policy decisions on global change issues. The program's scientific objectives are to monitor, understand, and, ultimately, predict global change. The strategy document identifies seven integrated and interdisciplinary elements of the program:

• *Biogeochemical dynamics.* The study of the sources, sinks, fluxes, and interactions among the mobile biogeochemical constituents within the Earth system and their influences (including global warming) on the life-sustaining envelope of the Earth.

• *Ecological systems and dynamics.* The study of how aquatic and terrestrial ecosystems both affect and respond to global change.

• *Climate and hydrologic systems.* The study of the physical processes that govern the climate and hydrologic systems central to global change, including the atmosphere, hydrosphere (oceans, surface and ground water, etc.), cryosphere (frozen regions), land surface, and biosphere.

• *Human interactions.* The study of the interface between natural processes and human activities. (The global environment is a crucial determinant of the human capacity for sustained development.)

Earth History

• *Earth-system history.* The study of past natural environment change as it is revealed in rocks, terrestrial and marine sediments, glaciers and ground ice, tree rings, geomorphic features (including the record of changes in sea level), or other manifestations of past environmental conditions. As past analogues of possible future global changes, the records contribute to the understanding of the present Earth system, to the discrimination between natural and anthropogenic change, and hence to the prediction of future global change.

• *Solid-Earth processes.* The study of solid-Earth processes that affect the life-supporting characteristics of the global environment and especially those processes that take place at the interfaces between the solid Earth and the atmosphere, hydrosphere, cryosphere, and biosphere.

• *Solar influences.* The study of variability in solar brightness and its impact on atmospheric density, chemistry, dynamics, ionizations, and climate.

This strategy document sent to the U.S. Congress

represents a crosscutting review and integration by the Office of Management and Budget of a number of initiatives by individual agencies with different purposes and characteristics in support of a national objective. This effort followed a procedure proposed by a committee of the presidents of the National Academy of Sciences, National Academy of Engineering, and Institute of Medicine and several of their respective councilors. . . .

The global changes clearly visible on the horizon are rooted in the scientific and technological advances that have unlocked many of the secrets of matter, energy, life processes, and information and made this knowledge accessible for human purposes. The options for society are three:

• permitting civilization to be snuffed out by savaging the global environment with the weaponry scientific knowledge has made available;

• allowing the global environment and civilization to be gradually suffocated by exponential population growth and by uncontrolled and inequitable transformation of natural resources into the goods and services that sustain and give meaning to life; and

• planning and constructing a more prosperous, just, and secure world.

The 1990s

The 1990s will be one of the more critical periods in the several million years of human evolution. If humans are to survive safely the changes that clearly lie ahead, each day must be marked by discrete progress toward a better world. Knowledge, the coin of scientific enterprise, is the *sine qua non* of such progress. However, the first step perhaps is to ''reaffirm a robust faith in the destiny of man,'' writes Pierre Teilhard de Chardin. It is the unique privilege and challenge of this generation to open this window of opportunity into that better world.

Thomas F. Malone is a Scholar in Residence at St. Joseph College in West Hartford, Connecticut and a member of the U.S. National Committee for the International Geosphere-Biosphere Program of the National Research Council in Washington, D.C. Robert Corell is Assistant Director for Geoscience for the National Science Foundation and Chairperson of the Working Group on the U.S. Global Change Research Program, Committee on Earth Sciences in Washington, D.C.

"Corporate America is awakening to the importance of clean air and proper waste disposal—and recognizing the opportunities that lie ahead."

Business Can Save the Environment

Michael Parrish

Corporate America is awakening to the importance of clean air and proper waste disposal—and recognizing the opportunities that lie ahead.

"In the old days, the hippie days, we used to have conferences and you would see a lot of beards," recalls Clarence G. Golueke. "Now you see a lot of suits and ties."

Golueke should know. Director of research and development for Cal Recovery Systems, a Richmond-based consulting firm, he's a veteran of four decades at UC Berkeley, teaching and developing environmentally sound solid-waste treatment schemes. During much of that time he was affably ignored, except by those foresighted conservationist longhairs.

But environmentalism has come into its own in the 1980s and now attracts professionals in suits from engineering, law, manufacturing and marketing. With this has come a far-reaching change in the attitude of U.S. businesses, particularly as corporate leaders have pondered the industries to be spawned in the next decade by an avalanche of new environmental regulations. Some opportunities are already clearly in sight.

The fall of the Berlin Wall, for example, was just more bad news for Robert Toering.

As a citizen he was pleased. But as president of a firm that makes shell casings for naval guns and tanks, he saw a bleak future for his corner of the defense business. Toering, president of the Norris division of NI Industries, in Vernon, had watched his sales dive in three years from $240 million to an expected $105 million to $110 million in 1989. "We've got to learn to make something other than bullets," he told himself again when he heard the news from Eastern Europe. And he pressed the search for ways to expand into civilian work. He didn't have to look very far.

One effect of current federal law is that by May 1990, metal-plating firms lacking approved treatment facilities must truck their liquid waste out of the Los Angeles basin, at considerable expense. Toering estimates that it would take two years and $7 million to build a commercial waste-metal treatment plant from scratch.

Toering just happens to have such a facility, however, running at only 15% of capacity. When he announced that it might become available, more than 400 Southern California companies gave him a call.

Toering also hopes to make containers for high-level radioactive waste. His machinery, which forms shell casings from single sheets of metal, could produce seamless drums that he says would hold up well "sitting out in the open for 50 or 100 years while they decide whether or not to use Yucca Mountain," the controversial proposed radiation waste dump in Nevada.

Looking Elsewhere

"I think every defense contractor is out there looking for non-defense business that might be appropriate for his company," says Toering. And having the right machines may not be the only advantage that defense contractors bring to environmental manufacturing.

"We're pretty good at dealing with the bureaucracy of the government," he points out, "so we're trying to find programs where that ability is an advantage."

Hughes Aircraft also looked in the mirror for opportunities in the booming environmental business.

Hughes scientists were studying ways to reduce emissions from their own buildings when the company took their ideas to the South Coast Air

Quality Management District, which is in the thick of its ambitious effort to clean up Southern California's smog. The district agreed to help fund seven Hughes projects.

"Now we can develop the solutions faster," says Verne Wochnick, Hughes senior liaison for legislative and regulatory affairs. "And by having them join us, we are also able to share that information a lot easier."

Other major companies see potential in the immense effort to clean up more than 1.5 million asbestos-plagued buildings around the country, 37,000 hazardous waste sites, more than 15,000 factories still discharging air pollutants and uncounted polluted ground water basins.

The big push behind these cleanups comes from federal, state and local regulations taking effect during the 1990s.

Take drinking water quality. The EPA [Environmental Protection Agency] is required to list—every three years, indefinitely—25 more contaminants that must be tested for and removed if necessary. As Jon G. DeBoer, of the American Water Works Assn., confided to a meeting of water industry executives, "If I had the money, I'd build a lab. I'd build a *string* of labs, across the country."

Water will also likely be far more expensive at the tap, providing another economic lure for innovation. Already some U.S. homes are connected to dual water delivery systems. One pours high-quality drinking water; the other, less treated water for lawns and cars.

Another growing market is under-the-tap water filters at home. Promoted as a reassurance to consumers who are suspicious of public water, the filters are also touted as a way to keep down the cost of maintaining city water pipes, since standards in the country's aging delivery pipes would not need to be drinking-water quality except at the tap.

"Major companies see potential in the immense effort to clean up more than 1.5 million asbestos-plagued buildings around the country."

"The profound change will come when water utilities get into the business of providing these units for residential, and probably commercial, use," predicts Neil Berlant, of L.A.-based Water Research Associates. "And they're already looking into it."

Berlant expects water prices to double or quadruple during the next three years and the home-filter business to grow from $3.5 billion in sales to more than $10 billion.

Other laws are pushing environmental businesses forward.

Many states have enacted or are drafting statutes to control the relentless stream of municipal trash, mostly by requiring large chunks of it to be recycled. A new California law requires a reduction of 25% in the state's municipal waste by 1995, and 50% by the year 2000, prompting a Los Angeles recycling ordinance passed in December 1989. In all, 30 states have passed recycling laws, 10 of which are mandatory. No matter its recent round of bad publicity, recycling is about to become part of the nation's everyday life.

"We are really going through a basic change," says Richard Chase, a partner in Recycle 2000, a San Marcos, CA-based consulting development company. "We're changing from a reliance on virgin materials to what's going to be a predominant reliance on recycled materials. . . . And it's definitely going to happen."

Toward Efficiency

Energy efficiency systems and planning—another growth field—takes various forms. In one incarnation, environmental consultants survey factories and office buildings to correct wasteful practices by replacing outmoded lights, insulation, and heating and cooling systems. They take their fee from the savings in overhead.

Larger-scale planning may be key to opening new international markets for U.S. environmental technology, particularly in Eastern Europe.

As one offshoot of an exchange begun in 1986, scientists and policy planners from the Soviet Union, the California Energy Commission, the Northwest Power Planning Council and the San Francisco office of the Natural Resources Defense Council, a U.S. environmental group, have been commuting between the two nations, studying Soviet energy use. They hope to find ways to end the Soviets' awesome inefficiency.

In Tallinn, capital of Estonia, the group is measuring the power used in a standard Soviet apartment, since the Soviets don't even know where household energy is used. Moreover, residents there sometimes have a hard time controlling the temperature in specific offices and apartments, since whole villages are often heated from one giant plant.

"It's not uncommon to see windows open in Moscow when it's 30 below," notes Robert K. Watson, an energy resource specialist with NRDC who is working on the project, "just because they've got those suckers cranked up so."

Two larger projects focus on a planning technique that has yet to become a household word in the United States, despite its use in some areas since shortly after the OPEC [Organization of Petroleum Exporting Countries] oil crisis of the 1970s.

It's called least-cost planning. The basic idea is that, all else being equal, it's better to meet increased energy demands with more efficient generators and appliances than simply to build another power plant.

A simple example, often used by environmentalists.

Forecasts show the need for a new power plant in the next 10 years. Yet planners might find that the efficiency of all the refrigerators expected to be sold in that area for the next decade could be improved enough so that no new plant was needed.

In fact, the Northwest Power Planning Council states of Washington, Oregon, Idaho and Montana have applied this philosophy, according to Edward Sheets, executive director of the council, whose least-cost plans are being tested in two Soviet republics.

Since 1979, Northwest utilities have spent more than $1 billion on energy-efficient programs, saving roughly the electrical output of one coal-fired generation plant.

"And all told," says Sheets, "the Northwest would have had to spend $1.4 billion *more* to get the same amount of power if it *had* built a coal plant.

"I guess there are two angles here," says Sheets. "First, there is a business opportunity for firms that can provide energy efficiency services. And secondly, we like to think that it's a benefit to the local economy if we can keep more dollars in consumer pockets by lowering their electric bills."

Sheets sees an increasingly good market in the Soviet Union and elsewhere for high-quality U.S. home insulation, energy-saving windows, lighting, and heating and cooling systems for buildings. In industry, he sees a significant market for efficient drive systems—pumps, motors, belts and all the machinery that makes a production line move.

"There is a business opportunity for firms than can provide energy efficiency services."

As part of the current study, the U.S. side has agreed to provide the Soviets technical support and economic development assistance, which Watson of NRDC describes as "a highfalutin way of saying that we're going to try to set up American industries who produce energy-efficient or energy-saving technologies, and try to get that technology exported to the Soviet Union."

"Least-cost planning really appealed to the Soviets," Sheets reports, though he's less optimistic about the Soviet republics as a market for U.S. technology. For one thing, he wonders whether they have the money to pay for it.

"My sense is that if they thought they could build it themselves, that would be their first choice," he says. "We found a great interest in joint ventures, a willingness to enter into production arrangements to produce U.S. technology. . . . Actual direct purchase

is problematic because of a real shortage of hard currency."

Other international markets may soon develop closer to home, in Mexico.

Richard Chase of Recycle 2000 has lately been in conversation with Mexican officials about setting up reprocessing plants for recyclable materials in Tijuana. Sooner or later all Southern Californians will have to separate their trash at home and office. Recyclable paper, metal, glass and plastic will go into one system. Organic trash will either be composted, burned or buried in a landfill.

Recyclables are reconstituted as raw materials, as pulp, metal ingots, plastics in pellet form. These are then made into more paper, cans and construction reinforcing rods, plastic flower pots and TV sets.

Recycling in Mexico

Chase sees several advantages in having these processes based just across the border. Mexico's lower wages—recycling is labor intensive—are only part of it.

"Paper mills, steel mills, aluminum smelters, glass factories—given the environmental and other situations in Southern California, it's difficult to locate those kinds of facilities here," says Chase.

"[In Baja California] you would have your raw material, a climate that's hospitable to economic development—and by that I don't mean hospitable toward pollution but hospitable toward industrial activities that produce jobs and export earnings—and you're sitting right next to the largest consumer marketplace in the world. It's all there."

Chase considers it absurd to ship recyclables to Asia, 10,000 miles rather than 120, as is done today. It also misses the chance to support a long-suffering neighbor.

"Certainly we have a bigger stake in the healthy economic development of Mexico," says Chase, "than in the economic benefit of Taiwan, Singapore or Indonesia."

Michael Parrish is a staff writer for the Los Angeles Times, *a Los Angeles daily newspaper.*

"In societies whose very existence depended upon knowing the earth... respect for the natural world... was surely inevitable."

viewpoint 97

Ancient Societies Demonstrate How to Preserve the Environment

Kirkpatrick Sale

In the beginning, as the Greeks saw it, when chaos settled into form there was a mighty sphere, floating free within the moist, gleaming embrace of the sky and its great swirling drifts of white cloud, a vibrant globe of green and blue and brown and gray, binding together in a holy, deep-breasted synchrony the temperatures of the sun, the gasses of the air, the chemicals of the sea, the minerals of the soil, and bearing the organized, self-contained, and almost purposeful aspect of a single organism, *alive*, a breathing, pulsing body that was, in the awed words of Plato, "a living creature, one and visible, containing within itself all living creatures."

To this the Greeks gave a name: Gaea, the earth mother. She was the mother of the heavens, Uranus, and of time, Cronus; of the Titans and the Cyclops; of the Meliae, the ash-tree spirits who were the progenitors of all humankind; the mother of all, first of the cosmos, creator of the creators. She became the symbol of all that was sacred and the source of all that was wise, and at the fissures and rifts in her surface—at Delphi, especially, and at Olympia and Dodona—she would impart her knowledge to those few mortals, the oracles, who knew how to hear it. . . .

Early Societies

The wisdom of the Greeks was not theirs alone. In fact, among the earliest societies it appears with such regularity across every continent, no matter what the climate or geography, and in every preliterate culture, that we may fairly think of it as a basic, almost innate, human perception. In virtually every hunter-gatherer society that archeologists have discovered from the paleolithic past, in almost every rudimentary society that anthropologists have

studied in recent centuries, one of the central deities—in many cases the primary god, worshipped before all others—was the earth.

There is no special mystery to it. In societies whose very existence depended upon knowing the earth and how to hunt its animals and forage for its foods—the way of life for 99 percent of human history—respect for the natural world and an appreciation of the land itself as sacred and inviolable was surely inevitable. That sensibility was literally so vital that it was embedded in some central place in each culture's myths and traditions and was embodied in each culture's supreme spirits and deities.

For these early human peoples, the world around and all its features—rivers, trees, clouds, springs, mountains—were regarded as alive, endowed with spirit and sensibility every bit as real as those of humans, and in fact of exactly the same type and quality as a human's: among the Iroquois this was called *orenda*, the invisible force inherent in all parts of the universe, and in certain Bantu languages the same presence is known as *mata*.

Animals had souls, of course, so in all hunting societies some form of ritual apology and forgiveness was necessary before the kill: hence the Navajo praying to the deer before the hunt, the Mbuti cleansing themselves by smoke each morning, the Naskapi pledging to the hunted, "You and I have the same mind and spirit." But plants and flowers and trees had spirits, too, every bit as sensate, so almost all early peoples had elaborate ceremonies connected with cutting and harvesting, asking exoneration for the painful removal of some of Mother Earth's children, and most had stories like the Ojibways', which speak of "the wailing of the trees under the axe," or like the ancient Chinese tales which mention cries of "pain and indignation" from fallen branches. Hence the well-nigh universal phenomenon that anthropologists, until recently, liked to dismiss as "tree-worshipping": treating certain local trees, or groves, or whole forests as especially sacred and sacrosanct, in innate recognition of the fundamental, life-sustaining function of arboreal life on earth. From the Celts in the West to the Yalta tribes in the East, and from the Finns in the North to the Greeks in the South, trees and forests occupied a special place of spiritual honor throughout ancient Europe. Indeed among northern German tribes the Teutonic word for *temple* actually meant forest, and in Greek the word *neos*, a holy sanctuary, implied not a human-built but a natural enclosure.

"Among such nature-based peoples there was no separation of the self from the world such as we have come to learn."

Among such nature-based peoples there was no separation of the self from the world such as we have come to learn, no division between the human (willed, thinking, superior) and the non-human (conditioned, insensate, inferior). Much of the world was highly mysterious, to be sure, and many phenomena were unexplainable, but there was at the same time a liberating, psychically healthy sense of wholeness, of oneness, of place. As anthropologist Jack Forbes has said about the early California Indian tribes:

> They perceived themselves as being deeply bound together with other people (and with the surrounding non-human forms of life) in a complex interconnected web of life, that is to say, a true community. . . . All creatures and all things were . . . brothers and sisters. From this idea came the basic principle of non-exploitation, of respect and reverence for all creatures.

Indicative of this bond is that for most of these societies the identity with the earth was so strong that their legends about creation commonly told of humanity itself emerging from a hole in the ground, or a cleft in the rocks, or the depths of a tree: the Mbuti in the Congolese rainforest, for example, say the very first human emerged from the inside of a mahogany tree, the Pueblo Indians that people climbed out of the "womb of the earth."

As a matter of fact we retain this identity in our languages today, though we, alas, no longer appreciate the association: the Indo-European word for earth, *dhghem*, is the root of the Latin *humanus*, the Old German *guman*, and the Old English *guman*, all of which meant "human." The only remnant of this sensibility I can think of today in our everyday language is *humus*, the rich, organic soil in which things grow best, though we no longer make the same connections the Latins did when we use the word.

It is natural but significant nonetheless that the deity of the earth in many societies was a woman, for the fecundity of both would be immediately obvious to any established society. This would be particularly true where, as was common until recently, the role of paternity was quite unknown and the woman's ability to give birth was as astonishing and wonderful—and necessary—as the earth's ability to regenerate itself in spring.

For the peoples of the Mediterranean and the Near East—as for the early Greeks—the Earth Goddess was at the center of spiritual constructs. Figures of "the mother goddess" are found in sacred shrines dating as far back as the Aurignacian cultures of 25,000 BC; excavations of Jarmo (6800 BC), Catal Hayuk (6500 BC), Halaf (5000 BC), Ur (4000 BC), and Elam (3000 BC) all indicate that female goddesses, and probably female priests as well, were dominant in their early religions. In Sumeria the goddess Nammu was "the mother who gave birth to heaven and earth"; in Egypt Isis was the "oldest of the old . . . from whom all becoming arose"; in Turkey the goddess Arinna was worshipped above all others, and "no other deity is as honored or great"; in Babylon Ishatar was the Queen of Heaven, "goddess of the universe [who] out of chaos brought us harmony." She was Cybele in Phrygia, Astarte in Phoenicia, Ashtoreth to the Hebrews, Athar in Syria. And her direct counterparts are found among the Irish, the Innuit Eskimos, the Japanese, the Iroquois, the Finns, the Khasis of India, the Lepcha of Sikkim, the Tallensi of West Africa. . . .

A Powerful Tradition

So powerful was this Gaean tradition, so rooted in what seems to have been more than twenty millennia of religious culture, that even the male-god Indo-Europeans who invaded the Mediterranean world in about 4500 BC and successfully imposed their values on many cultures in their path could not displace it. Male deities were introduced with apparently greater frequency after this period—the Greek pantheon shifted, to take but one example, and Zeus, Adonis, and the like began appearing from about 2000 BC—but at no time were the female deities entirely supplanted, even among the ancient Hebrews. It was not until fairly late on that Judaism, then Christianity, and then Islam finally succeeded in effectively purging most forms of goddess worship from the religious cultures of the area.

Even then, however, even with the triumph of male monotheism throughout most of the Mediterranean and European worlds, even with the displacement of earth-worship for various abstract kinds of sky-worship, and even with the placement of the human (male) above all other creatures of the world—*even then* the notion of an animate earth did not completely die, certainly not among the general mass of people, religious believers or not. For all but a few, no matter what the culture or god, the world and its parts still were regarded as endowed with life and spirit and purpose, sometimes knowable to humans, or discernible, more often not. Rivers and waves and clouds and winds, obviously, were living, and trees and flowers and grasses, and fire and lightning and rain and snow—these all could be seen to move, after all—but also stones and clods of earth and mountains. In the words of historian Morris Berman:

> The view of nature which predominated in the West down to the eve of the Scientific Revolution was that of an enchanted world. Rocks, trees, rivers, and clouds were all seen as wondrous, alive, and human beings felt at home in this environment. The cosmos, in short, was a place of *belonging*. A member of this cosmos was not an alienated observer of it but a direct participant in its drama. His personal destiny was bound up with its destiny, and this relationship gave meaning to his life.

In all the long stretch of human history, it seems, from our very beginnings as tribal beings 30,000 years ago right down through classical and medieval times, until sometime in the last 400 years, the people of this planet saw themselves as inhabitants within a world alive. . . .

As benevolent as she is, however, Gaea is capable of revenge.

The Mycenaean civilization that flourished on the Aegean islands and coasts in the second millennium before Christ, say from 1600 to 1000 BC, inspired the Homeric stories, those legends of great cities and heroic dynasties, and even they failed to do justice to the complexity and grandeur of that early culture. . . .

It was a sophisticated society, with written records and a developed economy—something like a hundred different agricultural and industrial occupations were listed in the Mycenaean records—and one that sustained a prosperous system of trade and a ruling stratum with elaborate buildings, extensive land and cattle holdings, and art and artifacts of considerable richness.

"In all the long stretch of human history . . . until sometime in the last 400 years, the people of this planet saw themselves as inhabitants within a world alive."

It seems that the Mycenaeans were not Greeks, strictly speaking, but they clearly adopted the Greek concept of the Earth Mother, Gaea, and sustained the elaborate Greek celebrations of her wisdom, creativity, sexuality, and fecundity; surviving artifacts show that Mycenaean shrines, probably the responsibility of a priestess caste, honored the generosity, the majesty, and the unpredictability of the goddess, her soil, her foods, her waters.

Yet somewhere, somehow, the poisons crept in. It might have been from *without*, from the so-called Dorians (probably the male-god Indo-Europeans) from the steppes of Europe, who, as art historian Vincent Scully puts it, suppressed "the old concept of the dominance of the goddess of the earth herself, seizing the sovereign power by virtue of their own thunder-wielding sky god, Zeus," and destroyed "the old, simple, almost vegetable unity between man and nature." Or it might have come from *within*, from the decadence and carelessness, the sheer hubris of cultures that in their latter days grow too large and distended (like the Egyptians, the Persians, the Romans, the Spanish, the Toltecs, and the modern Americans, among many), for it is then that they become more concerned with exploitation and domination than nurturance and sustainability, with the riches of ores rather than the riches of the soil, with preserving bureaucracy and hierarchy rather than ecosystems and habitats.

Forgotten Lessons

Whatever the reason, the ways of Gaea were forgotten. Over the years the Mycenaeans systematically cut down the holly, cypress, olive, pine, and sycamore trees that originally covered the Mediterranean slopes, using the wood for fuel and lumber—and often as much for export, and empty riches, as for themselves. The deforested hills, unreplenished, collapsed, their topsoils and minerals washed away in the torrential Mediterranean rains, and great gouges eroded into once-fertile hillsides. Herding of goats, cattle, and swine as well as sheep became a common practice, quite heedless of the multiple effects on the countryside. It wasn't bad enough that the animals' hooves destroyed groundcover and compacted the soils, and that their teeth devoured leaves and twigs in addition to grasses, but the herders even took to setting fire to the forests to open up more areas for their flocks.

The devastation was swift and thorough, indelibly fresh in Plato's mind even seven or eight centuries later: "What now remains compared with what then existed," he wrote, "is like the skeleton of a sick man, all the fat and soft earth having been wasted away, and only the bare framework of the land being left."

And thus descended the Greek Dark Ages. The Mycenaean culture collapsed, apparently within the astonishingly short period of two generations. For the next 500 years—a considerable stretch of time, equal to the one that separates us from Columbus—Greece suffered the consequences of its heedless rapaciousness. . . .

The Mycenaean Greeks were not the only ones through history who, having abandoned the worship and having forgotten the lessons of Gaea, were taught to their dismay the hard lessons of ecological hubris. Later on the Romans, whose cumulative assaults on the Mediterranean ecology were almost certainly a central factor in the collapse of their empire—and the Sumerians, the Harappans, the Mayans, the Chinese of at least the T'ang and Han dynasties, and numerous other imperial peoples who matched their dominance of humans with their dominance of nature, were forced to learn these inescapable truths.

> "In no previous society did the abandonment of Gaea reach the scale it reached in Europe in the centuries after the Renaissance."

But in no previous society did the abandonment of Gaea reach the scale it reached in Europe in the centuries after the Renaissance, the period of which we today are the exuberant consummation. For with the development of that branch of learning which usurped the word "science"—in the classical world it meant knowledge of all kinds, in the European world it was reserved for the study of a separate thing called "the natural world"—and which has dominated most intellectual and social life since the 16th century virtually all animistic, all venerative, all religious conceptions of the earth were deposed. In their stead came a new vision supported by the incontrovertible findings of physics, chemistry, mechanics, astronomy, and mathematics: the scientific worldview.

The new perception held—better than that, it *proved*—that the earth, the universe beyond it, and all within it operated according to certain clear, calculable, and unchanging laws, not by the whims of any living, sentient being. It showed that these laws were, far from being divinely created or spiritually inspired, capable of mundane scientific measurement, prediction, and replication, even scientific manipulation and control. It demonstrated that the objects of the universe, from the smallest stone to the earth's orb itself and the planets beyond, were not animate or purposeful, with individual souls and wills and spirits, but were nothing more than combinations of certain chemical and mechanical properties. It established beyond all doubt that there are not one but *two* worlds, the mechanical and inert one out there, made up of a random collection of insensate atoms, and the human one within, where thought and purpose and consciousness reside.

It achieved, in Schiller's matchless phrase, *"die Entgotterung der Natur"*—the "de-godding" of nature.

Bacon, Descartes, Newton, Galileo, all of the masterful minds of 16th- and 17th-century science, swept away, in only a few generations, the accumulated nonsense of the animistic past, much of which still lingered on even in the Europe of that time. To think of the cosmos as alive, to identify the dead matter of the earth with the organic spirit of human beings, was childish, barbarian, naive. If there was an image for the cosmos, it was not that of a goddess or any other being but something like what Newton spoke of as a giant clock, a Cosmick Machine, its many parts moving in an ordered, kinetic, mechanical way. As 17th-century physicist Robert Hooke put it, the scientific revolution enabled humankind "to discover all the secret workings of Nature, almost in the same manner as we do those that are the productions of Art and are manag'd by Wheels, and Engines, and Springs." And if God was allowed to play a part—for indeed these were all nominal Christians—he was given a role as little more than a clock-winder: "It seems probable to me," Newton wrote in 1730, "that God in the beginning formed matter in solid, massy, hard, impenetrable, movable particles, of such sizes and figures, and with such other properties and in such proportion to space as most conduced to the end for which He formed them."

Slowly and powerfully, with a growth both geometric and relentless, the ideas of the scientific paradigm transformed completely the attitudes of Western society toward nature and the cosmos. Nature was no longer either beautiful or scary but merely *there*, not to be worshipped or celebrated, but more often than not to be *used*. . . .

Consequences

Is that too harsh? Take as an example Europe's treatment of the New World that opened up at the same time as the rise of science and the nation-states that nurtured it. Two continents, pristine jewels of unimagined glories, were perceived as nothing but empty spaces for unwanted populations, repositories of wanted ores, tracts of trees to fell and fields to plow, virgin territories with no other purpose but to be *worked*. . . .

Kirkpatrick Sale is a writer and secretary of the E.F. Schumacher Society, an organization that advocates replacing nations and political boundaries with small communities and natural boundaries.

Ancient Societies Were Environmentally Destructive

Jared Diamond

Every part of the earth is sacred to my people. Every shining pine needle, every sandy shore, every mist in the dark woods, every clearing and humming insect is holy in the memory and experience of my people.... The white man ... is a stranger who comes in the night and takes from the land whatever he needs. The earth is not his brother but his enemy.... Continue to contaminate your bed, and you will one night suffocate in your own waste.

—Chief Seattle of the Duwamish people,
in a letter written in 1855 to
President Franklin Pierce

Environmentalists sickened by the damage that industrial societies are wreaking on the world often look to the past as a golden age. When Europeans began to settle America, the air and rivers were pure, the landscape green, the Great Plains teeming with bison. Today we breathe smog, worry about toxic chemicals in our drinking water, pave over the landscape, and rarely see any large wild animal. Worse is surely to come. By the time my infant sons reach retirement age, half the world's species will be extinct, the air radioactive, the seas polluted with oil.

Undoubtedly, one simple reason for our worsening mess is that modern technology has far more power to cause havoc than did the stone axes of the past. But a change in attitudes may also have contributed. Unlike modern city dwellers, at least some "primitive" peoples depend on and revere their local environment. Stories abound of how such peoples are in effect practicing conservationists, and we're only beginning to realize how sophisticated their policies are.

Well-intentioned foreign experts have made deserts out of large areas of Africa, for example. In those

Jared Diamond, "The Golden Age That Never Was," *Discover*, December 1988. Jared Diamond/© 1988 Discover Publications.

same areas local herders had thrived for uncounted millennia by making annual nomadic migrations that ensured the land never became overgrazed. Or, as a New Guinea tribesman once explained to me, "It's our custom that if a hunter one day kills a pigeon in one direction from the village, he waits a week before hunting pigeons again, then goes in the opposite direction."

Nostalgia

The nostalgia for a lost golden age extends beyond the environmentalist view; it's part of a larger, historical tendency to see the past as golden in many other respects. A famous exponent of this outlook was the eighteenth-century French philosopher Jean-Jacques Rousseau, whose *Discourse on the Origin of Inequality* traced our degeneration from a shining past to the human misery that Rousseau saw around him. When eighteenth-century European explorers encountered preindustrial peoples like Polynesians and American Indians, those peoples became idealized in European salons as "noble savages" living in a continued golden age, untouched by such curses of civilization as religious intolerance, political tyranny, and social inequality.

Even now the days of classical Greece and Rome are widely considered to be the golden age of Western civilization. Ironically, the Greeks and Romans also saw themselves as degenerates from a golden past. Half-conscious, I could still recite those lines by Ovid that I memorized in tenth-grade Latin: "Aurea prima sata est aetas, quae vindice nullo ..." ("First came the golden age, when men were honest and righteous of their own free will ..."). Ovid went on to contrast those virtues with the rampant treachery and warfare of his own times. I have no doubt that any humans still alive in the radioactive soup of the twenty-second century will write equally nostalgically about our era.

Given this widespread belief in a golden age, some

recent discoveries by archeologists and paleontologists have come as a shock. It's now clear that preindustrial societies have been exterminating species, destroying habitats, and undermining their own existence for thousands of years. And some of the best documented examples involve Polynesians and American Indians, the very peoples most often cited as exemplars of environmentalism. Needless to say, this revisionist view is hotly contested, not only in the halls of academia but also among lay people in Hawaii, New Zealand, and other areas with large Polynesian or Indian minorities.

Are the new "discoveries" just one more piece of racist pseudoscience by which white settlers seek to justify dispossessing indigenous peoples? How can they be reconciled with all the evidence for conservationist practices by existing preindustrial peoples? If the findings are true, can we use them as case histories to help us predict the fate that our own environmental policies may bring upon us? Can they explain some otherwise mysterious collapses of ancient civilizations, like that of the Maya or the Easter Islanders?

Before we can answer these controversial questions, we need to understand the new evidence belying the assumed past golden age of environmentalism. Let's first consider evidence for past waves of exterminations, then evidence for past destruction of habitats.

The Moa

When British colonists began to settle New Zealand in the 1800s, their plows uncovered bones of large birds that were then already extinct but that the Maori (the Polynesian settlers of New Zealand) remembered by the name *moa*. From complete skeletons, eggshells, and even feathers and pieces of skin, we have a good idea of what moas must have looked like alive: flightless, ostrich-like birds up to ten feet tall, divided among a dozen or two dozen species. Fossils and biochemical evidence indicate that moa ancestors had reached New Zealand millions of years previously. When and why, after surviving for so long, did the birds finally become extinct?

Until recently New Zealanders took it as dogma that the Maori were conservationists and didn't exterminate the moas. Instead, they believed, the birds became extinct from natural causes, such as changes in climate; at most, the Maori might have given the coup de grace to populations already on the verge of extinction. Three sets of discoveries have demolished this conviction.

First, radiocarbon dating of moa bones proves that when the Maori reached New Zealand around A.D. 1000 most, if not all, known moa species were still in existence. So were dozens of other New Zealand bird species that ornithologists now know only from fossil bones, including species of large geese, ducks,

swans, and eagles. Within roughly five centuries all the moas, plus these several dozen other bird species, were extinct. It would be an incredible coincidence if every individual of dozens of species that had occupied New Zealand for millions of years chose to drop dead at the precise geologic time when humans first arrived.

"Extinction waves also appear to have followed human colonization of every island where life had evolved in the absence of humans."

Second, more than a hundred large archeological sites are known—some of them covering dozens of acres—where Maori cut up prodigious numbers of moas, cooked them in earth ovens, and discarded the remains. They ate the meat, used the skins for clothing, fashioned bones into fishhooks and jewelry, and blew out the eggs and used them as water containers. During the nineteenth century moa bones were carted away from these sites by the wagonload. The number of moa skeletons in known Maori moa-hunting sites is estimated to be between 100,000 and 500,000, about ten times the number of moas likely to have been alive in New Zealand at any instant. Maori must have been slaughtering moas for many generations.

Finally, details of radiocarbon dates from New Zealand's South Island, where most of the known moa-hunting sites are located, suggest a fascinating pattern. Apparently, the oldest sites are in the north, dating from around A.D. 1150. As one moves southward sites become progressively younger; those farthest south date from around 1450. Thus Maori colonists may have arrived near the island's northern end and gradually spread southward, hunting moas to extinction as they advanced.

Having never seen humans before, moas must have been easy to kill; perhaps a hunter could just walk up to one and club it to death. The Maori practice of taking the eggs prevented moa populations from recovering. Less than a century may have been required to exterminate the moas at any one site. Within 300 years, when the wave of Maori colonists reached the south end of South Island, New Zealand's once-thriving moa populations were reduced to piles of skeletons in the earth, and memories passed on from generation to generation of Maori. A few centuries of hunting had sufficed to end millions of years of moa history.

Throughout Polynesia archeologists have found bones of extinct birds at sites of the first settlers, testifying to collisions like those of Maori and moas. On all the main islands of Hawaii, for example, paleontologists Storrs Olson and Helen James of the

Smithsonian Institution have identified fossil bird species that disappeared during Polynesian settlement. Their finds include not only small honeycreepers, which are related to species that are still present, but also bizarre flightless geese and ibis, species with no living close relatives at all.

Hawaii is notorious for its bird extinctions following European settlement, but this earlier wave of extinctions was unknown until Olson and James began publishing their discoveries in 1982. It's now known that before Captain Cook's arrival at least 50 species of Hawaiian birds—nearly one-tenth the number of bird species breeding on mainland North America—had already become extinct. That's not to say that all these birds were hunted out of existence. Although big geese, like the moas, were probably indeed exterminated by overhunting, small songbirds were more likely eliminated either by rats that arrived with the first Hawaiians or by the destruction of forests that Hawaiians cleared to gain land for agriculture.

I don't want to leave the impression that Polynesians were in any way unique as preindustrial exterminators. Their effects are particularly well documented, but extinction waves also appear to have followed human colonization of every island where life had evolved in the absence of humans. Nor were birds the only victims: mammals, lizards, frogs, snails, and even large insects vanished as well—thousands of species when one adds up all oceanic islands. Olson describes these insular extinctions as "one of the swiftest and most profound biological catastrophes in the history of the world.". . .

Easter Island

From this evidence that the golden age was tarnished by exterminations of species, let's now turn to the evidence for destruction of habitats. Two dramatic examples involve famous archeological puzzles: the giant stone statues of Easter Island and the abandoned pueblos of the southwestern United States.

An aura of mystery has clung to Easter Island ever since it and its Polynesian inhabitants were "discovered" by the Dutch explorer Jakob Roggeveen in 1722. Lying in the Pacific Ocean 2,300 miles west of Chile, Easter Island is one of the world's most isolated scraps of land. Hundreds of statues, weighing as much as 85 tons and up to 37 feet tall, were carved from volcanic quarries, transported several miles, and raised to an upright position on platforms, by people without metal or wheels and with no power source other than human muscle. Even more statues remain unfinished in the quarries or lie finished but abandoned between the quarries and platforms. The scene today is as if the carvers and movers had suddenly walked off the job, leaving an eerily silent landscape.

When Roggeveen arrived, many statues were still standing, though new ones were no longer being carved. By 1840 all the erected statues had been deliberately toppled by the Easter Islanders themselves. How were such huge statues transported and erected, why were they eventually toppled, and why had carving ceased?

"Recent discoveries . . . are making the supposed golden age of environmentalism look increasingly mythical."

The first of those questions was answered when living Easter Islanders showed Thor Heyerdahl how their ancestors had used logs as rollers to transport the statues and then as levers to erect them. The other questions were solved by subsequent archeological and paleontological studies that revealed Easter Island's gruesome history. When Polynesians settled the island around A.D. 400, it was covered by forest. They gradually proceeded to clear the land in order to plant gardens and to obtain logs for canoes and for erecting statues. By 1500 the human population had risen to about 7,000 (more than 150 people per square mile), some 1,000 statues had been carved, and at least 324 of those statues had been erected. But the forest had been destroyed so thoroughly that not a single tree survived.

An immediate result of this self-inflicted ecological disaster was that the islanders no longer had the logs they needed to transport and erect statues, so carving ceased. But deforestation also led to soil erosion and hence lower crop yields; and the lack of timber meant that the people could not build canoes and so had less protein available to them from fishing. These two indirect consequences brought starvation, as the population was now greater than Easter Island could support.

Island society collapsed in a holocaust of internecine warfare and cannibalism. A warrior class took over; spear points manufactured in huge quantities came to litter the landscape; the defeated were eaten or enslaved; rival clans pulled down each other's statues; and people took to living in caves for self-protection. What had once been a lush island supporting one of the world's most remarkable civilizations deteriorated into the Easter Island of today: a lonely grassland littered with fallen statues, supporting less than one third its former population.

The Anasazi

Our other case study of preindustrial habitat destruction involves the collapse of one of the most advanced Indian civilizations of North America. When Spanish explorers reached the Southwest, they found gigantic multistory dwellings standing uninhabited in the middle of treeless desert. The dwelling at Chaco Canyon National Historical Park in New Mexico had more than 600 rooms and was five stories high, more than 650 feet long, and more than 300 feet wide, making it the largest building ever erected in North America up to that time. Navajo in the region knew of the vanished builders only as *Anasazi*, "the Ancient Ones."

Archeologists subsequently established that the construction of the Chaco pueblos began shortly after A.D. 900 and ceased in the twelfth century. Why did the Anasazi erect a city in a barren wasteland, of all places? Where did they obtain their firewood, or the 200,000 sixteen-foot-long wooden beams that supported the roofs? Why did they then abandon the city that they had built at such enormous effort?

The conventional view, analogous to the claim that New Zealand's moas died out from natural changes in climate, attributes the abandonment of Chaco Canyon to a drought. However, a different interpretation emerges from the work of paleoecologists Julio Betancourt and Thomas Van Devender, who used an ingenious technique to decipher changes in Chaco vegetation through time. . . .

"We can read about all the ecological disasters of the past; the Anasazi couldn't."

Betancourt and Van Devender were able to reconstruct the following course of events: At the time the Chaco pueblos were erected, they were surrounded not by barren desert but by piñon and juniper woodland, with ponderosa pine forests nearby. This at once solves the mystery of where the firewood and timber came from, and it disposes of the apparent paradox of an "advanced" civilization rising from the desert.

As occupation continued at Chaco, however, the woodland and forest were cleared until the environment became the treeless wasteland that it remains today. The Indians then had to go over 10 miles to get firewood and over 25 miles to get pine logs. When the pine forests were gone, they built an elaborate road system to haul spruce and fir logs from mountain slopes some 50 miles away, relying on nothing more than their own muscle to do so.

The Anasazi had also built irrigation systems to concentrate available water into valley bottoms. But as deforestation caused increasing erosion and water runoff, and as irrigation channels gradually dug gullies into the ground, the water table may finally have dropped below the level of the Anasazi fields, making irrigation without pumps impossible. Thus,

while drought may have made some contribution to the Anasazi abandonment of Chaco Canyon, a self-inflicted ecological disaster was a major factor.

These are some of the recent discoveries that are making the supposed golden age of environmentalism look increasingly mythical. Let's now go back to the larger issues I raised at the outset. First, how can these discoveries of past environmental damage be reconciled with accounts of conservationist practices by so many more recent preindustrial peoples? Obviously, not all species have been exterminated, and not all habitats have been destroyed, so the golden age couldn't have been all black.

I suggest the following answer. It's still true that small, long-established societies tend to evolve conservationist practices, because they have had plenty of time to get to know their local environment and to perceive their self-interest. The damage is likely to occur when people suddenly colonize an unfamiliar environment (like the first Maori and Easter Islanders); or when they advance along a new frontier (like the first Indians to reach America) and can simply move beyond when they've damaged the region behind; or when they acquire a new technology whose destructive power they haven't had time to appreciate (like modern New Guineans, now devastating pigeon populations with shotguns). And some habitats and species are more susceptible to damage than others—such as a dry, unforgiving desert environment, or flightless birds that have never seen humans. . . .

Tragic failures become moral sins only if one should have known better from the outset. In that regard there are two big differences between us and eleventh-century Anasazi: scientific understanding and literacy. We know, and they didn't know, how to draw graphs that plot sustainable resource population size as a function of resource-harvesting rate. We can read about all the ecological disasters of the past; the Anasazi couldn't. Yet we continue to hunt whales and clear tropical rain forest as if no one had ever hunted moas or cleared piñon-juniper woodland.

Today's Blindness

The past was still a golden age, but of ignorance, while the present is an Iron Age of willful blindness. If we continue on our present course, future explorers coming upon New York's abandoned skyscrapers rising from a concrete wasteland will wonder what Ancient Ones built those steel pueblos, why we picked such a desolate site, and why our society collapsed.

Jared Diamond is a science writer who contributes regularly to Discover.

"Deep ecology goes beyond a limited, piecemeal, shallow approach to environmental problems."

Deep Ecology Is Necessary to Save the Environment

Bill Devall and George Sessions

The term *deep ecology* was coined by Arne Naess in his 1973 article, "The Shallow and the Deep, Long-Range Ecology Movements." Naess was attempting to describe the deeper, more spiritual approach to Nature exemplified in the writings of Aldo Leopold and Rachel Carson. He thought that this deeper approach resulted from a more sensitive openness to ourselves and nonhuman life around us. The essence of deep ecology is to keep asking more searching questions about human life, society, and Nature as in the Western philosophical tradition of Socrates. As examples of this deep questioning, Naess points out "that we ask why and how, where others do not. For instance, ecology as a science does not ask what kind of a society would be the best for maintaining a particular ecosystem—that is considered a question for value theory, for politics, for ethics." Thus deep ecology goes beyond the so-called factual scientific level to the level of self and Earth wisdom.

Deep ecology goes beyond a limited, piecemeal, shallow approach to environmental problems and attempts to articulate a comprehensive religious and philosophical worldview. The foundations of deep ecology are the basic intuitions and experiencing of ourselves and Nature which comprise ecological consciousness. Certain outlooks on politics and public policy flow naturally from this consciousness. . . .

Many of these questions are perennial philosophical and religious questions faced by humans in all cultures over the ages. What does it mean to be a unique human individual? How can the individual self maintain and increase its uniqueness while also being an inseparable aspect of the whole system wherein there are no sharp breaks between self and the *other*? An ecological perspective, in this deeper sense, results in what Theodore Roszak calls "an awakening of wholes greater than the sum of their parts. In spirit, the discipline is contemplative and therapeutic."

An Alternative to Dominance

Ecological consciousness and deep ecology are in sharp contrast with the dominant worldview of technocratic-industrial societies which regards humans as isolated and fundamentally separate from the rest of Nature, as superior to, and in charge of, the rest of creation. But the view of humans as separate and superior to the rest of Nature is only part of larger cultural patterns. For thousands of years, Western culture has become increasingly obsessed with the idea of *dominance*: with dominance of humans over nonhuman Nature, masculine over the feminine, wealthy and powerful over the poor, with the dominance of the West over non-Western cultures. Deep ecological consciousness allows us to see through these erroneous and dangerous illusions.

For deep ecology, the study of our place in the Earth household includes the study of ourselves as part of the organic whole. Going beyond a narrowly materialist scientific understanding of reality, the spiritual and the material aspects of reality fuse together. While the leading intellectuals of the dominant worldview have tended to view religion as "just superstition," and have looked upon ancient spiritual practice and enlightenment, such as found in Zen Buddhism, as essentially subjective, the search for deep ecological consciousness is the search for a more objective consciousness and state of being through an active, deep questioning and meditative process and way of life.

Many people have asked these deeper questions and cultivated ecological consciousness within the context of different spiritual traditions—Christianity,

Excerpted with permission from *Deep Ecology: Living as if Nature Mattered* by Bill Devall and George Sessions (Gibbs Smith, Publisher, 1985).

Taoism, Buddhism, and Native American rituals, for example. While differing greatly in other regards, many in these traditions agree with the basic principles of deep ecology.

Warwick Fox, an Australian philosopher, has succinctly expressed the central intuition of deep ecology: "It is the idea that we can make no firm ontological divide in the field of existence: That there is no bifurcation in reality between the human and the non-human realms . . . to the extent that we perceive boundaries, we fall short of deep ecological consciousness."

From this most basic insight or characteristic of deep ecological consciousness, Arne Naess has developed two *ultimate norms* or intuitions which are themselves not derivable from other principles or intuitions. They are arrived at by the deep questioning process and reveal the importance of moving to the philosophical and religious level of wisdom. They cannot be validated, of course, by the methodology of modern science based on its usual mechanistic assumptions and its very narrow definition of data. These ultimate norms are *self-realization* and *biocentric equality*.

"All things in the biosphere have an equal right to live and blossom."

In keeping with the spiritual traditions of many of the world's religions, the deep ecology norm of self-realization goes beyond the modern Western *self* which is defined as an isolated ego striving primarily for hedonistic gratification or for a narrow sense of individual salvation in this life or the next. This socially programmed sense of the narrow self or social self dislocates us, and leaves us prey to whatever fad or fashion is prevalent in our society or social reference group. We are thus robbed of beginning the search for our unique spiritual/biological personhood. Spiritual growth, or unfolding, begins when we cease to understand or see ourselves as isolated and narrow competing egos and begin to identify with other humans from our family and friends to, eventually, our species. But the deep ecology sense of self requires a further maturity and growth, an identification which goes beyond humanity to include the nonhuman world. We must see beyond our narrow contemporary cultural assumptions and values, and the conventional wisdom of our time and place, and this is best achieved by the meditative deep questioning process. Only in this way can we hope to attain full mature personhood and uniqueness.

A nurturing nondominating society can help in the "real work" of becoming a whole person. The "real work" can be summarized symbolically as the realization of "self-in-Self" where "Self" stands for

organic wholeness. This process of the full unfolding of the self can also be summarized by the phrase, "No one is saved until we are all saved," where the phrase "one" includes not only me, an individual human, but all humans, whales, grizzly bears, whole rain forest ecosystems, mountains and rivers, the tiniest microbes in the soil, and so on.

Biocentric Equality

The intuition of biocentric equality is that all things in the biosphere have an equal right to live and blossom and to reach their own individual forms of unfolding and self-realization within the larger Self-realization. This basic intuition is that all organisms and entities in the ecosphere, as parts of the interrelated whole, are equal in intrinsic worth. Naess suggests that biocentric equality as an intuition is true in principle, although in the process of living, all species use each other as food, shelter, etc. Mutual predation is a biological fact of life, and many of the world's religions have struggled with the spiritual implications of this. Some animal liberationists who attempt to side-step this problem by advocating vegetarianism are forced to say that the entire plant kingdom including rain forests have no right to their own existence. This evasion flies in the face of the basic intuition of equality. Aldo Leopold expressed this intuition when he said humans are "plain citizens" of the biotic community, not lord and master over all other species.

Biocentric equality is intimately related to the all-inclusive Self-realization in the sense that if we harm the rest of Nature then we are harming ourselves. There are no boundaries and everything is interrelated. But insofar as we perceive things as individual organisms or entities, the insight draws us to respect all human and nonhuman individuals in their own right as parts of the whole without feeling the need to set up hierarchies of species with humans at the top.

The practical implications of this intuition or norm suggest that we should live with minimum rather than maximum impact on other species and on the Earth in general. Thus we see another aspect of our guiding principle: "simple in means, rich in ends.". . .

A fuller discussion of the biocentric norm as it unfolds itself in practice begins with the realization that we, as individual humans, and as communities of humans, have vital needs which go beyond such basics as food, water, and shelter to include love, play, creative expression, intimate relationships with a particular landscape (or Nature taken in its entirety) as well as intimate relationships with other humans, and the vital need for spiritual growth, for becoming a mature human being.

Our vital material needs are probably more simple than many realize. In technocratic-industrial societies there is overwhelming propaganda and advertising which encourages false needs and destructive desires designed to foster increased production and consumption of goods. Most of this actually diverts us from facing reality in an objective way and from beginning the "real work" of spiritual growth and maturity.

Many people who do not see themselves as supporters of deep ecology nevertheless recognize an overriding, vital human need for a healthy and high-quality natural environment for humans, if not for all life, with minimum intrusion of toxic waste, nuclear radiation from human enterprises, minimum acid rain and smog, and enough free-flowing wilderness so humans can get in touch with their sources, the natural rhythms and the flow of time and place.

Drawing from the minority tradition and from the wisdom of many who have offered the insight of interconnectedness, we recognize that deep ecologists can offer suggestions for gaining maturity and encouraging the processes of harmony with Nature, but that there is no grand solution which is guaranteed to save us from ourselves.

The ultimate norms of deep ecology suggest a view of the nature of reality and our place as an individual (many in the one) in the larger scheme of things. They cannot be fully grasped intellectually but are ultimately experiential. . . . As a brief summary of our position thus far, Figure 1 summarizes the contrast between the dominant worldview and deep ecology.

Figure 1

Dominant Worldview	Deep Ecology
Dominance over Nature	Harmony with Nature
Natural environment as resource for humans	All Nature has intrinsic worth/biospecies equality
Material/economic growth for growing human population	Elegantly simple material needs (material goals serving the larger goal of self-realization)
Belief in ample resource reserves	Earth "supplies" limited
High technological progress and solutions	Appropriate technology; nondominating science
Consumerism	Doing with enough/recycling
National/centralized community	Minority tradition/bioregion

In April 1984, during the advent of spring and John Muir's birthday, George Sessions and Arne Naess summarized fifteen years of thinking on the principles of deep ecology while camping in Death Valley, California. In this great and special place, they articulated these principles in a literal, somewhat neutral way, hoping that they would be understood and accepted by persons coming from different philosophical and religious positions.

Readers are encouraged to elaborate their own versions of deep ecology, clarify key concepts and think through the consequences of acting from these principles.

Basic Principles

1. The well-being and flourishing of human and nonhuman Life on Earth have value in themselves (synonyms: intrinsic value, inherent value). These values are independent of the usefulness of the nonhuman world for human purposes.

2. Richness and diversity of life forms contribute to the realization of these values and are also values in themselves.

Vital Needs

3. Humans have no right to reduce this richness and diversity except to satisfy *vital* needs.

4. The flourishing of human life and cultures is compatible with a substantial decrease of the human population. The flourishing of nonhuman life requires such a decrease.

5. Present human interference with the nonhuman world is excessive, and the situation is rapidly worsening.

6. Policies must therefore be changed. These policies affect basic economic, technological, and ideological structures. The resulting state of affairs will be deeply different from the present.

7. The ideological change is mainly that of appreciating *life quality* (dwelling in situations of inherent value) rather than adhering to an increasingly higher standard of living. There will be a profound awareness of the difference between big and great.

8. Those who subscribe to the foregoing points have an obligation directly or indirectly to try to implement the necessary changes. . . .

The following excerpts are from an interview with Arne Naess conducted at the Zen Center of Los Angeles in April 1982. It was originally published as an interview in *Ten Directions*. In the interview, Naess further discusses the major perspective of deep ecology.

"The essence of deep ecology is to ask deeper questions. The adjective 'deep' stresses that we ask why and how, where others do not. For instance, ecology as a science does not ask what kind of a society would be the best for maintaining a particular ecosystem—that is considered a question for value theory, for politics, for ethics. As long as ecologists keep narrowly to their science, they do not ask such questions. What we need today is a tremendous expansion of ecological thinking in what I call ecosophy. *Sophy* comes from the Greek term *sophia*, 'wisdom,' which relates to ethics, norms, rules, and practice. Ecosophy, or deep ecology, then, involves a shift from science to wisdom.

"For example, we need to ask questions like, Why

do we think that economic growth and high levels of consumption are so important? The conventional answer would be to point to the economic consequences of not having economic growth. But in deep ecology, we ask whether the present society fulfills basic human needs like love and security and access to nature, and, in so doing, we question our society's underlying assumptions. We ask which society, which education, which form of religion, is beneficial for all life on the planet as a whole, and then we ask further what we need to do in order to make the necessary changes. We are not limited to a scientific approach; we have an obligation to verbalize a total view.

"Of course, total views may differ. Buddhism, for example, provides a fitting background or context for deep ecology, certain Christian groups have formed platforms of action in favor of deep ecology, and I myself have worked out my own philosophy, which I call ecosophy. In general, however, people do not question deeply enough to explicate or make clear a total view. If they did, most would agree with saving the planet from the destruction that's in progress. A total view, such as deep ecology, can provide a single motivating force for all the activities and movements aimed at saving the planet from human exploitation and domination.

Fundamental Values

". . . It's easier for deep ecologists than for others because we have certain fundamental values, a fundamental view of what's meaningful in life, what's worth maintaining, which makes it completely clear that we're opposed to further development for the sake of increased domination and an increased standard of living. The material standard of living should be drastically reduced and the quality of life, in the sense of basic satisfaction in the depths of one's heart or soul, should be maintained or increased. This view is intuitive, as are all important views, in the sense that it can't be proven. As Aristotle said, it shows a lack of education to try to prove everything, because you have to have a starting point. You can't prove the methodology of science, you can't prove logic, because logic presupposes fundamental premises.

"All the sciences are fragmentary and incomplete in relation to basic rules and norms, so it's very shallow to think that science can solve our problems. Without basic norms, there is no science.

". . . People can then oppose nuclear power without having to read thick books and without knowing the myriad facts that are used in newspapers and periodicals. And they must also find others who feel the same and form circles of friends who give one another confidence and support in living in a way that the majority find ridiculous, naive, stupid and simplistic. But in order to do that, one must already have enough self-confidence to

follow one's intuition—a quality very much lacking in broad sections of the populace. Most people follow the trends and advertisements and become philosophical and ethical cripples.

"There is a basic intuition in deep ecology that we have no right to destroy other living beings without sufficient reason. Another norm is that, with maturity, human beings will experience joy when other life forms experience joy and sorrow when other life forms experience sorrow. Not only will we feel sad when our brother or a dog or a cat feels sad, but we will grieve when living beings, including landscapes, are destroyed. In our civilization, we have vast means of destruction at our disposal but extremely little maturity in our feelings. Only a very narrow range of feelings have interested most human beings until now.

"Most people in deep ecology have had the feeling . . . that they are connected with something greater than their ego."

"For deep ecology, there is a core democracy in the biosphere. . . . In deep ecology, we have the goal not only of stabilizing human population but also of reducing it to a sustainable minimum without revolution or dictatorship. I should think we must have no more than 100 million people if we are to have the variety of cultures we had one hundred years ago. Because we need the conservation of human cultures, just as we need the conservation of animal species. . . .

Now I see the secret of the making of the best persons. It is to grow in the open air, and to eat and sleep with the earth.

—*Walt Whitman*, Leaves of Grass

Bill Devall teaches at Humboldt State University in Arcata, California, and is a member of the environmentalist groups Earth First! and the Sierra Club. George Sessions teaches philosophy at Sierra College in Rocklin, California, and is editor of the International Ecophilosophy Newsletter.

"The writings of some deep ecologists leave me unclear as to what they really believe and how they expect their philosophy to be lived."

viewpoint 100

Deep Ecology Is Impractical

P.S. Elder

Many of us read the ringing declarations of the deep ecologist with a thrill of agreement. We know our world is in trouble and instinctively feel that our materialism, drive for domination and abuse of technology are at the root of it.

The diagnosis of deep ecology seems right at the general level. The human obsession with continual economic expansion and mastering nature by brute scientific force have led us toward disaster. So in some areas has population pressure. Our precious earth has limited resources and, at least in the First World, mindless consumerism threatens its ecological integrity. Materialism also interferes with our self-realization and estranges us from each other. We need to develop cooperative, decentralized institutions which will use only *appropriate technology* to achieve our goal of sustainable, convivial societies around the entire world.

To accomplish these reforms, deep ecologists say, we need a transformation of consciousness. We must stop being anthropocentric and see nature not simply as a storehouse of resources suitable for human exploitation but as intrinsically valuable. We must empathize with and respect all living things. All species are of equal worth, or for David Bennett and Richard Sylvan,

> intrinsic value is equally distributed. This projection of egalitarian or impartiality principles, usually restricted to humans, to the whole of life in the natural sphere, is a central principle of deep ecology and is called biocentric egalitarianism.

There is also a strong belief that wilderness is essential to humankind's health if not survival. In fact, Christopher Manes goes so far as to say that "[w]ilderness is the only safeguard of freedom".

It is here that I stop. I have questions. Am I to understand deep ecologists through the ordinary

meaning of their words? My problem is that some of the statements, as ordinary language, just seem silly. Have I misunderstood them? Since some of the best thinkers in this field are philosophically inclined, one might expect a careful use of language.

If, on the other hand, deep ecologists seek only to communicate a general principle through metaphor and poetry, how can we understand what to do in our daily lives?

Are All Species Equal?

Consider the claim of biocentric or biological egalitarianism (all species are created equal). As a metaphor, biocentric egalitarianism may help us to point out the unnecessary harm humankind has caused to natural ecosystems. In a limited sense, it is also literally true. Each type of organism serves an interdependent function in a splendidly complex and diverse ecosphere. Each in its own place contributes and the notion of a higher or lower form of contribution to the system's stability and splendour seems out of place in this holistic awareness.

In an everyday way, however, biocentric egalitarianism makes little sense. I do not see how we are to actualize the belief that all species are equal. So many of our mundane activities result in the deliberate killing of other organisms. Must we stop doing these things?

I can see that this theory would not inhibit us from killing bacteria and viruses which threaten our life or health. The principle of self defence would justify the use of many drugs against these beasties. But what about drugs like penicillin which require the sacrifice of innocent living molds? Can we ethically produce such compounds under species egalitarianism?

Let us think about other natural functions and their justification under biological egalitarianism. How about eating?

Even if all species are created equal, we must eat

P.S. Elder, "Is Deep Ecology the Way?" *Alternatives*, April/May 1988. Subscriptions available from Faculty of Environmental Studies, University of Waterloo, Waterloo, Ont., Canada, N2L 3G1 for $17.50 (institutions $35).

to live, so we all surely have the right to kill to eat. When faced with a carrot, a cow and a Canadian, though, which can we eat? Why? Does the concept of intrinsic, equal worth mean that our choice doesn't matter? Surely the deep ecologists cannot advocate a hierarchy of intrinsic worth, with humans above most other species, for this is the very arrogance they decry. If they do adopt a hierarchy, how can we understand a species egalitarianism that blows hot and cold at the same time?

Perhaps we must use more than intrinsic worth to help us decide what to eat. Instrumental worth could be relevant. Which of these organisms, if left to live, could do the most good? But immediately the question has to be asked: good for what or whom? (And who would decide?) Given the framework of equal intrinsic worth, that which is good for humanity cannot be the criterion. Yet acceptance of the notion of equality of value in the ecosphere leaves little for instrumental measurement to do; instrumentality may not be the route to understanding.

Suppose we wanted to use instrumentality to make our choice. Suppose further that the Canadian were lazy, shiftless and anthropocentric to boot. If the cow and carrot were splendid specimens of their type (and after all, are there not more people than cows in the world?), what would the deep ecologist say?

What, then, should a creature like us, evolved as an omnivore, eat? The carrot, the cow, or the Canadian? Why?

The answer that we must not kill and eat the person is obvious for all sane people, deep or shallow, but its clarity makes one wonder just when deep ecologists want to invoke species egalitarianism.

"Are we entitled to kill a person about to chop down an ancient tree, in the way we are thought to be when the same person raises the axe against a child?"

Again, are we entitled to kill a person about to chop down an ancient tree, in the way we are thought to be when the same person raises the axe against a child? Why? And does the instrumental benefit obtained from the tree alter the entitlement?

I suspect that the characteristics of personhood as described by anthropocentrists—the self-conscious capacity to have hopes and wishes about the future, to weigh alternatives, freely choose among them and appreciate their attainment—are also relevant to deep ecologists. So they should be. The problem is to know when, and how, they relate to species

egalitarianism. Perhaps the need to eat, properly understood, gives us the right to hunt and kill, so long as we do so with restraint and respect for the chain of being. But one doesn't have to be a deep ecologist to accept this. I am living proof of that.

Do deep ecologists insist, in addition, that we eat only what we are prepared to kill, clean and cook with our very own hands? We would surely have a greater understanding of life and death if we lacked the insulation of the slaughterhouse from the bawling beast. But anyone willing to kill whales, porpoises and monkeys for food (with restraint and respect) is justified in doing so under this criterion.

Why, indeed, should these particular animals have any special status compared with other animals? Or must deep ecologists be vegetarians? Yet species egalitarianism also seems to reject any line dividing animal from vegetable, does it not? Therefore we can eat everything or nothing.

Presumably deep ecologists don't want to use a principle such as survival of the fittest as justification for human actions either, for it gives too much to the techno-maniacs. Anything we can do is justified under this principle, which may explain action but cannot justify it.

Evolution

A "real" believer in species egalitarianism could say that each species has an equal right as part of nature to manipulate the environment for its own benefit. (Ninety-nine percent of all species past and present have already become extinct, few because of human intervention.) If all have this right, and if there are winners and losers, hard cheese. It's the "natural way". Humans just happen to have a greater ability, through science, to occupy niches and to displace other species.

Thus, species egalitarianism is a two-edged sword—it can argue for conclusions antithetical to deep ecology. Which edge should we use and why?

Perhaps this is what Henryk Skolimowski means when he says that "[d]eep ecology simply has not come to terms with the idea of evolution. . . ."

What criterion remains to tell us what to eat? Naturalness of the food source? Again, we evolved as omnivores. Even cannibalism has been practiced at some times and places (not only by stone age tribes). Surely a position claiming either logical or emotional appeal has to give us some guidance on such basic matters.

The deep ecologists' treatment of wilderness raises another problem. Wilderness is important to me but I ask: do they romanticize paradise lost when they wax lyrical about its primordial importance? Must we merely preserve its last vestiges? (still a heroic task, for economic humans). Or are the "deeps" seriously prescribing a return to an "all natural" world? Some of them seem to imply this in their generalized principles, if not in their prescriptions.

Are deep ecologists anti-urban as their North American literature suggests? Do they accept the idea of an autonomous network of small villages and towns? Do they even accept sedentary agriculture? If so, how much? Farming involves clearing the wilderness. Are hunting and gathering the only acceptable means of subsistence? Are we to dismantle the cities, replant the wilderness and live the message as Christopher Manes writes, that "the Earth works without it [technology], bearing fruit, yielding shelter, proffering freedom"?

Is it ungenerous to ask what we should do about the (presumably) billions of people who could not be supported by the world as desired by the deep ecologists?

If deep ecologists had it to do over again, would the present English countryside be permitted? (I applaud the notion that considerable primeval forest would have been preserved.)

"Some people seem to think we should eschew anything emerging from the industrial revolution."

I believe that some of the greatest flowering of the human spirit has taken place in urban settings and that some cities (most notably those shaped in pre-automotive, pre-high-rise times) fostered this flourishing. Indeed, it can be argued that urbanization was a necessary pre-condition for some of our greatest achievements. Would not deep ecologists disagree?

Again, deep ecologists are (properly) very skeptical of modern technology. Is scientific method to blame, or, as one of my acquaintances appears to believe, is rational thought? Are we to reject either or both? Indeed, is curiosity not so basic to humans that science is inevitable? Manes suspects science must be anthropocentric, presumably in a non-trivial sense, and this raises a question about whether any human can avoid anthropocentrism in day to day living.

Some people seem to think we should eschew anything emerging from the industrial revolution (no steam or internal conbustion engines, let alone electricity, no mass production). They bemoan the passing of nomadic ways of life or medieval agriculture. In fact, Manes even says that technology is incompatible with human freedom; is this extreme view representative of the "deeps"? Unless a very restrictive meaning of technology is meant here and not "the means by which material things are produced", this *cri de coeur* cannot be taken literally and seriously at the same time.

Less radically, do the principles of the soft energy path advocates guide our search for acceptable technology? Can we add E.F. Schumacher? If so, I heartily agree with the "deeps", but again derive this position without becoming one.

Like Arne Naess, I believe argumentation must stop somewhere. Perhaps belief in species egalitarianism or intrinsic value is so basic it need not be justified. Either you believe it or you don't. After all, empathy is a prerequisite for ethics (although belief in species egalitarianism does not necessarily follow). But argument about what follows from an intrinsic value theory is certainly valid, even if one is asked to accept deep ecology's tenets as a religion.

There are reasons to decry rationalists who reject the legitimacy of feeling, intuition and experience in reaching new insights. We must respect the whole person, including emotion and intuition. (I leave the interesting psychological question whether intuition is partly the unconscious but rational processing of life experience and knowledge.) But there is a difference between discovering and justifying an idea. (Am I misnaming the thing by calling it an idea?) If I reach a position in my gut, what do I have but reasoned (ethical) argument to separate the benign gut feelings from the fascist ones? I immediately stress that this is just a contrast to make my point. I do not believe that deep ecologists are fascists.

A position resting on strong feelings, insulated from criticism on the ground that justification is unnecessary, had better be pretty non-controversial. We don't have to look very far in history to find examples of monstrous evil which rested on such foundations. What would deep ecologists say to an individual who claimed intrinsic value, or attributed it to the state, and held this belief to be above intellectual justification? After all, the corollary of there being no need for rational justification is that reasoned criticism of it is useless. Either you share this higher state of awareness or you don't.

Deep Ecologists and People

Let me summarize by saying that I desire a co-operative, decentralized, small scale, tolerant society which respects all life and which avoids activities threatening the peaceful, sustained carrying capacity of the earth. It would follow the soft energy path and employ organic farming methods. It would permit urbanization, subject to these guiding principles. It would be socialist, I think, but as long as we are visualizing utopia, we can imagine the non-exploitative private ownership of the means of production mediated as much by the "just price" as by supply and demand. Given our present situation, I freely acknowledge that I have no idea whether achieving this is possible.

But I also believe, in the words of John Passmore, that "the pollution of (North) American rivers is a small price to pay if the alternative is increased starvation in developing countries". The world is not simply a resource to be exploited, yet it is legitimately a natural resource. Accepting Passmore's remark as an ethical, not an empirical, statement, I suspect that many deep ecologists would disagree. From my sketchy knowledge, I am inclined to think that some of them don't like people very much. Indeed, Stephanie Mills states that the argument that deep ecology may express profound misanthropy is "worth considering".

"I am inclined to think that some . . . [deep ecologists] don't like people very much."

Thinking this through has also made me disagree with deep ecology's claim that shallow ecologists can be merely reformists. It would be interesting to know what environmental or social policies they want which an anthropocentric, egalitarian, decentralist, democratic, shallow ecologist could not support. Personally, I feel closer to being a utopian than a tinkerer.

Nothing above is meant as a personal attack on the integrity or sincerity of deep ecologists. Nor is this piece meant as a *reductio ad absurdum* tirade. My problem is that the writings of deep ecologists leave me unclear as to what they really believe and how they expect their philosophy to be lived. I want to accept a new vision, a new paradigm based on respect for all life, but I can't apply the general teachings of deep ecology to my own life without answers to some simple (I hope not simple-minded) questions.

I end with one of the original eco-philosophers. Addressing himself to deep ecologists, Skolimowski says:

> You fellows are doing a tremendous job. . . . The world has heard you. . . . But now you have to go deeper than you have so far. After all, you claim to be a *deep ecology* movement. So be deep. Don't stay on the level of propagandistic arguments.

A parting note. When I showed this draft to a deep ecologist friend, he replied that "your exposure to positivist scientific literature inhibits your response to poetry and holistic understanding of nature." Since "law sharpens the mind by narrowing it", I have a hunch that he's at least partly right. Even poetry, however, must pay some lip service to the logical principle of non-contradiction—a prerequisite to communication.

P.S. Elder is a professor of law in the faculty of environmental design at the University of Calgary in Calgary, Canada.

organizations

The Acid Rain Foundation, Inc.
1410 Varsity Dr.
Raleigh, NC 27606
(919) 828-9443

The Foundation was established to raise the level of public awareness about acid rain. It publishes the newsletter *Update* quarterly and the *Resource Directory* annually.

Air & Waste Management Association
PO Box 2861
Pittsburgh, PA 15230
(412) 232-3444

This organization consists of industrialists and others who seek economically feasible solutions to the problems of air pollution and hazardous waste management. Its publications include the *Directory of Government Air Pollution Agencies* and the monthly *Journal of the Air & Waste Management Association.*

American Association of Zoo Keepers, Inc. (AAZK)
National Headquarters
635 Gage Blvd.
Topeka, KS 66606
(913) 272-5821

AAZK is an organization of zoo keepers and other interested persons from the U.S., Canada, and eighteen other countries. Its goal is to promote the best possible care for exotic animals in captivity. Its monthly journal, *Animal Keeper's Forum*, carries updates on current legislation affecting zoo animals.

American Council on Science and Health (ACSH)
1995 Broadway, 18th Floor
New York, NY 10023-5860
(212) 362-7044

ACSH provides consumers with information on the relationship between chemicals, foods, nutrition, life-style factors, the environment, and human health. ACSH contends that many recent health scares—such as the concerns over traces of dioxin in the environment—are based on misinformation and exaggeration. It works to counter special interest groups which it believes practice "toxic terrorism over unproven health scares." Its publications include *Dioxin in the Environment, PCBs: Is the Cure Worth the Cost?, Cancer in the U.S.: Is There an Epidemic?,* and *Irradiated Foods.*

American Forestry Association (AFA)
PO Box 2000
Washington, DC 20013
(202) 667-3300

AFA, founded in 1875, is the nation's oldest citizen conservation organization. It works to protect and preserve America's trees. It also sponsors environmental and forestry educational programs. It publishes the magazine *American Forests* and the newsletter *Urban Forest Forum* bimonthly. AFA also publishes *Resource Hotline*, a biweekly policy and legislative newsletter, and the occasional *White Papers* series, including topics such as "Forest Effects of Air Pollution" and the "Save Our Trees Citizen Action Guide."

American Nuclear Society
555 N. Kensington Ave.
La Grange Park, IL 60525
(708) 352-6611

The Society works to reassure the American public that nuclear energy is a safe and efficient power source. It publishes the monthly *Nuclear News* and the series *Nuclear Power and the Environment: Questions and Answers.*

American Tunaboat Association
1 Tuna Lane
San Diego, CA 92101
(619) 233-6405

The Association lobbies for and represents the interests of American tuna vessels. It contends that the tuna industry's fishing practices are humane and do not threaten dolphins. It distributes the pamphlets *What's Going On Here? The Tuna-Porpoise Question* and *Fishing the Eastern Tropical Pacific: The Tuna/Dolphin Issue,* as well as the press release *The Protection and Rescue of Porpoise by the U.S. Tuna Purse Seine Fleet.*

American Wilderness Alliance
7500 E. Arapahoe Rd., Suite 355
Englewood, CO 80112
(303) 771-0380

The Alliance lobbies to protect publicly owned wildlands. It promotes dialogues between opposing sides to solve environmental policy questions. It publishes the quarterly newsletter *It's Time to Go Wild* and the magazine *Wild America.*

The Bio-Integral Resource Center
PO Box 7414
Berkeley, CA 94707
(415) 524-2567

The Center promotes integrated pest management, a strategy of controlling pests while taking into account any possible effects on the entire ecosystem. It recommends avoiding the use of pesticides and provides information on the least-toxic methods to eliminate pests. The Center maintains a library and a laboratory, and publishes the technical newsletter *The IPM Practitioner* and the *Common Sense Pest Control Quarterly,* written for the general public.

Center for Environmental Information, Inc. (CEI)
99 Court St.
Rochester, NY 14604-1824
(716) 546-3796

CEI distributes up-to-date and comprehensive information on environmental issues. Its publications include the bimonthly newsletter *CEI Sphere* and the monthly bulletins *Acid Precipitation Digest* and *Global Climate Change Digest*.

Center for Holistic Resource Management
800 Rio Grande Blvd. NW, Suite 12
Albuquerque, NM 87104
(505) 242-9272

The Center promotes holistic management, a model for solving environmental problems which takes the entire ecosystem into account. This model is used by farmers and ranchers to improve their land while maintaining their production goals. They work to be independent of chemicals and huge machinery. The Center publishes *The Savory Letter* quarterly.

Citizens for a Better Environment (CBE)
33 E. Congress St., Suite 523
Chicago, IL 60605
(312) 939-1530

CBE advocates the prevention of toxic hazards by using economic incentives to reduce or eliminate the use of toxins by industry. CBE opposes incineration of solid wastes. Its publications include the quarterly *Review*.

Citizens Clearinghouse for Hazardous Wastes, Inc. (CCHW)
PO Box 926
Arlington, VA 22216
(703) 276-7070

CCHW was founded by Lois Gibbs, leader of protests by the residents of Love Canal, a toxic waste site in upstate New York. CCHW distributes information, organizes at the grassroots level, and serves as a crisis center for those who fear their health has been endangered by pollution. CCHW calls for a complete halt to the production of hazardous wastes and a thorough cleanup of contaminated sites. It publishes two newsletters, *Action Bulletin* and *Everyone's Backyard*.

Critical Mass Energy Project
Public Citizen
215 Pennsylvania Ave. SE
Washington, DC 20003
(202) 546-4996

The Project, founded by consumer activist Ralph Nader, has been working to end reliance on nuclear power and to promote environmentally sound alternatives since 1974. It publishes the *Annual Nuclear Power Safety Report* and numerous pamphlets.

Earth First!
PO Box 7
Canton, NY 13617
(315) 379-9940

Earth First! uses civil disobedience and direct action to preserve wilderness and natural diversity. Some of its best-known actions include spiking trees to make them more difficult to cut down and dressing as bears in order to protest the destruction of forests. It publishes *Earth First! The Radical Environmental Journal* eight times a year.

Edison Electric Institute
1111 19th St. NW
Washington, DC 20036-3691.
(202) 778-6400

Edison Electric Institute is an association of electric companies which acts as a liaison between electric utilities and the federal government. Its publications include *Acid Rain: The Creation of an Issue, The Energy-Environment Game,* and *How Clean Is Clean? Clean-Up Standards for Groundwater and Soil.*

Environmental Defense Fund (EDF)
257 Park Ave. S.
New York, NY 10010
(212) 505-2100

EDF conducts research and lobbies on environmental issues. To correct environmental problems, it promotes economic incentives such as allowing farmers who conserve water to resell it for a profit to cities in need. EDF publishes the bimonthly newsletter *EDF Letter*.

Exxon Corporation
PO Box 101
Florham Park, NJ 07932
(201) 765-7000

Exxon is a multinational corporation that produces and distributes oil. Exxon has been involved in oil spills and oil cleanups and is researching methods of recycling plastics. It publishes *The Lamp* quarterly.

Friends of the Earth
218 D St. SE
Washington, DC 20003
(202) 544-2600

This organization works globally to influence public policy in order to protect the environment. It has successfully opposed the construction of nuclear power plants and helped preserve wildlife sanctuaries. It publishes the bimonthly magazine *Not Man Apart*.

The Garbage Project
Bureau of Applied Resources and Anthropology
University of Arizona
Tucson, AZ 85721

The Project examines landfills and conducts studies on the garbage Americans produce. It maintains that Americans do not create more waste now than they have in the past. It believes that plastics and styrofoam do not pose a major threat to the environment, and that the best methods to correct the solid waste problem already exist, such as dumping or burning garbage. Its publications include *The Phoenix Recycling Project* and *Inside Landfills*.

Greenpeace
1432 U St. NW
Washington, DC 20009
(202) 462-1177

Greenpeace opposes nuclear energy and the use of toxins and supports ocean and wildlife preservation. It uses controversial direct action techniques and strives for media coverage of its actions in an effort to educate the public. It publishes the bimonthly magazine *Greenpeace* and many books, including *Radiation and Health, Coastline,* and *The Greenpeace Book on Antarctica*.

The Heritage Foundation
214 Massachusetts Ave. NE
Washington, DC 20002
(202)546-4400

The Heritage Foundation is a conservative public policy think tank. It advocates free-market incentives to reduce pollution. Its publications include the quarterly magazine *Policy Review* as well as the booklets *The World Bank's Environmental Disasters* and *Protecting the Environment: A Free-Market Strategy*.

Institute for Alternative Agriculture, Inc.
9200 Edmonston Rd., Suite 117
Greenbelt, MD 20770
(301) 441-8777

The Institute encourages the adoption of resource-conserving and environmentally sound farming methods. It opposes the use of chemical fertilizers and pesticides. Its publications include the monthly newsletters *Alternative Agriculture News* and *Alternative Agriculture Resources Report*, as well as the quarterly *American Journal of Alternative Agriculture*.

Monsanto Chemical Company
800 N. Lindbergh Blvd.
St. Louis, MO 63167
(314) 694-1000

Monsanto is a major producer of agricultural pesticides and
herbicides, such as Roundup and Lasso. Monsanto began a program
to reduce air pollution and wastewater emissions from its plants
following the 1984 accident at a Union Carbide plant in Bhopal,
India, which released poisonous gas and was responsible for
numerous deaths. Its publications include *Your Right-to-Know,
Monsanto Pledges to Reduce Air Emissions,* and various
Backgrounders, including "Progress Report on Monsanto's 90
Percent Reduction Program."

National Environmental Development Association (NEDA)
1440 New York Ave. NW, Suite 300
Washington, DC 20005
(202) 638-1230

NEDA consists of leaders in the oil, chemical, paper, mining, and
automobile industries as well as labor and agriculture. NEDA
believes the interests of the environment and the economy must be
balanced in the development of environmental policy. It supports
free-market solutions to environmental problems. Its newsletter,
Balance, is published quarterly.

National Ground Water Information Center
National Water Well Association
6375 Riverside Dr.
Dublin, OH 43017
(614) 761-1711

The Center distributes information to the well-water industry as
well as to concerned individuals on all issues related to groundwater, including chemical and oil spills and toxic wastes. It
contends that groundwater is a safe drinking source, since less than
one percent of it has been contaminated. Its publications include
*Impact of Agricultural Activities on Ground Water, Ground Water
Pollution Control,* and *A Standardized System for Evaluating Waste
Disposal Sites.*

National Recycling Coalition
1101 30th St. NW, Suite 304
Washington, DC 20007
(202) 625-6406

The Coalition promotes recycling as a method of reducing
environmental pollution. It works for legislation, education, and
industrial policies which will foster recycling. It publishes a
quarterly newsletter and the magazine *Resource Recycling.*

National Resources Defense Council (NRDC)
40 W. 20th St.
New York, NY 10011
(212) 727-2700

NRDC addresses all environmental concerns, from the destruction
of tropical rain forests to toxic wastes. It has worked with the Soviet
Academy of Sciences to demonstrate how efficient production and
use of energy can reduce the greenhouse effect. It publishes *The
Amicus Journal* and the reports *Pesticide Alert: A Guide to Pesticides
in Fruits and Vegetables, Right Train, Wrong Track: EPA's
Mismanagement of Superfund,* among others.

National Rifle Association (NRA)
Hunter Services Division
1600 Rhode Island Ave. NW
Washington, DC 20036
(202) 828-6246

The NRA lobbies to protect the right of the individual to own and
use firearms. It distributes literature that argues that hunting is a
vital part of animal conservation. It publishes two monthly
magazines, *The American Hunter* and *The American Rifleman.* It also
publishes numerous brochures, including *Improving Access to Private
Land.*

National Solid Wastes Management Association
1730 Rhode Island Ave. NW, Suite 1000
Washington, DC 20036
(202) 659-4613

The Association is a trade organization of industries involved in
garbage collection, recycling, landfills, and treatment and disposal
of hazardous and medical wastes. It lobbies for laws that are
environmentally sound but still allow communities to dispose of
their waste. It publishes the monthly magazine *Waste Age* and the
newsletter *Recycling Times.*

Population Renewal Office
36 W. 59th St.
Kansas City, MO 64113
(816) 363-6980

This organization opposes efforts to reduce the world's population.
It maintains that the earth has the resources to support many more
people. It further contends that a declining world population is
more dangerous to human survival than overpopulation. It
publishes brochures and articles on a variety of topics specific to
population, such as "Out of Africa: Some Population Truths."

Rainforest Action Network
301 Broadway
San Francisco, CA 94133
(415) 398-4404

The Network takes actions ranging from boycotts and protests to
sponsoring scientific forums in order to fight the destruction of
tropical forests. It publishes the quarterly *World Rainforest Report.*
Send a postcard for a free information packet on tropical forests.

Sierra Club
Public Affairs
730 Polk St.
San Francisco, CA 94109
(415) 776-2211

The Club, one of the country's leading conservation organizations,
was founded in 1892 by John Muir to explore and protect the wild
places of the earth. It lobbies for legislation to protect the
environment from such problems as acid rain and hazardous
wastes. Its publications include the magazine *Sierra.* It is also a
book publisher. Among its recent titles are *Whatever Happened to
Ecology?, The Whale War,* and *Corporate Crime and Violence: Big
Business Power and the Abuse of the Public Trust.*

3M
Environmental Engineering and Pollution Control Dept.
PO Box 33331, Building 21-2W
St. Paul, MN 55133
(612) 778-4791

3M is a multinational corporation that manufactures a variety of
products, from electronic circuits to pharmaceuticals to tape. 3M
has voluntarily worked since 1975 to lower its release of pollutants.
Its publications include the brochures *Invitation to Innovation,
Expanding Our Commitment to Clean Air,* and *Technology at Work for
a Better Environment.*

Trans-Species Unlimited
PO Box 1553
Williamsport, PA 17703
(717) 322-3252

Trans-Species Unlimited believes that the human is just one of
many species inhabiting the earth and as such does not have
dominion over other species. It objects to animals being kept in
captivity in zoos and opposes hunting and fishing. It publishes
numerous brochures, including *What Can I Do for Animals?,* and the
quarterly newsletter *One World.*

Union of Concerned Scientists (UCS)
26 Church St.
Cambridge, MA 02238
(617) 547-5552

UCS is concerned about the impact of advanced technology on society. It makes recommendations to improve the safety of atomic energy. It also conducts research on alternative energy sources. Its publications include the bimonthly magazine *Catalyst* and the quarterly *NUCLEUS.*

U.S. Environmental Protection Agency (EPA)
Office of Information and Public Affairs
Washington, DC 20207
(301) 492-6580

The EPA is the primary agency of the U.S. government responsible for implementing federal laws designed to protect the environment. Among its many publications are *Indoor Air Quality, Acid Deposition: Long-Term Trends, Agricultural Chemicals in Ground Water: Proposed Pesticide Strategies,* and *Atmospheric Ozone Research and Its Policy Implications.*

U.S. Fish and Wildlife Service
Office of Public Affairs
Department of the Interior
Washington, DC 20240
(202) 343-5634

The mission of the Service is to conserve and protect America's fish and wildlife. It operates wildlife refuges and research centers. Its publications include *Effects of Acid Precipitation on Aquatic Resources* and *Community Models for Wildlife Impact Assessment.*

Worldwatch Institute
1776 Massachusetts Ave. NW
Washington, DC 20036
(202) 452-1999

The Institute serves as a resource center on topics such as population growth, depletion of the ozone layer, reforestation, and other environmental issues. Its publications include the bimonthly *World Watch* magazine and the annual *State of the World.* Its *Worldwatch Paper Series* has focused on such topics as "Defusing the Toxics Threat: Controlling Pesticides and Industrial Waste," "Global Warming: A Worldwide Strategy," and "Population Policies for a New Economic Era."

Zero Population Growth (ZPG)
1400 16th St. NW, Suite 320
Washington, DC 20036
(202) 332-2200

ZPG lobbies to reduce population growth in order to ensure adequate resources and prevent environmental destruction. It publishes the book *USA by Numbers* and numerous pamphlets, such as *Global Warming: A Primer.*

bibliography

Acid Rain

Carl E. Bagge — "A Tale of UFOs and Other Random Anxieties," *Vital Speeches of the Day*, September 1, 1986.

Sharon Begley — "Who'll Stop the Acid Rain?" *Newsweek*, March 24, 1986.

Warren T. Brookes — "Acid Rain Fails the Acid Test," *Conservative Chronicle*, August 23, 1989. Available from *Conservative Chronicle*, Box 11297, Des Moines, IA 50340-1297.

Warren T. Brookes — "Does Acid Rain Prevent Global Warming?" *Conservative Chronicle*, September 27, 1989. Available from *Conservative Chronicle*, Box 11297, Des Moines, IA 50340-1297.

William Morle Brown — "Hysteria About Acid Rain," *Fortune*, April 14, 1986.

Derek Burney — "Canada and the U.S. in a Global Context," *Vital Speeches of the Day*, November 1, 1989.

Betsy Carpenter — "What Goes Up Must Come Down?" *U.S. News & World Report*, July 25, 1988.

Elizabeth Drummey — "Is Acid Rain Falling on Our Heads?" *The New American*, March 27, 1989.

Edison Electric Institute — *Acid Rain: Answers to Your Questions*. Washington, DC: Edison Electric Institute, 1988. Available from Edison Electric Institute, 1111 19th St. NW, Washington, DC 20036-3691.

Stephen L. Feldman and Roger K. Raufer — *Acid Rain Emissions Trading: Implementing a Market Approach to Pollution Control*. Totowa, NJ: Rowman and Littlefield, 1988.

Denise Grady — "Something Fishy About Acid Rain..." *Time*, May 9, 1988.

Jon R. Luoma — "Forests Are Dying but Is Acid Rain Really to Blame?" *Audubon*, March 1987.

Merrill McLouglin — "Our Dirty Air," *U.S. News & World Report*, June 12, 1989.

Volker A. Mohnen — "The Challenge of Acid Rain," *Scientific American*, August 1988.

Robert E. Norton — "Yes, They Mind if We Smoke," *U.S. News & World Report*, July 25, 1988.

James L. Regens and Robert W. Rycroft — *The Acid Rain Controversy*. Pittsburgh, PA: University of Pittsburgh Press, 1988.

Jurgen Schmandt and Hilliard Roderick, eds. — *Acid Rain and Friendly Neighbors*. Durham, NC: Duke Press Policy Studies, 1986.

Daniel Seligman — "April Fooling," *Fortune*, May 11, 1987.

Tim Smart — "The Earth's Alarm Bells Are Ringing," *Business Week*, July 11, 1988.

Calvin Trillin — "Uncivil Liberties," *The Nation*, August 15-22, 1987.

Air Pollution

Sharon Begley — "A Long Summer of Smog," *Newsweek*, August 29, 1988.

Alan S. Blinder — "Two Cheers for Bush's Plan to Clean Up the Clean Air Act," *Business Week*, July 10, 1989.

Vicky Cahan — "This Is One Game of Chicken Detroit Can't Win," *Business Week*, September 4, 1989.

Betsy Carpenter — "The Newest Health Hazard: Breathing," *U.S. News & World Report*, June 12, 1989.

George J. Church — "Smell That Fresh Air!" *Time*, June 26, 1989.

Brian J. Cook — *Bureaucratic Politics and Regulatory Reform: The EPA and Emissions Trading*. New York: Greenwood Press, 1988.

Lodwrick M. Cook — "Breathing Easier in the Future," *Los Angeles Times*, January 6, 1990.

Michael Duffy — "First Hot Air, Then Clean Air," *Time*, July 31, 1989.

Edmund Faltermeyer — "Air: How Clean Is Clean Enough?" *Fortune*, July 17, 1989.

Marsha Freeman — " 'Clean Air' Will Finish Off U.S. Electric Power, " *21st Century Science & Technology*, September/October 1989. Available from 21st Century Science Associates, PO Box 65473, Washington, DC 20035.

Kent Jeffreys — "Two Cheers for Bush's Clean Air Plan," The Heritage Foundation *Backgrounder*, July 10, 1989. Available from The Heritage Foundation, 214 Massachusetts Ave. NE, Washington, DC 20002.

James J. Kilpatrick — "Clean Air Bill? Don't Hold Your Breath," *Conservative Chronicle*, January 24, 1990. Available from *Conservative Chronicle*, Box 11297, Des Moines, IA 50340-1297.

Merrill McLouglin — "Our Dirty Air," *U.S. News & World Report*, June 12, 1989.

Kenneth Mellanby, ed.	*Air Pollution, Acid Rain, and the Environment.* New York: Elsevier Science Publications, 1988.
Constantine S. Nicandros	"Adversarial Politics," *Vital Speeches of the Day*, May 1, 1988.
Joanne Silberner	"How a Breath of Fresh Air Can Hurt You," *U.S. News & World Report*, August 29-September 5, 1988.
S. Fred Singer	"Purity Can't Be Achieved," *The New York Times*, April 22, 1989.
Alan Weisman	"L.A. Fights for Breath," *The New York Times Magazine*, July 30, 1989.
David Woodruff	"Detroit's Big Worry for the 1990s," *Business Week*, September 4, 1989.

American Forests

Thomas A. Barron	"Mismanaging Public Lands," *The New York Times*, February 29, 1988.
Chris Bolgiano	"Yellowstone and the Let-Burn Policy," *American Forests*, January/February 1989.
Howard Burnett and Robert Barbee	"Lodgepole and the Yellowstone Fires," *American Forests*, February 1990.
Alston Chase	*Playing God in Yellowstone: The Destruction of America's First National Park.* Boston: Atlantic Monthly Press, 1986.
Frederick W. Cubbage and Richard W. Haynes	"Forest Resources, Free Markets, and Public Policy," *Forum for Applied Research and Public Policy*, Spring 1988. Available from the University of North Carolina Press, PO Box 2288, Chapel Hill, NC 27515-2288.
Steve H. Hanke	"Privatize the National Forests," *The Wall Street Journal*, August 22, 1988.
Marty Longan	"New Recreation Strategy for the National Forests," *American Forests*, March/April 1988.
William Penn Mott Jr.	"Searching for the Right Balance," *The New York Times*, July 5, 1987.
National Parks and Conservation Association	*Investing in Park Futures: The National Park System Plan: A Blueprint for Tomorrow.* Washington, DC: National Parks and Conservation Association, 1988.
Randal O'Toole	"The Forest Service's Catch-22," *The Washington Monthly*, January 1990.
Cass Peterson	"A Battle Over Leaves of Grass," *The Washington Post National Weekly Edition*, January 18-24, 1988.
Gordon Robinson	*The Forest and the Trees: A Guide to Excellent Forestry.* Washington, DC: Island Press, 1988.
Michael Satchell	"Yellowstone Lives!" *U.S. News & World Report*, May 15, 1989.
Bob Secter and Maura Dolan	"Controversy Still Smolders at Yellowstone," *Los Angeles Times*, May 22, 1989.
Richard West Sellars	"The Parks' Dilemma—Birds and Bees or Beautiful Vistas?" *The Washington Post National Weekly Edition*, June 12-18, 1989.
William E. Shands	"Beyond Multiple Use: Managing National Forests for Distinctive Values," *American Forests*, March/April 1988.
Lawrence Solomon	"Save the Forests—Sell the Trees," *The Wall Street Journal*, August 25, 1989.

Wallace Stegner	"Land of Many Uses and Abuses," *Los Angeles Times*, November 20, 1988.
David Rains Wallace	"The Next Four National Parks: Why We Need Them. How to Get Them," *Mother Jones*, July/August 1989.
Tom Wicker	"Stripping America's Forests," *The New York Times*, March 21, 1989.

Food Safety

Accuracy In Media	"Confessions of a Radical Disinformer," *AIM Report*, October-B 1989. Available from Accuracy In Media, Inc., 1275 K St. NW, Suite 1150, Washington, DC 20005.
Rod Benson	"Learning to Use Fewer Chemicals on the Farm," *In These Times*, August 2-29, 1989.
Warren T. Brookes	"Are Rat Tests Dangerous to Your Health?" *Conservative Chronicle*, October 11, 1989. Available from *Conservative Chronicle*, Box 11297, Des Moines, IA 50340-1297.
Consumer Reports	"Alar: Not Gone, Not Forgotten," May 1989.
Donald L. Dahlsten and Richard Garcia, eds.	*Eradication of Exotic Pests.* New Haven, CT: Yale University Press, 1989.
Edith Efron	"Nature's Carcinogens Are Everywhere," *Consumers' Research Magazine*, May 1989.
Susan Gilbert	"America Tackles the Pesticide Crisis," *The New York Times Magazine*, October 8, 1989.
Ron Givens	"A Scare in the Corn Belt," *Newsweek*, March 6, 1989.
Edward Groth III	"The Alar Debate," *Consumers' Research Magazine*, July 1989.
Pamela Jones	*Pesticides and Food Safety*, 1989. Pamphlet available from American Council on Science and Health, Food Safety Division, 1995 Broadway, 16th Floor, New York, NY 10023-5860.
Daniel E. Koshland	"Alar in Apples," *Science*, May 19, 1989.
Richard Krumme	"Why Are Rats and Actresses Dictating U.S. Food Supply?" *Successful Farming*, June 1989.
Lisa Lefferts	"The Truth About Seafood," *Garbage*, September/October 1989.
Michael Pittam	"'Too Much Fuss About Pesticides'—A Reply," *Priorities*, Winter 1990. Available from American Council on Science and Health, 1995 Broadway, 16th Floor, New York, NY 10023-5860.
Janet Raloff	"Pesticide/Food Risk Greatest Under Age 6," *Science News*, March 4, 1989.
Leslie Roberts	"Alar: The Numbers Game," *Science*, March 17, 1989.
Jim Schwab	"The Attraction Is Chemical," *The Nation*, October 16, 1989.
Kenneth R. Sheets	"Nature vs. Nurture on the Farm," *U.S. News & World Report*, September 18, 1989.
Frank E. Young	"Weighing Good Safety Risks," *FDA Consumer*, September 1989.

Garbage

James Barron
"Now the Recyclable Trash Is Overwhelming New York," *The New York Times*, December 10, 1989.

Deborah Boerner
"Paper or Plastic," *American Forests*, February 1990.

William Booth
"Sometimes a Little Degradation Is Desirable," *The Washington Post National Weekly Edition*, August 14-20, 1989.

Susan Boyd, Burks Lapham, and Cynthia McGrath, eds.
Waste: Choices for Communities. Washington, DC: CONCERN, 1988.

David K. Bulloch
"Sun, Fun, Sand, Sea—And, Again, Pollution," *The New York Times*, June 24, 1989.

James Cook
"Garbage into Gold," *Forbes*, January 22, 1990.

William J. Cook
"A Lot of Rubbish," *U.S. News & World Report*, December 25, 1989/January 1, 1990.

Terry B. Friedman and Marian W. LaFollette
"Soon No Site Will Be Off-Limits for Garbage Disposal," *Los Angeles Times*, May 8, 1987.

Barbara Goldoftas
"Recycling: Coming of Age," *Technology Review*, November/December 1987.

Allen Hershkowitz and Eugene Salerni
Garbage Management in Japan: Leading the Way. New York: INFORM, 1987.

Michael deCourcy Hinds
"In Sorting Trash, Householders Get Little Help from Industry," *The New York Times*, July 29, 1989.

John Langone
"A Stinking Mess," *Time*, January 2, 1989.

George Melloan
"Waste Disposal and the 'Environmental Evangelists,'" *The Wall Street Journal*, July 26, 1988.

David Morris
"Garbage Imperialism Must Stop: Let's Force Cities to Keep Wastes in Their Own Backyards," *Los Angeles Times*, May 18, 1987.

Homer Neal and J.R. Schubel
Solid Waste Management and the Environment: The Mounting Garbage and Trash Crisis. Englewood Cliffs, NJ: Prentice Hall, 1987.

Newsday
Rush to Burn: Solving America's Garbage Crisis? Washington, DC: Island Press, 1989.

Cynthia Pollock-Shea
"Recycling Urban Wastes: Solving the Garbage Glut," *USA Today*, July 1988.

William D. Ruckelshaus
"The Politics of Waste Disposal," *The Wall Street Journal*, September 5, 1989.

Stratford P. Sherman
"Trashing a $150 Billion Business," *Fortune*, August 28, 1989.

Greenhouse Effect

John A. Ahladas
"Global Warming: Fact or Science Fiction?" *Vital Speeches of the Day*, April 1, 1989.

Robert James Bidinotto
"What Is the Truth About Global Warming?" *Reader's Digest*, February 1990.

Warren T. Brookes
"The Global Warming Panic," *Forbes*, December 25, 1989.

Betsy Carpenter
"A Faulty Greenhouse?" *U.S. News & World Report*, December 25, 1989/January 1, 1990.

Dean Edward
The Challenge of Global Warming. Washington, DC: Island Press in cooperation with the National Resources Defense Council, 1989.

Michael H. Glantz
"Regional Impacts of Global Warming," *The World & I*, January 1989.

David Goeller
"The Prophet of Global Warming," *Environmental Action*, November/December 1989.

Bill McKibben
"Is the World Getting Hotter?" *The New York Review of Books*, December 8, 1988.

Janet Marinelli
"Global Warming: It's Not 'Them,' It's 'Us,'" *Garbage*, November/December 1989.

Michael E. Murphy
"What the Greenhouse Effect Portends," *America*, December 30, 1989.

Martin Parry
"Impact of Warming on Agriculture," *Forum for Applied Research and Public Policy*, Winter 1989. Available from The University of North Carolina Press, PO Box 2288, Chapel Hill, NC 27515-2288.

Peter Rogers and Myron Fiering
"Climate Change: Do We Know Enough to Act?" *Forum for Applied Research and Public Policy*, Winter 1989. Available from The University of North Carolina Press, PO Box 2288, Chapel Hill, NC 27515-2288.

Dick Russell
"The Endless Simmer," *In These Times*, January 11-17, 1989.

Stephen H. Schneider
Global Warming: Are We Entering the Greenhouse Century? San Francisco: Sierra Club Books, 1989.

Stephen H. Schneider
"Global Warming: Is It Real?" *Forum for Applied Research and Public Policy*, Winter 1989. Available from The University of North Carolina Press, PO Box 2288, Chapel Hill, NC 27515-2288.

Jane S. Shaw and Richard L. Stroup
"Getting Warmer?" *National Review*, July 14, 1989.

James G. Titus
"Impact of Warming on Sea Level," *Forum for Applied Research and Public Policy*, Winter 1989. Available from The University of North Carolina Press, PO Box 2288, Chapel Hill, NC 27515-2288.

Union of Concerned Scientists
Briefing Paper: The Greenhouse Effect, April 1989. Pamphlet available from the Union of Concerned Scientists, Publications Department BP, 26 Church St., Cambridge, MA 02238.

Timothy E. Wirth
"Addressing the Challenge of Climate Change," *American Forests*, December 1988.

Nuclear Power

Brian Ahlberg
"A Comeback for Nuclear Power," *Utne Reader*, November/December 1988.

Joseph R. Biden Jr.
"Restoring Confidence in Nuclear Energy," *Issues in Science and Technology*, Spring 1989.

Council on Scientific Affairs
"Medical Perspective on Nuclear Power," *Journal of the American Medical Association*, November 17, 1989.

John Graham
"Can Innovation Save Nuclear Power?" *The World & I*, April 1989.

Paul E. Gray
"Nuclear Reactors Everyone Will Love," *The Wall Street Journal*, August 17, 1989.

Dan Grossman and Seth Shulman — "A Nuclear Dump: The Experiment Begins," *Discover*, March 1989.

Jack Horan — "World Nuclear Power Operators Unite," *The Bulletin of the Atomic Scientists*, April 1989.

Tom Knudson — "Rancho Seco Decked Again," *The Bulletin of the Atomic Scientists*, December 1989.

Joseph G. Morone and Edward J. Woodhouse — *The Demise of Nuclear Energy?* New Haven, CT: Yale University Press, 1989.

The New York Times — "Revive the Atom," December 8, 1989.

M.F. Perutz — "Is Britain 'Befouled?'" *The New York Review of Books*, November 23, 1989.

Thomas H. Pigford — "Three Mile Island: The Good News," *The New York Times*, March 28, 1989.

Dan W. Reicher and Caroline Petti — "Why the Rush on Nuclear Waste?" *The New York Times*, July 13, 1988.

Marilynne Robinson — *Mother Country: Britain, the Welfare State, and Nuclear Pollution.* New York: Farrar, Straus & Giroux, 1989.

John Sillin — "Nuclear Medicine for Energy Ills," *The Wall Street Journal*, September 21, 1988.

Henry N. Wagner and Linda E. Ketchum — *Living with Radiation.* Baltimore: The Johns Hopkins University Press, 1989.

Matthew L. Wald — "Finding a Burial Place for Nuclear Wastes Grows More Difficult," *The New York Times*, December 5, 1989.

Matthew L. Wald — "Renewed Debate on Nuclear Power," *The New York Times*, October 23, 1989.

Harvey Wasserman — "Shut Down But Not Out," *The Progressive*, August 1988.

Tom Wicker — "Just One More Flop," *The New York Times*, December 8, 1989.

Population

David E. Bloom and Neil G. Bennett — "Future Shock," *The New Republic*, June 19, 1989.

Lester Brown — "Analyzing the Demographic Trap," *State of the World.* New York: W.W. Norton, 1987.

John Cavanaugh O'Keefe — "Peace with All Creation," *HLI Reports*, February 1990. Available from Human Life International, 7845 E Airpark Rd., Gaithersburg, MD 20819.

Paul Demeny — "World Population Trends," *Current History*, January 1989.

R. Scott Fosler — "Demographics of the 90s," *Vital Speeches of the Day*, July 1, 1989.

Carl Haub — "The World Population Crisis Was Forgotten, but Not Gone," *The Washington Post National Weekly Edition*, September 5-11, 1988.

Jacqueline Kasun — *The War Against Population: The Economics and Ideology of Population Control.* San Francisco: Ignatius Press, 1988.

Tony Kaye — "The Birth Dearth: Conservatives Conceive a Population Crisis," *Utne Reader*, May/June 1988.

Flora Lewis — "We Are Five Billion Now," *The New York Times*, May 18, 1987.

William McGurn — "Let 'Em In: The Argument for Immigrants," *The Wall Street Journal*, November 10, 1989.

Donella H. Meadows — "Futures Terrible and Terrific," *Los Angeles Times*, January 29, 1989.

Jane Menkin, ed. — *World Population and U.S. Policy.* New York: W.W. Norton, 1986.

William Peterson — "Staying Alive," *The American Scholar*, Winter 1988.

Guy Richards — "How to Get the Poor Some Help," *The Humanist*, March/April 1986.

Nafis Sadik — "How to Handle Population Growth," *The New York Times*, May 16, 1987.

Utne Reader — "The Population Bomb: An Explosive Issue for the Environmental Movement," May/June 1988.

Ben J. Wattenberg — *The Birth Dearth*. New York: Pharos Books, 1987.

Ben J. Wattenberg — "World's Population Bomb May Be a Dud," *Los Angeles Times*, June 3, 1987.

K.C. Zachariah and My T. Vu — *World Population Projections, 1987-88 Edition: Short-and Long-Term Estimates.* Baltimore: The Johns Hopkins University Press, published for the World Bank, 1988.

Protecting the Environment

Joan Bavaria — "An Environmental Code for Corporations," *Issues in Science and Technology*, Winter 1989/1990.

Melvin A. Benarde — *Our Precarious Habitat.* New York: John Wiley & Sons, 1989.

Lester Brown, Christopher Flavin, and Sandra Postel — "A Global Plan to Save Our Planet's Environment," *USA Today*, January 1990.

Phillip C. Cato — "The Management of the Biosphere," *Vital Speeches of the Day*, November 15, 1989.

Pat Costner and Dave Rapaport — "What Works," *Greenpeace*, January/February 1990.

Trip Gabriel — "The White House," *The New York Times Magazine*, August 13, 1989.

James Goldsmith — "The Environment," *Vital Speeches of the Day*, January 15, 1990.

Hal Harvey — "Rethinking National Security," *Utne Reader*, January/February 1990.

Robin Knight and Eleni Dimmler — "The Greening of Europe's Industries," *U.S. News & World Report*, June 5, 1989.

H. Jeffrey Leonard — *Pollution and the Struggle for the World Product.* Cambridge, UK: Cambridge University Press, 1988.

James Lovelock — *The Ages of Gaia.* New York: W.W. Norton & Co., 1988.

Bill McKibben — *The End of Nature.* New York: Random House, 1989.

Norman Myers — "Environment and Security," *Foreign Policy*, Spring 1989.

Robert Ornstein and Paul Ehrlich — *New World New Mind.* New York: Doubleday, 1989.

Carol W. Rendall — "Global Environmental Threats," *The World & I*, January 1990.

Dick Russell — "We Are All Losing the War," *The Nation*, March 27, 1989.

Thomas A. Sancton — "The Fight to Save the Planet," *Time*, December 18, 1989.

R. Emmett Tyrrell Jr. — "The Real Environmentalist," *The American Spectator*, September 1989.

Murray Weidenbaum	"Protecting the Environment," *Society*, November/December 1989.
David Whitacre	"Environmentalists Emerging," *Vital Speeches of the Day*, January 15, 1990.

Rain Forests

James Brooke	"Saving Scraps of the Rain Forest May Be Pointless, Naturalists Say," *The New York Times*, November 14, 1989.
Ellen B. Geld	"Will Farming Destroy Brazil's Amazon Basin?" *The Wall Street Journal*, January 13, 1989.
Neil Gross	"Charging Japan with Crimes Against the Earth," *Business Week*, October 9, 1989.
Susanna Hecht and Alexander Cockburn	"Defenders of the Amazon," *The Nation*, May 22, 1989.
Marius Jacobs	*The Tropical Rain Forest: A First Encounter*. New York: Springer-Verlag, 1988.
H. Jeffery Leonard	"Environmentalist Hysteria May Hasten Amazon's Destruction," *The Wall Street Journal*, October 16, 1987.
Eugene Linden	"Playing with Fire," *Time*, September 18, 1989.
Marc Margolis	"Amazon Ablaze," *World Monitor*, February 1989.
The New York Times	"Rain Forest Worth More if Uncut, Study Says," July 4, 1989.
Teresa Opheim	"Can Brazil Nut Ice Cream Save the Amazon?" *Utne Reader*, January/February 1990.
Diana Page	"Debt-for-Nature Swaps," *International Environmental Affairs*, Fall 1989. Available from the University Press of New England, 17½ Lebanon St., Hanover, NH 03755.
T.M. Pasca	"The Politics of Tropical Deforestation," *American Forests*, November/December 1988.
Sandra Postel	"Global View of a Tropical Disaster," *American Forests*, November/December 1988.
Mev Puleo	"The Struggle Continues," *Maryknoll*, January 1990. Available from the Catholic Foreign Mission Society of America Inc., Maryknoll, NY 10545.
John F. Richards and Richard P. Tucker, eds.	*World Deforestation in the Twentieth Century*. Durham, NC: Duke University Press, 1988.
Jonathan Schell	"Our Fragile Earth," *Discover*, October 1989.
Karl Schoenberger	"A Lust for Trees, a Love of Wood," *Los Angeles Times*, December 20, 1989.
Roger D. Stone	"The Global Stakes of Tropical Deforestation," *USA Today*, March 1988.
E.O. Wilson, ed.	*Biodiversity*. Washington, DC: National Academy Press, 1988.

Regulations and the Environment

Doug Bandow, ed.	*Protecting the Environment: A Free Market Strategy*. Washington, DC: The Heritage Foundation, 1986.
David Bollier and Joan Claybrook	*Freedom from Harm: The Civilizing Influence of Health, Safety and Environmental Regulation*. New York: Public Citizen and Democracy Project, 1986.
Barry Commoner	"Why We Have Failed," *Greenpeace*, September/October 1989.
Thomas d'Aquino	"Environment and Economy," *Vital Speeches of the Day*, August 1, 1989.
Gregg Easterbrook	"Cleaning Up," *Newsweek*, July 24, 1989.
Sheldon K. Friedlander	"Pollution Prevention," *Environment*, May 1989.
Scott Harshbarger	"Prosecuting Environmental Crimes," *Vital Speeches of the Day*, October 1, 1989.
Lawrence Gregory Hines	*The Market, Energy, and the Environment*. Boston: Allyn and Bacon, Inc., 1988.
Laurence R. Jahn	"Maintaining Nature's Delicate Balance," *USA Today*, November 1989.
Kent Jeffreys	"The 'Private' Approach Works," *The World & I*, June 1989.
Jeremy Main	"Here Comes the Big New Cleanup," *Fortune*, November 1988.
Michael J. Mandel	"The Right to Pollute Shouldn't Be for Sale," *Business Week*, May 22, 1989.
The New Republic	"Grime and Punishment," February 20, 1989.
Constantine S. Nicandros	"Adversarial Politics," *Vital Speeches of the Day*, May 1, 1988.
Fred L. Smith Jr.	"A Flawed Environmental Policy," *USA Today*, September 1988.
Robert N. Stavins	"Clean Profits: Using Economic Incentives to Protect the Environment," *Policy Review*, Spring 1989.
Robert N. Stavins	"Harnessing Market Forces to Protect the Environment," *Environment*, January/February 1989.
Dick Thompson	"What's the Cure for Burnout?" *Time*, December 25, 1989.

Toxic Waste

American Council on Science and Health	*Dioxin in the Environment: Its Effect on Human Health*, October 1988. Pamphlet available from the American Council on Science and Health, 1995 Broadway, 16th Floor, New York, NY 10023-5860.
Betsy Carpenter	"Superfund, Superflop," *U.S. News & World Report*, February 6, 1989.
Liane Clorfene Casten	"A Town Is Being Poisoned," *The Nation*, March 19, 1988.
Lee Clarke	*Acceptable Risk? Making Decisions in a Toxic Environment*. Berkeley: University of California Press, 1989.
Michael R. Edelstein	*Contaminated Communities: The Social and Psychological Impacts of Residential Toxic Exposure*. Boulder, CO: Westview Press, 1988.
Stuart Gold	"Occidental Petroleum: Politics, Pollution and Profit," *Multinational Monitor*, July/August 1989.
Joel S. Hirschhorn	"Cutting Production of Hazardous Waste," *Technology Review*, April 1988.
John Holusha	"Putting a Torch to Toxic Waste," *The New York Times*, June 21, 1989.

William D. Marbach | "What to Do with Our Waste," *Newsweek*, July 27, 1987.

John M. Mendeloff | *The Dilemma of Toxic Substance Regulation*. Cambridge, MA: MIT Press, 1988.

Warren R. Muir and Joanna D. Underwood | "Eliminating Toxic Waste," *The New York Times*, August 1, 1987.

William W. Nazaroff and Anthony V. Nero Jr., eds. | *Radon and Its Decay Products in Indoor Air*. New York: John Wiley and Sons, 1988.

Stephanie Pollack and Seth Shulman | "Toxic Responsibility," *The Atlantic Monthly*, March 1989.

Lewis Regenstein | *How to Survive in America the Poisoned*. Washington, DC: Acropolis Books, 1986.

Dick Russell | "Welcome to Dioxinville, Arkansas," *In These Times*, March 9-15, 1988.

Michael Satchell | "Uncle Sam's Toxic Folly," *U.S. News & World Report*, March 27, 1989.

Sally Squires | "Do We Really Have to Be Scared to Death of Radon?" *The Washington Post National Weekly Edition*, October 17-23, 1988.

Rochelle Stanfield | "New Technologies Aim to Make Toxic Wastes Permanently Harmless," *The New York Times*, July 19, 1988.

Judith Stone | "Toxic Avengers," *Discover*, August 1989.

Water Pollution

Jerry Adler | "Our Befouled Beaches," *Newsweek*, July 27, 1987.

American Chemical Society | *Evaluation of Pesticides in Ground Water*. Washington, DC: American Chemical Society, 1986.

Marc Beauchamp | "Whiskey's for Drinking, Water's for Fighting Over," *Forbes*, July 29, 1989.

David K. Bulloch | *The Wasted Ocean*. New York: Lyons & Burford Publishers, 1989.

Alan Burdick | "Hype Tide," *The New Republic*, June 12, 1989.

Vincent Carroll | "How the West Is Watered," *Reason*, July 1986.

Robert Gotlieb | *A Life of Its Own: The Politics and Power of Water*. San Diego: Harcourt Brace Jovanovich, 1988.

Robert Kourik | "Greywater: Why Throw It Away?" *Garbage*, January/February 1990.

Wesley Marx | "Cry of the American Coast," *Reader's Digest*, December 1988.

Tom Morganthau | "Don't Go Near the Water," *Newsweek*, August 1, 1988.

Kristine M. Napier | *Assessing the Quality of America's Water*. New York: American Council on Science and Health, December 1988. Available from the American Council on Science and Health, 1995 Broadway, 16th Floor, New York, NY 10023-5860.

The New Republic | "America's Issue," January 26, 1987.

Charles Osterberg | "Deep Ocean: The Safest Dump," *The New York Times*, June 14, 1989.

Jim Palmer | *Endangered Rivers and the Conservation Movement*. Berkeley: University of California Press, 1986.

William Sander | "Shooting the Political Rapids of Western Water," *The Wall Street Journal*, April 13, 1987.

Michael Satchell | "Fight for Pigeon River," *U.S. News & World Report*, December 4, 1989.

C.J. Silas | "Gaining the Environmental Initiative," *Vital Speeches of the Day*, October 15, 1989.

Tim Smart | "Costly Cleanups at the Gas Pump," *Business Week*, April 20, 1987.

Wildlife

Stephen Chapman | "How Can We Save Africa's Dying Elephants?" *Conservative Chronicle*, August 16, 1987. Available from *Conservative Chronicle*, Box 11297, Des Moines, IA 50340-1297.

Chicken of the Sea | *What's Going On Here? The Tuna-Porpoise Question*, 1981. Pamphlet available from the American Tunaboat Association, 1 Tuna Lane, San Diego, CA 92101-5896.

Merritt Clifton | "How Trapping Affects the Forest," *The Animals' Agenda*, November 1989.

Andrew Davis | "The Slaughter of Dolphins," *The Nation*, November 14, 1988.

Daniel J. Decker and Gary R. Goff, eds. | *Valuing Wildlife: Economic and Social Perspectives*. Boulder, CO: Westview Press, 1987.

Roger L. DiSilvestro | *The Endangered Kingdom: The Struggle to Save America's Wildlife*. New York: John Wiley and Sons, 1989.

Michael W. Fox | "The Captive Panther," *The Animals' Agenda*, September/October 1988.

Melissa Greene | "No Rms, Jungle Vu," *The Atlantic Monthly*, December 1987.

Ted Gup | "Trail of Shame: Elephants Face a Grim Struggle Against Greed and Deceit," *Time*, October 16, 1989.

Jerry Howard | "Brave New Zoos," *New Age Journal*, January/February 1990.

James J. Kilpatrick | "Fanaticism in Any Form Has Small Appeal," *Conservative Chronicle*, December 13, 1989. Available from *Conservative Chronicle*, Box 11297, Des Moines, IA 5034-1297

Aldo Leopold | *Game Management*. Madison: University of Wisconsin Press, 1986.

People for the Ethical Treatment of Animals | "Zoos: Pitiful Prisons." Fact sheet available from People for the Ethical Treatment of Animals, PO Box 42516, Washington, DC 20015.

Jane Perlez | "Global Trade in Ivory Is Banned to Protect the African Elephant," *The New York Times*, October 17, 1989.

Christie Prescott-Allen and Robert Prescott-Allen | *The First Resource: Wild Species in the North American Economy*. New Haven, CT: Yale University Press, 1986.

George Reiger | "We Aren't Thoughtless Thugs," *U.S. News & World Report*, February 5, 1990.

Michael Satchell | "The American Hunter Under Fire," *U.S. News & World Report*, February 5, 1990.

Randy T. Simmons and Urs P. Kreuter | "Banning Ivory Trade Endangers Elephants," Human Events, October 28, 1989. Available from *Human Events* Inc., 422 First St. SE, Washington, DC 20003.

index